Genius of the Dance

JAN. 13. 1956.

Twenty-five years ago this week Anna Pavlova died
after a career that had made her name a legend. A te—
gramme on Thursday, introduced here by DONALD
who has helped to prepare it, will throw light on he—

THE young people of today cannot possibly assess the quality of a dancer who died twenty-five years ago any more than they can determine the comparative ability of Denis Compton and Dr. Grace. Yet any schoolboy will tell you that 'W.G.' was a Great Man; and any schoolgirl, swooning in adoration of Fonteyn, Markova, and Elvin, will recount for you in the same bated breath the glories of Anna Pavlova.

The reason of course is that she was a genius. It falls to some people to make such an impact on their own generation that they become part of the world's folk-lore. Pavlova was one of that rare company.

She was born in Petrograd, probably about 1880, and died of double pneumonia at The Hague on January 23, 1931. Between these dates she lived a life of incessant work, a life that is fully documented. So there can rarely have been such a store of research material available to the earnest seeker after truth. To dramatise her life would surely be easy, as well as rewarding, because she lived drama—every minute of the day. No need to search for appropriate background music because it existed perpetually in the foreground of her work. The décor was already designed; the recurring scenery of practice hall, theatre, and hotel room. The characters were known, all they required was a play. And it was just this biographical play that was envisaged by Patricia Foy, the producer of *Music for You*. It was to be a major programme, involving the resources of the Television Drama Department, and Paul Tabori was chosen to write the script. He is Hungarian by birth, cosmopolitan in experience, and a knowledgeable fellow in the lively arts. After weeks of research we went to France with the object of seeking out those members of the Russian colony in Paris who had known and worked with the dancer at various stages of her career. It turned out to be a bizarre pilgrimage.

The Old Lady of Montmartre

One recalls, for example, sitting on a hard stool in a draughty practice room somewhere on the slopes of Montmartre. There is the traditional 'barre,' mirrors along one wall and, above an ancient stone fire-place, a life-size bust of Pavlova as the Swan, wings and all. A tiny old lady sits opposite, erect and slim, her beautiful face carved apparently out of a walnut shell. She is a Countess, and over eighty, yet she still demonstrates ballet to her daily class. The talk is a sort of rich *consommé* of Russian, French, and English, with a word or two of German dropped in for seasoning. Someone asks: 'Tell us, Countess, what made Pavlova supreme? What was her greatest gift?'

A brief pause and then the answer comes in one word: 'Talent.'

It gradually became clear to us that to present the true life-story of Anna Pavlova was quite impossible. Everybody agreed on her supremacy, but disagreed about everything else. It is not, for example, completely certain that she was ever married. Victor Emilionovitch Dandre, her manager, life-long friend and reputed husband, never mentioned their wedding in his biography, while others state explicitly that it never took place. Again, the late Oliveroff, a dancer with her Company, tells in his book how 'Madame' and the famous opera singer Mary Garden toured together and were intimate friends for years. So we wrote to Miss Garden, who courteously and surprisingly replied that to her own great sorrow she and Pavlova had never met.

Scores of similar inconsistencies not only forced us to change our plan but provided us with a new one. Instead of an inaccurate biography we are presenting the eight ages of Anna Pavlova as told by eight composite personalities whom we have called, generically, the Maid, the Countess, the Princess,

the Baron, the American, the Impresario, the Choreographer, and the Dancer. Each describes in turn a different stage of her career and colours it with his own opinions, prejudices, and enthusiasms, the narrative in each case becoming a dramatised flash-back.

The changing fashions and settings will mark the passing years; the ballets and divertissements introduced at different stages are those danced by Pavlova at that time—and to dance them we have Alicia Markova.

One of the triumphs of Pavlova's art: 'The Death of the Swan,' from the painting by Sir John Lavery, R.A., now in the Tate Gallery

PLIER   TO BEND
SE JETER   TO JUMP
SE TOURNER   TO TURN - TO REVOLVE
BATTEMENT   BEATING - STAMPING
ÉPAULE   SHOOLDER
PORT   -   CARRIAGE - BEARING.

Svetlana Beriosova (as Swanhilda) and David Blair (as Franz) in *Coppélia* (Petipa-Ivanov, St. Petersburg, 1884) as presented by the Sadler Wells Theatre Ballet in 1952. Ballet as an international synthesis: a ballerina born in Lithuania and trained in the Russian school in New York, Paris and London dances for an English company the role of a Polish maiden in a ballet based on a story by a German writer, devised in Paris in 1870 for the last great French dancer of the nineteenth century, and later produced in a new version in Russia at the very beginning of the renaissance in ballet.

AN ANATOMY
OF BALLET

FERNAU HALL

With 85 illustrations
including many from the
Mander-Mitchenson Theatre Collection
and with numerous
drawings

LONDON
ANDREW MELROSE

Andrew Melrose Limited
London New York Toronto
Melbourne Sydney Cape Town

First published 1953

Set in eleven point Monotype Bembo
one point leaded

Printed in Great Britain
by The Anchor Press, Ltd.,
Tiptree, Essex

To

MY MOTHER and MY WIFE

Preface

WHEN THE art of ballet was reborn in Europe at the beginning of the eighteenth century, opera was already established as one of the major branches of the theatre, and for the next 200 years ballet developed mainly as an adjunct to opera: the theatres in which opera and ballet were performed were sometimes called opera-houses, but never ballet-houses.

During the twentieth century the status of ballet changed considerably. Large numbers of independent ballet companies were formed, and productions of new ballets far outnumbered productions of new operas. In countries without a strong tradition of native opera (notably England, the British Dominions and the United States) ballet has put down deep roots in the last few decades of this century: in these countries even the bad new ballets (of which there are an unconscionable number) have a quality of self-assurance only to be found in the best of the new native operas. In countries with an old tradition of native opera, ballet still takes second place in the State and municipal opera-houses, but there is now a tendency for independent ballet companies to be formed, and one may expect this tendency to grow stronger in the future.

In spite of serious deficiencies in the quality of new ballets and in the standard of performance of established ballets, the art of ballet retains its hold on the public in the second half of the twentieth century, and is as characteristic of this century as the film and television.

The enormous expansion in ballet in the twentieth century has inevitably led to a good deal of diversification, with the emergence of types of ballet which differ from each other quite as much as grand opera differs from revue and musical comedy. Nevertheless we still use a single word to describe all the different types of ballet; the resultant confusion has made it very difficult for the public to build up standards of discrimination, and is reflected all too clearly in the artistic policies of the various ballet companies.

In this book I have attempted to classify ballets and ballet companies into their main types, and also to show how these types have evolved in the twentieth century. Only in this way can we hope to understand the violent contrasts in the quality of the new ballets produced (and the standard of performance in established ballets) between company and company and from one period to another; in fact one of the primary aims of this book is to investigate the conditions needed for the maintenance of a high standard of creation and performance, and what happens when these conditions are not present.

Modern ballet dates from about 1875, and Part I deals with the renaissance that began at this time in the Imperial Russian Ballet and continued in the Diaghilev Ballet. This is a subject which has been dealt with in a large number of books, but until recently we have been too close to this period to see it in perspective, and the importance of the developments in the period before the formation of the Diaghilev Ballet has been largely underestimated.

Parts II and III refer only to the twentieth century. The expansion of ballet in the twentieth century led to such diversification that I have found it advisable to deal separately with ballets and ballet companies. Part II deals with choreographers and their achievements, for it is choreography alone which distinguishes ballet from the other arts of the theatre. Part III deals with ballet companies and the artistic policies they embody.

The division of the book between Parts II and III introduces certain difficulties, for the development of choreography has been deeply influenced by the development of ballet companies, and vice versa: it is in fact the interaction between the two which largely determines the shape of ballet history. Though certain sections of Part II cannot be fully understood except in relation to the corresponding sections of Part III, I have found it desirable to retain this arrangement of the book, for any other arrangement raises even greater difficulties.

In *Modern English Ballet* I dealt with ballet in one country against the background of world ballet history; there the main emphasis was on aspects of ballet peculiar to England. In this book the main emphasis is on those aspects of ballet which succeed each other in time and are to some extent common to ballet in all countries, irrespective of differences in technique and in national character and cultural traditions. The sections of this book dealing with English ballet overlap to some extent with the corresponding sections of *Modern English Ballet* (though the treatment is different), and I have therefore curtailed these sections. On the other hand there are few things more infuriating to a reader than a long series of references to another book—particularly if he has not read it—and I have thought it best to preserve continuity at a few points by including summaries of material in *Modern English Ballet*.

I am very conscious of the dangers and difficulties involved in an attempt to analyse the creative process in choreography and the development of organizations as complex as ballet companies. All those with practical experience of ballet know that the quality of the work seen by the public depends to a very large extent on intangible factors which matter very much to choreographers and dancers, but find little place in histories of ballet. As the tools of his trade the choreographer has living, creative individuals, not chisels or brushes, and in the study of ballet we must take into account the whole range of human personality, behaviour and consciousness. Since our knowledge of these matters is still very limited, we cannot hope to account for every aspect of the development of ballet in this century. I have done my best to survey the whole extent of this uncharted territory, but I have left many blanks which I hope others will fill in.

Believing as I do that the art of ballet can retain its vitality only if there are institutions which permit (and indeed encourage) artists with important new ideas to come to maturity, I have devoted myself mainly to an analysis of the creative potentialities of each type of ballet and ballet company. In so far as this analysis is valid I hope that it will help important new ideas to emerge in the future.

TABLE OF CONTENTS

		page
Preface		7
Introduction—Maîtres de Ballet, Patrons, Theatrical Managers and Ballet Companies up to 1875		19
1.	Court Companies and Commercial Companies	19
2.	Weaver in London	20
3.	Sallé: Paris and London	21
4.	Noverre: Paris, London, Stuttgart, Vienna	23
5.	Didelot: London and St. Petersburg	27
6.	Milan: Vigano and Blasis	30
7.	Paris: the So-called Romantic Ballet	33
8.	Perrot: Paris, London, St. Petersburg	35
9.	Bournonville in Copenhagen	39
10.	General Degeneration	40

PART I

THE RENAISSANCE (1875–1929)

1.	Degeneration in Russia	47
2.	The Renaissance Begins	53
3.	*The Sleeping Beauty*	58
4.	*Le Lac des Cygnes* in St. Petersburg	61
5.	Mamontov, Benois, Diaghilev and Volkonsky	63
6.	Fokine	65
7.	Diaghilev's First Paris Seasons	66
8.	The Permanent Diaghilev Company	69
9.	Diaghilev Re-forms his Company	73
10.	The Cocktail Period	79

PART II

TYPES OF CHOREOGRAPHY

page

A. Michel Fokine: Renaissance of Classical Romanticism   87

B. Expressionism   97
  Vaslav Nijinsky   103
  Dalcroze, Laban and Wigman   116
  Léonide Massine   126
  Jean Borlin   135
  Bronislava Nijinska   138
  Martha Graham   141
  Kurt Jooss   149
  Ninette de Valois   152

C. Post-Expressionist Pseudo-Classicism   160
  Bronislava Nijinska   160
  George Balanchine   162
  Serge Lifar   176
  Frederick Ashton   185

D. Antony Tudor: Post-Expressionist Classicism   200

E. Birgit Åkesson: Post-Expressionist Free Dance   220

F. The Innocent Eye   227
  Agnes de Mille   228
  Frank Staff   239
  Jerome Robbins   241
  Roland Petit   246
  John Cranko   252

G. Russia since 1917   259

H. India   265
  (a) Classical Styles   265
  (b) Folk Dances   273

H. India—(contd.)   page
    (c) Modern Indian Ballet   273
         Ruth St. Denis   275
         Rabindranath Tagore   278
         Anna Pavlova   279
         Uday Shankar   281
         Menaka   286
         Ballet in Bombay   288
         Krishna Kutty   290

I. Spain   294
    (a) Flamenco   294
    (b) Regional Dances   301
    (c) Spanish Ballet   302

J. Yugoslavia   307

PART III

TYPES OF BALLET COMPANY IN THE TWENTIETH CENTURY

A. Old-established State Ballets Surviving into the Twentieth Century   315
    Paris Opéra   317
    Royal Danish Ballet   321

B. Ballet Companies Formed in the Twentieth Century   325
    1. The Dancer's Company   327
        (a) The Individualistic Classical Dancer's Company   327
             Anna Pavlova   328
             Anton Dolin (Markova-Dolin B., Festival B.)   334
             Ram Gopal   343
        (b) The Expressionist Free Dancer's Company   346
             Isadora Duncan   346
             Mary Wigman   349
             Martha Graham   350

B. Ballet Companies Formed in the Twentieth Century—(*contd.*)   *page*

        (*c*) The Rich Dancer's Company   352

            Ida Rubinstein   353

            Mona Inglesby (International B.)   354

            Mrinalini Sarabhai   357

      2. The Choreographer's Company   360

        (*a*) Subsidized Companies   362

            Kurt Jooss   362

            Ninette de Valois (Vic-Wells B., Sadlers Wells B., Sadlers Wells Theatre B.)   364

            George Balanchine (American B., New York City B.)   377

        (*b*) Unsubsidized Companies   385

            Michel Fokine   385

            Antony Tudor (Dance Theatre, London B.)   386

            Roland Petit (Ballets de Paris)   388

      3. The Creative Company   391

            Rolf de Maré's Ballets-Suédois   392

            Marie Rambert's Ballet Club (also B. Rambert)   394

            Margaret Barr's Dance Drama Group   399

      4. The Hybrid Company   402

            Ballets Russes de Monte Carlo No. 2 (Blum-de Basil-Massine)   402

            Ballets Russes de Monte Carlo No. 3 (Blum-Massine-Denham)   412

            Ballet Theatre   417

            Ballets des Champs-Élysées   424

      5. The Patron-Manager's Company: Grand Ballet du Marquis de Cuevas   427

Conclusion   431

Biographical note on author   441

Line drawings   443

Index   445

LIST OF ILLUSTRATIONS

Beriosova and David Blair in *Coppélia*   *photo Roger Wood*   *frontispiece*

Marie Sallé   *from an etching by Larmessin after a painting by Lancret*   *facing page* 32

Didelot and Mlle Théodore in *Amphion and Thalia*   *print by Rowlandson*   33

Vigano and Maria Medina in the opera *Arianna*   *drawing by Schadow*   33

Cerito at Her Majesty's Theatre   *Mander-Mitchenson Th. Coll.*   48

Brudefærden i Hardanger (Bournonville)   49

Giselle in London with Grisi and Perrot   *Mander-Mitchenson Th. Coll.*   49

Pavlova and Nicolas Legat in *Le Lac des Cygnes*   64

Nijinsky in *Le Pavillon d'Armide*   *Mander-Mitchenson Th. Coll.*   65

Diaghilev in 1927   *Mander-Mitchenson Th. Coll.*   65

The Diaghilev Ballet rehearsing   *Mander-Mitchenson Th. Coll.*   65

Petrouchka with Karsavina and Bolm   *Mander-Mitchenson Th. Coll.*   80

Le Train Bleu with Sokolova and Dolin   *Mander-Mitchenson Th. Coll.*   81

La Chatte with Lifar   *Mander-Mitchenson Th. Coll.*   81

Schéhérazade with Karsavina and Nijinsky   *Mander-Mitchenson Th. Coll.*   96

Les Sylphides with Karsavina   *Mander-Mitchenson Th. Coll.*   97

L'Oiseau de Feu with Karsavina and Bolm   *Mander-Mitchenson Th. Coll.*   97

Isadora Duncan   *photo Elvira* 112

L'Après-Midi d'un Faune with Nijinsky   *Mander-Mitchenson Th. Coll.*   113

Le Sacre du Printemps   *Mander Mitchenson Th. Coll.*   113

Rudolf von Laban   *photo Suse Byk* 128

Mary Wigman   *photo S. Enkelmann* 128

Les Présages with Verchinina   *Mander-Mitchenson Th. Coll.*   129

La Boutique Fantasque with Danilova and Massine   129
    Mander-Mitchenson Th. Coll.

L'Homme et Son Désir   *photo Isabey* 144

Martha Graham   *Mander-Mitchenson Th. Coll.* 144

The Rake's Progress with Markova and Harold Turner   145
    photo J. W. Debenham

The Green Table   *photo Roger Wood* 145

Les Biches with Nikitina and Lifar   *Mander-Mitchenson Th. Coll.* 160

La Chatte with Lifar   160

Serenade with Nicolas Magallanes, Diana Adams and Melissa Hayden
photo Roger Wood facing page 161

The Firebird (Balanchine) with Maria Tallchief and Francisco Moncion 161
photo Roger Wood

Bacchus et Ariane (Lifar) with Spessivsteva and Lifar *photo Lipnitzki* 176

Lifar in *Icare* *Mander-Mitchenson Th. Coll.* 176

Margot Fonteyn in *Façade* *photo Anthony* 177

Homage to the Queen with Violetta Elvin and John Hart *photo Roger Wood* 177

The Planets with Maude Lloyd, Antony Tudor and Kyra Nijinska 208
photo J. W. Debenham

Jardin aux Lilas with Hugh Laing, Peggy van Praagh, Antony Tudor and
Maude Lloyd *photo Malcolm Dunbar* 208

Dark Elegies with Antony Tudor, Maude Lloyd, Peggy van Praagh,
Agnes de Mille and Walter Gore *photo Houston Rogers* 209

Nora Kaye in *Pillar of Fire* *photo Roger Wood* 209

Birgit Åkesson in *Movement* *photo Flodquist* 224

Rodeo with Allyn McLerie *photo Roger Wood* 225

Oklahoma! (the dream ballet) *photo Angus McBean* 225

Peter and the Wolf with Celia Franca, Walter Gore, Lulu Dukes and Leo
Kersley *photo Ramsey & Muspratt* 240

Fancy Free with Jerome Robbins *photo Roger Wood* 241

The Age of Anxiety *photo Roger Wood* 241

Carmen with Roland Petit and Renée Jeanmaire *photo Paul Wilson* 256

Les Demoiselles de la Nuit *photo Roger Wood* 257

Pineapple Poll with Elaine Fifield and David Poole *photo Roger Wood* 257

Taras Bulba with Sergueyev 272

Romeo and Juliet with Ulanova and Sergueyev 272
photo supplied by Gala Films Ltd.

Mrinalini (Marianne Balchin) in a Kathak dance *photo Helga Sharland* 273

Krishna Kutty in *The Art of Kathakali*, with commentary by Shirin Vajifdar 273
photo Helga Sharland

Ruth St. Denis *Mander-Mitchenson Th. Coll.* 288

Pavlova as Radha *photo E. O. Hoppé* 288

Uday Shankar and Simkie *photo Apers* 288

Menaka *photo S. Enkelmann* 288

The Boon with Krishna Kutty and Roshan Vajifdar *photo Paul Wilson* 289

Antonio in a Flamenco dance *photo Roger Wood* 304

Argentina *Mander-Mitchenson Th. Coll.* *facing page* 304

Yugoslav national dance *Oro* in *The Legend of Ohrid* 305

The Fountain of Bakhchisaraï with Zlata Lanović, Oscar Harmoš and Ana Roje 305

The Royal Danish Ballet: *La Sylphide* with Anna Tychsen and Hans Beck 336

The Paris Opéra: Carlotta Zambelli and Albert Aveline *photo Roosen* 336

The Festival Ballet: *Symphony for Fun* with Noël Rossana, John Gilpin and Anita Landa *photo Paul Wilson* 337

Pavlova and Mordkin *Mander-Mitchenson Th. Coll.* 337

Isadora Duncan with her pupils *Mander-Mitchenson Th. Coll.* 352

Mary Wigman with her dance-group *Mander-Mitchenson Th. Coll.* 352

The International Ballet: *Giselle* with Mona Inglesby 353
photo Tunbridge-Sedgwick

Ida Rubinstein as Cleopatra *Mander-Mitchenson Th. Coll.* 353

Margot Fonteyn as Odette in *Le Lac des Cygnes* *photo Roger Wood* 368

The Vic-Wells Ballet: *Checkmate* with June Brae and Harold Turner 369
photo Studio Iris

The London Ballet: Peggy van Praagh in *Soirée Musicale* *photo Anthony* 369

The Ballets-Suédois: *La Maison des Fous* 384

The Marie Rambert Dancers in class (1930) *Mander-Mitchenson Th. Coll.* 384

The de Basil-Massine company in 1936 385

René Blum and Massine 385

The Blum-de Basil-Massine company: *Les Présages* with Baronova and Lichine *Mander-Mitchenson Th. Coll.* 400

The de Basil-Massine company: *Schéhérazade* with Shabelevsky 400
Mander-Mitchenson Th. Coll.

The Blum company: *L'Épreuve d'Amour* *Mander-Mitchenson Th. Coll.* 401

The Denham Ballet Russe de Monte Carlo: *Danses Concertantes* with Danilova and Franklin *photo Richard Tucker* 401

Ballet Theatre: *Pillar of Fire* with Lucia Chase and Nora Kaye 416
photo Roger Wood

Ballet Theatre: *Undertow* with Hugh Laing and Nora Kaye 416
photo Roger Wood

The Ballets des Champs-Élysees: *Le Jeune Homme et la Mort* with Jean Babilée and Nathalie Philippart *photo Roger Wood* 417

The Grand Ballet du Marquis de Cuevas: *Night Shadow* with Éthery Pagava and George Skibine *photo Roger Wood* 417

Introduction

Maîtres de Ballet, Patrons, Theatrical Managers and Ballet Companies up to 1875

1. COURT COMPANIES AND COMMERCIAL COMPANIES

UP TO the beginning of the nineteenth century maîtres de ballet[1] had a Hobson's choice between two main types of ballet company. On the one hand there were the court ballets, maintained as one section of the court operas, subsidized from the Privy Purse, and administered by a court official: these companies were of great importance as preservers of tradition, for they kept alive a repertoire of old ballets and thus prevented the achievements of past generations from being lost; but they tended to be riddled with intrigue and to resist tenaciously any artistic progress. On the other hand there were ballet companies employed by theatrical managers[2] in control of commercial theatres: when supported by a manager of courage and vision and led by a great maître de ballet this type of company was responsible for major advances in the art of ballet, but its achievements were ephemeral because the company ceased to exist when the manager retired, or for some reason was forced to abandon his theatre or change his policy. The great maîtres de ballet usually worked with both types of company, moving from one country to another in search of reasonably satisfactory conditions of work.

During the nineteenth century there was a strong tendency for the court ballets to change their character and become semi-commercial: this was the result of profound changes in social relationships and patterns of thought and behaviour which followed the French Revolution and accompanied the industrial revolution. In the nineteenth century a court ballet seemed an anachronism—as indeed it was. Nevertheless this anachronism was of vital importance as a repository of tradition; since there was no satisfactory system

---

[1] Before the twentieth century "maître de ballet" signified teacher, choreographer and producer of revivals (régisseur).

[2] The corresponding Continental term is "impresario". For some time there has been a tendency for managers working in the field of ballet, opera and music in England and the United States to describe themselves as "impresarios", while in the field of drama the American term equivalent to "manager" is now "producer". The theatrical manager assumes financial responsibility for the productions he presents, and should not be confused with the business manager of the twentieth-century ballet company—who is simply employed by the company on a salary or percentage basis.

of recording ballet this art would have died out completely but for the survival of a few court ballets. The semi-commercial type of State ballet unfortunately tended to combine the disadvantage of both the other types.

We are concerned here only with ballet in the modern sense of the word— the self-sufficient ballet d'action, the mute equivalent of opera and drama—and not with earlier theatrical forms such as ballet de cour, masque, ballet à entrées and opera-ballet, in which danced divertissements were only one element in a miscellaneous entertainment.

2. WEAVER IN LONDON

As early as the second half of the seventeenth century various books[1] suggested the possibility of a new type of ballet which, like the pantomimes of ancient Rome, would consist of mime and expressive dancing, and would be capable of expressing a story without the help of words. These ideas became fashionable in the second decade of the eighteenth century, and a number of works[2] were published making similar suggestions—among them one by the English dancing master John Weaver (1673–1760). It is significant that Weaver was the only one of these writers professionally concerned with dancing, and it was this English dancing master who created the first pantomime-ballets putting into practice the theories expressed in the various books; in England, without a State ballet, Weaver had a freedom of action denied to his professional colleagues in France.

In 1702 Weaver composed the grotesque ballet *The Cheats of Scapin; or, the Tavern Bilkers*. It was no accident that the first self-sufficient English ballet was a comedy: the Elizabethan jig[3] had established a strong tradition of highly expressive professional comedy dancing, and during the seventeenth century the growing emphasis on the pantomimic and virtuosic elements in stage dancing gradually drew attention away from the sung dialogue and made it unnecessary. The result was that although technique and expressiveness improved, the dancing entertainments became rather formless. What Weaver did was to re-introduce a definite plot without re-introducing the sung dialogue of

---

[1] Abbé Michel de Pure, *Idée des Spectacles Anciens et Nouveaux* (Paris, 1669); Isaac Vossius, *De Poematum cantu et viribus Rythmi* (Oxford, 1673); C. F. Menestrier, *Des Ballets Anciens et Modernes selon les Règles du Théâtre* (Paris, 1682).

[2] Pierre Jean Burette, *Treize Mémoires sur la Gymnastique des Anciens* (1710); John Weaver, *Essay towards an History of Dancing* (1712); Niccolo Calliachi, *De Ludis Scenicis Mimorum et Pantomimium* (1713); Abbé Jean Baptiste du Bos, *Réflexions sur la Poésie et sur la Peinture* (1719).

[3] The stage jig was a relatively short comic piece (normally performed as an after-piece at the end of a play) in which the performers sang their lines to one or more well-known tunes, and danced at the same time. (*Cf.* C. R. Baskerville, *The Elizabethan Jig and Related Song Drama*, pp. 77–163). The stage jig led forward to opera as well as to ballet.

the Elizabethan and Jacobean jigs. Like his predecessors he made considerable use of ideas from the Commedia dell'Arte.

Weaver next moved on to serious large-scale pantomime-ballets inspired by the pantomimes of ancient Rome, beginning with *The Loves of Mars and Venus* and *Perseus and Andromeda*; between 1717 and 1733 he produced a series of such pantomime-ballets, taking as his themes precisely those myths used by the Greek pantomime dancers working in ancient Rome.[1] The principal dancers employed by Weaver were the English danseuse Hester Santlow and the great French dancer Louis Dupré; Weaver himself danced only demi-caractère and grotesque rôles; the corps de ballet was English. Performances were given either at Drury Lane Theatre or Lincoln's Inn Fields Theatre. Weaver founded a tradition which continues to the present day in the Christmas pantomime, but unfortunately the self-sufficient pantomime-ballet or ballet d'action did not survive in England for lack of a court ballet company to preserve it during periods of decadence, and had to be revived from time to time by foreign maîtres de ballet.

3. SALLÉ: PARIS AND LONDON

The next important stage in the evolution of the ballet d'action came about through the collaboration of a French dancer-choreographer of genius (Marie Sallé, 1705–56) and a great English theatrical manager and mime (John Rich, ca. 1692–1761).

During nearly fifty years of theatrical management—first at Lincoln's Inn Fields and then at the theatre which he constructed at Covent Garden—Rich produced a large number of plays and ballad operas, but he had his greatest and most consistent success in the field of pantomime. Like other managers of the day he imported French dancers from Paris: while still in her 'teens Sallé danced in divertissements inserted between the acts of plays produced by Rich and also in his pantomimes. One such pantomime was *Apollo and Daphne, or the Burgomaster Tricked* (1726): Marie Sallé danced the part of Apollo (in the guise of Pierrot) and her sister danced Daphne, while in the divertissement which ended the pantomime Marie Sallé danced Zephire and her brother danced Flore.

Sallé was trained by the leading danseuse of the Paris Opéra, Françoise Prévost, but rather than dance at the Opéra she preferred to dance at Covent

[1] Pantomime originated in Magna Graecia, in South Italy, and later it became immensely popular in Rome; the great pantomime dancers working in Rome were nearly all Greeks. The pantomime dancers used those themes of Graeco-Roman mythology which were best suited for choreographic representation. A choir sang the words, while the pantomime dancers represented all the rôles.

Garden for Rich and in Paris at the fair theatre managed by her uncle Francisque Moylin, one of the most successful Harlequins and managers among the *forains* of the day. All such managers had a hard time in Paris because of the opposition of the directors of the Comédie Française and the Opéra (who intervened to get fair theatres closed down whenever their competition became serious), and it was partly for this reason that the ballet d'action was evolved in London rather than Paris.[1]

Sallé joined the Paris Opéra in 1727. She had the powerful support of her teacher Prévost, and, in spite of intrigues against her, went rapidly to the top in company with Camargo (another Prévost pupil). Though Sallé had great success with critics and the public, the rigid conventions of the Opéra gave her little scope for creative work, and in 1730 she returned to Rich in London. By this time she had aroused the interest of some of the greatest French writers of the day: they understood what she was trying to do, and gave her what support they could. Fontenelle, for example, wrote for her a letter of introduction to Montesquieu in London explaining why she had been driven to leave the Opéra:

> The charming dancing and above all the strict morals of the little *Aristide* have displeased her companions, which is normal, and even the masters, which would be senseless, if they did not have mistresses among her companions.[2]

She returned to the Opéra in 1731. Conditions were just as crippling as before, and after less than a year she left once again. This time she stayed in Paris, and made an attempt to show up the Opéra by dancing with the Comédiens Italiens (who performed a French adaptation of Commedia dell'Arte). She began rehearsals with them, and news of this caused great excitement in Paris; but at the last minute M. de Maurepas, Master of the King's Household, warned Sallé that if she did not abandon her project of dancing with the Italiens she would go to prison. Sallé reacted to this piece of news by returning to London, taking with her as her partner the brilliant young Opéra dancer Malter. (Her brother had just died.)

The company which Rich assembled to support her was a strong one. Apart from Sallé and Malter it included the great French danseur Louis Dupré and a number of lesser-known French and English dancers of both sexes. Working with this company Sallé composed two ballets d'action, *Pygmalion*

---

[1] The managers of patent theatres in London were just as ruthless in invoking their patents to suppress dangerous competition as their opposite numbers in Paris, but in London it was possible for a man like Rich to get control of a patent, whereas in Paris it would have been unthinkable for a man like Moylin to be allowed to buy the concession of a subsidized Royal institution like the Opéra.

[2] *Oevres complètes de Fontenelle* (1758), Vol. XI, p. 121—quoted by Emile Dacier, *Mlle Sallé* (Paris 1909), p. 59.

and *Bacchus et Ariane*, which took London by storm and represented a turning-point in ballet history. In Sallé's own dancing in these ballets we can trace the emergence of the great French tradition of the ballet d'action. In *Bacchus et Ariane* the London correspondent of the *Mercure de France* found

> the expressions and sentiments . . . of the profoundest grief, despair and utter dejection; in a word, all the great passions perfectly declaimed by means of dances, attitudes and gestures suggested by the position of a woman who is abandoned by the man she loves.[1]

Noverre later gave the highest possible praise to Sallé's "simple and touching graces", describing her dancing as full of feeling, lightness and finesse and her facial expressions as "noble, sensitive and *spirituelle*".[2]

Unfortunately Sallé, through no fault of her own, became embroiled in the existing war between two operatic factions in London. In an effort to prop up his declining fortunes Handel introduced ballets starring her into his operas, and this led to her being hissed when she danced in a ballet of her own composition in Handel's opera *Alcina* (1735). This regrettable cabal (very characteristic of the London theatre of the day) caused Sallé to abandon the idea of continuing her career in London; she returned to the Opéra, but found no opportunity of making the major reforms needed to establish a sound tradition of ballet at this institution, and accordingly retired on a pension from the King five years later, at the ridiculously early age of thirty-three. In spite of all obstacles, however, she managed during her last five years at the Opéra to compose a number of dramatic pas de deux and also some whole scenes of dancing in various operas which were in effect ballets d'action, thus continuing the genre she had established in London with the help of John Rich.

4. NOVERRE: PARIS, LONDON, STUTTGART, VIENNA

As Emile Dacier has pointed out,[3] Noverre was well aware of the importance of these scenes of dancing composed by Sallé. Jean Georges Noverre (1727–1809), the next genius of the ballet d'action, was profoundly influenced by Sallé. He did not begin to frequent the Opéra until 1745, five years after her retirement from the Opéra, but at this time she was still appearing in command per-

---

[1] *Mercure de France*, March 16, 1734 (as translated by H. Saxe Wyndham in *Annals of Covent Garden Theatre*, Vol. I, p. 44).
[2] *Lettres sur les Arts Imitateurs* (Paris, 1807), Vol. II, p. 103.
[3] Emile Dacier, *Mlle Sallé*, p. 172; *see also* Noverre, *Lettres sur les Arts Imitateurs* (Paris, 1807). Vol. I, p. 271.

formances at the royal theatre at Versailles, and he often watched her daily practices at her home.[1]

Noverre also came into contact with the new Anglo-French tradition of ballet-pantomime through his teacher Louis Dupré, who had danced in the ballet-pantomimes of both Weaver and Sallé. Moreover, Noverre had an invaluable opportunity of working under the direct guidance of Sallé herself when the manager Jean Monnet obtained the concession for the Opéra Comique at the Foire St. Laurent in 1743, and included among his productions ballets composed by Dupré, Lany and Sallé. These productions had music by the greatest French composer of the day (Rameau), costumes by the greatest French designer-painter of the day (Boucher), and libretti by Favart (the father of French opéra comique). Noverre, aged sixteen, was brought in by his teacher Dupré, and was one of the small company of dancers taking part in this memorable season. Monnet's productions (vaudevilles, parodies, operas, short ballets, etc.) had a vitality sadly lacking at the Opéra, and attracted the public away from the Opéra; the Opéra reacted in its usual fashion, arranging for Monnet's concession to be cancelled and thus crippling the development of the ballet d'action in France.

In 1752 Monnet once again obtained the concession of the Opéra Comique, and this time employed as his maître de ballet Noverre. Noverre composed for Monnet a number of large-scale spectacular ballets, one of which (*Ballet Chinois*) had enormous success and made Noverre famous—though he was slow in coming to maturity as a choreographer, and his ballets were still little more than large-scale divertissements. When Garrick brought him to London in 1753 Noverre might well have been inspired by the greater freedom of work in London and by the London audience (not to mention Garrick's superb miming) to come to maturity as a composer of ballets d'action, just as Sallé had done two decades earlier; but the anti-French feeling in London caused by the war between England and France made it impossible for Noverre to make satisfactory contact with the audience, and creative work was impossible under such conditions. He actually composed his first ballet d'action in Lyons, after leaving London. In Lyons, however, opportunities for balletic composition were meagre, and Noverre did not reach full maturity until 1760, when he was given the post of maître de ballet by the Duke of Württemberg and began to work under almost ideal conditions. Then at last he was able to put to good use what he had learned from Sallé and Garrick.

Noverre's stay at Stuttgart was of great historical importance, for he established there—beyond the reach of the Opéra—a magnificent French company, attracting almost all the best French dancers and training them to interpret rôles in ballets d'action rather than exploit their virtuosity and per-

[1] Noverre, *Lettres sur les Arts Imitateurs*, Vol. II, p. 103.

sonality. (Like Russian ballet in the twentieth century, French ballet could only come to full maturity outside France.) Noverre's company included twenty principal dancers and a corps de ballet of 100. One of Noverre's best pupils at Stuttgart was the danseuse Nancy Lévier, who later had sensational success as the heroine of Angiolini's great ballet *Semiramide*.

Duke Carl Eugen was fanatically devoted to the theatre. He lavished all the resources of his country on magnificent productions of opera and ballet, and employed many of the finest artists of the day: in addition to Noverre these included the Italian composer Jommelli, the Italian stage designer and machinist Servandoni, and the French designer Boquet. The performances were staged entirely for the benefit of Carl Eugen and his guests from all over Europe; the people of Württemberg (who paid for them) saw little of them. Naturally they began to complain bitterly, and eventually Carl Eugen had to cut down his outrageously extravagant expenditure; nevertheless his support of Noverre for several years made him one of the most important patrons in the whole history of ballet. But for him Noverre could never have created *Medée et Jason*, and his famous *Letters* might have been only of academic interest. Carl Eugen was only one of a large number of German princes who spent money lavishly on all the arts at this time: his distinction was that he spent his money on a man of genius.

At the same time that Noverre was coming to maturity in Stuttgart, Count Durazzo, Intendant of the Austrian Imperial Theatres, was making theatrical history by helping Gluck to revolutionize opera and commissioning ballets d'action of the highest interest from the maître de ballet Gasparo Angiolini (1722–96), the composer Gluck, and the librettist Calzabigi (who was just as interested in the reform of ballet as the reform of opera, and had, in fact, written a book on the subject). Durazzo was a personage unique in theatrical history— a director of court theatres who had not only the vision and judgment to bring together in a well-balanced team the most important creative artists of the day, but also the ability to provide them with satisfactory conditions of work and protect them from the intrigues which normally kill all creative vitality in a State theatre. The quality of Durazzo's work can be judged from the fact that Angiolini, while working as a member of a team at Vienna, was able to produce two ballets *Don Juan* and *Semiramide* which challenged comparison with the best of Noverre's ballets, whereas working in other cities Angiolini was quite unable to compete with Noverre. (Noverre was the type of universal genius who matures slowly but achieves such mastery of all branches of his subject that he needs no guidance—only adequate financial support and freedom from sabotage.)

After Angiolini left Vienna for St. Petersburg, Durazzo brought Noverre to Vienna (1767), showing admirable artistic understanding by allowing Noverre to bring with him from Stuttgart a number of his best dancers and pupils; the two Imperial theatres of Vienna already had good-sized ballet companies, but Noverre could not put his ideas into practice without dancers trained by him and accustomed to the interpretation of dramatic rôles in his ballets.

From the beginning of his career Noverre had dreamed of becoming maître de ballet of the Paris Opéra; this was natural enough, for Noverre was born in Paris and grew up there. When his Austrian pupil Marie Antoinette[1] became Queen of France he at last had the opportunity of realizing this dream; Marie Antoinette did, in fact, obtain this appointment for him, and then very wisely the King of France appointed a new administrator of the Opéra with the task of introducing an impartial régime and breaking down the rigid patterns of intrigue which ensured that opportunities bore little or no relation to talent. Unfortunately the efforts of the new administrator and of Noverre himself were almost powerless against the intrigues within the Opéra; Noverre's projects for ballets were either ruthlessly distorted or rejected outright, arrangements were made for his productions to be viciously attacked in the Press, dancers refused to take the rôles he assigned to them, new ballets had to be performed with old scenery, and so on. Noverre tried to conciliate his attackers by making a large number of concessions, but without effect. His worst enemy was Maximilien Gardel, who had expected to be the next maître de ballet by right of seniority. It made no difference to Gardel that Noverre was a genius; to Gardel he was a "foreigner", and no trick was too mean for Gardel to use to drive Noverre to leave. To make things worse, Noverre had no chance to show the full range of his talents with the dancers of the Opéra, whose idea of dancing was something completely physical, and who had no idea of the interpretation of rôles—nor any desire to learn anything about this.

The intrigues against Noverre succeeded, as they were bound to do: Noverre's opponents knew every trick of the game, and it is always much easier to destroy an artist's creative ability than to foster it. After three years Noverre gave up the unequal fight and began to make arrangements for his retirement.

After leaving the Opéra Noverre came once again to England (1781), and enjoyed an Indian summer during which he revived all the greatest ballets of his long career as well as producing a number of new ones. He had enormous success with the London public—in spite of the fact that England and France were once again at war—and attracted to London all the best dancers of the day, just as before he had attracted them to Stuttgart. Noverre's old friend Garrick had just retired, but Noverre was supported in turn by two theatrical managers (Taylor and O'Reilly) and worked happily at two of the most important London theatres, Drury Lane and the King's Theatre.

[1] In addition to his appointment as maître de ballet of the Austrian Imperial theatres Noverre was dancing master to the Austrian Imperial family.

By the time Noverre retired (1794) the ballet d'action was firmly established at a number of the principal opera-houses of Europe; even the Paris Opéra was beginning to follow the lead given by Noverre. The tradition established by Weaver, Sallé, Hilverding,[1] Noverre and Angiolini was continued by a number of outstanding maîtres de ballet—all of them pupils of Noverre or Angiolini or both. Unfortunately the new generation of maîtres de ballet had to struggle against exactly the same obstacles as their teachers, for the organization of the theatre was ill-adapted to the preservation of a great tradition of ballet. Only one of the great maîtres de ballet of the generation which followed Noverre (Vigano) was able to make a career for himself in the leading opera-house of his own country, and this was due to the fortunate accident that an admirer left him a fortune; the other great maîtres de ballet had to look outside the capitals of their own countries for the recognition and support they deserved.

5. DIDELOT: LONDON AND ST. PETERSBURG

Jean Dauberval (1742–1806) was the first great maître de ballet to carry on the Noverre tradition. He seemed to be in a very strong position, for he made a great name for himself as a dancer at the Paris Opéra, and was appointed assistant maître de ballet there; but the maître de ballet of the Paris Opéra, Pierre Gardel, intrigued against Dauberval just as his brother Maximilien had intrigued against Noverre, and in despair of finding any opportunity of putting his ideas into practice at the Opéra Dauberval retired from the Opéra with a pension in 1783. He returned to Bordeaux and succeeded in making this city a ballet centre of some importance, in spite of the fact that the resources of the municipal theatre were much less than those available in Paris. He specialized in a genre of pathetic comedy which was his own invention; and his most famous ballet *La Fille Mal Gardée* (1786) still survives in various versions.

Noverre's greatest pupil was probably Charles Didelot (1767–1836). Didelot was trained first by Dauberval (who was twenty-five years his senior), then by Noverre, and then by Auguste Vestris (the greatest male dancer of the day). Didelot became a dancer of outstanding ability, and was engaged by Noverre during the latter's final period in London: in this way Didelot was able to assimilate Noverre's ideas and methods of composition. Though Didelot danced at the Paris Opéra with great success as a guest artist, his exceptional talent aroused the usual intrigues against him, and he was not taken into the permanent company. He had his first chance to compose ballets in London while dancing for Noverre there, and had such success that he was commissioned to compose a number of ballets in London after Noverre's retirement.

[1] Angiolini's teacher.

Like Sallé, Didelot came to maturity as a maître de ballet in London, backed by the manager of the King's Theatre and encouraged and stimulated by the London audience. His ballet *Zéphire et Flore* (composed in London in 1796) made him famous, and represented a major step forward in the development of the ballet d'action.

Didelot brought together in a new synthesis the contributions to ballet of his three great teachers, Noverre, Dauberval and Vestris. From Noverre he took the basic idea of the ballet d'action; from Dauberval he took ideas for comedy in ballet; and from Vestris (who was devoted to pure dancing) he learned to avoid Noverre's mistake of over-weighting ballets with mime at the expense of dancing. Noverre had made London the centre of the ballet world when he arrived there for the second time in 1781, and under Didelot it kept this position up to the beginning of the nineteenth century.

Both Drury Lane and Covent Garden had resident corps de ballet, and an academy of dancing was founded in London to provide dancers for the various London theatres, though soloists were still imported from France. The ballet d'action tradition continued by Noverre and Didelot in London was as much English as French; in fact Didelot introduced scenes of comedy into his serious ballets in a manner which was typically English and quite foreign to French theatrical traditions. If an English court ballet had been founded at this time, with Didelot as director, England would undoubtedly have continued to be a major centre of ballet, even if the quality of the new ballets declined in the same way as elsewhere. But the English monarchs missed the opportunity, and ballet in England lost most of its artistic importance after the departure of Didelot.

In 1801 Didelot accepted an invitation to go to St. Petersburg; he composed some ballets there in the next ten years, but his creative output was limited by the fact that he had not been officially appointed maître de ballet, and there were in fact two official maîtres de ballet over his head—Valberg (Wahlberg?) and Auguste. Didelot was also crippled by the fact that there were very few dancers in Russia capable of doing justice to his ideas. He therefore concentrated mainly on teaching; by about 1807 some wonderful artists were beginning to emerge from the Imperial school, and he began serious creative work with a production of his London masterpiece *Zéphire et Flore* and a new version of Noverre's masterpiece *Medée et Jason*.

Didelot left St. Petersburg in 1811, hoping to achieve the recognition which was his due in Paris by producing *Zéphire et Flore* at the Opéra: needless to say he encountered the most vicious intrigues (led by Pierre Gardel, who was jealous of the fame of *Zéphire et Flore*), and negotiations dragged on for years. Finally Didelot was granted permission to produce his ballet at the Opéra on condition that he payed all the expenses out of his own pocket *in advance*! The ballet was a great success, and he was offered an engagement at the Opéra. Very wisely he declined this invitation: he could hardly hope to succeed where Noverre and Dauberval had failed.

Intentionally or not, Didelot made possible his return to Russia under favourable conditions by leaving Russia when he did. The standard of choreography and teaching declined considerably in his absence, and when he returned in 1815 he was able to force the Director of the Imperial Theatres (Prince Tufiakin) to agree to a contract which gave him complete control of the ballet. Didelot was at last reasonably safe from intrigue, and composed a long series of fine ballets with the help of the wonderful dancers emerging from the school. Russian ballet now reached such a high standard that there was no need to import soloists from abroad, though the Directorate of the Imperial Theatres forced Didelot to import a few male dancers; the Russian ballerinas were so far superior to those available elsewhere that there could be no question of importing any ballerinas. There were a number of great artists among the Russian dancers of the day—above all the incomparable Istomina, celebrated by Pushkin in *Eugene Onegin*.[1] Didelot was very proud of his Russian pupils, and became to a considerable extent Russianized, though he never learned to speak Russian well. (This was unnecessary, for all well-educated Russians spoke French, and some spoke French better than Russian.) Didelot even composed Russian ballets based on poems by Pushkin; in fact the great tradition of Russian ballet dates from this period.

In spite of his iron-clad contract Didelot suffered considerably from the persecution of successive Directors of the Imperial Theatres: these were titled gentlemen whose appointment came about as the net resultant of court intrigues, and who had no particular knowledge of, or liking for, the theatre. Prince Tufiakin (who was interested chiefly in having affairs with the danseuses) soon began to regret bitterly his decision to recall Didelot, for the great maître de ballet insisted on doing things his own way, and resisted any interference from corrupt and ignorant court officials like Tufiakin.

Tufiakin's successor, Prince Gagarin, was even more fanatical in his persecution of Didelot; he could not simply dismiss Didelot (who had a strong contract and was the idol of the dancers and the public), but in 1829, two years after his appointment, he devised a peculiarly mean and cynical trick for bringing low the great man. One day he remarked to Didelot that the corps de ballet dancers were slow in changing their clothes; Didelot paid little attention to this remark, and at once Gagarin ordered Didelot to be arrested. In this way he forced Didelot to resign. Didelot was broken-hearted: by this time he was completely Russianized, and the Russian ballet was his own creation. Excluded

---

[1] In most cases I have transliterated Russian names phonetically, using the corresponding English spelling, but where a name is very well known (e.g. Eugene Onegin, Tchaikovsky, Nijinsky, Petrouchka) I have retained the familiar spelling.

from the ballet, he lost interest in life, and finally died in Kiev in 1837: in effect he had been murdered by Gagarin. His dismissal had very serious consequences, and Russian ballet degenerated rapidly, though Didelot's work had been done so well that some of the great tradition survived. (His ballet *Zéphire et Flore* survived in the repertoire in St. Petersburg right up to the beginning of the twentieth century.)

Though no giant like Didelot, the Italian maître de ballet Vincenzo Galeotti (1733–1816) did for the Royal Danish Ballet what Didelot did for the Imperial Russian Ballet. Galeotti studied first under Angiolini and then under Noverre; having no opportunity of making a career for himself in his native Florence he went to Copenhagen, where he became maître de ballet of the Royal Ballet in 1775. He worked steadily in Copenhagen for forty-one years, giving the Royal Danish Ballet a solid grounding in the great tradition of the ballet d'action—a tradition which it has never lost. He died in harness at the age of eighty-three, having just completed his last ballet *Macbeth*.

6. MILAN: VIGANO AND BLASIS

In spite of the fact that Italians have a remarkable national flair for classical dancing—the classical technique was largely developed by Italian maîtres de ballet working in France, and a high proportion of the greatest ballerinas have been Italian—the concentration on vocal acrobatics in Italian opera-houses in the eighteenth century led to the almost complete elimination of dancing from these theatres. Milan, however, was for a variety of political reasons very much under the influence of French taste, and when Noverre introduced the ballet d'action to Milan in 1771[1] the Milanese gave it a warm welcome: his ballet *Medée et Jason* made a particularly strong impression. From this time onwards Milan has remained the main centre of Italian ballet.

Noverre worked at the court theatre of Milan, the Teatro Ducale. The destruction of this theatre in 1776 led to the construction of a new theatre to take its place, La Scala, which was opened in 1778. La Scala was not a court theatre, though it was constructed on land donated by Maria Teresa, Empress of Austria and Duchess of Milan: it was in fact constructed, controlled and subsidized by the holders of the season tickets of its boxes. Every box was owned by a small group of wealthy people, each of whom was entitled to the use of the box at one performance of each production during the season. The actual management was delegated by the society of box-owners to commercial

---

[1] Northern Italy, including Milan, was under Austrian rule at this time. Noverre produced ballets in Milan during the period 1771–75 while still in the service of the Austrian Imperial family. During this same period Angiolini produced ballets at Venice and Padua as well as Milan; there seemed to be no interest in ballet in the more southerly parts of Italy.

impresarios. From 1806 to 1918 La Scala was a semi-state theatre, being owned and subsidized by its joint proprietors, the government (later the municipality) and the box-owners. Since each production was only given often enough to be seen by each of the box-owners, there was no provision for maintaining a repertoire of old ballets as in the court theatres: the system worked well enough for opera (which can always be revived from the score when required) but it was quite unsuited to ballet. As a result La Scala was able to maintain a tradition of classical dancing, but not of ballet.

A very large number of maîtres de ballet were employed at La Scala from 1778 onwards (including Angiolini from 1780 to 1782), but none of them was employed for long: what the box-owners wanted was variety. In fact conditions were hopelessly unsuitable for the emergence of an Italian tradition of ballet d'action until Salvatore Vigano (1769–1821) was appointed maître de ballet in 1812: with the fortune left him by his admirer he was able to put his ideas into action without having to worry about the complex patterns of intrigue which plagued his predecessors.

Vigano came of a dancing family (his father was maître de ballet in Naples), but he first came into contact with the ballet d'action when Dauberval took him to London during Noverre's final period there. Like Didelot, Vigano assimilated the achievements of Noverre and Dauberval and then struck out in a new direction: during his years of creative activity at La Scala (1812–21) he made Milan the equal of St. Petersburg as a home of ballet, and these two cities were rival centres of the ballet world. Though inspired by Anglo-French models his *coreodrammi* were far in advance of anything to be seen in France or England at this time.

Vigano's contribution to the art of ballet was to efface the sharp distinction between dancing and mime, and to make every movement fully expressive of the emotion of the moment and the character of the rôle portrayed by the dancer, while preserving harmony between the interlocking movements of all the different characters on the stage: from a technical point of view his revolutionary advances in choreography anticipated the corresponding advances made in opera by Verdi towards the end of the nineteenth century in *Otello* and *Falstaff*. Naturally Vigano's new style required a great deal of rehearsal, for every tiny detail had to be worked out gradually by a process of trial and error and patiently taught to the dancers. (Verdi took three years to compose *Otello*, working quietly in his study; Vigano worked with equal patience and determination on his ballets at La Scala, using live dancers and spending many weeks on a single scene.)

Vigano was a master of every element of ballet and theatrical technique, and his productions were *Gesamtkunstwerke* (works of arts with every detail taking its proper place in a harmonious total effect) such as the world has rarely seen. His designer was Sanquirico, perhaps the finest of all the nineteenth-century stage designers—Sanquirico, who reigned at La Scala from 1806 to 1832 and was one of its chief glories. Vigano's choreographic ideas were so complex that he did not usually attempt to commission the music for them from a single composer (though he commissioned the first version of *Prometeo*[1] from Beethoven): his normal practice was to select exactly the music which fitted his ideas from existing music by any one of a number of composers (Haydn, Mozart, Beethoven, Rossini, Sponini, etc.) and if necessary to compose melodies himself. If constructed in a crude manner such a patchwork would have been intolerably "bitty"; but Vigano was a very skilful musician, and won the respect of the most sensitive spectators.

Vigano's achievements at La Scala were backed up by the foundation of a school attached to the theatre—the Imperial and Royal Academy of Dancing and Pantomime. The students of the school provided a steady stream of dancers to the theatre, though by no means all the dancers in the Scala company came from the school; like other great maîtres de ballet Vigano attracted to his company the finest dancers from all the schools. A considerable number of fine artists came to maturity through being rehearsed by him and dancing in his ballets—notably Antonia Miller, Antonia Pallerini, Maria Bummel-Vigano, Giulia Vigano, Carlo Blasis and Salvatore Taglioni. Nevertheless Stendhal regretted that Vigano did not have at his disposal the leading dancers of the Paris Opéra, feeling that the combination of the best French dancing and Vigano's choreographic genius would produce a perfect ensemble.

Though Vigano's genius was fully recognized in Italy during his lifetime, and his death was deeply mourned, the organization of La Scala made it impossible for his ballets to remain in the repertoire for long after his death. After his ballets had disappeared from the repertoire La Scala ceased to have major importance as a home of ballet, though its school continued to turn out good dancers, and the demand for dancers from La Scala encouraged teachers to continue working in private schools in Milan: the dancers emerging from the Scala school and the private schools of Milan provided stars for most of the opera-houses of Europe (including La Scala) during the second half of the nineteenth century.

By far the most important of the Milan teachers was Carlo Blasis (1797–1878), who developed a new Italian school out of the existing French school: Blasis' own original contribution was a wonderful purity of line and a harmonious balance between the angles of the limbs.[2] Blasis' early training was entirely French (under Dauberval in Bordeaux and Pierre Gardel at the Paris Opéra), and though he was born in Italy he was billed in Italy as a "ballerino francese" when first he danced there.

---

[1] Vigano produced his first version of *Prometeo* in 1801, before he came to La Scala.
[2] *See* Carlo Blasis, *The Code of Terpsichore* (London, 1830), p. 97.

Marie Sallé in Paris in 1732

Above: Didelot and Mlle Théodore in *Amphion and Thalia* at the Pantheon, London (1791)

Salvatore Vigano and his wife Maria Medina in the opera *Arianna* (on tour in Central Europe *ca.* 1795)

Blasis, who had enormous talent as a dancer, had such success at the Paris Opéra that he aroused the usual jealous intrigues against himself, and left in disgust. For fourteen years he performed in Italy as a solo dancer (mainly at La Scala), but then a leg injury made him abandon dancing and concentrate on teaching and choreography. He acquired such fame through his teaching and his books that he was appointed Director of the Scala Academy in 1838. During the next fifteen years he trained a large number of great dancers, both at the Scala Academy and at his private school.

7. PARIS: THE SO-CALLED ROMANTIC BALLET

The death of Vigano in 1821 and the enforced retirement of Didelot in 1829 brought to an end the golden age of the ballet d'action. The thirties and forties of the nineteenth century saw a tremendous increase in the quantity of ballet, but the popularity of ballet was based almost entirely on the star-appeal of a few great ballerinas; male dancing almost ceased to exist, and the average standard of choreography remained at a low level.

In this new period the Paris Opéra, which had previously been moribund—giving innumerable repeat performances of ballets which had been dull even to start with—suddenly became a centre of lively activity because of the changes brought about by the new Director, Dr. Louis Véron. The July Revolution of 1830 brought to the throne of France the "bourgeois monarch" Louis Philippe, and in the new political climate the State abandoned many of the traditional attributes of royalty, including the royal ballet. Even in the eighteenth century the concession for the Opéra had been farmed out by the King to private impresarios, but he did not hesitate to change directors when things went badly, and the fact that he often ordered command performances at the private royal theatre at Versailles naturally had its effect on the artistic policy of the Opéra. Moreover, the Opéra came under the general control of the royal official in charge of the King's Household and the Département of Paris; this official appointed an Inspector-General of the Opéra to supervise all the internal and external affairs of the Opéra. After 1830 the Opéra continued to receive its subsidy, but it had no direct connection with the court, and its directors had no need to take into consideration the taste of the monarch.

Dr. Véron (who got his start in business selling patent medicine) ran the Opéra on a strictly commercial basis, exploiting the star system to the utmost and making so much money that he was able to retire with a fortune after four years. Dr. Véron's policy in regard to opera took the form of encouraging romantic operas with even more lavish ballets and scenic spectacle than was already the fashion in Paris; he took over the Opéra in 1831, and in the same year produced Meyerbeer's first Paris opera, *Robert le Diable*, with libretto by Scribe and a mysterious ballet scene in which Taglioni led a number of white-clad nuns in a haunted abbey. The ballet scene in this opera gave rise in the following year to the production of a whole ballet in similar vein, *La Sylphide*, with choreography by Taglioni's father, Filippo Taglioni. This type of super-natural romanticism, which had originated in Macpherson's *Ossian* (1762), and in the horrific novels of English writers like "Monk" Lewis and Mrs. Radcliffe, was already somewhat old-fashioned; but the Paris Opéra had been cut off from the major developments in ballet for so long that the stilted and conventional romanticism of *La Sylphide* and its numerous progeny seemed to the patrons of the Opéra a daring innovation. (Much the same thing happened a century later, when Lifar introduced the late-Diaghilev style.) Though this period is commonly known as the Romantic Ballet, the ballets produced at the Opéra during the period represented a pseudo-classical adaptation of roman-ticism rather than romanticism itself; the stories were romantic, but every detail of choreography, music, décor and costume was regulated by formula, and there was no place for the daring flights of imagination which were typical of genuine romanticism. In fact the so-called romantic ballets of this period stood in much the same relationship to the genuinely romantic ballets of men like Vigano and Didelot that the stodgy Meyerbeer opera *Robert le Diable* stood to Weber's opera *Der Freischütz*.[1]

Though the standard of choreography at the Opéra was low, Véron and his successors did break through the crippling system of casting through intrigue and seniority, and employed at the Opéra all the greatest ballerinas of the day —Taglioni, Cerito, Grisi, Elssler and Grahn. Not one of these great dancers was trained at the Opéra, where the French school was beginning to fossilize.[2] One effect of the introduction of a new system of commercial management was to make it almost impossible for the Opéra to preserve ballets in its repertoire, but it had the great merit of bringing some fresh air into the dusty corridors of this institution.

Like many theatre directors in the twentieth century, Dr. Véron and his successors at the Opéra had little understanding of choreography, and were content to present the great ballerinas of the day in starring vehicles which were designed simply to show the technique and personality of the star in question:

[1] The great maîtres de ballet were keenly sensitive to changes in the Zeitgeist, and the romantic tendencies which began to appear in English and German literature in the second half of the eighteenth century (becoming dominant in the early years of the nineteenth century) were clearly apparent in the ballets d'action of Didelot, Vigano and Galeotti early in the nineteenth century.

[2] Marie Taglioni was the daughter of a Milanese maître de ballet and was trained by him: Grisi and Cerito were dancers trained in Milan by Blasis, Guillet and others; Grahn was a Danish dancer trained by Bournonville; Elssler was a Viennese dancer trained first by the French teacher Aumer in Vienna and then for five years in Italy as she toured with an Italian company.

the stories were cut to a pattern, the characters were flat and stereotyped, the male dancer was reduced to a mere support, the corps de ballet was used mainly to decorate the stage, and the music was appallingly banal. This star-system paid well for a time, but in the long run it almost killed the art of ballet.

8. PERROT: PARIS, LONDON, ST. PETERSBURG

It was almost by accident that the Opéra presented in 1841 *Giselle*, in which the standard of choreography was far above the usual level. Jules Perrot (1810–90), the man responsible for the high standard of choreography in *Giselle*, had managed to make contact with the great tradition of the ballet d'action partly through his teacher August Vestris (who had danced in the ballets of Noverre in Stuttgart and in Paris), and partly through the Didelot ballet *Zéphire et Flore* (which was revived in 1834 at the Opéra to provide a suitable vehicle for the combined talents of Taglioni and Perrot).[1] Being a great male dancer the young Perrot was an anachronism, and for this reason it was necessary to revive an old ballet to find for him a male rôle of any importance. In spite of his great success at the Opéra, Perrot was disgusted by the intrigues within it and left in despair in 1835, like others among the most sensitive of the Opéra dancers from Sallé onwards. But it was not merely intrigue which induced him to leave; he had fallen under the spell of the Istrian dancer Carlotta Grisi (whom he had met in Naples in 1833) and wanted to join her. She had already been trained in the French school in Milan by Blasis and Guillet, though she had rather neglected her technique after leaving La Scala; Perrot took her in hand and made her the greatest interpretative artist of the day.

Perrot and Grisi had great success in London, Vienna, Munich, Naples and Milan, appearing mainly in pas de deux composed by Perrot himself. In 1840 the two great dancers reached Paris, where they danced in an opera-ballet *Le Zingaro*, produced at the Théâtre de la Renaissance by Anténor Joly (who had built the theatre two years previously). Joly had already infuriated the Comédie Française by his successful production of Victor Hugo's pioneer romantic drama *Ruy Blas*, and his production of *Le Zingaro* with Perrot and Grisi was no less distasteful to the Opéra: as usual arrangements were rapidly made to have his theatre closed.

Grisi was now taken on at the Opéra; Perrot was not taken on, being in disgrace for leaving in 1835. It is not known exactly how Perrot came to be entrusted with the most important sections of the choreography of *Giselle* (including the whole of Grisi's rôle): Beaumont suggests that this may have

[1] He also seems in some way to have made contact with the Vigano tradition of *coreodramma* —perhaps through Grisi, who began her training at the Scala school when the Vigano tradition was not quite extinct.

been due to the intervention of the composer Adam, who was on very friendly terms with both Perrot and Grisi.[1] Certainly Grisi would have done everything in her power to arrange for her own rôle to be composed by Perrot, for she knew that he alone could show her talents to best advantage. Whatever the true explanation, the Director of the Opéra (Léon Pillet) took care to give the credit for the ballet to Coralli rather than to Perrot, who had had the effrontery to walk out six years previously.

In its book *Giselle* was to the last degree conventional. The second act (which represented an adaptation by the professional librettist Saint-Georges of a suggestion by Gautier) was based on the formula of the ballet blanc which had been standard ever since the production of *La Sylphide* in 1832. The first act (for which Saint-Georges was entirely responsible) followed the same formula as the first act of *La Sylphide*—a formula which could be traced back to the pastoral comedies of Dauberval, such as *La Fille Mal Gardée*. The mad scene at the end of the first act was similar to the mad scene in act I of Milon's ballet *Nina ou la Folle par Amour*, produced at the Opéra in 1813: this mad scene was in turn related to the mad scenes which were extremely common in the operas of the day.[2]

In spite of the conventionality of the book Perrot managed to treat the theme of the ballet with delightful freshness and spontaneity, and Grisi at last won in Paris the recognition due to her outstanding talents. Pillet now invited Perrot to discuss further productions; like many other theatre directors, however, he thought he knew exactly what the public wanted, and tried to force on Perrot trivial themes which would, in fact, have given no suitable opportunities to either Perrot or Grisi. Once again Perrot left the Opéra in disgust— this time never to return.

Giselle stood out in a very striking manner from the rest of the Opéra repertoire, just as *Zéphire et Flore* had done, and it was kept in the regular repertoire up to 1849, with Grisi invariably in the title rôle. After the retirement of Grisi the only dancer considered worthy of succeeding her in the title rôle was the French dancer Zina Richard, who had been trained in Russia and came to maturity in Russia under the eye of Perrot himself. Other Russian-trained ballerinas who continued the Perrot tradition in Paris were Muravieva (for whom *Giselle* was revived at the Opéra in 1863) and Grantsova (for whom it was revived at the Opéra in 1866). After 1868 *Giselle* was dropped from the Opéra repertoire, and the Opéra version was lost completely: the organization of the Opéra on a semi-commercial basis made impossible the preservation of even the greatest ballet created there.

[1] *The Ballet Called Giselle*, p. 23.
[2] The reason for the popularity of mad scenes in opera was the excuse they provided for elaborate displays of coloratura singing.

In London Perrot found the support he needed from Benjamin Lumley, manager of Her Majesty's Theatre. This remarkable man was by far the greatest operatic impresario of the day: he made London the centre of the operatic world, and even the directors of La Scala tried to lure him to Milan. He was no less successful in the field of ballet, employing Perrot as his maître de ballet from 1842 to 1848 and making London the centre of the ballet world once again. By the time he wrote his memoirs (*Reminiscences of the Opera,* 1864) ballet had degenerated and fallen out of favour, and he wrote relatively little of his relationship with Perrot; but they seem to have worked together in a friendly and creative way, just as Rich and Sallé had done over a century earlier. It was Lumley who suggested to Perrot the idea of *Esmeralda,* one of Perrot's finest ballets:

> I myself originally proposed the subject to Perrot, who at first rejected it as impracticable. Eventually, however, Perrot altered his opinion, and I frequently sat up with him the greater part of the night, in order to assist and encourage him in his labours.[1]

Another ballet which Lumley suggested to Perrot was *Faust.* Pleased with the great success in London of Perrot's new version of *Giselle* (a ballet based on a Yugoslav legend described by Heine), Lumley commissioned the book of a Faust ballet from Heine. Unfortunately Heine's script proved quite impracticable: even today audiences would not tolerate many of the incidents devised by Heine.[2] (Later Perrot made his own adaptation of the Faust legend and produced a highly successful ballet with this theme at La Scala.)

Unfortunately the best efforts of Perrot and Lumley did not suffice to retain the interest of the fickle and fashionable audience of the day in ballets d'action for more than a few years: all the public wanted was novelty, and this Lumley and Perrot provided with such items as *Le Pas de Quatre,* bringing together four of the greatest ballerinas of the day.

Perhaps Lumley's basic mistake was in bringing over Pugni from Paris as composer for the ballets: Lumley showed shrewd judgment in weighing up the musical value of the new operas of the day, but he accepted the idea current at the time that ballet music did not need to have the same stature as other types of music. He wrote of Pugni's music for *Esmeralda* that "for this style of composition his talents seem to have been peculiarly fitted".[3] In fact they were quite inadequate. At the beginning of the ballet, for example, the story demands blood-curdling music to suggest the ferocity and unruly gaiety of the Beggars, but Pugni's waltz is as pretty and respectable as Gounod's music for the Walpurgisnacht ballet in the opera *Faust.* There were good composers living at this

---

[1] Benjamin Lumley, *Reminiscences of the Opera,* p. 85.
[2] A translation of this script was published in London in 1952.
[3] Benjamin Lumley, *Reminiscences of the Opera,* p. 85.

time in various European countries, but because of the decadence of ballet none of them took any interest in this medium, and there were no composers of any stature working in England. The great success of a ballet produced in 1936 to the music of Berlioz (*La Symphonie Fantastique*) suggests that ballet in England might have taken a very different course if Lumley had invited Berlioz to London instead of Pugni. Even Adam would have been far preferable: one could not expect any audience to listen to many repetitions of a Pugni score. (*Esmeralda* has in fact remained in the repertoire in Russia up to the present day, because of the brilliance of the choreography, but this could only happen in a subsidized State ballet.)

All the great ballerinas of Perrot's day understood very well the difference between the quality of Perrot's choreography and that of nearly all other contemporary maîtres de ballet, and delighted to dance in his ballets whenever they had the chance to do so. When Elssler reached St. Petersburg in 1848 she hastened to make arrangements for Perrot to be invited to come there: corrupt versions of his ballets were being produced in Russia, but she preferred the real thing, and after Perrot arrived she danced almost entirely in his ballets. The same was true of Grisi, who succeeded Elssler in St. Petersburg in 1850.

Perrot had great success in Russia, producing his best ballets (*Esmeralda*, *Catarina*, *Faust*, *Giselle*, etc.) for Elssler and Grisi. The standard of training and performance of the Russian danseuses had declined since the enforced retirement of Didelot, but the Russian ballerinas were enormously stimulated by the work of Perrot himself in class and in rehearsal. A number of fine Russian danseuses came to maturity at this time—among them Prikhunova, whose grace and poetic arm-movements were worthy of Grisi.

In spite of his success in Russia, Perrot (like Noverre and Didelot before him) longed for recognition in his native Paris, and in 1851 he left Russia, apparently for good. At the Paris Opéra, however, the intrigues were just as hostile to talent as ever before, and Perrot found himself ruthlessly excluded. He therefore returned to St. Petersburg. In his absence the feeble ballets produced by Mazilier had emphasized the high quality of Perrot's compositions, and he had no difficulty in obtaining re-appointment as maître de ballet.

For a while things went well with Perrot, but after 1854 he began to suffer increasing persecution from the Director of the Imperial Theatres, Guédéonov —who hated Perrot for the same reasons that Tufiakin had hated Didelot, and did his best to force Perrot to resign. Instead of creating new ballets Perrot found himself ordered to spend his time rehearsing old ballets (work which an assistant might well have done) and producing trivial divertissements for insertion into Italian operas. This persecution had serious effects on Perrot, whose choreography had a lyrical and spontaneous quality, and who could not create except under good conditions. By nature he was adaptable and versatile

—in London he had shown himself perfectly willing to co-operate with Lumley by composing ballets such as *Le Pas de Quatre*—and at the command of Guédéonov he composed light-weight divertissements such as *La Débutante* and *La Rose, la Violette et le Papillon*. But there were some concessions he would not make, and Guédéonov hated him for his artistic integrity and independence of spirit. Things became even worse for Perrot in 1857, when Guédéonov retired after twenty-five years' service and was replaced by Saburov, who combined lack of interest in the theatre with intense interest in the danseuses: in fact his morals were much the same as those of the notorious Prince Tufiakin. Two years after Saburov's appointment Perrot was driven to despair by Saburov's stupidity and his tactics of persecution, and left Russia—in spite of the fact that he was only forty-eight, and could look for no other opportunities to continue his career outside Russia. After his departure ballet in Russia degenerated just as it did elsewhere in Europe.

9. BOURNONVILLE IN COPENHAGEN

The career of Auguste Bournonville (1805–79) moved on a parallel course to that of Perrot. He assimilated the ballet d'action tradition from his father, Antoine Bournonville (who was a pupil of Noverre, and was premier danseur under Galeotti in the Royal Danish Ballet); from Auguste Vestris, whose pupil he was at the same time as Perrot; and from the Galeotti ballets surviving in the Royal Danish Ballet's repertoire when he joined the company in 1830, after four years in the Paris Opéra. Bournonville became the absolute dictator of the Royal Danish Ballet, introducing the Vestris school of classical dancing and training a number of great dancers—notably Lucile Grahn. At the same time he began to compose a long series of ballets d'action strong enough to endure without loss of vitality long after his death: about ten of them still form the core of the Royal Danish repertoire. Though Bournonville had no successors of comparable stature, he had pupils well able to preserve the Vestris school of dancing, the choreography of his ballets, the proper spirit of execution of these ballets, and a tradition of powerful dramatic mime. Fortunately the Royal Danish Ballet, being a court ballet with a generous subsidy, was able to preserve its repertoire irrespective of the state of popular interest in ballet or the popularity of individual ballets.

Bournonville himself, however, suffered very much from the decline in popular interest. In the fifties of the nineteenth century, when Bournonville had been at work in Copenhagen for over two decades, Danish ballet began to suffer from the same influences that were destroying ballet in other European countries. Despairing of ballet in Denmark, Bournonville resigned his post in

Copenhagen; he went to Vienna in 1855 and Stockholm in 1860 in search of a more stimulating atmosphere and a more lively interest in ballet. His search was in vain, and he returned to Copenhagen in 1864. There he tried to re-awaken interest in ballet by all sorts of desperate means, and in fact his charming little ballet *Livjægerne paa Amager* (1871) had great success with the public. In 1874 he went to St. Petersburg and Moscow, hoping to get commissions for ballets. His efforts were in vain, and he returned once again to Copenhagen, drawing on the experiences of his Russian trip for his last ballet *Fra Sibirien til Moskou* (1877).

Bournonville's varied talents—his mastery of characterization and dramatic construction, his flair for national dances and complex patterns of group movement, his sense of humour, and his gift for keeping up interest by modulating from one mood to another—were seen at the their best in ballets such as *La Sylphide* (1836), *Brudefærden i Hardanger* (1853) and *Et Folkesagn* (1854): together with the corresponding ballets of Perrot these ballets represented a late flowering of real choreographic romanticism. Right at the beginning of his career as a maître de ballet Bournonville broke away violently from Filippo Taglioni's production of *La Sylphide*: he made the Sylphide herself into a capricious and delightful creature, built up the rôle of the hero James, adapted authentic Scottish dances to the ballet-technique without sacrificing their essential qualities, and made the witch Madge into a powerful figure who dominated the stage in gruesome triumph at the final curtain. In *Brudefærden i Hardanger* he showed an equally strong feeling for the essential qualities of Norwegian dances, while in *Et Folkesagn* he tackled with great success a theme drawn from Danish folklore; among the many admirably contrasted rôles in the latter ballet there was a grotesque fairy Viderik who combined pathos and humour and to some extent anticipated Chaplin's Tramp.

10. GENERAL DEGENERATION

Bournonville died in 1879, two years after composing his last ballet; Perrot lived on until 1892, vegetating for thirty-five years after his enforced retirement. Both Bournonville and Perrot were completely out of place in the high-Victorian world. This was a period of tremendous achievement in practical activities such as science, industry, trade, exploration, politics and scholarship, but it had little use for real ballet, which is essentially poetic. A few great poets (such as Gerard Manley Hopkins in England) managed to do fine work, but only at the cost of breaking away violently from Victorian habits of thought and feeling and immersing themselves in a private world. This was not possible in ballet, which does not exist except in contact with the public. The middle and late Victorians loved ballet-dancing after their own fashion; from the middle of the nineteenth century right up to the second decade of the twentieth century ballet-dancing meant a frivolous and rather naughty entertainment provided by buxom girls in short skirts whose off-stage virtue was (rightly or wrongly) considered far from impregnable.

The decline in choreography was inevitably accompanied by a decline in the quality of dancing. Only three countries—Italy, Russia and Denmark—retained the great tradition of classical dancing established in the first half of the nineteenth century by Vestris, Didelot, Vigano, Blasis, Bournonville and Perrot; in France the French school degenerated so catastrophically that the stars of the Opéra had invariably to be imported from Russia or Italy.

The degeneration of the French school in France was not due to any lack of talent among French dancers. When given a fair chance French dancers have always shown themselves the equal of those of any other nationality, and it is no accident that the technical language of ballet is French, just as the technical language of music is Italian.

During the second half of the nineteenth century there was one French dancer, Léontine Beaugrand (b. 1842), who combined great talent with enormous strength of character, and managed to revive the French tradition of classical dancing in spite of obstacles which would have broken the heart of almost any other artist. She stood out from her contemporaries at the Opéra in the most violent manner, yet was passed over when due for promotion, and was only given solo rôles when someone fell ill; in 1863 her contract was not renewed, and it was only because the maître de ballet Saint-Léon needed a dancer with an excellent technique for a number in his new ballet *Diavolina*, and put pressure on the Director of the Opéra (Émile Perrin), that the decision to retire her was revoked. She then learned the principal rôle in *Diavolina* in secret, and when the creator of the rôle (Muravieva) returned to Russia she took it over with great success; in fact, she inspired Nuitter to devise for her the ballet *Coppélia*. Nevertheless the Director of the Opéra once again passed over Beaugrand and imported the Russo-German dancer Grantsova to dance the principal rôle in this extremely French ballet. Rehearsals dragged on for three years, and Grantsova left without dancing in the ballet. Yet again Beaugrand was passed over, the rôle being given to the sixteen-year-old Italian dancer Bozacchi at the première in 1870. The latter died during the Siege of Paris, and Beaugrand finally danced Swanhilda in 1871, bringing to the rôle which had been devised for her such qualities of wit, vivacity and rhythmic precision that she had enormous success. Needless to say she was given no further opportunities worthy of her talents—when *Sylvia* was produced in 1877 she was again passed over in favour of the Italian dancer Sangalli—and in 1880 her contract was not renewed, in spite of the fact that she was only thirty-eight and dancing better than ever. Relying only on her ability as a dancer, and lacking an influential protector, she had no chance against the intrigues characteristic of the Opéra. Her premature retirement dealt a death-blow to the French school of classical dancing and the French tradition of the ballet d'action.[1]

During the forties and fifties there were a number of important developments in Italian dancing. At the beginning of this period the French school was far superior to the Italian school, and Blasis' version of the French school soon came to dominate Italian dancing. Blasis trained an amazing number of great dancers, and under his leadership (later also under that of his pupils Giovanni Lepri and Cattarina Beretta, who became teachers) ballet technique went ahead rapidly. The Blasis school became considerably Italianized, and was so influential that after the middle of the century one cannot draw any clear distinction between the Blasis school and the Italian (or Milanese) school.

During the fifties there was a renaissance in Italian ballet which has unfortunately been rather neglected by ballet historians. No great Italian choreographers appeared, but the influence of Perrot was strong, and there were a large number of good dancers and mimes (both male and female) who joined together in small touring companies and took ballet all over Italy. Often these companies had Perrot ballets in their repertoire: in 1854, for example, the American ballerina Augusta Maywood joined a company managed by the Lasiná brothers which had in its repertoire *Esmeralda, Catarina, Giselle* and *Faust*.[2]

Towards the end of the fifties Italian ballet began to degenerate. A new type of ballet appeared in which the whole emphasis was on tasteless spectacle, and the dancers began to concentrate more and more on *tours de force*. At the same time touring companies began to find life very difficult, for the star singers demanded such enormous salaries that theatrical managers had little money to spare for dancers, and Italian dancers had to seek their careers outside Italy. Ballet might well have disappeared from the Italian stage if it had not been for the enormous success of the grandiose but empty spectacles which Luigi Manzotti originated at Turin (*Sieba*, 1876) and continued at La Scala, Milan—notably in *Excelsior* (1881), *Amor* (1886) and *Sport* (1897).

Milan retained a tradition of dancing but not of ballet; it was only at the court theatres of Russia and Denmark that the great tradition of the ballet d'action survived. Theoretically the renaissance might have occurred either in Russia or in Denmark: it actually took place in Russia as part of a tremendous wave of achievement in all the arts which began as early as the second decade

---

[1] Full details of Beaugrand's career are given by L. de Fourcaud in *Léontine Beaugrand* (Paris, 1881). After her enforced retirement she was not even invited to teach at the Opéra school.

[2] For details of Maywood's remarkable career in Italy *see* M. H. Winter, "Augusta Maywood", in *Chronicles of the American Dance* (ed. Paul Magriel), p. 134.

of the nineteenth century in literature, and culminated in ballet, which is of course a synthesis of several arts. Though the renaissance in ballet took a characteristically Russian form, it would have been scarcely possible without certain vital elements of the great ballet tradition which were preserved in Denmark and Italy and imported into Russia from these countries.

PART I

The Renaissance (1875–1929)

1. DEGENERATION IN RUSSIA

THE BALLETS produced by Marius Petipa (1822–1910) in St. Petersburg in the second half of the nineteenth century were the choreographic equivalent of *opera seria*, hundreds of examples of which were produced by Italian composers (inside and outside Italy) in the second half of the seventeenth century and the first half of the eighteenth century. In the Petipa ballets (as in *opera seria*) all the different elements going to make up the work were clamped within rigid moulds: the ballerina ruled the stage just as the castrato had done, with the variation and the adage taking the place of the da capo aria. No dramatic unity or natural flow of action was possible, for the sequence of set-pieces was determined by a formula, and the libretto consequently bore no relation to psychology, probability or human experience of any kind. (For one thing, every story had to be twisted to provide a happy ending.) The rôles were carefully tailored to fit the requirements of the ballerinas; if they did not like them they did not hesitate to alter them. Isolated numbers might achieve some artistic value, when conditions were exceptionally favourable, but the ballets as a whole had no more organic unity than *opera seria*. (It is worth remembering that even Handel would scarcely be remembered today if he had not broken away from *opera seria*, while Mozart, one of the greatest of all opera composers, was defeated when he attempted *opera seria* in *La Clemenza di Tito*.) The formulas used in both *opera seria* and the Petipa ballets were not completely arbitrary—they arose through a kind of fossilization of the methods of good composers and choreographers—but they were applied in a completely arbitrary way.

Petipa's name bulks large in histories of ballet (and in contemporary repertoires) not so much because of the quality of his choreography but rather because of his unique position as a link with the past. After the final departure of Saint-Léon in 1869 he was in effect the only maître de ballet in Russia, and after the retirement of Bournonville in 1877 he was the only active maître de ballet worthy of the name in the whole world. Some of his assistants were allowed by him to achieve a certain measure of fame, but he kept firm control of all choreography in Russia right up to his enforced retirement in 1903, at the age of eighty-one—still full of vitality and busy with projects for new ballets. Petipa emerged into the twentieth century as a choreographic coelocanth, a direct link with the middle of the nineteenth century. For this reason twentieth-century Russians tended to admire him quite uncritically, and regarded his ballets as "classics", making no distinction between the Perrot heritage and the Petipa heritage; they even regarded *Giselle* as a Petipa ballet. (In the programmes of the Maryinsky, the Diaghilev company and the Pavlova company, *Giselle* was attributed to Petipa, and this is still the custom in Russia.) This attitude to Petipa was exported from Russia, and in the West an understanding of the real character of Petipa's work has been still further obscured by the extremely narrow and unrepresentative selection of the Perrot and Petipa ballets which are shown to the public.

Though Petipa in his youth had engagements as premier danseur and maître de ballet in Nantes, Bordeaux and Madrid,[1] he made little mark in Western Europe. He arrived in St. Petersburg in 1847, and was taken on by the Imperial Ballet as premier danseur. Apart from his work as solo dancer he assisted his father Jean Petipa and the German maître de ballet Frederick on the production of a new ballet *Paquita* and the revival of the Mazilier ballet *Le Diable Amoureux*; when Fanny Elssler arrived, he began to prepare for her the Perrot ballet *Esmeralda*, of which the title rôle was one of her favourite parts. Elssler, however, succeeded in having Perrot himself brought to St. Petersburg, and the arrival of the great maître de ballet naturally put an end to Petipa's work in choreography. The next few years were of great importance to Petipa, for they gave him his first opportunity of making contact with the great tradition of the ballet d'action and studying the methods of composition of a great choreographer. Petipa danced leading rôles in the Perrot ballets, and in 1854 acted as Perrot's assistant in the production of *Faust*.

During the 1858–59 season, with Perrot on the point of departure, Petipa began to compose ballets once again and was appointed maître de ballet. But Arthur Saint-Léon (1815–70) took the opportunity presented by Perrot's departure to come to Russia, and for the next decade dominated ballet in Russia so effectively that Petipa had no chance to establish himself. Saint-Léon's talent as a choreographer was far inferior to Perrot's, but—unlike Perrot—he had no artistic scruples to prevent him from accommodating himself to every whim of the Directorate and influential court circles. Petipa had little to learn from Saint-Léon's choreography (except a few hints on the balletization of national dances), but he learned a great deal from Saint-Léon's technique as a courtier: he could not fail to notice the marked difference in the treatment given to Perrot and Saint-Léon. In later years Petipa showed himself even more skilful than Saint-Léon in coping with court intrigue.

[1] The ballets produced by Petipa in Madrid had Spanish themes, and showed Petipa's superficial adaptability: *Carmen et son Toreador*, *La Perle de Seville*, *Départ pour une Corride*, etc. In Russia he drew on his memories of Spain for the ballet *Don Quixote* (which has little to do with the *Don Quixote* of Cervantes) and for a number of divertissements in other ballets.

Fanny Cerito at Her Majesty's Theatre, London, *ca.* 1839
(as seen from the stage box)

Brudefærden i Hardanger (Wedding Voyage in Hardanger—Bournonville, Copenhagen 1853). The man at the back is probably Bournonville

Below: Giselle (Perrot-Coralli Paris, 1841). New version produced by Perrot in London in 1842, with Grisi as Giselle and Perrot as Albrecht

Though Saint-Léon continued to arrange ballets in Russia up to 1869, Petipa was given a chance in 1862 to compose a full-scale ballet, *La Fille du Pharaon*: this came about through the determination of Saburov to provide something new and striking for the benefit of Rosati, whose "protector"[1] he was. Saburov lost interest in the project when his feelings towards Rosati began to cool, but Petipa managed to persuade Saburov to let him continue with the project. In spite of serious defects this lavish spectacle was a success, largely because of its topical interest in connection with the excavations in Egypt; from now on Petipa continued to compose ballets regularly, and after the final departure of Saint-Léon he was in sole command of all ballet in Russia. Unfortunately for Petipa the public was turning away from ballet: he did his best to outdo Saint-Léon by devising striking novelties to catch public interest (e.g. filling the stage with a huge golden cage from the inside of which dancers were "flown" on wires) but he had far more failures than successes. Ballet became less and less popular; at some periods the frequency of performances was reduced to one per week or even less, and sometimes the house was largely filled with "paper". Fortunately for Petipa the Imperial Theatres were not run on commercial lines, and the ballet continued to receive its subsidy in spite of its lack of popular support.

Though Petipa was strongly influenced by Perrot, and appeared to be carrying on the great tradition of Didelot and Perrot, in fact he reduced this tradition to a lifeless formula. We cannot, however, lay the blame for this regimentation of ballet entirely on Petipa's shoulders: the process was already far advanced in his youth. Bournonville and Perrot were only able to do good work by swimming against the tide, and Saint-Léon continued the process of regimentation in Russia while Petipa was making his first important attempts at choreography. Petipa did no more than carry to its logical conclusion a process which was already nearly complete.

Superficially Petipa's ballets were romantic—they had highly romantic plots—but all the stories were modified to have a happy ending, and the treatment with its complete absence of mystery and imagination was not in the least romantic; the Petipa ballets were, in fact, pseudo-classical in style.

---

[1] In the Imperial Russian Ballet, as in most old-established State ballets, the opportunities given to a ballerina at any time depended to a large extent on the influence exerted by the man whose mistress she was at that time. Talent was also necessary, but it could only operate within the patterns established in other ways. Lydia Kyaksht in her memoirs (*Romantic Recollections*) describes how the ballerina Kshessinskaya became the absolute ruler of the Imperial Ballet during the time she was the favourite of the Tsar's son: "Every whim of hers was gratified the instant she expressed it." She even secured the dismissal of the Director of the Imperial Theatres when he was rash enough to give some orders which did not meet with her approval. People were surprised when Kshessinskaya continued to secure leading rôles after the Crown Prince became Tsar and thought it best to break off his relationship with her. But Kshessinskaya was a very talented dancer who deserved leading rôles—and in any case this fascinating person had not one but several Grand Dukes as her devoted admirers.

After his experience of working with Perrot, Petipa had no illusions about the artistic quality of his work: he knew very well that the "divertissementation" of ballet carried out by him represented a perversion of the great tradition. It is impossible not to sympathize with him when he replied to the criticisms of Bournonville in 1874 by saying that he entirely agreed with them, but was forced by the "blasé public" and "superior authority" to stage productions which he despised.

The pressure put on Petipa from above and below was very great, and it is to his credit that he was able to salvage some artistic standards. Though the new ballets were of poor quality, and the standard of dancing declined steadily after the enforced retirement of Perrot, Petipa was lucky enough to have the services of the great Swedish teacher Christian Johannsen (1817–1903), who had been trained by both Bournonvilles (father and son) in Stockholm, and preserved much of the Vestris style. (Petipa himself had little talent as a teacher: in this respect he differed violently from the great maîtres de ballet who preceded him in Russia.)

Petipa's greatest achievements were to be found not in his own ballets but in the fine Perrot ballets which he succeeded in keeping in the repertoire— *Giselle, Faust, Catarina, Le Corsaire*,[1] *Esmeralda* and *Ondine*.[2] Up to 1890 he preserved his revered master's choreography with admirable fidelity; in fact he did for Perrot what Perrot could not do for himself. Fortunately Petipa had exactly the right kind of talent for this task. A maître de ballet with great creative power and originality would have committed suicide rather than work under these conditions; Petipa, however, took everything in his stride, refusing to allow his optimism and good humour to be affected by the stupidity of the Directorate, the indifference of the public and the repeated failure of ballets in which he had done his best to please everyone.

The degeneration of choreography was to be seen particularly clearly in Petipa's treatment of the music. When composing a dance Petipa took very little interest in the theme of the ballet or the character of the rôle portrayed by the artist: what mattered to him was making the most striking effect possible with the particular technical accomplishments, physique and personality of the ballerina who was to dance the rôle. The relationship between the music and the steps interested him very little: he used the music as a means of fixing the tempo and metre of the dance, ignoring to a large extent its peculiarities of phrasing, melody, rhythm, etc. He had every inducement to treat the music in this way, for the Directors of the Imperial Theatres were accustomed to commission the music from staff composers whose work was of very slight musical

---

[1] This was originally a Mazilier ballet, but Perrot revised it considerably when he produced it in Russia.

[2] Known as *The Naïade and the Fisherman* in Russia.

value. Pugni had shown a certain amount of talent both in opera and ballet before he arrived in Russia in 1848, but in the process of grinding out dozens of scores for conventional ballets (in his capacity as official ballet composer to the Imperial Theatres) he lost all his creative powers—which at the best of times had been very limited; his successors Minkus and Drigo never had the chance of being anything but hack composers. The dreary nature of their work can best be realized by comparison with the remarkable operas by Russian composers (Glinka, Dargomizhky, Balakirev, Mussorgsky, Borodin, Rimsky-Korsakov) which were produced at the Imperial opera houses during the whole of the Petipa epoch. Unfortunately the formulas for ballet were so rigid that it was considered that only specialists could write ballet music; no one expected ballet music to have the qualities looked for in other types of music.

It is important to remember that Petipa's choreography was not normally devised to fit the music: to all intents and purposes the choreography and the music were created independently of each other, just as were the other elements in the ballet (décor, costumes, orchestration, etc.). Before giving his instructions to the composer, Petipa worked out the ballet in elaborate detail, deciding which solos were to be given to the various ballerinas and making plans for the mimed scenes, processions, group dances, etc. He then ordered music from the composer to fit this project, specifying for each dance, mimed scene or procession the number of bars, the time-signature and the tempo, together with a vague indication of the character of the various scenes (lively, sad, gay, etc.). He made no specific demands for the evocation of distinct moods or the exact delineation of the character of the personages, knowing quite well that the composers were incapable of such refinements. When he started to rehearse a dance he knew the steps he wanted to use, suited to the particular soloist in question, and fitted these steps in a rough-and-ready manner to the music. Sometimes they fitted quite well, but they were quite likely to fit badly. Their actual relationships to the music worried him very little: his main concern was that the steps should fit the *bars* of the music, and should end at the same time as the music with an appropriate climax. He worked to a piano score provided by the composer, and took no interest in the orchestration (which was sometimes quite out of harmony with the dances he arranged). This method of composition was very convenient for Petipa—it enabled him to plan the whole ballet down to its smallest details on paper, and made it unnecessary for him to tackle any difficult musical problems during rehearsal—but at the same time it prevented him from realizing to the full his own modest potentialities as a choreographer.[1]

---

[1] I do not mean to suggest that Petipa did not study the score before starting rehearsal. He studied the score carefully, checking that it fitted his specifications exactly. If it did not he sent it back for alteration.

In fact he found considerable difficulty in putting together enchaînements of dance-steps, and was accustomed to watch the classes of Johannsen and other teachers in a desperate search for ideas. While his assistant Ivanov lived he made considerable use of his inventive powers even in ballets which were attributed wholly to Petipa on the programme, and after Ivanov's death he used Nicolas Legat in the same way.

The incongruity between music and dancing was sometimes so blatant that one would swear Petipa was perversely determined to prevent his artists from having a chance to dance in a noble and expressive manner; but such perversity was as foreign to Petipa as its opposite (musical sensitivity). Incongruities arose naturally from the methods of composition in use, and (like the corresponding incongruities in English Christmas pantomimes) were taken for granted by everyone as a part of the general mix-up. In fact people were not even aware of them as incongruities: they were thought to be as much a normal part of ballet as the fifth position and tights.

By the middle of the seventies ballet had sunk to a very low level in Russia. The best dancers did not bother about daily classes,[1] and the average standard of technique was feeble. The style of dancing was winsome and affected: the danseuses paid little attention to the interpretation of their rôles, being mainly concerned in casting alluring smiles and roguish glances at their friends in the audience; their gestures and their facial expressions were arch and coy, while their arms drooped in a soft sentimental manner. Male dancing was unimportant, except in character rôles; the main task of the serious male dancer was to support the ballerina. The corps de ballet dancers worked in a careless manner, dragging their feet and hardly bothering to use their arms. Ballet was treated by the public as something of small importance compared with the drama and opera. In fact it was considered as being rather questionable from the moral point of view, and the relatively small number of fanatical balletomanes who attended the performances were known to be interested in the personal charms of their favourite ballerinas rather than in ballet in general. One of the few remaining attractions of the ballet was the legs of danseuses: shoulders and bosoms were also important, but it was only at the ballet that the female leg was shown in public in quantity. To quote Alexandre Benois (who was a balletomane himself, being as a boy of fourteen a staunch admirer of the corporal charms of Marie Petipa):

> The balletomanes formed a special clan of their own and had the reputation of being hopelessly incorrigible cranks; they were looked upon as somewhat eccentric and slightly depraved. . . . The ballet . . . where people were only busy with such

[1] It was not until 1895 that Johannsen instituted the famous *Classe de Perfection* (continued after his retirement by his favourite pupil Nicolas Legat) at which the dancers of the company continued their training after graduation from the school.

nonsense as dancing, and in very scanty costumes at that, was considered unworthy of the attention of serious people. One of the chief reproaches made against the Tsar's Government was that it patronized and encouraged the ballet . . . Grown-ups talked about it in the same vein, as when they spoke of the circus or the operette.[1]

It was the custom to take children to the ballet, particularly to the matinées at Christmas, Carnival and Easter, just as in England it was the custom to take the children to the Christmas pantomimes which were the English equivalent of the Russian ballets of this period. Both in Russia and England parents believed that the children would not understand those aspects of the show which were not suitable for children.

Though the degeneration of ballet in Western Europe was probably inevitable, this was by no means true of Russia. The nineteenth century in Russia had far more in common with the Italian Renaissance and the Elizabethan age of England than with the Victorian age of Western Europe. There was no sharp break in artistic development, such as happened in Western Europe at the middle of the century. Russian literature, founded by Pushkin, Lermontov and Gogol early in the nineteenth century, continued to show splendid vitality in the second half of the century: Western Europe had few novelists to compare with Turgueniev, Goncharov, Saltykov-Shchedrin. Tolstoy and Dostoyevsky, and the novels of Dostoyevsky (1821–81) represent the beginning of twentieth-century literature. In Russian opera and instrumental music development was continuous from its beginnings in the work of Glinka (1803–57) to the work of Stravinsky in the twentieth century. The development of Russian drama was less continuous, but Ostrovsky was writing great plays like *The Storm* and *The Forest* at a time when the drama of Western Europe (Ibsen apart) was unworthy of serious attention. The degeneration in ballet at a time when great achievements were being made in other branches of Russian art was caused by the deliberate action of a series of corrupt and stupid men who took advantage of their position as Director of the Imperial Theatres to persecute Didelot and Perrot.[2]

2. THE RENAISSANCE BEGINS

In Moscow the ballet tradition was weaker than in St. Petersburg, and the standard of dancing and choreography much lower; but in Moscow (far from the court) conventions were not quite so rigid as in St. Petersburg, and it was

---

[1] *Reminiscences of the Russian Ballet*, pp. 47–48.

[2] The great Russian writers of the nineteenth century suffered much the same sort of persecution as Didelot and Perrot, but they were able to continue work to some extent in spite of all obstacles. Didelot and Perrot, in contrast, depended entirely on official support, for there were no commercial theatres with important ballet companies in Russia.

here that the renaissance in European ballet began in 1875 when V. P. Beguichev (Intendant of the Moscow Imperial Theatres) commissioned his friend Tchaikovsky to compose the music for a ballet *Le Lac des Cygnes*.

Tchaikovsky (1840–93) had a great liking for ballet—as early as 1870 he had conceived the idea of composing a ballet *Cendrillon*—and he now had the stimulus of a mythological theme which strongly appealed to him. (As Grace Roberts points out,[1] he probably had a good deal to do with the preparation of the book of the ballet, even though in the programme it was attributed to his friend Beguichev and the dancer and régisseur V. F. Geltser.) Tchaikovsky found in the theme an outlet for many of his deepest feelings, and was inspired to write wonderfully evocative ballet music of a new kind, much closer in style to Wagner's operas than to the conventional ballet music of the day.

As Beaumont makes clear,[2] Moscow had no choreographers or dancers capable of doing justice to the poetic theme and music of *Le Lac des Cygnes*. The choreographer Reisinger could make nothing of the music, and hacked it about in an effort to make it resemble the conventional ballet music with which he was familiar. He even had the dancers compose their own variations, and all the dances were produced collectively. The key rôle of Odette-Odile was danced by a certain Karpakova, who had little talent and obviously obtained the part through intrigue. Inevitably the production was a failure. It was revived in Moscow in 1880 and 1882, with new choreography by Olaf Hansen, and then fell into oblivion. No further progress was possible in Moscow, in the absence of choreographers and dancers corresponding to Tchaikovsky in stature.

The next important stage in the renaissance of ballet was reached in St. Petersburg through the appointment in 1881 as Director of the Imperial Theatres, for the first time in generations, of a man with a certain amount of taste and judgment—I. A. Vsevolozhky (1835–1909).

Paradoxically, the renaissance of ballet in Russia was facilitated by the low level to which it had fallen. By this time Petipa was very set in his ways, and was strongly resistant to new ideas; but the failure of successive new ballets and the decline in popular support for the ballet brought him to a position in 1885 where he read of his resignation in the newspapers, and thought that his career was finished. Vsevolozhky, the new Director, deliberately allowed Petipa to feel himself in grave danger so that he would be more amenable to the changes which he wished to introduce.

Vsevolozhky was a man of a very different stamp from his predecessors. He was a cultured, well-educated and polished diplomat with some talent for drawing and a real flair for the theatre. Disliking existing tendencies in the opera and the drama, he decided to concentrate all his attention on the ballet.

[1] Grace Roberts, *Borzoi Book of Ballets*, p. 305.
[2] C. W. Beaumont, *The Ballet Called Swan-Lake*, p. 13.

Though he was very conservative in his outlook, and by no means a Durazzo, he had a definite artistic policy, and by putting it into effect he started a chain of events which went far beyond anything he planned.

Vsevolozhky's first innovations were to suppress the post, held by Minkus, of ballet composer to the Imperial Theatres, and to commission a production (with choreography by Petipa and his assistant Ivanov) of the ballet *Coppélia*, with music by Delibes. This ballet had been produced at the Paris Opéra as early as 1870 by Saint-Léon, but without a strong push from Vsevolozhky Petipa might never have got round to producing it; for the fact that the music had been composed to fit a project devised by another choreographer meant that Petipa had to solve difficult problems in rehearsal. The score by Delibes, though rather sugary, had real musical quality, and this production prepared the way for the production of Tchaikovsky ballets in St. Petersburg.

Vsevolozhky's next innovation was to order Petipa to take into the Imperial Ballet and give the leading rôles to the Italian dancers who were beginning to appear in the pleasure-gardens of St. Petersburg. This order was extremely distasteful to Petipa, who preferred to work only with dancers trained in *his* school (i.e. the Imperial Russian school of which he was director); but he had to obey. The Italian dancers were creating a sensation in Russia, for technically they were far stronger than the Russians, and some of them had strong personalities and powerful dramatic gifts: the old Franco-Danish style used in Russia was pitifully inadequate compared with the Italian style of these virtuosi.

Most of the Italians were pupils of either Cattarina Beretta of Milan or Giovanni Lepri of Florence, and had been trained in Italianized versions of the Blasis school. The Russian dancers admired the superior technical skill of the Italian dancers, and set out to imitate it, but were not blind to the defects of their dancing.

The Lepri pupil Enrico Cecchetti (1850–1928) began to visit St. Petersburg in 1874, and in 1886 came to St. Petersburg at the head of an Italian company, with Limido as his prima ballerina. This company gave performances in a theatre in the Arcadia pleasure-garden. The Manzotti ballets performed by this company were in the usual grandiloquent Italian style of the day, but the dancing of Limido introduced the Russians to a pure classical style which they had to take very seriously. Nicolas Legat has recorded the powerful impression made on him by Cecchetti and Limido:

> The only male dancer of the group was Enrico Cecchetti. He was about forty-five[1] years of age when he came to Russia, and at the very height of his career, but too old to modify his school of *tours de force* or round out his dexterity with the dignity and poise which were then the outstanding attributes of the Russian school.

[1] Cecchetti was actually thirty-six at the time.

The first time I saw him dance was at a music-hall in the pleasure-garden Arcadia. I was sixteen at the time. To say that I was amazed by what appeared then to be the amazing virtuosity of the little Italian, would be putting it mildly. I came out literally staggered. Eight pirouettes! And on the stage of the Maryinsky and in the theatre school our dancers were content with four. Cecchetti was partnering Limido, and these two made a perfect combination. They were both very small, but graceful and well built. Limido was in my opinion the greatest of all the Italians, and one of the greatest dancers of all time. In pure technique she excelled all others, and it was well-nigh incredible that when she came to Russia she was already fifty years of age.[1]

Limido was too old to make a career for herself in St. Petersburg, but Cecchetti remained, and had great influence both as a dancer and as a teacher. Other Italians who stayed in St. Petersburg and had great influence were the ballerinas Zucchi, dell'Era, Brianza and Legnani. Brianza and Cecchetti created a sensation in 1890 when they both danced in the première of *The Sleeping Beauty*—Brianza as Princess Aurora and Cecchetti as the Blue Bird and Carabosse.

During the next two decades there were several parallel tendencies in classical dancing in Russia. A number of ambitious young dancers graduating from the Maryinsky school from 1888 onwards set out to master the secrets of the brilliant technique of the Italians (both Lepri-trained and Beretta-trained) and to equal or even surpass them technically, while retaining the virtues of the French and Franco-Danish schools. By far the most important of these pioneers was Nicolas Legat (1869–1937), who became a great dancer and a teacher of genius. He took over the class of perfection established in 1895 by the Bournonville pupil Johannsen (who retired after sixty years' work in Russia) and created a new, characteristically Russian school quite distinct from existing schools. Legat himself has admirably described what happened:

> We accepted it [the Italian school] but we also very quickly saw its limitations. So we added to it, embellished it, ennobled it. We rendered it more pliable, more sympathetic, more subtle, more personal. We adapted it to individual possibilities and to individual genius. Into the Italian school we poured the rich, life-giving, inspiring force of the *russkaya dusha* [Russian soul or spirit] . . . The *élan*[2] manifested by the great dancers of the Russian school was born of supreme and merciless training, training in *taste* as well as in steps and movements.[3]

It is quite likely that much of the richness of the Legat school was due to the fact that it represented to some extent a cross-breeding of two

---

[1] *The Story of the Russian School*, p. 17.
[2] Defined by Legat as "a combination of fire, passion and enthusiasm".
[3] Nicolas Legat, "What is 'Élan' in Dancing", *The Dancing Times*, February, 1937.

stocks descended from a common ancestor (the Franco-Danish and Franco-Italian schools), leading to a recovery in a relatively pure state of the virtues of the old French school of Vestris. At the same time the young Russian dancers (led by Legat) added to the new school characteristically Peterburgian qualities of poetry, simplicity, psychological truth in characterization, depth of feeling and classical restraint. (Though these qualities were to be found in all the best Russian art since the time of Pushkin, most of them were more characteristic of the "Westernizing" art of St. Petersburg than of the "Russianizing" art of Moscow.)

Alongside the new Russian school of Legat, Cecchetti continued to teach his Italianized version of the Blasis school; this had its own characteristic virtues —notably in the purity and balance of its line—but differed fundamentally from the Legat school in many respects, above all in its attitude to routine. Legat, following the example of Johannsen, made each class a fresh experience for his pupils, developing the mind, feelings, imagination and taste as well as the body, whereas Cecchetti continued the Italian custom of using a high proportion of standard exercises, and relied on a weekly sequence of these to ensure the balanced training of all the muscles.

The Cecchetti method has survived up to the present day in relatively pure form as a result of the initiative of C. W. Beaumont, who codified it in London in the early twenties of the twentieth century in the two volumes of the famous *Manual of Classical Dancing (Cecchetti Method)* which he prepared in collaboration with Idzikovsky, Cecchetti himself and Cecchetti's favourite English pupil Margaret Craske.

The Legat system was not suitable for codification in this manner, for it demanded that each class should be an act of imaginative creation by the teacher and that each pupil should be treated differently. In fact Legat pupils all over the world teach the Russian school by methods that vary a good deal from teacher to teacher. Towards the end of his life Legat realized the importance of developing a clear-cut system which could be taught to teachers, in spite of its subtlety and flexibility, and fortunately succeeded in transmitting this system to his favourite London pupil, Ana Roje, in the four years preceding his death in 1937.[1]

All but one of the Italians who came to Russia in the eighties and nineties of the nineteenth century remained very Italian. The exception was Legnani. This great artist went for training to Nicolas Legat (in spite of the fact that she was older than him) and became considerably Russianized; she created the rôle of Odette-Odile in the St. Petersburg production of *Le Lac des Cygnes*, and had major influence on the Russian dancers who graduated from the Maryinsky

[1] *See* below, p. 309.

after 1887 and matured into some of the greatest dancers the world has ever seen.[1]

In Moscow conditions were much less favourable for a renaissance in ballet than in St. Petersburg, and progress was slow after the remarkable initiative which led to the first production of *Le Lac des Cygnes* in 1875. In fact the creative forces corresponding to those which transformed the Maryinsky in St. Petersburg led in Moscow to the formation of the Moscow Art Theatre and its epoch-making productions of plays by Chekhov.

3. THE SLEEPING BEAUTY

The fact that *The Sleeping Beauty* was the first ballet to give good opportunities at the Maryinsky to both Brianza and Cecchetti was not the only reason for the extraordinary impact of this ballet. Vsevolozhky introduced in this ballet two other revolutionary innovations: he supervised all the different components of the production so that there was a certain amount of harmony between them, and he commissioned the music for it from Tchaikovsky.

Not only did Vsevolozhky control all the details of this production: he wrote the book and designed the costumes. The book had many defects, and the colours of his costumes were rather insipid, but the mere fact that the different elements of the ballet fitted together gave it a certain atmosphere of poetry completely absent from its predecessors. Even though the harmony achieved by Vsevolozhky did not go very far (the décors, by Rollin and others, were just as stodgy as ever) it was enough to inspire the young painter Alexandre Benois (*b.* 1870) with the idea of ballet as a *Gesamtkunstwerk*[2]—a work of art in which every detail harmonizes with every other detail and contributes its due effect to the work as a whole. (Wagner had already been working towards a similar ideal in opera, and had made propaganda for it in his writings.)

Tchaikovsky's music made a profound impression in St. Petersburg. He was already recognized there as a great theatre composer—his opera *Eugene Onegin*, produced at the Maryinsky a decade previously, had been an enormous success —and his score for *The Sleeping Beauty* did much to re-establish the idea that

[1] The most distinguished of the danseuses were Preobazhenskaya (graduation of 1889), Kshessinskaya (1890), Trefilova (1894), Astafieva (1895), Vil, Vaganova (1897), Yegorova (1898), Sedova (1898), Pavlova (1899), Karsavina (1900), Lydia Kyaksht (1900), Bronislava Nijinska (1908), Lopukhova (1909) and Spessivsteva (1913). The most distinguished of the danseurs were Nicolas Legat (1888), George Kyaksht (1891), Sergei Legat (1894), Obukhov (1895), Fokine (1898), Bolm (1904), Koslov, Gavrilov, Nijinsky (1908), Boris Romanov (1909), and Vladimirov (1911). Apart from these artists there were many fine dancers who would have been stars in almost any other company.

[2] For convenience I use Wagner's term in this book, though Wagner was far from being the inventor of the idea. It was fully expounded by the French Encyclopédistes before 1760, and Noverre applied it to ballet in *Lettres sur les Arts Imitateurs*, Vol. I, p. 383.

a ballet could be a major work of art. In this ballet the signs of a renaissance in Russian ballet were unmistakable, even though the ballet was deliberately designed to exploit the talents of an Italian ballerina. (The great exponents of the new Russian school were just beginning to emerge as soloists.)

Though *The Sleeping Beauty* was far superior to its predecessors in some respects, it was inferior to them in others. It was no part of Vsevolozhky's plan to make ballet into a major art, the equivalent of opera and drama. Vsevolozhky's idea was to make ballet into a light entertainment—the Russian equivalent of the ballet de cour at the time of Louis XIV (who is the prototype of King Florestan XXIV in *The Sleeping Beauty*).

Since the Tsar's family went to the ballet to be amused, to be captivated, to relax from grave thoughts and affairs of state, it was clearly not the place for dramas or gloomy scenes of poverty and suffering. In His Imperial Majesty's theatre everything had to be gay, festive and free from care, especially free from care. The ballet, therefore, needed a clever master of ceremonies, prepared to surprise Their Majesties with a pleasant novelty, rather than a choreographer.[1]

In putting his ideas into effect Vsevolozhky did not encourage Petipa to improve his methods of composition; on the contrary, he forced Petipa to abandon his last remaining contacts with the great tradition of Perrot.

In all previous Petipa ballets the plot had been of minor importance, and few dances had any expressive function in the development of the action. In *The Sleeping Beauty* the action was lost to sight almost entirely, the mimed scenes were dragged out quite unnecessarily, and the dances were scattered through the ballet in a highly arbitrary way. Structurally, the ballet fell well behind its predecessors.[2]

Petipa (now a man of sixty-eight) did not allow the fact that he was working with a great composer to affect his methods of composition: he planned the ballet in elaborate detail and gave Tchaikovsky his usual specifications as to the number of bars, the tempo and the time signature for each episode. In addition, however, he took advantage of Tchaikovsky's skill as a composer to make certain demands for changes in mood. Tchaikovsky adapted himself with extraordinary ease to these rigid demands, writing music that not only conformed to specification but was full of wit, fantasy and spontaneity. For various personal reasons he seemed to enjoy being imprisoned in this strait-

---

[1] Yuri Slonimsky, *Marius Petipa* (Dance Index), p. 116.

[2] One of the main reasons why *Aurora's Wedding* (the Diaghilev version of the last act of *The Sleeping Beauty*) was successful, after the relatively cool reception given to the ballet in its entirety by London audiences, was that the last act does not pretend to be anything more than a suite of divertissements, and the weaknesses in Petipa's treatment of the theme are therefore not apparent.

jacket, and wrote some excellent music for *The Sleeping Beauty*—though the theme did not inspire him as profoundly as that of *Le Lac des Cygnes*.

Tchaikovsky was interested in the symbolism of the theme, and treated it on the plane of fantasy, introducing where possible a number of nuances of feeling and flashes of wit and poetry. Petipa, however, was much too set in his ways to change his style to harmonize with the music: he treated the theme with the same rather pompous and prosaic solemnity that one finds in his other ballets, and excluded all fantasy. The dances consisted of his usual enchaînements in which everything was designed to allow the soloist in question to make an effect of bravura and virtuosity. (Petipa was so little sensitive to the nuances in the music that he used almost the same arm movements and steps for two variations with strongly contrasted music.) Even the title rôle had almost no individuality: Princess Aurora was no more than a series of dances tailored to fit the technique and personality of Brianza (apart from certain pas d'action in Act I).[1]

After composing almost exclusively for ballerinas for a great many years Petipa was unable to accommodate himself to the existence of fine male dancers: in *The Sleeping Beauty* Cecchetti composed his own variation, and in later ballets Petipa often had Nicolas Legat compose the male solos.

Petipa followed *The Sleeping Beauty* with a number of spectacular ballets in similar style, with music by hack composers. In 1892, however, Vsevolozhky and Petipa commissioned from Tchaikovsky a second ballet, *Casse-Noisette*. Because of the limitations of their artistic outlook and their misunderstanding of the nature of Tchaikovsky's talent, they provided him with a feeble theme in which he could find no poetic symbolism. He did his best to conquer his dislike of the theme, but was only partially successful, and one cannot compare his score for this ballet with the best of his ballet music—though of course it was far superior to the hack-work of Minkus, Drigo, Krotkov, etc. Ivanov, to whom the choreography was entrusted after Petipa fell ill, was baffled by the dreary theme even more than Tchaikovsky.

Like Queen Victoria, Petipa lived too long; and he treated his unfortunate assistant Ivanov in much the same fashion that Victoria treated the Prince of Wales (the future Edward VII). Lev Ivanov (1834–1901) had much the same opportunities as Petipa of familiarizing himself with the methods of composition of the great Perrot while dancing solo rôles for Perrot, and since he was far more imaginative and musical than Petipa he was in a much better position to grasp the real meaning of Perrot's work. Undoubtedly he would have achieved wonders if Petipa had given him a fair chance. But Petipa saw

[1] Petipa would be bewildered by contemporary productions in which ballerinas with physique and temperament very different from those of Brianza try to make something positive out of this rôle. Whenever Petipa made a change in casting he changed the choreography as well; he had no illusions about the permanent value of any one of his arrangements of steps.

to it that Ivanov worked very closely under his supervision, and deprived Ivanov of the chance of working on themes that would have inspired him; everything that Ivanov did had to be submitted to Petipa for approval, and Petipa himself worked out the projects for Ivanov's ballets.

Casse-Noisette gives us a few hints of the ballets which Tchaikovsky and Ivanov might have produced in collaboration if Vsevolozhky and Petipa had given them a free hand—notably the grand pas de deux of the Sugar-Plum Fairy and her Cavalier, which is far more musical than anything achieved by Petipa in this vein. Most of the ballet, however, is very dull and conventional.

4. *LE LAC DES CYGNES* IN ST. PETERSBURG

Tchaikovsky's scores for *The Sleeping Beauty* and *Casse-Noisette* aroused Vsevolozhky's interest in the idea of reviving *Le Lac des Cygnes* in St. Petersburg. Tchaikovsky was delighted at the prospect; since he attributed the failure of the Moscow productions to defects (!) in the music he was prepared to re-write the music to fit the requirements of Petipa, but died before he could do this.

Fortunately Petipa entrusted Act II[1] to Ivanov: we may perhaps assume that Petipa was daunted by the exceptionally "symphonic" nature of the music for this act, and preferred to avoid the difficult problems which he would have had to face in rehearsal. The theme and the music of this act exactly suited the talents and temperament of Ivanov, and he was inspired to compose the first major Russian ballet since the retirement of Didelot. Though the structure of the Act (as roughed out by Petipa) conformed to the formula for the balletic equivalent of *opera seria*, Ivanov dared for once to break right away from the Petipa style, and composed dance-images that were the choreographic equivalent of the music: as in the ballets of Perrot, the different movements expressed the moods and character of each personage, and the corps de ballet was used as an integral part of the danced action. Normally Petipa might have been expected to assert his authority by interfering with Ivanov's work and crippling his invention, but Act II had to be prepared very hurriedly for a memorial concert to Tchaikovsky, and so Ivanov was able to show his real talent for the first and last time. This Act (together with its sequel Act IV) prepared the way for a renaissance in choreography after Ivanov's death.

When Petipa put the whole ballet into production he made drastic alterations in its structure in order to make it conform as far as possible to the standard pattern established by him in *The Sleeping Beauty* to meet the requirements of Vsevolozhky. Not only did he alter the book: he had Drigo alter the music so

---

[1] Petipa decided to call Act II "Act I, Scene 2", but for convenience I have retained the division into acts of the original Moscow production.

as to make it lighter in texture and closer to conventional ballet music. When Petipa arranged the choreography for Act I he made no attempt to provide a fitting prelude to Tchaikovsky's poetic fantasy, contenting himself with conventional dances and mime scenes that might have belonged to any of his other ballets. In Act III, however, he broke away from his usual lazy habits, composing enchaînements which definitely belonged to the music and had some relation to the action: moreover he probably assigned much of the work on the solos to Ivanov, as was his habit. On the other hand Petipa made little attempt to give dramatic verisimilitude to the mimed action of Act III. As Beaumont points out,[1] some of the action is ludicrous: it is extremely ill-mannered of Rothbart to sit on the Prince's throne, and one would hardly expect the cunning Magician to explain his plot to Odile in full view of the assembled guests and the Queen.

Unlike the other Petipa ballets, Le Lac des Cygnes is genuinely romantic, and has the tragic ending typical of Tchaikovsky.[2] Petipa could not provide the usual happy ending without remodelling the whole ballet, but he did what he could to take away the sadness of the ending by providing a happy apotheosis. If Le Lac des Cygnes still holds the stage as one of the most important items in the balletic heritage from the nineteenth century, this is in spite of Petipa, Drigo, Reisinger e tutti quanti.

The special quality of the St. Petersburg production of Le Lac des Cygnes was due to a number of fortunate accidents. In the other ballets which followed The Sleeping Beauty Petipa's choreography continued the tendencies established in The Sleeping Beauty, and the last vestiges of the artistic principles of Perrot were abandoned. Petipa himself was well aware of the significance of these tendencies: as Slonimsky points out,[3] Petipa made clear his final renunciation of the principles of his master by concluding his notes on the revival of Le Corsaire in 1891 with the words "Corsaire by Saint-Georges and Mazilier, but not by Perrot." (After 1890 Petipa and his assistants carried out all revivals with great ruthlessness, changing or cutting everything that did not fit in with the style of The Sleeping Beauty: this style, as Petipa well knew, was much closer to that of Mazilier than that of Perrot.)

---

[1] *The Ballet Called Swan-Lake*, pp. 128–9.
[2] The legend takes different forms in various parts of Europe: in Russia, for example, there is a folk-song *The Two Swans* which ends with the Prince dropping his white-feathered arrow instead of shooting the swans. We cannot be certain whether Tchaikovsky selected a tragic version of the legend or adapted a non-tragic version to suit his temperament.
[3] *Marius Petipa* (Dance Index), p. 119.

5. MAMONTOV, BENOIS, DIAGHILEV AND VOLKONSKY

The next important stage in the renaissance of ballet was reached in Moscow through the commissioning by Savva Mamontov (a rich Moscow merchant who ran a private theatre where he presented operas by Russian nationalist composers) of distinguished contemporary Russian easel painters to design the décors and costumes for his productions, avoiding the professional stage designers. Two of these painters, Korovin and Golovin, showed a remarkable flair for stage design: they used the stage as a canvas, employing colours with a freedom never before seen in stage design.

In 1898 Mamontov brought his company to St. Petersburg, and its décors made a very strong impression on the group of painters associated with Benois and Sergei Diaghilev (1872–1929). Though the St. Petersburg artists did not approve entirely of the work of the Muscovite artists in the field of ballet,[1] finding it insufficiently poetic for this medium, they learned from Korovin and Golovin that stage décor could rise to a high artistic level.

In 1898 the Benois-Diaghilev circle of artists was also stimulated by the foundation by Diaghilev of a magazine *Mir Iskustva* (The World of Art) with funds provided partly by the great patron Savva Mamontov and partly by Princess Tenishev. This magazine rapidly became the focus of all the most important trends in Russian art.

One of the contributors to *Mir Iskustva* was Prince Volkonsky, and his appointment in 1899 as Director of the Imperial Theatres seemed likely to inaugurate a new period of rapid progress at the Maryinsky. Volkonsky was a man of very wide culture, an expert in every aspect of the theatre, and progressive in his ideas: his appointment opened the way for the reform of ballet by the brilliant members of the Benois-Diaghilev circle (which was also the Editorial Board of *Mir Iskustva*). Volkonsky knew too much about intrigues within the Imperial Theatres to push ahead too fast, and as a first step gave Diaghilev the job of editing the Annual of the Imperial Theatres—which he did surpassingly well, with the collaboration of the *Mir Iskustva* circle. But the *Mir Iskustva* circle (including Diaghilev himself) had all been interested in ballet by Benois, and they pressed Volkonsky to allow them to put their ideas into practice on the production of a ballet *Sylvia* (the second ballet composed by Delibes for the Paris Opéra). In 1900 Volkonsky consented, assigning the décor

---

[1] As the result of the great success of their work for Mamontov, Korovin and Golovin received many commissions for productions at the Imperial Theatres in Moscow and St. Petersburg, and became the most important designers for opera and ballet in these theatres. Friendly relations developed between the two Moscow designers and the Benois-Diaghilev circle, and Diaghilev commissioned décors and costumes from both of them in the early years of the Diaghilev ballet.

and costumes to various members of the *Mir Iskustva* circle, and putting Diaghilev in charge to co-ordinate details and act as liaison between the creative artists and the members of the Maryinsky staff.

Inevitably the appointment of Diaghilev caused opposition among the higher grades of the Imperial Theatres Directorate, and they protested against the assignment of such important work to a "junior assistant". In order to cope with this intrigue Volkonsky decided to ask Diaghilev to let the production be in the name of the Directorate (i.e. Volkonsky) rather than in Diaghilev's name, though Diaghilev would continue in fact to control the production. Diaghilev then showed the childish wilfulness and arrogance which were later to cripple his career over and over again. (He often behaved more like a spoiled child than a grown man.) Instead of allowing Volkonsky to make haste slowly and allow the staff of the Imperial Theatres Directorate and the Maryinsky Theatre gradually to get used to working with real artists, Diaghilev insisted on retaining power in name as well as in fact: he even tried to blackmail Volkonsky by refusing to edit the Annual for the following year, and went over his head to appeal directly to the Tsar via a Grand Duke who was hoping to get Volkonsky's job. Volkonsky went so far as to call on Diaghilev with his assistant Teliakovsky in an effort to patch things up—their interests were identical, and they were surrounded by enemies—but Diaghilev remained obdurate. He paid for his arrogance very quickly: one of his many enemies secured an order from the Tsar dismissing him in a humiliating way. A few months later Volkonsky himself resigned: the occasion for this was a fine which he imposed on the all-powerful ballerina Kshessinskaya, knowing quite well that this would have violent repercussions. In fact he had no heart to continue in his post without the collaboration of the *Mir Iskustva* artists. (Diaghilev had persuaded them to withdraw their services from Volkonsky.)

The dismissal of Diaghilev, and the subsequent resignation of Volkonsky, made further progress almost impossible at the Maryinsky. Diaghilev abandoned ballet completely for a number of years, immersing himself in painting and music. Volkonsky's successor Teliakovsky, a retired cavalry officer, was a man very different from Volkonsky; his attitude to ballet can be judged from the fact that when Benois approached him with a project for an eighteenth-century ballet *Le Pavillon d'Armide*, he insisted to Benois that there should be plenty of waltzes: "Waltzes create the success of ballet".[1] Teliakovsky com-

---

[1] *Reminiscences of the Russian Ballet*, p. 226. In justice to Teliakovsky I must add that he was a very much better director than most of his predecessors. His treatment of drama was quite intelligent—Komisarjevsky pays a high tribute to him in his memoirs *Myself and the Theatre*—and he commissioned a number of fine productions of Russian operas utilizing the talents of men like Korovin, Golovin and Meyerhold. In ballet his authority was weakened by the same sort of intrigues that caused Volkonsky to resign; Kshessinskaya made life very difficult for him at times. After the violent dispute between Diaghilev and the Imperial Theatres Directorate one could hardly expect Teliakovsky to climb down and welcome back the arrogant Diaghilev.

Le Lac des Cygnes (Petipa–Ivanov, St. Petersburg, 1895) with
Pavlova as Odette and Nicolas Legat as Prince Siegfried
(*ca.* 1910)

Left: Nijinsky making his spectacular sideways leap as René de Beaugency in the Diaghilev Ballet's 1909 production of *Le Pavillon d'Armide* (Fokine, St. Petersburg, 1907)

Diaghilev in 1927

Below: the Diaghilev Ballet rehearsing in 1911. *In the foreground:* Stravinsky, Fokine, Karsavina

missioned décors and costumes for plays, operas, and ballets from the *Mir Iskustva* artists separately, but he avoided letting them take charge of a production as a whole, and would have nothing to do with Diaghilev.

6. FOKINE

By this time all but one of the elements needed for a complete renaissance of ballet were present in St. Petersburg. The missing element was good choreography. Petipa still continued to dominate ballet up to 1903, when his ballet *The Magic Mirror* was a fiasco, and he resigned in 1904.[1] His resignation made little difference to the standard of choreography: Gorsky, from Moscow,[2] was crude, melodramatic and unpoetic even by the St. Petersburg standards of the day, and Nicolas Legat (like Blasis) poured all his creative powers into his teaching. There were many criticisms of the décor and costumes of the ballets presented at the Maryinsky at this time in *Mir Iskustva*, but neither Diaghilev nor any of his collaborators seemed to realize that there was anything fundamentally wrong with the choreography of the day: their interests were confined to décor, costumes and music. This was easy to understand: the Petipa style had been established for so long that no other was imaginable except to a choreographer of genius like Fokine.

Fokine worked for some time on his own, with no contact with the Benois-Diaghilev group. He was a teacher at the Imperial School, and from 1905 onwards acquired experience arranging ballets for the Annual Display of the Senior Pupils; later he began to compose ballets for charity performances at the Maryinsky and elsewhere with the dancers of the Maryinsky company. His work was outstanding in its originality and poetic intensity, and he rapidly acquired fame in St. Petersburg.

It was not until 1907, however, that a ballet was produced which combined the new ideas of décor, costume and music of the Benois-Diaghilev group and Fokine's new ideas of choreography into a *Gesamtkunstwerk*. This ballet (*Le Pavillon d'Armide*) was staged at the Maryinsky as a normal repertoire production through much the same sort of accident that led to the production of *Giselle* at the Paris Opéra. Fokine heard about the existence of Benois' project

[1] According to Petipa the demonstrations against *The Magic Mirror* were organized by Teliakovsky to get rid of him. Whether or not this was true, *The Magic Mirror* was a bad ballet, with all the faults of *The Sleeping Beauty* in exaggerated form.

[2] Gorsky was sent to Moscow after being trained in St. Petersburg. Muscovite ballet had been of minor importance for some considerable time, and the misfits and failures of St. Petersburg were usually sent to Moscow. Gorsky made some small innovations in Moscow, making the mime more melodramatic and improving the construction, but his style of choreography was much the same as that of Petipa.

for *Le Pavillon d'Armide* from the composer Cherepnin (from whom Benois had commissioned the music for this ballet) and produced one scene of the ballet for a Pupils' Display; this interested Kuprensky (Director of the Production Department of the Maryinsky) to make arrangements in Teliakovsky's absence for a production of the whole ballet, as a normal contribution to the repertoire. At first he gave Benois and Fokine every facility, presumably hoping to secure prestige for himself; but after Teliakovsky's return he suddenly changed his attitude and began to put every possible obstacle in their way. Evidently Teliakovsky had realized Kuprensky's aims and administered a severe reprimand. Kuprensky hoped to provoke Benois into doing something rash, which would give him an excuse to liquidate the production; but Benois kept his temper; and the work went ahead in spite of obstacles until a week before the première, when the star of the ballet (Kshessinskaya) suddenly refused to dance in it. This was a severe blow, and could easily have wrecked the production; but Pavlova—braving the anger of the Directorate—stepped into the breach. Finally, as a last resort, the Directorate sought to ensure the failure of the ballet by arranging for it to be shown after a *complete* performance of *Le Lac des Cygnes*—by which time the audience and the critics would be too tired to appreciate it. Benois hit back with an article in the Press, denouncing the Directorate, and in fact the ballet, postponed to a later date and presented under good conditions, was a great success. But it was quite obvious to Benois, Diaghilev and Fokine that there was no future for their ideas within the Maryinsky.

7. DIAGHILEV'S FIRST PARIS SEASONS

In 1907 Diaghilev began work once again as an impresario, presenting concerts of Russian music in Paris. In 1908 he brought to Paris Meyerhold's production of the opera *Boris Godunov* with Chaliapine in the title rôle. For this venture he had the financial support and powerful influence of the Grand Duke Vladimir Alexandrovitch, who had for years taken a keen interest in the work of Diaghilev and his associates. Thanks to this august patronage Diaghilev secured the use of the Hermitage Theatre (the private Imperial theatre within the Hermitage Palace) for the storage and display of costumes and the painting of scenery. The success of *Boris Godunov* encouraged Diaghilev to return in 1909 with a combined season of opera and ballet. He was promised a lavish subsidy from the Grand Duke, the use of the Hermitage Theatre for rehearsals, and the loan of Maryinsky décors and costumes. The death of the Grand Duke and a quarrel between Diaghilev and the all-powerful Kshessinskaya (who was furious to find that she would have to share the limelight in Paris with Pavlova) put Diaghilev in a very difficult position: he lost the subsidy, the Hermitage and the loan of costumes and décors from the Maryinsky. Fortunately Diaghilev had other wealthy friends who provided him with the money he needed—notably Prince Dolgarukov-Argutinky in Russia and Madame Sert in Paris: in those spacious days, when both income tax and death duties were low, rich people could give away large sums almost without noticing it.

The change in arrangements enforced by the loss of Imperial patronage turned out to be for the best: Benois and Bakst designed new costumes and décors for the Paris visit, and all those associated with the productions (Diaghilev, Fokine and the designers) took the opportunity of bringing every detail of the productions into harmony with the others. From a financial point of view the season belonged to a completely different world from that of today: Diaghilev brought a large opera company, a large ballet company and a complete stage staff all the way from Moscow and St. Petersburg to Paris for twelve performances only!

During this season Diaghilev brought to Paris little that was new: what he brought was the best of what was available in St. Petersburg. *Le Pavillon d'Armide* was already in the Maryinsky repertoire, though Benois and Fokine took the opportunity of making a few revisions suggested by their experience in the Maryinsky production. Fokine revived two ballets which he had produced with Maryinsky dancers for charity performances—*Chopiniana* (renamed *Les Sylphides*) and *Une Nuit d'Égypte* (renamed *Cléopâtre*); these were given new décors and costumes by Benois and Bakst respectively.[1] For the latter ballet Diaghilev insisted on the introduction of music by other composers in place of some of Arensky's music which he disliked, but the new pieces of music were chosen to reduce to a minimum the necessary alteration in the choreography. The existing Maryinsky production of the opera *Prince Igor*[2] included a scene of ballet with "Polovstian" dances composed by Ivanov: for the Paris season Fokine composed new "Polovstian" dances which were much better than the original, though he kept their outline much the same. The only completely new item was *Le Festin*, a suite of divertissements of minor importance which was intended to give a certain Russian flavour to the programmes.

The overwhelming success of the 1909 season took Diaghilev and his associates by surprise: the eight performances of *Boris Godunov* with Chaliapine in 1908 had made a good impression, but the inhabitants of Western Europe had some acquaintance with good operas and good singing. The Russian ballets, on the other hand, seemed like a completely new branch of art, and the

[1] For the charity performances décor and costumes borrowed from the Maryinsky scenestore and wardrobe were used.
[2] On later pages *Prince Igor* refers only to the Polovstian Dances, not to the opera as a whole.

Maryinsky soloists seemed to belong to a completely different world from the dancers to be seen in the West. By this time people in Western Europe had completely forgotten that ballet could be taken seriously.

One serious weakness of the Diaghilev "équipe" which planned and supervised this remarkable season was the lack of a musician equal in stature to the others: Cherepnin was an academic composer producing works of sound craftsmanship, but he had no place in the Diaghilev circle. Diaghilev filled this gap before the next Paris visit by discovering Stravinsky, and this discovery led to the production in Paris in 1910 of *L'Oiseau de Feu*. This ballet, together with *Schéhérazade* (devised by Benois on the basis of existing music by Rimsky-Korsakov), represented the first important new ballets produced by the Diaghilev équipe under the leadership of Diaghilev. (The other novelty of 1910, *Carnaval*, had been composed by Fokine for production as the entertainment at a ball.) With the production of *Schéhérazade* and above all of *L'Oiseau de Feu* the Diaghilev Ballet began to emerge as something distinct from the Maryinsky; up to then Diaghilev had presented works which, but for the obstructiveness of Teliakovsky, would certainly have been part of the Maryinsky repertoire.

At this time there was no Diaghilev company in the sense of a body of dancers employed permanently by him. The dancers and the choreographer were all members of the Imperial Russian Ballet and could only dance for Diaghilev during their long summer holidays. What was permanent was the group of friends associated with Benois and Diaghilev which planned the ballets: this had originated nearly two decades previously in the regular meetings of Benois' school friends. Diaghilev was the driving force in the group: it was he who found means of coping with every obstacle, collected the money from patrons, and galvanized the others into activity; he also took a major part in the selection of the music, having had some training as a musician. Benois took the lead in devising the books of the ballets, and designed the décors and costumes for a number of them; Diaghilev gave him the official title of "Artistic Director". Bakst was a designer of remarkable versatility and (like Benois) took part in the production of some of the ballets. Stravinsky not only wrote the music but originated the themes of some of the most important of the Diaghilev ballets. Fokine, on the other hand, worked to some extent outside the group, and was not a member of the inner circle; a number of the most important Diaghilev productions were originally produced by Fokine on his own.

Most of the Diaghilev productions suffered to some extent from the fact that Diaghilev and his équipe thought much more in terms of costumes, décor and book than in terms of choreography: this arose from the fact that they had been working in the theatre for some time before they came into contact with a choreographer whose work was comparable in stature to their own.[1]

Diaghilev's leadership was not always tactful, and sometimes he behaved so badly that the équipe nearly disintegrated. In 1910, for example, he insulted Benois in a wilful and childish manner by ascribing *Schéhérazade* in the programme to Bakst, though it had been devised by Benois. The members of the équipe put up with such treatment from Diaghilev because of the wonderful opportunities they received through working with him; but it caused a great deal of unnecessary friction.

Diaghilev found great difficulty in raising the money needed for the 1910 tour; this was finally found for him in Paris by Gabriel Astruc, who became the business manager of the company.

8. THE PERMANENT DIAGHILEV COMPANY

The year 1911 was of decisive importance in the history of the Diaghilev company. In February of that year, while Nijinsky was appearing at the Maryinsky, Diaghilev encouraged him to behave in such an arrogant manner (refusing to apologize after a minor scandal about a costume) that his expulsion followed automatically. Nijinsky had to leave Russia at once to avoid arrest, and Diaghilev went with him. Diaghilev then organized a company on a permanent basis, with a small nucleus of dancers constantly employed by him and the rest fitting in the Diaghilev tours with their obligations to the Imperial Theatres. (Ballerinas did not have to give more than a certain number of performances per year, and could choose their own dates to some extent.)

Another important event of 1911 was the first visit of the company to London. The first season at Covent Garden (June–July) was so fabulously successful that Diaghilev arranged a return visit for a longer season in the Autumn, bringing together in honour of the occasion three of the greatest ballerinas of the Maryinsky—Kshessinskaya, Pavlova and Karsavina.

In London the Diaghilev company encountered an audience far larger and more reliable than anywhere else: houses were sold out every night, and if the artists had been available the seasons might have extended almost indefinitely. To quote Anatole Bourman:

> It was as though we were in our beloved Russia, so understanding and hospitable were our audiences, who shortly made themselves acquainted with the

[1] The ballets were described in the programme as being "by" the author of the book, as if they were plays to which music and dancing had been added (e.g. "Le Pavillon d'Armide—ballet en trois scènes d'Alexandre Benois.") This terminology had a long tradition behind it. At the Paris Opéra, for example, royalties were paid to the author of the book but not to the choreographer, and in order to provide some money for the latter it was usual to attribute the book partly to him.

names of every member of the company. Piles of telegrams, congratulatory messages, flowers and gifts waited for us after every appearance.[1]

The large and reliable London audience became the principal support of the company, making it possible for Diaghilev to hold the company together on a permanent basis. So long as Diaghilev maintained a high artistic standard he was able to count on the London seasons to bring in a great deal of money and relieve the company of the strain of continual touring. He was now fortunate enough to have as his business manager the wealthy Baron Gunsbourg, who paid all expenses without worrying about whether or not he got them back from the box-office receipts; but even the Baron's fortune would not have been enough to maintain the company without the London seasons.

The major artistic event of 1911 was the production of *Petrouchka*. The miraculous quality of this ballet—a perfect example of a *Gesamtkunstwerk*—was due to the fact that each great artist concerned was able to give full expression to his own creative ideas and yet harmonize them with the general conception and those of the other members of the team.

The details of the genesis of *Petrouchka* are of great interest as showing the process of collaboration within the Diaghilev ballet in its most creative period. The ballet originated as a short piano piece—a burlesque duel between a puppet and an orchestra—which took shape in Stravinsky's mind long before he committed it to paper. In fact he did not write it down until he had told Diaghilev about a project for a ballet based on a pagan rite (i.e. *Le Sacre du Printemps*) and had been urged by Diaghilev to begin work on this ballet. When he played the puppet-piece to Diaghilev (who was expecting music for *Sacre*) Diaghilev saw its possibilities as the basis for a ballet. He and Stravinsky both saw the ballet in terms of the strange atmosphere of the Russian Punch and Judy show. Diaghilev then wrote to Benois, asking him to "make the ballet" which he and Stravinsky had in mind. Benois was feeling very bitter because of Diaghilev's bad behaviour over *Schéhérazade*, but the project appealed to him strongly, and he agreed to take it on. He wrote the now-familiar story of the three puppets and the Charlatan, and placed the scenes at a fair in St. Petersburg—one of his dearest childhood memories. The actual details of the production were worked out by Benois and Stravinsky in collaboration, though Diaghilev supplied some of the details (e.g. the coachmen and grooms). When Fokine started rehearsals Benois supervised every detail, and in fact the wonderful crowd movements were partly his work; the dances were, of course, entirely the work of Fokine. At first Fokine disliked the music (which in 1911 sounded almost unbearably discordant) but later he came to terms with it, and excelled himself in his choreography for this ballet.

[1] *The Tragedy of Nijinsky*, p. 204.

Diaghilev's rôle in the creation of this ballet did not seem very important in comparison with the contributions of Stravinsky, Benois and Fokine, but in fact it was of great importance. He saw the possibilities in Stravinsky's piano piece, and brought together the right team; he then gave them freedom to work out their ideas, taking on his shoulders all the humdrum technical details of running a ballet company (a full-time job in itself).

Petrouchka was the last important ballet with choreography by Fokine. He had brought about a renaissance of the romantic ballet, but romanticism itself was moribund, and a rough beast was slouching towards Europe to be born. Fokine, a classical romanticist belonging in spirit to the early decades of the nineteenth century, was completely out of sympathy with the new expressionist tendencies which were making themselves felt in all the arts at this time. In fact he was as out of place in the first half of the twentieth century as Perrot and Bournonville had been in the second half of the nineteenth.

It is hard to disentangle the motives underlying Diaghilev's artistic policy at this time. On the one hand he saw clearly that Fokine was repeating himself, and that there were new ideas in the air which found no expression in Fokine's work—whereas he sensed that Nijinsky had in him the potentiality of coming to grips with these ideas. Under these circumstances it was natural enough for him to foster Nijinsky's development as a choreographer alongside Fokine. On the other hand Diaghilev's treatment of Fokine suggested that Diaghilev was influenced equally strongly by the fact that Nijinsky was very much under his domination, having had no experience of choreography outside the Diaghilev company—whereas Fokine had become established as a choreographer before he met Diaghilev, and maintained his own point of view on artistic matters. Diaghilev was already seeking to establish for himself a position of absolute power.

In fact Diaghilev subjected Fokine to a good deal of humiliation, apparently doing everything in his power to force Fokine to leave the company, short of actually cancelling his contract. He refused to allow Fokine sufficient rehearsal time for *Daphnis et Chloë*, pretending that the company was fully occupied with *Faune*; he would not allow new costumes to be made for *Daphnis et Chloë*, and the dancers had to dress their hair the best they could, whereas for *Faune* he provided beautiful new costumes and golden wigs. Because of the difficulties put in Fokine's path by Diaghilev the ballet was still unfinished when it was due for production, and then Diaghilev tried to persuade Fokine to cancel the production. Never an easy-going person, Fokine refused to be intimidated, and finished the ballet in a tremendous rush of activity.

Fokine also suffered from the fact that the Nijinsky ballet with its expressionist tendencies was in tune with the times, whereas his own style was losing its appeal: he saw the new Nijinsky ballet making a tremendous impression at a time when his own new ballets made only a tepid impression. He was incapable of sympathizing with the new trends, in spite of the fact that they had grown out of his own work on *Petrouchka*; to him they represented the destruction of everything he had laboured for years to create. He finally decided to leave in 1912, after thinking over the matter for a long time. It cost him a great deal to resign, for to a large extent the Diaghilev Ballet was his creation, and life outside it was unimaginable. In fact he had everything to lose and little to gain by leaving. If Diaghilev had made any real effort to soothe his wounded feelings he could have retained him. When Diaghilev chose to exert his charm he was irresistible: he could charm a tiger out of its skin. But he made no such effort.

This arrogant and wilful action by Diaghilev was the first of a number of irrevocable mistakes made by him which ended up by destroying the Diaghilev Ballet as an artistic enterprise of major importance. By this time Diaghilev was beginning to think of the company as *his* creation, ignoring the fact that the work of the company was only the culmination of a renaissance which had begun nearly four decades previously. His attitude of mind is shown by a remark he made to Benois when the latter expressed the fear that they might lose Fokine: "That's not so great a calamity. What is a ballet-master? I could make a ballet-master out of this ink-well if I wanted to."[1] Though Diaghilev's encouragement of Nijinsky was of great importance, and though Fokine belonged unmistakably to the past rather than the future, the departure of Fokine broke a vital link with tradition: the company needed both Fokine and Nijinsky for healthy development.

In the short run, however, Diaghilev's decision not to retain Fokine had no ill effects. In fact in 1913 Diaghilev achieved a further triumph in *Le Sacre du Printemps*, a ballet in which the harmony of all the elements was almost as perfect as in *Petrouchka*—in spite of the fact that *Sacre* was so far ahead of its time that very few were capable of understanding its full significance until after the First World War. In the two years which separated *Petrouchka* from *Sacre* the Diaghilev company moved from the early nineteenth century far into the twentieth century.

Even more destructive was the decision taken by Diaghilev to dismiss Nijinsky after the latter's marriage. If Diaghilev had dismissed Nijinsky in a moment of jealous fury immediately after receiving the news of his marriage, this would have meant very little: such behaviour would have been natural enough, and the quarrel could have been patched up eventually in the Russian manner, like Diaghilev's disputes with Benois. In fact, however, Diaghilev waited until he had formed a liaison with another man before dismissing Nijinsky, sending his brutal telegram of dismissal *three months* after the latter's

[1] A. Benois, *Reminiscences of the Russian Ballet*, p. 318.

marriage. He then devoted himself to revenge, using every ounce of his influence and energy to ruin Nijinsky. When Nijinsky tried to commission a décor from Bakst, the latter refused, on Diaghilev's instructions, and quoted Diaghilev's words to him: "As high as Nijinsky stands now, as low am I going to thrust him." When Lady Ripon forced Diaghilev to employ Nijinsky for the London season of 1914, Diaghilev ordered the company to insult him by ignoring him completely. Diaghilev's ruthless persecution of Nijinsky had serious effects on Nijinsky in the long run—effects which harmed Diaghilev just as much as they did Nijinsky.

Though Diaghilev tried to convince himself that Nijinsky was no more indispensable than anyone else in the company, the permanent touring company had been built around Nijinsky, and without his dancing it was like Hamlet without the Prince. As a choreographer Nijinsky was no less indispensable: he was the first great pioneer of expressionist choreography, and by dismissing him Diaghilev deprived his company of the avant-garde position it had won with *Sacre*. In fact Diaghilev was put into a position where he had to choose between destroying the artistic impetus of his company and satisfying his thirst for revenge. He chose the latter. This was a crime of truly heroic dimensions: it arose from a tragic flaw in Diaghilev's character—his *hybris*, or overweening pride—and the results followed with the remorseless logic of a Greek tragedy.

By this time Diaghilev had in his charge most of the artistically significant aspects of Russian ballet in the twentieth century—the culmination of four decades of great achievement by a series of great artists. To some extent this concentration was due to the fact that only outside Russia could the leading Russian artists find the freedom they needed to put their idea into practice, but it must not be forgotten that Diaghilev himself had been instrumental in bringing about the resignation of Volkonsky (thus handing the Imperial Theatres over to Teliakovsky), and it was Diaghilev who made it necessary for Nijinsky to live outside Russia. When Diaghilev treated the ballet company he had formed as if it were his own property, he acted in the same irresponsible manner as Napoleon squandering the lives of French soldiers in the Russian campaign and the Hundred Days which ended at Waterloo. The comparison with Napoleon is illuminating: with both these great men it is hard to disentangle their constructive achievements from their work of destruction.

9. DIAGHILEV RE-FORMS HIS COMPANY

During the early years of the war Diaghilev found it impossible to get continuous bookings in neutral countries, and the company dispersed. In 1915, however, he signed a contract with Otto Kahn (the great American patron of the arts who at this time dominated the Metropolitan Opera in New York) to bring the company to the United States. In fact, Diaghilev had no company at the time, but on the strength of his American contract he began a series of Herculean efforts to bring together some sort of a company. Under strong pressure from Otto Kahn he even made arrangements for the release of Nijinsky from internment in Hungary.

Unfortunately the release of Nijinsky came too late for him to take part in the first New York season (in January, 1916) at the Century Theatre.[1] The company that appeared at the Century Theatre was far inferior to the pre-War company: there was only one first-rate soloist (Lopukhova), and exacting rôles had to be given to dancers quite incapable of doing justice to them. Moreover there was no-one in the company capable of rehearsing the ballets in such a way as to restore to them their previous quality. Diaghilev had banked on the fact that because the American public had never seen his pre-War company it would have no standards; but the American public had seen Pavlova and Mordkin, and after the novelty had worn off the attendances at the Century Theatre began to decline. Some months later, when the company returned from a tour to appear at the Metropolitan, the subscribers began to complain bitterly.

The arrival of Nijinsky and Bolm at the Metropolitan changed everything. Nijinsky had been given a build-up such as no dancer had ever had before, but he lived up to it. Bolm too was a tower of strength. The dancers were now rehearsed by maîtres de ballet who knew how to give the choreography its proper value, there was a nucleus of first-rate soloists, and the season was a great success.

Relations between Diaghilev and Nijinsky were inevitably strained. Diaghilev could no longer afford to insult Nijinsky as he had done under similar circumstances in London in 1914, for the continued existence of his company depended entirely on his retaining the Metropolitan contract: America was the only neutral country where at this time it was possible to tour for any length of time. Diaghilev was polite to Nijinsky and his wife, but could not reconcile himself to the fact that Nijinsky was now a married man with a mind of his own. In fact Nijinsky had matured considerably since their last meeting, whereas Diaghilev was still in many respects a spoiled child. When Nijinsky tried to interest Diaghilev in two projects for new ballets (*Tyl Eulenspiegel* and *Mephisto Valse*) Diaghilev showed no interest: he was now grooming Massine to take Nijinsky's place, both as dancer and choreographer. Relations between Diaghilev and Nijinsky were also embittered by the fact that Nijinsky had won

---

[1] The opera season was still in progress at the Metropolitan when the company arrived, and so Otto Kahn leased the Century Theatre in order to give the company a New York season prior to its tour.

a law-suit against Diaghilev for back salary, and Kahn had arranged for the sum owed by Diaghilev to Nijinsky to be paid back in weekly instalments from the receipts.

Kahn was pleased with the success of the second New York season, and decided to arrange another Russian season for the following year, with a tour to follow. The first tour had lost money, and the second tour was also bound to lose money, for at this time ballet was very little known "on the road" in the United States; but Otto Kahn was thinking of the future, and considered that the loss was fully justified. Being well aware of the bitterness between Diaghilev and Nijinsky, he had no confidence in their working well together under the strain of continuous touring, and decided to arrange for the company to come without Diaghilev, putting the company under the joint management of Nijinsky and Bolm while the company was in America; from Kahn's point of view Nijinsky was indispensable but Diaghilev was not. Diaghilev accepted this humiliating arrangement, for the American contract was essential to the continuing existence of his company, and Kahn refused to sign a contract unless it included a clause stipulating that Diaghilev would not return to the United States while his company was there. In effect the Metropolitan Opera rented the company from Diaghilev and put it in the charge of Nijinsky and Bolm. Diaghilev decided to treat the American tour simply as a means of raising money, and went on working in Spain with Massine and a small group of dancers.

Since Nijinsky was co-director he was able to put into production his ballet *Tyl Eulenspiegel*, in spite of the fact that Diaghilev took no interest in it. This was the first important ballet produced anywhere in the world since Nijinsky's dismissal. (At this time the Diaghilev Ballet had no serious competitors.) Nijinsky had profited well from his years of creative work under the guidance of Diaghilev, and produced a *Gesamtkunstwerk* that was worthy of comparison with the productions staged by Diaghilev in the golden age of the Diaghilev company (1909–13), in spite of serious defects caused by the short time available for rehearsals.

Kahn's initiative in putting the company under the joint direction of Nijinsky and Bolm seemed sensible enough on the face of it: Nijinsky had the sensitive understanding of artistic trends needed to formulate a progressive artistic policy, while Bolm had the well-balanced temperament and the long practical experience needed for the detailed management of a ballet company. In fact, however, the division of power between two directors was fatal to the smooth running of the company, for it encouraged intrigues and the formation of factions. The bitter conflicts which resulted were bad for Nijinsky, who was already showing the first symptoms of the mental illness which later overcame him.

After the long American tour Nijinsky returned with the rest of the company to Spain, and for a time things seemed to go well, with the whole company re-united under the leadership of Diaghilev. But Diaghilev was still unable to reconcile himself to a new relationship with Nijinsky, and it was not long before bitter disputes broke out again.

The return of Nijinsky to the company during 1916–17 was forced on Diaghilev by impresarios, and had no effect on his artistic policy. He now based all his plans on the choreography of Massine, showing no interest in Nijinsky's plans for future ballets or even in revivals of *Sacre* and *Tyl Eulenspiegel*. Nijinsky left the company after its South American tour, and succumbed to mental illness soon afterwards.

The period 1916–20 was the Indian Summer of the Diaghilev Ballet. Apart from Nijinsky's appearances in his own rôles in the period 1916–17 and his production of *Tyl Eulenspiegel*, this period saw the emergence of Massine as a fine character dancer and a choreographer of outstanding ability. For a time, indeed, Diaghilev's plans for replacing Nijinsky seemed to work very well. Diaghilev had shown uncanny insight in selecting Massine, for the latter had had relatively little ballet training when Diaghilev discovered him in the drama section of the Imperial Theatre School in Moscow in 1913; in 1915 Massine composed his first ballet, and in 1917 he began to compose a series of ballets of such power and vitality that they restored the Diaghilev company almost to its pre-War position of artistic leadership.

After the Russian revolution of October, 1917, nearly all the greatest Russian dancers left Russia, and Diaghilev was able to strengthen his company enormously by taking some of them into his employment. The strengthened company began a London season in September, 1918, at the Coliseum, a variety theatre managed by Sir Oswald Stoll: there it provided one ballet from its repertoire as part of a variety bill. Later it moved to the Alhambra for a normal ballet season. In fact it appeared almost continuously[1] in London at various theatres for well over a year—one of the most extraordinary ballet seasons in theatrical history. If Diaghilev had been able to maintain a satisfactory artistic policy he could have taken advantage of the traditional fidelity and enthusiasm of the London audience to build a solid basis for his company in the post-War world.

Unfortunately Diaghilev had cut himself off by his own mistakes from any possibility of building for the future. He put all his faith in Massine, commissioning from this young choreographer with no roots in the Maryinsky a very large number of ballets. Massine's vein of neo-classical expressionism was soon worked out, and his creative powers began to fade very obviously in 1920. In that year he had a number of bitter disputes with Diaghilev and left him. His

[1] The record-breaking London season was interrupted by a few performances in Manchester.

departure left Diaghilev without a choreographer; even if he had remained, however, it is likely that his new ballets would have been disappointing.

The year 1921 began with Diaghilev apparently in full command of the situation: Massine's rôles were danced by the talented and versatile Woizikovsky, and the company was strengthened by the return of Lopukhova. Diaghilev's attempt to stage an expressionist ballet *Chout* without a choreographer[1] was not a success, but he had an exciting novelty in the shape of a traditional Spanish Cuadro Flamenco[2] and a superb repertoire. The London season which began in May continued until the end of July with good houses, and Diaghilev signed a contract to return later in the year for a season lasting at least six months with a lavish production of *The Sleeping Princess* (*The Sleeping Beauty*). In fact the prospects of the company seemed very bright. By the end of the year, however, Diaghilev was broken in health and spirit, and deeply in debt, while his company was in ruins. Eventually he managed to patch together some of the pieces, but Humpty Dumpty was never the same again.

It is easy to understand the grave mistake made by Diaghilev and Sir Oswald Stoll (who financed *The Sleeping Princess*) in over-estimating the drawing power of this production. Sir Oswald Stoll could not have known about the serious choreographic deficiencies of *The Sleeping Princess* (as compared with the other Maryinsky classics produced by Diaghilev, such as *Giselle* and *Le Lac des Cygnes*), while Diaghilev had never shown the same profound understanding of choreography that he showed for music and décor. After the long Russian ballet season of 1918–19 it was natural enough to think that an all-star production of *The Sleeping Princess* (originally designed to exploit the star-appeal of a large number of Italian and Russian ballerinas) would have the same spectacular success as the original Maryinsky production, particularly if provided with lavish settings and costumes by the world-famous Bakst.

The mistake made by Diaghilev in preparing his plans for *The Sleeping Princess* was not in itself very serious: all impresarios must gamble on their estimate of audience reactions, and cannot expect to achieve anything important without taking risks and making mistakes. Diaghilev, however, turned what might have been a temporary reverse into a major disaster by his refusal to face the fact that he had made a mistake. In this way he destroyed his company, just as Napoleon destroyed the Grande Armée in Russia. As soon as it was obvious that *The Sleeping Princess* was losing money heavily, Sir Oswald Stoll sensibly asked Diaghilev to vary the programmes with ballets from the general repertoire of the company. If Diaghilev had accepted this suggestion the season might have eclipsed even the miraculous season of 1918–19, for the company now

---

[1] The author-designer of the ballet, Larionov, produced it himself with the help of the dancer Slavinsky.
[2] *See* below, p. 298.

included a number of the greatest stars of the Maryinsky (including Spessivsteva, Trefilova and Yegorova). Instead, Diaghilev put off a decision for a whole fortnight. This infuriated Sir Oswald Stoll—who had already been annoyed by Diaghilev's childish habit of spending huge sums on items not covered by the original estimates without troubling to find out whether such additional items were really important. Sir Oswald Stoll therefore decided to withdraw the production. The settings and costumes were seized for debt, and Diaghilev left the country hurriedly. He could not now come back to England (where he owed a great deal of money) and this made it extremely difficult for him to re-establish his company; by this time the London season was all-important financially to him.

Diaghilev's failure to adapt himself to the realities of the situation when the show began to lose money heavily was not due only to his vanity and obstinacy; he was afraid that even if he alternated *The Sleeping Princess* with other ballets the season might not run long enough to pay back the enormously inflated costs of production of *The Sleeping Princess*, and then the décors and costumes of the other ballets might be seized for debt along with those of *The Sleeping Princess*. In fact this was a risk which he had to take if he wanted to maintain his company at a high standard. The Diaghilev of 1909 would probably have had the flexibility of mind and the daring to take this risk. By putting off the decision until too late the Diaghilev of 1921 made disaster a certainty. He soon had no money to pay salaries, and the stars dispersed.

At the end of 1922 a generous patron paid off Diaghilev's enormous debts, and in 1923 he was fortunate enough to obtain a contract which enabled the company to spend four months of every year at Monte Carlo. During January and April they gave three performances each week of the ballets in the repertoire, while during February and March the corps de ballet danced in the operas produced during the opera season. The Monte Carlo theatre was not large, and salaries were correspondingly low, but the company lived rent free at Monte Carlo, and conditions were ideal for the preparation of new ballets.

During the period 1922–23 Diaghilev was forced, in spite of himself, to stage two important expressionist ballets which continued trends which he had abandoned when he dismissed Nijinsky: both ballets had been devised by Stravinsky some years previously, but up to now Diaghilev had managed to avoid staging them, and he did not give them anything like the same sympathetic treatment that he had been giving the Massine ballets. *Le Renard* (with book and music by Stravinsky, décor by Larionov, and choreography by Nijinska in a style inspired by the work of her brother) was a ballet of exceptional interest, in spite of certain defects: audiences were unprepared for its uncompromising expressionism (Nijinsky's *Sacre* and *Tyl Eulenspiegel* having been dropped from the repertoire) and Diaghilev withdrew the ballet soon after its première without giving it a fair chance to establish itself in the repertoire. In the case of *Les Noces* (with décor and costumes by Larionov's wife Goncharova) he held up production for a long time, making ruthless changes in Stravinsky's project which ruined some of Stravinsky's most important ideas. Stravinsky had worked on his own in Switzerland during the war, and had devised some new methods of staging in his production *L'Histoire du Soldat*: he deliberately broke the theatrical illusion by placing musicians, actors, singers and dancers on the stage together. Diaghilev had no interest in *L'Histoire du Soldat* because (like *Tyl Eulenspiegel*) it had been produced independently of him, and he became furious when Stravinsky reminded him that the ideas he wanted to use in *Les Noces* had succeeded admirably in *L'Histoire du Soldat*. The final production of *Les Noces* was a rather unhappy compromise between Stravinsky's bold project and a more conventional ballet: the four pianos were visible at the sides of the stage, but the musicians playing the percussion and the singers were put in the orchestra pit. This broke up the harmony of music and movement intended by Stravinsky and gave the production an air of deliberate iconoclasm which was never intended by him. (Though Stravinsky's ideas often seemed strange at first, they were invariably extremely logical, and when properly executed came to seem quite natural in the course of time.)

10. THE COCKTAIL PERIOD

In *Les Noces* Diaghilev broke away to some extent from the *Gesamtkunstwerk* principle which he had taken over from Benois and which up to then had been basic in all his productions. After *Les Noces* he abandoned this principle completely: instead of making each production as perfect an embodiment of its basic ideas as possible, and educating the public to appreciate it, he now gave the new ballets an illusion of novelty by introducing into each ballet a deliberately arbitrary mixture of different styles in the various elements of the ballet, and treating the theme of the ballet as of no importance.

In a moment of terrifying honesty in 1924, Diaghilev analysed the nature of his new policy. To Lydia Lopukhova he described himself as a maker of cocktails: "I am a bar-tender, and have invented certain cocktails. Now other people come and steal my recipes; certainly they have not the right."[1]

The illusion of novelty created by the deliberately arbitrary mixture of disparate elements faded rapidly, and once Diaghilev started this policy he had to keep staging new ballets in rapid succession. Choreography was of relatively small importance in the cocktails, which relied for their effect mainly on the décors and costumes designed by the avant-garde painters of the day. What

[1] A. L. Haskell, *Balletomania*, p. 183.

Diaghilev demanded of the choreography was that it should be unobtrusive—neither noticeably banal nor yet so unusual as to present any difficulties to the audience.

Diaghilev may well have introduced the cocktail ballet as a desperate expedient in 1923, when he was cut off from London and worried by the competition of the expressionist ballets of the Ballets-Suédois—the first serious competition he had experienced. He now found himelf caught up in a vicious circle: because of his artistic policy he could no longer retain the services of the leading dancers of the day, and the resultant decline in the quality of performance of the older ballets in the repertoire forced Diaghilev to rely more and more heavily on the ephemeral appeal of new cocktail ballets (in which the quality of dancing was of much less importance than what Hollywood was later to call a gimmick). The cocktail ballets appealed only to a narrow sophisticated public, and in his efforts to cater to the taste of this public Diaghilev found himself reduced to being a follower of fashion rather than an artistic leader.

His relationship with the London public was now quite different. After long negotiations he was able to bring the company to the Coliseum in November, 1924, performing one ballet at a time in a variety bill, and in this way he was able to pay back part of his debt. He did the same for two separate seasons in 1925, and finally he was able to bring his company to His Majesty's Theatre in the summer of 1926 for a six-weeks' season of pure ballet. But this season and those which followed were very different from those of 1911–14 and 1918–21. The cocktail ballets had a relatively narrow appeal in London, and the theatre was sometimes half empty. People came to see the novelties, but were not much interested in coming to see ballets over and over again.

Now, for the first time, Diaghilev allowed his personal prejudices to have a deleterious effect on his artistic policy. In the new ballets he gave excessive prominence to male dancing, and almost ceased to provide any sympathetic rôles for danseuses.

In default of real ballerinas,[1] he had to give rôles to dancers which were far beyond their capacity. Danilova, for example, had to dance very exacting rôles before she was ready for them, and was often given rôles which did not suit her temperament. Nikitina had great potentialities but was pushed too hard and never realized them. Lifar had unmistakable talent, but danced every rôle exactly alike, and never matured artistically. In fact the new ballets gave none of the dancers any opportunity to mature: all they learned was a rather shallow kind of sophistication.

Diaghilev's new artistic policy did more than deprive him of the services

[1] According to André Levinson (*La Danse d' Aujourd 'Hui*, p. 10) there were at least ten of the stars of the Maryinsky dancing outside Russia at this time—not one of them in the Diaghilev company.

ouchka (Fokine, Paris, 1911) with Karsavina as the Ballerina and Bolm as the Blackamoor

Le Train Bleu (Nijinska, Paris, 1924) with Sokolova and Dolin

Below: La Chatte (Balanchine, Monte Carlo, 1927) with Lifar as the Young Man

of the greatest dancers of the day (apart from occasional appearances as guest artists); it led inevitably to the dispersal of his équipe—the artists responsible for the invention and planning of ballets like *Petrouchka*, *Le Sacre du Printemps*, *Le Renard* and *Les Noces*. Instead of being surrounded by artists of the stature of Benois, Bakst, Stravinsky, Larionov and Goncharova, Diaghilev was now surrounded by well-groomed nonentities. Ballets were no longer produced by creative artists working as a team: Diaghilev commissioned the different elements of the new ballet in an almost arbitrary way, bothering only to see that the final result on the stage had a slick sophistication. His new associates found that they could persuade him to adopt almost any suggestion, no matter how ridiculous, if they told him that he was getting old and could not understand new tendencies.

The most important member of the Diaghilev entourage in the cocktail period was Boris Kokhno. Diaghilev commissioned from him the books of most of the new ballets, and entrusted him with the general supervision of the productions. (Diaghilev himself became more and more bored with ballet, and ceased to concern himself with the details of production.) To quote C. W. Beaumont, Kokhno

> was both friend and secretary, and came to exert an increasing influence on the nature of Diaghilev's productions . . . He urged Diaghilev along the path of the chic and the "amusing"; he persuaded him to be always le dernier cri; unfortunately, few things stale more quickly than the sensation of a night or a week.[1]

The dancers saw much more of him than they did of Diaghilev: according to Lifar (whose pen is clearly sharpened by jealousy)

> he would even lay the law down to the dancers and the corps de ballet in regard to choreography. Kokhno's permanent attendance at rehearsals, his authoritarian suggestions and categorical demands, his somewhat haughty manner towards the members of the company, and his obvious intimacy with Diaghilev (he would "thou" him in public, and call him Seriozha) gave birth to many rumours that Kokhno was designated to succeed Sergei Pavlovich . . . The artists were on the whole somewhat afraid of Kokhno and did not like him, considering that his influence contributed to Diaghilev's aloofness.[2]

Though Kokhno's influence was undoubtedly of real importance it should not be overestimated. Diaghilev was inevitably driven towards the production of cocktail ballets for a narrow sophisticated public by the fact that he had deprived himself of the possibility of creating ballets of high quality for a broad

---

[1] *The Diaghilev Ballet in London*, p. 227.
[2] *Diaghilev*, p. 314.

A.A.O.B—F

public. In these new circumstances he had no use for people like Benois, Larionov and Stravinsky, who were accustomed to maintain high artistic standards and had minds of their own; he therefore surrounded himself with young men like Kokhno and Balanchine, who had never known the Diaghilev ballet in its great days and adapted themselves easily to the new artistic policy. Diaghilev would never have accepted Kokhno's suggestions and scripts for ballets if Kokhno's attitude to ballet had not been in harmony with his own.

Diaghilev's attitude to ballet in his cocktail period was shown very clearly in his treatment of Constant Lambert's ballet *Roméo et Juliette*. Lambert wrote music for this ballet which in spite of a certain modish harshness had a gentle, almost naïve lyricism, and he tried to persuade Diaghilev to commission the décor from Christopher Wood, whose *faux-naïf* style was perfectly in harmony with Lambert's music. Diaghilev refused to do this, preferring to make Lambert's music and the Shakespeare story ingredients in a cocktail of which the other ingredients consisted of surrealist décor and costumes by Gabo and Pevsner. Lambert was enraged by Diaghilev's treatment of his ideas (which made nonsense of them) and quarrelled bitterly with Diaghilev: though Lambert was still only a student at the Royal College of Music he understood very well the importance of harmony between the elements in a ballet, and refused to accept Diaghilev's cynical outlook. The final ballet was little more than a series of puerile stunts in which the story was almost ignored.

The production of *Ode* in 1928 (vividly described by Nicolas Nabokov in his book *Old Friends and New Music*) illustrated even more clearly Diaghilev's outlook in his cocktail period. This ballet began as a cantata—a setting by Nabokov of a didactic poem by the eighteenth-century Russian poet Lomonosov entitled *Ode to the Majesty of God on the Occasion of the Appearance of the Great Northern Lights*. Diaghilev was interested in the poem because it contained references to the Empress Elizabeth, from whom the Diaghilev family was supposed to be descended, and he commissioned Kokhno to work out a didactic-allegorical story for a ballet based on the cantata. He commissioned the décor and costumes for the ballet from the surrealist painter Pavel Chelichev, whose wildly fantastic décors he had admired in Berlin. Chelichev took little interest in the story of the ballet (which offered no scope to his surrealist ideas) and used the ballet simply as a pretext for the display of a number of experimental stage effects, including projected scenery (then very much the rage in Central Europe) and a trick-film (already used in ballet as early as 1925 in *Relâche*). Chelichev's experiments had no connection at all with Nabokov's music, which was gentle, lyrical and somewhat old-fashioned, in harmony with the naïve language of the poem. To quote Nabokov:

from the outset there were three different and in a way irreconcilable points of view on the *Ode* project. First there was Diaghilev's notion about a grand Elizabethan period piece, a tribute to the epoch of the great Russian court-poet Lomonosov; second there was Tchelitchev's view of *Ode* as a modern, surrealist experiment; and third there was my music, which did not fit into either of the first two categories.[1]

Once Massine began work on the choreography a fourth irreconcilable element was added to the existing three. Apart from one or two lyrical dances, Massine's cerebral pseudo-classicism had nothing to do with the romantic mood of Nabokov's music and the story of the ballet. Diaghilev came to a rehearsal and became angry because the movements were not as he wanted them. "What Massine is doing," he told Nabokov, "is modern, cold, angular stuff that has nothing to do with your music."[2] But he did nothing about getting the choreography altered: in fact he stopped coming to rehearsals, and when Nabokov mentioned the ballet to him he changed the subject. Kokhno now took over supervision of the production. Chelichev refused even to speak to Nabokov, who was understandably puzzled when he was called in to time a film shot of young men wearing fencing masks diving in slow motion.

Up to the last few days before the first night Diaghilev showed no interest in the production, in spite of the fantastic complexity of the scenic arrangements. Three days before the première he suddenly took command, and from then on worked day and night to co-ordinate every detail: presumably he had let things get into what seemed hopeless confusion before taking over in order to make his achievement in securing a smooth-running performance seem impressively Napoleonic.

His relations with composers were rather different from his relations with designers. He had a high degree of professional *expertise* in music, and his flair in detecting promise in young composers was almost infallible. For this reason he was able to offer his audiences music by unknown composers that was invariably competent, even if it fell far below the standard set by Stravinsky before 1923. In décor Diaghilev was much less enterprising, commissioning work from all the most famous avant-garde painters of the day in turn, irrespective of whether or not they had any feeling for the theatre. Results were sometimes amazingly good, but they were just as likely to be disappointing.

Diaghilev's declining years were tragic. Critics and audiences were inclined to be cool to his cocktail ballets, and he had to keep up a stream of new productions to replace the old cocktails, whose appeal declined with terrifying speed. Diaghilev himself became so bored with his cocktails that he kept away

[1] Nicolas Nabokov, *Old Friends and New Music*, p. 77.
[2] *Ibid*, p. 89.

from ballet for long periods, and tried without success to find a substitute for ballet in books. Raskolnikov, the hero of Dostoyevsky's novel *Crime and Punishment*, could choose between the Neva and Siberia, but Diaghilev had no Sonia to help him: being a diabetic, he drifted towards death through refusing to pay any attention to the orders of his doctors.

Towards the end of his life Diaghilev sought an escape from his cocktails by making plans for the revival of Maryinsky "classics", and he was delighted to have the chance in 1929 of presenting the great Spessivtseva in London in Act II of *Le Lac des Cygnes*. No matter how far Diaghilev's artistic policy degenerated, he never lost his admiration for great classical dancing; by keeping such great ballets as *Le Lac des Cygnes*, *Les Sylphides*, *Petrouchka* and *Prince Igor* alive in his repertoire, he preserved the great tradition of the ballet d'action, and made possible many important new developments after his death.

On the other hand the cocktail tradition established by Diaghilev had grave consequences. The type of ballet to which Diaghilev devoted his great talents and enormous energy during the last six years of his life was naturally continued by the people who worked for him during this period, and rapidly came to dominate world ballet.

PART II

Types of Choreography

THE TWENTIETH CENTURY began with a violent revolt against a moribund tradition of pseudo-classicism, which by then had been unchallenged for nearly half a century. One wing of this revolt, led by Fokine, retained the classical technique as a basis for choreography. The other wing, inspired by the work of Isadora Duncan, broke away completely from the classical technique. During the last half-century these two movements have influenced each other in many ways, but still retain their autonomy.

At the same time that this revolt was getting under way some form of expressionism was beginning to emerge in all the arts, and it rapidly became the dominating tendency in choreography. The free dance became completely expressionist, and (with one important exception) has remained so ever since. Developments in ballet based on the classical technique have been rather more complex.

The significance of the major trends in choreography in the twentieth century has been obscured by the general tendency to regard the developments within each major branch of theatrical dancing as being *sui generis*. In fact the major developments in the free dance (and even in Indian and Spanish dancing) can best be understood in relation to corresponding developments in ballet based on the classical technique.

A

Michel Fokine (1880–1942):

Renaissance of Classical Romanticism

FOKINE'S CAREER was perhaps the most tragic in the whole history of ballet. Being a choreographer of genius, he was able almost single-handed to clear away the encrustation of half a century of dead convention and re-establish ballet as a living art: in his best ballets Fokine revived the great tradition of Vigano, Didelot and Perrot, and at the same time looked forward to the second half of the twentieth century. But he had the misfortune to be born at a time when the whole world of art was moving into a new epoch, in which all the values which Fokine prized were at a discount. The art of ballet was just as subject to the Zeitgeist as any other, and so after a few years of brilliant achievement Fokine found himself adrift in a world where he was a complete stranger. He could not ignore the world around him—in fact he had been greatly stimulated at the beginning of his career by one of the pioneers of the new epoch, Isadora Duncan, and in one of his own ballets he did much to prepare the way for the new epoch in ballet—but he could never fully adapt himself to the new epoch, and the bitter conflicts inside him between old and new quickly destroyed his creative powers.

It is characteristic of Fokine that all his finest ballets were composed by him in a single burst of creative excitement: he could not do well except when he worked freely and rapidly, following the dictates of his daemon. Normally the most charming of men, he became ruthless and sometimes even cruel when he began to compose ballets; he had to work fast and freely if he was to do good work, and reacted violently to any stupidity or lack of sensitivity which held him back. All the best of his early productions—Pavlova's solo *Le Cygne* (*The Dying Swan*), *Chopiniana* (*Les Sylphides*) and *Carnaval*—were composed by him very hurriedly for charity performances; *Carnaval* was practically complete in *one* rehearsal, and many of the groups in *Chopiniana* were worked out by him on stage as the overture was playing for the first performance. His work for Diaghilev followed the same pattern: the most successful of his Diaghilev ballets—*Prince Igor, Schéhérazade, Le Spectre de la*

Rose and *Petrouchka*—were composed by Fokine very rapidly after they had been planned in detail by others; *Prince Igor*, in spite of its complexity, was composed by Fokine in eight rehearsals. Though Diaghilev may be blamed for excluding Fokine from the teams which planned these ballets—Fokine would certainly have widened his range of understanding by participating in the preliminary discussions—Diaghilev's policy was to a large extent justified by Fokine's temperament.

The only successful ballet in which Fokine had a large share in preparing the book was *L'Oiseau de Feu*. The story of this ballet was put together by Fokine from a number of unrelated fairy tales, and was rather unsatisfactory, for it gave relatively little scope to Fokine's special gifts as a choreographer except in the rôle of Fire-Bird itself. Karsavina's wonderful performance in this rôle, Stravinsky's miraculously dramatic music, and the exciting costumes, décor and lighting made the ballet a moderate success with the public, but it lacked the shattering inevitability of Fokine's best ballets.

The "Indian" and "Greek" ballets produced by Fokine for Diaghilev were the product of much study and long preparation, and on the whole were so lacking in spontaneity and poetry that they made relatively little impression. From the beginning of his career as a choreographer—before even he saw the "Greek" dances of Isadora Duncan—Fokine had been fascinated by the idea of producing a "Greek" ballet. In 1904, before he had had any experience in choreography, he made plans for a "Greek" ballet *Daphnis et Chloë*, submitting a scenario for this ballet to the Directorate of the Imperial Theatres (which of course was not interested). Refusing to be discouraged, Fokine managed to put some of his ideas into effect in *Acis et Galathée*, a new version of an Ivanov ballet which he arranged for a Pupils' Display; in this production he made his first tentative attempt to make the dancers depart from their classroom technique and move through poses drawn from Greek paintings. Two years later, after the appearance of Duncan in Russia, he produced another "Greek" ballet *Eunice* which aroused the violent disapproval of the older balletomanes because the dancers appeared in Duncanish chitons instead of the conventional tutus, and made use of Duncanish gestures far removed from the academic technique. (*Eunice* took the form of a Greek processional dance, and was given a single performance at the Maryinsky in aid of charity; the soloists were Pavlova, Kshessinskaya and Gerdt.) In 1911 Diaghilev planned to put *Daphnis et Chloë* into production, using Fokine's 1904 libretto; but Diaghilev disapproved of this libretto because it gave equal prominence to the boy and the girl, whereas he wanted a ballet in which Nijinsky starred on his own. He therefore decided to produce another "Greek" ballet *Narcisse*, on a theme suggested by Bakst. *Narcisse* had a *succès d'estime*, largely because of the charming costumes and décor; Fokine's choreography made little impression on the imagination or the memory of the public—except for a few poetic passages in the solos for Nijinsky (Narcisse), Nijinska (the chief Bacchante) and Karsavina (Echo). The ballet began with a group dance of frogs, goblins and miscellaneous forest denizens in Fokine's most naïve neo-Petipan manner. The goblins in *L'Oiseau de Feu* were made bearable by Stravinsky's music, but the Cherepnin goblins were excessively banal.

Le Dieu Bleu had its origin in Fokine's enthusiasm for Oriental dancing, stimulated by the visit of the Royal Siamese dancers to St. Petersburg in 1900. Unfortunately the Siamese classical style (with its emphasis on slow arm movements and limited variety of leg movements) blends very badly with the ballet technique, and Fokine's study of Indian painting and sculpture was equally misleading: the choreography which resulted was much too insipid and stilted to hold the stage, and the ballet was soon dropped from the repertoire.

Much the same was true of *Daphnis et Chloë*, put into production by Diaghilev (after a year's delay) in the same season as *Le Dieu Bleu*. Though the choreography had a certain tepid charm, its sentimentality and lack of integration with the music prevented the ballet from staying long in the repertoire in spite of the success of Ravel's music. (The music had real interest as a tone poem, but much of it was little suited for choreography.)

In his exotic melodramas (*Cléopâtre, Schéhérazade, Islamey, Thamar* and *La Légende de Joseph*), Fokine kept fairly closely to the Maryinsky tradition. These ballets were works of skilled craftsmanship, with Fokine applying to Russian nationalist music the principles of dramatic construction embodied in the ballets of the Maryinsky repertoire. Though Fokine avoided conventional gestures entirely in his mime scenes, and composed dances more exotic and less academic than any arranged by Petipa, he kept well within the Petipa framework. Petipa praised highly Fokine's first essays in choreography, and one may easily imagine him being even more impressed with this group of ballets. He would certainly have been enthusiastic about Fokine's favourite device for a climax—a mass spectacle with line upon line of dancers all making simple movements that combined together in contrapuntal patterns to create an effect of constantly increasing excitement. (Petipa himself had quite a flair for mass dances covering the whole stage, but Fokine far surpassed him.) In the same way Fokine's refusal to insert dances except at points where they arose naturally out of the action would have seemed to Petipa a return to the principles of balletic construction he had learned from Perrot. One might almost say that Fokine's exotic melodramas were the ballets which should have been produced at the Maryinsky at the time when Russian composers were writing the music on which they were based.[1]

---

[1] *Le Légende de Joseph* had music specially composed by Richard Strauss, but was of the same choreographic type as the others.

In spite of Fokine's skilled craftsmanship (which enabled him to produce exactly what was expected of him by the authors of the books of these ballets) he was unable to overcome the defects of their obsolete structure, and after *Thamar* it was clear that their style had no further possibilities of development. By this time Fokine was repeating himself in a distressingly obvious manner. *Thamar* was a weaker version of *Schéhérazade*, just as *Papillons* was a weaker version of *Carnaval*. Diaghilev had no illusions about the artistic value of ballets like *Schéhérazade*: he revived *Schéhérazade* in the twenties in order to make money, but roared with laughter when he watched it.

The "Oriental" dances in these ballets (apart from the Lesghinka in *Thamar*) had the same weaknesses as the "Indian" dances in *Le Dieu Bleu*. Even Fokine's magnificent ballet *Prince Igor* was to some extent crippled by the insipid "Persian" dances, in which the women spent their time languorously waving scarves. Undoubtedly Fokine was hampered by his lack of knowledge of real Oriental dances: the fiery dances of his Polovstian warriors and girls were based on Russian, Ukrainian and gypsy dances, all of which were easily available to Fokine in the Maryinsky repertoire and in the St. Petersburg cafés. (Later Fokine went to the Caucausus and studied the authentic dances of the different peoples of this region: his little-known ballet *Danses Caucasiennes* was based on these studies.)

Fokine showed his real genius in ballets of a very different sort. The most important of Fokine's early productions was the solo *Le Cygne* (*The Dying Swan*), composed by him for Pavlova to perform at a charity show in 1905. Though Fokine took a few hints from Ivanov's choreography for *Le Lac des Cygnes*, he was inspired by Pavlova's genius as a dancer and the Saint-Saëns music to make a decisive break with the conventional Petipa style. In its direct and lyrical expression of passionate feeling this dance is genuinely romantic: the arm movements with their wonderful contrasts of tension and line could belong to no other rôle.

Pavlova also inspired Fokine's most important contribution to the art of ballet, *Les Sylphides* (1908); this was entirely his own creation, whereas *Prince Igor* represented a new version of the dances arranged for a Maryinsky production of the opera by Ivanov, and *Petrouchka* was devised by the Diaghilev équipe.

The manner in which *Les Sylphides* came into existence shows clearly the peculiar nature of Fokine's talent. He was too much imbued with the Maryinsky tradition to plan such a revolutionary ballet in advance; the idea grew gradually from stage to stage, taking its own shape freely and spontaneously with a minimum of conscious planning. This ballet—rightly regarded as one of the most poetic ever composed—was evolved by Fokine in a few rehearsals for a Pupils' Display as an expansion of a classical pas de deux in the Taglioni style arranged by Fokine for Pavlova and Obukhov as part of a suite of items in various styles. In working out the structure of the new version Fokine may well have been influenced by descriptions of the Perrot *Pas de Quatre*, and he was certainly influenced by Perrot's style of choreography: the best passages in the ballet suggest Grisi dancing for Perrot. (Several Perrot ballets were in the Maryinsky repertoire at this time.) On the other hand the groups taken up by the corps de ballet and the soloists, some of the stage patterns, and two of the solos seem to have been influenced by the ballet *La Sylphide*, which was still in the Maryinsky repertoire in Fokine's youth.[1]

It is not difficult to pick holes in *Les Sylphides*: the ballet shows the faults almost inevitable in view of the way in which it came into existence. Fokine was like Perrot and Ivanov in relying on inspiration coming to him as he listened to the music, but—unlike Perrot—he could not subjugate his daemon to the task of planning a long ballet. Only in the Pas de Deux and the Prélude do we find Fokine and his daemon working happily together, inspired by Pavlova's extraordinary gifts. The Prélude is the least difficult of all the solos from a technical point of view, but it makes greater demands on the dancer's sense of style and poetic feeling than almost any other rôle. The two Mazurkas and the Valse, on the other hand, show a certain uneasy mixture between the romantic style of the Prélude and Pas de Deux and a more conventional academic style.

In creating this ballet Fokine intended to evoke the spirit of the Taglioni period and was therefore perfectly justified in using the same sort of enchaîne-ments that Taglioni danced. But Taglioni danced to conventional "ballet music" by composers like Schneitzhoeffer and Labarre, and Fokine composed his ballet to music by a great romantic composer of the period of the romantic ballet. No typical maître de ballet of the Taglioni period would have dreamed of composing a ballet to Chopin's music, for it was completely unsuitable for the type of choreography then in use; Fokine, having learned from Duncan that music by Chopin could in fact be danced, was inspired by Chopin's music to produce a new type of poetic choreography which inaugu-rated a new era in ballet. Being highly musical, Fokine showed himself sensitive to all the nuances of rubato in the music, but he was not content just to reproduce these nuances in the dancing: he placed the accents of the dancing with great subtlety so that the movements evoke a series of feelings too fleeting to describe but clearly apparent in a good performance.

The choreography of this ballet illustrated with the utmost clarity Fokine's ideas on the treatment of music by the choreographer: "Music is not the mere

[1] Marie Taglioni stayed in St. Petersburg for five years, appearing often in a large number of ballets arranged for her by her father Filippo Taglioni (including *La Sylphide*), and left a vivid memory behind her.

accompaniment of a rhythmic step, but an organic part of the dance: the quality of choreographic inspiration is determined by the quality of the music."[1] In an interview with Arnold Haskell he explained the spontaneous way in which his images grew out of the music: "Once the score has become part of me images are formed, which I occasionally fix in little drawings. That is the general plan, but the fantasy comes during rehearsals."[2]

In its structure and in its classicism and abstraction *Les Sylphides* looks forward to the second half of the twentieth century, in spite of its convincing and harmonious evocation of a particular period in the middle of the nineteenth century. *Petrouchka*, in contrast, looks back to the beginning of the nineteenth century (the period of the ballet) and at the same time was the first ballet to reflect the expressionism which dominated ballet in the two decades which followed its composition. (Like all great artists Fokine took what he needed from the past to make an assault on the future.)

When Benois and his collaborators prepared the project for *Petrouchka* they worked with such complete understanding of the period of the ballet that not only is all the local colour completely right for the period, but the very construction of the ballet belongs to the early years of the nineteenth century. Structurally the ballet has affinities with the *coreodrammi* composed by Vigano in Milan between 1809 and 1819, and it has even more striking affinities with the ballets produced by Didelot in St. Petersburg between 1816 and 1829. It does not require much stretch of the imagination to picture a ballet similar to *Petrouchka* being produced in Russia at about the period chosen for this ballet, with book by Pushkin and music by Glinka. Benois was capable of sentimentality and naïve melodrama when devising exotic ballets placed in ancient Egypt or the mysterious Orient, but in his own favourite place and period his artistic judgment was infallible. Even Stravinsky's music is perfectly appropriate to the period, for it is based on traditional airs and dances which might quite well have been heard at the period. Fokine had already had experience working with Benois on a period ballet (*Le Pavillon d'Armide*), and he collaborated even more effectively on *Petrouchka*, working in the very city of the ballet. (Some of the traditional "Butter Week" customs shown in the ballet still survived in St. Petersburg at this time.)

The title rôle of the ballet, however, belongs unmistakably to the first half of the twentieth century, both musically and choreographically. This rôle has strong elements of expressionism, and foreshadows all the major developments in choreography in the next two decades.

Propert lays great stress on Nijinsky's contribution to the creation of this rôle: "The part is all his own, for Fokine had given him complete freedom in

---

[1] Quoted by Tamara Karsavina in *Theatre Street*, p. 169.
[2] *Balletomania*, p. 138.

the making of it. Here at last among the puppets of the ballet we have a living individuality." This statement should not be taken to mean that the choreography was entirely Nijinsky's: on the contrary, at this period Nijinsky had no experience of choreography, and was incapable of such an achievement. It does, however, draw attention to the process of collaboration between choreographer and dancer which is characteristic of the finest choreography. The choreographer cannot create something organic and emotionally expressive except by working through the understanding, personality and technique of the dancer who creates the rôle, and the dancer cannot bring the movements to life unless he is allowed to do them in a way which feels right to him. During rehearsal there is a continuous process of mutual stimulation: the choreographer devises an image, the dancer seizes upon it and builds it up (under the guidance of the choreographer) into something which satisfies his own conception of the rôle, and this in turn inspires the choreographer to create another image in a similar or contrasted mood.

Nijinsky was God's gift to any choreographer, for he not only brought out every nuance of feeling asked by the choreographer, but fitted the various aspects of the rôle together into an organic unity and added something magical of his own. His versatility was so phenomenal that there seemed no mood or character which he could not assume to perfection, but for a number of reasons the rôle of *Petrouchka* appealed exceptionally strongly, and he made it into one of the most powerful myths of our time.[1]

The conditions prevailing at the time Fokine arranged this rôle—Stravinsky's expressionist music, a powerful theme which could only be expressed in dancing, and Nijinsky coming to the full maturity of his genius as a dancer—were so favourable that Fokine was inspired to create choreography which stands apart from everything else composed by him. Though only a highly trained classical dancer could perform the movements, they break away from the classical mould in almost every detail; at the same time they have a completely satisfying unity and harmony of their own. In the composition of this rôle Fokine abandoned his usual distinction between dancing and mime, creating movements that are highly dramatic and yet have the formal perfection normally associated with dancing.

Petrouchka was Fokine's last important ballet. He was completely unable to understand the impulses which drove Nijinsky to create a new style with none of the qualities of grace, spontaneity, freedom and lyricism which were the glories of the great Russian tradition of romantic ballet. From Fokine's point of view Nijinsky was setting out to destroy ballet.

To a certain extent Fokine's bitter feelings were justified: the rise of expressionism did mean the neglect of much that was wonderful in the classical-

[1] *See* below, p. 112.

romantic tradition revived by him. In the major ballets of the next period there was no place for the qualities which Fokine valued above all, and sought to cultivate in his dancers—qualities summed up in two words which he often used in rehearsal: "naslazhdaïtess" (do it with enjoyment) and "laskovo" (caressingly).[1] But there was no holding back the tide. Fokinian romanticism was moribund by 1913, and the only way forward led through expressionism.

Genius in retreat is always a melancholy sight, and Fokine's declining years were tragic. He met adversity with courage, refusing to see merit in any aspect of expressionism or to admit any difference in quality between the masterpieces composed by him up to 1911 and his later works; in fact he embarrassed friends and admirers by expecting them to be just as much impressed by his mediocre new compositions as by revivals of his masterpieces.

In Russia during the First World War he had relatively little opportunity for composition, for the Maryinsky almost ceased to produce new ballets— though he composed some ballets for charity performances as in the past. In the United States (where he lived after 1919) he had had even less opportunity for creative work. Twice he formed companies of his own, but the conditions under which he worked were very frustrating for a man of his passionate temperament.[2]

His most ambitious American ballet was Les Elfes, composed in 1924 for his own American Ballet and later revived for the third Ballets Russes de Monte Carlo. Superficially Les Elfes was an abstract ballet of the same general type as Les Sylphides, but choreographically the two ballets had nothing in common: where Les Sylphides was poetic and mysterious, Les Elfes was sentimental and rather flashily spectacular. In default of dancers like Pavlova, Nijinsky and Karsavina, capable of creating imaginative effects with simple means, Fokine did his best to make some sort of theatrical effect by bringing together enchaîne-ments of difficult classroom steps which had little to do with Mendelssohn's music (Overture to a Midsummer Night's Dream) and had no poetry in them. (Like all good choreographers, Fokine would not abide dullness on the stage, and if he could not grip the audience in one way he would do it in another.)

It was not until 1936, when Fokine was on a visit to France to compose ballets for Ida Rubinstein,[3] that he came into contact with René Blum and was made artistic director of a ballet company which gave him some chance of reviving his fading creative powers. The Blum company was young and inexperienced, and had no great ballerinas, but it was at least a permanent professional company with some contact with the great Russian tradition of noble and expressive dancing.

---

[1] Irving Deakin, Ballet Profile, p. 91.
[2] See below, p. 385.
[3] See below, p. 353.

Fokine's most important creation for the Blum company was the "chinoiserie" ballet *L'Épreuve d'Amour* (1936). Here the frivolous theme of the ballet and Mozart's equally frivolous music ruled out any attempt at the grand romantic manner, and Fokine was able to come to terms with the limited talent available to him and his own limited powers of creation. Very skilfully he concealed the limitations of the company's soloists by making considerable use of properties (such as wands and a Chinese dragon) and picturesque group movements of the corps de ballet. Only one solo rôle was of much importance —that of the Butterfly, in which Fokine exploited the charm, lightness and technical skill of Kirsova by giving her enchaînements of considerable virtuosity, making no call on qualities of imagination and emotional depth which she did not possess. In fact the ballet as a whole was a fine example of skilful craftsmanship, and coming as it did at a time when ballet was degenerating rapidly, it received rather excessive praise. (Obukhov's admirable performance in one of the smaller rôles gave some hint of the ballet which Fokine might have composed for the early Diaghilev company.)

In spite of its serious deficiencies *L'Épreuve d'Amour* had a certain lightness of touch and spontaneity which recalled the Fokine of happier days, and was sadly lacking in the other ballets composed by Fokine at this time. *Don Juan* (1937) was a mime-play in which dancing had little place: here Fokine used a ponderous and prosaic type of mime which contrasted in the most depressing manner with the imaginative, fast-moving and expressive dance-mime of ballets like *L'Oiseau de Feu* and *Petrouchka*. (The original *Don Juan* of Angiolini might well have been in a style like that of Fokine's ballet, but this did not make the ponderousness of Fokine's *Don Juan* any the more acceptable.)

Other ballets composed by Fokine at this time showed much the same defects as *Don Juan*. In *Paganini*, composed for de Basil in 1939, he attempted to outdo the expressionists at their own game, using such devices as transparent violins lit from inside; but *Paganini* was crude and clumsy in comparison with *La Symphonie Fantastique* (1936) of which the mood was somewhat similar. (Massine was never a genius like Fokine, but expressionism was his native tongue.) It was characteristic of Fokine that he attempted expressionism after it was already moribund.

Cendrillon (composed for de Basil in 1939) and *Barbe-Bleu* (composed for Ballet Theatre in 1941) were fairy-tale ballets even less worthy of Fokine's talents. The humour in these ballets was slapstick clowning of the most ponderous sort, and Fokine's attempts at contemporaneity (e.g. the introduction of acrobatics) were embarrassingly out of date. *Cendrillon* was even booed by the Covent Garden gallery, in spite of the enormous admiration which English audiences had for Fokine's great ballets.

Fortunately Fokine's compositions of his declining years soon fell out of the repertoire, and the memory of his genius is kept green by innumerable performances of his masterpieces, above all *Les Sylphides* and *Petrouchka*. These retain a few shreds of their former glory, even when performed (with the choreography altered almost beyond recognition) by dancers with little understanding of the style of the two ballets or their changing moods.

Schéhérazade (Fokine, Paris, 1910) with Karsavina as Zobeïde and
Nijinsky as the Favourite Slave

Les Sylphides (Fokine, St. Petersburg, 1908) as presented by the Diaghilev Ballet at Covent Garden in June, 1911. Karsavina in the centre

L'Oiseau de Feu (Fokine, Paris, 1910) with Karsavina as the Firebird and Bolm as Ivan Tsarevich

B

Expressionism

EXPRESSIONISM MAY be defined as a type of art in which the main emphasis is placed on the creation of images expressing the intense emotions of the artist *at all costs*, usually through violent distortion and a considerable degree of simplification. (The latter process leads towards abstraction—a characteristically expressionist form of abstraction which differs profoundly from other types.) Though the word expressionism is modern, painters and sculptors have created works that may properly be called expressionist at many different periods and in many different countries (e.g. the paintings of El Greco, Bosch and Grunewald, the Caprichos of Goya, Romanesque sculpture, and nearly all American Indian, Polynesian and African Negro sculpture). Expressionism is by no means the same thing as romanticism, but these two have much in common, and the expressionism of the twentieth century corresponds in many ways to the romanticism of the nineteenth. (Much of modern expressionism grew out of late romanticism.)

Modern expressionism began to emerge in all the arts towards the end of the nineteenth century and in the early years of the twentieth. In painting, van Gogh, Gauguin and Toulouse-Lautrec were important pioneers of expressionism, while Picasso's revolutionary innovations were to a large extent inspired by a number of characteristically expressionist types of art—mediaeval Catalonian frescoes, Romanesque sculpture, the paintings of El Greco, Negro sculpture, etc.[1] Rodin moved strongly towards expressionism, his head of Balzac being characteristically expressionist: it is no accident that he was one of the first to appreciate Isadora Duncan, and rushed to the defence of *L'Après-Midi d'un Faune* when this early example of balletic expressionism came under attack from Calmette.

In music expressionism emerged during the second decade of the twentieth century in the compositions of Schönberg and Stravinsky. Though Schönberg wrote in an international idiom his expressionism was as characteristically Central European as Stravinsky's expressionism was Russian. Schönberg began

---

[1] Picasso's Analytical Cubism may to some extent be regarded as an abstract type of expressionism.

his career as a typical exponent of late-German romanticism: then what Mosco Carner calls his "monomanic urge for unrestricted self-expression" led him over a period of years to "an intensification and elaboration of Wagnerian chromaticism until the emotional pressure reached so high a degree that in his subsequent expressionist period it destroyed the functional relation of the chromatic note to its diatonic 'parent'."[1] Schönberg's expressionism took clear shape in 1909 with his "monodrama" *Erwartung*, a setting for solo voice and orchestra of a typically hysterical German expressionist poem; but the master-piece of expressionist opera was beyond question *Wozzeck*, composed by Schönberg's pupil Alban Berg between 1914 and 1920 and first produced in 1925. Stravinsky, independently of Schönberg, moved in a somewhat similar direction, but his work was strongly conditioned by his roots in Russian nationalist music (he was a pupil of Rimsky-Korsakov), and reached maturity in the scores provided by him for a series of intensely Russian expressionist ballets—*Petrouchka*[2] (1911), *Le Sacre du Printemps* (1913), *Le Renard* (1922) and *Les Noces* (1923).

A number of German-speaking poets began to write expressionist poetry during the first and second decades of the twentieth century; in Western Europe, however, poets were little affected by expressionism. Kafka was the major pioneer of the expressionist novel in Central Europe. James Joyce's *Ulysses* (written during the First World War) showed strong expressionist tendencies, and one might perhaps describe its successor *Finnegans Wake* as the expressionist novel to end all expressionist novels in English, though certain American writers continue to find stimulus in this genre.

In the drama expressionism began to emerge toward the end of the nineteenth century in the last plays of the Norwegian dramatist Ibsen and (a few years later) in the dream plays of the Swedish dramatist Strindberg; these dramatists reached toward expressionism in an effort to break through the limitations of their own naturalism, whereas the German dramatist Wedekind showed expressionist tendencies from the start; his plays from *Earth–Spirit* (1895) onwards were unmistakably expressionist.

Stanislavsky's first dramatic productions in Moscow (in the early years of the twentieth century) were strongly expressionist, with the main emphasis on striking and mysterious scenic effects produced with the aid of décor and lighting. Such productions were in fact a highly subjective expression of the ideas and feelings of the producer. Later, however, he became dissatisfied with this type of production because it suppressed the creative powers of the actors and failed to do justice to the full meaning of the play; and he went on to create a

---

[1] *The Listener*, Dec. 27, 1951, p. 1118.
[2] The music for the title rôle of *Petrouchka* was strongly expressionist, even though this was only slightly true of the rest of the ballet.

new type of poetic realism which gave full scope to the individuality of the actors, and was admirably adapted to the plays of Chekhov and Gorky which were the chief glories of the Moscow Art Theatre.

On the other hand Stanislavsky's pupil Meyerhold developed very strongly in an expressionist direction, interpreting plays in a violently individual and distorted manner which Stanislavsky did not like because it reduced actors to puppets.[1] In the confused aftermath of the Revolution expressionism became dominant in the Russian theatre, and Meyerhold had great influence: the subtle and poetic realism of the Moscow Art Theatre seemed to have little relevance to the violence characteristic of life at this time.

Stanislavsky's favourite pupil Vakhtangov succeeded in combining an expressionist freedom of treatment with respect for the individuality and creative powers of the actors: his violent and ecstatic production of The Dybbuk (1918) for the Jewish theatre Habima was a landmark in expressionist theatre. No less important was his gay, witty and colourful production of the Gozzi fairy-tale Turandot for the Vakhtangov Theatre in 1923, just before his untimely death. In both productions he combined together first-rate acting, singing and dancing into a new kind of synthesis: for this reason, and also because of his respect for the creative powers of his actors, these productions kept their vitality indefinitely just like good ballets, instead of dating after a few years like other expressionist productions. (The Vakhtangov productions of The Dybbuk and Turandot still remain in the repertoires of Habima[2] and the Vakhtangov Theatre respectively.) If Vakhtangov had lived expressionism in the theatre might well have developed on very different lines.

In Germany the first unmistakably expressionist production was Reinhardt's production of Ibsen's play Ghosts in Berlin in 1906, with décor and costumes by the pioneer expressionist painter Edvard Munch and boldly expressionist lighting. (In the last scene the mood of despair was heightened by shadows of the mother and son cast on the walls by a hanging lamp.)

The Norwegian Munch was the father of Central European expressionist painting; this developed into a distinct school with characteristics different from those of expressionist painting in Paris and Moscow. The paintings produced by Munch up to his nervous breakdown in 1907 had a hysterical violence which gave them a strong appeal in Central Europe (where his influence began to be felt after about 1902), and most of the features of Central European expressionist painting can be traced back to him. In Central Europe there was close contact between painting and the theatre: not only did the painters design the

---

[1] Stanislavsky founded an experimental studio of the Moscow Art Theatre in 1905 and put Meyerhold in charge, but he dissolved the studio when he found Meyerhold developing on lines which he (Stanislavsky) knew from bitter experience would lead to the destruction of imaginative acting. (Cf. David Magarshack, Stanislavsky, p. 274).

[2] Habima settled down in Tel-Aviv in 1928, after a long period of touring the world.

décor and costumes and advise on lighting, but in some cases even wrote the plays. (The painter Kokoschka was one of the men writing plays for the Stormbühne, formed in Berlin in 1910 for the presentation of expressionist plays in expressionist style.)

After the war Central Europe was the scene of widespread misery, starvation, disillusion and social disintegration which followed the military defeat, the blockade and the inflation; under these conditions hysterical expressionism of the Munch type seemed the only thing which could really express people's feelings, and it made rapid progress in every branch of art. In the theatre progress was particularly rapid: public interest in expressionism was so strong that it enabled expressionist dramatists, writers, designers, composers and choreographers to gain control of scores of theatres owned and subsidized by the states and municipalities.

In Central Europe theatrical expressionism developed in much the same direction as in Russia, and in fact many of the expressionist plays written in Germany were also produced in Russia. At a feverish pace the leading dramatists (particularly Kaiser and Toller), the leading producers (particularly Reinhardt, Jessner and Fehling) and the leading designers worked together to develop a type of drama in which every detail of text, speech, gesture, movement, décor, costumes, lighting and music was completely expressionist. Every element in the production was designed to make the most violent and immediate impact on the audience; contrasts were as sharp as possible, and characterization and themes were simplified to the last degree. The plays were written in a rapid series of short scenes, with telegraphic dialogue that dispensed with prepositions, adjectives, pronouns and even verbs. The characters were personified abstractions with names like "Engineer", "Workman", "The Poet", "Man", "Him", "Her", "X", and so on. Acting full of subtle nuances of psychology and poetic implication, in the Stanislavsky manner, was quite unsuitable for such plays, and (as in Russia) producers demanded a rhetorical style (derived from that used by Wedekind when acting in his own plays) that never pretended to be anything but acting. "The new acting was speeded up to a prodigious tempo. Movements were jittery and gestures unpredictable, delivery jerky and shrill."[1] Every possible distortion of real-life behaviour was considered desirable in order to heighten the emotional impact of the production. Violent distortion was equally de rigeur in the décor: walls leaned over at impossible angles, in order to give the impression of a nightmare world, and sometimes the natural forms were distorted in such a way as to take the shape of a symbol. The lighting departed as far as possible from any suggestion of natural illumination: powerful spotlights concentrated the whole attention of the audience on the part of the stage in use at any time, leaving the rest of the stage in complete darkness, and scenes normally finished with a blackout.

[1] Mordecai Gorelik, *New Theatres for Old*, p. 253.

In dancing the pioneer of expressionism was the American genius Isadora Duncan (1878–1927), who came to Europe to seek a career at the end of the nineteenth century. She came at exactly the right time, when the art of ballet was almost dead and dancing was no longer considered a major art capable of making an impression on sensitive, intelligent people. She embodied in herself the myth, common to romanticism and expressionism, of the inspired artist who breaks all the conventional restraints on human expression and brings about the triumph of spontaneous emotion. She had little technique, and relied on improvisation under the stimulus of great music, giving the freest possible expression to her own individuality. She was also a pioneer in dancing barefoot, in short and filmy costumes which left bare parts of the body normally covered, and worked all alone on the stage against a background of plain blue curtains; but none of these innovations would have made such an impact if her dancing had not had a new and exciting quality of spontaneity and poetic intensity.

Technically her dancing was very limited. Her leg movements were confined to a walk, a run, a kick of one knee up in front, a corresponding kick of one heel up behind, and so on. Her vocabulary of gesture was wider, including broad movements leading to upraised arms, movements inspired by those shown on ancient Greek vase paintings, stylized imitations of natural gestures such as those used in playing the harp or gathering flowers, gestures like those of a conductor indicating the shape of a melody or rhythm, and so on. Generally the symbolism she used was very simple and straightforward. But she had a warm and magnetic personality and great emotional power which enabled her to stir audiences to their very depths with these simple movements.

Sometimes she felt impelled to tackle projects beyond the capacity of her means of expression, but in her best items there was complete harmony between idea and image. Karsavina describes this aspect of her dancing with great sympathy and understanding:

> When she interpreted *The Elysian Fields*[1] her artistic means were not only adequate but raised to the same level of supreme and absolute beauty as the music of Gluck itself. She moved with those wonderful steps of hers with a simplicity and a detachment that could only come with the intuition of genius itself. She seemed to float, a complete vision of peace and harmony, the very embodiment of the classical spirit that was her ideal.[2]

Though Karsavina was a classically trained dancer she fell under Duncan's spell as soon as she saw her:

---

[1] A scene from Gluck's opera *Orfeo*; Duncan danced almost the whole of this opera, taking different rôles in turn and suggesting by her gestures the actions of the invisible characters.
[2] *Theatre Street*, p. 171.

It never occurred to me that there was the slightest hostility between her art and our own. There seemed room for both, and each had much that it could learn to advantage from the other.[1]

Duncan had enormous influence wherever she appeared. In each country certain aspects of her dancing—those aspects which were in harmony with the national temperament and cultural traditions—made a particularly strong impression, and gave rise to national styles of the free dance.

In England, France and the United States she inspired styles of natural movement which kept fairly closely to her own limited technique; in addition, however, the "Revived Greek" style invented by Ruby Ginner in England developed a fairly complex technique, and in the United States various schools of the free dance developed very elaborate techniques.

In Russia Duncan's arrival coincided with a crucial stage in a renaissance in ballet, and she had great influence on the architects of this renaissance—Fokine, Pavlova, Diaghilev, Nijinsky, Karsavina and many others. Though in Russia her influence on dancing and choreography was not as obvious as in other countries, being only one of a number of important factors in the renaissance of ballet, it was profound and lasting. She also had a powerful influence on Stanislavsky and through him on the whole of the subsequent development of the art of theatrical production, both in Russia and in other countries influenced by Russian methods. (She proved to Stanislavsky that movement could be just as expressive as speech, and was just as important in the presentation of the theme of a play.) At the invitation of Lunacharsky Duncan came to Moscow in 1921 and established a school there, but by this time her ideas had been fully assimilated in Russia, and her direct influence on the Soviet theatre was slight.

In Central Europe during the first decade of the twentieth century Duncan made an impression greater than any other dancer at any time. There her dancing did much to stimulate the formation of a considerable number of styles of free dancing which continued some of the fundamental principles of her dancing (e.g. respect for the expression of the individuality of each dancer and creation through improvisation) and many of its technical features (bare feet, bare legs, reliance on "natural" movements such as walking and running, and so on). Inevitably these schools were influenced by the prevailing tendencies in Central European expressionism, and developed a hysterical quality not to be found in Duncan's work; on the other hand they made very considerable technical progress, expanding her vocabulary of movement in many directions.

---

[1] *Theatre Street*, p. 171.

VASLAV NIJINSKY (1890–1950)

We have four independent accounts of the genesis and production of Nijinsky's first ballet *L'Après-Midi d'un Faune*. Romola Nijinska gives the entire credit to Nijinsky himself. She describes Nijinsky as saying to Diaghilev one day: "I have in mind a choreographic poem, not a ballet, which I would like to do. My idea of Greece is utterly different from Bakst's and Fokine's." This suggestion (according to Romola Nijinska) interested and amused Diaghilev, and he asked Nijinsky: "Why not work on it?" Nijinsky replied: "I have done so, and the whole *oeuvre* is already quite clear. Of course I should like to have the music composed for it."[1] This undoubtedly represents Nijinsky's own view of what happened: in his *Diary* he wrote: "I created the whole ballet alone."[2]

Lifar gives Nijinsky almost no credit at all. He mentions Bakst as teaching Nijinsky "la plastique antique" but describes the ballet as

> a work inspired and created by Diaghilev. . . . The idea of *Faune* came to Diaghilev for the first time in 1911 at Venice. It is he who showed Nijinsky the angular "plastique" of the central figure. . . . He was responsible for the whole composition of *Faune*, from the poses of the nymphs, reproducing the dances of antiquity, to the final gesture, and including the halting of the dancing on the crescendo of the orchestra.[3]

Lifar became Diaghilev's constant companion towards the end of the latter's life, and this account probably reflects Diaghilev's view of what happened.

Stravinsky gives Diaghilev credit for the original idea, but attributes the rest of the production entirely to Bakst:

> At the suggestion of Bakst, who was obsessed by ancient Greece, this tableau [suggested by Diaghilev] was to be presented as an animated bas-relief, with the figures in profile. Bakst dominated this production. Besides creating the decorative setting and the beautiful costumes, he inspired the choreography even to the slightest movements.[4]

According to Fokine the title rôle—i.e. the greater part of the choreography —was stolen from one of his own compositions, with which Nijinsky was familiar through being rehearsed in it:

[1] *Nijinsky*, p. 149.
[2] *The Diary of Vaslav Nijinsky*, p. 151.
[3] *Histoire du Ballet Russe*, pp. 213–14.
[4] *Chronicle of My Life*, p. 64.

Nijinsky's own rôle, with its oblique movement, is lifted straight out of the Bacchanale from *Tannhaüser*, which I arranged for Karsavina and him. The same archaic poses, only he substituted for the final embrace the act of onanism which I find most displeasing.[1]

It is clear that none of these accounts gives the whole story, and one may assume that Diaghilev, Bakst, Fokine and Nijinsky all had a share in determining the final shape of the ballet. Certainly Nijinsky was not yet ready to compose a ballet entirely on his own. He had been cut off from the world by Diaghilev, and had been dominated by Diaghilev in every respect: even his own dancing had been profoundly influenced by Diaghilev, who saw in Nijinsky potentialities which could never be realized at the Maryinsky. On the other hand the efforts by Lifar, Stravinsky, Fokine and others to reduce to insignificance Nijinsky's contribution to the choreography are wide of the mark. When later attempts were made by Diaghilev and members of his équipe to "dictate" ballets to choreographers without much creative ability (e.g. the attempt by Larionov to produce the ballet *Chout* with Slavinsky) results were very disappointing, and certain aspects of the choreography of *Faune* were in violent contrast to the ideas of Diaghilev, Bakst and Fokine.

From the very start Nijinsky showed himself to be a choreographer of a very different type from Fokine. Before starting rehearsals he insisted on being provided with a studio, a pianist and a dancer, in order that he might work out his own ideas in privacy. Much as he admired Diaghilev, he felt the need to shut himself in for a while and make his own mistakes, until he had clarified his ideas to some extent. For two months he worked in Paris with the dancer Gavrilov, refusing to show anything to Diaghilev until he had solved some of the problems involved and was ready to start rehearsals with the company. Once rehearsals started Bakst undoubtedly played a very active part in determining the details of the groups, and Nijinsky relied heavily on Diaghilev's advice in solving the innumerable difficult problems which emerged in so revolutionary a ballet. It is also clear that Diaghilev was responsible for the theme of the ballet: Nijinsky did not even know until after the ballet was finished that Debussy's music (which Diaghilev persuaded him to use) was based on a poem by Mallarmé which also provided the theme of the ballet. Reluctantly Nijinsky agreed to use the Debussy music, though its shimmering impressionism and smooth curves ran counter to the jagged, staccato expressionist movements (derived from those of the title rôle of *Petrouchka*) which he wanted to use. Fortunately Diaghilev and Nijinsky saw eye to eye about using dancing to suggest a series of moods rather than making it one element in the treatment of a story: from the very beginning of his career Nijinsky treated

---

[1] Interview quoted by Haskell in *Balletomania*, p. 139.

dancing as a normal means of expression rather than as something inserted into a mimed story.

There were wonderful moments in *Faune* where the various ideas of Bakst, Diaghilev, Fokine and Nijinsky came together in harmony with Debussy's score and created effects of great poetic intensity; but there were also a great many passages where the ballet seemed no more than the exposition of a formula, something as dry and intellectual as a theorem in geometry: the sudden changes of front by the corps de ballet when they came to the side of the stage were particularly disturbing. Even at its least harmonious, however, the ballet retained its unique atmosphere, and as a whole it was a fine piece of theatre which deserved its persistent success.

Diaghilev's influence was much less marked in Nijinsky's next ballet *Les Jeux*. From Nijinsky's point of view this ballet was as much an experiment as *Faune*: profoundly influenced by the theories of Dalcroze,[1] Nijinsky tried to arrange independent movements of the various limbs of the dancers to fit every detail of the counterpoint of the music. The treatment of the theme was even more abstract than in *Faune*: though the dancers wore tennis clothes and made use of properties such as a tennis racket, the movements of the dancers had no connection with those used in tennis, and sport was used as a symbol for something else. (The playful aspects of sport were used ironically to symbolize a particularly frivolous kind of perverted love.) In order to bring out the abstract, expressionist character of his ballet Nijinsky froze the faces of his dancers into mask-like immobility, and prevented the emergence of any romantic lyricism by avoiding extended movements of the arms and half-clenching the hands. In general the movements showed the same emphasis on angularity as those of *Faune*.

Unfortunately there was little harmony between the theme chosen by Nijinsky and the experiments he was determined to make in the style of movement and the treatment of the music. Having highly trained dancers at his disposal Nijinsky was able to go a long way in his application of Dalcrozian ideas; but the result on the stage had a frigid cerebral quality which detracted very seriously from the atmosphere he wished to create. In spite of its lack of success, however, this ballet had great historical importance as the first ballet with a definitely contemporary theme and the first to show a characteristically expressionist treatment of the music.

In *Le Sacre du Printemps*, Nijinsky broke away from Diaghilev's direct

---

[1] Diaghilev had been much impressed by the work of Dalcroze at Hellerau, and had asked Dalcroze to send him one of his best pupils to give the Diaghilev company training in Eurhythmics. Dalcroze sent Marie Rambert. Though the lessons were very unpopular with the company and were soon discontinued, the Dalcrozian ideas she brought with her had considerable influence on Nijinsky. She acted as Nijinsky's adviser when he worked out his Dalcrozian treatment of the music in *Le Sacre du Printemps*.

influence, and worked on the choreography without his help, though of course
he was indirectly affected by Diaghilev's general artistic leadership, just as were
Stravinsky and Roerich. The ballet in fact represented a fusion of the ideas of
Stravinsky, Roerich[1] and Nijinsky collaborating together on a theme (originally
devised by Stravinsky) which meant a great deal to all of them. Their treatment
of the theme combined a high degree of abstraction with enormous primitive
violence: *Le Sacre du Printemps* was in fact the first great expressionist ballet,
foreshadowing nearly all the characteristic features of post-War expressionism
in both ballet and the free dance. It had much in common with *Les Demoiselles
d'Avignon* (1905–6), the great painting in which Picasso brought together
elements from Negro sculpture and the paintings of Cézanne and El Greco and
launched a new school of painting; both the Picasso painting and the Diaghilev
ballet bewildered most of those who saw them for the first time. Though *Le
Sacre du Printemps* and *Les Demoiselles d'Avignon* now seem to have been far
ahead of their time, they were actually very much of their time: the great artists
responsible for them showed themselves more sensitive to significant trends in
thought and feeling than their contemporaries, and so the full importance of
their work was not apparent for many years.

Nijinsky's choreography for *Le Sacre du Printemps* was from the point of
view of artistic evolution almost the exact equivalent of the music, and naturally
aroused the same feelings of revulsion and bewilderment in the audience and
critics. Even today a good performance of the score of *Le Sacre du Printemps*
in a concert-hall is disturbing, in spite of the enormous developments in stridency
and atonality in the last four decades: its demoniacal violence gives some hint
of the effect on the audience of 1913 of the music, the choreography and the
décor and costumes all together.

In *Le Sacre du Printemps* Nijinsky developed still further the Dalcrozian
ideas of *Les Jeux*, but instead of running counter to the theme they were
completely in harmony with it.

The best eye-witness account is that given by Propert:

> *Le Sacre du Printemps* was as profoundly moving as its predecessor was halting
> and ineffectual. But here, instead of clockwork tennis players, we were watching
> men and women, primitive and unreasoning, helpless in the clutch of some im-
> placable being whose nature they but dimly understood, but of whose merciless
> power they were horribly aware . . . I think that only Russians could have wanted to,
> or dared to use such a theme. I am sure no company but Diaghilev's could have
> carried it through. It demanded a very alert intelligence on their part to follow the

---

[1] Roerich's designs for costume and make-up were admirably in harmony with the rest
of the production, but his décors were relatively insipid: Diaghilev would have done well to
commission the décor from Picasso. At this time, however, the avant-garde Parisian painters
took no interest in ballet.

flight of Nijinsky's imagination, and a musical perception so keen that they could distinguish their allotted parts in a score of amazing complexity, in which as many as three and sometimes even four, themes in unrelated keys are running concurrently. . . . The dancing throughout was determined by the music. The weight and quality of sound was reflected faithfully in varying numbers of the dancers and the intensity of their movements, and even in the colour of their dresses. The scarlet groups would instantly dominate the stage in some passages of horns and trumpets, while violins or flutes carried the sense of white or grey or orderly ritual or quavering uncertainty.[1]

Each movement was intended to suggest the Stone Age, and so broke away completely from the classical technique.

There was no dancing on the point of the toes, no pirouettes or entrechats. Instead, we saw contorted limbs, toes turned inwards, and heads bent stiffly sideways. Instead of arms moving in rippling curves we saw them strained rigidly downwards or as rigidly bent at the elbow, and instead of the silence of the feet that had seemed scarcely to touch the ground they flew over, we heard the stamping and shuffling of insistent shoes.[2]

The hands of the dancers were normally clenched into fists—as in Les Jeux, but more strongly.

There were many innovations in the use of groups. At certain moments half a dozen dancers moved shoulder to shoulder without touching each other, executing intricate movements in complex rhythms with the utmost precision. The various choreographic themes introduced into Act I were brought together in the finale of this act, with a wide circle of women moving to the main theme of the music and smaller groups of men moving inside the big circle to the other themes present in the music.

Though in style Nijinsky's expressionist choreography was the counterpart of Stravinsky's expressionist music, much of it lacked the maturity, economy and homogeneity of the music. By this time Stravinsky (aged thirty-one) was a highly experienced composer; he had been maturing steadily ever since he became Rimsky-Korsakov's pupil in 1902, and through working with Fokine on L'Oiseau de Feu and Petrouchka had acquired mastery over every aspect of composition for ballet. Nijinsky, in contrast, had only begun his career as a choreographer the year before, and was tackling a score which in its rhythms and in many other respects was probably the most difficult ever written. (Even today the most skilled conductors think twice before tackling Sacre.) Stravinsky's comments on choreography are usually infuriatingly obtuse (he ignores every

[1] W. A. Propert, The Russian Ballet in Western Europe—1909–1920, p. 79.
[2] Ibid., p. 80.

aspect of choreography except its relationship to the music) but he had some justification for describing Nijinsky's choreography as being "very laboured" instead of being "a plastic realization flowing simply and naturally from what the music demanded".[1] There were times when Nijinsky's choreography lost all connection with the theme, and became a mere application of Dalcrozian ideas, as mechanical and cerebral as anything in *Les Jeux*. This was not due to Nijinsky's precise, expressionist technique of dealing with the music—the music in fact demanded treatment of this sort, Fokinian lyricism being completely out of place—but rather to the fact that the movements were without significance in themselves. In the best scenes, however, the dancing had such power that Nijinsky's expressionist treatment of the music seemed perfectly natural. This was true, for example, of the storm scene ("terrified women thrown, as if by centrifugal force, out of the turning swarming crowd, lashed by the orchestra's whip, snapped up by the instrumental cyclone.")[2] It was most of all true of the magnificent dance of the Chosen Maiden, the climax of the ballet. This long, exhausting and complex dance—almost a ballet in miniature—had such irresistible power and inevitability that (as danced by Marie Piltz) it silenced even the rioting crowd of the first night. Her angular, grotesque and ecstatic movements, full of violent dynamic contrasts, showed for the first time the intensity of which balletic expressionism was capable.

The première of *Sacre* left the spectators dazed and frightened, but during subsequent performances people began to realize the tremendous sincerity and integrity which had gone into its composition, and it even began to arouse enthusiasm. Unfortunately it was taken out of the repertoire after three performances in Paris and three in London, because of Diaghilev's quarrel with Nijinsky, and so it was not possible for contemporary audiences and critics to realize that the apparently iconoclastic details of the choreography arose naturally and inevitably out of previous developments in choreography, just as Stravinsky's musical innovations were already latent in his score for *Petrouchka*. The dance of the Chosen Maiden, for example, was foreshadowed by the dances of Petrouchka both technically and emotionally. In many types of folk dance, and above all in the most primitive type of European folk dance (Morris dancing), one may find precedents for Nijinsky's exact reproduction of the rhythms of the music and his emphasis on the contact of feet with the ground.

Because of Diaghilev's quarrel with Nijinsky only one of the subsequent ballets planned by Nijinsky was ever put into production, but he talked over his plans with his sister Bronislava, and in this way some of his ideas came to affect the course of ballet history.

While crossing to South America in 1913 Nijinsky, in a natural reaction to

[1] *Chronicle of My Life*, p. 83.
[2] E. Vuillermoz, *La Revue Musicale*, June 15 1913.

the violent expressionism of *Sacre*, began to plan an abstract classical ballet to the music of Bach. It is likely that this project was inspired by another project for a Bach ballet (having as its theme the triumph of Apollo) which Benois and Diaghilev had worked on together during the interval between the end of the Paris season and the departure of the company for South America. Nijinsky's ideas were slightly different: he planned to dispense with all story, and asked the help of the company's conductor René Baton to help him find appropriate music among Bach chaconnes, preludes, etc. Baton played for him day after day on the ship while he worked out the choreography. (Diaghilev was not on the boat, his nerve having failed at the last moment: he had a neurotic fear of being drowned, and hated sea voyages.)

Romola Nijinska describes a few of the many ballets planned by Nijinsky after their marriage. The most important of these projects, *Tyl Eulenspiegel*, was planned by Nijinsky while he was interned during the war in Hungary; this was later put into production with the Diaghilev Ballet. *Mephisto Valse* was planned in 1916, while the Nijinskys were staying in Vienna on their way to America; it was based on an episode in the Faust story, and was to be in classical style. Nijinsky made arrangements to produce this ballet with the Diaghilev Ballet, but rehearsals had to be abandoned because of an accident sustained by him, and he never produced it. After completing the project for *Mephisto Valse*, Nijinsky began to work on a project for a Japanese ballet; for a long time he had been fascinated by Japanese dancing, and had composed solo dances for himself in a style inspired by Japanese prints.

Little attention has been paid to *Tyl Eulenspiegel* in books on European ballet because it was never seen in Europe, and Diaghilev had every inducement to disparage a ballet produced without any help from him[1] at a time when Nijinsky was co-director of his company in his stead. (Diaghilev never saw the ballet, and made no effort to revive it in later years.) Fortunately Paul Magriel has cleared away misapprehensions about *Tyl Eulenspiegel* by bringing together in a monograph published by Dance Index a number of reports on this ballet by Americans who either worked on the New York production or saw it from the front. These accounts make clear that *Tyl Eulenspiegel*, with all its faults, was an expressionist comedy fully worthy of the choreographer of *Sacre*. Nijinsky was cruelly hampered by the fact that the company did not arrive in New York until two weeks before the opening night of its season; to make things worse, Diaghilev retained sixteen of the most experienced members of the company in Europe, sending inexperienced dancers in their place. Knowing

---

[1] Diaghilev's behaviour was often neurotic, but particularly so in regard to works composed by members of his équipe independently of him. He would invariably refuse even to talk about such works, and would have nothing to do with them even if he thereby did great injury to himself. (He treated Stravinsky's *L'Histoire du Soldat*, for example, exactly as he did *Tyl Eulenspiegel*.)

Nijinsky's slow methods of composition, Diaghilev was able to foresee that Nijinsky would have a very difficult time, and would be unable to achieve a satisfactory production of the two ballets he had contracted to produce. In fact Nijinsky did not even have a clear two weeks at his disposal to work on his new ballets: part of this time had to be spent on polishing up the other ballets in the repertoire and teaching their parts to the new members of the company, while as a further blow Nijinsky strained his ankle at the first costume rehearsal of *Tyl*. As a result *Tyl* had to be postponed to the last week of the season, and at the première parts of it were improvised by the corps de ballet.

Nijinsky's own rôle—that of Tyl himself—was a very different matter. He had had a long time to prepare this rôle, and poured all his genius into his interpretation of it. He made Tyl into the comic equivalent of Petrouchka, altering the ending to make Tyl appear above the heads of the crowds mourning his death: Tyl's mocking laugh was the comic equivalent of Petrouchka's cry of despair. There were no precedents in either the Maryinsky or Diaghilev repertoires for an expressionist comedy ballet like *Tyl Eulenspiegel*; it is likely that Nijinsky was influenced in his choreography by the work of the brilliant English grotesque dancer Little Tich (whom he admired intensely) and by the films of Chaplin (whom he rightly regarded as a genius).

Though *Tyl Eulenspiegel* was just as expressionist as *Sacre*, it represented a very different type of expressionism, inspired by Gothic sculpture, Gothic architecture, the paintings of Breughel and Bosch, early German wood-cuts, and in fact the whole art of the Middle Ages. According to the American critic Carl van Vechten (who was familiar with the Diaghilev company at its pre-War best and had seen the première of *Sacre*), Nijinsky's achievement in this rôle surpassed anything he had yet done:

> The keynote of Nijinsky's interpretation was gaiety. He was as utterly picaresque as the work itself; he reincarnated the spirit of *Gil Blas*; indeed, a new quality crept into stage expression through this characterization.[1]

Nijinsky's performance was hampered by his injured ankle (he omitted some of the more difficult steps he had planned), but even at less than his best Nijinsky was still supreme among the male dancers of his time.

The whole of Nijinsky's development as choreographer was deeply influenced by his personal relationship with Diaghilev, which dominated his life from 1909 onwards. Diaghilev did not lead Nijinsky astray: Nijinsky was already having an affair with a rich prince when he was introduced to Diaghilev. He had drifted into homosexuality (much to his friend Bourman's disgust) partly because after a childhood of bitter poverty, insecurity and humiliation

---

[1] Dance Index monograph *Nijinsky* (ed. Paul Magriel), p. 11.

he was offered the most dazzling luxury. If we can believe Nijinsky's *Diary* (written after he had begun to go mad) Diaghilev took advantage of the fact that Nijinsky was ill during the first Paris season to persuade him to come to live with him.[1] Earlier in the *Diary* he wrote:

> I did not like Diaghilev, but lived with him; I hated Diaghilev from the first day of our acquaintance, because I knew his power.[2]

We need not accept Nijinsky's violent statement that he hated Diaghilev from the beginning—this was written after he had suffered very severely at the hands of Diaghilev, and tended to blame everything on him—but there is good reason to think that their relationship became distasteful to Nijinsky fairly soon.

From the start Diaghilev seems to have been aware (consciously or unconsciously) of the danger of losing Nijinsky, and did his best to cut him off from the world: Nijinsky lost contact with all his friends and even with his own family. Nijinsky profited enormously from his association with Diaghilev, one of the most cultured men alive, and admired him intensely; but he chafed at being made a puppet, with no chance of having a life of his own. In fact Nijinsky was put in the same position as the child of over-possessive and over-protective parents, and reacted in the same way that sensitive children often do in such a situation, hiding his real self behind a mask of taciturnity and polite banality. He seemed to consist of two people—a man of genius on the stage, and a charming but shallow youth off-stage.

This neurotic division in Nijinsky's personality originated during his first two years at the Maryinsky school, when he was viciously persecuted by his fellow-students—who despised him because he was Polish and very poor, and were jealous of him because he was much better than any of them at dancing. Nijinsky tried to keep out of trouble by being as unobtrusive as possible, hiding his sensitivity and making no complaints, no matter how badly he was treated. It was only when he was in dancing-class or dancing on the stage that he had no need to fear persecution, and could express himself with perfect freedom. When he came under Diaghilev's domination he reverted to the attitude of his childhood, hiding his feelings under a mask when in private life but giving them full expression in his dancing and choreography.

Though the changes in Nijinsky's personal relationship with Diaghilev profoundly affected his ballets and did much to determine the shape they took, they do not account for their artistic quality. Lionel Trilling has dealt with this point with admirable clarity in *The Liberal Imagination*:

[1] *The Diary of Vaslav Nijinsky*, p. 148.
[2] *Ibid*, p. 62.

Nothing is so characteristic of the artist as his power of shaping his work, of subjugating his raw material, however aberrant it may be from what one may call normality, to the consistency of nature. It would be impossible to deny that whatever disease or mutilation the artist may suffer is an element in his production which has its effect on every part of it, but disease and mutilation are available to us all—life provides them with prodigious generosity. What makes the artist is his power to shape the material of pain we all have.[1]

The first signs of Nijinsky's revolt can be seen two years after the beginning of his intimate relationship with Diaghilev, in his interpretation of the rôle of Petrouchka. The rôle appealed to him very strongly because he saw in it the image of his own position: he too was a puppet, with every detail of his life controlled by strings in the hands of a puppet-master (Diaghilev). Nijinsky lost himself in all his rôles, but the transformation he achieved in *Petrouchka* was so complete as to be terrifying: as Beaumont says, he was not so much a dancer imitating a puppet, but a puppet that sometimes aped a human being.

He seemed to have limbs of wood and a face made of plaster ... Only now and again did he make you aware that beneath this façade there was a tiny spark of human life, which you caught sight of by accident, as though it were something you were not meant to see ... [He was a] wretched puppet—beaten, humiliated and the sport of its fellows—a victim of cruel injustice which moved by jerks and starts and hardly left the ground.[2]

In private life Nijinsky was sometimes very like Petrouchka, suddenly making a witty and acute remark which seemed an accident because of its contrast with his usual polite inanities. The rôle of Petrouchka mattered so much to him that each performance of it was a harrowing experience for him, and he had a strong tendency to forget what came next—something quite astonishing in a dancer of genius. (Fokine had to stay in the wings and prompt him when his mind went blank.)

In Nijinsky's first ballet *L'Après-Midi d'un Faune* his revolt was obscured by the fact that the theme, the shape of the ballet as a whole and many of the details of the choreography were devised by Diaghilev and Bakst. But even here his conception of the theme, built up by him without knowledge of the Mallarmé poem, clearly reflects an early stage in the growth of his understanding of his own emotional life. According to Nijinsky's conception of the theme (reproduced by Romola Nijinska in her biography) the ballet is a drama of adolescence:

[1] P. 175.
[2] *Complete Book of Ballets*, p. 722.

Isadora Duncan

L'Après-Midi d'un Faune (Nijinsky, Paris, 1912) with Nijinsky as the Faun

Le Sacre du Printemps (Nijinsky, Paris, 1913)

the initial awakening of the emotional and sexual instincts and their reaction. The day-dreams, the longings of a modern schoolboy are similar to the half-voiced desires of those primitive creatures, the ancestors of man, part animal, part male human being.[1]

In this conception one can see dawning in Nijinsky an understanding of the unconscious factors in his own emotional and sexual development: his conception of the theme of the ballet was very different from Diaghilev's, who saw the ballet simply as "the erotic gambols of a faun importuning nymphs". (When he danced the Faun Nijinsky naturally stressed his own adolescent interpretation of the rôle, and this was also apparent in many details of his choreography.)

Les Jeux was devised by Nijinsky himself, and represented in disguised form a bitter attack on Diaghilev. In devising the theme of this ballet Nijinsky showed the same combination of subtlety and boldness that he had used, while a schoolboy at the Maryinsky, in planning the theft of examination questions. In his *Diary* he wrote:

> *Jeux* is the life of which Diaghilev dreamed. He wanted to have two boys as lovers . . . In the ballet, the two girls represent the two boys and the young man is Diaghilev. I changed the characters, as love between three men could not be represented on the stage.[2]

Though the satirical element in *Les Jeux* was heavily disguised, Nijinsky's use of expressionism for satirical purpose was prophetic: this proved later to be the genre for which expressionism based on the ballet technique is best suited.

It is significant that in the rôles arranged for himself in both *Faune* and *Les Jeux* Nijinsky made no use of his incomparable elevation and his extraordinary feeling for dynamic subtleties of movement. Movement was lacking in both these ballets, which to a large extent consisted of a series of poses joined together in the simplest possible manner. There was nothing in the themes which demanded this treatment: in fact one might well expect a faun or a tennis player to indulge in violent movements, including leaps. Presumably Nijinsky was impressed by the fact that in *Petrouchka* the subjection of the leading figure was expressed choreographically by close contact with the ground and staccato, hemmed-in movements, and felt that he could not indulge in elevation and free movements until he had won his own freedom.

Sacre represented a decisive stage in Nijinsky's growth towards maturity and self-knowledge. For the first time he worked in complete independence of Diaghilev, tackling a score of the greatest imaginable complexity with fanatical

[1] *Nijinsky*, p. 147.
[2] *The Diary of Vaslav Nijinsky*, p. 154.
A.A.O.B—H

determination to make every detail as he wanted it. A very large number of rehearsals was necessary, but in view of the complexity of the score and the complete novelty of the movements the number was by no means excessive. The intellectual effort required to come to terms with this score in the extremely precise way chosen by Nijinsky was enormous,[1] even though he had considerable assistance in analysing the music from Stravinsky and Marie Rambert. Stravinsky thought the extremely lengthy and laboured efforts by Nijinsky to get his dancers to perform small phrases exactly as he wanted them the mark of a man without musicality,[2] but Stravinsky's ideas in this matter were based only on Fokine's methods of work: Nijinsky's methods were in fact almost exactly the same as those of Vigano, who was a highly trained musician.

Nijinsky's treatment of the dancers in rehearsal was completely expressionist. The atmosphere was very different from that prevailing in Fokine's rehearsals, where the work went ahead very rapidly.

> Nijinsky rehearsed like an inexhaustible demon until he nearly dropped in his tracks. Jumps were no longer completed with slightly flexed knees, but flat-footed and straight-legged in a fashion to preclude the possibility of lightness . . . With every leap we landed heavily enough to jar every organ in us. Our heads throbbed with pain.[3]

When Nijinsky's friend Bourman complained he became furious and replied: "The steps are mine. They will stay. Go back and dance them. . . ."[3]

Nijinsky's revolt against Diaghilev emerged clearly in his treatment of the Chosen Maiden—a rôle with many affinities with the Petrouchka rôle in which Nijinsky first gave expression to his revolt. By this time, however, Nijinsky had matured considerably, and instead of showing the Chosen Maiden as a helpless puppet he made her accept her fate in a mood combining terror, ecstasy and self-dedication. The choreographer who composed this rôle was a very different person from the puppet of 1911, and a break with Diaghilev was bound to come sooner or later.

The choreography of *Sacre* was characteristically expressionist in its suppression of individuality in all the rôles except one central rôle with which the choreographer identified himself. Though the dancers moved more freely in space than the dancers in *Faune* or *Les Jeux*, their movements were still tied rigidly to the music. Every note in the music had a corresponding movement,

---

[1] Nijinsky's choreography was so complex that he attempted to record it as he went along with a notation which he had himself invented; but the records became so unwieldy that he gave up the idea, and relied on his memory in the normal way.
[2] *Chronicle of My Life*, p. 83.
[3] Anatole Bourman, *The Tragedy of Nijinsky*, p. 245.

and when the dancers were combined into groups they had to move with complete unanimity, as if parts of a machine: there was no place for the expression of individual personality as demanded by the great Maryinsky tradition. This suppression of individuality was quite out of place in *Les Jeux*, and even in *Sacre* (where it fitted the theme) Nijinsky's fanaticism in the application of his theories at times created a feeling of almost unbearable oppression in the spectators. In this fanatical determination to make the dancers into automatons one can see a reflection of the intensity of the emotions felt by Nijinsky about his position: the same symptom was later to become characteristic of Central European expressionism, and had a somewhat similar psychological origin.

Nijinsky was now mature enough to visualize a break with Diaghilev, but he could have had no illusions about the difficulty of persuading Diaghilev to make any change in the nature of their relationship. The violence of Diaghilev's jealous possessiveness had been made clear to Nijinsky on a number of occasions. Diaghilev's actions to obtain or retain something he wanted had the overwhelming quality of a force of nature. Arguments meant nothing to him when his mind was made up, and Nijinsky could do nothing but wait for a favourable opportunity.

The opportunity came when the company sailed for South America without Diaghilev. If we can believe Bourman's account of this voyage[1] Nijinsky married Romola Pulszky on the rebound from Loda Klementovich, a dancer in the company who had become engaged to Bourman. Certainly Romola Pulszky was just as bewildered by Nijinsky's offer of marriage as anyone else, in spite of the fact that she had been pursuing him for a long time. To many people Nijinsky's sudden marriage to a woman with whom he had exchanged only a few words (they had no language in common) seemed the act of an imbecile, but in fact it was a perfectly logical and sensible thing to do. Not even Diaghilev could defy the marriage bond, sanctified by thousands of years of tradition.

In his choreography for his next ballet *Tyl Eulenspiegel* Nijinsky gave clear expression to his joy at achieving independence. (He had no wish to leave the Diaghilev Ballet, but he was determined to break loose from Diaghilev.) In composing his own rôle he made for the first time full use of his wonderful elevation, moving freely in both space and time. Now he felt no need to abolish the individuality of the artists and tie their movements rigidly to the music. The whole atmosphere of this ballet was joyful and optimistic. Though Nijinsky's interpretation of Tyl resembled his interpretation of Petrouchka in being the hero of a myth of death and rebirth, the emphasis in Tyl was on mockery and release from bondage rather than on repression. The prisoner had at last burst out of his cage and was trying his wings.

[1] A. Bourman, *The Tragedy of Nijinsky*, p. 257.

This analysis of the various stages in Nijinsky's struggle against Diaghilev is important because it throws light on later developments in expressionism, but it helps us to understand only one aspect of Nijinsky's ballets. Like all genuine works of art they are full of ambiguity, and have a variety of apparent and latent meanings in addition to the classic rebellion against the father-figure.

Nearly all the important developments in ballet based on the classical technique in the years of the First World War and in the twenties and early thirties were derived directly or indirectly from Nijinsky's ballets. These ballets had the defects characteristic of expressionism, but they were good of their kind, and represented an essential stage in the development of ballet in the twentieth century.

DALCROZE, LABAN AND WIGMAN

The crucial experiments leading toward the formation in Central Europe of a technically complex form of expressionist free dance were made by Émile Jaques-Dalcroze (1865–1950), Rudolf von Laban (b. 1879) and Mary Wigman (b. 1886) between about 1905 (when Laban opened his first school) and 1918 (when Wigman gave her first public recital). It is not possible to distinguish clearly between the contributions of these three, for they had considerable influence on each other.

Dalcroze is generally thought of as a teacher of music and a composer, but from the very beginning he had contact with the theatre. When he was only twenty he interrupted his studies to accept an engagement for a short time as musical director of a theatre in Algiers (where he was much stimulated by Arab music and dancing), and when he established his institute at Hellerau he included in it an experimental theatre where Appia staged some of his most important pioneer productions.

Dalcroze was born in Vienna, with a Swiss father and a German mother, and was very much a cosmopolitan Central European. He studied music in Geneva, Paris and Venice, became professor of music in Geneva, and then went to Hellerau near Dresden in Germany, at the invitation of the brothers Wolf and Harald Dohrn, to start the "College of Music and Rhythm" in buildings specially constructed for him. He became interested in dancing through his attempts to correct defects in the sense of rhythm of music students by means of specially devised exercises in bodily movement. Gradually these exercises became more and more complex, embodying not only the rhythm of the music, but also its phrasing, melody, counterpoint and structure. The actual spatial shape of the movements devised by Dalcroze was strongly influenced by the dancing of Duncan, though from a musical point of view his movements were far more complex: different parts of the body moved in counter-rhythms, and different themes in the music were sometimes represented by different groups of dancers. (Dalcroze succeeded in building up compositions in which he showed all the elements in the structure of complex musical forms such as the fugue.)

Laban was even more a man of the theatre than Dalcroze, and just as much a cosmopolitan Central European. He was born in Bratislava when this Slovakian town was part of the Austro-Hungarian Empire, and his ancestors belonged to several of the different nations of the Empire. While still a boy he gained experience at the State Theatre of Bratislava as assistant stage manager, and at the age of fifteen he formed a "dance-dramatic club". He was then sent by his father to Paris to study architecture, but he soon branched out in Paris into stage-design, drama and dancing, and formed a small troupe of dancers which he presented in a revue. He also studied Arab and Negro dances in North Africa, and in Paris came into contact with Delsarte's theories and methods of training.

Delsartism played a very important part in the evolution of the free dance, and we must therefore examine François Delsarte's position in the history of the theatre. Delsarte (1811–70) was one of a line of teachers of acting who sought to raise the general standard of acting by codifying the expression of different emotions and temperaments. Some sort of codification was known in the seventeenth century, but it developed into a very complex and rigid system in the eighteenth century—the Age of Reason, when all art was expected to conform to a theory about the passions. (A typical eighteenth-century attitude to the passions can be studied in the writings of Noverre.) The most complete description of eighteenth-century ideas on the codification of acting is that given by Aaron Hill (an English teacher of acting, theatrical manager and playwright) in his book *An Essay on the Art of Acting* (1746). He listed ten dramatic passions—Joy, Grief, Fear, Anger, Pity, Scorn, Hatred, Jealousy, Wonder and Love[1]—and prescribed appropriate movements, postures and facial expressions for each. Joy, for example, should cause the actor to observe that

> his forehead appears open and raised, his eye smiling and sparkling, his neck will be stretched and erect, without stiffness, as if it would add new height to his stature; his chest will be inflated, and majestically tautened; his back-bone erect, and all the joints of his arms, wrists, fingers, knees and ankles will be high-strung and braced boldly.

[1] These standard passions correspond with extraordinary precision to the *rasas* of classical Indian *abhinaya*. (*See* p. 266, below.)

Many of the eighteenth-century writers on the art of acting (e.g. Riccoboni, John Hill, Garrick, Saint-Albine, Lessing) were too familiar with the dullness caused by acting based on detailed rules to attempt to codify acting in this way, but Aaron Hill's manual (and others of similar character) had considerable influence; even in the nineteenth century Aaron Hill's book was revised and re-issued, and new manuals of a similar character were written.

In France tragic actors were particularly prone to a stilted, rhetorical style of delivery and movement, and Delsarte, disgusted by the stilted style of his day, undertook a lengthy, detailed and scientific study of the way various kinds of people actually do behave under the stress of emotion: he observed people of every possible age and type in all sorts of circumstances, and then classified his observations in an attempt to discover general laws for the guidance of actors and singers. In his formulation of general laws he suffered from the fact that the science of psychology was still in an embryonic state, and he looked for guidance to existing theatrical traditions, books such as Aaron Hill's on the training in acting, and also the ancient Roman treatises on rhetoric which influenced the Elizabethans.

Delsarte went much further than his European predecessors in the elaboration of precise and detailed rules for facial expression, gesture and bodily movements suitable for the expression of different emotions and characters. These detailed rules were incorporated in a general philosophy of movement: the personality was divided into three different aspects (intellectual, emotional and physical) and these aspects were assigned in a very complicated way to different parts of the body. Various general types of movement were attributed to different degrees of emotion: violent emotions, for example, were held to demand "the method of opposition", with the limbs and head moving in opposite directions at the same time. In order to enable actors and singers to put his laws into practice Delsarte developed exercises in freedom and relaxation for the different muscles, the idea being to teach each part of the body to express the appropriate idea or emotion in ways prescribed by Delsarte's laws.

Delsarte had a number of famous actors and singers as his pupils, and exerted enormous influence in France: by a strange paradox the late-Romantics seemed to feel a need for strict rules to give form to their rather over-ripe emotions. (At this same period Schumann took to writing fugues, Liszt wrote a Prelude and Fugue on BACH, and even Wagner studied Palestrina.) Gradually, however, Delsarte's rules became just as stultifying as the mechanical rhetoric against which he had revolted, and his system declined considerably in influence in France—though his pupils continued to teach it well into the twentieth century. Equally rigid traditional systems of conventional gestures and facial expressions and movements had given good results in the pantomime dancing of ancient Rome, and are still a vital part of the classical dance-drama of India, Bali,

China and Japan; but Delsarte's codifications eventually proved to be little suited for the rapidly changing world of Victorian Europe.

In the twentieth century Delsarte's principles appealed strongly to the pioneers of expressionist dancing. In breaking away from all traditional patterns of movement they badly needed some rules to give form to their dancing—without some rules dancing is impossible—and so they seized on Delsarte's system with delight. In Russia Volkonsky was much influenced by Delsarte; he passed on some of Delsarte's ideas to Fokine, who applied them in choreography, and in this way they reached Nijinsky. (As often happens when a gifted Russian artist takes up a foreign idea, Fokine transformed Delsartism into something different from, and in many respects better than, the original.)

Delsartism became very popular in the United States towards the end of the nineteenth century,[1] and had considerable influence on the two leading American pioneers of the free dance—Isadora Duncan and Ruth St. Denis.

The Delsarte system appealed very strongly to Laban (with his interest in philosophy and mathematics and his training in architecture); he studied it deeply, and made it the basis for his experiments and his teaching in his various schools.

The year 1913 was a crucial one in the history of the expressionist free dance. In that year Wigman (having broken away from Dalcroze the year previously) was introduced to Laban by the wife of the German expressionist painter Nolde, and was persuaded by Laban to come and work at his school at Ascona in Switzerland. Wigman brought with her Dalcroze's technique of rhythmic movement and the results of his elaborate studies in different methods of associating music and movement; moreover she was a gifted dancer and choreographer, and was able to bring together ideas from many different sources to form dances which were a spontaneous expression of her personality and the particular mood of the dance. In the autumn of 1913 Wigman composed her first major work—*Hexentanz* (Witch-Dance)—performed in silence, and full of demoniacal expressionist violence.

During the War years Laban kept his school going in Switzerland, working in collaboration with Wigman and other pupils on the elaboration of his theories. After the end of the War the expressionist free dance shared in the general upsurge of expressionist art in Central Europe, becoming a mass movement instead of the study of a few specialists. The two most influential leaders were Laban and Wigman: these two moved in very different directions after Wigman left Laban in 1919, and from then on the free dancers tended to belong to either the Laban camp or the Wigman camp. The teachings and compositions of Laban and Wigman had similar roots, and to a visitor from Western

[1] Delsarte left no complete description of his method, but his scattered writings were collected together in *Delsarte System of Oratory* (New York, 1893). A number of his pupils and pupils of his pupils have written books expounding his system—e.g. Rose Meller O'Neill, *The Science and Art of Speech and Gesture* (London, n. d.)

Europe the differences between them would have appeared of small importance; nevertheless they meant a great deal to the young people of Central Europe flocking into the free dance in their thousands at this period.

Laban is above all a philosopher, a man of intellect—the chief theoretician of the free dance. He conceives a dance as something constructed by the dancer out of space, time and weight through the application of certain scientific laws. In treating dancing as a construction out of space, time and weight Laban moved along the same path as a number of artists during the second decade of the twentieth century, and in particular the Suprematists in Moscow (a group of architects, engineers and painters, who worked together during the period 1913–17). The leading members of this group, Naum Gabo and Antoine Pevsner, described themselves as constructivists after issuing a Manifesto in 1920; this Manifesto began with the words, "To communicate the reality of life, art should be based on the two fundamental elements: space and time."[1]

In his teaching and his choreography Laban combined the new ideas about abstraction emerging at this time with Delsarte's theories about the analysis of movement and the relation of different types of movement to emotion and character. What one might call the constructivist element in Laban's theories found typical expression in large-scale "movement-choir" productions such as *Titan*, which had no music, employed large numbers of dancers, and lasted an entire evening. Laban worked out each detail of the complex interlocking patterns with the care of a mathematician or architect; often he moved the groups over flights of steps in order to give more variety to the patterns in space. By means of his movement-notation he was able to send choreography to a great many separate groups of dancers in different cities and bring them together without any rehearsal for gigantic spectacles such as the Parade of Industries in Vienna, with 10,000 participants. (A demonstration on a similar scale at the 1936 Olympic Games frightened the Nazis, for it gave evidence of a highly organized mass movement independent of them, and they made Laban a virtual prisoner in a castle; he managed to escape to Paris, but had to leave all his records behind.)

When Laban tackled a dramatic theme he made use of Delsarte's theories in an expressionist way, presenting the story by means of grotesque and violently exaggerated mime. His debt to Delsarte can be seen clearly in his book *The Mastery of Movement on the Stage*, particularly in passages such as the following:

> The emotion of love might be evoked by the image of a floating goddess who, speaking in terms of effort-thinking, indulges in all the three motion factors of space,

[1] Gabo and Pevsner fell into disfavour with the Soviet authorities in 1922 and left Russia. (*Cf.* Herbert Read, *The Philosophy of Modern Art*, p. 229.)

time and weight. Her movements will be flexible, sustained and light. But hatred, with its hard impact upon reality, could be symbolized by the image of a thrusting demon who, in his typical acts of movement, fights against all three motion factors of space, time and weight. His motions will be direct, quick and strong . . .[1]

Laban's own style of choreography is clearly evoked by his description of the movements of a charitable person:

> One can imagine a softly gliding good Samaritan quick to succour, or one desperately wringing his hands uncertain what to do, or a third charitably flicking the dust from the unfortunate victim, and fluttering excitably about him.[2]

Even more influential than Laban's productions were his ideas, disseminated through Central Europe through his lectures, articles and books and the work of his pupils. Perhaps the most enduring of all his achievements was his movement notation, which showed his various gifts at their best. This system (the Laban Kinetographie) treats the human body as an object moving in space and time, and makes no assumptions about the actual technique of dancing in use: it applies just as well to classical ballet as to the various schools of the free dance (or the movements of men at work); the Dance Notation Bureau in New York exists to teach and develop this system, and has considerable influence in the United States.

Many pupils have found Laban stimulating as a teacher, for he has the habit of throwing out innumerable ideas: some are banal, some are hopelessly impractical, but every now and then there is an idea which rings a bell with a particular auditor and opens out for him all sorts of new possibilities which he can explore for himself.

Year after year Laban applied his formulas to the production of ballets, bringing together his usual vocabulary of punching, floating, pressing, slashing, dabbing, flicking, sliding and wringing movements. In England his influence was very strong at a Manchester dance school (the Art of Movement Studio), and in 1950 graduates of this school formed themselves into a company which they called British Dance Theatre. The "ballets" performed by this group were of great historical interest, for (apart from a few of the more familiar Jooss mannerisms) they reproduced the Laban style of the early twenties. English audiences were bewildered by these performances, which had no apparent connection with the art of dancing. The performers executed their punching, stabbing and flicking movements with the greatest solemnity and concentration, their faces frozen in a typically expressionist grimace: the period flavour was as authentic as that of a revival of the film *The Cabinet of Dr. Caligari.*

[1] P. 125.
[2] P. 127.

Though Wigman had been considerably influenced by Laban, and applied in her choreography and teaching a great many of his theories, she reacted away from his intellectual methods of composition; normally she composed her solo dances in the manner of Duncan as a spontaneous expression of mood or emotion, and in her teaching she laid great stress on improvisation. This did not mean that the Laban formulas played no part in Wigmanesque compositions: the pupil was supposed to master them so well that they did not hamper improvisation. Much of Wigman's work (particularly her group compositions) was as cerebral as any of Laban's, but her best solos had an element of ecstasy and spontaneity absent from Laban's compositions.

Wigman stood out from nearly all her contemporaries in having a strong personality and great dramatic ability; in dances which suited her personality and her technique she was devastatingly effective. This was true particularly of her demoniacal rôles: no one could equal her in the expression of horror, and this gave her much the same influence in the aftermath of the First World War as Munch. But her face was always twisted into a grimace (unless she wore a mask), her hands were always strained, and she was incapable of any kind of lyricism or femininity. (Her dancing had a completely masculine strength: there was nothing to suggest that she was a woman.) In rôles which did not suit her temperament, she could be as ludicrous as Munch trying to suggest "Carefree Youth" and "Masculine Vigour" in his group of large paintings *The Bathers*.

Laban and Wigman spent much of their time teaching in their various schools, and nearly all the other leading free dancers set up schools of their own, until free-dance schools were almost as common in Central Europe as ballet schools were later to become in England. Next to the Laban and Wigman schools the most important school was Hellerau-Laxenburg: when the First World War began Dalcroze returned to Switzerland, and his Hellerau school (under the direction of the German dancer Valeria Kratina) moved to Laxenburg, near Vienna. From here Dalcrozian ideas flowed out to the other schools, while at the same time the Hellerau-Laxenburg style was influenced by the work done by Laban and Wigman and their respective pupils. The director of the Hellerau-Laxenburg dance group was Rosalia Chladek; as dancer and choreographer she had considerable influence.

The pupils at all the free-dance schools of Central Europe worked with ferocious intensity, but their chances of achieving anything valuable were very slight, for what they learned was not so much an integrated dance-technique as a set of mannerisms which the teacher had developed as an expression of his or her own personality. In the long run the combination and re-combination of these mannerisms tended to become insufferable even in the dancing of the teacher: when reproduced by a pupil they meant nothing at all. Since each movement was more or less arbitrary, there could be no absolute standard of perfection in its execution, and the pupils suffered from having no definite mark at which to aim (as a classical dancer has). Composition was even more difficult, for it was impossible to make any real distinction between choreography and dance-technique, and the creative efforts of the pupil could only be feeble copies of those of the teacher.

The theory behind this teaching was very different. In theory the teacher avoided set exercises as much as possible, building up each class as a series of variations on a few original themes. This was linked up with the method of composition of the free dancer, who (in theory) is not limited to any one set of standard movements, and creates movements quite freely to express any mood or character. Instead of equipping the pupil with a vocabulary of standard steps the teacher set out to train the pupil in a variety of different qualities, tempi and rhythms of movement, so that he could create a variety of dances for himself and tackle any movement a choreographer might require of him—even a classical step. This theory was of great importance in widening the range of choreography, but it was based on a fallacy. In fact the "freedom" of the free dancer proved to be illusory, for the vocabulary of movement available to him —consisting as it did of the mannerisms of his teachers—was extremely limited. The dancer's means of getting about the stage were limited to walking and running steps, his leaps were clumsy, and the effects gained by emphasizing effort and contact with the floor were very limited in comparison with those achieved by a classically trained dancer with elevation and the concealment of effort.

One serious weakness which the expressionist free dance shared with the Petipa type of ballet was the dichotomy between dancing and mime. Every possible effort was made by free dancers to conceal this dichotomy: conventional ballet mime derived from the Commedia dell'Arte was suppressed, and naturalistic gestures were repeated over and over again in a broad and rhythmic manner in an attempt to make them pass as dance movements. Nevertheless the final result remained a lumpy mixture of mime and classroom movements, just as it had done in Petipa's day. (Truly expressive dances are created from dance-images, and a choreographer cannot create these except when he is creating with the whole of his personality: it was precisely this wholeness that the neurotic free dancers found most difficult of achievement.)

It was perhaps an unconscious awareness of this dichotomy which induced nearly all the free-dance groups to devote much attention to pure abstraction. Some of the abstract items were interpretations of music inspired by the work of Duncan and Dalcroze; some were danced to percussion accompaniment (either played by members of the group in the wings or produced by dancers as an integral part of their performance); and some were performed in silence. In the purely abstract items the absence of any dramatic interest made a number of deficiencies in the dance-techniques of the various schools disastrously obvious. (Pure abstraction makes greater demands for subtlety in dynamic control and purity of line than any other genre, and is completely unsuitable for expressionist treatment.)

Each school of the expressionist free dance reflected very closely the temperament and physique of the dancer who created it and also the artistic climate of the period when the style reached its definitive form. For this reason the dances and ballets composed in any one style began to "date" after a few years even when performed by the creator of the style, and dances composed by disciples "dated" almost before they were composed. Only those with sufficient independence of mind, originality and creative power to invent a new style and a new dance-technique suited to their own personality and physique and the Zeitgeist of their own day could hope to achieve anything valuable. In other words it was not enough to have great talent: one had to be a genius or nothing.

Another fundamental weakness of the expressionist free dance as a whole was its failure to cope satisfactorily with the problem of strain. All the different schools put great emphasis on the control of tension in the various parts of the body, in theory providing for a continuous range of tension from the greatest possible strain to complete relaxation in the different muscles, and keeping the muscles of the different parts of the body independent of each other in this respect. In fact the expressionist free dancers were much too typically expressionist to be able to tackle even the relatively simple problems involved in the distribution of tension in the classical technique (which demands that the top half of the trunk, the arms, the shoulders and the head should be controlled with the bare minimum of effort needed to maintain good posture, in complete independence of the violent efforts being made by the legs to move the body about the stage). The free dancers learned to relax their whole bodies until they collapsed like an empty sack, and could tense every muscle like a professional strong man, but they could not achieve the flexible economy of effort which is needed to achieve nuances of expression in emotions less violent than horror, despair or fury.

This failure to cope with the problem of strain became very obvious in the late twenties, when the expressionist free dancers began to tackle certain aspects of the classical technique. Some of them tried to learn separate classical steps as an integral whole (avoiding the fragmentary exercises characteristic of classical training). With long practice they were able to get the outline more or less right, but they could never give the steps the right delicacy of phrasing, for they put the same effort into all the different sections of the step, instead of building up to the climax in the proper way. Those who took complete classical classes did much better, but they rarely succeeded in doing away with signs of strain in their hands and faces. Free dancers normally held their hands in a rather stiff and stylized manner that concealed the tension in the hands and was not obtrusive in their normal work, but stood out very clearly in a classical step; and much the same was true of their facial expressions. Only a few free dancers with exceptional versatility and the chance of having good classical classes at a relatively early age have succeeded in coping adequately with the use of hands and faces in classical steps.

In spite of the deficiencies in the free dance which caused the free dancers to make efforts to master some aspects of the classical technique, they continued to regard their own style as far superior aesthetically to ballets based on the classical technique. They thought of their own work as an art of movement devised for purposes of expression or communication, in contrast to dancing based on the classical technique, which they regarded as a series of pictures— a charming spectacle but no more. This criticism was based on a complete misunderstanding of the fundamental principles of classical dancing. All good classical dancing (whether Indian, Balinese, Japanese or European) is a powerful means of communication, and the "pictures" have an important function in this communication: they represent a point of climax in the phrase, arising naturally out of the movement and giving it a precision and expressive power which it would not otherwise have. The "pictures" correspond roughly to the planes in a painting: they may be emphasized or smoothed over, but they cannot be ignored without taking away all vitality from the work. The "picture" to which the free dancers object is one of a large number of optical illusions which the classically trained dancer has to learn to create, in order to project the dance up to the back of the gallery; it is as artificial and as necessary as the full tone of the opera singer. Even the full pointe (perhaps the greatest bug-bear of the free dancers) is no more and no less artificial than e.g. the barefoot pirouette of the Wigman dancer balanced on the edge of one big toe.

These arrogant and prejudiced criticisms of the classical ballet by free dancers represented the normal assertiveness of a young art struggling for a place in the sun. Though most of the work done by the free dancers was extremely bad, the new ballets based on the classical technique were also very disappointing during the hey-day of the Central European free dance (roughly from the middle of the twenties to the seizure of power by the Nazis in 1933). During this period the best of the new solo dances and ballets in free style were well able to stand comparison with the best of the new work based on the classical technique.

With all its deficiencies the expressionist free dance represented a genuine contribution to the art of the dance, and was infinitely more vital than the sentimental and conventional ballets based on the classical technique which the opera houses of Central Europe were producing before they were invaded by the free dancers. Good ballets had been produced in Central Europe at various

times during the last two centuries, but nearly always by foreign maîtres de
ballet. The expressionist free dance was completely indigenous, and though it
ceased to progress after 1933 and seemed to have little relevance to the aftermath
of the Second World War, we can see now that what it did achieve in its own
period was of great importance. To use the language of biological evolution,
the free dance was a progressive movement, in spite of its serious deficiencies,
because in its hey-day it was related to the needs of the human process in
Central Europe, and contained the seeds of its future transformation.[1]

In the United States the free dance originated independently from much the
same roots as the Central European free dance, and has developed in a very
similar way: there is an American equivalent for almost every aspect of the
Central European free dance, either as the result of a process of parallel development (similar causes producing similar effects), or through the introduction of
ideas from Central Europe by immigrant dancers and American dancers who
went to Central Europe for training. Nevertheless the American free dance has
remained characteristically American ever since it was founded by Isadora
Duncan: it assimilated from the Central European free dance and from the
classical technique only those elements which fitted in with its own established
patterns.[2]

LÉONIDE MASSINE (b. 1896)

Massine's early career had something of the quality of a fairy tale. When
Diaghilev discovered him, in 1913, he was a student of seventeen at the Imperial
Theatre School in Moscow, training to be an actor: at this time there was no
sharp distinction between the training of actors and dancers at the Moscow
school. With his short legs Massine seemed debarred from a career as a dancer,
and when Diaghilev discovered him his dance-technique was relatively slight.
Nevertheless Diaghilev picked on this youth to efface the achievements of
Nijinsky, both as dancer and choreographer!

Though Diaghilev's aim was of course unrealizable, Massine developed
with amazing speed in the favourable artistic climate provided for him by
Diaghilev, and became a character dancer and a choreographer of outstanding
ability. As a dancer he developed such stage presence, personality and dramatic
sense that he was able to dominate the stage without apparent effort, and the

---

[1] Cf. Julian Huxley, "The Human Phase" (No. VI in a series of lectures "The Process of
Evolution"), The Listener, Nov. 22, 1951.
[2] See below, p. 143.

deficiencies of his technique were not apparent in the character rôles which he composed for himself. As a choreographer he composed a number of ballets so solidly constructed that they have taken their place in the standard international repertoire.

Unlike Fokine and Nijinsky he did not have to struggle to discover a style in harmony with the artistic trends of the day and his own temperament. He started work at a time when expressionism was the only possible style for a sensitive choreographer, and this style suited his temperament very well. The pioneer work had already been done by Nijinsky, and Massine was able to stand on Nijinsky's shoulders. He was enormously helped by the advice of Larionov, to whom Diaghilev entrusted him to complete his cultural education: Larionov, a brilliant expressionist painter and designer with a penchant for grotesque buffoonery and satire, helped Massine to develop as a choreographer along these lines. Among other things he introduced Massine to the drawings of Callot, and so helped him to acquire a feeling for the Italy of the seventeenth and eighteenth centuries.

The tragic and extremely iconoclastic expressionism of *Sacre* no longer fitted the mood of the times after the outbreak of the 1914–18 War. Immediately after *Sacre* Diaghilev, Benois and Nijinsky had contemplated a return to a more classical style, and Picasso pointed the way with his neo-classical style of painting inspired by the work of Ingres. Massine therefore developed a grotesque style which was definitely expressionist in feeling and yet made much greater use of classroom steps than Nijinsky's style.

Massine's first ballet, *Soleil de Nuit* (1915), was composed by him when he was only nineteen, and was little more than a suite of balletized Russian dances. It was skilfully composed, and showed that Massine had real talent for composition. His first important ballet was *Les Femmes de Bonne Humeur* (1917), and here he developed his characteristic style of neo-classical expressionism. He made considerable use of classical steps, establishing in this way a period atmosphere appropriate to a ballet based on a comedy by Goldoni; but he used the classical steps in a definitely expressionist way, exaggerating every angle and giving the whole ballet a jittery sort of animation, fitting some movement to every note of the music. The characterization was simplified in a characteristically expressionist way, and the grotesque buffoonery of some of the humour showed clearly the influence of Larionov. (The humour in Goldoni's original play was much more subtle.)

Though *Les Femmes de Bonne Humeur* was a great success in its own day, and retained much of its popular appeal during the early years of the de Basil company, it fell flat when revived by the de Cuevas company in 1950, in spite of a remarkable performance by René Bon as Battista: like a great many expressionist productions this ballet "dated" very badly. After three decades the unceasing ant-like industry of the dancers seemed fussy and irritating, giving the same feeling of straining after effect as typical German expressionist productions. The whole ballet seemed to consist of a series of distorted classroom steps fitted to the music with great intelligence but no imagination: everything was prosaic, whereas dancing by its very nature must be poetic.

Parade (1917) was of little importance from the point of view of choreography. It was devised by Cocteau, Satie and Picasso as a piece of nonsense somewhat in the Dada[1] manner, and Massine was completely at sea in this atmosphere: though he had a strong feeling for grotesque, expressionist satire he could not accommodate himself to the sophisticated nonsense in which Picasso made fun of Cubism and Satie composed a score including parts for typewriters.

La Boutique Fantasque (1919) has been severely criticized and with good reason: in comparison with other Massine ballets the structure was weak (the ballet was to a large extent a suite of divertissements) and there were a number of severe lapses of taste. Nevertheless, this ballet had a vitality which did not fade with the passage of time: unlike *Les Femmes de Bonne Humeur* it contained an element of fantasy essential to ballet, and its choreography showed many touches of delightfully spontaneous invention.

Boutique was a new version of an old German ballet *Die Puppenfee* which had been revived in 1902 in St. Petersburg with choreography by Serge and Nicolas Legat and décor and costumes by Bakst. In typically expressionist fashion (following the example of Meyerhold and other Muscovite expressionist producers) Massine produced an extremely personal version of the old ballet by twisting and distorting it in a hundred different ways so as to make it express his own view of the old ballet: in effect *Boutique* is an expressionist satire of the Petipa style. Massine inserted a rôle for himself (the Can-Can Dancer) which had a typically expressionist grotesque humour: his face was made up dead white, with thick black eyebrows, and his movements were wildly eccentric, with emphasis on peculiar hand movements. The rôle suited him very well, and was a great success with the public: from now on a great many Massine ballets included as one of their main characters a variation of this rôle. Even the miller, the hero of the Spanish ballet *Le Tricorne*, was partly derived from the grotesque Can-Can Dancer.

The "clou" of *Le Tricorne* (also composed in 1919) is the famous Farruca; everything else (except the Jota finale) is insipid by comparison. This dance was based on a real Flamenco Farruca improvised one day by the gypsy Felix for the benefit of Massine and Diaghilev. Flamenco usually loses much of its fire when crystallized into a set dance performed to set music, but Massine

---

[1] Dada was an international style (characterized by the most violent and provocative nonsense) which emerged during the First World War as a protest against the horrors of war.

Rudolf von Laban

Below: Mary Wigman

Above: Les Présages (Massine, Monte Carlo, 1932) with Verchinina as Action (*on the left*)

La Boutique Fantasque (Massine, London, 1919) with Danilova and Massine as the Cancan Dancers adapted the dance to Falla's music and the ballet technique with such skill, and performed the dance with such a fine understanding of the dynamics of a Farruca, that he might well have been a gypsy himself. This was possible for him because (except for Kathakali) Flamenco is the most expressionist of all traditional styles, and the Farruca—with its emphasis on violent contrasts between quick and slow tempi and bold and subtle movements—is the most expressionist aspect of Flamenco. With his expressionist background and temperament Massine was perfectly equipped to achieve profound understanding of the Farruca. He did not show anything like the same sympathy for other types of Spanish dancing. The rôle of the Miller's Wife, for example, was rather characterless, and this was also true of much of the group dancing—with the important exception of the Jota finale, which was worthy of Fokine.

The Farruca in *Le Tricorne* represented the highest point of Massine's achievement in his early years as a choreographer. He was now only twenty-three, but had produced no less than seven full-scale ballets in four years. Whether he realized it or not he needed to cease creative work and give his ideas a chance to mature. But he was the only choreographer of the company: Diaghilev made no effort to foster another choreographer and kept him hard at work.[1] Inevitably he began to repeat himself, just as Fokine had done. This was apparent to some extent even in *Pulcinella* (1920), an Italianate expressionist period ballet with admirable harmony between book, music, choreography and décor; it was obvious in *Le Astuzie Feminili*,[2] an opera ballet in which there was a very laboured attempt to recapture the mood of *Les Femmes de Bonne Humeur*.

In 1921 Diaghilev commissioned from Massine a new version of *Le Sacre du Printemps*, a ballet for which Diaghilev had the highest regard. Diaghilev now seemed to be losing his grip to some extent, for he made a serious error of judgment in giving *Sacre* to Massine. (Bronislava Nijinska could have revived her brother's choreography with real understanding, but Diaghilev presumably was still anxious to efface the memory of Nijinsky.)

Though Massine had a marked talent for grotesque, satirical neo-classical expressionism, he was unfitted by temperament to tackle the terror, ecstasy and mystery of *Sacre*. He tried to assert his individuality by making the ballet more

---

[1] In justice to Diaghilev I must add that even if he had given Massine more time for reflection we cannot be certain that Massine's career as a choreographer would not have followed much the same curve. All the expressionist choreographers of Massine's generation seemed to feel a pressing need to work at a tremendous rate; in this way they rapidly exhausted their creative powers, and ceased to make any progress while they were still relatively young. On the other hand Massine did manage to absorb new ideas many years later, and created three important ballets in the period 1932-6. This suggests that the loss of his creative powers after 1919 was not inevitable.

[2] The first two acts were pure opera; the third act contained a long suite of divertissements which was later performed separately under the name *Cimarosiana*.

abstract and cutting out all references to folk-lore, but the incidents which he added had a triviality quite unworthy of the theme.

> Massine's version is not in the main different from the original, despite the most ambitious declarations to the contrary . . . What names will you give to Massine's battle scene in which some of the dancers bind their arms and knock each other down, while their comrades, in symmetrical groups, "play at theatre" by bringing up to their eyes both fists joined in the form of a lorgnette?[1]

Massine's failure to come to grips with the theme was particularly apparent in the dance of the Chosen Maiden. In an attempt to establish his superiority to Nijinsky (who had subjected himself to the music) Massine adopted the clever but inartistic device of making the rhythms and phrasing of the dance completely different from the rhythms and phrasing of the music.[2] Since the rhythms and phrasing of both were extremely complicated, the relationship between the two had no meaning, and Sokolova (though a very gifted artist) had no chance to establish an atmosphere of ecstasy and terror as Marie Piltz had done. Sokolova's dance was tremendously effective theatrically, but it had little to do with *Sacre*.

Massine left Diaghilev after the production of *Sacre* (which he found a great strain); on his own, however, he was no more successful in finding the right outlet for his creative abilities than when under the tutelage of Diaghilev. No further progress was possible in his own sort of grotesque expressionist comedy, and he could not find another style. The ballets he arranged for the Soirées de Paris of Count Etienne de Beaumont in 1924 showed the same defects as *Les Femmes de Bonne Humeur*: the same constant striving to force as many steps into the music as it would hold, the same cerebral distortion of the academic steps. In *Le Beau Danube* (first produced for this season) he made a serious attempt to correct these weaknesses in his style, and to some extent succeeded. Unfortunately this ballet suffered from a puerile plot: the sentimental story and conventional characters made little appeal to Massine, and he produced a ballet that rarely rose above the level of musical comedy. He later produced an expanded version of this ballet for de Basil, and reproductions of this expanded version have been commissioned by a number of ballet companies. Because he is a skilled craftsman with an eye for frustrated talent and knows how to get the

---

[1] E. Vuillermoz, *La Revue Musicale*, Feb., 1921.
[2] In a brilliant article in *Footnotes to the Ballet* (ed. Caryl Brahms) (p. 225–6) Sokolova explained how she managed to keep the dance more or less in step with the orchestra. She rehearsed it for hours with a metronome, so as to fix the tempo; in performance she took her cue to begin from the first beat of the conductor, then ignored the music except for three pauses where she was instructed by Massine to meet the orchestra on two beats. If either she or the orchestra were early or late, she "faked" things by missing or adding one movement. She had to "fake" at every performance except two, but nobody could possibly have known about this except Massine and herself.

best out of dancers, a production of *Le Beau Danube* usually stands out from the other ballets in the stodgy repertoires of the companies that commission ballets from Massine, but it shows very little of his real quality: like other expressionists he is not really at home in Ruritania.

Massine began to work for Diaghilev again in 1925, and became one of the small group of choreographers whom Diaghilev used to set his dancers in movement during the unhappy years when he abandoned most of his ideals and produced only cocktail ballets. Under these circumstances Massine had no chance of finding his way back to the creative fire of his youth.

The formation of the Blum-de Basil-Massine company in 1932, with Massine as maître de ballet,[1] gave him the chance of putting into production some projects on which he had begun work while still with Diaghilev. These were his early symphonic ballets, inspired partly by the ideas of music-interpretation which had been worked out in turn by Duncan, Dalcroze and Nijinsky, and partly by the expressionist solo dances and group items of Central Europe. Ideas drawn from these two sources were blended together by Massine in a confused and confusing manner in the first of the symphonic ballets, *Les Présages* (which had a number of different dancers representing abstractions like "Fate" and "Frivolity"). At times the ballet was quite embarrassingly naïve and pretentious, like the vast majority of its Central European counterparts; but Massine was fortunate in having at his disposal Verchinina, a great artist who had had training in the free dance after being trained in the classical technique. She made it possible for Massine to put on the stage Labanist ideas far more poetically and effectively than Laban himself could have done: her performances in *Les Présages* (and also in the next symphonic ballet *Choreartium*) made a very powerful impression on all who saw them, and lifted those parts of the ballet in which she appeared to a new plane. The movements she executed were completely "free dance" in style, but she performed them with a classical economy of effort and purity of line which made them quite different from anything to be seen in Central Europe at this time.

Unfortunately Massine could not succeed in welding together the different elements in these ballets into an organic whole: the abstract symbolism was arbitrary and inconsistent, and fitted in badly with the long series of pseudo-classical enchaînements which he fitted with great care to the counterpoint of the music. The passages of music interpretation were clearly influenced by the work of this nature done by Nijinska and Balanchine, but Massine seemed determined to outdo them by achieving a far greater complexity of counterpoint. He succeeded in this aim, but his aridly intellectual methods of composition made it impossible for him to achieve any of the dignity and power of his best expressionist work.

[1] Massine succeeded to this position after Balanchine left.

His second symphonic ballet, *Choreartium* (1933), avoided most of the faults of taste of *Les Présages*, and had a wonderful slow movement in which Verchinina was given full opportunity to show her remarkable talent: this movement was in effect a solo for her, accompanied by the corps de ballet, and was an expressionist ballet in miniature in lyrical "free-dance" style. The other three scenes of *Choreartium* had some fine moments, but they showed the same rather unsatisfactory mixture of styles as *Les Présages*. The slow movement was clearly a scene of lamentation; the rest of the ballet was largely abstract.

In his third symphonic ballet, *La Symphonie Fantastique* (1936), he had the great advantage of music written to a romantic story and perfectly suitable for expressionist treatment: for once, his great skill in composition was controlled and directed by his imagination. Massine himself must have realized the importance in his career of this ballet, for he spent three years on its composition. The ballet was very unequal, with dull and pretentious passages alternating with imaginative ones; but "The March to the Scaffold" was almost perfect from beginning to end. This scene was complete in itself, and represented one of the two or three finest expressionist ballets ever composed. The theme gave full opportunity to Massine's gift for grotesque satire and his feeling for the style of a period. Nothing was simply copied from free-dance productions or his own earlier work, and there were no conventional pseudo-classical enchaînements; every detail arose naturally and inevitably from the theme, the costumes and the music, and was perfectly suited both to Massine's twentieth-century expressionism and to the nineteenth-century romanticism of Berlioz. Though the scene was full of the usual expressionist effects—violent contrasts of action and tempo, use of masses of uniformly clad dancers moving with complete unanimity, concentration on a single mood of horror and despair—there was none of the hysterical straining after effect typical of the corresponding Central European productions, and none of Massine's habitual fussiness. The most striking effects were achieved with extraordinary economy of means: the vertical jumps of the lines of judges, flashing their red stockings and flapping their robes, were fully worthy of the lithographs by Daumier and Forain which inspired Massine's treatment of this scene. Perhaps the most striking feature of this scene was its concentration: in contrast to nearly all other Massine ballets there was no padding, and the build-up to the climax when the Prisoner was executed had the same admirable speed and inevitability as the last scene of *Petrouchka*.

This scene was the finest long passage of choreography composed by Massine; unfortunately, however, it came too late in his career to provide a stepping-stone to further achievements. By this time expressionism had exhausted most of its potentialities, and no longer corresponded to the state of the Zeitgeist. Like many other fine expressionist choreographers, Massine seemed to pour all his creative powers into certain magnificent scenes in a few ballets and then have no more to say. His subsequent symphonic ballets had the same faults as the first two symphonic ballets in exaggerated form, and lacked anything to compare with Verchinina's striking solos. Many of his later ballets (e.g. *Gaieté Parisienne*) were no more than glorified cabaret numbers, bringing together in a commercial formula (with a great deal of padding) ideas from the most popular of his earlier ballets. The dancing in *Tristan Fou* (1944) was of such stupefying banality that it failed to distract the attention of the audience away from Dali's surrealist décor. Much the same was true of *Clock Symphony* (1948), composed for the Sadlers Wells Ballet: here Massine, in a desperate search for new effects, tried to create an effect of originality by using a pair of human legs to suggest the pendulum of a clock. The whole of the choreography for *Clock Symphony* was roughly on this level of invention.

Not all the ballets composed by Massine in the forties and early fifties were as distressingly bad as *Tristan Fou* and *Clock Symphony*. *Mam'zelle Angot* (composed in 1943 for Ballet Theatre, and revived in 1947 for the Sadlers Wells Ballet) showed a good deal of skilful craftsmanship, particularly in the counterpoint of movements by different groups of dancers; but every detail of the choreography represented a repetition (in sentimentalized form) of previous material composed by him. Clearly the sentimental theme and the correspondingly sugary music (both taken from the original operetta by Lecocq) made little or no appeal to Massine's expressionist temperament.

Donald of the Burthens (composed in 1951 for the Sadlers Wells Ballet) was an ambitious attempt by Massine to repeat the success of *Le Tricorne*. The ballet was based on a Scottish legend, it was furnished with music by a Scottish composer based on Scottish traditional tunes, the décor and costumes were commissioned from the two leading avant-garde Scottish painters, and Massine studied Scottish dancing for two years before starting work on the choreography; leaving nothing to chance, he even had his Scottish teachers supervise the execution of the Scottish steps by the company, and brought in a piper and a singer of "mouth-music" to perform on the stage as part of the musical accompaniment.

Clearly the legend of *Donald of the Burthens* (a variant of the Faust story) appealed to Massine because of the possibilities it presented for expressionist treatment—possibilities at least as great as the story of *Le Tricorne*. Unfortunately for Massine, however, the Highland dancing on which he based most of his choreography is one of the least expressionist of all highly developed traditional styles. It demands in the performer all the classical virtues—restraint, meticulous attention to detail, exact balance between the parts, perfection of line and rhythm, impersonality, and so on. The Highlanders are highly emotional people, but in their traditional art-forms (e.g. dancing and Pibroch bagpipe music) they delight in holding the expression of their emotions within extremely strict rules. Guided by his Scottish teachers Massine used the traditional steps with some skill, and expanded them into elaborate counterpoint in his usual cerebral manner; but when he tried to distort the traditional steps in order to build up Donald's character and express his feelings, the result was discordant and meaningless—neither fish, flesh nor caller herring. The traditional dances were effective only when they kept closely to traditional patterns, and even then they were less effective than the real thing performed by traditional dancers.

The ballet was saved from complete failure by Beryl Grey's intelligent performance in the rôle of Death. Massine's choreography for this rôle was to the last degree hackneyed and cerebral: Death used the turned-in knees, angular arms and stiff, twisted hands made all too familiar by every expressionist choreographer since the composition of *Petrouchka*. Nevertheless Beryl Grey, helped by her studies in the free dance under Audrey de Vos, brought such understanding and intensity to her interpretation of these hackneyed movements that from time to time she made the ballet come to life.

The ballet was constructed by Massine on the same lines as a typical Petipa ballet, with the last act consisting of a series of divertissements performed for the benefit of the King and Queen, and the ballet ended in a grand finale bringing in the whole cast. Unfortunately the legend chosen by Massine did not have the happy ending favoured by Petipa: in order to make possible the usual grand finale Massine inserted the death of Donald after the divertissements, and then had Death lead the entire cast (apart, of course, from Donald) in a series of Scottish dances. This provided a happy and colourful finale, but it made nonsense of the legend: even at his worst Petipa never provided a spectacle quite as ludicrous as Death in red all-over tights and pointe shoes taking part in a series of Scottish dances working up to a cheerful climax.

The extraordinary lack of taste and judgment shown by Massine in *Donald of the Burthens* can partly be understood if one takes into account the fact that to a choreographer of his generation expressionism is not a style of art: it is art itself. Romantic artists saw the whole of artistic creation up to their own day as aspects of romanticism (for Mendelssohn, even Bach was a mystic, a "Gothic" master of music); and expressionists looked at other styles in an equally subjective manner. Massine, a thorough expressionist, saw nothing incongruous in making the austere, classical dances of the Scottish Highlands the basis for an expressionist ballet.

On the other hand it is impossible to believe that he did not see the incongruity between his expressionist theme and his spectacular finale. In 1919, in the hey-day of expressionism, Massine had gaily satirized the moribund Petipa-style ballets of the nineteenth century in *La Boutique Fantasque*. He was now faced with a situation in which his natural style offered no further possibilities of development and had lost its appeal to the public, whereas the Petipa-style ballets popularized by Diaghilev and Pavlova had become more reliable box-office attractions than most types of modern ballet. It is therefore easily understandable that he should attempt to ensure the success of *Donald of the Burthens* (his most ambitious production for over a decade) by giving it the shape of a Petipa ballet—even though this shape was completely unsuitable to the theme and represented the most violent possible departure from the aesthetic ideals of his youth. In fact such a hotch-potch had no more chance of success than Petipa's attempt to repeat the success of *The Sleeping Beauty* with *The Magic Mirror*; and *Donald of the Burthens* did not remain long in the repertoire.

JEAN BORLIN (1893–1930)

Borlin is the type and image of all expressionist choreographers: every feature normal to the career of such a choreographer is to be found in his short career.

While still in the Swedish Royal Ballet Borlin came under the influence of Fokine, who came to Stockholm in 1911 to produce several of his ballets for the Opera. Borlin (aged eighteen) was then only in the corps de ballet, and was becoming very bored with ballet; but Fokine brought a breath of fresh air into the banal repertoire, and Borlin became tremendously enthusiastic. His efforts to wring every possible ounce of emotion and theatrical effect out of Fokine's choreography for *Cléopâtre* (in which Borlin danced the part of a Faun) were typically expressionist in their fanaticism. Fokine described him as a fair youth who

crossed the stage with great bounds, landed with all his force and glided over the boards among a group of bacchantes. What character! What ecstasy! The fanatical sacrifice of a bruised body in order to produce the maximum of choreographic effect.[1]

This was two years before Nijinsky produced *Sacre*—yet Borlin, in remote Stockholm, was already feeling his way towards expressionism.

Borlin now became interested in the native dances of many countries and in particular in African Negro dances. Gradually he made his way up through

[1] Michel Fokine, *Borlin—Mon Elève* (quoted by C. W. Beaumont in *Conplete Book of Ballets*, p. 815.)

the various ranks of the Royal Ballet, and in 1918 would have been made premier danseur if he had not left to study under Fokine in Copenhagen.

It was at this time that Rolf de Maré decided to form a ballet company, taking Borlin as maître de ballet, choreographer and premier danseur. Borlin started his career as choreographer with much the same disadvantages and advantages as Massine. Like Massine he had been trained in a school where the style was far from satisfactory, and the repertoire of the Swedish Royal Opera House was even more depressing than that of the Bolshoy Theatre. Like Massine he had the opportunity to work with Fokine and learn from him some of the craft of composition. Like Massine he had the advice and encouragement of an artistic director fully acquainted with all the latest tendencies in all the arts. Unlike Massine, however, Borlin did not find himself dancing in a company with a repertoire containing a wonderful variety of great ballets based on the classical technique. Borlin had to create the entire repertoire of the Ballets-Suédois himself. Following the example of Nijinsky, and encouraged by Rolf de Maré (who was one of the very first to buy paintings by Picasso), he broke away violently from the classical tradition: by the time he began work as a choreographer the neo-classical expressionism of Massine had lost all its novelty, and in Central Europe the free dancers were developing a new technique with few links with the classical technique.

Before bringing the company to Paris for its opening season Rolf de Maré brought Borlin to Paris on a "reconnaissance"—a recital of solo dances. The most striking of these dances was *Sculpture Nègre*, a violently expressionist dance inspired by African Negro dances; Borlin converted his body into the shape of a piece of expressionist Negro sculpture by means of a mask covering his entire head and padded tights, and danced in front of a backcloth (designed by Paul Colin) in the style of African Bushmen rock-paintings. Other items included a Dervish dance, and evocations of the past based on his study of painting and sculpture.

Borlin's first three ballets for the company were *Jeux* (a new version of the Nijinsky ballet), *Iberia* (based on his study of Spanish dances) and *La Nuit de St. Jean* (based on Swedish folk-dances). In *La Maison des Fous* he took advantage of a typically expressionist theme (a scene in a mad-house) to make a complete break with tradition: many of the mad characters danced in bare feet, and used movements which had something in common with contemporary experimental work in Central Europe.

The most important ballet of the first year of the company's existence was *El Greco*, based not so much on traditional Spanish dances as on the expressionism of El Greco's paintings: upraised arms were used in the El Greco manner to suggest a mood of exaltation.

During the next three years Borlin worked at a killing pace, rehearsing ambitious new ballets, dancing the principal rôles in most of the ballets in the repertoire, rehearsing new dancers to take the place of the departing members (a heavy task, for such departures were frequent), taking classes, and so on. Some idea of the strain under which he worked can be judged from the fact that when he reached the première of *L'Homme et Son Désir*—a long and complex ballet in which he had the principal rôle and was on stage the whole time—he had had no time to rehearse his own rôle.

L'Homme et Son Désir had much in common with the expressionist dramas which were beginning to reach the stage in Germany. The central figure was Man in the abstract, robbed of personality by night and sleep; his dreams were represented by vague figures in faceless masks. He performed a dance of obsession, then seized the veil of The Woman and gradually became wrapped in it as he unwrapped it from The Woman. The three chief characters (The Man, The Woman and The Other Woman) danced in bare feet. The Man was nearly nude, and danced on one of a number of levels: this was the first time rostrums were used in this way in Paris, though they were later to become almost a cliché in Central Europe. (Jessner used so many steps and rostrums in his dramatic productions that people began to talk of *Jessnertreppen*.) The details of this ballet were determined to a large extent by the author of the book (Paul Claudel), the composer (Darius Milhaud), and the designer (Andrée Parr), but the theme was one which fitted in very well with Borlin's own expressionist tendencies. It is possible that the use of movement in profile in this ballet was suggested by *L'Après-Midi d'un Faune*.

The influence of the pre-War expressionism associated with Nijinsky was clear in *Offerlunden*, an attempt at a Scandinavian *Sacre du Printemps*. (This was produced in 1922, the year following Diaghilev's revival of *Sacre*.) The idea behind *Offerlunden* was bold and interesting—the Viking ancestors of the Scandinavian dancers were undoubtedly just as violent and barbaric as the ancestors of the Russians—but the result on the stage was very different: the formal patterns of Scandinavian dances provided no basis for an evocation of Scandinavian paganism.

La Création du Monde was an important production in the most uncompromising expressionist style. Borlin had contemplated producing a Negro ballet ever since he composed the dance *Sculpture Nègre*. This ballet was like much of the expressionist drama in that the décor and costumes dominated the production. Léger's costumes made dancing out of the question except for The Man and The Woman: crocodiles and insects dragged huge carapaces, animals walked on hands and knees, herons walked on stilts, and other birds were represented by danseuses whose stiff costumes allowed only the tips of their pointes to be seen. At the beginning of the ballet all the dancers were concentrated in a shapeless mass in very dim lighting, and after its creation each creature took only a few steps before merging with the mass again. It was only when the two leading figures began to perform the dance of desire that the mass of dancers moved faster and faster, working up to a frenzied climax.

Like other expressionists of this period, Borlin and his associates found it perfectly natural to load a heavy weight of symbolism on themes which at other periods would have been treated as a useful opportunity for light relief. *Skating Rink*, for example, was based on the movements of skaters and those of dancers at apache balls, but the ballet was made into a sombre expressionist dance-drama, with an overwhelming abstract décor by Léger and an attempt to make the whirling of the skaters into a symbol for the "vortex of life itself. At the end of the ballet gradually the discarded lover is caught up in the swirling mass, while the newcomer carries off his mistress, consenting or filled with anguish."[1] In later years dozens of dramas of this type were produced in Central Europe—among them Laban's *La Nuit* and the Jooss ballet *Big City*.

Not all the ballets produced by the Ballets-Suédois were expressionist: apart from ballets based on Swedish folk-lore Borlin paid tribute to his teacher Fokine in a new version of *Chopiniana*. His last production was the Dada ballet *Relâche*. This was devised by the leading Dada painter Picabia: all the details were worked out by Picabia while the company was on tour in the United States, and Borlin had only a small share in the production.

The intolerable strain under which Borlin worked had its inevitable result. He had a nervous breakdown, and with the dissolution of the Ballets-Suédois his career ended—though he continued to give recitals at which the fading of his powers was clearly apparent. We must not take it for granted that if the strain had been less his career would have been longer and his choreography more perfect. Like all the expressionists he was driven by his daemon to work at high pressure, avoiding so far as possible any relaxation. From the moment when he began to bruise his body in his urge to squeeze the last ounce out of his rôle as a Faun in Fokine's production of *Cléopâtre* he dedicated himself to creative activity with a fanaticism that was completely typical of the expressionism of this period.

BRONISLAVA NIJINSKA (*b.* 1891)

Bronislava Nijinska entered the Imperial School two years after her brother; they were trained by different teachers at the school, but she had lessons from her brother during the summer holidays, and continued to be strongly under his influence right up to the time when she was separated from him by the War.

[1] C. W. Beaumont, *Complete Book of Ballets*, p. 828.

Though Nijinska was a dancer with a splendid technique and remarkable powers of expression (she graduated from the Imperial School in 1908 with first prize for dancing and was soon given solo rôles at the Maryinsky), Diaghilev did not want to include her in the company which he took to Paris because of her peculiar features. (Maryinsky ballerinas were never expected to be conventionally beautiful, but Nijinska's face was exceptionally strange.) Nevertheless Nijinsky managed to persuade Diaghilev to include his beloved sister in the company, and she took part in all subsequent seasons right up to Nijinsky's break with Diaghilev. When Nijinsky was dismissed from the Maryinsky she resigned in sympathy, and became part of the permanent nucleus of the Diaghilev company.

She had a hard time at first in the company, for her peculiar face made her unsuitable for "straight" parts in relatively conventional ballets. She came into her own with the production of *Petrouchka*, for in this ballet her features were perfectly acceptable: she danced first the Street Dancer, then the Ballerina, and was made Karsavina's understudy.

Nijinsky gave her a small but important part in *Faune*: her face was ideal for expressionist ballets. He intended to create for her the leading rôle of the Chosen Maiden in *Sacre* (her strong technique, expressive powers and sympathy for Nijinsky's ideas made her the ideal interpreter for this exacting rôle), but she infuriated Nijinsky by telling him that she could not dance the rôle since she was expecting a baby. (Fortunately for Nijinsky Marie Piltz proved an admirable substitute for Nijinska; at this time the Diaghilev company could call on all the best Maryinsky dancers, and had great reserves of talent.)

When Nijinsky was dismissed by Diaghilev Nijinska left Diaghilev and acted as her brother's assistant in organizing the company with which Nijinsky appeared at the Palace Theatre in London in 1914. (She went to Russia on her own to choose dancers for the company.) Though Diaghilev put tremendous pressure on her to prevent her appearing with her brother (he moved heaven and earth in the law courts, seeking to prove that she was under contract to him), Nijinska with great courage stood by her brother and appeared as his principal danseuse.

After this ill-fated season she returned to Russia, composing her first ballet in St. Petersburg. In 1920 she moved to Kiev, where she started a school, and began to compose dances and small ballets for her pupils. After Massine left Diaghilev in 1921, Diaghilev had no maître de ballet, and sent for Nijinska to take charge of the revival of *The Sleeping Beauty*.

The failure of *The Sleeping Beauty* made it necessary for Diaghilev to undertake once again the production of new ballets, and he put into production *Le Renard*, an expressionist ballet which Stravinsky had devised as far back as 1917. Stravinsky's music (for instruments and voices) was strongly expressionist in its harsh inhumanity, and Larionov devised suitably violent expressionist décor and costumes. Nijinska could find little inspiration in Massine's neo-classical expressionist style, which was already moribund when he left the company, and she tried to evolve an eclectic expressionist style of her own by bringing together elements from the three of her brother's ballets which were familiar to her, and combining these with the acrobatics which were just coming into fashion in Russia (in both drama and ballet) at the time she left. The mixture was not entirely convincing, but the new ballet had far more originality and vitality than many other ballets of the period, and included a fine satirical rôle for Nijinska herself, which she danced superbly.

A year later Diaghilev put into production another expressionist ballet devised and composed by Stravinsky during the war, *Les Noces*. The idea for the ballet had come to Stravinsky in 1914, immediately after the production of *Sacre*, and the ballet was related to *Sacre* in many ways.

Much of Nijinska's choreography for *Les Noces* was based on Nijinsky's work in his first three ballets. The precise Dalcrozian treatment of the music in *Les Noces*, with counterpoint in the music represented by contrapuntal movements on the stage, was derived from *Les Jeux* and *Sacre*; many of the details of the choreography (e.g. solid groups moving in mechanical unison, clenched fists, feet pounding on the ground) were derived from *Sacre*, while other details (e.g. the fresco-like profile positions of the body, and the parallel foot-positions) were derived from *Faune*. But her aims were rather different from Nijinsky's: she took very little interest in the meaning of the words of the songs, concentrating her main interest on abstract patterns and making very little use of solo dancing. To a large extent she used the bodies of the dancers as building blocks, constructing quasi-architectural groups and then breaking them down.[1]

This attempt at an abstract expressionist choreography was perfectly justified by Stravinsky's music, and was of the highest interest. Unfortunately for Nijinska the rather crude expressionist idiom in which she worked was too limited and too lacking in nuances to support an abstract ballet lasting twenty-three minutes, and her deafness made it difficult for her to create new movements in harmony with the music; it was only at intervals that the ballet really came to terms with the music. In typical expressionist fashion Nijinska made no concessions whatever to the audience: she composed the patterns she felt were right, and bothered not at all if anyone else liked them. In fact there were some expressionists who liked the patterns very much, though the ballet never achieved wide popularity. In spite of its defects *Les Noces* was in some ways the most interesting ballet of the twenties. It represented a revival of Nijinsky's full-blooded expressionism by a choreographer who fully understood this style, and was in fact the last ballet of major importance produced by Diaghilev.

[1] Goleizovsky had begun to do this in Moscow before Nijinska left Russia: it was a characteristic expression of Russian constructivism. (*See* p. 260 below.)

Though balletic expressionism as a whole had many unexplored possibilities, *Les Noces* marked the end of the road for Nijinska. Even if Diaghilev had not adopted a "cocktail" policy immediately after the production of *Les Noces*, it is unlikely that Nijinska would have continued in this direction. She lacked her brother's ability to strike into new territory, and in *Les Noces* she had exhausted all the possibilities of the material at her disposal. In her later ballets she abandoned expressionism and never returned to it, even when she had a company of her own.

Nijinska, though possessed of a very real creative talent, had the misfortune to be born into a period when talent was not enough. In a less tortured period she would have composed a large number of excellent ballets in the accepted style of the day: the character dance *The Three Ivans* which she added to her revival of *The Sleeping Princess* in 1921 was one of the finest things in the ballet, and became a high-light of the one-act ballet *Aurora's Wedding*.

MARTHA GRAHAM (b. ca. 1903)

Like other great American artists of her time Isadora Duncan needed to come to Europe to discover her own potentialities and reach maturity. It was relatively easy to make a clean break with the past in the United States, where the ballet tradition was too feeble to exert much influence, but at the same time it was impossible for her to construct a new style without making contact with the major artistic tendencies of Europe. In Europe she found it difficult at first to make the contacts she needed, for she knew no one and had no introductions. Gradually, however, her dancing attracted the interest of distinguished artists and writers; from them she absorbed ideas with the facility of genius, and her dancing matured with astonishing speed, until it was able to compete with the best that the classical tradition could offer at the time (e.g. Pavlova in *Giselle*).

Though Duncan profited enormously from these European influences she never ceased to be characteristically American: only an American girl of her generation could have created a new form of dancing with such qualities of spontaneity, optimism, child-like simplicity, assurance, expansiveness of movement and exuberant vitality.

In spite of the essential Americanism of her dancing Duncan did not have in the United States such a violent impact as she had in Central Europe; the unique quality of her genius could only be appreciated by comparison with the moribund quality of the traditional ballet. After the failure of her debut in Chicago in 1899 she did not return to the United States until 1909. By this time she had become the most famous dancer in all Europe, but at first she had a cool reception in her native land. She persisted in her attempts to win American audiences, and eventually had considerable success; she was still a great artist, but a tendency to embonpoint made it more difficult for her to make the same overwhelming impact as in her youth. (She returned to the United States in 1911, 1917 and 1922.)

Though her influence in the United States came later than in Europe, it was just as pervasive when it got under way. By the early twenties barefoot "Greek" or "Nature" dancing in Duncanish tunics was all the rage in girls' schools, and there were a fair number of ambitious girls who began to give concert recitals in public, just as Duncan had done. Inevitably, however, the attractiveness to the public of these performances was very limited, and their artistic value was no greater than that of similar attempts in other countries to follow in the footsteps of Isadora. Real progress was impossible without a much greater theatrical understanding and a much more highly developed technique. Denishawn, though not the only school of the free dance at this time, was by far the most advanced in these two respects, and its influence was accordingly decisive on the evolution of the American free dance.

The career of Ruth St. Denis (*b.* 1877) is described in a later section.[1] As a free dancer her influence in the United States was of the same order as that of Duncan herself. She evolved from Delsartism and a few glimpses of Oriental dances a free style which to Western eyes seemed completely Oriental, though it was very unlike the real thing.[2] In 1914 she joined forces with Ted Shawn (*b.* 1891), who was in the process of evolving a free style of his own from the simpler aspects of the classical ballet technique and various types of folk-dances and national dances. Though he was only twenty-three he had already had considerable stage experience and teaching experience, and had even composed dances for a film.

Unlike Ruth St. Denis, Ted Shawn was keenly interested in dance-technique and in authentic traditional dances, and based his compositions on authentic originals (American Indian, Spanish, Negro, American folk-dances, and so on.) Because of his tall stature he avoided the pure ballet technique himself, but he appreciated its value for others. At the Denishawn School Ruth St. Denis and Ted Shawn taught the styles in which they had specialized, and composed items in these styles for the performing groups formed out of their students. In addition, however, they brought to the school specialist teachers of Delsartism, Dalcroze Eurhythmics, and a form of "Greek" dancing, and the training included a modified form of the classical ballet technique performed in bare feet. Being

---

[1] *See* p. 275 below.
[2] Some glimpses of a typical St. Denis composition are preserved in the banquet scene of the film *Intolerance* (1918).

keenly interested in technique, Ted Shawn did far more teaching than Ruth St. Denis.

The full-size Denishawn company and the various smaller variety groups were reasonably successful in the theatre. For sixteen years the Denishawn company toured the United States, and there was a successful Oriental tour in 1925–26; during this period Ruth St. Denis and Ted Shawn continued to arrange solos, pas de deux, group dances and ballets. By 1931 (when Ruth St. Denis and Ted Shawn parted company) Denishawn had become a commercial enterprise of considerable magnitude.

Though the various elements in the Denishawn training were much the same as those brought together by Laban, Ruth St. Denis and Ted Shawn worked for a long time in complete independence of contemporary developments in Central Europe,[1] and made little attempt to evolve an integrated technique out of these various elements. The Denishawn School was conceived by its founders as a "University of the Dance" at which the students could study different types of dancing just as they could take different subjects at a university. Their productions for the company were to a large extent based on their own work as soloists, and reflected this same "university" conception of departmentalized dancing. Ted Shawn, for example, composed (apart from many solos for himself) an American Indian dance-drama *The Feather of the Dawn* (with himself in the leading rôle, performing a version of a traditional eagle dance) and an "Aztec" dance-drama *Xochitl* (with leading rôles danced by Martha Graham and either himself or one of his male students). Ruth St. Denis composed a large number of solos, group dances and ballets in her usual "Oriental" style, taking subjects and costumes from India, Japan, Greece, China, Siam, Cambodia, etc. She also composed abstract music-interpretations inspired by the work of Isadora Duncan in this genre. (In the latter she was assisted by Doris Humphrey, who later composed music-interpretations on her own for the Denishawn company.)

From the very beginning Martha Graham stood out in a marked manner from the other Denishawn dancers. After joining the school in 1916 she studied mainly with Shawn, and three years later he gave her the leading female rôle in his Aztec dance-drama *Xochitl*. Whatever her rôle (a unit in a music-interpretation, a Japanese girl arranging flowers, or a ferocious Aztec maiden) she brought to her dancing an intensity which was in strong contrast to the prettyprettiness around her. Like Jean Borlin working for Fokine, she put every ounce of energy into her interpretations, and began to give the first indications of the magnetic personality, dramatic power and stage presence which were

[1] In the last year of Denishawn's existence (1931) Ted Shawn went to Germany to study the Central European free dance, and arranged for a German teacher (Margaret Wallman) to teach at the Denishawn School. It was just at this time that Wigman toured in the United States and the influence of the Central European free dance became powerful in this country.

later to enable her to draw all eyes to herself the moment she stepped on a stage. Though she learned much from her Denishawn experiences, she was much too much of an expressionist to be happy for long in the Denishawn atmosphere, and in 1923 she left the company to start working on her own, in collaboration with the composer-accompanist Louis Horst. (The latter, musical director of Denishawn, had ideas very similar to Martha Graham, and left Denishawn soon after her.)

By this time expressionism had established itself in the American theatre. One of the earliest and most important expressionist productions in America was Nijinsky's ballet *Tyl Eulenspiegel*: though this was performed by the Diaghilev Ballet, it was produced especially for America, with décor and costumes by the young American designer Robert Edmund Jones. In spite of defects inevitable in such a hurried production (which caused it to have a very mixed reception in the press) it made a profound impression on many who saw it. Carl van Vechten quotes with approval Margaret Wycherly's comment after the first performance:

> She felt he [Nijinsky] had for the first time leaped into the hearts of the great American public, whose appreciation of his subtler art as expressed in *Narcisse*, *Petrouchka* and even *Schéhérazade*, had been more moderate.[1]

Inspired by Nijinsky's expressionism Robert Edmund Jones became one of the most important pioneers of expressionist stage design. He wrote of his experience with Nijinsky:

> The great artist who taught me so much now exists apart ... I dwell for the last time upon my strange, magical shattering experience and remember once more what it has meant to me ... It has given me a heightened and broadened sense of life. It has taught me to be true to my own inner dream, to live by this dream, never to betray it.[2]

During the early twenties expressionism made rapid progress in the United States, attracting the attention of most of the leading dramatists and producers. Eugene O'Neill's *The Emperor Jones* (1920), with its flashbacks and drum accompaniment, showed strong expressionist tendencies, and the same was true of his play *The Hairy Ape* (1922). John Howard Lawson's *Roger Bloomer* and Elmer Rice's *The Adding Machine* (both 1923) kept rather closer to German prototypes of expressionist drama.

Expressionism was very much in the air when Martha Graham broke away

---

[1] Dance Index monograph, *Nijinsky*, p. 11.
[2] Article by Robert Edmund Jones in above monograph, p. 60.

L'Homme et Son Désir
(Borlin, Paris, 1921) with
Borlin as The Man

Below: Martha Graham

The Rake's Progress (de Valois, London, 1935) with Markova as the Betrayed Girl
and Harold Turner as the Rake

The Green Table (Jooss, Paris, 1932): The Gentlemen in Black

from Denishawn, and as soon as she had achieved for herself financial independence by getting a job teaching at the Eastman School of Music she began to make experiments leading towards the creation of an integrated expressionist style of free dancing. In other words she began in the middle twenties to do for the American free dance what Dalcroze, Laban, Wigman and others had done for the Central European free dance some years previously. Her technique grew from similar roots and inevitably moved in a similar direction, but the expressionism she evolved was a complete projection of her own personality, and was as American as the skyscraper and the blues. When Wigman, Kreutzberg and other German free dancers began to tour in America the Graham style was already solidly established, and when the Wigman pupil Hanya Holm started a branch of the Wigman school in the United States in 1931, she found it expedient to adapt the Wigman style considerably to conform to American ideas which were to a large extent derived from the work of Martha Graham.

When Martha Graham gave her first recital in New York in 1926 with her pupils, she had not yet fully established her own style, and many of her items were composed in various Denishawn exotic styles. (They included, rather surprisingly, "Oriental" items such as *Three Gopi Maidens*; it was only later that the influence of Ted Shawn showed itself in items based on American Indian material.) She was one of a dozen or more recital dancers giving recitals at long intervals, working hard for months in order to prepare a number of new dances and gather together enough money to give a single performance. But she stood out from the others because of her extraordinary personality, and as she perfected her expressionist style and technique she became unmistakably the leader of a new movement. Though a number of other dancers followed her lead and some of them had striking success, she alone was able to expand her New York recitals into Broadway seasons of a fortnight or more, and sometimes to take her group on coast-to-coast tours under the management of a commerical impresario. (In the United States the free dancers had a far more difficult time than in Central Europe, for there were no American State-subsidized theatres, and it was almost impossible for the avant-garde dancers to break into the commercial theatre.)

One of the most striking and typically expressionist features of the Graham technique was the impulse starting at the centre of the body and following out to the end of the limbs. Impulses of this kind (derived from the teachings of Delsarte) were equally characteristic of the Wigman technique and other Central European schools, but Graham gave them an individual flavour by putting great emphasis on what she called a "percussive attack". She also considerably developed the Delsartian technique for falling to the ground in a smooth and controlled manner, and (like her Central European contem-

A.A.O.B.—K

poraries) broke away from the classical technique by emphasizing the effort needed to do movements and the impact created by her feet striking the ground. She kept making experiments on herself and her pupils, trying out new movements and working hard on those which seemed to offer the greatest possibilities. Her own physique played a large part in these experiments: over and over again she discovered ways of making her body perform movements unlike any seen before. Throughout her career she maintained her leadership as a technical innovator, and inevitably had great influence on the various styles which came into existence during the late twenties and the thirties. The depression which began in 1929, causing far greater unemployment and misery than any previous economic crisis, gave much the same stimulus to the American free dance as defeat, blockade and inflation had done to the Central European free dance a decade earlier; the number of teachers, pupils and recital dancers doubled and re-doubled, and for the first time free dancers were able to make an appeal to the general public. It made little difference whether or not the themes of the dances were "socially significant"—though very often they were: what mattered was that people were shaken up so badly that they were prepared to take an interest in new forms of theatre, even in dances designed to say something instead of providing light entertainment.

Martha Graham was as much a pioneer in her choice of themes as in her technical innovations. Agnes de Mille describes this aspect of Graham's work with her habitual dry humour:

> She was doing dances of revolt and protest in the posh days of 1929. She was using religious ritual and American folkways when revolution became the young radicals' artistic line in 1931-33 . . . [Soon] she was through with folkways and making experiments in psychology, and while other concerts were padded with "American suites" and "Dust Bowl Ballads" Graham began to turn out her superb satires "Every Soul is a Circus" and "Punch and the Judy". . . . The dance world seethed with satire and Martha concerned herself with woman as artist and then woman as woman, inaugurating her poetic tragedies "Letter to the World", "Deaths and Entrances" and "Salem Shore" and developing the first use of the spoken word in relation to dance pattern.[1] Everyone else began to do biographies: Graham delved deeper and deeper into anthropology—"Dark Meadow". She began to search Greek mythology for the key to woman's present discomforts—"Labyrinth", "Cave of the Heart" "Night Journey".[2]

Notwithstanding the great interest of her themes and her technical innovations Graham would never have reached her unique position in the American,

[1] In fact Graham was by no means the first to arrange dances to the spoken word. Duncan and Ruth St. Denis had done this a generation earlier, and in Central Europe the free dance was used by producers of expressionist dramas at an early stage in the development of this genre.
[2] *Dance to the Piper*, pp. 135-36.

theatre if she had not had such a magnetic personality that she could dominate an audience even when her experiments had led her up a blind alley. In the United States the majority of the recital dancers were intelligent, well-educated, idealistic and tremendously hard-working artists, willing to slave away year after year to put on dance recitals at long intervals, with relatively little popular support: like all other expressionists they were only interested in what they felt to be "truth", and had no interest in "beauty" or making concessions to popular taste. They were proud of their austerity, and felt no need of making contact with the general theatre public. In fact they developed a Puritan revulsion to the glamour of the theatre, preferring to describe their performances as "concerts" or "recitals": they regarded the theatre as the home of trivial spectacles such as ballet. ("Ballet" was a term of abuse among them.) One branch of the free dance developed as part of the curriculum of schools and colleges. To a large extent this estrangement from the theatre was due to the commercial organization of the American theatre—many of the best brains in the drama likewise found it necessary to work in educational establishments and in semi-amateur little theatres—but it fitted in very well with the *Weltanschauung* of the American free dancers. They devoted their lives to the dance with almost a religious sense of dedication, and felt no necessity to make their work theatrically effective.[1] When they did work in the commercial theatre—above all in musicals— they accepted the ironclad conventions of such productions with the same whole-hearted fanaticism that they pursued high art in their concert recitals.

Martha Graham's outlook was very different in some ways, though the *Weltanschauung* of the free dancers was to a large extent derived from her own work. Unlike most of her contemporaries, she had developed a fine feeling for the theatre before she began to compose her own dances, and she was able to build up a fairly large audience for her work in the theatre without making any concessions. Sometimes in her experiments she broke certain fundamental laws of the theatre, with unfortunate results, but this happened through her intense desire to explore new territory, not to any lack of theatrical feeling. Normally her work was intensely theatrical (in the good sense of the word) and was just as capable of winning over a general audience as any other type of theatrical dancing. Even those who felt little sympathy for expressionism or were discomfited by certain deficiencies in her dancing could not deny her importance. People might like her or dislike her, but no one could remain indifferent to her. In her style of dancing Graham incarnated the expressionist ideal, just as the acting of Edmund Kean incarnated the romantic ideal a century earlier. (The

---

[1] Though the organization of theatres in Central Europe made it far easier for free dancers to make contact with the general public, they suffered from a somewhat similar lack of contact with theatrical traditions. This was very obvious in such details as costumes and make-up, which were often crude and ugly even when they were intended to be more or less "straight".

two ideals are surprisingly similar: much that was written about Kean applies equally well to Graham.)[1]

By far the most serious deficiency in her dancing was her failure (in common with other expressionist dancers of her generation) to cope with the problem of strain: the complexity and intensity of her inner conflicts made it impossible for her to relax, though her technique included many exercises in relaxation derived from the work of Delsarte. Even in quiet passages clearly intended to create a lyrical effect her hands continued to reflect a soul in torment. At no time did her hands (or those of her pupils) fall into an easy and spontaneous line; either they were contorted in sympathy with some violent movement or deliberately held in some stylized position similar in character to the self-conscious positions used by Jooss dancers. The hands of a dancer are as significant as the brushwork of a painter: faking is impossible, the hands show with perfect clarity whether the artist is expressing himself freely and harmoniously with the whole of his psyche or whether various impulses are warring against each other inside him. The strains which appear in the hands of dancers affect the movement of the whole body no less powerfully than the hands, though not in so obvious a manner. (It is possible that Graham's predilection for properties which she handled while dancing may be related to her inability to cope with the strain appearing in her hands.)

It is important to realize that the expressionist dancer-choreographer has to face a far more difficult problem than the expressionist painter or dramatist. The violent inner conflicts which eventually drove van Gogh to madness, Strindberg and Munch to nervous breakdowns, and Ernst Toller to suicide did not prevent these expressionist artists from achieving a very high degree of integration and fulfilment in their creative work, carried out with the aid of brushes and paint or pen and paper. Dancer-choreographers, on the other hand, have to work with their own bodies and with bodies controlled by personalities different from their own: one can imagine van Gogh's misery if he had had to take into account the complex personality and need for self-fulfilment of each of his tubes of paint! Being a thoroughbred expressionist dancer-choreographer Graham was held back from full realization of her own potentialities by the inescapable limitations of her medium. Nevertheless she did achieve a great deal in spite of these limitations, and thereby considerably enriched American culture. By her persistent determination to discover new types of movement and new themes she sometimes lost a great deal of time, and she experienced much bitterness and frustration when things went badly; but she saved herself

---

[1] *Cf.* Coleridge's famous comment, "To see Kean was to read Shakespeare by flashes of lightning", and Hazlitt's less sympathetic comment, "Kean is all effort, all violence, all extreme passion; he is possessed of a fury, a demon that leaves him no repose."

from the fossilization to which expressionism is more liable than almost any other genre, and kept her own type of theatrical expressionism alive long after other types had become moribund.

KURT JOOSS (*b.* 1901)

One of the many advantages which Jooss had over his Central European contemporaries was his lengthy association with the distinguished teacher Sigurd Leeder. Though Leeder worked in close collaboration with Jooss, and his methods of teaching were closely linked with Jooss' style as a choreographer, he maintained some independence of outlook, and the Jooss–Leeder technique had a certain objective value of its own, quite apart from the ballets which Jooss composed. (By this I do not mean that the Jooss–Leeder technique differed from the Wigman technique in being completely free from arbitrary mannerisms.)

Jooss was originally trained by Laban, and later became Laban's principal dancer and assistant teacher and choreographer. In the early twenties Jooss remained strongly under Laban's influence and composed ballets in a style close to Laban's. After several years' experience in the production of ballets with his own group Jooss began to realize the limitations of the Laban style as a basis for work in the theatre, and therefore abandoned creative work for a period (1926–27), during which he studied on his own in Paris and Vienna. The most powerful influence experienced by him during this period seems to have been the Diaghilev Ballet, for immediately after the death of Diaghilev he began to produce a series of new versions of Diaghilev ballets with his new group at the Essen municipal theatres. The ballets selected by him for production were *Petrouchka*, *Le Bal*, *Prince Igor*, *La Boutique Fantasque*, *Le Fils Prodigue* and *Pulcinella*.[1] The choice of ballets was significant: Jooss was clearly attracted by the grotesque satirical expressionism of Massine's choreography for *La Boutique Fantasque* and *Pulcinella*, and Fokine's tragically expressionist choreography for the title rôle in *Petrouchka*. The choreography of the other Diaghilev ballets could not be described as expressionist, but each of them had themes suitable for expressionist treatment (in contrast to other Diaghilev ballets such as *Les Sylphides* and *Le Spectre de la Rose*, which demanded lyrical treatment). Jooss was by no means a pioneer in producing free-dance versions of Diaghilev ballets: other choreographers were doing the same thing at other German opera-houses. (In 1927, for example, Maudrik produced *L'Oiseau de Feu* at the State

---

[1] He also produced *Coppélia*; this was not in the Diaghilev repertoire, but was in the repertoire of a number of State ballets (including the Paris Opéra) and the Pavlova company.

Opera in Berlin, and Georgi produced *Petrouchka* and *Pulcinella* at the Stadt-theater in Hanover.)

During this same period (the late twenties and early thirties) Jooss and Leeder worked hard with the Essen dance group to assimilate some aspects of the classical technique. This was a tendency common to a number of the leaders of the Central European free dance at the time. As early as 1928 the recital dancer Kreutzberg had added a considerable amount of training in the classical technique to his free-dance training, and the Berlin State Opera had begun to present ballets in which some sections were in free style and other sections were made up from classical steps.

Jooss and Leeder came to grips with the classical technique in their own way, attempting to expand their own technique to include certain carefully selected classical steps such as the *grand jeté en tournant* without taking over the academic training which prepares the classical dancer for such steps by teaching separately all the elements from which they are built up.[1] In some ways this attempt to tackle the classical technique the wrong way round was a mistake (the dancers had to spend an enormous amount of work in mastering quite simple things); but it was a fortunate mistake, for it made possible a valuable extension in the whole range of movement of the Jooss dancers: they learned to soar through the air and land with ease and grace, and the line of their bodies became far more precise and harmonious. Jooss and Leeder still avoided the "pictures" and tip-toe balance characteristic of the classical technique, concentrating on securing a smooth continuity of movement with no sharp accents, but within their chosen sector of the classical technique they secured admirable suppleness of *plié* and control of movement into the floor.

At the same time that the Jooss dancers expanded their vocabulary of movement Jooss himself profited considerably from his experience in coming to grips with a traditional technique with clear-cut standards of perfection: his choreography gained solidity and precision through being confined within self-imposed limitations, in the same way that Munch profited from the technical limitations imposed by the techniques of lithography and wood-engraving. (Munch's work in these media was on the whole far more satisfying than his oil-paintings; for much the same reasons the black-and-white work of Georg Grosz and Käthe Kollwitz and the wood-carvings of Barlach were far superior to the mass of expressionist art in less exacting media.)

In his masterpiece *The Green Table* (1932) Jooss tackled a contemporary theme which gave magnificent scope to his talent for grotesque satire: he poured into this ballet everything he had learned from Laban, from the expressionist drama and from the Diaghilev Ballet, and brought together in this ballet

---

[1] Some years later Jooss and Leeder found it desirable to make use of a standard Cecchetti "barre" (connected series of exercises at the barre).

the best solo dances and episodes from ballets composed by him in the previous decade. Though the result was to some extent lacking in homogeneity, and had a number of weak passages, it was constructed with remarkable skill, and the best scenes were superlatively good. Unlike nearly all other ballets in free style, *The Green Table* could stand comparison with the best of the ballets based on traditional classical techniques, and proved capable of attracting audiences outside Central Europe. (The world-wide tours of the Ballets Jooss were based almost entirely on this ballet.)

The weakest scenes in the ballet were those in which Jooss joined together his chosen vocabulary of classical steps according to Laban formulas, working in a coldly intellectual way; the rôle of Death, consisting of the repetition at intolerable length of a few stodgy "motto" movements of the type used by Laban, was also very inexpressive. (Death's sudden appearances were stage-managed by Jooss with great skill, but the actual choreography for the rôle was lamentably crude.) On the other hand the best scenes had enormous vitality, and showed few of the familiar defects of the expressionist free dance. This was particularly true of the opening and closing scenes (the Peace Conference), which never failed to make a strong impression on audiences. Here the stiff formal gestures of the white-gloved hands of the diplomats combined to form a miniature ballet that was completely satisfying—whereas normally the hands of free dancers have a stiff self-conscious quality which is distressing to anyone familiar with the flexible and expressive hands of great classical dancers.

Having put all his best ideas into *The Green Table* Jooss was left with nothing fresh to say: nearly all his subsequent productions were new versions of pre-1932 Jooss ballets, revived by Jooss with choreography in the manner of *The Green Table* but without the extraordinary imaginative sweep of his masterpiece. After *The Green Table* Jooss repeated himself just as Massine had done after *La Boutique Fantasque*. *Big City*, considerably influenced by Laban ballets such as *La Nuit*, stood out by the brilliance of its construction, but the sentimental over-simplification of the plot and characterization and the poverty of ideas in the choreography put this ballet in a very different class to *The Green Table*. The other ballets were cerebral and wearisome applications of Laban formulas: each character was given a "motto" step and repeated this step *ad nauseam*, and the ballets as a whole were padded out to large dimensions in a misguided attempt to give them heroic stature.

Thanks to the universal success of *The Green Table* Jooss was able to keep his company together and make contact with audiences in many different countries during his long period as a refugee from the Nazis. But the expressionism of the other ballets in the repertoire began to "date" very seriously in the forties, and this was also true of the weaker passages of *The Green Table*; with the fading away of popular support Jooss was forced to dissolve his company in 1947. Fortunately, however, the defeat of the Nazis made it possible for him to return to Essen in 1950. When his new group began to perform in Germany in 1952, with *The Green Table* as the centre of its repertoire, this ballet (little known in Germany up to then) began to take its rightful place as the *Petrouchka* of German ballet.

Unfortunately the ballets composed by Jooss for his new group had the same defects as those composed by him in England in the thirties and forties. After the War there was a strong reaction in Germany away from the expressionist free dance towards ballets based on the classical technique: Jooss did his best to come to terms with this movement of public taste by including a relatively high proportion of adapted classical steps in his choreography, but he used them in the same monotonous and inexpressive way as before, and his dancers showed in their movements a ponderous, self-conscious quality destructive of the *élan* characteristic of the classical tradition. An attempt by Jooss to escape from this dilemma by returning to the crude constructivist style of the twenties (in the "Barbed-Wire" scene of *Journey in the Fog*) was equally unsuccessful. The new group was disbanded by Jooss in 1953, after a season in London.

NINETTE DE VALOIS (*b.* 1898)

During the period when Ninette de Valois was a permanent member of the Diaghilev company (1923–25) she was rehearsed in new ballets by three different choreographers (Nijinska, Massine and Balanchine) and danced in the best ballets of Fokine and Massine (not to mention Petipa). Judging by her account of her experiences in her book *Invitation to the Ballet* the works which made the strongest impression on her were Massine's early neo-classical expressionist ballets *Les Femmes de Bonne Humeur*, *La Boutique Fantasque* and *Le Tricorne*.[1] She writes of Massine's work with a reverence she does not show for any other choreographer, describing him as a genius, the choreographer who more than anyone expresses the modern age:

> Of Massine it is harder to speak [than of Fokine], for he is of the modern choreographers. Dynamic still in achievement and experiment,[2] his mind has the characteristic architectural tendency of today. But to the writer this man spells the word genius, not the genius of fiction but the genius of fact; that infinite capacity for

[1] P. 163. She gave practical expression to her admiration for Massine by commissioning a series of ballets from him at Covent Garden. He is the only guest choreographer to be honoured in this manner.

[2] The book was first published in 1937.

taking pains, power of analysis and concentration, and further, imagination and judgment as opposed to originality and flair.[1]

The emphasis on "analysis and concentration" as opposed to "originality and flair" is profoundly significant. Ninette de Valois was strongly attracted to the intellectual, Laban-Jooss wing of expressionism: as one might expect she praises Jooss but had little use for Wigman or Graham. She writes about Jooss with exceptional sympathy and understanding; though she is aware of his weaknesses she is very much alive to the fine qualities of his best work:

> One must pay special homage to the mind and matter of Kurt Jooss. This artist has such remarkable natural gifts that one can only deplore their restricted medium. He has the apparent visual tastelessness that is often to be found in those whose creative ability is unguided, but he has contributed to movement (both in the balletic and the dance sense) some choreography of real importance . . . When he cares to dispense with a display of superficial knowledge of the classical school he shows a theatre-craft, an originality and a technique of mass orchestration that is extremely satisfying and formal in construction.[1]

A third choreographer of whom she writes with sympathy and enthusiasm is Jean Borlin, whose expressionist ballet *El Greco* she praises very highly:

> *El Greco* and *Les Vierges Folles* were two works that in their own line were utterly satisfactory, the former having a nobility and simplicity about it that struck an unusual and courageous note at that time.[2]

She writes of Fokine with much less understanding and sympathy, praising him for precisely those qualities which were of least importance in his best work ("a great and extremely logical mind . . . a sense of fitting climax and harmonic choreographic orchestration which is rare today"), and ignoring his poetic lyricism and spontaneity. Characteristically, she praises *Les Sylphides* for its "continuity and rational dramatic development". Like the romantic composers who admired in composers of earlier periods qualities typical of the romantic period, Ninette de Valois admired in *Les Sylphides* qualities typical of her own intellectual wing of expressionism but not in the least typical of *Les Sylphides*, with its rapidly improvised and rather haphazard structure.[3]

The influences of Massine, Borlin and the Laban-Jooss intellectual wing of

[1] P. 178.
[2] P. 179. The description of *El Greco* as being unusual and courageous in striking a note of nobility and simplicity presumably refers to the artistic policy of the Diaghilev company after the production of *Les Noces*.
[3] When the prima ballerina dances the Prélude and the Pas de Deux, the order of the solos is changed to give her a rest between items, but the ballet is just as effective as when she combines the Mazurka and the Pas de Deux, and the solos are danced in the usual order. Few people even notice that a change has been made in the order of the solos.

the Central European free dance are very obvious in the major ballets of Ninette de Valois. Other important influences are the teachings of Dalcroze (she had two years' training in Dalcroze Eurhythmics) and the "plastic" movements used by Dalcroze and his assistants in dance-compositions. (These "plastic" compositions of Dalcroze were to a large extent inspired by the work of Duncan, but they were also influenced by parallel developments in other schools of the free dance.)[1]

After leaving Diaghilev she found an opportunity for trying out her expressionist ideas in solo dances for herself (notably an admirable solo *Pride*), in group movements for the actors in Terence Gray's avant-garde expressionist productions at the Festival Theatre, Cambridge, and in the dances and stylized acting of the actors and dancers in productions of the poetic plays of W. B. Yeats (supervised by Yeats himself) at the Abbey Theatre in Dublin. The "plastic" movements she used in this work were much closer to Dalcroze and Laban than to the classical technique. At the same time, however, she ran a ballet school in London, the Academy of Choreographic Art, where "plastic" movements formed only a relatively small part of the training. In 1928 she moved her school to the Old Vic at the invitation of Lilian Baylis, and presented her pupils once a year in small-scale academic divertissements that were very different from the expressionist work she was doing in other theatres. These pupils became the corps de ballet of the Vic-Wells Ballet when Lilian Baylis decided to add ballet performances to her long-established performances of drama and opera in English, and invited Ninette de Valois to become director of the ballet section of her organization.

After the formation of the Vic-Wells Ballet Ninette de Valois continued to show the same marked dichotomy in her compositions as before. For the Vic-Wells Ballet (appearing at Sadlers Wells and the Old Vic) she arranged a large number of insipid divertissement ballets which seemed designed for performance by schoolgirls at end-of-term displays, whereas for the Camargo Society productions in the West End she composed dance-dramas in a violently expressionist style, much closer to Borlin and Laban than Massine. This dichotomy was due in part to the fact that the Vic-Wells Ballet was weak in personnel at this time, whereas the Camargo Society was able to call on all the best dancers resident in London; but a similar dichotomy can be seen throughout her career, and in fact in the careers of nearly all expressionist choreographers. When such choreographers move outside their own genre and attempt to compose light-hearted entertainments, they seemed to lose their grip, and resort to the most conventional and sentimental ideas.

---

[1] Dalcroze did his best to prevent his work from being recognized as a style of dancing, describing it not as dancing but "moving plastic". (*See* his article "The Technique of Moving Plastic", reproduced in *Eurhythmics, Art and Education*, pp. 14–47.)

The first large-scale ballet composed by Ninette de Valois was *La Création du Monde*, a new version of the Borlin ballet which she produced for the Camargo Society in 1931. In this production she watered down to some extent the uncompromising expressionist violence of the original: she treated the theme in a relatively straightforward dramatic manner, she avoided reproducing de Maré's violently expressionist lighting, and the costumes and décor (commissioned by her from E. Wolfe) were almost ludicrously tame in comparison with Léger's devastating originals. Nevertheless *La Création du Monde* gave good opportunities to Ninette de Valois' special gifts as choreographer, and was far more alive and original than any other English ballet of the period. She was of course helped by her memories of Borlin's original choreography and the careful planning of the ballet by Blaise Cendrars, Milhaud, Léger, Borlin and de Maré. On the other hand attempts at new versions of old ballets very often come to grief; and Ninette de Valois showed a fine understanding of her own talents when she selected this particular ballet for production. *La Création du Monde* was later taken into the repertoire of the Vic-Wells Ballet, but it did not fit in very well with the rest of the repertoire. This was in many ways the most important ballet composed by Ninette de Valois in the early years of the Vic-Wells company; it was praised by the critics, and at the time she regarded it as her finest ballet; nevertheless she took it out of the repertoire and revived it only once (in 1934).

A few months after producing *La Création du Monde* Ninette produced for the Camargo Society *Job*, a "masque for dancing" devised by Geoffrey Keynes on the basis of the famous illustrated book by William Blake. The project for the ballet and the music (commissioned by Geoffrey Keynes from Vaughan Williams) were based on English traditions and were not particularly expressionist, but Ninette de Valois based her production on various aspects of the expressionist free dance. At certain points the original project, the score and the expressionist choreography found common ground, and then results were satisfactory. This was particularly true of the violently grotesque Labanist dances of Job's Comforters and the allegorical figures War, Pestilence and Famine: these characters wore masks and used their hands with admirably stylized viciousness. Satan himself was nearly nude, and danced in bare feet using typically free-dance steps: Dolin made this part vivid and dynamic, his acrobatic style lending itself well to the expressionist choreography.

On the other hand the group dances, in a rather insipid Dalcrozian "plastic" style, were very disappointing: the music (inspired by English folk-dance tunes) clearly demanded something much less gentle and ladylike. The production also suffered from long passages in which nothing much happened, the dancers either standing in tableaux inspired by Blake drawings or walking slowly to form another tableau. At such times the ballet was very dull, all interest being concentrated in the music. This dullness was due in part to faults in the original project of Geoffrey Keynes, but another choreographer might have coped more successfully with the defects of the project—if necessary asking Vaughan Williams to cut or alter the music. Because of these defects the ballet did not realize more than a small fraction of the potentialities of the theme and the music, and never became really popular. Nevertheless the best of the expressionist episodes had great vitality, and the ballet has been successfully revived on a number of occasions by the Vic-Wells Ballet and its successor the Sadlers Wells Ballet.

Ninette de Valois showed her affinity with the intellectual wing of expressionism by the way in which she tackled the choreography of these ballets, working out all details in a notebook before starting rehearsal and then teaching the movements to the dancers exactly as she had planned them. In the usual expressionist Dalcrozian manner she tied each movement to a definite note in the score and assigned some movement to each note, mechanically accompanying repetitions in the music with repetitions on the stage even if this was visually unsatisfactory. Her expressionist treatment of the music was reasonably satisfactory when withers were to be wrung, but it was totally unsuited to the non-expressionist ballets which she composed in large numbers, and helped to make them depressingly prosaic and monotonous.

Most of the ballets composed by Ninette de Valois for the Vic-Wells Ballet after *Job* continued the insipid and sentimental manner of her earlier productions. Even when she produced new versions of Borlin ballets she selected the most innocuous ballets in the Ballets-Suédois repertoire, notably *The Wise and Foolish Virgins* (*Les Vierges Folles*). The original had a stilted, doll-like charm because of its skilful adaptation of Swedish peasant costumes and naïve folk-traditions,[1] but this charm was lost in the "plastic" English version, for Ninette de Valois had little feeling for rural naïveté. Like other expressionists, she needed a grotesque or satirical theme to stimulate her imagination. In the Paris of Toulouse-Lautrec she found a certain amount of stimulus, composing for the Ballet Club a comedy-ballet *Bar aux Folies-Bergères* (1934) which showed considerable influence from the Massine ballet *La Boutique Fantasque* (though it lacked the magic and expressionist vigour of *Boutique*). But it was not until 1935 that Ninette de Valois found an expressionist theme which gave full opportunities to her talent: this was *The Rake's Progress*, devised by the composer Gavin Gordon on the basis of the famous series of prints by Hogarth. In this ballet Ninette de Valois was able to bring together influences from Massine (*Les Femmes de Bonne Humeur*), Jooss (*The Green Table*) and Borlin (*La Maison des Fous*): the mixture of styles in her

---

[1] This ballet was the most popular one in the repertoire of the Ballets-Suédois, being given more performances than any other.

choreography was not fully satisfying, but the ballet was admirably constructed and was a great success in spite of certain weaknesses.

The first scene was the least successful of all the scenes in the ballet: the mime was rather ponderous and the Betrayed Girl was given a "motto" theme of a crude and conventional type in the Laban-Jooss manner. (She expressed embarrassment by trotting on her pointes and hiding her face with her hand.) Only in the dancing lesson did the first scene come to life. Obviously the trouble with this scene was that there was nothing in the action to give much scope to the choreographer's expressionist talents. Such opportunities were plentiful in Scene II (a house of ill-fame), Scene IV (a gaming-house) and Scene VI (a mad-house), and the choreographer took good advantage of them. In Scenes II and IV the grotesque, satirical expressionism of the choreography combined together elements from the early ballets of Massine and from the Jooss ballet *The Green Table*, though it never reached the level of the best passages in these ballets. Scene VI (which owed much to Borlin and the free dance of the early twenties) was even more typically expressionist with its series of madmen dancing semi-nude with bare feet: two of the mad dances in this scene (that of the Gentleman with the Rope and that of the Rake himself) represented the peak of Ninette de Valois' achievement as a choreographer. Unfortunately, however, the impact of these dances was dulled by the inordinate padding of this scene: after the concentration of the previous scenes the ballet needed to build up rapidly to a climax.

Though *The Rake's Progress* was to Ninette de Valois what *The Green Table* was to Jooss and "The March to the Scaffold" to Massine, and remained solidly in the repertoire of the Vic-Wells Ballet from the time it was composed, it did not appear to good advantage when revived at Covent Garden for the Sadlers Wells Ballet: the décors (by Rex Whistler) did not suit the large Covent Garden stage, and the dancers cast in the leading rôles gave performances that were insipid compared with the best of the pre-War performances. On the other hand the revival at Sadlers Wells for the Sadlers Wells Theatre Ballet, with David Blair in the title rôle,[1] was a great success. Though by this time good new choreography in expressionist style was hardly possible, a fine example of expressionist ballet from an earlier period retained all its power to grip an audience.

Checkmate (1937) was almost as perfect a *Gesamtkunstwerk* as *The Rake's Progress*, with admirable expressionist décor and costumes by McKnight Kauffer and violently rhythmic music by Arthur Bliss combining together with the choreography to produce a harmonious synthesis; but in this ballet certain faults which had been of small importance in *The Rake's Progress* (notably padding and sentimentality in the female rôles) were very prominent. *Checkmate* sprang to life whenever the Red Knight (Harold Turner) or the

[1] *See* below, p. 372.

Black Queen (June Brae) had a solo or danced together: inspired by the dancing of these two admirable artists Ninette de Valois composed two rôles that were full of vitality and character, and showed a fine understanding of Massine's work in developing a neo-classical style of expressionism. Moreover the last scene, in which Ninette de Valois skilfully marshalled large groups of dancers carrying staves in dim expressionist lighting, had the remorseless horror characteristic of the best expressionist group choreography for both free dancers and classically trained dancers. Unfortunately, however, these admirable episodes were separated by long passages of Kitsch[1] in which the atmosphere of the ballet was dissipated.

After *Checkmate* Ninette de Valois composed ballets at longer and longer intervals, devoting herself almost entirely to administration. *Promenade*, composed in 1943 at a difficult period when Ashton was in the Forces and the technique of the company was suffering from the strain of war-time touring, consisted of a series of academic enchaînements mixed together with mimed passages that had no connection with the dancing; the ballet was clearly inspired by Massine's *Le Beau Danube*, but lacked even the sentimental and commercialized charm of that ballet.

After *Promenade* Ninette de Valois abandoned choreography completely for a long time. No doubt she was influenced by the fact that ever since *Checkmate* her ballets had had very limited success with critics and the public, and also by the apparent swing of public taste away from expressionism. (Helpmann's melodramatic mime plays *Hamlet* and *Miracle in the Gorbals* were successful, but his completely expressionist production *Adam Zero*—with its central figure Man moving through the stages of life, accompanied by all the usual expressionist stage devices—was a failure.)[2]

She returned to choreography in 1950 to stage Roberto Gerhardt's ballet *Don Quixote*. This had been accepted for production some time previously, but the actual production was delayed several times. In the normal way Frederick Ashton, the company's staff choreographer, would have staged *Don Quixote*, but the expressionist theme was completely unsuitable for his style of composition, and presumably this was the reason why in the end Ninette de Valois decided to arrange the ballet herself. (Helpmann was the obvious choice for this ballet; it is not clear why it was not assigned to him.)

Though the expressionism of Ninette de Valois' choreography for *Don Quixote* was much less naïve than Helpmann's expressionism in *Adam Zero*, it belonged just as clearly to the early twenties, and bewildered audiences and

---

[1] An untranslatable German word for something which is sentimental and trite.

[2] It is typical of the artistic backwardness of the Sadlers Wells Ballet at this time that an artist as intelligent as Helpmann should have thought that he was being daringly modern when (working on a script by Michael Benthall) he resurrected the most hackneyed devices of the expressionist drama of the twenties.

critics unfamiliar with the work done in Central Europe at this period. There was hardly anything in the choreography that could be recognized as dancing: the various characters indulged in a curious sort of slow and portentous mime which conveyed nothing of Roberto Gerhardt's theme—a particular interpretation of the Don Quixote story on which Gerhardt (a distinguished Catalan composer) had been working for many years. In one typical scene the whole emphasis was concentrated on a rope hanging from the flies, which Don Quixote kept swinging about the stage: if the dancers had any idea of the significance of what they were doing they gave no sign of it. Though Gerhardt's music (the first major ballet score by a disciple of Schönberg) was perfectly suitable for expressionist choreography, the movements bore almost as little relation to the rhythm and phrasing of the music as Massine's version of the dance of the Chosen Maiden. (This ignoring of the music was just as typically expressionist as the opposite tendency to follow it with pedantic accuracy: one reason why the expressionist choreographers were seldom able to arrange satisfactory neo-classical enchaînements was that they could not achieve in their treatment of the music a happy medium between these two extremes.)

Don Quixote was as unsuccessful as *Adam Zero*, and made painfully clear the moribund state of balletic expressionism. Even in the thirties expressionism was on the decline: the fine expressionist ballets produced by Jooss, Massine and Ninette de Valois in the period 1932–36 represented the swan-song of a period that was almost over.

C

Post-Expressionist Pseudo-Classicism

FOR THE cocktail ballets produced by Diaghilev after 1923 all creative styles of choreography were unsuitable. The most advanced of contemporary styles, the Nijinsky type of expressionism, had only a limited appeal to audiences, and in any case was no longer a novelty. Some sort of a return to the past was obviously necessary; Fokinian romanticism was now very passé, and the obvious solution to this problem was a return to the Petipa type of pseudo-classicism. On the other hand straightforward choreography in the Petipa manner would not have fitted in very well with the avant-garde décor, costumes and music, and Diaghilev's choreographers therefore gave this familiar style a flavour of sophistication and novelty by distorting it in an expressionist direction and adding to it a few typically expressionist avant-garde devices. As in the Petipa ballets, the choreographers made little attempt to come to grips with the theme of the ballets: this would have been as out of place as a serious discussion at a cocktail party.

BRONISLAVA NIJINSKA (b. 1891)

The first of the post-expressionist pseudo-classical ballets, *Les Biches* (1924), was to some extent a transitional ballet, for its theme was derived from Nijinsky's expressionist ballet *Les Jeux*, and Nijinska made some attempt to come to grips with the theme: her viciously satirical treatment of the hostess of the party (who toyed with a long pearl necklace and flaunted an almost equally long cigarette-holder) was closer in spirit to the expressionist work being done in Central Europe and Russia at this time than to the innocuous style demanded by Diaghilev. For most of the ballet, however, the element of violent satire was kept firmly in the background, and the whole emphasis was put on a series of solos and group dances in pseudo-classical style. There was little attempt at characterization, and no attempt at logical construction: dance followed dance

Above: *Les Biches* (Nijin-ka, Monte Carlo, 1924) with Nikitina and Lifar

La Chatte (Balanchine, Monte Carlo, 1927) with Lifar as the young man

Above: Serenade (Balanchine, New York, 1935) as performed by the New York City Ballet in 1950 with Nicolas Magallanes, Diana Adams and Melissa Hayden

The Firebird (Balanchine, New York, 1950) with Maria Tallchief as the Firebird and Francisco Moncion as Ivan Tsarevich. (New version of Fokine ballet *L'Oiseau de Feu*)

with deliberate inconsequence, as in a suite of divertissements.[1] The general effect was as if someone had taken a novel by Firbank, removed some of the wit, cleaned up the references to sexual perversion, and converted the novel into an operetta.

The most effective part of *Les Biches* was the rôle of the girl in blue doublet and white gloves, originally danced by Vera Nemchinova. This rôle perfectly suited her rather frigid style: she walked across the stage on pointes, moving her shoulders up and down in a way which suggested cool sophistication. It was the success of this rôle which more than anything created a vogue for pseudo-classicism.

In her next two ballets (*Les Tentations de la Bergère* and *Les Facheux*) Nijinska found herself in a difficult position. Both ballets were supposed to have a certain amount of period flavour—the former was based on music by Montéclair (1662–1724) and the latter on a play by Molière—but there was no attempt to treat their stories seriously, and the costumes and décors (by Braque and Juan Gris respectively) belonged quite as much to the twentieth-century École de Paris as to the eighteenth century. Nijinska's attempts to adapt the pseudo-classical style of *Les Biches* to these period cocktails were not very successful.

Her next ballet was *Le Train Bleu* (1924). Though related to the expressionist-acrobatic ballets then being produced in Russia, it conformed perfectly to Diaghilev's requirements for a cocktail ballet. *Le Train Bleu* was inspired by Anton Dolin's talent for acrobatics, and existed chiefly to give him a chance to show this talent. Other rôles included suggestions of swimming, golf, tennis, beach games, the music hall, slow-motion effects in the cinema, etc.

Nijinska then left Diaghilev for two years; her place was taken by Massine, who continued on the same path. His most successful pseudo-classical ballet was *Les Matelots*, a knockabout entertainment involving three sailors.

In 1926 Nijinska returned to Diaghilev to compose the choreography for *Roméo et Juliette*, a highly characteristic cocktail ballet. The story of *Roméo et Juliette* was adapted in a flippant manner to provide a skeleton on which to hang a series of dances. The ballet began with a class, with the dancers in practice dress performing under the eyes of the teacher. The teacher then taught a pas de deux to two of the dancers who came late. After an entr'acte (in which only the feet of the dancers could be seen performing exercises) the ballet continued with five episodes from Shakespeare's play *Romeo and Juliet*. The idea for such an anti-illusory treatment of the story was derived from various expressionist experiments of a similar character in Russia, but Nijinska's choreography was pseudo-classical rather than expressionist. In this respect *Roméo et Juliette* was highly typical of the period.

---

[1] According to Russian terminology a divertissement is a suite of short, varied items; I have followed the English practice of regarding each separate item as a divertissement.

From now on Diaghilev made little use of Nijinska as a choreographer, though he was glad to use her as a maître de ballet. She therefore began to work for a number of other companies, continuing to use the pseudo-classical style she had developed for Diaghilev. The next step was obvious. She had been powerfully influenced by the theories of Dalcroze, and had applied them in the expressionist ballet *Les Noces*, which was effectively abstract; the next step was clearly the composition of a Dalcrozian music-interpretation in pseudo-classical style. Diaghilev was opposed to such abstract ballets (he relied in preparing his cocktails on a jarring conflict between the theme and its treatment, and without a theme no such conflict was possible), and so Nijinska had to wait until 1928 for the chance of composing an abstract pseudo-classical ballet. This was the first version of *La Valse*, arranged for Ida Rubinstein at Monte Carlo. In this ballet (based on Ravel's famous choreographic poem) the dancers wore neutral costumes (i.e. tights) and performed a series of academic entrées.

In 1931 Nijinska composed two further abstract pseudo-classical ballets for Ida Rubinstein, *Étude de Bach* and *Variations de Beethoven*; the latter ballet had some slight suggestion of different periods, but the former was completely abstract. Since then she has arranged a number of abstract ballets of this type. All have the same cerebral quality: the steps are fitted to the music with characteristically expressionist mechanical precision, giving an effect of depressing pedantry to the choreography—particularly when a great many repetitions of a musical theme are reflected by exact repetitions of the step chosen to represent this theme. (Repetition in dancing is something very different from repetition in music.)

Apart from the abstract ballets she arranged a considerable number of story ballets, all in her habitual pseudo-classical style. Though she was no longer under the compulsion of adapting herself to Diaghilev's requirements she seemed to find it natural to continue with the style she had devised for him, just as she had continued with her brother's style in her early period with Diaghilev, in spite of the fact that ten years of violent change had elapsed since Nijinsky had created this style.

GEORGE BALANCHINE (*b.* 1904)

Balanchine joined the Maryinsky school in 1914, at the age of ten, and graduated in 1921 at a time when in revolutionary Russia the most violent expressionism seemed the only possible style in every branch of art, and the heritage from the past seemed either of small importance or a feudal relic to be scrapped as soon as possible. In this same year (1921) the avant-garde expressionist dancer and choreographer Goleizovsky gave a recital in Petrograd with some of his dancers, presenting a number of highly erotic items such as *Salome* and *L'Après-Midi d'un Faune* almost without benefit of costumes. This concert performance enormously impressed Balanchine, and he joined in the battle between the traditionalists and expressionists in Petrograd. In 1923, when still only nineteen and a corps de ballet dancer at the Maryinsky,[1] he staged an evening of ballet in the old Duma amphitheatre with the help of some of the Maryinsky students. This was intended to be the first of a series of performances, but the directors of the Maryinsky opposed the enterprise, and Balanchine was forced to abandon it after one performance. Nevertheless expressionism was in the air in Petrograd, and considering Balanchine's youth and inexperience he found a surprisingly large number of opportunities for composition. Apart from composing dances in a number of plays (including the expressionist play by Ernst Toller *Broken Bow* at the Mikhailovsky Theatre, the great State theatre which was the dramatic equivalent of the Maryinsky), he even managed to produce a small ballet at the Maryinsky, *Enigma*.

In Irving Deakin's admirably full account of this period in Balanchine's career we see events entirely through the eyes of twenty-year-old Balanchine:

> As in the reception accorded Fokine a decade and a half earlier, it was the "old guard" that turned Balanchine down, while it was youth that supported him. . . . There were no more "Evenings of the Young Ballet". . . . *Enigma* . . . was hissed off the stage as being too revolutionary, and the powerful critic Volynsky, who had been kindly disposed towards the young Balanchine heretofore, damned him.[2]

One would imagine from this account that Balanchine was the only representative of "modernism" in Petrograd, surrounded by a lot of old fogies. This was very far from the truth. In fact the tide was running so strongly towards expressionism that the great traditions of the past were in grave danger, even though in Petrograd expressionism did not make quite such an overwhelming appeal as in Moscow, and the directors of the Maryinsky were doing their best to preserve the heritage of the past.[3]

During the winter of 1924 the Maryinsky tenor V. Dmitriev (who was very interested in Balanchine's work) began to plan a tour for the following summer vacation[4] with a small company of dancers led by Balanchine, hoping to take

---

[1] At this time it was called the Petrograd State Academic Theatre for Opera and Ballet. Later it was named after Kirov. But for a long time Leningraders continued to call it the Maryinsky, just as they persisted in talking of the 5th of October Prospect as the "Nevsky".

[2] *Ballet Profile*, p. 138. Volynsky was actually artistic director of the Maryinsky at this time.

[3] *See* below, p. 261.

[4] *See* below, p. 328. Tours of small groups during the summer vacation were the usual thing for Maryinsky dancers.

the dancers to Siberia and if possible to China. But he did not get the necessary documents in time for such a long tour, and instead he took the company to Germany. (At this time relations between Russia and Germany were close and friendly.) He took the company on a tour of German spas, and then managed to book it at the Empire Theatre in London. He next obtained an audition for the dancers with Diaghilev in Paris, and Diaghilev engaged three of them— Balanchine, Danilova and Tamara Geva. At this time Diaghilev enjoyed great prestige in Russia, and it is easy to understand why the artists were anxious to join him.

Diaghilev, for his part, was very interested in the new trends in the theatre in Russia: he had kept up his friendship with Meyerhold and Tairov, and had a fairly good idea of what was going on. He was glad to have in Balanchine a choreographer familiar with the latest developments, and the departure of Nijinska left him without a choreographer soon after Balanchine joined the company. But he was too cautious to risk the fate of his company by putting his faith in an untried young choreographer; instead, he persuaded Massine to return, and commissioned two ballets from him before he gave Balanchine his first chance.

Balanchine's first ballet, *Barabau*, composed in 1926 after he had been with Diaghilev for a year, was disappointing: the crude slapstick humour (akin to the early experiments in *grotesk* in Central Europe) was far below even the relatively naïve standard of *Les Biches* and *Les Matelots* (which were at least witty from time to time). Though Balanchine clearly had some talent, he was completely lacking in the contact with tradition which enabled Nijinska to give her cocktail ballets some elegance of form, while *Barabau* could not hope to make up for its lack of form by overwhelming sincerity and intensity, as did the great expressionist ballets.

Nevertheless Diaghilev had powerful reasons for favouring Balanchine. By temperament and background he fitted in much better than Massine and Nijinska with the cocktail period; Diaghilev was now losing contact with nearly all the old members of his équipe (Benois, Stravinsky, Larionov, Goncharova) and surrounding himself with young people who were unlikely to dispute his authority. He therefore commissioned a further ballet from Nijinska (*Roméo et Juliette*); this gave Balanchine an opportunity to study Nijinska's methods of composition (he was already familiar with Massine's) and helped him to profit from his study of her ballet *Les Biches*, which was still in the repertoire. He profited from these studies sufficiently for Diaghilev's purposes, and Diaghilev made him his resident choreographer, though he still continued to employ Massine and Nijinska. (During the period 1926–29 he commissioned nine ballets from Balanchine, as compared with five from Massine, two from Nijinska and one from Lifar.)

Balanchine found no difficulty in adapting himself to the artistic climate of the Diaghilev ballet during its declining years. Unlike Massine and Nijinska, he had no contact with the glories of the pre-War period, and neither Fokine's romanticism nor Nijinsky's passionately sincere expressionism meant anything to him; on the other hand the acrobatic expressionism with which he was familiar could be adapted without conflict or sacrifice to the task of providing a sauce piquante for pseudo-classicism. He was taught by Diaghilev to work on his own without bothering about the décor and costumes (which would have nothing to do with the theme or the choreography) and to take only the most flippant interest in the theme of the ballet (which would emerge in the programme notes but hardly anywhere else). Pseudo-classicism became Balanchine's natural style, whereas in the pseudo-classicism of Massine and Nijinska one could always feel a certain conflict between the ideals of the choreographers and the genre in which they worked.

Though pseudo-classicism was quite unsuitable for the treatment of serious themes or for full-blooded satire, it did lend itself to some extent to playful satire, and Balanchine gave proof of real talent in one or two witty dances, such as the hornpipe in *The Triumph of Neptune* and the big pas de deux in *Les Deux Mendiants*. Unfortunately he lacked the sense of style and organizing ability to maintain this wit for a whole ballet; *The Triumph of Neptune*, for example, was based on the English "juvenile drama" and offered wonderful opportunities for a balletic interpretation of the rich traditions of the English Christmas pantomime, but Balanchine showed no more understanding of these traditions than he did of the great Maryinsky tradition, and produced a rather insipid spectacle in which the witty dances were surrounded by a mass of sentimentality.

La Chatte was far more typical of Balanchine's work at this period. This ballet was based on a fable by Æsop which was turned on its head and made almost incomprehensible in order to give the leading rôle to a man (Lifar). Balanchine composed for this ballet a series of dances (made up of his usual mixture of slightly distorted classroom steps and acrobatics) which had almost nothing to do with the story and nothing whatever to do with the mysterious abstract style of the décor (constructed in transparent talc by the two Bauhaus artists Gabo and Pevsner).

La Chatte was typical of the period in having a cast consisting of seven men and one woman. In *Apollon Musagète* Balanchine reverted to a pseudo-classical style more akin to Petipa's, with a preponderance of women and a minimum of acrobatics. In doing so he was probably influenced by Stravinsky's neo-classical music, for in composing this score (commissioned by Elizabeth Sprague Coolidge for a festival of contemporary music in Washington with choreography by Adolph Bolm) Stravinsky had deliberately returned to the forms of the eighteenth century, making use of diatonic harmony and long string melodies.

After disposing of his theme (Apollo the master of the Muses, inspiring each of them to her own art) in the prologue, Stravinsky composed a work which was effectively abstract; and Balanchine followed the lead given by Stravinsky. From this point the transition to a completely abstract ballet was easy and obvious, but (as already mentioned) Diaghilev had his own reasons for opposing this step, and Balanchine himself seemed to feel no particular impulse to move in this direction, in spite of the lead given by Nijinska.

Balanchine's last ballet for Diaghilev, *The Prodigal Son* (1939), was, if possible, even more typical of the late-Diaghilev period than *La Chatte*. The main emphasis was on one male rôle (danced by Lifar) supported by a corps de ballet of twelve other men. There was only one female rôle of any consequence (the Siren) and this was made quite remarkably repulsive. Compared with a masterpiece like *Petrouchka* this ballet was of negligible value, for its mythological theme was used largely as an excuse for a series of stunts (such as a revue-like suggestion of a boat-journey), while the main emphasis was concentrated on a long pas de deux of relatively crude Goleizovskian eroticism and a melodramatic climax in which the hero dragged himself at great length across the stage with the aid of a stick: in fact there was little in the ballet which could be described as dancing. Nevertheless it had the great merit of being completely consistent in its perverse sensationalism; unlike later attempts at this genre it had the courage of its convictions, and succeeded triumphantly in holding the attention of the audience. Here one could see Diaghilev bringing all his genius as an artistic director to bear on the problems involved in making palatable to a limited and sophisticated audience something which was in essence tasteless and crude; he succeeded so well that of all the Diaghilev cocktail ballets *The Prodigal Son* is one of the very few which can stand revival.

Without Diaghilev Balanchine never again achieved this level of consistent and sophisticated sensationalism. After the death of Diaghilev he continued to work in collaboration with Diaghilev's assistant and librettist Kokhno, and composed cocktail ballets of the same type as those produced by him during his years with Diaghilev. *Cotillon*, for example (composed in 1932 for the Blum-de Basil Ballets Russes), had a book by Kokhno and was very similar to *Le Bal* (also with book by Kokhno), the last but one of the ballets which Balanchine composed for Diaghilev. *La Concurrence* was clearly devised as a prelude for a spectacular climax in which all three of the baby ballerinas of the company performed their spectacular fouettés in a kind of competition. *Cotillon* had as its climax the performance of fouettés by Toumanova alone. Both these ballets consisted of a series of numbers strung together with deliberate inconsequence, after the manner of *Les Biches*. Balanchine produced several similar ballets in 1933 for Les Ballets 1933, still working in collaboration with Kokhno and the designer Bérard.

He continued in the same vein in the United States when established at the head of the American Ballet, but he also arranged for this company *Serenade* (1934), roughly half-way in style between Massine's first symphonic ballet *Les Présages* (composed in 1932 when Balanchine and Massine were both working at Monte Carlo for René Blum's new company) and the purely abstract music-interpretation ballets composed by Nijinska in 1931 for Ida Rubinstein. The abstract parts of *Serenade* were much closer to Nijinska than to Massine: as in *Apollon Musagète* Balanchine avoided Massine's complicated counterpoint, confining himself for the most part to simple and repetitive academic steps fitted to the obvious theme of the music. On the other hand he made use from time to time of episodes of melodramatic mime which in their vague and pretentious symbolism recalled both the weaker passages of *Les Présages* (which had been composed by Massine to a Tchaikovsky symphony similar in feeling to the Tchaikovsky *Serenade for Strings* used by Balanchine) and some of the episodes in Balanchine's own cocktail ballets of the type of *Le Bal* and *Cotillon*. Balanchine still fought shy of pure abstraction: when he produced new versions of *Serenade* in later years he used much more mime of the *Présages-Cotillon* type than in the first version, and he waited until 1941 before composing his first purely abstract ballet. Since then he has concentrated heavily on this style, using it for roughly half his new productions.

It is possible to discuss these ballets en masse, for they all resemble each other very closely, in spite of the fact that the music to which they are arranged varies very widely in style and period; it seems to make very little difference to Balanchine whether he is working on music by Bach, Mozart, Bizet, Tchaikovsky or Stravinsky, for he uses exactly the same type of enchaînement and stage pattern for each.

The most interesting feature in these ballets is Balanchine's skilful technique of changing his groups from one geometrical pattern to another with such speed and economy that sometimes it is almost impossible to see how he does it. Such changes of pattern are common in European folk-dances, and Balanchine seems to have studied these dances with sympathy and understanding.

In other respects the ballets are quite staggeringly conventional. The enchaînements keep close to Petipa's most stereotyped manner: with the devastating honesty that is typical of Balanchine he admits that a great deal of his choreography is based on passages in Petipa ballets which are unknown in the West but which he remembers from his youth at the Maryinsky.[1]

Balanchine's treatment of the music represents a compromise between Petipa's usual technique and the Dalcrozian technique characteristic of expressionism; both these techniques are quite unsuitable for the classical music normally used by Balanchine in his abstract ballets, and his blend of the two

[1] Lecture to London Ballet Circle, June, 1950.

techniques often causes effects of distressing banality on the stage. He starts rehearsal with only a rough outline of the ballet in his mind, and works out the details on the spur of the moment after listening to the music; he sets the steps and the arm movements to the individual *notes* of the music, ignoring the melody, rhythm and phrasing almost completely. (In this way he is able to use the same sort of enchaînements for widely different types of music.) He differs from Petipa, however, in taking no account of the small connecting-up steps which good choreographers use as a preparation for the big steps. There are no nuances or subtle gradients of emphasis in Balanchine's phrases. He tries to achieve an effect of great brilliance by joining together (without connecting-up steps) all the most difficult and spectacular steps, but this crudity of phrasing makes it impossible for the dancer to do full justice to any of the big steps. She moves in a curiously cramped manner, never soaring through the air, never making full use of the stage and never taking her movements "through the floor" in the way needed to give emphasis to the movements away from the floor. The result is a soul-destroying dullness. This point is emphasized in an acute analysis of Balanchine's style by "The Sitter-Out" in *The Dancing Times*:

> The neo-classical ballets of Balanchine . . . are lacking in what one may term a canon of the classical dance; each pose and *pas* in the vocabulary of movement is worth doing properly and in the right place. In most of Balanchine's ballets the auxiliary steps such as *glissades*, *chassés*, *temps liés* etc. are missing. Their place is taken by endless running steps, taking the dancers from pose to pose, beat to pirouette, leap to jump, or just over the stage with monotonous regularity.[1]

Balanchine is probably aware of the dullness, conventionality and repetitiousness of his ballets. Indeed, he seems to take pride in these qualities, no doubt regarding them as a normal feature of classicism.[2] His view of the classical tradition as something stereotyped, repetitious and mechanical is characteristically expressionist: it is exactly that of the free dancers of Europe and America—who tend to regard classicism as essentially cold and formal.

In harmony with this conception of classicism Balanchine makes no attempt to give interest to his music-visualizations by representing the counterpoint of the music in a complicated Dalcrozian manner or working out spatial patterns forming a kind of extra voice to the counterpoint of the music. Normally he confines himself to the most obvious type of visualization, and does not shrink from any amount of repetition. If the corps de ballet are lined up in couples across the stage and two of the principals cross between one of

---

[1] July, 1952.
[2] At the London Ballet Circle lecture previously quoted he said, "I am a very dull teacher"; his demonstration class for the Imperial Society of Teachers of Dancing amply confirmed this statement.

the static couples, one can be certain that they will not rest until they have passed between every couple on the stage.

Though the inordinate repetitiousness of Balanchine's classic ballets is liable to reduce the spectator to a state of semi-coma, it has the merit of permitting economy in the use of standard steps and gives the spectator an illusion of architectural form. When disciples of Balanchine try to avoid the repetitiousness of his ballets and delight the eye with constantly changing patterns of steps, the resultant effect of confusion is far more distressing than Balanchinian repetitiousness. In fact there is no half-way point between confusion and dullness: pseudo-classicism, like expressionism, is much too crude and inflexible a style to provide a suitable basis for abstract composition, where nuances are all-important.

Balanchine's debt to Petipa is particularly clear in his attitude to male dancers. Normally the male dancer has the same subordinate rôle in Balanchine's "classic ballets" as in the Petipa ballets: if he appears at all, it is to support the ballerina. Sometimes Balanchine brings on a line of male dancers and tries to use them to form the same type of symmetrical patterns as the danseuses, but male dancers do not take kindly to becoming units in a sentimental picture, and the result is somewhat embarrassing, both to them and to the audience.

Perhaps feeling slightly bored with his own "classic ballets", Balanchine composed in 1952 a ballet *Metamorphoses* (based on Hindemith's composition *Symphonic Metamorphoses on Themes by Carl Maria von Weber*), in which he returned to the acrobatics, expressionist distortions and constructivist costumes typical of the early twenties in Russia; he also included as light relief a comedy rôle for Tanaquil LeClercq very similar to the one he had already given her in *Bourrée Fantasque*. His attitude to male dancing emerged exceptionally clearly in the rôle he allotted to Tanaquil LeClercq's partner, Todd Bolender. The latter, dressed as a beetle, remained on the ground (crawling or prostrate) throughout a long pas de deux; as one witty spectator remarked at the New York première, Balanchine "reduced the male partner to the lowest possible level at which he might still function as a partner to the ballerina".[1]

Balanchine's view of the classical tradition does not extend to much variety in arm movements and positions. The whole emphasis of his choreography is on leg movements: the arms keep to a few fixed positions and move from one to another in a stilted manner. Sometimes he emphasizes this stilted quality by having a line of dancers stand or kneel *sur place* and simply move their arms from one standard position to another. In the same way he tends to keep the dancers facing straight to the front, their faces fixed in a painfully rigid smile. The general atmosphere is at times rather similar to that of a variety chorus, instructed by the producer to lay emphasis on "eyes and teeth".

[1] Quoted by Lillian Moore in "New York Notes" in *The Dancing Times*, January, 1953.

When Balanchine arranged *Trumpet Concerto* for the Sadlers Wells Theatre Ballet he cast a strange side-light on his aesthetic outlook. Presumably because the trumpet has military associations he elected to give this "classic ballet" a military flavour: the dancers were dressed in the familiar semi-military costumes of the precision dancers of variety and revue, and from time to time Balanchine introduced military associations into his choreography by suggestions of salutes and military evolutions. It was unwise of him to challenge comparison with the Tiller Girls, for they do this sort of thing much better than ballet dancers. Their whole training is directed towards split-second timing, perfect uniformity of facial expression and style and dead-straight lines—and in fact their evolutions are sometimes more complex than anything attempted by Balanchine. *Trumpet Concerto* was aesthetically inferior to a Tiller Girl number, for it was composed to unsuitable music by Haydn, and the ballet dancers had to struggle to obtain certain effects which Tiller Girls achieve with ease.

The ballet *Le Palais de Cristal*[1] which he arranged for the Paris Opéra in 1947 was no less revealing of Balanchine's aesthetic outlook. For this ballet (based on Bizet's symphony) he adopted much the same plan as in *La Concurrence*, building up to a climax in which he staged a competition between the four stars of the Opéra, each performing the *tours de force* which she did best. In Paris Balanchine could choose between two strongly established traditions: the Italian tradition (that used in the Opéra school) and the Russian tradition taught by the leading Parisian teachers (Preobazhenskaya, Kniasev, Yegorova, etc.) to the best of the Opéra dancers. Balanchine showed his lack of contact with the great Russian tradition by concentrating on the Italian tradition at the Opéra.

In many respects the style used by Balanchine in his "classic ballets" was highly typical of post-expressionist pseudo-classicism. Influences from Petipa were strong, and the style was firmly based on the classical technique, but Balanchine's enchaînements had a dry, clipped, mechanical quality that recalled the productions of the cerebral wing of the expressionist free dance in Central Europe. If Laban had devoted himself to the classical technique instead of the free dance one could imagine him composing enchaînements very similar to these.

The American audiences which welcomed the "classic ballets" which Balanchine began to arrange for the Ballet Russe de Monte Carlo in 1943 obeyed a healthy instinct. Massine's turgid and over-complicated expressionism had by this time exhausted its appeal. The great success of Fokine's Ballet Theatre production of *Les Sylphides* (in spite of its serious defects) showed clearly the trend in popular taste. As the danger of war passed into the real thing, with

---

[1] Balanchine produced a new version of this ballet for the New York City Ballet under the name *Symphony in C*.

all its tragedies and anxieties, people began to feel a need for a kind of art which would help them to stand up to their experiences by showing them a world of order, security and permanence—in satisfying contrast to the strain, messiness and insecurity of their everyday world.[1] Balanchine's ballets had the desired qualities of simplicity and order, and were accepted at their face value as "classic ballets". The need was so great that their defects were ignored, being accepted as a normal element in classical ballet.

Balanchine's story ballets differ in no essential respect from his abstract ballets. He is well aware of this, and made his ideas on the subject clear in an article on the nature of choreography:

> The important thing in ballet is the movement itself, as it is sound which is important in a symphony. A ballet may contain a story, but the visual spectacle, not the story, is the essential element. . . . As in music, the audience should be prepared to enjoy the movements regardless of the story. . . . Choreographic movement is an end in itself, and its only purpose is to create the impression of intensity and beauty.[2]

In his *Notes on Choreography* in *The Dance Encyclopedia* he wrote in very similar language. We look in vain in either article for any mention of the problems involved in the exposition of a theme: to Balanchine this subject is clearly of minor importance in choreography. When he tackles a theme he adopts the same technique as Petipa, confining the exposition of the theme to passages of mime, and devoting himself to the composition of dances which have only the most tenuous connection with the theme or the character and mood of the protagonist. The great achievements of Ivanov, Fokine, Nijinsky, Massine and

[1] Much the same thing happened in England in the eighteenth century, when wars were frequent and the strain of life very great. It was this period that gave birth to Georgian architecture and the corresponding American colonial style, with its wonderful harmony of proportions and classical simplicity; it also gave birth to the art of ballet in the modern sense of the word.

[2] *Dance News* (New York), May, 1945. This statement brings together in a curious salad ideas drawn from Dalcroze, Laban, Nijinska and Gautier; the emphasis on "movement" is typical both of Laban and Nijinska. In an article published in Laban's magazine *Schrifttanz* (April, 1930) Nijinska expressed partial agreement with Laban's theories, referring to a study published by her in Kiev in 1920, *The School of Movement, School of Choreography*. In this study she wrote: "Modern choreography must introduce movement into the technique of the dance. In the same way that colour is the material of painting and sound that of music, that of dancing is movement. Only it can move the spectator, for rhythm lives in movement alone. Movement is not only the passage from one position to another, but something more. . . . In the schools of classical dancing one studies only certain fixed steps, but the secret of creating the dance between the positions is unknown both to the teacher and the dancer. Great dancers like Nijinsky and Pavlova have aroused our enthusiasm because they possess this secret; in their inner self real movement was stronger than the position. Naturally this was sub-conscious, and came from their genius, not the 'school.' " (Quoted by Pierre Michaut in *Le Ballet Contemporain*, p. 26). In fact, Nijinska was wrong in asserting that "the secret of creating the dance between the positions is unknown both to the dancer and the teacher". Emphasis on expressive arm movements is one of the most characteristic features of the Legat system, and in this respect both Nijinsky and Pavlova owed a great deal to Legat.

Tudor in developing expressive dance-imagery have no meaning for Balanchine: for him a story ballet consists of spectacular dancing plus mime.

Balanchine's archaic ideas on balletic structure inevitably land him in difficulties when he tackles a ballet with a logical and continuous dramatic theme, and while working in Europe he nearly always confined himself to divertissement ballets of the *Cotillon* type, in which the deficiencies of his choreographic technique were not obvious. He continued to compose divertissement ballets in the United States for a while, but audiences there had had little chance to build up standards of discrimination, and eventually he began to take the risk of composing dramatic ballets.

His first major attempt at a dramatic ballet in the United States was his choreographic production of the Gluck opera *Orphée et Euridice* at the Metropolitan. This production was really a late-Diaghilevian cocktail, for Chelichev's surrealist décors and costumes and Balanchine's extremely tortuous expressionist choreography had nothing to do with the classical simplicity and directness of Gluck's music.

Opera seemed to have a strong attraction for Balanchine, and in 1946 he produced for the Ballet Russe de Monte Carlo a ballet *Night Shadow* based on Bellini's opera *La Sonnambula*. This avoided the tortuous obscurity of *Orphée et Euridice*, but fell into the opposite extreme of monotony and sentimentality, and was just as far from the spirit of the music as the earlier ballet. The ballet began with a long ballroom scene, with a divertissement consisting of a series of very insipid entrées; there was also a good deal of melodramatic mime, with characters staring at each other for long periods. (Clearly Balanchine found great difficulty in filling out the music.) All this was (as in many Balanchine story ballets) no more than a prelude to a long spectacular pas d'action, the raison d'être of the ballet. In this pas de deux the somnambulist walked across the stage on pointe (like the girl in blue in *Les Biches*), and the poet steered her as if he were driving a car. The scene was theatrically effective, though padded out to quite excessive length; choreographically it was negligible, being more suitable for a variety show than a ballet.

Characteristically, Balanchine ended the ballet with a cheap stunt of the sort that was common in the early days of expressionism: after being carried across the stage by four men the dead body of the poet was deposited into the arms of the somnambulist, and the slender girl then walked off with it single-handed. This was strongly reminiscent of the ending of *The Prodigal Son*.

In his second ballet based on the Orpheus myth (*Orpheus*) Balanchine took the theme far more seriously, and clearly did his best to come to grips with it. Unfortunately his pseudo-classical style and lack of dramatic sense prevented him from getting anywhere near the intensity of Stravinsky's wonderful score; much of the choreography had only the vaguest connection with the music, and often he seemed hard put to it to think of any movements to fill out the music. The abstract-surrealist properties provided for him by Isamo Noguchi (who had developed his style of décor working for Martha Graham) also seemed to baffle Balanchine, for he made little effort to integrate them into his choreography: Orpheus, for example, spent a good deal of time holding a mask high in the air, or else walking about with it in a solemn manner.

As in *The Prodigal Son* and *Night Shadow* the whole choreography of *Orpheus* was subordinated to one long and spectacular pas d'action for the two chief characters, a pas de deux which for Balanchine was clearly the raison d'être of the ballet. In *Orpheus* Balanchine made the pas de deux so much like the corresponding pas de deux in *The Prodigal Son* that at times it seemed a new version of it: its clever eroticism unfortunately made nonsense of the myth, being out of key with the rest of the ballet.

Balanchine's new version of the Fokine ballet *L'Oiseau de Feu* was of great interest, for it defined to within a millimetre Balanchine's relationship to the great Russian ballet tradition. Since Balanchine considered Fokine a poor choreographer, he decided to make new versions of the Stravinsky ballets in which the mistakes made by Fokine would be corrected.[1] He was influenced in this decision by Stravinsky's criticisms of Fokine's work on these ballets and by the changes Stravinsky made in the scores.

Balanchine's *Firebird* had much the same character as typical Hollywood re-makes of Continental films, reflecting an almost unbelievable insensitivity to the characteristic qualities of the original. Though much of Fokine's original choreography was skilful rather than inspired, the ballet as a whole was immensely convincing because Fokine adjusted every tiny detail of movement and music to create exactly the effect required by the story at any moment; the various scenes were linked together with great care for atmosphere, suspense and climax; and the characterization was superb. Balanchine's "improvements" took the form of cutting out almost every element of fantasy and poetry from Fokine's ballet, and weakening its dramatic structure so as to kill all suspense and climax. One of his typical "improvements" was to cut out completely the magical scene where Ivan waves the magic feather and the Firebird comes to his aid, forcing the demons to follow her in a wild dance until finally they sink to the ground in slumber.

His treatment of the climax was equally characteristic. In Fokine's ballet this is a moment of great tension; the demons are asleep, and Ivan (with typical fairy-tale cruelty) teases Koscheï like a cat with a mouse before finally throwing high in the air the egg which contains Koscheï's soul; the breaking of the egg causes

---

[1] In the lecture to the London Ballet Circle previously quoted Balanchine stated that he had learned some technical lessons from Fokine, such as the building up of finales, but he expressed a low opinion of Fokine's choreography in general.

the destruction of Koscheï in a clap of thunder and a black-out, in the best fairy-tale tradition. Balanchine replaced this scene with an amateurish attempt at a spectacular finale of the type used by Fokine in *Schéhérazade* and *Prince Igor*, with the whole stage covered with demons lined up in neat parallel rows and making gestures of stupefying banality. There was no build-up of climax, and Balanchine finally brought the scene to an end by having Ivan move across to Koscheï and dispatch him with his sword.

Balanchine's changes in the structure of the ballet were to some extent made necessary by Stravinsky's changes in the music: every bar of Stravinsky's original score had been worked out by him to fit Fokine's requirements of characterization and subtle changes of mood and action, and his new version was much less satisfactory from a choreographic point of view. But Balanchine could have used the original score had he wished to do so.

As in his other dramatic ballets Balanchine concentrated all his attention on a spectacular pas d'action, the long solo of the Firebird. This solo he arranged for his wife Maria Tallchief with sensitive feeling for her limitations and capabilities: in his understanding of the personality and technique of a ballerina Balanchine showed himself a worthy disciple of Petipa. In this case Balanchine took advantage of the fact that the ballerina's hands had a tendency to be stiff (with a broken line at the wrist) to make this mannerism into the leitmotiv of the rôle, so that the dancer was seen to better advantage than ever before. Unfortunately Balanchine exploited this excellent idea up to and past the limit, dragging out the dance long after all the possibilites of the material had been exhausted.

Balanchine's new version of Act II of *Le Lac des Cygnes* was a very different matter. The Ivanov choreography of the original was much closer to Balanchine's natural pseudo-classical style than the Fokine style of *L'Oiseau de Feu*, and though the programme note claimed that "Balanchine's choreography is not Ivanov's choreography" he retained a great deal of the latter in his new version. For the most part he confined himself to making the stage-patterns of the corps-de-ballet movements more complex, introducing the same sort of patterns that he used in his "classic ballets". These changes had the merit of concealing to some extent the lack of lyricism in the dancing of the corps de ballet, and were so much in harmony with the Ivanov style that Ivanov himself might conceivably have approved of them. Balanchine made only a few changes in the rôle of Odette: these seemed quite arbitrary, for they were no better adapted to the style of the ballerina (Maria Tallchief) than the original movements, and in most cases were less expressive; on the other hand he usually retained the original phrasing, so that the ballerina had good opportunities to show the full extent of her talents. In fact Balanchine produced Maria Tallchief so well in the rôle of Odette that she gave the performance of her life: she could not compare with the greatest of the Russians, but she showed a fine simplicity, avoiding the mannerisms which had disfigured her work in the past.

Though Balanchine's version of *Lac* was sharply criticized both in the United States and in England, it was better by far than most productions of Maryinsky and Diaghilev ballets by American companies; the modifications made by him were not much more serious than those made by him when he revised the ballet to suit the limited Diaghilev company of the twenties, and were of the same order as those made by Petipa when he revived his own ballets at the Maryinsky.

Unfortunately Balanchine's relatively competent production of *Lac* did not signify any growth in his understanding of the classical tradition: the completely new items added by him to *Lac* (a pas de trois and a pas de neuf) were quite out of harmony with the rest of the ballet, and the new "classic ballets" composed by him at this period had exactly the same fault as the earlier ballets of this type.

It is not necessary to rely only on deduction from his ballets to build up a picture of Balanchine's aesthetic outlook. Sometimes he takes the trouble to explain it in detail, with a straightforward honesty which takes one's breath away. At a lecture-demonstration in New York he explained that

> Ballets to me is like butterflies—I like to see new ones each year. Sometimes the gesture or rhythm becomes more important but you use practically the same steps in new surroundings. The life of a ballet is not long. A ballet lives two years and then it is nice to see something else.[1]

This was exactly the attitude to ballet in general and choreography in particular of Diaghilev in his cocktail period: though there have been innumerable changes in the ballet world since 1929 Balanchine himself remains essentially the same man that worked for Diaghilev.

By a curious twist of fate Balanchine has become to some extent the Laban of America. Martha Graham became the American counterpart of Wigman, but theatrical conditions in America did not permit the emergence in America of anything corresponding to the Laban wing of the expressionist free dance of Central Europe, with its emphasis on patterns of group movement rather than on highly emotional solo dancing. To a large extent Balanchine's "classic ballets" filled this gap. His cerebral attitude to dancing is similar to Laban's, and he has been indirectly influenced by Laban in many ways: it is significant that he thinks highly of Laban's Dance Notation. His influence among young American choreographers showed the same sudden increase after 1943 as did that of Laban in Central Europe after 1918.

[1] September, 1951 (YMHA-YWHA). Quoted by Arthur Todd in *Ballet Today*, October, 1951.

The sequence of events leading from the European hegira of the American genius Isadora Duncan to the innovations of Fokine, Dalcroze, Laban, Nijinsky, Nijinska and Goleizovsky, and eventually after four decades to the emergence of Balanchine's pseudo-classicism as the dominant American style of choreography, is one of the strangest in ballet history. Nevertheless this train of events has its own inner logic, and is by no means unique. In France, for example, a fairly similar sequence of events leads from Perrot to Lifar.

SERGE LIFAR (*b.* 1905)

Though Lifar and Balanchine were almost exact contemporaries, and reached the Diaghilev company at roughly the same period (Lifar in 1923, Balanchine in 1924), their backgrounds in Russia were very different. Balanchine had had the full Maryinsky training and two years in the Maryinsky company before joining Diaghilev, whereas Lifar had had only one month's training in Nijinska's school in Kiev. To all intents and purposes Lifar was a child of the Diaghilev ballet in its cocktail period, and owed a great deal to Balanchine—who was resident choreographer during practically the whole of Lifar's career as a Diaghilev soloist, and provided him with his best rôles.

When Nijinska sent for five of her favourite pupils in 1923 Lifar managed to join the party in place of one of the pupils who had vanished, and Diaghilev (who was hard-pressed for dancers at the time) took him on in spite of the fact that he was almost untrained. He danced in the corps de ballet, and for two years picked up what he could in the daily company classes. His progress was slow, for company classes—intended for fully trained dancers—are bad for untrained dancers: the latter attempt difficult steps before mastering the elements from which these steps are built up, and inevitably acquire bad habits. Lifar first began to make real progress in 1925, when he spent his summer holidays studying with Cecchetti, and in later years he spent what time he could perfecting his technique under this great teacher. (Cecchetti died in 1928.) Lifar was twenty when he had his first Cecchetti lesson, and could not hope to acquire the all-round technique of Maryinsky dancers who progressed slowly through seven years of graduated training, starting at the age of ten; nevertheless his body was loose, he worked very hard, he had great talent, and his progress was astonishingly fast. He began to receive small parts in 1925, and by 1927 he was the star of the company, with ballets created specially for him. His deficiencies were of small importance in the cocktail ballets of the day, and in any case he was by 1925 the rising star: Diaghilev saw to it that the choreographers provided him rôles that gave him the opportunity to shine in those steps which he did

Bacchus et Ariane (Lifar, Paris, 1931) with Spessivsteva as Ariane and Lifar as Bacchus

Below: Lifar in the title role of his ballet *Icare* (Paris, 1935)

Margot Fonteyn *ca.* 1937 performin
the Polka of *Façade* (Ashton, Londo
1931)

Below: *Homage to the Queen* (Ashto
London, 1953) with Violetta Elv
(*centre*) as Queen of the Waters a
John Hart as her consort

best. Since he started to dance at the same time that he started training he had a good opportunity to build up a striking stage personality. The rôle he portrayed was always Serge Lifar, but this was exactly what was demanded of him. At this period his face and body had the beauty of a Slav Apollo, and Diaghilev took full advantage of this in his productions.

During his years with the Diaghilev company Lifar had many opportunities to make contact with surviving remnants of the golden age of the company. The major Nijinsky ballets had been scrapped, but the repertoire included at various times all the best Fokine ballets—*Les Sylphides, Petrouchka, Prince Igor, L'Oiseau de Feu, Le Carnaval, Le Spectre de la Rose*—and the best of the Petipa-Ivanov ballets, *Le Lac des Cygnes*. It also included the best of Massine's grotesque expressionist ballets and Nijinska's masterpiece *Les Noces*. The dancers included such fine artists as Karsavina, Lopukhova, Spessivsteva, Sokolova, Massine, Idzikovsky and Woizikovsky, even though these were never all present at one time. The great Russian tradition was overshadowed by the cocktail ballets, but it was by no means extinct.

On the other hand the change in Diaghilev's artistic policy which occurred in 1924 was so violent that to a young man of Lifar's generation the golden age of the company was almost as remote as the age of Noverre, and seemed to have just as little relevance to the composition of new ballets. When Lifar started to compose new ballets in 1929 he inevitably made use of the fashionable pseudo-classical style which was characteristic of the Diaghilev ballet in the cocktail period.

Diaghilev did not use Lifar as a choreographer until the last year of his life. Since 1925 Diaghilev had been ringing the changes on three experienced choreographers, and Lifar had his hands full as a dancer. By 1929, however, Diaghilev had run through almost all the leading painters of the École de Paris, the Bauhaus and Russian constructivism, and decided as a last resort to go back to the acrobatic expressionism of the early twenties with a new version of *Le Renard*. (Such a step was fairly obvious after *Le Pas d'Acier* and *La Chatte*.) In order to make the new version of *Le Renard* seem a real novelty he devised a new gimmick—the use of a double cast of dancers and professional acrobats—and commissioned new choreography from Lifar. Lifar's first experiment in choreography, in the early stages of *Zéphire et Flore* (1925), had not been very promising, and Diaghilev took the precaution of putting him under the tutelage of Larionov for the production of the new version of *Le Renard*. Lifar's choreography was of small importance in the production, in which classically trained dancers tried to outdo real acrobats with imitation acrobatics based on the classical technique. The mixture was hardly a success from the point of view of the spectator, but it provided Diaghilev with some useful publicity.

Lifar's entry into the Paris Opéra came about through the same kind of

A.A.O.B.—M

lucky break that made possible his entry into the Diaghilev company. Balanchine had been engaged by the Director of the Opéra, Jaques Rouché, to produce a ballet *Les Créatures de Promethée*, but fell ill after arranging some of the scenes, and Lifar was commissioned to complete the ballet. Lifar took a hint from the last ballets arranged by Balanchine for Diaghilev (with himself as star) and made the ballet very largely a vehicle for the expression of his own personality: he was on the stage the whole time, taking part in each episode and dominating the stage by his violent athleticism. This ballet pleased the Director of the Opéra, and a few months later Lifar was appointed maître de ballet at the Opéra. He showed a flair worthy of Petipa at keeping his end up in the complex intrigues of a State ballet (his experiences in the last years of the Diaghilev company had been a valuable preparation for this), and soon consolidated his position so effectively that it became unassailable. Fortunately for Lifar, his acrobatic pseudo-classicism (though very conventional by Diaghilevian standards) came as a breath of fresh air in the Opéra, where the ballets were so dreary that any change could only be for the better.

Bacchus et Ariane (1931) was typical of the ballets composed by Lifar at this period. He gave hardly any dancing to the corps de ballet, and concentrated everything on Bacchus (himself) and Ariane (Spessivsteva). Their costumes were typical of the Diaghilev cocktail period—both wore short jerkins and gloves, while Lifar wore boots—and Lifar composed for himself a series of his usual acrobatic feats and violent gestures. Spessivsteva, with all the great Russian tradition behind her, was able to infuse some dance-quality into Lifar's clumsy enchaînements, but Lifar made no attempt at fluidity or phrasing of any kind.

Though Lifar seemed to the aficionados of the Opéra to be a daring innovator, he was in fact a strict traditionalist. It was as natural for him to dance and compose in a violent and staccato manner as it was for Spessivsteva to dance in a noble and poetic manner. Lifar was in much the same position as the distinguished English writer Mark Benney, brought up by his parents to be a burglar; unlike Mark Benney, however, he showed no impulse to rebel against his conditioning. As a dancer he had come strongly under the influence of the acrobatic expressionism which Balanchine brought from Russia in 1924, fostering violence and the pointing-up of technical difficulties rather than nobility, poetry, economy, fluidity, restraint and the art which conceals art. At the same time the fact that Lifar began serious training when he was already a full-grown man with powerful muscles encouraged him to concentrate on *tours de force*, and to gain his effects by the exertion of his full strength at all times rather than through economy of effort and perfect co-ordination between different muscles. Lifar, being impressionable, made both his dancing and his choreography into a perfect expression of the artistic climate of the Diaghilev ballet during its cocktail period. He sought for the most striking effect at each moment, paying no attention to characterization, atmosphere or the gradual build-up of effects by devices of construction. Though his limbs (carefully trained by Cecchetti) took up the pure lines of the classical technique, his outlook was that of an acrobat.

During 1932 Lifar abandoned the composition of new ballets and devoted himself to the staging of new versions of Diaghilev ballets. In his cavalier treatment of these ballets he continued the policy established by Diaghilev in his declining years (when inferior new versions of *L'Après-Midi d'un Faune*, *Le Sacre du Printemps* and *Le Renard* were produced); it is rather doubtful, however, if Diaghilev would have countenanced the production of Lifarian versions of *Le Spectre de la Rose*, *Les Sylphides* and *Giselle*—the very ballets for which Lifar's style was least suitable. Lifar's "improvements" on Fokine and Perrot anticipated by many years Balanchine's "improvements" on *L'Oiseau de Feu*, though the effects were less disastrous because of the presence of Spessivtseva at the head of the company; she did not allow her incomparably poetic and mysterious interpretations to be affected by the odd things happening around her. She left the Opéra after the production of *Giselle*, before Lifar had had time to stage his fourth revival—a suite of extracts from *The Sleeping Beauty* under the name *Divertissement de Tchaikovsky*.

In his production of *Giselle* Lifar built up his own rôle (Albrecht) by various means until it was just as prominent as that of Giselle. After Spessivtseva left he built up his rôle still further (until the ballet should obviously have been called *Serge*) and danced the rôle with his usual staccato violence. At the Maryinsky *Giselle* had been regarded as something holy, and no dancer would have dreamed of altering any detail of it. Though Lifar had a fine opportunity of familiarizing himself with the Maryinsky tradition while working with Spessivtseva (one of the greatest products of the Maryinsky), and though he was working at the very theatre where *Giselle* had been created, he made no effort to keep his modifications within the style of the period. His melodramatic staging of Albrecht's entrance in Act II showed clearly his attitude to the great Russian and French traditions: he made this entrance into the most prominent episode in the Act, dragging it out by walking slowly across the stage towing a cloak several yards long, and carrying a bunch of flowers almost as large as himself.

One could hardly expect a post-expressionist pseudo-classicist like Lifar to understand the romantic lyricism of Perrot and Fokine, but he had a much better chance of making a good showing when he staged a suite of extracts from the pseudo-classical Petipa ballet *The Sleeping Beauty*. (He could not stage the complete ballet because of the prejudice against Tchaikovsky among French musicians.) Strangely enough Lifar seemed to understand Petipa just as little as

he understood Perrot or Fokine: he altered the relationship between the movements and the music in all the entreés (not just his own) so that the steps had the
chopped-up quality of his own dancing. Petipa's original arrangements were
not particularly musical, but Lifar's seemed specially designed to prevent the
dancers from achieving the particular effects of climax and contrast intended by
Petipa. It was hard to see what Lifar was aiming at in these modifications, for
they added nothing, and in fact reduced all the enchaînements to the same
monotonous level: even when adapting existing choreography and working
with ballerinas he still thought in terms of his own physique and his own style
of dancing. Though he had assimilated Balanchine's style of composition *for
Lifar*, he had failed to assimilate from Balanchine the Maryinsky tradition of
composing dances to suit the sex, physique, technique and personality of the
dancer chosen for the rôle.

In 1935 he arranged a new version of the Nijinsky ballet *L'Après-Midi d'un
Faune*: characteristically, he transformed this ballet into a Lifarian pas seul for
himself.

Icare (1936) was the first of a series of ballets with themes drawn from
Greek, Roman and Jewish antiquity. In this ballet Lifar showed himself for the
first time as a master of publicity.

> Preceded by interviews, declarations and polemics on the relations between
> dancing and music, and even a manifesto published by Serge Lifar, *Icare* was launched
> in an atmosphere of discussion of ideas, as a bold experiment, inspired by a pioneer
> spirit, by the passion for renewal which animates its author.[1]

Lifar's methods of publicity had great success, and his claims to have effected
a revolution in choreography were widely accepted, in spite of the fact that
every ingredient in the ballet was hackneyed. His greatest "innovation"—the
use as an accompaniment of pure percussion music based on the dance movements—had been used by Laban soon after Lifar was born, and had been the
favourite practice of Wigman for nearly two decades.

Lifar could not have studied the methods of the Central European free
dancers with any assiduity, for the rhythms which he assigned to J. E. Szyfer for
orchestration had the maddening banality and repetitiveness of the singing of
a small child. Lifar's choreography consisted for the most part of a series of
repetitions of a single classroom step, followed by a series of repetitions of
another step: the percussion section of the orchestra simply hammered out the
obvious rhythms of each step in turn.

Icare was almost as much a pas seul as Lifar's production of *Faune*; the other
characters had only the simplest movements to make, and Lifar often had the

---

[1] Pierre Michaut, *Le Ballet Contemporain*, p. 135.

stage to himself. His acting (above all his death-agony) had the hysterical over-emphasis characteristic of expressionism at its worst, and was completely unsuitable for a classical myth.

This hysterical expressionism was only one of a number of aspects of Lifar's work which suggested that he would have been perfectly at home in Central Europe in the early twenties. *Le Manifeste du Chorégraphe*, which he issued as part of his publicity campaign before the production of *Icare*, might have been written by almost any young Central European dancer about 1920[1] (apart from his use of the word "ballet" rather than "Tanz"). What is surprising is that he succeeded in getting people to accept such hackneyed ideas as novel. (The Concours organized by the Archives Internationals de la Danse in 1932 had brought to Paris a considerable number of expressionist free-dance groups, including the Ballets Jooss performing *The Green Table*.)

After the production of *Icare* Lifar issued a new manifesto *The Path of Icarus*, in which he claimed that "*Icare* opened up vast new horizons . . . to the new forms of the ballet, or more generally . . . to the art of the dance". Later in the manifesto he described himself as "proposing a new method, a method which should . . . inaugurate a new era in the history of the dance". Since the new era had exhausted nearly all its possibilities before Lifar decided to put it under new management, it is hardly surprising that it did not last very long. He actually composed two ballets in direct line of succession from *Icare*—*David Triomphant* (1937) and *Le Cantique des Cantiques* (1938): the former had a purely percussive accompaniment, the latter had percussion supplemented by the wails of the Ondes Martenot. Lifar's other two Graeco-Roman ballets—*Alexandre le Grand* (1937) and *Aeneas* (1938)—strayed rather far from the path of Icarus, being arranged to pre-existing music.

These mythological ballets resembled each other just as much as the "classic ballets" of Balanchine. All emphasis was concentrated on Lifar's rôle, which was so often the same, whatever the name attached to it: an arrogant lonely figure, performing a small vocabulary of staccato leaps and violent gestures, and beating out rhythms with a concentration worthy of a better cause.

Even the most solid technique could not have survived such a regime for long without injury, and Lifar's rapidly acquired technique degenerated with disconcerting rapidity. By the end of the thirties his movements had lost much of their grace and lightness, and he no longer evoked a Slav Apollo.

The Blum-de Basil-Massine company appeared in Paris in 1933 and 1934, but from then on neither this company nor its two daughter companies found

[1] Typical items in the manifesto were the following: "Ballet does not need to borrow its rhythmic patterns from the music. . . . Ballet can exist free from all musical accompaniment. . . . In the event that ballet is tied to music, the rhythmic basis must be that of the choreographer and not that of the musician. . . . A choreographic theatre, free and independent, must be created."

it possible to visit Paris; for various financial reasons a season at a commercial theatre was almost certain to show a loss, and the large State-subsidized theatres made no effort to bring the touring companies to Paris. (In all countries the State ballets tend to discourage effective competition.) As a result London completely effaced Paris as a world centre of ballet, and Paris became a backwater. Lifar, free from effective competition, was able to go on arranging the same dull ballet under many different names from year to year, without suffering any loss in prestige or authority.

The deadlock was broken in 1939, when the Blum-Massine company appeared in Paris and made a profound impression, in spite of many weaknesses in its repertoire and personnel. The outbreak of war freed Lifar from any further danger of competition, but the 1939 visit gave him food for thought; moreover he had had a chance to make contact with an artistic climate very different from anything he had experienced under Diaghilev when he danced in the Blum-Massine Monte Carlo company as a guest artist in 1938, and saw Massine working in a company of which he was artistic director. Lifar now began to arrange ballets which showed some influences from his various recent experiences, working in various genres and giving opportunities to dancers other than himself. For the first time his ballets showed an attempt at the assembly of solos, pas de deux, pas de trois, group dances, etc., into some sort of composition.

Nevertheless his outlook on ballet was still fundamentally the same, and so were the details of his choreography: he still showed little understanding of the use of dance-imagery for the creation of character and the evocation of mood or atmosphere. The deficiencies of his style were very obvious when he followed the example of Nijinska and arranged an abstract ballet *Suite en Blanc* (based on extracts from the score by Lalo for the ballet *Namouna*). The extracts from Lalo's score had no continuity, and Lifar arranged the ballet as a suite of divertissements, adapting each entrée to the style and technique of the dancers in question. He was now capable of varying to some extent the vocabulary of steps he used in order to suit the various dancers, but his method of building up enchaînements was still as clumsy as ever, preventing dancers from achieving any vitality or fluidity in their work; his abstract style was appreciably different from Balanchine's abstract style, but it had almost exactly the same defects.

In the dramatic ballets to which Lifar had devoted himself up to this time the deficiencies of his style were disguised to some extent by the development of the action. In an abstract ballet like *Suite en Blanc* these deficiencies showed up very clearly, and it was perhaps for this reason that from now on Lifar avoided abstraction almost entirely.

At the time of the Liberation Lifar left the Opéra, and in 1946 he joined the Nouveau Ballet de Monte Carlo as artistic director and principal choreographer. This was a period of feverish activity in all spheres of French life, with creative impulses which had been dammed up during the Occupation bursting forth with tremendous energy. The Opéra (where all creative work was at a standstill) seemed intolerably dull to the best dancers of the company, and nearly all of these left, joining Lifar in Monte Carlo, Roland Petit in Paris or each in turn.

At Monte Carlo Lifar found himself in a very favourable position for escaping from his limitations and moving in new directions. He had a remarkable group of soloists at his disposal, and his authority was even more absolute than at the Opéra (where it was limited to some extent by the tradition of casting according to official rank and a very complicated web of intrigue and protection). Moreover the spirit of the times was strongly in favour of daring experiments.

Undoubtedly Lifar made a genuine attempt to rise to the occasion. Though he spent much of his time on the composition of pas de deux in his familiar manner and on a new version of *Suite en Blanc* (under the name of *Noir et Blanc*), he also spent two years on the most ambitious project of his career. *Chota Roustaveli* (1946) was in four acts, lasting an entire evening, and was provided with music by three composers of three different nationalities (Honegger, Harsanyi and Cherepnin). The ballet was based on the Georgian epic *The Knight in the Tiger's Skin* and the life of its author (Chota Roustaveli).

Lifar's failure to come to grips with the theme was on the same grandiose scale as the project itself. The construction of the ballet was so clumsy that it was impossible to make head or tail of it. The poet himself—Lifar standing on a pedestal and pretending to read (with magniloquent gestures) from a copy of the poem—got inextricably mixed up with the story of the poem. All the choreography was in the familiar Lifarian vein, and since this was spread over four acts it became unbearably tedious: at no point did Lifar show much feeling for period, place, character or mood. The music by the three different composers did not fit together, and helped to deprive the ballet of any unity it might otherwise have had.

In 1948 Lifar returned to the Opéra; at first his position was ambiguous (he was allowed to work as maître de ballet but not to dance) but he soon re-established his previous unassailable position, and continued in the path established by him during the War years. His technique of composition was now far less clumsy than before the War, and the competition of foreign ballet companies visiting Paris and two new French companies (both presenting ballets by Roland Petit) made it advisable for him to ensure some variety in his subjects and methods of treatment. (He even composed for a small temporary group of dancers a circus ballet *L'Ecuyère* which showed great influence from the Petit ballet *Les Forains* and was in fact quite as good as that overrated ballet.[1])

The ballets composed by Lifar after his return to the Opéra avoided most

[1] *See* p. 247 below.

of the crude defects of his early years, but they still showed in exaggerated form all the characteristic defects of post-expressionist pseudo-classicism, and he persisted in dancing in them in spite of the fact that his dancing was sometimes a parody of what it had been in his youth.

The comparison between Balanchine and Lifar is instructive, for they are both products of the Diaghilev cocktail period. Balanchine may be regarded as a tree with roots in three different types of soil—the Petipa tradition of the pre-revolutionary Maryinsky, the acrobatic expressionism of post-revolutionary Russia, and the post-expressionist pseudo-classicism of Nijinska and Massine. None of these soils had much fertility, and Balanchine's growth was accordingly limited, but he was able to some extent to make up the deficiencies of one soil from the nutriments available in the others. Lifar, on the other hand, had no roots in any soil: he may perhaps be regarded as a graft on the Balanchine tree. After some years of work as a choreographer Lifar began to realize that his productions had serious deficiencies, and tried to put down roots in various places—early German expressionism, Nijinska's pseudo-classical abstraction, the 1938 productions of Massine for the Ballets Russes de Monte Carlo, and even the work of Roland Petit. Though his ballets changed their outward shape under the impact of these influences, they did not change their real nature in any way: in the fifties Lifar was just as rootless as in the twenties, with little contact with the cultural traditions of Russia, France, Germany or any other country. (His treatment of the French ballet *Giselle* illustrated one result of this lack of tradition.)

Lifar's influence on French choreography has inevitably been overwhelming. Before he joined the Opéra the productions there (apart from the great classical ballets starring Spessivsteva) were so sentimental and old-fashioned that few people took them seriously. Lifar succeeded in making the Opéra fashionable once again, and showed such a flair for publicity that his productions continued to attract attention, in spite of a marked disparity between his claims and his achievements. During the whole period of Lifar's early career at the Opéra, from 1929 to the Liberation, Paris was cut off from important foreign companies except on very rare occasions; even when there were visits from important foreign companies (in 1933, 1934, 1937 and 1939) the seasons were short and bulked very small in comparison with the Opéra's weekly performances. Through his official position, his productions at the Opéra, his articles and books, and his many personal contacts, Lifar exerted a profound influence on every aspect of French ballet, and young choreographers naturally modelled themselves on him. To the young Frenchmen the Lifarian style was not a style at all—it was the natural and obvious way of composing a ballet in France. Even when Lifar was away from the Opera (in the period following the Liberation) the young French choreographers—with one important exception—

still used his style. They were dimly aware that other styles existed, but these other styles had no more meaning for them than Fokine's style had for Lifar when he joined the Diaghilev ballet.

Though the Heavens may fall, Lifar remains immutably and indubitably Lifar. In 1952, sixteen years after proclaiming that *Icare* should inaugurate a new era in the history of the dance, we find him listing three of his own ballets (*Icare, Oriane et le Prince d'Amour* and *Lucifer*) among the six most remarkable ballets of the twentieth century, in conjunction with two Fokine ballets (*Petrouchka* and *Daphnis et Chloë*) and Nijinsky's greatest ballet (*Le Sacre du Printemps*).[1]

This supreme self-confidence is often found among the great innovators in all branches of art: we find it in Blake, Berlioz, Wagner and Cézanne, just as we do in Noverre, Duncan and Fokine. Without it such artists could hardly survive the frustration they encounter during the desperate years when they struggle for recognition. But it is also found in men like Lifar, who suffer little or no frustration, and whose talents are of a different order.

FREDERICK ASHTON (*b.* 1906)

Though Ashton's career has been similar in many respects to those of Balanchine and Lifar, he enjoyed a number of important advantages over them:

(*a*) He was working in his own country, and therefore benefited from the fact that his instinctive way of doing things was likely to be understood by his dancers and easily appreciated by the public.

(*b*) He worked in companies in which he had almost complete freedom of action, but in which he was not the sole choreographer and did not have the responsibility of building up a balanced repertoire; he could therefore concentrate on the type of ballet which suited him best.

(*c*) Throughout his career he had the stimulus of the London audience, famous for its ability to bring out the best in dancers and choreographers.

(*d*) For most of his career he was able to build his ballets around Margot Fonteyn; Lifar had Spessivtseva, Chauviré, Jeanmaire, Marchand and Vyroubova, but he had little feeling for female dancing, whereas Ashton thought almost entirely in feminine terms.

(*e*) During his early formative years at the Ballet Club he had the stimulus of working alongside a choreographer of genius who was just beginning his

[1] Serge Lifar, "My Two Latest Creations", *Opera Ballet Music-Hall in the World*, Vol. I, No. 2.

career: Ashton could learn nothing from Tudor (whose style was quite different from his own), but Tudor's rapid progress put Ashton on his mettle.

(*f*) He came into such close contact with the Diaghilev ballet that he was able to assimilate its atmosphere and the methods of composition of the Diaghilev choreographers, but he never actually joined the company, and so escaped the intensive conditioning to which all the Diaghilev choreographers were subjected during the cocktail period of this company.

With all these advantages Ashton found it fairly easy to adapt the late-Diaghilev style to English conditions, and in due course to evolve a style of his own. Pseudo-classicism is by its nature essentially cosmopolitan, but Ashton—being an Englishman working in England—was able to give it a certain recognizably English flavour. In harmony with English taste he cut down considerably the elements of expressionism, and gave the Petipan element much less of an expressionist twist than either Balanchine or Lifar. This avoidance of expressionism helped him to gain popularity in England, where only the best expressionism arouses enthusiasm, and anything less than the best makes little impression. (The hysterical expressionism of Wigman, for example, was coldly received, and she learned to avoid England in her tours.)

Like Balanchine and Lifar, Ashton knew the Diaghilev company only in its cocktail period. Apart from studying the performances when the company came to London he had indirect contact with Russian ballet through Marie Rambert (his teacher, patron and artistic mentor); through the Russian designer Sophie Fedorovitch (who designed the décor and costumes for his first ballet in 1926, and subsequently collaborated with him on many different occasions); and finally through Bronislava Nijinska (who was choreographer and maître de ballet of the Ida Rubinstein company, which he joined in 1927). Each of these three women were themselves strongly influenced by the artistic outlook of the Diaghilev ballet in its final period; Ashton himself assimilated this outlook so well from them (and from members of the Diaghilev entourage whom he met through them) that Diaghilev was pleased with his work when he saw it. But for Diaghilev's death in 1929 he would almost certainly have commissioned one or more ballets from Ashton.

Ashton composed his first ballet in 1926 (a small satirical sketch in a revue), but he did not begin to form a style of his own until he had spent twelve months under Nijinska in the Ida Rubinstein company (1927–28). During this period Nijinska composed a number of ballets in the pseudo-classical style she had evolved for Diaghilev. This experience made a strong impression on Ashton: not only could he study her methods of composition, but he could understand how she achieved her effects in those of her ballets which remained in the Diaghilev repertoire—above all *Les Biches*. (It is very difficult for an inexperienced choreographer to analyse a ballet when he only sees it in performance:

young composers would have the same difficulty if they had no access to scores.) Massine also composed two ballets for Ida Rubinstein at this period, but Ashton does not seem to have been much affected by these ballets.

The other major influence on Ashton was Balanchine. Ashton was never rehearsed by him, but he was able to study his methods of composition by watching him rehearse the Diaghilev company, and was also able to see many of his ballets in performance. Ashton later modelled his own methods of composition more on those of Balanchine than those of Nijinska: no doubt he was influenced by the fact that Balanchine was Diaghilev's favourite choreographer during the whole of the period when Ashton was in contact with the Diaghilev company.

In 1930 Marie Rambert began to stage regular performances with the Marie Rambert Dancers (later transformed into the Ballet Club), and Ashton rapidly composed a number of ballets for this company in order to build up its repertoire. (Marie Rambert also staged ballets like *Les Sylphides*, a short version of *Le Lac des Cygnes* and *Aurora's Wedding*, but these were totally unsuited to the tiny stage of the Mercury Theatre.) Like Ninette de Valois, Ashton reserved his most important ballets for Camargo Society performances, since at these performances he could supplement the Ballet Club dancers with other dancers available in London (including even Lopukhova), and he also had the advantage of a large stage, a large West-End audience, good publicity, etc.

Pomona, composed by Ashton in 1930 for the Camargo Society, showed considerable influence from the ballets composed by Nijinska for Ida Rubinstein and also from Balanchine's ballet *Apollon Musagète*. Ashton made little effort to establish a theme, confining himself to putting together pseudo-classical enchaînements to fit the music. There was no attempt at characterization and very little at the evocation of mood. This ballet was twice revived by the Vic-Wells Ballet but failed to establish itself in the repertoire; nevertheless it has historical interest as the first of a series of semi-abstract ballets through which Ashton carried forward a number of favourite enchaînements and patterns of group movement.

Façade, composed in 1931 for the Camargo Society, was Ashton's first important comedy ballet, and in many ways his best. Here the main influence was Balanchine. Ashton made no attempt at homogeneity of style or solid construction; instead, he took a number of pieces from the piano suite adapted by Walton from the original *Façade* (a recitation of Edith Sitwell poems accompanied by music specially composed by Walton) and improvised comedy numbers for one, two, three or four dances to fit the mood of each piece. Some of his improvisations were successful: "Polka", for example, had much the same gaiety and wit as the best comedy dances in Balanchine's ballet *Le Triomphe de Neptune*; "Tango" was a grotesque parody of a ballroom tango;

and "Popular Song" was a clever skit on bored tap-dancers playing second-rate variety dates. But there were other scenes (such as "Yodelling Song") where the dancing was quite pointless and the humour was scarcely up to the level of a good charade. In fact the whole ballet gave the impression of having been strung together rather carelessly in a great hurry.

C. W. Beaumont, reviewing the first performance, criticized it severely as belonging to the music-hall rather than to ballet.[1] His criticisms were fully justified: only at rare moments did the choreography show any feeling for the sophisticated wit of Edith Sitwell's words and Walton's music. If the whole ballet had been on the level of the Polka, and the Sitwell words had been used as well as the Walton music,[2] the ballet would have been something very different. Unfortunately everything in Ashton's past experience predisposed him to refrain from any attempt at a harmonious ensemble.

In spite of its serious defects, *Façade* had some fine moments, it was more original than most other English ballets of the day, and the choreographer was well served by the décor, costumes and music. This ballet is one of the very few English ballets to form part of the repertoire of several different companies.[3]

Mercury, arranged by Ashton in 1931 for the Ballet Club, was a misguided attempt at a new version of one of the dreariest of Massine's cocktail ballets; Ashton's choreography contained no dancing worthy of the name, and the ballet was merely a series of undistinguished poses and arm movements.

In *Les Masques*, composed for the Ballet Club in 1933, Ashton applied himself for the first time to the style used by Nijinska in *Les Biches* and continued by Balanchine in a number of ballets. *Les Masques* (with clever-clever décor and costumes by Sophie Fedorovitch) was a deliberately pointless cocktail ballet which would have fitted perfectly into the late Diaghilev repertoire. Some of the details (such as the celluloid muff carried by the heroine) recalled details in Diaghilev cocktail ballets such as *La Chatte*, while other details recalled the Balanchine ballets *Le Bal* (1929) and *Cotillon* (1932). The resemblances to *Cotillon* were particularly striking, for most of the two ballets were based on the same Chabrier music.

At the end of 1933 Ashton composed for the Vic-Wells Ballet *Les Rendez-vous*, a ballet similar in structure and mood to *Mozartiana*, which Balanchine had composed for Les Ballets 1933 earlier in the year. (Normally Ashton tended to look for inspiration to the ballets he had seen most recently.) The theme common to *Les Rendezvous* and *Mozartiana* was ostentatiously trivial in the cocktail manner: individuals and small groups of people keep meeting

---

[1] Review of Camargo Society performance of June, 1930, in *Dancing World*.
[2] The music loses much of its point without the counter-rhythms of the words; the meanings of the words are less important than their sound-values and rhythms.
[3] It is performed by the Rambert Ballet, the Sadlers Wells Ballet and the Sadlers Wells Theatre Ballet.

each other in a public place. Most of Ashton's choreography was insipid and pointless, but one pas de trois showed that under favourable circumstances his pseudo-classical style was capable of supporting the composition of dances with attractive qualities of playful gaiety and charm; the music had a sparkling melody with an insistent rhythm, and he managed to discover enchaînements which brought out these qualities. If he had had the judgment to recognize the difference between this dance and his usual choreography, and the inventiveness to build out from it to the rest of *Les Rendezvous* (as Fokine built out from the Pas de Deux when he composed *Chopiniana*), Ashton could have made *Les Rendezvous* a ballet strong enough to win a permanent place in the repertoire. As in *Façade*, however, Ashton showed no interest in homogeneity: he improvised the ballet from phrase to phrase, and left the shape of the ballet as a whole to look after itself. Like Balanchine and Lifar, he had the habit of seizing on any step which the music suggested and fitting it in with previous steps, regardless of the theme of the ballet; if no steps suggested themselves to Ashton when he listened to the music he was inclined to ask the dancers to play about and make use of any of their improvisations which caught his fancy. He also had the Balanchinian and Lifarian habit of bringing forward considerable material from earlier ballets. (This repetitiousness, highly characteristic of twentieth-century pseudo-classicism, is partly due to the bewilderment and frustration of dancers in rehearsal when faced with instructions from the choreographer so vague that they can be interpreted in a thousand different ways: in such circumstances dancers inevitably tend to reproduce something from a previous ballet, in the hope that this is what the choreographer means.)

In 1935, after joining the Vic-Wells Ballet as resident choreographer, Ashton celebrated his appointment by composing his first large-scale ballet, *Le Baiser de la Fée*. This was a new version of a ballet composed by Nijinska in 1928, at a time when Ashton was dancing in the Rubinstein company. In this ballet, which had a definite story, Ashton found that his previous experience in cocktail ballets was of little use in distinguishing between characters and building up a dramatic structure. Like Balanchine and Lifar he made no effort to come to grips with the problems involved in a story ballet, giving the dancers his habitual type of enchaînement and relying on a few passages of mime in conjunction with the décor, the costumes and the synopsis in the programme to keep the audience abreast of the story. His choreography in general avoided the crude technical faults of the choreography of Balanchine and Lifar, but its virtues were almost entirely negative: it did not achieve even the bravura with which Petipa would have decorated such a theme.

During the next few years Ashton arranged a number of other romantic ballets in rather similar style—e.g. *Apparitions*, *Nocturne* and *Horoscope*. Though Margot Fonteyn gave the promise of great talent in her performance in *Le*

Baiser de la Fée, and later rose to fame by giving the best performance in Act I of *Giselle* since Spessivsteva, Ashton made very limited use of her talents, giving her in each ballet the same sort of enchaînements and demanding of her the expression of the same wistful mood. All these ballets had considerable success when first performed, but gradually lost their appeal and were deleted from the repertoire.

After the War new productions were badly needed to build up the repertoire of the second company and strengthen the repertoire of the main company. Ninette de Valois therefore commissioned Ashton to revive a number of the thirty-five ballets composed by him between 1926 and 1941 (*Valses Nobles et Sentimentales, Nocturne, Apparitions, A Wedding Bouquet* and *Dante Sonata*), but none of these ballets established themselves permanently in the post-war repertoire.[1] In fact only two of Ashton's pre-War ballets showed any enduring vitality after the War: these were two comedy ballets (*Façade* and *Les Patineurs*) which had remained in the repertoire since they were first produced.

Les Patineurs (1937) had much the same value in programme-building as *Façade*. It was in effect a *grand divertissement*—a series of dances suggesting scattered episodes during an evening on the ice. Constant Lambert put together various pieces by Meyerbeer to make a well-balanced and sparkling score, perfectly adapted to the theme, and Ashton found the music so suitable for his favourite type of enchaînement that he was able to keep up a reasonably high technical standard of choreography and even link the various episodes together to some extent. Unlike Balanchine and Lifar, he seemed to feel no need to give his enchaînements an effect of spurious originality by making them clipped and jerky in the expressionist manner; though the dances in *Les Patineurs* were highly conventional they did give the dancers a chance to move, and preserved some of the animation of the music. In fact the dancers had some chance to put individuality into their rôles, just as the Maryinsky dancers used to do in Petipa ballets.

Les Patineurs stood out from all other Ashton ballets in having one rôle (that of the champion skater) which gave real opportunities to a male dancer —opportunities which Harold Turner exploited to the utmost. (Normally Ashton showed little interest in male dancing.)

Ashton went through a bad time between the middle of 1938 and the beginning of 1940. He had exhausted all the potentialities of his own brand of pseudo-classicism, and began to repeat himself in an obvious and clumsy manner. *Cupid and Psyche*, the only ballet produced by him in 1939, was a failure, and was taken off after a few days.

The outbreak of war and the subsequent growth of strong currents of

[1] For some reason *Apparitions* was revived again in 1952–53, though there was no evidence that it was markedly more popular than the other Ashton revivals.

popular feeling encouraged Ashton to try his hand for the first time at expressionism. In *Dante Sonata* (1940) he used many of the clichés of the hysterical expressionism of Central Europe in the early twenties—bare feet, masses of bodies crawling on the ground, agonized gestures, and so on. Unlike Ninette de Valois, however, he showed no understanding of the technique of the free dance, and the movements in detail had nothing of the pungency of the best of the expressionist choreography in *La Création du Monde, Job, The Rake's Progress* and *Checkmate*.

Dante Sonata was a considerable success at the time, for its hysterical emotionalism provided a pleasant contrast with the rather insipid quality of the rest of the repertoire, and the style was new to the English audiences of the day. After a few years, however, the defects of the choreography became painfully obvious, and the ballet was dropped from the repertoire.

In spite of the success with the public of *Dante Sonata* at its first production, Ashton sensibly avoided any further attempts at this genre: he had little talent for it, and he had used up all his ideas in *Dante Sonata*. On the other hand he could scarcely go back to the manner of *Cupid and Psyche*. In this dilemma he decided to try his hand at an abstract ballet in the Massine symphonic manner —*The Wanderer*. This ballet was not a success: Ashton lacked Massine's talent for massing large groups of dancers in contrapuntal patterns, and the genre was quite familiar in England, so that both critics and the public had some standard of comparison. To make things worse Massine himself had exhausted all the potentialities of the genre some years earlier; in his desperate search for novelty at any cost Ashton was driven to make crude and repetitious use of religious symbols such as the Crucifixion—a device previously used by Massine.

Ashton was then called up into the Forces. The enforced rest from choreography and the change in his environment were invaluable to him. By 1938 he had exhausted all the potentialities of his own style, and the plumes he borrowed in 1940–41 were very tattered before they reached him; now, however, he had a great deal of time to think about the future and plan a ballet which would enable him to re-establish his position in competition with Helpmann (who had emerged as a choreographer of some stature in his absence).

When he returned from the Forces in 1946 he put his plans into action in *Symphonic Variations*. This began as a semi-abstract ballet with a large cast, and a vague mythological theme connected with the re-birth of life in the Spring: presumably he intended to treat the theme in somewhat the same manner as in *The Wanderer*. In rehearsal, however, he sensibly jettisoned all the symbolism and all the corps de ballet, limiting the cast to the six best soloists; in this way he avoided the worst defects of *The Wanderer*. The César Franck music suited very well his favourite type of enchaînement, and he brought together all his favourite enchaînements from *Pomona* onwards, being helped to use them in a spontaneous way by his long rest from choreography; in addition he composed some new enchaînements in similar style. His choreography fitted the music in a facile way, but it showed far more respect for the phrasing, melody and rhythm than the choreography of the abstract ballets of Balanchine and Lifar. Because of its spontaneity and relative musicality *Symphonic Variations* was a success with the public, and became part of the permanent repertoire—the only serious Ashton ballet to do so.

The success of *Symphonic Variations* consolidated Ashton's position as chief Sadlers Wells choreographer; since Ninette de Valois had by now ceased to arrange ballets, and since she gave no further commissions to Helpmann, Ashton was now in fact the only resident choreographer working with the main company. In due course his special position was emphasized by the fact that he was made associate artistic director. His influence before the war had been very great; now that the Sadlers Wells Ballet was recognized as one of the greatest companies in the world, and was established at Covent Garden with a large subsidy and no competition from international Ballet-Russe companies, Ashton's influence became as dominant in England as Lifar's in France.

Unlike Lifar and Balanchine, Ashton showed little tendency to issue manifestos, preferring to let his work speak for itself. That is not to say that he was backward in pushing his work to the fore: he simply adapted himself to English ideas about the appropriate way in which a person should speak of his own work. In a B.B.C. feature dealing with the technique of ballet he let other speakers do most of the talking, and pointed out that choreographers vary enormously in their methods; he could speak only for himself. His main interest, he said, was "the re-statement of classicism in a personal way which I feel to be essential". At the end of the programme he summed up his attitude to ballet in language very similar to Balanchine's: "If modern ballet is to survive *dancing* must be paramount: the subject-matter is less important than this."[1]

Though Ashton's public statements on his attitude to ballet are rare and rather vague, his colleague William Chappell (who has been strongly influenced by his ballets) has described with admirable clarity the aesthetic outlook which they incorporate:

> As long as dancing takes precedence over miming and acting it is unimportant whether the plot is complex, the theme is slight, or there is no subject at all other than something indicated or suggested by the costumes and décor . . . The value of a ballet scenario lies in the amount of atmosphere it helps to produce. Finally, and above all else, the raison d'être of a ballet lies in its creator's ability to discover fascinating and unusual movements for his dancers.[2]

---

[1] *Techniques*: No. 3, *Ballet* (Home Service, . . . March 1948).
[2] *Studies in Ballet*, pp. 33–34.

Chappell is expressing his personal views, but these were moulded over a long period of years during which he danced in Ashton's ballets and designed décor and costumes for Ashton. His suggestion that the theme of a ballet might only be "indicated" by the costumes and décor is clearly based on personal experience; in fact Chappell is so much under the influence of Ashton's ballets that though he invariably writes about ballet in general his remarks apply only to the ballets of Ashton, Lifar, Balanchine and their imitators. It never seems to occur to Chappell that any other types of ballet exist.

Later in the same book he makes clear Ashton's attitude to the themes of his ballet:

> In the wordless musical world of the ballet certain gestures can give the key to the shape and meaning of the work offered. The choreographer will point his theme by these and then give himself up to evolving his dances. . . . First and foremost a choreographer is bent on making a dance movement musically and aesthetically correct, and . . . it is only a short mime passage or a slight repeated gesture superimposed on the general line of the choreography that give the meaning necessary to explain the ballet's theme.[1]

His description of the theme of a ballet as something "superimposed on the general line of the choreography" after it is "musically and aesthetically correct" has an epic simplicity for which we owe him much gratitude. The odd thing is that he means to praise Caesar, not to bury him.

Both Ashton's broadcast and Chappell's book belong to the halcyon period immediately after the War, when the Sadlers Wells Ballet had just moved to Covent Garden, ballet was booming, *Symphonic Variations* was a triumphant success with critics and the public, and pseudo-classicism seemed to be carrying all before it. This style subsequently maintained its dominating position, but the growing coolness of the public and critics would not have encouraged quite such a confident attitude to problems of choreography a few years later.

The special circumstances which made it possible for Ashton to score a popular success with *Symphonic Variations* were by their very nature non-recurring, and his subsequent ballets showed the same faults as those produced by him in the late thirties and early forties. The War had interrupted the trends which were firmly established in the period 1938–42, but had not abolished them.

In 1947 Ashton produced only one ballet, *Valses Nobles et Sentimentales*— an abstract version of his Ballet Club ballet *Valentine's Eve*. This was composed for the junior company. In 1948 he composed for the senior company another abstract work, *Scènes de Ballet*. This began in a style fairly closely imitated from

---

[1] *Ibid*, p. 115.
A.A.O.B.—N

Balanchine's "classic ballet" style, with dancers moving in neat lines and making clipped movements tied mechanically to the music; after a few minutes, however, Ashton seemed to lose interest in this style, and reverted to his usual manner. Unfortunately Stravinsky's brittle parodistic music was little suited to Ashton's usual enchaînements, and he seemed to find great difficulty in filling up the music: from time to time there were clumsy lifts and awkward transitions quite foreign to his usual style.

From now on these awkward passages became common in Ashton's choreography; he seemed to find it more and more difficult to find steps to fill up the music, which now he treated as an enemy. He suffered very much from the fact that he used up his steps very quickly: Balanchine, working in a country where ideas about classical ballet were largely formed on his own ballets, was able to economize steps by repeating them ad nauseam, but Ashton had no such advantages. The strain on him was particularly heavy in abstract ballets with no passages of mime, and he abandoned this genre after *Scènes de Ballet.*

In *Don Juan* (produced at the end of 1948) Ashton attempted to compose a mysterious ballet of the type favoured by Kokhno and Cocteau, taking as his theme a version by Swinburne of some verses by Gautier. The title rôle was acted by Helpmann in the melodramatic style already used by him in his own ballets; one of the two leading female rôles, La Mort Amoureuse, was clearly inspired by the numerous glamorous Death-figures in contemporary French ballets and films. Ashton attempted to give an illusion of novelty to his choreography for the rôle by inserting into it the type of acrobatic double-work[1] favoured by Lifar and Balanchine; but these circus-tricks did not suit Ashton's style, and he used them in a clumsy way. At one moment, for example, he had two men lift La Mort Amoureuse (who meanwhile did the splits in the air) and balance her across one shoulder of Don Juan; after a few moments of precarious balancing she was helped down, and the ballet continued. Ashton clearly intended this lift to look difficult and exciting, but it only looked difficult.

In *Cinderella* Ashton composed the most ambitious ballet of his career up to then—a multi-act ballet in the Petipa manner, lasting an entire evening. Having often found himself at a loss in preceding ballets for steps to fill out the music, he made things easy for himself in *Cinderella* by making the dancing very conventional and concentrating on the slapstick comedy. He leaned heavily on the English pantomime tradition, arranging for the Ugly Sisters to be acted by men (himself and Helpmann), and building up these rôles at the expense of Cinderella's. The heroine had only two dances of any importance in the whole long ballet—one in Act I and one in Act II. Ashton kept all his best

---

[1] "Double-work" is the usual name in England for sequences of movement in which the man supports the woman. The Russian name for this is "adagio", and this is the term normally used in the United States.

ideas for the dances, and gave them fluidity and grace in his best manner. Else-where, however, he reduced the myth to sentimental triviality by treating it without any element of poetic fantasy. The Ugly Sisters succeeded in holding the attention of the audience by using the familiar technique of the Panto Dame, but from a choreographic point of view their rôles were very dull. In an effort to give the ballet symbolic significance Ashton made the incident of the striking of midnight as melodramatic as possible, arranging for the Jester to be raised high in the air at each stroke; but the effect was as laboured and unconvincing as his acrobatic lifts in *Don Juan*.

Ashton treated Prokofiev's music with the same insensitivity with which Petipa treated Tchaikovsky's score for *The Sleeping Beauty*. The *Cinderella* score had been originally commissioned for production at the Bolshoy in Moscow, and Prokofiev had coped with the stylistic requirements of choreography at this theatre by writing in the style of Tchaikovsky. His score fell below the standard of Tchaikovsky's best ballet music, but it was quite as good as much of Tchaikovsky's work, and showed admirable feeling for character and mood; Prokofiev adapted himself to the task in hand with the wit and intelligence one might have expected from the composer of *Classical Symphony*. This music was perfectly adaptable to Ashton's usual type of enchaînement, and in fact he tackled it with considerable skill when he composed Cinderella's broom dance. Elsewhere, however, he paid very little attention to the nuances of the music, and this gave the dances a monotonous and curiously arbitrary quality: it was obvious that at any moment he could have used other steps just as easily.

Cinderella was produced in December, 1949, just in time for the pantomime season; Ashton then waited over a year before composing another ballet at Covent Garden. (The long American tour of the company made difficult the production of new ballets in 1950.) In New York, however, Ashton produced for the New York City Ballet *Illuminations* (1950). In theory this was based on Benjamin Britten's settings of prose poems by Rimbaud, but Ashton's choreo-graphy was so remote in feeling and in detail from both Rimbaud and Britten that the ballet was in fact quite as arbitrary as any late-Diaghilevian cocktail. (A typical gimmick was the introduction of a danseuse with one foot bare and the other shod in a pointe shoe.) Apparently feeling the need to assert his avant-gardisme in New York in competition with Balanchine, Ashton made a determined attempt at Goleizovskian eroticism wrapped up in obscene symbolism.

In 1951 Ashton produced at Covent Garden a new version of the Fokine ballet *Daphnis et Chloë*. This ballet presented severe problems of style to the choreographer. Fokine had devised it for production in a neo-Greek manner, using poses taken from Greek vase-paintings, while Ravel composed in a score whose texture was mainly impressionist but which included certain sections showing strong influence from the nationalist Russian scores of the ballets *Prince Igor* and *Schéhérazade*. Fokine himself failed to achieve a fully satisfactory style for the ballet, but at least his neo-Greek style had a certain homogeneity; Ashton, on the other hand, wavered uncertainly between a number of different styles, and there were long passages where the music went on playing but the choreographer seemed to have no idea what to do with the dancers. The group dance of the shepherds in Scene I was adapted from a Macedonian dance which had been performed in London the previous Summer by Yugoslav folk-dancers, but Ashton made nonsense of the traditional steps by having men perform them in a mincing, balletic manner, with carefully pointed feet. The dance of Daphnis in the dance contest in Scene I was a particularly unhappy attempt at the Lifar style: Daphnis performed a series of jerky steps and leaps with no connection with each other and even less with the music. Ashton seemed to give up completely when he had to bring on Pan and his nymphs: there was nothing in the movements of these characters to suggest that they were in any way supernatural.

In the second scene (the Pirates' Anchorage) Ravel's music showed influences from *Prince Igor*, and Ashton took advantage of this to introduce group dances very similar to those in *Prince Igor*. He was also inspired by Ravel's music to compose a Polovstian dance for the Pirate Chief which had energy and ferocity, and Alexander Grant made the most of every chance given to him. (Such chances for male dancers were very rare at Covent Garden.)

After the Polovstian dances the choreography lost all impetus, and became so insipid that the main weight of the ballet seemed to be concentrated in the orchestra pit. The ballet would have been greatly improved by severe cutting, but Ravel's executors would not permit any alteration in his score.

A few months later Ashton tackled an even more difficult project—the ballet *Tiresias*, with book and music by Constant Lambert. Both the book and the score had many defects, and Ashton failed so completely to cope with the problems presented by them that the ballet was a disastrous failure. For once critics and the public were unanimous: not since Ashton produced *Cupid and Psyche* in 1939 had any Sadlers Wells ballet misfired so lamentably. The details of Ashton's choreography were not much worse than corresponding details in *Don Juan* and *Daphnis et Chloë*, but *Tiresias* came at the end of a series of bad ballets, and it was padded out to enormous dimensions: the ballet lasted over an hour. It was as if a blinding light had been focused on Ashton's deficiencies as a choreographer, throwing each one of them into sharp relief.

The theme of *Tiresias*, put together by Constant Lambert from a number of Cretan myths, was similar in some respects to the themes of the mythological ballets composed by Lifar in the middle thirties—and Ashton took Lifar's style as a model when he began the choreography of the first scene. As in *Scènes de*

Ballet, however, he gradually lost interest in his adopted style, and found himself faced with enormous expanses of music with no apparent idea of how to come to grips with them. Episode by episode the ballet dragged its slow length along, with the ending seeming to recede further and further into the remote future.

In his desperate search for some way of giving interest to his choreography Ashton fell into one fault of taste after another. In Scene II, for example, the two snakes crawled over each other in a laboriously erotic manner which would have been less boring if it had not been so monotonous, while the unfortunate Neophyte had to spend most of her time waving a wand from side to side, like a Boy Scout learning semaphore. In Scene III there was a long and dull scene in which Hera and Zeus, standing uncomfortably on pillars, conducted a conversation in arbitrary and incomprehensible gestures. At no point in the ballet did the movements give the dancers any chance to establish character or mood, and the attempts at the suggestion of myth and ritual were as wooden as anything in the corresponding Lifar ballets.

Perhaps the oddest thing about *Tiresias* was that it was given its first production at a gala performance in aid of the Ballet Benevolent Fund: it should have been obvious some weeks earlier that *Tiresias* would be unsuitable for a gala. Margot Fonteyn did wonders in vitalizing her rôle in Scene II; but Scenes I and III were almost devoid of interest.

Ashton's choreography for the film *Tales of Hoffman* belongs to this same period, and had the same defects as his work in the field of "live" ballet. At no point in the film did Ashton create dance-images expressive of the characters and moods of the personages involved, and this made the film as a whole into a bewildering succession of shots with little or no relation to the singing or each other. In fact there were passages when the film could be best enjoyed by a spectator with his eyes shut. Massine's superb acting in one of the central rôles, with its professional assurance and complete grasp of the film medium, showed very clearly what was wrong with Ashton's choreography.

From 1946 onwards Ashton moved in a vicious circle. The responsible nature of his position as chief choreographer and associate artistic director of the Sadlers Wells Ballet, established at Covent Garden with the assistance of a Government subsidy, made it essential for him to tackle ballets with ambitious themes and exacting modern scores. Though Ashton had shown real talent in the playfully satirical divertissement ballets *Façade* and *Les Patineurs*, his pseudo-classical style was much too limited and inflexible for the type of ballet he tackled after *Symphonic Variations*, and in his attempts to maintain his reputation and establish an impression of novelty he drifted steadily away from the style which suited him best. *Tiresias* showed in the clearest possible form not only the inherent deficiencies of Ashton's style but of pseudo-classicism in general.

In 1952 Ashton was able to escape from this vicious circle by producing a new version of *Sylvia*. This ballet (originally produced at the Paris Opéra by Mérante in 1876) had music by Delibes, and clearly demanded nothing more than an imitation of the Petipa style, without any expressionist devices. Ashton did exactly this, showing considerable skill in achieving a balance between pure dances, pas d'action and mime scenes: clearly he had for once taken care to study the music and the script very carefully. The actual result on the stage fell below the standard achieved by Petipa at his best (e.g. in Act III of *Le Lac des Cygnes*), and Act I of *Sylvia* was quite remarkably dull and clumsy; even Margot Fonteyn for once seemed to abandon in despair any attempt to inject some vitality and musicality into her enchaînements; but Acts II and III were worthy of comparison with Petipa's routine ballets such as *Raymonda* (which has a theme similar to that of *Sylvia*).

On the other hand Ashton's choreography was very insipid by comparison with Delibes' music, which provided him with a large number of opportunities which he failed to take. Perrot, for example, would have made something striking out of the Bacchic dance performed by the chaste nymph Sylvia in order to lure Orion into drinking himself into a stupor; the dance actually performed by Sylvia in Ashton's production was quite lacking in tension and climax, and would scarcely have lured a party of schoolgirls into drinking some cocoa. The famous pizzicato was even more disappointing. Here one could have relied on Petipa to provide the ballerina with the opportunity for a dazzling display of *posés*, *relevés*, *battements frappés*, beats and so on; Ashton, however, put together a few simple steps with none of the sparkle demanded by the music. Only in one dance did Ashton show that he had really mastered the music: the pas de deux of Sylvia and Aminta in Act III was arranged with some understanding of the possibilities inherent in combinations of steps, and Margot Fonteyn took full advantage of the opportunities provided her.

As in *Cinderella*, Ashton seemed to be aware of a certain lack of vitality in his choreography, and sought to liven up the enormously long ballet with some crude mimed buffoonery, making the god Eros into a figure of low comedy. Alexander Grant succeeded in arousing some laughter in this rôle, but his buffoonery was completely out of harmony with the rest of the ballet.

With all its faults *Sylvia* held the stage better than any of Ashton's ballets since *Symphonic Variations*. Clearly Ashton would have been quite at home in the second half of the nineteenth century working at the Paris Opéra or the Maryinsky, and would have been well advised to continue along the same road, producing a series of new versions of nineteenth-century ballets. Unfortunately for Ashton, however, *Sylvia* was almost unique in having music of some value: only a Pavlova could have induced modern audiences to accept the music of other typical ballets of this period.

No doubt this was one of the main reasons why Ashton followed the example of Balanchine and began in 1952 to make changes in the productions of Maryinsky ballets by the two Sadlers Wells companies: he introduced two new dances into the Sadlers Wells Ballet's production of *Le Lac des Cygnes*, and provided new choreography for the last act of the Theatre Ballet's production of *Casse-Noisette*. The changes in *Le Lac des Cygnes* were relatively minor ones, but the changes he made in *Casse-Noisette* ensured the complete destruction of the work of Ivanov. Though Ivanov was not at his best in *Casse-Noisette*, Ashton's new choreography was markedly inferior, and the destruction of part of a composition by the first great Russian choreographer for no apparent reason was hard to accept.

In 1953 Ashton attempted to escape from the limitations of his style in a different direction. *Homage to the Queen* (first produced at Covent Garden on Coronation Day) was clearly inspired by *Les Éléments* (1847), the third ballet produced by Perrot in London as a display-piece for several ballerinas. Here Ashton was following a well-beaten path: several choreographers had already produced new versions of *Le Pas de Quatre*, and Fokine had produced a new version of *Les Éléments* in 1937.

From a purely structural point of view Ashton's version was more satisfying than Fokine's, for the latter was arranged to highly unsuitable music by Bach. (As I wrote at the time, Fokine's treatment of the Bach fugues was "obvious to the point of banality".[1]) Ashton's ballet, in contrast, gained by the fact that it had music specially composed for it (by Malcolm Arnold); it did not pretend to be anything more than a suite of divertissements in different moods, with an obvious break for applause after each number. On the other hand it was disfigured by the same desperate search for novelty at all costs that appeared in *Scènes de Ballet* and *Don Juan*: the Queen of the Earth, for example, was given a long series of supported hops on pointe which enabled Nadia Nerina to show the strength of her feet but nothing else, while Margot Fonteyn (Queen of the Air) was carried around the stage upside-down in a lift to which only this great artist could have given some hint of grace and airiness. As usual Ashton managed to pull himself together at one point and compose a solo showing real invention: Violetta Elvin (Queen of the Waters) performed sinuous arm movements suggestive of waves with admirable style and feeling, showing an unsuspected aspect of her talent. But this fine solo stood out from the rest of the ballet in the most violent manner. Clearly the archaistic style in which Ashton worked could only stimulate him for a short period at a time, and he was still caught between the horns of his familiar dilemma.

[1] "Symphonic Ballet", *Dancing Times*, August, 1937.

D

Antony Tudor (*b.* 1908): Post-Expressionist Classicism

BEING MERELY a sophisticated mixture of previous styles, post-expressionist pseudo-classicism contained no possibilities of development, and remained much the same from one decade to the next. For a long time it dominated the ballet world almost completely, though eventually critics and the public began to show signs of becoming tired of the repetition of the same devices.

Meanwhile Antony Tudor, without benefit of publicity and with only a bare minimum of resources (little money, a tiny stage, and only a handful of fully-trained dancers), was creating a new classical style which corresponded in a much more profound way to popular current of thought and feeling. Like Isadora Duncan, he had no difficulty in making contact with the public—in spite of his great originality—whenever he had the chance of showing his work under reasonably satisfactory conditions. Though he was constantly frustrated by the organization of the ballet world, and succeeded in putting on the stage only a minority of his projects, he managed to mature steadily for many years.

Tudor's position in ballet history is similar in many respects to that of Fokine. Tudor's task was easier than Fokine's, for balletic pseudo-classicism had been re-established for only eight years when Tudor began his career as a choreographer; on the other hand the pseudo-classicism of the twentieth century was to a considerable extent a continuation of the pseudo-classicism which dominated the second half of the nineteenth century. In the repertoires of the major ballet companies the two styles were treated with equal awe, and every effort was made to establish them as the twin classical styles of modern times and of the past respectively.

In the early thirties, when Tudor started as a choreographer, the ballet world was in a very confused state. Diaghilev's cocktail policy during the last six years of his life had considerably weakened the links with the past. Fokine's neo-romanticism was still popular, but his ballets were often badly performed, and his style seemed to belong to some remote pre-War epoch. Expressionism still showed considerable vitality among free dancers, but Diaghilev had commissioned no expressionist ballet since 1923, and the pseudo-classical choreographers fostered by him used the stylistic devices of expressionism purely for their shock value. It was possible to see two major nineteenth-century ballets (*Giselle* and *Le Lac des Cygnes*), but these were lumped together with *Aurora's Wedding* and *Les Sylphides* as "classical ballets", and normally all "classical ballets" were performed in much the same style.

With the sure instinct of genius Tudor found a path to the future through this confusion of styles, taking what he needed from Perrot, Fokine and various expressionist choreographers and ignoring completely the three fashionable pseudo-classical styles which dominated the ballet world during the thirties and forties.

He was born just in time to make contact with the best of the Maryinsky and early-Diaghilev traditions before they faded out. Three of the greatest Maryinsky ballerinas—Pavlova, Karsavina and Spessivsteva—were still active in his youth, and Karsavina even danced at the Ballet Club. He saw a number of the best Fokine ballets performed by the Diaghilev and Blum-de Basil-Massine companies—even though these companies did not always have the ballerinas to do justice to them—and he also saw two major Fokine compositions performed by the great artist who inspired them (Pavlova). *Giselle* was to be seen with ideal performances in the principal rôle by Pavlova and Spessivsteva, whatever the defects of the rest of the production. Male dancing of comparable quality was harder to find, but Massine, Woizikovsky and Shabelevsky gave superb performances in character rôles.

Tudor also had the opportunity of studying the major expressionist productions of Nijinsky, Massine, Nijinska, Jooss and Ninette de Valois. Nevertheless, expressionism had passed its peak and was showing signs of exhaustion: Tudor was able to take what he needed from expressionism (even to the extent of composing whole ballets in expressionist style) without catching the expressionist virus. Fortunately Nicolas Legat was teaching in London throughout the formative years of Tudor's career as a choreographer, and so he was able to learn the secrets of the Russian school through watching it being taught by the great teacher who was its chief architect: it is impossible to exaggerate the value of this to Tudor when he undertook the revival of real classicism in choreography.

Another major influence on his development was Oriental dancing, now to be seen in London almost for the first time. (Uday Shankar visited London for the first time in 1931; the classical dances of Japan were first shown in London by Rikuhei Umemoto in 1933.)

Tudor's first ballet, *Cross-Gartered*, produced for the Ballet Club in 1931, showed influences from both Fokine and Massine. The choreography was not

particularly original, but the ballet was solidly constructed, the different characters were clearly distinguished from each other, and the style (based on Elizabethan dances) was homogeneous. What was remarkable about this ballet was
that it was produced by Tudor two years after he started training, and it showed
no influence whatever from Diaghilev's cocktail period, in spite of the strong
late-Diaghilevian influence at the Ballet Club. Tudor earned his living at the
Ballet Club by doing an enormous amount of work with easy versatility—
taking classes, giving private lessons, painting scenery, doing choreography,
playing for rehearsals, and combining the rôles of dancer, stage manager and
electrician at performances. From the very beginning, however, he had decided
to be a choreographer, and he set out to master every detail of the craft of
composition. He had Fokine's ability to improvise movements full of poetry
and atmosphere, but—unlike Fokine—he was able to keep his spontaneity and
imaginative vitality when he prepared a ballet carefully in advance. In contrast
to the expressionists and pseudo-classicists, he seemed to feel no need to assert
his originality and individuality. His early ballets showed him trying out
different styles and subjects, learning as much from his failures as his successes:
each ballet had something of the character of an experiment, and he worked out
every detail of music, costume, décor and lighting so that it would contribute
its share of the total effect. (From the very beginning he returned to the ideal of
a *Gesamtkunstwerk* which Diaghilev had abandoned and which the pseudo-
classical choreographers had learned to regard as naïve.) Because of the
thoroughness of his method of composition each ballet had solidity, and nearly
all of them remained in the repertoire.

His second ballet, *Lysistrata* (1932), was so solidly constructed that it made
most existing ballets by English choreographers seem like casual suites of
divertissements (which is exactly what they were). Neither its general style
nor its dramatic structure were strikingly original, but Tudor gave clear signs
of a powerful and original talent in his characterization of Lysistrata, who
dominated the ballet: the dance-movements which he gave her built up a picture
of a delightfully feminine person similar to the heroine of the Aristophanes
play which inspired Tudor's ballet. The ballet as a whole had considerable
charm and remained in the repertoire right up to the time Tudor left the Ballet
Club.

In *Atalanta of the East* (1933) Tudor followed the example of Fokine by
composing an Indian ballet. The stimulus for this was provided by the visit of
Uday Shankar two years before. Tudor showed his exceptional musical sensitivity by recognizing the impossibility of setting Indian movements to Western
music, and choosing as the accompaniment for his ballet a setting of Oriental
melodies for Western instruments. This style was too foreign to Tudor and his
dancers for him to achieve a fully satisfying synthesis of East and West, but he

learned a great deal about expressive arm movements in his experiments with mudras. These experiments gave Tudor glimpses of a new world of dance-imagery. He began to see how dance-images could be used to express all the feelings which are too deep and subtle for words, and to move towards a style of his own.

The fact that *Atalanta of the East* was set in a remote country enabled Tudor to achieve the measure of objectivity and distance from his subject which he needed in order to give full expression to his ideas. From the very beginning his outlook was genuinely classical: in contrast to the expressionists (who sought to make their images an expression of their own individual feelings) Tudor sought to step away from his own feelings and give his characters objective reality as part of a self-sufficient whole. He therefore found it natural to work in a number of different genres, trying out different ways of achieving this objectivity.

In *The Planets* (1934) he tried out three different modes of abstraction, choosing three items from Holst's suite *The Planets* which were suitable for the different genres he had in mind.

The first scene, *Venus*, was not very successful, but it had great interest as the prototype of the Proustian genre which later became very important in his work. In this scene he made considerable use of movements which remained fairly close to standard classroom steps, and the atmosphere was romantic and lyrical. The chief rôle was that of a young girl on the verge of adolescence, for whom Tudor composed movements that were tender and diffident: she moved as if in a dream. Unfortunately the images used by Tudor were not very expressive; apparently he needed the support of a definite period and story to come to grips with the experience underlying this scene.

The style of the next scene, *Mars*, was completely expressionist—so much so that it was easy to imagine the scene being danced by free dancers. Here the major influences were *The Green Table* (performed in London the previous year) and *Le Sacre du Printemps*. Fists were clenched, faces were rigid and expressionless, and movements were jagged and tied mechanically to the pounding rhythms of the music. The Mortal Born under Mars dominated the scene in the same way that Death dominated the stage in *The Green Table*, though Tudor's choreography owed nothing to the crude and unconvincing movements created by Jooss for Death. The four Followers of Mars were helpless puppets, crushed by Mars into soulless uniformity and showing only the most violent emotions. Even the Mortal Born under Mars was lacking in individuality: though he dominated the stage, he too was a puppet in the grip of blind, inhuman forces.

Though *Mars* was admirably successful within the limits of the genre, serious expressionism made relatively little appeal to Tudor, and he never returned to this genre. Nevertheless the experience of composing an expressionist scene was of great importance to him: in this way he came to understand expressionism from the inside, and was able to use the stylistic discoveries of the expressionists for his own purposes.

His most important achievement in *The Planets* was the rôle of the Mortal Born under Neptune in the final scene. Here he combined hand and arm movements inspired by Indian mudras with relatively classical leg movements, forming images of the utmost precision for the expression of ideas and feelings seldom if ever before expressed in dancing: the mood was highly abstract—the suggestion of man reaching out into new regions of space and thought—and yet the projection of the mood was vivid and exciting. In some curious manner Tudor managed to combine a suggestion of the slow wheeling of planets in space with a suggestion of the intuitive inspiration of the mystic.

In the finale of *The Descent of Hebe* (1936) Tudor came to grips with another aspect of abstraction—the technique of music-interpretation first developed by Duncan and Dalcroze and then taken over by the free dancers. In the final scene of *The Descent of Hebe* Tudor applied Dalcrozian ideas to the classical technique in a completely new way, making his visualization of a fugue the finale of a dramatic ballet. He emphasized the formal nature of his choreography by keeping the dancers moving in straight lines between ground-rows representing clouds—a device probably inspired by *l'Après-Midi d'un Faune*—and yet the effect of the patterns was full of animation and human feeling. In contrast to the expressionists, he seemed to feel no need to reduce his dancers to robots when he used them for the creation of abstract patterns.

In this scene Tudor showed for the first time his extraordinary musical gifts. Fokine had already shown, in *Les Sylphides*, how dance-images could be formed in which the varying relationship between the rhythm and phrasing of the dancing and the rhythm and phrasing of the music was used for expressive purposes. Tudor considerably developed this technique, making use of a flexible relationship between music and dancing for a hundred different purposes. Normally his aim was the expression of nuances of mood, but in the finale of *The Descent of Hebe* his aim was the adaptation of the musical structure of Bloch's fugue to the laws of dancing and the special requirements of this scene as a finale to a dramatic ballet, bringing together all the characters in a musical resolution of the action. He solved the problems involved in this adaptation with such success that the visual fugue gave a delightful impression of spontaneity and inevitability, though in fact the relations between the dancing and the music were very complex.

In 1936, two years after the production of *The Planets*, Tudor was ready to solve the problems which eluded him in the first scene of this ballet. Instead of using the abstract style of *The Planets* he secured the necessary measure of distance from his theme by setting it in the past. To some extent, however, *Jardin aux Lilas* was abstract: Tudor made no effort to tell a straightforward story in the manner of a play, preferring to show various aspects of a crisis in the relationship between four people and to control the flow of time to suit his own purposes. The ballet gave almost the impression of a dream, with simple every-day actions such as the shaking of hands combining with dance-images of great power and technical complexity in a tissue of movements that had rare poetic intensity.

It was not possible to recognize in *Jardin aux Lilas* the influence of any other ballet: by this time Tudor had formed his own style, and all the movements seemed to belong only to this ballet. The most obvious influences were those of Proust and Bergson: Tudor adapted to ballet Bergsonian ideas about time, memory, consciousness and determinism, in the same way that Proust adapted them to the novel. Like Proust, Tudor showed a remarkably delicate sensitivity to the impressions and moods of different types of person; like Proust, he gave his images the freshness of the experiences of childhood and of a certain type of vivid dream.[1] Tudor seemed able to go straight to the heart of experience, avoiding all the stereotyped patterns established by previous choreographers, and his work so successful that this ballet has been taken into the repertoires of no less than five companies.[2] *Jardin aux Lilas* has achieved much wider fame than any other English ballet.

Tudor's technique of controlling the flow of time in *Jardin aux Lilas* owed something to films, but it owed still more to the technique developed by Proust in his great novel *À la Recherche du Temps Perdu*. At some moments Tudor slowed down the flow of time to make clear the implications of certain gestures; and at one moment he even stopped it entirely, in order to make clear Caroline's feelings at the moment when she realizes that she will never see her lover again. Like Proust, Tudor was concerned not only with the feelings and inner conflicts of his characters but of the ambience in which they moved: he used a series of short entrances by members of the corps de ballet (playing separate rôles as guests at the garden-party) to build up a dream-like atmosphere surrounding the four main characters.

Like Proust, Tudor showed a strong feeling for the past as something alive and significant. For this reason he found it perfectly natural to use movements relatively close to standard classroom steps as part of the texture of a ballet which broke away violently from previous models. Sometimes in *Jardin aux*

---

[1] *Cf.* Bergson, *Time and Free Will*, p. 8: "How do you become aware of a deep passion, once it has taken hold of you, if not by perceiving that the same objects no longer impress you in the same manner? All your sensations and all your ideas seem to brighten up: it is like child-hood back again. We experience something of the kind in certain dreams. . . ."

[2] Rambert Ballet, London Ballet, Ballet Theatre, Royal Swedish Ballet and New York City Ballet.

Lilas he used the classical technique as a symbol for the forces of convention, driving Caroline into a marriage of convenience and destroying natural human feelings; at other times he used the elevation steps of the classical technique—with the wonderful control in the air which they provide—to symbolize a desperate but fruitless attempt to break away from social convention.

In previous ballets (notably in *Lysistrata* and *The Descent of Hebe*) Tudor had shown a fine talent for creating convincing female rôles: in *Jardin aux Lilas* this talent flowered into a truly Proustian capacity for understanding feminine psychology and creating fully rounded female characters. The two female principals of *Jardin aux Lilas* are admirably contrasted, and both have an extraordinary vitality and truth. In fact, for the first time in the twentieth century, a choreographer succeeded in emulating the achievements of good dramatists, novelists and film directors in presenting characters with all their inner conflicts, mixed emotions and unpredictable changes of mood.

Certain aspects of *Jardin aux Lilas* suggested a strong influence from the second volume of Proust's novel, *Un Amour de Swann*, even though the characters and incidents in the ballet were quite different from those of the novel. The lilacs of the décor which did so much to establish the atmosphere of the ballet were possibly inspired by those in Swann's garden; and the main theme of Chausson's *Poème* for violin and orchestra (which Tudor used as the music of the ballet) might easily have been the "petite phrase" which haunted Swann and was associated in his mind with Odette.

The only serious weakness of *Jardin aux Lilas* was Tudor's treatment of the two principal male rôles: these were only lightly sketched in, and had little of the poetic intensity of the leading female rôles. (This did not matter in the case of the Bridegroom, superbly mimed by Tudor himself—it seemed natural that this character should hide his feelings and behave with frigid conventionality—but it represented a weakness in the treatment of the rôle of Caroline's lover.) In fact Tudor was hampered in his teatment of male rôles by the deficiencies of his own technique and the technical deficiencies and emotional immaturity of his principal male dancer, Hugh Laing. Fortunately the lack of solidity in the part of Caroline's lover was compensated by the superb performance of Peggy van Praagh in the complex and exacting rôle of "The Woman in his Past". She was able to realize Tudor's ideas with perfect understanding and imaginative intensity, and he was able to work out all his ideas on her, even if the danseuses to whom he later assigned the movements were unable to do justice to them.

In spite of the strong influence of Bergson and Proust on *Jardin aux Lilas* it was completely English in feeling. This quality was hard to define, though obvious to the spectator. It emerged in Tudor's acceptance of tradition as something fresh and living—something that took its place in the centre of his imagery without in any way hampering him from saying anything he had to say. It was also evident in the complete economy of effort at all times: some of the most striking effects were obtained with a minimum of movement, and this was particularly true of his own rôle. The romantic atmosphere of the lilac-drenched garden was at the same time typically Proustian and typically English. (Much of this atmosphere emerged through Tudor's skilful marshalling of a large number of small details of costume, grouping and above all lighting; with his long practical experience of lighting he was able to plan the choreography so that it would make its due effect in combination with specific lighting effects, which in effect formed part of the choreography.)

In certain important respects *Jardin aux Lilas* was classical in the manner of Stendhal rather than Proustian: Tudor avoided precisely those unclassical aspects of Proust (his impressionist prolixity and his expressionist tendency to confuse his own experiences with those of the narrator of his novel) in which Proust showed himself a child of his time. Proust's prolixity, in particular, was due to the fact that his medium (words) was not suited to the depiction of the complex moods and sensations which formed the material of his novel. As Bergson says,

> the word with well-defined outlines, the rough and ready word, which stores up the stable, common, and consequently impersonal element in the impressions of mankind, overwhelms or at least covers over the fugitive impressions of our individual consciousness.[1]

In *Jardin aux Lilas* Tudor used a type of dance-imagery which enabled him to pin down fugitive feelings and impressions with admirable economy and precision, constructing a carefully planned sequence of episodes which gave a picture of the cross-currents of emotion joining together four people at a crisis in their lives: there was nothing in his economical choreography to compare with the tortuous labyrinth of Proust's endless paragraphs. In the same way Tudor maintained an austere classical detachment from his theme, giving himself (as in nearly all his ballets) a relatively small rôle, and building up this rôle into a self-sufficient whole with no apparent connection with his own personality.

His next ballet, *Dark Elegies* (1937), was unmistakably a work of genius,[2]

---

[1] *Time and Free Will*, p. 132.

[2] The ballet showed its full stature for the first time at the end of 1938, when Tudor produced it with his own company, the London Ballet. American and English critics unfamiliar with the work of this company have treated *Pillar of Fire* as Tudor's greatest ballet, but in fact *Pillar of Fire* was less satisfactory as a whole than the London Ballet production of *Dark Elegies*. John Martin's statement that *Dark Elegies* has "nothing like the same appeal as *Jardin aux Lilas*" (*World Book of Modern Ballet*, p. 70) applies only to the Ballet Theatre productions of the two ballets: *Dark Elegies* was in fact the most popular ballet in the repertoire of the London Ballet.

even when produced by the Ballet Rambert[1] under very unsatisfactory conditions. Certain sections (the first song, the storm scene and the ending) were completely successful, and it was possible to see the potentialities of the other sections through the inadequate performances. In this ballet Tudor took over many of the discoveries of the expressionists during the previous fifteen years and used them in a completely new way. *Dark Elegies* broke away from all existing models quite as strongly as *Le Sacre du Printemps*, yet it had deep roots in tradition, and was completely classical in feeling.

Tudor gave extraordinary power to his theme (parents mourning the death of their children) by treating it in the reserved, near-abstract manner of the Neptune scene in *The Planets* rather than in the dramatic manner of *Jardin aux Lilas*. Like many painters, sculptors and composers he seemed to find that his artistic development demanded that he should swing between the poles of abstraction and realism.

Before composing *Dark Elegies* he experimented for two years to clarify the types of movement he wanted to use, and to work out certain key images which later became focal points in the ballet. (During these experiments he used only dancers who were able to seize his ideas quickly and give them imaginative expression.) When he began work with the whole company he created auxiliary images, adapting himself when necessary to the personality and technique of the dancer in question. (He had used a similar technique of composition on *Jardin aux Lilas*, but he perfected it while working on *Dark Elegies*.)

Since *Dark Elegies* was far more abstract than *Jardin aux Lilas* he had to take even greater care of nuances of line, rhythm and feeling in the performance of all the dancers. He also had to make the male characters strong enough to balance the female characters. He worked with great imagination on both these problems, and solved them brilliantly.

Many influences from expressionism could be traced in *Dark Elegies*. The semi-circular groups of kneeling women showed affinities with similar groups in the Martha Graham theatre piece *Primitive Mysteries*: this was never shown in London, but it is likely that Tudor heard about Martha Graham's work from Agnes de Mille.[2] The flat hands of the dancers in some of the passages recall the stylized position of the hands in nearly all expressionist works, from *Petrouchka* onwards, and now and again Tudor used a modified form of the Delsartian impulse. The circular representation of a storm recalled the storm scene in *Le Sacre du Printemps*, and the upraised arm of the dancer of the first song in *Dark Elegies* also recalled a position of the Chosen Virgin in *Sacre*.

In spite of these expressionist details the general feeling of *Dark Elegies* was

[1] When the Ballet Club appeared in the West End in one of its annual seasons Marie Rambert called it the Ballet Rambert. *Dark Elegies* was first produced in the West End, and only later at the Mercury Theatre.

[2] *Cf.* Agnes de Mille, *Dance to the Piper*, p. 220.

Planets (Tudor, London, 1934) with Maude Lloyd (Attendant on Neptune), Antony Tudor (Planet Neptune) and Kyra Nijinska (Mortal Born Under Neptune)

in aux Lilas (Tudor, London, 1936) with Hugh Laing as Her Lover, Peggy van Praagh as The *man* in His Past, Antony Tudor as The Man She Must Marry, and Maude Lloyd as Caroline

not in the least expressionist. They took their place in a web of imagery in which each movement seemed to belong to *Dark Elegies* and to no other ballet. (Apart from expressionist ideas, Tudor took many ideas from Kabuki, tap-dancing, folk-dances, etc.)

There was a significant contrast between the endings of *Dark Elegies* and of the expressionist ballet *Le Sacre du Printemps* (with which *Dark Elegies* had certain affinities). *Sacre* ended with a paroxysm—the violent death of the Chosen Virgin. *Elegies* had a quiet ending, with the dancers walking off in pairs one behind the other. The last person to leave the stage (Peggy van Praagh) moved offstage quite slowly, with subdued *jetés* that had a sad, lyrical poetry very rare in ballet. This quiet ending was typical of Tudor, and reflected his classical outlook.

The first version of *Dark Elegies* was produced by Tudor under great difficulties: Tudor had to use a number of dancers who could understand very little of his ideas, and Marie Rambert interfered in the casting. The season ended with quarrels even more bitter than usual, and Tudor left the company—something he had wanted to do for a long time. The future was dark for him, but he knew that he could not make any further progress without breaking away from the Ballet Club and establishing a professional company of his own.

Between 1938 and 1941 *Dark Elegies* was superbly danced by Tudor's own company, the London Ballet. Tudor did a great deal of work on the choreography, altering all the weak passages and achieving a remarkably high standard of expressiveness in all the dances. In fact this ballet became for the London Ballet what *The Three Sisters* was to the Moscow Art Theatre. In spite of the fact that it was based on a cycle of songs sung in German,[1] *Dark Elegies* as performed by the London Ballet was as English as Purcell's opera *Dido and Aeneas*: the feelings evoked by Tudor had much the same simplicity and directness as Dido's Lament. Though the ballet was unlike any previous ballet in many ways, and baffled the critics completely at its first performance, it soon won its way into the hearts of the public. It made a very strong impression on the dancers of Tudor's company, who came to maturity dancing in it.

During the next few years Tudor's development was severely limited by the fact that he had to spend his energy struggling desperately to raise money and make bricks without straw. In some respects his position was like that of Nijinsky after the latter's break with Diaghilev.

In June, 1937, Tudor produced *Gallant Assembly* for his newly formed company Dance Theatre. This was an attempt at an eighteenth-century ballet with a vicious type of satirical humour that Tudor had never used before. Here Tudor seemed to be applying to ballet Bergsonian ideas about the nature of

---

[1] *Dark Elegies* was composed by Tudor to Mahler's *Kindertotenlieder*—songs for the death of children.

comedy. (In his famous book *Le Rire* Bergson described laughter as arising when a person behaved as a mechanical puppet, reacting in a rigid manner to events, rather than as a flexible, integrated individual who is sensitive to changes in the world around him.) Tudor treated the "Aristocrats in Love" as puppets, performing formal movements in a stiff expressionist manner, and making ludicrous obscene gestures; here one could see some influence from Massine's Italianate expressionist ballets. The Hired Performers (also in love) danced period movements in a relatively smooth, lyrical manner. Clearly Tudor intended the humour to arise from the contrast between the two types of love. This attempt at humour was ponderous and unsuccessful: as in the first scene of *The Planets*, he was trying out a new style with considerable potentialities, and later profited considerably from this work even though at the time it did not express what he intended.

After Tudor had struggled unsuccessfully for a year to raise the capital for putting his company on a permanent basis he composed a ballet *Judgment of Paris*, commissioned by Agnes de Mille for a show at the Westminster Theatre. This ballet was even more bitter than *Gallant Assembly*, and (within its limits) was completely successful. The theme of the ballet (suggested by Hugh Laing) was a satirical version of the classical myth evoked by the title of the ballet, with the figures of mythology transposed into characters in a brothel. In atmosphere the ballet had much in common with Kurt Weill's expressionist version of *The Beggar's Opera*, and Tudor used Weill's music for his ballet. Tudor's choreography was completely expressionist: the action was presented through naturalistic mime, and the "dances" of the prostitutes were as amateurish as they would have been in real life.

In spite of its prosaic naturalism *Judgment of Paris* was saved from banality by the Swiftian *saeva indignatio* of Tudor's satire, the perfect harmony between all the elements of the ballet, and the solid dramatic structure. In this ballet Tudor returned to the play-like dramatic structure which had been normal in ballet up to the time of Fokine and Nijinsky, and which Tudor himself had used in *Lysistrata*.

To make its proper effect *Judgment of Paris* needed to be performed by the prostitutes with a sordid viciousness that was slightly outside the range of the dancers in the London Ballet, though the ballet provided useful contrast in the repertoire of this company. Many years later, in 1950, Paula Hinton (admirably rehearsed by Walter Gore) gave one of the prostitutes all the vulgarity needed in the rôle, and made the ballet extremely funny; the same thing happened in 1952, when Margaret Scott and Joyce Graeme re-joined the Rambert Ballet as guest artists to dance in this ballet for two special performances at the Lyric, Hammersmith.

In many ways *Judgment of Paris* was the antithesis of *Dark Elegies*, and it was hardly surprising that the artists who achieved such a fine interpretation of the lyrical and tragic quality of *Elegies* found it difficult to adjust themselves to the sordid naturalism of *Judgment*. In *Elegies* Tudor used typical movements from expressionist ballets in a new way, so that they created an effect which was noble and classical: in *Judgment*, on the other hand, he composed a completely expressionist ballet without making use of any movements from previous expressionist ballets.

Even when Tudor had his own company at Toynbee Hall he was still hampered by lack of capital and the necessity of building up a balanced repertoire: instead of moving on from *Jardin aux Lilas* and *Dark Elegies* he had to devote himself to divertissement ballets like *Soirée Musicale* and *Gala Performance*.

One of Tudor's new productions at Toynbee Hall—*Mercury*, a scene added to *The Planets*—gave some hint of what he might have achieved if he had found a patron or impresario. This scene was experimental in the way that the first three scenes had been. In it Tudor suggested the volatility of Mercury by the use of extremely fast and complicated counter-rhythms and quick darting movements. The effect was exhilarating, though as baffling at first as the rhythms in *Les Noces*.

The saddest aspect of Tudor's period at the head of the London Ballet was that he had no opportunity of putting *Pillar of Fire* into rehearsal. This ballet was devised by Tudor for soloists who had come to maturity under his care in *Jardin aux Lilas* and *Dark Elegies*, and undoubtedly would have surpassed even *Dark Elegies*.

Tudor joined Ballet Theatre in 1939, but delayed producing *Pillar of Fire* until Nora Kaye was sufficiently mature to do justice to the central rôle of Hagar. The ballet was actually produced in 1942, and was immediately recognized in the United States as a masterpiece, though it suffered severely from the fact that Tudor had to adapt it to a company very different from the one for which it was intended. While producing *Jardin aux Lilas* for Ballet Theatre in 1940 he had found it necessary to make his effects in a bold theatrical way, ignoring nuances of mood which were beyond the scope of the dancers at his disposal, and this experience naturally affected him when he came to produce *Pillar of Fire*. Fortunately he had three sensitive artists at his disposal—Nora Kaye, Hugh Laing and himself—and he composed rôles for these artists so strong that they were able to carry the main weight of the ballet on their shoulders.

In style *Pillar of Fire* represented a fusion of *Jardin aux Lilas* and *Dark Elegies*. Tudor used the classical technique for symbolic purposes in much the same way as in *Jardin*, but he composed dance-images drawing on the full range of movement used by him in *Elegies*. Though the structure of *Pillar of Fire* was based on that of *Jardin*, Tudor evolved a large number of new devices in order to deal with the complex theme of the later ballet. This was particularly true of his devices for controlling the flow of time. In *Pillar of Fire* the psychic transformations in the heroine required the passage of considerable time—perhaps several months—and Tudor chose to represent these transformations choreographically, instead of letting the audience imagine them happening during intervals between scenes, as in a play. He therefore found it essential to use a much higher degree of abstraction than in *Jardin*, even though—as in *Jardin*—he established the factual, individual quality of Hagar's experience by means of naturalistic details such as the smoothing of a dress. The contrast between these everyday gestures and the glorious breadth and rhythmic power of the dance-images had something of the same poignant quality as the similar contrasts in Shakespeare's plays between full-blooded rhetoric and prosaic statements such as Lear's "Pray you, undo this button: thank you, sir." As in *Jardin* and *Elegies*, the solos, pas de deux, pas de trois, etc., emerged in a natural way as part of the exposition of the theme: at no time did they take shape as self-sufficient dances (like the solos in pseudo-classical ballets), though some of the dancing demanded a very high degree of technical skill.

The extreme technical complexity underlying the apparent ease and spontaneity of *Pillar of Fire* was made clear when Nora Kaye danced in this ballet after Tudor and Hugh Laing had left Ballet Theatre. Tudor's partnering had been so perfect that it was never possible to see how Nora Kaye achieved her effects: the images emerged in a simple and easy manner, and the whole emphasis was on the emotional effect intended by the choreographer at each moment. When Nora Kaye danced with another partner there were split-seconds of hesitation when one could see her prepare for some particularly difficult lift or turn, and then it was obvious that the Tudor choreography demanded in the ballerina almost unbelievable strength and control—in fact more strength and control than many of the dazzling effects in ballets by Petipa or post-expressionist pseudo-classicists.

Though Nora Kaye danced superbly in *Pillar of Fire*, and Tudor was able to make the most exacting demands on her technique, she never achieved the same degree of maturity and subtlety that Tudor was able to obtain from his best London ballerinas (Peggy van Praagh and Gerd Larsen[1]). This was no discredit to Nora Kaye: with her background she inevitably tackled the rôle in a quasi-expressionistic manner, and concentrated on giving the most powerful possible expression to those aspects of the rôle which were within her emotional range.

In the two leading male rôles Hugh Laing and Tudor himself went far

---

[1] Gerd Larsen later became fairly well known through dancing small parts with the Sadlers Wells Ballet, but was always badly miscast, and had no chance to display the remarkable talent she had shown in *Dark Elegies*.

beyond anything they had previously achieved. Hugh Laing had only a relatively short part, but he danced it with such intensity that it changed the whole atmosphere of the ballet, as in fact the theme required. Tudor had continued to mature as a dancer step by step with his development as a choreographer, and in *Pillar of Fire* he was able to give himself enchaînements far more technically difficult than ever before. His rôle was extremely difficult from the point of view of interpretation, for he had to suggest not only the real man with whom Hagar was in love but the ideal man of her fevered imagination. Tudor achieved this with such complete success that his performance looked quite simple, and dominated the stage to exactly the extent required by the theme at any moment: in fact his rôle was so exacting that no dancer could replace him in it.

Pillar of Fire was not in the least experimental. Tudor knew from experience exactly how to obtain the effects he had in mind, and presented the tangled feelings of Hagar with supreme economy and precision of imagery: stage by stage Hagar's feelings of love, hatred, jealousy and self-contempt were laid bare, and then her gradual development towards self-knowledge and emotional maturity.

One important reason why Tudor chose Schönberg's tone-poem *Verklärte Nacht* as the basis for a ballet was clearly the fact that the theme of the poem which inspired the music appealed strongly to Tudor; but the period and style of Schönberg's late-romantic music were also important to Tudor. In his satirical expressionist ballet *Judgment of Paris* he had used jazzy music from the hey-day of expressionism, even though the costumes suggested a rather earlier period. In his serious ballets with a classical feeling (i.e. *Jardin aux Lilas, Dark Elegies* and *Pillar of Fire*) he found it essential to achieve some distance from his theme by setting it in the past—not a remote past, but a past sufficiently close to seem disturbingly actual without having the chaotic banality of contemporary life. The past which suited him best was the end of the nineteenth century, and characteristic music of this period—by Mahler, Chausson and Schönberg—helped him to come to grips with his theme in the concrete and precise manner habitual to him.

Even though Schönberg's music had never been intended as a basis for choreography, and in fact seemed to the lay ear almost undanceable, Tudor seemed to find it admirably suited to his purpose. He made use of a subtle and extremely flexible technique for adjusting the tempi, rhythms, phrasing and dynamics of his choreography to the corresponding features of the music without doing violence to the latter.

What he did was to absorb the music with all its nuances and then work out the structure of his ballet in such a way that the music fitted into it as one of its elements. This sensitive and imaginative technique was similar to that used by

Fokine in ballets like *Les Sylphides*, *Carnaval* and *Spectre de la Rose*; it was very different from the cerebral methods used by Benois in working out the plot of *Schéhérazade*.

The fact that the music employed by Tudor in *Pillar of Fire* and his other serious ballets had a somewhat overstuffed, late-Romantic texture, while his own style of composition was severely classical, did not worry him: he used the texture of the music as one element in his composition, just as he used period costumes, romantic lighting and occasional naturalistic gestures. In fact his classicism had so many elements of romanticism in it that he might be called a romantic classicist—like nearly all the great choreographers using the classical technique from Noverre onwards.

By this time Tudor was completely master of his medium. If he still absorbed new ideas of movement from the ballets of other choreographers and from traditional styles of dancing, he assimilated these ideas so perfectly that it was impossible to trace their influence. On the other hand he was clearly absorbing a variety of ideas from philosophy and psychology, and widening his understanding of human nature. In *Pillar of Fire* he used his heroine Hagar to some extent in the same way that Proust used his narrator, giving form to the flux of images by showing events more or less with the emotional colouring they had for Hagar. Here one could see the influence on Tudor of Bergson's ideas about consciousness and Proust's application of these theories (together with the similar theories of Proust's teacher Darlu).

The influence of Freud on Tudor was no less profound. Tudor belonged to the generation which grew up at a time when the ideas of Freud were just becoming part of the cultural environment of every civilized human being, and Tudor assimilated these ideas as naturally as he assimilated Darwin's ideas about evolution. When he came to tackle a theme like that of *Pillar of Fire*, he inevitably made use of Freudian ideas in his treatment of the theme. The fact that Freud's work enabled Tudor to understand the torments suffered by Hagar more clearly than he would otherwise have done in no way cramped his imaginative grasp of the theme: far from treating Hagar as an extract from a psychiatrist's case-book he made her into a fully rounded individual, with something of the magical quality that invests the figures of mythology.

Two years after *Pillar of Fire*, in 1944, Tudor composed *Undertow*. This lacked the mature perfection of *Pillar of Fire*, but went beyond it in some respects, and opened up a number of new paths.

In devising the structure of *Undertow* Tudor was clearly influenced by *À la Recherche du Temps Perdu*. The Transgressor—the central figure of the ballet—was the equivalent of the narrator of Proust's novel, all events being shown entirely as they appeared to him. The prologue of the ballet (in which the Transgressor is born, and grows into a child in love with its mother and jealous of its father) corresponded to the first volume of the novel, *Du Côté de Chez Swann*, which shows the entire childhood of the narrator (who is obsessively in love with his mother and regards his father with cool respect). The main scene of the ballet consisted of a series of linked episodes which corresponded in a general way to the central volumes of the novel, though the events and the characters were completely different. The epilogue of the ballet (in which The Transgressor re-lives the memory of the events leading up to his crime) corresponded to the last volume of the novel, *Le Temps Retrouvé*.

Tudor showed great skill in adapting the structure of the long novel to the requirements of a ballet of normal length and to his own theme (which differed considerably from Proust's, even though the two themes moved in much the same direction). In Proust's novel the narrator is the alter ego of Proust himself, and the whole long novel leads up to the point in *Le Temps Retrouvé* where the narrator succeeds in making contact with the creative powers locked in his unconscious. At last he is able to recapture his memories of the past: his resistances and repressions are resolved, and he is a whole person, no longer tormented by doubts, hesitations, anxiety and the fear of death. The narrator finds the key to the past in insignificant details on which he stumbles almost by accident. Things are very different in Tudor's ballet: the Transgressor is lifted out of his miasma of fear, guilt and repression by the terrifying experience of the murder, and then comes to maturity by living through the memories of the past and seeing them with new understanding. But his moment of self-discovery —like that of Oedipus—comes too late. The Transgressor was the tragic counterpart of Hagar, who also reached maturity after a harrowing experience but had not been marked down by the Fates for destruction.[1]

In style *Undertow* was a very strange mixture. Roughly half the ballet—the rôle of the Transgressor, who was on stage almost the whole time—was composed in a style related to that of the Proustian dramatic ballets *Jardin aux Lilas* and *Pillar of Fire*. The other half of the ballet was composed in an expressionist style related to that of *Judgment of Paris*.

Though Tudor was justified in making a clear distinction between the style of the dancing of the Transgressor and that of characters who had no existence except as fragments of the Transgressor's consciousness, he carried this distinction to such lengths that even the rôle of the Transgressor suffered: one would have thought that only in his vaguest dreams would the Transgressor see the people around him in such a simplified form. The latter were in fact

---

[1] Tudor almost never provides audiences with a programme-note giving a synopsis of his ballets, and gives only a hint of the theme in the title and in the descriptions attached to the names of some of the characters. For this reason spectators are liable to vary widely in their interpretation of his ballets. John Martin, for example, gives an interpretation of *Undertow* very different from mine (*World Book of Modern Ballet*, p. 90). One interpretation does not of course exclude another: Tudor's dance-imagery is so complex and evocative that his ballets have several different levels of meaning.

realized just as fully as their counterparts in *Judgment of Paris*, but they *appeared* thin by comparison with the extraordinary length and complexity of the central rôle; it was almost as if Tudor had pinned labels to them saying "Lecherous Old Man", "Gold-Digger" and so on.

The rôle of Transgressor was built up by Tudor with hundreds of vivid details of imagery until it took on the disturbing and contradictory reality of a character in a great novel or play: in other words Tudor succeeded in doing for a male character what he had already done for female characters in *Jardin aux Lilas* and *Pillar of Fire*. Hugh Laing lacked Tudor's own extraordinary ability to dominate the stage without making any movement, but he was perfectly cast in the rôle, he was very carefully rehearsed by Tudor, and he danced the rôle with such sensitivity and understanding that he made the defects of the ballet as a whole seem of small importance. He was particularly good in the long and difficult solo of remembrance at the beginning of the epilogue: here Tudor moved into completely new territory, and the effort of imagination demanded of Laing was equivalent to that demanded of Peggy van Praagh when Tudor began to compose the first solo of *Dark Elegies*. The darting, flickering quality of his movements suggested admirably the sudden movement of his mind through his memories of past experiences.

Only at one point did Tudor make a bridge between the two halves of his ballet. This was in the terrifying erotic pas de deux of Medusa and the Transgressor, ending up with the murder of the former by the latter. In this pas de deux Tudor blended his two styles, arranging for Medusa to develop greater and greater powers of fascination step by step with the gathering tempest in the soul of the Transgressor, until at last the conflicting emotions within him (love-hatred, attraction-repulsion) reached an unbearable intensity. One interesting aspect of this pas de deux was Tudor's use of the woman's leg (extended in the normal balletic way with a straight knee and a well-pointed toe) as a symbol of male passion. This distortion of ballet tradition was completely foreign to his normal style of choreography, but it represented a characteristically expressionist view of the classical technique: Agnes de Mille, for example, describes the classical danseuse as regarding the tautening of her back and leg in exactly this way.[1] Here one could see Tudor taking an American idea which was normally unconscious and making it disturbingly explicit, in much the same way that Lorca made explicit Spanish ideas on sex and religion.[2]

Clearly Tudor intended to provide *Undertow* with a quiet ending similar in general character to the endings of his other great serious ballets (*Jardin aux Lilas, Dark Elegies* and *Pillar of Fire*), making a few simple movements, perfectly timed and adjusted with great care to harmonize with the concluding phrases

---

[1] *Dance to the Piper*, p. 59. *See* also below, p. 230.
[2] *Cf.* Arturo Barea, *Lorca: The Poet and his People*, pp. 30–52.

of the music, serve to resolve in a satisfying manner the conflicts of the ballet. In *Undertow*, hampered by a certain lack of poetry in the finale of the music and by the awkward mixture of styles in the choreography, he was led astray into the use of properties which did not marry well with the dancing, and the significance of the ending was by no means clear to the audience. (Presumably the properties thrown on to the stage were intended to have the same function as the objects in Proust's novel—the bun, the paving-stone and so on—which bring back the memory of the past to the narrator.)

As in Nijinsky's *Sacre* and *Tyl Eulenspiegel*, the minor rôles in *Undertow* showed serious defects, but these were amply compensated by the extraordinary power and magnitude of the central rôle. Like *Sacre* and *Tyl Eulenspiegel*, *Undertow* aroused bitter controversies, and was quickly dropped from the repertoire.

There were violent changes in Ballet Theatre in the next few years, and it was not until 1948 that Tudor was given the chance to compose another ambitious ballet. He chose to compose a work of enormous length—a semi-abstract ballet in roughly the same genre as *Dark Elegies*, based on Mahler's symphony *Das Lied von der Erde*. Mahler's symphony takes the form of a very elaborate setting of a group of poems by the Chinese poet Li Po, and Tudor's choreography was also based to some extent on these poems, though (as in *Dark Elegies*) he took into account the generalized mood of the music rather than the detailed meanings of the words.

No ballet was composed in stranger circumstances than *Shadow of the Wind*. Tudor had the habit when composing exacting serious ballets of leaving a few details to the last moment, but what happened with *Shadow of the Wind* was something very different: according to Agnes de Mille,[1] forty-eight hours before the first performance forty-eight minutes of the music remained to be set.

The choreography inevitably varied even more in quality than that of *Undertow*: cutting a symphony was impossible, and Tudor had to arrange long scenes for dancers with no possibility of their being able to understand his abstract style. In the best passages, however, he created effects of unearthly beauty—images floating in a world of their own outside time and space. Like the *Mercury* scene which he added to *The Planets* in 1939, the magical passages in *Shadow of the Wind* gave hints of new worlds of fantasy which Tudor might have explored if he had had the chance to work under good conditions.

Tudor then left Ballet Theatre, which was rapidly losing all the qualities which had attracted to it Tudor himself and a number of distinguished dancers such as Hugh Laing, Nora Kaye and Diana Adams, who did their best work in his ballets. The latter artists joined New York City Ballet, and in due course this organization commissioned some ballets from Tudor: unfortunately the

[1] *Dance to the Piper*, p. 176.

artistic climate of the New York City Ballet was no more stimulating to Tudor than that of Ballet Theatre in its declining years.

In some ways the most puzzling of all the ballets composed by Tudor in the United States was *La Gloire*, produced by him in 1952 for the New York City Ballet. In this ballet he took up the theme of the fading actress, jealous of a young rival, which was very much in the air at the time (having been used both in a film and in a play); this theme was suggested by Lincoln Kirstein, director-general of the company. As one might expect, Tudor gave the principal rôles to Hugh Laing, Nora Kaye and Diana Adams. In its structure *La Gloire* was of the highest interest, with Tudor showing his familiar mastery over the flow of time: he telescoped together three different performances by the fading actress and a number of scenes in the wings, and presented a death-scene in such an ambiguous way that it was hard to say whether it took place in the ballet or in the play within the ballet. On the other hand the underlying theme of the ballet remained obscure, and the texture of the choreography showed a bewildering mixture of satirical expressionism, parodies of other ballets and academic classicism.

Tudor's experiences in the United States were very different from those of his contemporary W. H. Auden, who came to the United States at about the same time. Auden (as Richard Hoggart has pointed out) was driven to go to the United States by his need for loneliness and isolation. Hoggart quotes Auden as saying that "the attractiveness of America to a writer is its openness and lack of tradition. In a way it's frightening. . . . There is no past. No tradition. No roots."[1] Tudor's needs as a creative artist were almost the exact opposite of those of Auden. He could not create except when he could establish roots stretching into the past: tradition was as all-important to him as it was to Proust. In his semi-abstract ballets his reliance on tradition was quite as absolute as in his Proustian dramatic ballets: *Dark Elegies*, for example, was to a considerable extent inspired by folk-dances, in the same way that Mahler based his songs on the German lieder tradition which had roots in folk-song and folk-dance. It was equally important for Tudor to work with dancers who could understand intuitively what he wanted their movements to express: often the most important aspects of interpretation cannot be described in words, and Tudor's outlook was so essentially English that it was very difficult for him to establish this *rapport* with American dancers. (Even a great artist like Nora Kaye could not achieve certain qualities of expression which were within the range of the youngest member of the London Ballet.)

After over a decade of residence in the United States Tudor was still completely English. In the United States he was like a fish on dry land: he could still move to some extent, but only with a disproportionate effort, and he could

[1] *Auden, An Introductory Essay*, p. 136.

no longer breathe properly or absorb nutriment. This was a question of temperament, not of race or nationality. If he had been born in the United States, he would have probably found his way to England in the wake of Henry James and T. S. Eliot. Though Tudor's work gave great pleasure to American audiences, his ballets were produced under very unsatisfactory conditions, and gave a very limited idea of what he was capable of doing when working with a company of English dancers selected by him. In view of the fact that after the War English companies began to take English ballet to the United States, one must consider that the ballets which Tudor failed to produce after 1939 because of his exile from England represented almost as great a loss to the United States as to England. The fact that America provided him for a time with the financial support that he looked for in vain in England does not make this loss any the less tragic.

Birgit Åkesson: Post-Expressionist Free Dance

BIRGIT ÅKESSON stands in much the same relationship to the free dance as Tudor to ballet based on the classical technique. Like Tudor, she came to maturity during the decline of expressionism, breaking away from expressionism to found a new style but retaining many of the most important innovations of the expressionists. Like Tudor, she worked completely alone, swimming doggedly against the tide and finding stimulus in work done in other arts rather than in the work of her contemporaries among dancers and choreographers. Unlike Tudor, however, she had no support from tradition, and her development was inevitably much slower than his.

She left Sweden in 1931 to study with Mary Wigman, who was then the most famous of all free dancers, and whose school at Dresden attracted dancers from all over the world. The students at the Wigman-Schule (nearly all of them girls) worshipped Mary Wigman as a goddess, and worked with the utmost fanaticism to mould themselves into her likeness. Birgit Åkesson had outstanding talent, and in spite of her youth and inexperience was chosen as one of the leading members of the Wigman dance group for the first American tour (1932); unlike her colleagues, however, she had a very strong personality of her own, and retained this in spite of the atmosphere of hysterical adulation which surrounded her. This gave her movements on the stage a striking individuality, but it also made her unpopular with Wigman, who took care to bring home to her the sacrilegious nature of her conduct by excluding her from the American tour.

After three years Birgit Åkesson became dissatisfied with Wigman's expressionism and came to Paris to work on her own. In Paris there was no teacher from whom she could learn anything useful to her, but the artistic climate was favourable for the creation of an individual style. She gave her first solo recital in 1934 at the Vieux Colombier. Inevitably her early compositions showed considerable Wigman influence, just as Martha Graham's early compositions were much influenced by Ruth St. Denis and Ted Shawn. Working very slowly, with many set-backs, Birgit Åkesson felt her way towards a new style which had no place for arbitrary movements or mannerisms. What she was seeking was a style with the classical virtues of restraint, economy of effort, perfection of line, and infinite subtlety of nuance, avoiding all the hysterical violence characteristic of expressionism.

Like other major innovators Birgit Åkesson had to create a new style and a new technique at the same time. She set out to make every part of her body poetic (i.e. capable of the greatest subtlety of movement and line), whatever the height of her body from the ground and whatever the position of her legs and feet. This required very great strength in her legs and back to give her the necessary control in the more difficult positions, and she developed this strength by means of hundreds of *pliés* in a wide variety of different positions of the feet. In working out these *pliés* she developed remarkable ease and assurance in her control of her back, though her hip positions were very different from the ballet positions developed to give just this control; her technique was in fact closer to that of Balinese classical dancing than ballet.

Her new style differed fundamentally from existing styles of the free dance in coping successfully with the problem of strain. At every moment her hands and her facial expression had the ease and spontaneity characteristic of good classical ballet, showing neither the knotted fingers nor the grimaces characteristic of expressionist dancing. Her face did not show much variety of expression—this was not demanded by the type of dances she was composing——but it had a subtle, mysterious look comparable with that of a great ballet dancer, and her hands seemed to grow in the most natural way from her arms, so that they formed an organic part of the movement without attracting special attention to themselves. This ease and harmony in her hands and face reflected an absence of undesirable tension in the whole of her body: no one can achieve such ease and harmony by conscious effort.[1] Like a good ballet dancer she combined a highly developed technical skill with spontaneity and ease: at each performance she reproduced to within a millimetre, yet without apparent effort, the images she had devised to create a certain effect on the audience when seen from the appropriate angle to the front.

In her mastery of strain and her co-ordination of all her movements with complete economy of effort she was much closer in spirit to Duncan than to Wigman, though she was born too late to see Duncan dance. She differed profoundly from Duncan, however, in placing no reliance on improvisation, and developing a highly complex technique which she could (and did) pass on to students.

One of the most important ways in which she freed herself from her expressionist background was the composition of movement studies based on

---

[1] *Cf.* Marie Rambert's attempt to give this ease and harmony to Agnes de Mille's features by pushing them into the appropriate positions: as Agnes de Mille found by looking in the mirror, her face then looked like a death-mask. (*Dance to the Piper*, p. 184.)

music by Bach—the least expressionist of composers. The style of her early movement studies was still Wigmanesque, but her work with Bach's music helped her move away from Wigman towards a classical style characterized by restraint, economy and harmony.

The first dance in which she succeeded in giving clear expression to her ideals was *Soir Bleu*. This was composed for performance in silence and was highly abstract in style, though each movement had a meaning which could to some extent be described in words. Birgit Åkesson was by no means a pioneer either in working without music or in developing in the direction of abstraction: both dancing without music and abstraction had formed part of the free dance ever since it was created by Isadora Duncan, and both were characteristic of the Wigman style (though Wigman usually accompanied her dances with specially composed percussion music). These trends in the free dance were the choreographic equivalent of parallel trends in painting and sculpture and also to some extent in poetry. What was new about *Soir Bleu* was that it was effective in its abstraction. By breaking away from expressionism Birgit Åkesson was able to do things which the expressionists had striven for in vain. There were no arbitrary mannerisms in the choreography: every movement had a poetic quality that enabled it to play its due part in the structure of the dance as a whole, and the movements had such a clear-cut pattern in time that the absence of music was not noticeable after the first few moments: in fact the movements seemed to create their own kind of visual music. For this reason, *Soir Bleu* was able to hold the attention of audiences and move them emotionally—whereas dances intended to be performed in silence are usually accompanied by a great deal of coughing and audible shuffling from the audience.

Soir Bleu was the plastic equivalent of mysterious lyrical poems like Donne's *Go and Catch a Falling Star* or Blake's *Tyger, Tyger Burning Bright*: each image had great precision, but the logic of their combination was far from obvious, and together they evoked feelings beyond the reach of more normal language. The images followed each other like the mudras in the *abhinaya*[1] of classical Indian dancing. First there was a suggestion of the atmosphere of early evening, with light stretching out great distances to the horizon. Then there was a sudden change of the point of view: the dancer became herself the light, and fell rapidly to the bottom of the sea. Her hands indicated the passage of a shoal of fishes; then she became one of the fishes; and so on. The tempo was slow, and each image was clearly established by repetition and variation before the next image appeared. As in the adages of classical ballet, the slow passages in the Kathakali style of India, and much of the classical dancing of Siam, Cambodia, Java, Bali and Japan, the slow passages in *Soir Bleu* held the attention of the audience by their purity of line and delicate nuances in the quality of movement. At certain

1 *See* below, p. 266.

moments *Soir Bleu* seemed like sculpture in movement rather than dancing in the ordinary sense of the word: each image of movement was based on a single striking position, and the images were connected up by relatively simple bridge passages.

One of the most striking features of Birgit Åkesson's dancing in *Soir Bleu* was its classical impersonality. She seemed to leave behind her own personality when she started to dance, and became the moods which she was interpreting. This loss of individuality and personality did not, as one might expect, lead to a loss of vitality: the images seemed to project themselves to the audience with their own energy, independently of the personality of the artist who created them. Even her face was something quite different from her offstage face.

Soir Bleu represented a turning point in Birgit Åkesson's career, and she retained it in her repertoire, though she made many changes in the details of the choreography as she matured artistically.

Another dance in the same genre as *Soir Bleu* was *Moon and Rain*. This dance did not have the same homogeneity and perfection of structure as *Soir Bleu*, but it had some striking images which pointed the way toward a new style. One such image was a rapid fluttering movement of the arms, suggesting a flag in the wind.

During the War Birgit Åkesson was confined in Sweden, and for various reasons found it very difficult to continue her career as a dancer. After the War she began intensive work again, and made studies leading towards a new style which eventually took shape in *Movement*. This dance was purely abstract, and the images it contained could not be explained at all in words: whereas in *Soir Bleu* the underlying meaning of the dance emerged in the combination of the images and the mysterious alteration in the point of view, in *Movement* the underlying meaning found direct expression in the images themselves.

From a technical point of view *Movement* represented a considerable advance on *Soir Bleu*. There was much greater variety in the type of movement, and most of the movements demanded a very high degree of muscular control. The dance began, for example, with the dancer balanced on one shoulder, one elbow and her head, with her legs and body high in the air; from this position she slowly brought one leg across in front of her body and placed her foot on the ground, moving on from this to quite different positions. These images could easily have appeared acrobatic, but in fact they induced the same feeling of ease and inevitability as the movements of a good classical dancer.

Movement also differed from *Soir Bleu* in the concentration of its imagery. It was no longer possible to distinguish between images and bridge passages: the images seemed to grow and develop in an organic way according to their own laws, like plants photographed by stop-motion cameras. In spite of the lack of any theme which could be described in words, *Movement* was not in the least cerebral, and compelled the attention of the spectator even more forcibly than *Soir Bleu*.

The tempi of *Movement* were far more varied than those of *Soir Bleu*, and from time to time Birgit Åkesson employed the rhythmic sound produced by her feet on the ground for expressive purposes. The device has long been characteristic of Indian dancing, and was an important feature of expressionist dancing from *Le Sacre du Printemps* onwards: Birgit Åkesson used it for her own purposes in a non-expressionist way, just as Tudor used expressionist devices in *Dark Elegies*.

In *Movement* Birgit Åkesson realized the dream which had haunted free dancers ever since the days of Duncan of a purely abstract dance which could stand by itself without the need for any theme describable in words. Laban has described the aspirations of free dancers towards abstraction, using language obviously influenced by the statements of abstract painters and sculptors on their aspirations:

> The modern or abstract dancer attempts to convey an insight into a strange spiritual world of his own. . . . Dance is for these artists a manifestation of those inner forces out of which the complications of human happenings grow. They are not interested in the situations, happenings and conflicts of practical life, not even in the enhanced form in which drama portrays such conflicts. They think that they can scoop deeper from the reality underlying the ordinary experience of life, and that dance is the language in which this deeper awareness is conveyed to the spectator. The plot of all abstract dances consists solely of the development of a characteristic movement-rhythm as it proceeds along certain parts in space. Modern dancers . . . see in these evolutions in space the messengers of ideas and emotions which surpass thought expressible in words. It is obvious that such movements conveying such inner experiences must be carefully selected and assembled into rhythms adequate for the inner sensation. This selection is the result of deep concentration and it might involve strenuous effort taking time to make. The mental or intellectual factor is restricted to the memorizing of the right series of movements which are the result of the selection. Sometimes a title is given to an abstract dance, which does not however indicate any content but solely a mood.[1]

Laban rightly points out that "all traditional folk dances and national dances are abstract in this sense". But folk-dances correspond to a relatively low degree of complexity of social organization and psychological differentiation. In the traditional classical dances of India, which correspond to a high level of civilization, there are a large number of highly complex items of pure dance (*nrtta*): by moving on from *Soir Bleu* to *Movement* Birgit Åkesson made a transition corresponding to the transition in Indian classical dancing from *natya* (a mixture of dramatic expression and pure dance) to *nrtta* (pure dance).[2]

[1] *The Mastery of Movement on the Stage*, p. 157.
[2] *See* below, p. 268.

Opposite: Birgit Åkesson in her dance *Movement* (Stockholm, 1949)

Rodeo (de Mille, New York, 1942—second version) with Allyn McLerie as the Cowgirl (*centre*)

Oklahoma!—the dream ballet *Laurie Makes Up Her Mind* (de Mille, New York, 1943) as produced in London in 1947. *Left:* Lulu Dukes. *Centre:* Marguerite Stewart

After completing the first version of *Movement* (1948) Birgit Åkesson began to feel the need of stimulus from other artists. This was natural enough, for she had been working in complete isolation for nearly a decade, and had been cooped up in Sweden throughout the war. She therefore went on a tour of a number of European countries and the United States, giving recitals and studying the new developments in dancing in the various countries. In New York she came into contact with the work of Martha Graham and Antony Tudor for the first time. Up to then ballet based on the classical technique had meant relatively little to her, but she recognized in the Tudor ballet *Pillar of Fire* the expression of an artistic sensibility which had to some extent been moving parallel to her own, and this ballet affected her deeply. Because her technique differed so greatly from the classical technique there could be no question of direct influence on her compositions, but she was greatly stimulated by Tudor's work.

One of the first results of Birgit Åkesson's tour was her decision to compose movement studies based on the music of Bartok. Her habit of composing her major works for performance in silence was not due to any puritanical objection to music, but simply to the fact that she had never succeeded in finding a composer who could create music that would harmonize with her movement-images. (Such music would have to differ violently from any existing type of music.) It was suggested to her in England that Bartok might suit her type of movement better than any other, and in fact she found this to be true when she composed two movement studies to items from *Microcosmos*. In these studies she worked out images of a new kind, such as one based on the opposition between a stiff arm and a strongly braced shoulder. She now began to employ a greater variety of tensions, particularly in the top half of her body, and also to expand her technical training to facilitate the new types of movement.

Though the Bartok music gave much greater scope to Birgit Åkesson than previous music used by her (notably music by Bach and Hindemith), her Bartok music-studies still had the character of preparatory studies for large-scale works in which she had complete freedom to establish her own rhythms and phrases; and it was not until she composed *Öga: sömn i dröm* (Eye: sleep in the dream), first performed at the Stockholm Royal Opera House in March, 1953, that she was able to give full expression to the new ideas engendered by the stimulus of her foreign tour. Like her earlier major compositions this dance was composed by her slowly and painfully, with many interruptions and blind alleys. The dance took her two years to complete, and lasted twenty minutes; the choreography was devised to make its effect in harmony with a lighting plot (here one could see the influence of the designer and lighting expert Peter Goffin, whom she met in England), and she worked on the dance in collaboration with the composer Karl-Birger Blomdahl and the poet Erik

Lindegren.[1] What one might call its spiritual content was much more complex than in her previous compositions: by means of contrapuntal movements of different parts of her body she gave expression to contrasting moods and inner conflicts.

Though for a number of reasons the most original Swedish artists seem to feel bound to escape from Sweden (at least for a time), it is perhaps possible to detect something characteristically Swedish in the very cosmopolitanism of the best Swedish artists—who assimilate the most advanced trends in European culture and then do something different. In this respect Birgit Åkesson shows some affinity to Strindberg. But in style and temperament she is poles removed from Swedish expressionists such as Strindberg and Borlin. A Parisian critic had some justification for describing her as "the Picasso of the dance", for her formative years were spent in Paris, and she stands apart from her contemporaries quite as much as Picasso; but her style is not in the least Picassian.

One can see many analogies between her dances and the great silent films produced in Sweden in the early twenties—particularly those directed by Stiller. To my mind, however, the artist to whom she shows the greatest affinity is Vermeer, in spite of the fact that she tends towards abstraction (to the extent that any dance performed by a living person can be abstract), whereas Vermeer's paintings give the illusion of naturalistic representation. Much the same mysterious paradoxes underly the work of the two artists. Both seem to need to achieve an inhuman detachment to give expression to themes of which humanity is the essence, both have a strong personality which is disguised as objectivity, and both reveal to us a world apart, conceding nothing to the spectator and yet establishing a powerful *rapport* with him. What Lawrence Gowing says of the paintings of Vermeer applies equally to the dances of Birgit Åkesson: "Every form is coolly, positively itself, and being so finds a deep alliance, an identity of nature with all its fellows."[2] In technique the two artists are remote from all their contemporaries, and both produce a very small number of works, each one representing the solution of some technical or emotional problem. Both show an extraordinary acute apprehension of space and a mystical attitude to light. The analogy between a painter and a dancer can take us only a certain distance, but it has the merit of illuminating certain aspects of Birgit Åkesson's work for which there are no precedents in the field of choreography.

---

[1] The title of the dance (*Öga: sömn i dröm*) is taken from the title of poem inspired by the dance and written by Erik Lindegren while the dance was still nameless.

[2] Lawrence Gowing, *Vermeer*, p. 45.

F

The Innocent Eye

FREE DANCERS had need of genius to make a successful rebellion against the past, and this was almost equally true of the classically trained dancers attempting to set up as choreographers in the confused aftermath of expressionism. These young choreographers naturally did their best to copy the style of the choreographers at the head of the leading ballet companies in the countries where ballet was most highly developed. In England, choreographers like Andrée Howard and Walter Gore modelled themselves on Frederick Ashton; in France, Janine Charrat and her contemporaries modelled themselves on Lifar; in the United States, William Dollar, John Taras, Todd Bolender and others modelled themselves on Balanchine. Unfortunately for the second generation, the originators of post-expressionist pseudo-classicism had exhausted nearly all the possibilities of the genre before the young people set to work, and the ballets of the latter reproduced in exaggerated form the defects of the former.

Fortunately, however, there was one genre—that of playful, gently satirical comedy—in which the first pseudo-classicists had had a certain amount of success, and a few young choreographers with real talent but no great originality found it possible for a time to do interesting work in this genre. These choreographers differed considerably from each other in temperament and background, but they all had one thing in common: they approached the dominant pseudo-classical style of their day from the outside, regarding it with fresh and innocent eyes. Two of them were Americans, approaching ballet by way of the expressionist free dance. Two were South Africans who began their training in South Africa, and made their first contact with professional ballet when they reached England. One was a Frenchman who grew up during the

War (when France was cut off from the rest of the ballet world) and began his career in the extraordinary period of effervescence after the Liberation, when everything seemed possible.

The success of the ballets produced by these choreographers depended on a delicate balance between naïveté and sophistication. At a certain stage in their careers they were able to tackle comic subjects in a playful light-hearted way, having learned enough about the ballet tradition to make fun of it and having acquired enough understanding of composition to put their ideas together in a reasonably satisfying way. The ballets produced by them at this stage in their careers had real charm, and added appreciably to the gaiety of nations.

But innocence is not a quality which can be retained for long in the ballet world; soon these choreographers began to realize that life is real and earnest, and were driven to tackle subjects for which their style was quite unsuitable. They were almost totally unable to assimilate anything from the ballets of Tudor, who was tackling serious themes with great success. The leading companies either ignored him or gave him only limited and temporary support: to the young choreographers he seemed a lonely outsider, achieving amazing effects in a highly personal style which had no relation to the main stream of choreography and completely defied analysis or imitation. Now and again the young choreographers tried to take some ideas from Tudor, but normally they kept to the fashionable pseudo-classical style of their day: this they used to tackle serious themes, with appalling results. It was as if Cole Porter tried to write a tragedy in blank verse, or Irving Berlin tried his hand at a symphony. In their laudable efforts to grow up the young choreographers lost their child-like spontaneity and directness, and found nothing to replace these admirable qualities.

This decline in creative power accompanying a growth in the sense of moral responsibility seems to be characteristic of new cultures in which the artist has no support from tradition. Something of the sort could be observed in e.g. the work of Gogol after he completed *Dead Souls*, the first great Russian novel—though of course the stature of Gogol was incomparably greater than that of the choreographers in question.

AGNES DE MILLE (*b.* 1908)

Agnes de Mille was born a decade earlier than any of the other innocent-eyed choreographers, and inevitably was much more strongly influenced by expressionism than them; in her youth expressionism seemed the only style of any artistic importance. Both in her limitations and her achievements she was as typical of her generation as Duncan and Graham were of their respective generations.

The most powerful influence experienced by her in her youth was that of films. The famous Cecil B. de Mille was her uncle, her father was employed by Cecil B. as one of his directors, and she grew up in such close contact with silent films that their visual language became almost as natural to her as normal speech. Though she suffered a number of set-backs in her career, she had many great advantages over her contemporaries: any choreographer might well have been jealous of the Sunday-evening film-shows at her father's home, where Charlie Chaplin was a frequent visitor, and often entertained Agnes de Mille and her sister with small improvised sketches. She describes Chaplin as "the greatest actor of his time",[1] but he was as much a dancer as an actor: if he had been trained in the classical technique he might have equalled Nijinsky, and his best films are like ballets in that they can be seen over and over again without losing any of their power to move the spectator.

Like many other American girls of her generation Agnes de Mille saw Isadora Duncan and Ruth St. Denis, and put on family shows in which she performed dances of her own composition inspired by their work—though her parents prohibited her from attending classes at her school where dances in the style of Duncan and St. Denis were taught. Like many other American girls of her generation she was swept off her feet by Pavlova, and determined to learn to dance like her.

When Agnes de Mille started ballet training at the Koslov school in Los Angeles she tackled it with typically expressionist *Sturm und Drang*. She was only allowed two lessons a week, and tried to compensate for this by practising on her own and working always with the most violent concentration and effort. Her private practice while her technique was still unformed gave her many faults which she never succeeded in entirely eradicating; more serious, however, was the wrong attitude which she developed towards the classical technique. Instead of it becoming for her a natural means of expression, it remained a distant and almost unattainable goal which could only be approached by superhuman efforts; one might almost say that it was for her an enemy to be conquered by brute force. With such an attitude to ballet, she never learned to understand the classical technique from the inside, and her execution of classical steps always had something self-conscious about it. This attitude did not prevent her from doing fine work as a dancer and a choreographer, but it put narrow limitations on the range of her work. Russian nobility and lyricism were completely outside her understanding: like her contemporaries in Central Europe she could only think of expression in terms of violent effort. She had seen Pavlova, and one of her teachers was an English girl who had been trained

[1] *Dance to the Piper*, p. 76.

by Pavlova—but Agnes de Mille could not discover any link between what Pavlova did on the stage and what went on in class.

Her failure to understand the classical tradition of ballet emerges very clearly in the chapter "Ballet and Sex" in her autobiography. Her conception of ballet was virile and completely physical, with no place for spiritual expression or for the grace, lyricism and delicacy characteristic of the feminine aspects of the classical tradition:

> The very physical stresses, the strengthening and bracing and tautening of her back and legs supply such a sense of driving power as to give her [the female classical dancer] the illusion of male potency.[1]

Agnes de Mille finished her ballet training in 1928 and came to New York to work on her own, becoming one of about a dozen recital dancers working in New York at this time. She had one great advantage over most of her contemporaries in possessing a private income, and so was able to spend all her time on her dancing. (It was impossible to make money giving recitals.) Though her outlook was much the same as that of the other recital dancers, she differed from them in basing her work on the classical technique: this was not due to her own choice but rather to that of her parents, who had sent her to a ballet school rather than to the Denishawn School (which was located in Los Angeles in her youth).

When she began to compose dances for herself she showed her attitude to the classical technique very clearly by using it merely as decorative trimming: her compositions were naturalistic character sketches in mime, clearly inspired by the acting in silent films. As she wrote in her autobiography, she was "using dance like costuming. The crux of the matter was the acted story."[2] Her instinct in this matter was sound: when she followed her instinct she usually made progress.

All the items composed by her in her first two years as a recital dancer were of this character, and many of them (the Degas studies *Stagefright* and *Ballet Class*, *Schuhplattltanz*, and *Audition*) became permanent features of her repertoire. The best of them was *Audition*, for this was based on personal experience, and gave an outlet for her sardonic sense of humour; she poured into this unpretentious but poignant item all the bitterness accumulated by her in dozens of fruitless auditions on Broadway. This was the only one of her items which showed any influence from Chaplin: it lacked the poetry, magic and rhythmic subtlety of Chaplin's work, but it showed a typically Chaplinesque mixture of pathos and humour. In this item (as in the Degas studies) the curiously self-

[1] *Dance to the Piper*, p. 59.
[2] I bid., p. 95.

conscious and brittle quality of her dancing did not injure the effect of the items as a whole; in fact it fitted in perfectly with the mood of each item.

By the time Agnes de Mille reached New York Martha Graham had already established herself as the leading figure among the free dancers. Louis Horst played for nearly all the recital dancers (including Agnes de Mille), and he urged Agnes de Mille to go and see Martha Graham. Finally she went. She was impressed, but not moved: at this time the Graham expressionist style was very new, and people took some time to get used to it. Gradually, however, Agnes de Mille came under the spell of Martha Graham—so much so that in her book *Dance to the Piper* she writes of her from the far side of idolatry. She watched classes, attended all performances, and begged Martha Graham to take her as a pupil. Martha Graham helped her with criticism and advice, but refused to teach her, taking the view that Agnes de Mille should develop on her own lines. Nevertheless her influence on Agnes de Mille was profound. Later on Agnes de Mille began to compose dances dealing with such Grahamish themes as the dust bowl of the Middle West and the habits of mind of the Brahmin families of Boston, doing her best to come to grips with the Graham style. These attempts at Grahamish expressionism were not very successful (the austerely abstract compositions would have been completely incomprehensible except for the elaborate programme notes) but they were important in widening her understanding of dance-movement as distinct from mime.

Giving recitals at long intervals with her own money did not satisfy Agnes de Mille as it did her contemporaries. She was not a de Mille for nothing: she wanted to break into the professional theatre and earn her living doing the work for which she had been trained. But there was no American ballet of any artistic value at this time, and producers of Broadway shows had no use for her work: she had the wrong sort of face, the wrong sort of body and—what was even worse—original ideas.

Her first chance to work in the professional theatre came when she was commissioned to arrange the dances in a Broadway musical comedy. She learned all about the seamy side of Broadway on this production: her work was sabotaged in every possible way, and eventually she was intrigued out of the show altogether.

Though she and her mother had a comfortable income, they had to keep up appearances in New York, and the recitals cost Agnes de Mille a great deal of money. She therefore decided to go to Europe, where recitals could be put on much more cheaply. This decision was of critical importance in her career. Like many other American recital dancers she was swindled in Paris, but she ended up in London, and there she found conditions ideal for making artistic progress. The cost of living was low, and she was able to give recitals at the Mercury Theatre so cheaply that eventually they paid for themselves. She attended classes at the Rambert School,[1] sometimes having private lessons from Antony Tudor, and became friendly with him and Hugh Laing. At her recitals Hugh Laing danced with her as her partner, while Tudor acted as stage manager. During the next six years Tudor had an enormous influence on her: though she could not assimilate his style, she learned to think of dancing based on the classical technique as a natural language of expression, and for the first time made contact with the great ballet tradition. (Without some contact with tradition no choreographer can hope to use the classical technique in an easy and spontaneous manner.)

At the beginning of 1937 she was chosen by Tudor to create the third solo at the première of *Dark Elegies*. Marie Rambert had consistently refused to let her dance with her company, though in fact she had more talent than many of the other dancers in the company, and some of the character rôles would have suited her very well; now, however, Tudor managed to persuade Marie Rambert to let her dance with the company as guest artist in the one ballet.

Tudor had good reason to insist on Agnes de Mille for *Dark Elegies*. The Rambert company was not run on a professional basis, and most of the dancers were semi-trained; Tudor had Peggy van Praagh and Maude Lloyd for two of the female solos, but he badly needed another experienced professional dancer for the third solo. He composed for Agnes de Mille a solo admirably suited to her temperament and physique, making it very angular and including a high proportion of expressionist elements.[2]

Though Agnes de Mille tackled this rôle with great sincerity and a high degree of intellectual understanding of what the movements were meant to express, she could not escape from the limitations imposed by her background, and performed the movements almost as if they had been composed by Martha Graham: she seemed to revel in the oddness of the movements instead of dancing them in a natural and spontaneous manner, and the classical tradition did not shine through them as it should have done. On the other hand she probably danced the rôle better than any other available dancer could have done, and she had every right to resent Marie Rambert's bitter criticism of her performance. She then left the Mercury Theatre and the Rambert School. Tudor and Hugh Laing left at the same time; the three pooled their resources and founded a small company (Dance Theatre), taking in the best of the Ballet Club dancers and a few others from the best of the London schools.

Dance Theatre performed in Oxford for one week in June, 1937, the programme consisting of the best of Tudor's existing ballets (plus one unsatisfactory new ballet) and the best of Agnes de Mille's repertoire of solos and pas de deux.

---

[1] The Rambert classes were held in the studio next door to the Mercury Theatre.
[2] Later he changed the dance considerably, making it more classical in feeling and bringing it into harmony with the first solo.

This arrangement suited both Tudor and Agnes de Mille. He had not yet composed sufficient ballets to fill up two programmes, and Agnes de Mille's items provided useful variety in the season. She benefited greatly from the fact that for the first time she could dance in conditions of relative comfort, free from the strain of rushing from one dance to the next as quickly as she could change costumes, while her morale was greatly strengthened by the fact that she was dancing as an equal among a wonderful group of dancers chosen by Tudor.

Though the quality of the show was very high, neither Tudor nor Agnes de Mille had contacts in the commercial theatre world, and no further bookings were obtained. Agnes de Mille then tried her luck in the United States, with results just as humiliating as before. Her work on the film *Romeo and Juliet* and the Broadway musical *Hooray for What* was considerably altered, and she was forced to leave the musical before it reached Broadway.

In April, 1938, Agnes de Mille presented a show in London in which for the first time she showed group items as well as her solos and pas de deux. The group consisted partly of members of Dance Theatre and partly of other English dancers.

By far the most important item was the short ballet *Rodeo*, the first important American ballet. In this ballet Agnes de Mille broke clean away from the limitations of her previous work. She had some highly trained dancers at her disposal—above all Peggy van Praagh—and she used them with astonishing skill and originality: it was as if she had grown up overnight. Though *Rodeo* was composed by Agnes de Mille in England, as the culmination of six years of work in England under the influence of Tudor, it was completely American in style and feeling. Through working away from the killing strain of New York, stimulated by the interesting work around her, she had been able to clarify her own ideas and develop an original American style. (Some American composers of her generation profited in a similar way from working in Paris under the influence of Nadia Boulanger.)

The actual movements were largely expressionist in feeling: the dancers represented horses of different kinds (bucking bronchos, colts, sedate cowponies and so on) and moved in a very unclassical manner, emphasizing the blows of their feet on the ground and arching their bodies strongly in the air. The general mood was one of gaiety and excitement. Peggy van Praagh was outstanding, bringing out the qualities of movement required by the choreography and yet giving to her movements the qualities of poise, economy, precision and clean line that are characteristic of the classical tradition; the combination of the vitality of the frontier and the mature talent of a great classically trained dancer was irresistible.

The structure of the ballet was just as original and effective as the detail of the choreography. Agnes de Mille built up the atmosphere of the rodeo by using a very rapid succession of short entrées. To some extent this technique was derived from *Jardin aux Lilas*, but it was also influenced by the rapid cutting of scenes of gathering tension in the silent films. The construction of the ballet was so solid and effective that it was hard to believe that *Rodeo* was Agnes de Mille's first important ballet.

After a show at the Westminster Theatre (in June, 1938), in which she danced in Tudor's ballet *Judgment of Paris*, she and Tudor parted company. In her autobiography she attributed this break partly to the fact that rival directors can never function happily together, but mainly to the fact that Tudor had gradually become convinced that their two styles were incompatible. Whatever the full explanation of this break, it clearly had a devastating effect on Agnes de Mille.

She arrived in the United States in good time to take part in the formation of Ballet Theatre. This company seemed to offer to its choreographers the opportunity of a lifetime—the freedom to produce whatever ballets they fancied, a large company, ample time for rehearsals, and no expense spared for décor and costume. For Agnes de Mille, however, Ballet Theatre offered nothing but frustration. Though she was by far the finest American choreographer, and though Richard Pleasant (manager of the company) asked her to make a list of all the ballets she wanted to produce, she found herself faced with the crippling proviso that she was not to dance in any of them. She fought hard against this decision, knowing very well that she herself was the only dancer in the company capable of giving a satisfactory interpretation of the central rôles in the comedy ballets she wanted to produce; but she was beating her head against a brick wall.[1]

For its first season Ballet Theatre commissioned from Agnes de Mille a ballet (based on *La Création du Monde*) for sixteen amateur Negro girls; this ballet never had a chance of success, for the amateurs lacked the power to project their work in a big theatre, and the company could not afford to keep them on the payroll for the sake of one ballet.

Things went badly with Ballet Theatre in 1940, and at the beginning of 1941 there was a slight change of policy: Agnes de Mille was commissioned to produce *Three Virgins and a Devil*, with herself in one of the leading rôles. But the change came too late. By this time Agnes de Mille was not the same person that arranged *Rodeo*. In *Three Virgins and a Devil* (based on a sketch she had produced in a London revue) she used a crude naturalistic mimed humour that was far inferior to the bitter irony of her early sketches like *Audition*, and could not compare in any way with the riotous danced humour of *Rodeo*. The ballet was supposed to be set in the Middle Ages, but her attempts at

[1] *See* below, p. 419.

mediaeval atmosphere were few and ineffectual. The structure of the ballet was lamentably weak. Though the ballet was a success with the public, she could not fail (after *Rodeo*) to be aware of the defects of her ballet. Eventually she "learned to tolerate *Virgins*"[1] but she insisted on its being taken out of the repertoire when the standard of performance declined.

In 1942 she received a commission from the Ballet Russe de Monte Carlo for an American ballet, and decided to produce an expanded version of *Rodeo*, with music specially composed by Aaron Copland. Fortunately for Agnes de Mille, this company was in a difficult position because of the decline in the appeal of Massine's ballets, the departure of Massine, and the vast increase in the competitive power of Ballet Theatre through its displacement of the Ballet Russe de Monte Carlo in the affections of the leading American impresario, S. Hurok. Under these circumstances Sergei Denham, director of the Ballet Russe de Monte Carlo, was forced to give Agnes de Mille the free hand she demanded.

Agnes de Mille realized that this was her big chance to establish her reputation, and set out to ensure the success of *Rodeo* at all costs. She went back to the style of her early solos (1929–32), devising a rather conventional story (akin to that of many Western films) of a tomboyish cow-girl who dresses and acts like a man in order to stay close to the head wrangler with whom she is in love; at the end of the ballet the heroine puts on girl's clothes and wins his love, just as in the films. Agnes de Mille made the cow-girl into the same diffident, clumsy figure that had already appeared in a number of her solo items, adapting this figure to the Wild Western atmosphere. In addition to the dances from the first version of *Rodeo* she included in the expanded version, as an interlude without much connection with the action, the square dance which she had included in the programme in London when the first version of *Rodeo* was performed; she retained the invitation to the audience to clap the beats, and added a caller.

Unfortunately the exciting quality of the first version was largely swamped in the sentimentality and padding of the expanded version. The ballet would have gained enormously by being cut by at least one-third; every effect was underlined and repeated so often that it lost all its poetry and much of its humour. Her efforts to return to the mimed humour of her early solos were only partially successful: she had grown out of this relatively crude type of humour when she composed the original version of *Rodeo*, and she could not recapture the spontaneity and naïveté of her early years. No doubt she was also influenced by the fact that she was working with cosmopolitan Russian and Polish male dancers and British and American male dancers who had largely absorbed the point of view of the cosmopolitan Slavs: instead of taking chances on their picking up

[1] *Dance to the Piper*, p. 240.

subtleties of danced humour she naturally preferred to rely on slapstick mime which would still make its point even if done in a rather blatant manner.

Another reason for the prolixity of the expanded version was the influence of *Billy the Kid*,[1] a pretentious cowboy ballet produced by Eugene Loring a few months after Agnes de Mille arranged the first version of *Rodeo* in London. One image which she used a great deal (a dancer standing with one knee in the air to suggest a cowboy on a horse) was too static to be of much use in a ballet, and far inferior to the delightfully dynamic movements of the original version of *Rodeo* and the corresponding movements in *Billy the Kid*.

In spite of its defects the second version of *Rodeo* retained some of the fine qualities of the first version, and was a great success with the public. It was the first American ballet to enjoy the same sort of success in the United States as the best ballets by foreign choreographers, and Agnes de Mille leaped into fame.

The great success of *Rodeo* induced the Theatre Guild to commission from Agnes de Mille the dances in the musical *Oklahoma!*, of which the mood was to be somewhat similar to that of *Rodeo*. Though the originators of *Oklahoma!* (the script writer Oscar Hammerstein II, the composer Richard Rodgers and the producer Rouben Mamoulian) were men of a very different stamp from those with whom Agnes de Mille had worked on previous musicals, they were all men with long experience in the ferociously competitive world of Broadway, and in view of the parlous financial position of the Theatre Guild it was essential that no unnecessary risks should be taken. *Oklahoma!* was technically better than its predecessors in that the songs and dances developed in a natural manner out of the action, but it kept strictly within the iron conventions of the musical comedy form, and Agnes de Mille introduced much the same proportion of "corn" into her choreography as Hammerstein into the script and Rodgers into the music. As George Amberg says, the production had more charm and less pretentiousness than the average musical; but there was nothing experimental about it.[2]

The climax of *Oklahoma!* was the dream ballet *Laurie Makes up her Mind*. Elsewhere in the production dancers were used in groups (apart from a few sudden entrances of soloists) as part of the local colour, but in the ballet the solo acting rôles were doubled by solo dancers, and the whole weight of the production was carried by the dancers for quite a long period.

The book of the ballet[3] was worked out by Agnes de Mille in great detail, and had much the same character as the scenarios of the silent films with which she became familiar in her youth. This script provided for a great deal of silent acting, but relatively little dancing: the ballet scene was in fact a continuation

[1] *See* below, p. 380.
[2] *Ballet in America*, p. 176.
[3] Quoted in full by George Amberg in *Ballet in America*, p. 176.

of the story of the show in mime, with a few decorative trimmings. Choreographically the most interesting episode was the scene where the dream-Judd attacks the dream-Laurie: here Agnes de Mille used the fall-and-recovery technique characteristic of the Doris Humphrey style of the free dance to suggest the slow-motion effect sometimes experienced in dreams. As in *Rodeo*, however, an interesting effect was spoiled by excessive repetition, so that the movement lost its value as a dance-image and became a bravura effect.

It is impossible to blame Agnes de Mille for any weaknesses in the choreography of *Oklahoma!*. She was working in a field where every detail was regulated by convention, and in fact she achieved a higher choreographic standard than that of any musical before or since. *Oklahoma!* was, of course, a tremendous success, and convinced the hard-headed business men promoting musicals of the desirability of employing the best available American choreographers and dancers. The relatively slight changes brought about by *Oklahoma!* were of great importance, for the musical (with all its artistic limitations) proved to be almost the only theatrical genre able to keep solvent during the later devastating rise in the cost of theatrical production on Broadway. Theatrical conditions made any progress beyond *Oklahoma!* impossible, and in fact some of the innovations of *Oklahoma!* were later abandoned; nevertheless this musical proved the commercial practicability of a show in which dances and songs are integrated with the action instead of being completely irrelevant, and this reform was never completely abandoned.

After *Oklahoma!* Agnes de Mille was in great demand as a choreographer of musicals, and developed a slick efficient style (based on her work in *Oklahoma!*) which combined certain elements of the classical technique and the free dance. (By this time a high proportion of American professional dancers had had training in both.) Though the work paid well and added much to her reputation, it was not fully satisfying artistically, and in 1948 she composed an ambitious ballet for Ballet Theatre, *Fall River Legend*.

Her choice of a serious theme was easy to understand. She was living in the age of anxiety just like everyone else (including Thurber's seal), and she could not go on indefinitely working in the cheerful comedy style of *Rodeo*—particularly as this was the style usually demanded of her in musicals.

As one might expect she tried to come to grips with her sombre theme by bringing together her habitual silent-film type of mime and the serious styles of the two choreographers whom she admired most—Graham and Tudor. This mixture proved very unsatisfactory; the different ingredients did not blend at all, and in her attempt to take over dance-images from Tudor ballets she exaggerated and vulgarized them almost beyond recognition.

Her misunderstanding of Tudor's style was particularly clear in her treatment of one of the dance-images of 'The Young Man from the House Opposite' in

Pillar of Fire. The Young Man made a slight rotating movement of one knee which in its context suggested with remarkable precision both his mood and the impact he made on Hagar: the gesture was able to carry these various implications because it had the "multiplane" quality of poetic dance-imagery. In *Fall River Legend* Agnes de Mille had the heroine Lizzie perform this gesture (in a crudely exaggerated form) over and over again, demonstrating Lizzie's erotic desires in the most blatant manner possible.

Other details of *Fall River Legend* were even more melodramatic. In order to make clear that Lizzie had committed murder, Agnes de Mille had her appear on the stage wearing a petticoat with an enormous red stain. She then had Lizzie express her guilt by uttering loud sobs and even screams.[1] In fact she had Nora Kaye stand on the stage for about ten minutes expressing harrowing grief by almost every device known to melodrama; at any moment one expected snow to start falling and a green spot to illuminate the black moustachios of the villain.

This concentration on violent emotional expression at all costs was of course typically expressionist; but even in the very early days of expressionism, in the second and third decades of this century, choreographers were rarely as naïve as Agnes de Mille in *Fall River Legend*. Her innocent eye (which caused her to regard her melodramatic clichés as daring innovations) was a fatal handicap outside her own restricted field of light comedy.

In *The Harvest According* (composed for Ballet Theatre in 1952) she made a far more intelligent attempt to tackle a serious subject. This ballet had a theme typical of the expressionist twenties—a child is born, troops go off to war, and so on—but Agnes de Mille gave the theme a certain individuality by placing it at the time of the American Civil War, and she brought together appropriate ideas from Martha Graham and Antony Tudor without any of the melodramatic stunts which disfigured *Fall River Legend*. On the other hand she showed surprisingly little interest in the rhythms of the music, and the movements never sprang to life: during the whole ballet they had the quality of a quiet introduction to something exciting which in fact never arrived.

From one point of view Agnes de Mille was unfortunate in the date of her birth. She battered away for years without success trying to break into the American theatre, and when at last she did break in she did so under rather unfavourable circumstances, so that younger choreographers benefited more from her achievements than she did herself. In other words she suffered in the same way as every other pioneer. From another point of view she was extremely lucky in being born when she was: she saw Chaplin, Pavlova and Duncan in the flesh, she worked alongside Martha Graham when this great

[1] This crude device had already been used by Jerome Robbins in *Facsimile*, also with Nora Kaye.

pioneer was coming to maturity, and then she worked alongside Tudor during the whole of his formative period. With such a succession of stimuli an artist with any sensitivity and creative power could hardly fail to do work of real interest.

FRANK STAFF (b. 1918)

Unlike most other male dancers of his generation Frank Staff had the advantage of starting his training while still a boy: he was in fact thirteen when he began training in Cape Town under Helen Webb in 1931. Maude Lloyd, one of the original members of the Ballet Club, also had her initial training under this teacher, and when she returned to Cape Town on a visit in 1932 Staff had some classes from her. In 1934 he followed Maude Lloyd's example by coming to London to continue his training at the Rambert School. Male dancers of any age were very rare in London in those days, and soon he began to dance with the Ballet Club and the Vic-Wells Ballet.[1] Though he danced at the Wells during two periods (1934–35 and 1938–39), his main interest was the Ballet Club.

By temperament he was close to Ashton, and had a technique which by contemporary English standards was quite solid; Ashton accordingly gave him the principal male rôle in Valentine's Eve (1935), the last ballet he composed for the Ballet Club. Andrée Howard, who continued in the same path as Ashton after the latter's departure, gave Staff important rôles in nearly all her ballets; two of her ballets (La Muse s'Amuse and La Fête Étrange) had him in the central rôle. He also danced important classical rôles in Marie Rambert's revivals of Diaghilev ballets, though he was really a character dancer. (The Ballet Club had no danseurs nobles after the departure of Harold Turner.) Staff danced no solo rôles in Tudor ballets while Tudor was with the Ballet Club.

He and Walter Gore were by far the most experienced male dancers remaining in the Ballet Club when Tudor and Hugh Laing left in 1937 to form Dance Theatre, and in 1938 Marie Rambert encouraged both Staff and Gore to start work as choreographers. Both began with new versions of old Ashton ballets, and showed strong influences from Ashton; neither showed any influence from Tudor. They belonged to the pseudo-classical wing of the Ballet Club which became dominant after the departure of Tudor.

Staff's first ballet The Tartans—a suite of Scottish dances—was only of minor interest, though it proved him to have a good ear for music and some feeling for composition.

[1] Nearly all the Ballet Club dancers took engagements at the Wells company from time to time. Performances were on different evenings and did not interfere with each other.

Czernyana (1939) showed more individuality, though this ballet owed a great deal to Ashton's *Façade*. Staff's approach was exactly the same as Ashton's: he took a series of short piano studies by Czerny and improvised items to fit them, paying no attention to the shape of the ballet as a whole. Some of the items were in the playfully satirical style of the best scenes of *Façade*, while others were in Ashton's vague romantic manner. The best item was *Étude Symphonique*, a vicious satire of the Massine symphonic ballets. This was exactly the sort of item that intimate sophisticated revues should include but almost never do. Consciously or not, Staff was reviving a very old tradition when he burlesqued the fashionable ballet of his day: English clowns and grotesque dancers have been doing this for two hundred years. If all the items had been as funny as *Étude Symphonique* the ballet would have been a delightful burlesque, even though its appeal was necessarily ephemeral; unfortunately, however, he tried to build the ballet up with a number of pseudo-classical abstract items which were depressingly conventional in the Ashton manner.

In 1940 the combination of a number of factors enabled him to compose a ballet (*Peter and the Wolf*) which was so witty and well-constructed that it remained at the centre of the Rambert repertoire for a long time. He was now sufficiently experienced to be able to come to grips with choreographic problems, but he had not lost the naïveté and spontaneity evident in the best satirical sketches of *Czernyana*, and Prokofiev provided him with a good story and witty music, both being admirably suited for choreography. No choreographer can fail completely with Prokofiev's fairy-tale, with its delightful mixture of naïveté and sophistication, and Staff rose to the occasion. *Peter and the Wolf* in fact gave an idea of the fine ballet Ashton might have made out of *Façade* if he had not been under the influence of the late-Diaghilevian fashion for cocktail ballets and had possessed a stronger feeling for balletic construction.

The early episodes of *Peter and the Wolf* were made excessively slow by the fact that Staff used as accompaniment a record of a concert performance of Prokofiev's "symphonic tale for children", complete with spoken commentary; but after the action got well under way the choreography developed a fine continuity and homogeneity, with humour that was often danced rather than mimed. Staff's naïve characterization of each personage with a few simple movements was exactly right for the fairy-tale theme and Prokofiev's music, and he showed a fine sense of timing in making his satirical points on exactly the right beats of the music. The ballet ended in a rousing finale in which the various characters moved diagonally across the stage in a fantastic procession which showed Staff's sense of humour at its most incisive. The humour of the ballet—above all that of the finale—wore very well, for nothing went on too long, and Staff achieved his effects with economy and precision. He showed himself very skilful at "throwing away" effects which other choreographers

Peter and the Wolf (Staff, Cambridge, 1940) with Celia Franca as the Bird,
Walter Gore as the Cat, Lulu Dukes as Peter and Leo Kersley as the Wolf

Fancy Free (Robbins, New York, 1944) with Jerome Robbins performing the solo of the First Sailor

The Age of Anxiety (Robbins, New York, 1950)

would have emphasized, and making capital out of sudden unexpected contrasts.

In his later ballets Staff fell so far below the level of *Peter and the Wolf* that in retrospect this success appeared as a happy accident. *Enigma Variations* (1940) was an attempt at pseudo-classical abstraction, partly inspired by the same symphonic ballets which Staff had satirized in *Czernyana*. Staff's own pseudo-classical style, derived from that of Ashton, was quite unsuitable for an abstract interpretation of the wide variety of moods of Elgar's music: in two variations he was inspired by Sylvia Hayden (who had been the baby ballerina in Tudor's company) to create flowing, lyrical movements, but most of the ballet showed little connection with the music. *Un Songe* (1945) was an even more pretentious and unsuccessful attempt at abstraction, with much of the dancing in silence, and some clumsy attempts at evoking mystery by the use of screens in the manner of Balanchine's ballet *Cotillon*. In *Lovers' Gallery* (composed for the Metropolitan Ballet in 1947) he made an attempt to return to comedy; but he had lost all the naïveté which enabled him to approach the story of *Peter and the Wolf* with such admirably childlike directness and simplicity, and his attempts at comedy were distressingly laboured.

His attempts at the representation of the Seven Deadly Sins in *Fanciulla delle Rose* (1948) were even more laboured, in spite of the fact that he had Beriosova as his ballerina.

In 1952 he composed for the New-Ballet company *Ballade* to the music of Fauré, seeking to interpret the changing moods of the music (as in *Enigma Variations*). The style he used was a curious mixture of *Les Sylphides*, *Giselle* and *Jardin aux Lilas*. From time to time Staff showed his musicality in some interesting contrapuntal rhythms, and he was fortunate in having in Constance Garfield a sensitive lyrical dancer; but the ballet dragged on and on, with a great deal of repetition, until there seemed no reason why it should ever end. Though Staff's abstract choreography lacked the serious technical defects of the attempts at this genre by most other pseudo-classical choreographers, it was also quite lacking in positive qualities.

JEROME ROBBINS (b. 1918)

Jerome Robbins profited enormously from the pioneer work of Agnes de Mille. He had no need to beat his head against brick walls: success came easily and soon.

Though the early careers of the two choreographers were very different, their approach to ballet was much the same, and eventually their careers ran parallel. Like Agnes de Mille, Jerome Robbins was completely typical of his generation: both choreographers stood out from their contemporaries in having exceptional talent, not in having an original outlook.

At the age of nineteen, in 1937, Jerome Robbins began his dancing career studying the free dance as an apprentice in the Dance Center of Gluck-Sandor and Felicia Sorel, occasionally playing a rôle at the Yiddish Art Theatre, and taking ballet lessons on the side. He then won a scholarship to the New Dance League, which provided him with further training in the free dance. Later he had training with many classical teachers, and also studied Spanish, Oriental and Interpretative dancing.

Though *Fancy Free* (1944) was his first ballet for a big company, he had valuable experience in choreography before he tackled this ballet. Beginning in 1938 (one year after he started training) and continuing right up to 1941 (after he had joined Ballet Theatre), he spent his summers dancing at Camp Tamiment, Pennsylvania, and there he was given the opportunity to create his first ballets: one was a satire on a French bedroom farce, the other a serious ballet, *Harlem Incident*. From the autumn of 1939 until the time that he joined Ballet Theatre in 1940 he danced in the chorus of a number of Broadway shows, including one that had choreography by Balanchine.

In Ballet Theatre his talent as a dancer was recognized, and he was given a number of important solo rôles. He was badly miscast as Petrouchka, but showed promise of a fine gift for comedy in solo rôles in ballets like *Three Virgins and a Devil*, *Bluebeard* and *Helen of Troy*, in spite of the poor quality of the choreography in these ballets. But he did not get a chance to show his real quality as a comedy dancer until he composed a rôle for himself in *Fancy Free*.

Fancy Free, produced in 1944, owed a great deal to the expanded version of *Rodeo* (1942) and the dream ballet in *Oklahoma!* (1943). The scenario prepared by Jerome Robbins for *Fancy Free*[1] was just as much like a film scenario as those used by Agnes de Mille, giving the precise details of action and mood (along with indications of the music) at each moment. But Jerome Robbins improved on Agnes de Mille by providing for the action to keep developing into dancing in a natural and spontaneous manner, and making three very complex dances the climax of the ballet. Robbins seemed to find no difficulty in planning every detail of the ballet in such a way as to create the *illusion* of spontaneity and natural behaviour in the final result on the stage, making use of a smooth transition through various degrees of stylization from naturalistic movements right up to formal solos using the full resources of the classical technique. There were no breaks in the texture of his ballets, as in the narrative ballets of Balanchine, Lifar and Ashton: the three sailors kept in character throughout,

---

[1] Quoted in full by George Amberg in *Ballet in America*.

being just as convincing when dancing as when smoking a cigarette or taking a drink.

In *Fancy Free* naïveté and sophistication were so delicately balanced that the ballet gave something of the same thrill as expert tight-rope walking: Jerome Robbins never put a foot wrong, avoiding all the pretentiousness and sentimentality that could very easily have swamped his playful satire. Clearly Robbins had learned much from musical films, in which the script-writers had to face much the same problems as Robbins; the influence of the carefree Fred Astaire-Ginger Rogers films was unmistakable.

Robbins' touch was particularly assured just at the points when one might have expected it to falter—i.e. in the elaborate solos of the three sailors. In these solos he was able to make use of his training in free dance, Oriental dance and Spanish dance in a natural way by having the sailors brag choreographically of their wide travels, introducing into their dancing fragments from a Siamese dance, a Farruca, a Samba, a tap dance, a limbering exercise, a Cancan, a Martha Graham dance and so on. Such eclecticism would have been fatal in a serious ballet—Robbins made no effort to weld the different elements together—but it was perfectly acceptable in the context.

In arranging the three sailor rôles Robbins took care to keep well within the limitations of typical American male dancers. In fact all three of the men who created these rôles (Harold Lang, John Kriza and Jerome Robbins himself) did so well that it was difficult to choose between them, and later these rôles were taken over successfully by other dancers. Robbins was so much a child of his time that he probably was not even aware of these limitations: he simply gave his artists the things which he knew they could do well and which fitted his conception of the ballet. In spite of the elaborate planning of *Fancy Free*, it gave the impression of having been composed by Robbins as naturally as a bird sings.

The three girls had little dancing to do, and their rôles were much less important than those of the sailors. This showed good sense on Robbins' part, for he seemed to be unable to give the girls the same convincing individuality as the sailors. Clearly he felt the male parts as an extension of his own style of dancing, and could not think himself inside the girls to the same extent.

Fancy Free represented an important stage in the development of American ballet. It was no better artistically than the first version of *Rodeo*, but it was better than the version of *Rodeo* shown in America, and it provided a standard against which other American ballets could be measured. Like the musical films which it closely resembled it could be shown in any country of the world without apology or reservations: it did not aim very high, but within its limits it was nearly perfect.

Unquestionably Robbins himself was aware of the close links between

Fancy Free and stage and film musicals. In the same year that he composed *Fancy Free* he expanded it into a successful stage musical *On the Town*. This launched him on his career as a free-lance choreographer, and he left Ballet Theatre for Broadway. A few years later he took the logical next step of converting *On the Town* into the highly successful film of the same name, composing new dances suited to the style and limitations of Gene Kelly.

Interplay, composed by Robbins in 1945 for Billy Rose's Concert Varieties at the Ziegfield Theatre and later taken into the Ballet Theatre repertoire, had many of the same qualities as *Fancy Free*, and might almost be considered as its sequel. The title chosen by Robbins was apt and witty: superficially the ballet had the appearance of a Balanchine "classic ballet", and "interplay" in its usual metaphorical meaning was quite suitable as the title of an abstract ballet. In reality, however, the ballet was not in the least abstract, being clearly inspired by competitive children's games, and its theme was clearly indicated by the literal meaning of "interplay": Robbins thus prepared the spectator for a playful ballet with a superficially abstract structure.

Interplay had something of the same quality as the *New Yorker* magazine at its best period. Robbins stood a little back from his theme, satirizing in a gentle way the typical American attitude to the classical technique. He showed American dancers approaching ballet in much the same mood that American tourists approach the antiquities of Europe, delighting in their old-fashioned quaintness. (After gambolling about like puppies the dancers decide to perform a kind of minuet: they perform this with studious correctness, but all the time they show their amusement at the quaintness of the steps.) Robbins stood only a small distance away from his theme, and was clearly almost as much affected by the attitudes he satirized as his dancers (who gave superbly natural performances). His mockery was completely lacking in the *saeva indignatio* shown by Tudor in *Undertow* produced the year before: *Interplay* had the charm and innocence of the children's games which inspired it.

After the success of the musical *On the Town* Jerome Robbins became a prominent choreographer of musicals, second only to Agnes de Mille in popularity with producers. He had grown up in close contact with Broadway, and seemed to find little difficulty in adapting himself to the iron conventions of the musical without sacrificing his spontaneity and verve: in his arrangements one did not feel any of the inner conflicts apparent in the choreography for musicals of Agnes de Mille. His spontaneity was admirably apparent in *High Button Shoes* (1947), in which he based his choreography on the Mack Sennett Keystone comedies. In detail the movements of the dancers were not of great interest, but Robbins achieved a gay equivalent of the surrealist extravagance of the film comedies by making use of a large number of exits and entrances in rapid succession.

Unfortunately Jerome Robbins could no more retain his innocent eye than Agnes de Mille or Frank Staff. The end of the War seemed to promise a period of relaxation, but in fact life became even more of a strain, particularly in New York (where relaxation has always been difficult). Jerome Robbins did the only possible thing for a sincere artist: he attempted to come to grips with the strains of his time by creating a ballet which incorporated them. In *Facsimile*, composed in 1946 for Ballet Theatre, he tackled a complex psychological theme of the type used by Tudor and Martha Graham, attempting to show by means of the changing relationships between three people the emotional impotence, frustration and empty sophistication of modern life. In such a theme Robbins was out of his depth, using Grahamish properties and a symbolic setting with distressing clumsiness, and failing completely in his efforts to combine Graham's expressionist style with Tudor's post-expressionist classicism. His desperate attempt at being avant-garde led him into melodramatic stunts such as having Nora Kaye sob out loud: this was presumably inspired by the current fashion for the use of spoken words among free dancers. It was easy to see that he meant the movements of the dancers to express emptiness, frivolity, despair and frustration, but his style was completely inadequate for the expression of such feelings: he was in the position of a writer trying to translate *The Waste Land* into Esperanto.

After joining the New York City Ballet in 1949, as associate artistic director, Jerome Robbins had a free hand to produce what ballets he pleased, and composed a series of ambitious ballets heavy with social significance. In *The Guests* he attempted to adapt the Balanchine style to the expression of conflicts between a majority and a minority group:[1] the dancers kept in straight lines, and performed academic steps in a cold and formal manner. Clearly Robbins meant these movements to suggest "the organized activities of a submissive and un-imaginative people" and to contrast them with the imaginative and individual-ized dancing of the two lovers in revolt against this mechanization of life; but he had the lovers dance in a pseudo-classical Balanchinian manner which was just as cerebral and frigid (though more complex) than that of the corps de ballet. The pretentious symbolism of the ballet—e.g. the distribution of masks by the leader—evoked memories of Balanchine's attempts at mystification in his cocktail ballets like *Le Bal* and *Cotillon*, and was out of key with the theme.

In *The Age of Anxiety* (1950) Robbins made another attempt to combine Tudor and Graham, this time in a ballet on a very large scale. The ballet was based partly on Leonard Bernstein's second symphony and partly on the dramatic poem by Auden (*The Age of Anxiety*) which inspired Bernstein's symphony. Auden's poem achieved a fairly high degree of obscurity, but it

[1] It was obvious that Robbins had anti-Semitism in his mind, but he was careful not to limit the symbolism to any particular aspect of discrimination by one group against another.

was pellucid in comparison with Robbins' ballet. Robbins placed everything
on a rarefied plane of abstraction, introducing Jungian archetypal myths such
as the dream journey to find happiness and yet falling back on images of the
utmost melodramatic crudity (e.g. having the dancers whip their other selves,
presumably to suggest masochism).

Only at one point did the choreography rise out of the morass of obscurity:
this was the scene of the Masque, in which the dancers broke into straightforward jitterbug dancing. Suddenly the hysterical expressionist *Weltschmerz* of
the earlier scenes disappeared: one could almost hear the dancers sigh with relief
as they came to grips with movements which were at least danceable, even if
they had little to do with Auden's poem or the latest researches in psychiatry.

In 1951 Robbins returned to psychological allegory with *The Cage*, in
which he attempted to show contemporary relations between the sexes in
terms of the sex-life of insects. Once again he gave Nora Kaye a hysterically
melodramatic rôle as the man-eating female, while the principal male dancer
had little to do except roll backwards and forwards on the stage. The ballet
had perhaps some documentary interest for psychiatrists interested in the study
of sado-masochism, but its artistic value was negligible.

In 1952 Robbins continued in this genre with *Ballade*, presenting clowns
and harlequins in a series of episodes of which the symbolism was so plati-
tudinous as to set the teeth on edge. By this time the sentimentality and banality
of his outlook was distressingly obvious.

In this same year he attempted in vain to repeat the success of *Interplay*
with *The Pied Piper*, a plotless ballet hurriedly composed at short notice to
Aaron Copland's clarinet concerto. Robbins used familiar expressionist devices
with considerable skill and ingenuity, presenting the ballet on a bare stage
without any wings or backcloth so that the complex lighting equipment used
by the company was visible; but he had to pad out a few comedy ideas to
enormous length to fill up the music of the concerto, and the ballet was very
repetitive. It was saved from dullness by Tanaquil LeClercq's admirable performance in a rather tenous comedy rôle which she built up with considerable
imagination. But not even this fine artist could disguise the fact that Robbins
had long ago exhausted all the possibilities of this type of zany humour.

ROLAND PETIT (b. 1924)

If one compares Roland Petit's achievements with those of the great French
maîtres de ballet of the eighteenth and nineteenth centuries they do not bulk
very large. Nevertheless his achievements were of great significance, for he

managed to break away from the Lifar style to some extent, and was the first French choreographer of any real stature to emerge for nearly a century.

After being trained at the Opéra school he entered the corps de ballet of the Opéra in 1939, at the age of fifteen. During the War years Paris was cut off from the rest of the ballet world, and his ideas of choreography were inevitably formed by the Lifar ballets (together with Lifar versions of older ballets) in which he danced. Petit had exceptional talent as a dancer, and gradually moved up through all the grades; but he was dissatisfied with the opportunities given him at the Opéra, and from 1940 onwards he danced in recitals with Janine Charrat (who composed the dances they performed).

Immediately after the Liberation of Paris (in the summer of 1944) Roland Petit resigned from the Opéra to seek a career on his own. This was a period when anything seemed possible in Paris: all the energies dammed up during the years of the Occupation burst out with the force of an explosion. In this atmosphere the fusty routine of the Opéra was insufferable to young and ambitious dancers, and a number of the most talented of the young dancers left the Opéra at about the same time as Petit. Meanwhile other talented dancers were returning to Paris from the cities where they had lived during the war. In fact conditions were more favourable for the formation of a new French company than for a century or more.

Petit began his career as a choreographer in the winter of 1944-45, composing dances for the joint recitals organized by Irène Lidova and Claude Giraud at the Théâtre Sarah Bernhardt under the name "Vendredis de la Danse". Material conditions were still very difficult—the theatres were still unheated, and the accompaniment was limited to one piano—but the dancers at these performances included some fine artists (among them Nina Vyroubova and Renée Jeanmaire) and the programmes were a great success with the public. They attracted the interest of Christian Bérard and Boris Kokhno, who devised a full-length ballet *Les Forains* for production with music by Sauguet and choreography by Petit.

Les Forains was in essentials a cocktail ballet of the same type that Boris Kokhno had devised for Balanchine: it consisted of a series of divertissements supposed to be presented by a troupe of strolling fair-ground entertainers. The various items (Siamese twins, a woman in a trance, an acrobat and so on) gave little scope for dancing, but this did not seem to worry Petit, who relied for the most part on rather obvious theatrical devices—though he arranged for himself as Master of Ceremonies a solo in which he effectively combined conjuring tricks with academic steps. He made no attempt to come to grips with the problems presented by a choreographic treatment of the theme; in fact he did not even seem to be aware of the existence of such problems. Most of his choreography was so tenuous that the ballet gave the impression of having been improvised in a single rehearsal. (We must remember that he was only twenty-one at the time.)

Nevertheless *Les Forains* stood out from the Lifar ballets performed at the Opéra because of the sincerity, charm and spontaneity of the artists taking part in it; and even the sentimentality of the tear-jerking finale (with the players mournfully packing their things and walking away) was a pleasant change from the aridity of Lifar's ballets. Above all, *Les Forains* was good theatre. Bérard's idea of having the players construct their booth on the stage was very effective, and the ballet was a big success with the public. As a result Roland Petit and his associates were encouraged to form a ballet company, the Compagnie des Champs-Élysées, with Boris Kokhno as artistic director and Petit as choreographer.

Roland Petit built up the repertoire of the new company by composing a number of new ballets—*Le Rendezvous, Le Déjeuner sur l'Herbe, La Fiancée du Diable*, and *Les Amours de Jupiter*. Some were better than others, but none of them showed any advance on *Les Forains*. Though Petit had real talent, it had little chance to mature in this late-Diaghilevian artistic climate revived by Kokhno, Cocteau and Bérard. *Le Rendezvous*, for example, had a book by Prévert in which he brought together all the pretentious symbolic figures he had already worked to death (in more ways than one) in the films he scripted for Carné: inevitably Petit could produce nothing better than a weak imitation of the films. *La Fiancée du Diable* had a book which was so banal in its romanticism (a mysterious château, a mysterious Bride, a mysterious Bridegroom who turned out to be the Devil, and so on) that it was almost an insult to the intelligence of the public, and had no meaning to a choreographer working in Paris in 1946. *Les Amours de Jupiter* had the advantage of a somewhat less hackneyed theme (Kokhno chose four episodes from the *Metamorphoses* of Ovid), and Petit showed considerable skill in treating the four scenes of seduction without undue obscenity; but the scenes were much more suited to revue than ballet. *Le Déjeuner sur l'Herbe* had no point whatever, and Petit's choreography was even more tenuous than usual.

In June, 1946, Kokhno commissioned from Cocteau a ballet *Le Jeune Homme et la Mort* in which he and Cocteau succeeded in going beyond anything Diaghilev had achieved in deliberately planned incongruity between the elements making up a ballet. The ballet was composed to jazz music which was used for the rehearsal, but not for the performances. Cocteau indicated to Petit the movements he wanted and Petit passed these on to the dancers, inserting from time to time a few academic steps (such as pirouettes and *grands jétés en tournant*) to maintain the illusion that the work was a ballet and not a clumsy adaptation of a Cocteau film. The mime was not completely naturalistic—Philippart did not in fact kick Babilée in the face, she only pretended to do so—but in general the acting was kept as sordid and naturalistic as possible. The climax of the work was reached when Babilée somehow managed to hang himself in a most convincingly naturalistic manner.

The gimmick in this ballet was the combination of sordid naturalistic acting with the noblest music that could be found (Bach's C Minor Passacaglia), every care being taken to prevent the choreography from having any relationship with the music. (The Bach music was not heard by the dancers until the first performance: the difference between the time taken to play the Passacaglia three times and the time taken by the ballet was absorbed by delaying the rise of the curtain for the appropriate time after the beginning of the music.)

In these cocktail ballets the choreography was of minor importance compared with the décor and the various gimmicks, and they gave Petit no opportunity of coming to maturity as a choreographer. Tired of being dominated by his associates, and frustrated in his own projects, he left the Compagnie des Champs-Élysées in January, 1948, to form his own company, the Ballets de Paris.

This was a turning-point in Petit's career. At last he had the freedom to work as he pleased, and by this time he had had the chance to study the ballets of his English and American contemporaries. The ballets of Ashton in particular seemed to make a strong impression on him. (He commissioned a ballet from Ashton for his new company.) Clearly Ashton's relatively fluid pseudo-classicism was more suited to Petit's temperament than Lifar's staccato style.

Petit's major production in the opening season of the Ballets de Paris, in May, 1948, was *Les Demoiselles de la Nuit*. This had a fairy-tale script by Anouilh which was well suited to Petit's style of choreography, and Petit devised the principal rôle (Agathe, the White Kitten) for Margot Fonteyn, who danced with the company as guest artist. (Petit admired her dancing, but was sensitive enough to realize that at Covent Garden she was never given the chance to show the full range of her talents.)

In composing this rôle Petit came to grips for the first time with the major problems of choreographic composition, and solved these problems with admirable inventiveness and assurance. Since Agathe wore a mask for much of the ballet, Petit was unable to rely on the dancer conveying the action by means of changing facial expressions, and he created dance images which successfully expressed the character of the rôle and the swiftly changing moods. Though Petit was undoubtedly influenced in devising the choreography by his conception of Margot Fonteyn's personality, the images he invented had validity apart from her superb performance. After Margot Fonteyn returned to Covent Garden, Colette Marchand took over the rôle and suddenly blossomed out as a dancer of extraordinary talent, giving every movement an enigmatic and unpredictable quality: her combination of femininity and felinity, of sweetness and ferocity, was quite irresistible.

The rest of the ballet was so far inferior to this rôle that it seemed to be the work of another choreographer. Petit made no effort to break away from the mannerisms and clichés of his earlier ballets: the Baron, for example, was simply Roland Petit in his usual rôle performing his favourite collection of classroom steps.

Nine months later Petit produced *Carmen*, which had much the same virtues and defects as *Les Demoiselles de la Nuit*. This ballet was completely dominated by Renée Jeanmaire's unforgettable performance in the title rôle. Choreographically this rôle was inferior to Agathe, for many of the steps had a vague arbitrary quality, and in the long bedroom scene (probably inspired by the pas de deux of the Transgressor and Medusa in *Undertow*) Petit treated the erotic symbolism without fantasy or mystery. But Jeanmaire danced the rôle with such purity of line and musicality that she transformed much of the crudity into poetry, and built up the rôle with hundreds of tiny nuances of expression until it challenged comparison with Bizet's own creation. In fact her contribution to the composition of the rôle was so great that it was impossible to imagine any other dancer performing it. She caught the imagination of the public with her performance of this rôle in the same way that Elssler swept people off their feet a century earlier with her Cachuca, and made the ballet *Carmen* so popular (in spite of its severe defects) that it was performed in London and New York every night for weeks on end.

The rest of the ballet was completely unworthy of the central rôle: Petit seemed to have made up his mind to do everything he could to vulgarize Bizet's opera. He transferred the music about with arbitrary perversity, constantly using music intended for one scene to accompany another scene for which it was quite unsuited. There was one particularly pointless scene in which he had the corps de ballet wave cigarettes in a circle and sing in chorus "L'Amour . . . L'Amour" to the tune of the habañera. Though he had broken away from Kokhno, Cocteau and Bérard he still seemed to think that it was naïve to treat Bizet's musical craftsmanship with respect, and to attempt to bring all the elements of a ballet into harmony.

He cast himself in the rôle of Don José, altering the character completely to conform to his usual self-consciously tragic rôle; as Pierre Michaut has pointed out, he seemed to think of Don José as a kind of Hamlet.[1] His attempt at creating a Spanish dance for himself was pathetically amateurish: he used the simple movements by which a Spanish dancer prepares for a spectacular step, and then omitted the spectacular step. Quite apart from the technical faults in the choreography, this dance was quite out of character, and had nothing to do with the action.

The subsequent ballets of Roland Petit had the defects of his two major

[1] *Le Ballet Contemporain*, p. 321.

ballets without anything corresponding to the wonderful central rôles of these ballets, and he showed himself unwilling to make any attempt to cope with the problems of composing a ballet as an organic whole. *L'Oeuf à la Coque*, composed at the same time as *Carmen*, was no more than a series of conventional music-hall numbers: the splendid artists of his company performed the high kicks and Cancan steps with a virtuosity and élan no music-hall dancer could emulate, but their talents were wasted on such hackneyed steps. Now and again they managed to insert an element of satire into their performance, but the choreography gave them little help in this respect. *Ballabile*, composed in 1950 for the Sadlers Wells Ballet, was also a cocktail ballet with no definite theme, though one could hardly call it abstract: it gave the effect of having been improvised by Petit in a mood of extreme cynicism. (He seemed to make a point of giving the dancers exactly the sort of enchaînements which they would find most difficult to perform.) Parts of it were clearly intended as a satire of Ashton's ballets, for he brought together many of Ashton's favourite mannerisms. Some sections were sentimental in the manner of *Les Forains*; others were no more than pseudo-classical enchaînements fitted vaguely to the music. Now and again there were passages of slap-stick clowning, such as the scene in which one of the men kept opening and closing his umbrella. The only rôle which showed any originality or inventiveness was the solo part created for Anne Negus and later taken over by Margaret Dale: the latter managed to find surprisingly many nuances of humour in this rather repetitive part, and whenever she was on the stage the ballet showed flashes of vitality.

From the beginning of his career Petit showed a fine ability to recognize talent in a danseuse and give it a chance to flower: he did a great deal to further the careers of a number of ballerinas who otherwise (as Michaut says) "would have consumed themselves in waiting".[1] On the other hand his Lifarian habit of building the principal male rôles in his ballets around his own personality prevented him from composing any male rôles comparable to the best of his female rôles, though he gave a few valuable opportunities to Jean Babilée, Serge Perrault and Gordon Hamilton.

Because of the frustration he suffered in the early years of his career while working in the Ballets des Champs-Élysées he never managed to compose a well-constructed light comedy of the same type as *Rodeo*, *Peter and the Wolf* and *Fancy Free*. He had at least as much talent for light comedy as Agnes de Mille, Frank Staff and Jerome Robbins, but by the time he had broken away from the archaic and pretentious late-Diaghilevian atmosphere of the Champs-Élysées company he had lost the innocence and spontaneity needed for this genre. His later attempts at playful comedy (*L'Oeuf à la Coque* and *Ballabile*) were damaged by an incongruous element of ferocious cynicism, and only a

[1] *Le Ballet Contemporain*, p. 323.

few flashes of wit and humour hinted at the comedy ballet which Petit might have composed in 1945 or 1946.

The dances and ballets he composed for the film *Hans Christian Andersen* were even more disappointing, for he confined himself to making a pastiche of the more banal episodes of earlier ballets (notably *Carmen*). He made no attempt to evoke any of the spirit of the Royal Danish Ballet (where the dancing sequences were supposed to take place), in spite of the fact that he had as one of his principal dancers the distinguished Danish premier danseur Erik Bruhn. It was painful to watch such fine artists as Renée Jeanmaire and Erik Bruhn struggling against Petit's tasteless and unimaginative choreography: they were in fact in exactly the same unhappy position as Danny Kaye, the hero of the film.

The new ballets composed by Petit in 1953 mainly continued in the same path as *L'Oeuf à la Coque* and *Ballabile*. *Ciné-Bijou*, for example, represented a lengthy and pretentious but ineffectual attempt at American jazz dancing. *Deuil en 24 Heures* was decorated with admirably colourful décors and costumes by Clavé, and the two leading male dancers (Serge Perrault and José Ferran) made their white spats flash across the stage with considerable verve; but the few comic ideas were worked to death, and much of the ballet seemed no more than a pretext to display a series of clever décors. *Le Loup* had a script by Anouilh and clearly was intended to repeat the success of *Les Demoiselles de la Nuit*: Petit himself showed to better advantage than ever before in the central rôle of the wolf, but this rôle was completely lacking in the poetic fantasy which distinguished the White Kitten, and the rest of the ballet had the same defects as Petit's other serious ballets. *The Lady in the Ice*, with book, décor and commentary by Orson Welles, was even less convincing in its pretentious symbolism than *Le Loup*: by now Petit had worn out his small stock of clichés.

JOHN CRANKO (*b.* 1927)

John Cranko began training at the age of fifteen in Cape Town in South Africa. Two years later, in 1944, he made his début with the Cape Town Ballet, and later began to work with the University Ballet, dancing leading rôles and arranging some ballets. He came to England in 1946 as one of a number of talented South African dancers who came to England to seek their fortune as soon as transport conditions became relatively normal after the end of the war. (Others who came at about this time were Nadia Nerina, Patricia Miller, Pamela Chrimes and David Poole.) Like the others Cranko joined the Sadlers Wells School and was soon taken into the newly formed junior company.

His development as a choreographer was strongly influenced by the atmosphere of the second company. Ninette de Valois had a policy of limiting its repertoire to the most flimsy sort of divertissement ballets; presumably she considered anything else beyond the capacity of the dancers, most of whom were aged about seventeen and had had no previous stage experience. The effect of this policy was to keep the company year after year in a state of almost pre-natal immaturity: the dancers acquired professional slickness but showed little tendency to develop artistically.

Cranko began his English career as a choreographer in 1947 with a short divertissement *Adieu*, a conventional romantic pas de deux originally arranged as the cabaret at a ball and later taken into the second company's repertoire. He also revived for the second company *Tritsch-Tratsch*, a pas de deux originally composed in South Africa. The latter was a cheerful trifle (involving two sailor-boys and a girl) that would have been suitable for a revue or a variety programme, but was hardly suitable for the repertoire of a ballet company. On the other hand it had vitality sadly lacking in the rest of the repertoire, and so became a permanent addition to the repertoire. It did not hint at any originality in Cranko, but it did show that he was capable of setting steps neatly to music.

Morceaux Enfantins, composed by him in the same year for the R.A.D. Production Club[1] with members of the second company, was a work of some promise, in view of the fact that Cranko was still only twenty and was composing his first full-scale ballet for a professional company. The ballet had severe defects: Cranko showed very little understanding of the devices by which episodes in a ballet can be linked up into an integrated whole, and there were long passages of completely pointless mime in which he seemed to be having a hard time to fill out the music. His style was inevitably based on that of Ashton. During most of the ballet he paid very little attention to the music, in spite of the fact that in *Tritsch-Tratsch* he had proved himself to have some ear for music.

Nevertheless there were isolated passages in this ballet which showed Cranko to have more talent than any of the other young choreographers receiving commissions from the junior company at about this time (Celia Franca, Anthony Burke, Alan Carter and Nancy McNaught). In particular Cranko composed one grotesque character rôle for Jane Shore which had individuality and gave this artist a chance to show her keen sense of humour, and towards the end of the ballet he arranged a group dance to the Gollywog's Cakewalk which showed real feeling for the rhythm and mood of the music. This ballet was taken into the Sadlers Wells Theatre Ballet's repertoire in 1948 with the title *Children's Corner*, and had a fair amount of success with the public.

It now seemed possible that Cranko might move on from *Children's Corner*

[1] At this period the R.A.D. Production Club arranged occasional Sunday performances at the Sadlers Wells Theatre in which ballets were staged by young choreographers. Very few young choreographers outside the Sadlers Wells organization had the funds to produce ballets for these performances, and to a large extent they were used as a testing-ground for young Sadlers Wells choreographers.

to a playful comedy ballet with an interesting theme and a clear-cut dramatic structure, just as Frank Staff moved on from the divertissement-ballet *Czernyana* to *Peter and the Wolf*. Cranko, however, seemed to feel that the time had come for him to tackle a really serious theme, and in 1949 he composed *Sea Change*, of which the theme was almost identical with that of *Dark Elegies*. Unfortunately this tragic theme was totally unsuited for Cranko's Ashtonian pseudo-classical style, and the music (Sibelius' *En Saga*) gave little support for the interpretation which Cranko put on it.

In his next ballet *Beauty and the Beast* (1949) he limited himself to two dancers—perhaps he realized the deficiencies of his choreographic technique as displayed in *Sea Change*—and chose a very simple fairy-tale theme. He treated this theme in the vague, somewhat sentimental manner which Ashton used for similar themes, but showed himself capable of finding movements well suited to the temperament and technique of his charming compatriot Patricia Miller—the only ballerina in the company at the time with any fluidity or lyricism in her movements. Even in this short ballet for two dancers Cranko seemed to find it necessary to use a great deal of padding: by this time the Ashton style was so exhausted that even to a naïve South African the style offered very little stimulus.

The following summer the New York City Ballet came to Covent Garden to repay the visit which the Sadlers Wells Ballet had paid to New York. Relations between the Sadlers Wells organization and the New York City Ballet were close and friendly: Balanchine arranged ballets for the two Sadlers Wells companies, and in return the resident choreographers of the two Sadlers Wells companies—Ashton and Cranko—arranged ballets for the New York City Ballet. (By this time Cranko's competitors had left the Sadlers Wells Theatre Ballet, and he was the official resident choreographer for the company, though he danced in the main company.)

Cranko had a very unhappy experience working with the New York City Ballet: his work in the genteel adolescent atmosphere of the Sadlers Wells Theatre Ballet was a poor preparation for the rather more sophisticated atmosphere of the New York City Ballet. The romantic subject on which he worked (the ballet was called *The Witch*) was very hackneyed, and his treatment of it was so crude and conventional that at times the ballet seemed almost like a parody of the genre. Once again Cranko avoided the difficulties presented by the highly unsuitable music (Ravel's second piano concerto) by ignoring the music almost completely: the movements looked as if they had been intended for quite different music (as in fact they had been). In his effort to adapt himself to the American company Cranko made use of a number of Balanchine's acrobatic tricks, showing particular fondness for one trick in which the danseuse is carried high in the air by two men; in fact one ballerina in *The Witch* did little else. Even less imaginative was Cranko's version of the erotic pas de deux of *Undertow*.

In spite of his unhappy experiences in the Balanchine-Kirstein company Cranko made his next production for the Sadlers Wells Theatre Ballet (*Pastorale*, 1950) a "classic ballet" in the Balanchine manner, basing his ballet on a Mozart Divertimento. There was a slight thread of story involving three pairs of shepherds and shepherdesses: like the other Theatre Ballet choreographers, Cranko seemed at this time to be working for an imaginary audience of schoolgirls carefully shielded from the drawings of Ronald Searle. In fact *Pastorale* was effectively abstract, and was as insipid as the abstract ballets of any of the other disciples of Balanchine—though more musical than Balanchine's own "classic ballets". According to Arnold Haskell,[1] this ballet was composed hurriedly to take the place of *The Witch*, but one can hardly suppose that it would have been much improved if more time had been spent on it; the chances of reviving dead horses are little affected by the time available for flogging them.

It was not until 1951 that Cranko justified to some extent the important position which had been given him by composing a comedy ballet *Pineapple Poll* which was something more than a haphazard suite of divertissements. This ballet was so much superior to the rest of the Sadlers Wells Theatre Ballet repertoire that it made a very strong impression on the long-suffering Theatre Ballet public: the demand for it became so great that programmes were altered in order to allow it to be given at almost every performance for the rest of the season, and it became for the second company what *Les Patineurs* was for the main company.

The motive behind the staging of this ballet was the very natural desire to take advantage of the fact that Sullivan's music had just entered the public domain. A period sailor ballet which was the first ballet to have music by Sullivan, based on one of Gilbert's Bab Ballads, and embellished with delightful period décor and costumes by Osbert Lancaster, could hardly fail completely; and Cranko, provided for the first time with a theme which was fully suited to his talents and his style of choreography, composed the finest ballet of his career. He made skilful use of the very limited talents of the company's prima ballerina Elaine Fifield, exploiting her hard, precise technique and making her doll-like ingenuousness an essential part of the rôle. None of the other rôles reached this level, but at least Cranko showed some awareness of the importance of characterization through movement, and the talented dancers of the company took full advantage of every slight opportunity given them to show personality and a sense of humour.

If one compared *Pineapple Poll* with other ballets in the same genre (in particular *Fancy Free*), instead of with the rest of the Theatre Ballet repertoire,

[1] *Foyer* No. 1 (Autumn, 1951), p. 39.

it was sadly disappointing. Working in the divertissement atmosphere of the
Theatre Ballet, Cranko had never found it necessary to come to grips with the
problems of balletic construction, and when the time came for him to plan
Pineapple Poll he failed to make the ballet build up or even to give himself
suitable choreographic opportunities. There was an enormous amount of
padding, and one whole scene (in which the girls slip on board the ship) was
completely redundant. Much of the humour was so crude that it was depressing
rather than funny: clearly Cranko had lost most of the naïveté and spontaneity
which distinguished the best of his choreography for *Children's Corner*. What
humour *Pineapple Poll* did possess was largely mimed, and there was hardly
any comedy dancing corresponding to the comic songs which are the raison
d'être of the Gilbert and Sullivan operas.

In his next ballet *Harlequin in April* (1951) he followed the example set by
Jerome Robbins in tackling a weighty theme with complex psychological and
mythological symbolism. His anonymous librettist provided him with a
remarkable mixture of symbols—the Fisher-King from Eliot's poem *The
Waste Land*, Harlequin, Pierrot, unicorns and so on.

Even a very great choreographer, working with appropriate music, would
have found it extremely difficult to make anything of this mixture of symbols;
Cranko's style of choreography was as completely unsuitable for such a theme as
that of Robbins, and the music was commissioned from Richard Arnell, who
was almost as much out of his element as Richard Rodgers would have been.

Like all pseudo-classical choreographers placed in a similar situation, Cranko
tried to solve the problems facing him by ignoring the music and filling the
stage with patterns which had only a tenuous relationship with the theme.
The whole ballet was just as obscure and pretentious as *The Age of Anxiety*,
though it was saved from complete failure by Piper's admirable décor and his
brilliant use of lighting. Tired of watching the incomprehensible choreography,
the eye of the spectator could enjoy the effects produced by changes of lighting
on the semi-transparent false proscenium and the ghostly apparitions of dancers
emerging from black curtains centre up-stage and moving down-stage through
mysterious side lighting. (These lighting effects were worthy of better choreography.) In his attempt to create the illusion of novelty Cranko followed the
example set by Helpmann of bringing in some of the most hackneyed devices
of the expressionist drama, such as changing the costume of the central figure
in view of the audience. (The trouble with all such devices is that they provide
little scope for dancing.)

In the Spring of 1952 Cranko composed his first ballet for the main company
—*Bonne-Bouche*, a comedy ballet obviously intended to repeat the success of
Pineapple Poll. The new ballet also had delectable décor and costumes by
Osbert Lancaster, but choreographically it was far inferior to its predecessor.

Carmen (Petit, Paris, 1949) with Roland Petit as Don José and Renée Jeanmaire as Carmen

Les Demoiselles de la Nu
(Petit, Paris, 1948): Agathe
the White Kitten

Below: Pineapple Poll (Cranko
London, 1951) with Elain
Fifield as Pineapple Poll an
David Poole as Jasper

Cranko devised the ballet with such little feeling for dramatic construction that over and over again he found himself covering the same ground, and the padding reached such enormous dimensions that the dancers had no chance of showing any wit in their movements. According to C. W. Beaumont,[1] the ballet was composed in only one month; but the texture of its choreography was so thin and conventional that the ballet might easily have been put together in a week or less.

Later in 1952 Cranko composed for the junior company a ballet *Reflection*, in much the same vein as *Harlequin in April*. *Reflection* had as its chief characters Narcissus, The Tender Child, The Aggressive Child, the Lovers, Echo and the Adolescents; it was clearly inspired by Tudor's so-called "psychological ballets" (*Jardin aux Lilas, Pillar of Fire* and *Undertow*) and by Robbins' attempts at this genre. Cranko's misunderstanding of Tudor was as profound as that of Robbins, and *Reflection* gave the impression of having been put together after a hasty reading-up of Freud, Jung and Adler. At no time did the jerky expressionist distortions of classroom movements give anything more than a summary indication of the traumas, complexes and fixations they were intended to convey: the desire to return to the womb, for example, was symbolized by Narcissus diving into the middle of a ring of dancers. This was repeated many times, like a Marx Brothers gag, but it was not funny even the first time. In the same way the relationship between Narcissus ("unable to project his emotions") and Echo ("who must absorb the personality of another in order to create an identity for herself") was symbolized by the rather obvious device of having Narcissus perform various steps which were copied exactly by Echo. The style of *Reflection* was very similar to that of *The Age of Anxiety*, and it was clear that Cranko was following in the same path as Robbins.

Early in 1953 Cranko composed for the main company *The Shadow*. Though most of this was arranged in the facile abstract manner of *Pastorale*, he followed the example set by Balanchine in *Serenade* of including a certain amount of melodramatic but obscure mime in order to give the ballet a certain amount of individuality. The gimmick he chose to use was the introduction of a man in black wearing an enormous black cloak with which he covered the principal danseuse (Beriosova) from time to time. Presumably Cranko took the idea partly from the Hans Andersen fairy-tale and partly from Jung's Shadow symbol; but he treated his shadow-figure with such banality that it emerged as something very like Von Rothbart in *Le Lac des Cygnes*, and at the première this similarity was rather unkindly emphasized by the substitution of Act II of *Lac* for *Ballet Imperial* as the first ballet on the programme.

Cranko's failure to do justice to his own talents was not due to any lack of ambition or drive: he brought these qualities with him from South Africa,

[1] *Ballet*, June, 1952, p. 33.
A.A.O.B—R

and held fast to them in Europe. What he lacked was the genius to break away from the pseudo-classical style in which he was brought up and form a completely new style of his own. On the other hand we must bear in mind that the possession of such genius might have wrecked his career: he went to the top inside the Sadlers Wells organization because he kept within its standard Ashtonian pseudo-classical style, and his development as a choreographer corresponded roughly to the course set for the Sadlers Wells Theatre Ballet. If he had been less impressionable and more original he might have received as little scope at Sadlers Wells as Tudor (who was employed there as a dancer, and was allowed to compose dances in operas, but received no commissions for ballets).

G

Russia Since 1917

SOVIET BALLET is a world apart, and the generalizations of this book apply to it only to a very limited extent. Adequate treatment of Soviet ballet in all its aspects would require a great deal of space: here we are concerned only with those aspects which are relevant to world ballet.

Perhaps the most astonishing thing about Soviet ballet is that in spite of its very high degree of isolation and the violent changes in social conditions in Russia from one period to the next it has followed a path parallel to that taken by ballet in Western countries.

On the eve of the Revolution the Maryinsky was to some extent an artistic backwater: nearly all its most creative impulses had been absorbed into the Diaghilev Ballet, and the repertoire was much the same as in the days of Petipa. Teliakovsky was still Director of the Imperial Theatres, and Fokine was still only an assistant maître de ballet. Though some of the ballets produced by Fokine for charity shows (e.g. *Cléopâtre*, *Chopiniana*, *Carnaval* and *Papillons*) had been taken into the repertoire, he had no direct influence on artistic policy, and the Maryinsky showed no interest in his more advanced productions for Diaghilev, such as the Stravinsky ballets *L'Oiseau de Feu* and *Petrouchka*.

On the other hand the new Russian tradition of classical dancing was maintained at a high level. Legat and other good teachers trained by him were active, and though Pavlova, Lydia Kyaksht, Nijinsky and Bronislava Nijinska had left the Maryinsky, there were many great dancers appearing on the stage of this theatre, giving fabulous performances in ballets like *Giselle*, *Esmeralda*, *Le Lac des Cygnes* and *Chopiniana*.

The effect of the Revolution was to cause a very serious break in the traditions of the Maryinsky. The school and the theatre closed, and did not re-open for a year. All the great Maryinsky dancers scattered over the face of the earth: some left in 1918, as soon as transport conditions made this possible, and others in the next two or three years. Fokine left in 1918, and Legat in 1922 after a period in Moscow. When the theatre reopened the remaining dancers found themselves in a bewildering and ambiguous position. There was a widespread feeling that ballet was a purely aristocratic art, with no more meaning for the workers of Soviet Russia than the jewellery of Fabergé: the ballet had been a department of the court, and audiences had in fact been very largely aristocratic.

It was largely thanks to the courage and good sense of the Commissar for Education, Lunacharsky, that the various Imperial theatres were made into State institutions and revived. Moreover Lunacharsky took care to put in charge of the theatres men with real knowledge and ability, capable of carrying on traditions and resisting the contemporary trends in the Russian theatre towards a complete break with the past. Akim Volynsky, the new artistic director of the Maryinsky, was a very erudite critic and historian who made far-reaching plans for the further development of the Maryinsky; unfortunately, however, his view of tradition was so limited that he was violently opposed to the work of Fokine, and he was therefore unable to maintain a proper balance between the maintenance and the renewal of tradition. (He was dismissed a few years later, his place being taken by Lopukhov.)

At this time the drama was dominated by various new types of expressionist productions, the work of men like Meyerhold, Tairov and Vakhtangov; but the Maryinsky and the Bolshoy continued to perform *Giselle*, *Le Lac des Cygnes*, *Casse-Noisette*, *The Sleeping Beauty*, *Esmeralda*, *Raymonda*, *Don Quixote*, *Vain Precautions*,[1] *The Hunch-Backed Horse* and so on. The standard of performance had dropped greatly (particularly at the Maryinsky—it did not have so far to fall at the Bolshoy), and to the young people of the time these ballets were dry as dust, with no artistic value and no meaning to the new Russia.

In accordance with the spirit of the times Lunacharsky gave the Maryinsky-trained choreographer Kasyan Goleizovsky permission to start an avant-garde dance group, the Moscow Kamerny (Chamber) Ballet. With this group Goleizovsky produced wildly iconoclastic solos and group dances in a barefoot free style, making considerable use of acrobatics, constructivist imitation of machinery, architectural groups, and an eroticism verging on obscenity; in some items the dancers appeared almost nude. In fact the work done by Goleizovsky was very similar to that being done at this time by the free-dance groups of Central Europe, though his acrobatics and constructivism were allied to Meyerhold's bio-mechanics and were highly typical of the Soviet theatre of the day. Goleizovsky also did a good deal of work in the music-hall, and largely effaced the distinction between ballet and music-hall. At the time this was considered a very artistic thing to do: the music-hall and the circus, being proletarian entertainments, were considered necessarily more vital and significant than the "bourgeois" theatre.[2] At first expressionism was excluded

---

[1] *La Fille Mal Gardée.*

[2] The extraordinary outlook of the time—similar in many ways to that prevailing in France during the French Revolution—is well reproduced in books on the Russian theatre written this time by Huntley Carter.

from the Maryinsky and the Bolshoy, but in due course training in acrobatics and the free dance was introduced into the schools attached to these theatres, and expressionist-constructivist ballets were produced. In 1924, for example, Goleizovsky staged a constructivist production of *Beautiful Joseph* (*La Légende de Joseph*) at the Maryinsky; and this trend acquired such momentum towards the end of the twenties that old ballets began to receive new expressionist-constructivist or "realistic" productions, and the classical tradition was in danger of complete extinction.

The fact that it did not disappear was largely due to the efforts of a small number of people at the Maryinsky—the artistic director Akim Volynsky, the chief choreographer Fedor Lopukhov (later also artistic director), the régisseur and teacher of boys Ponomaryev, and the teacher of senior girls Agrippina Vaganova (artistic director in succession to Lopukhov after 1930 and later still director of all ballet training in the Soviet Union). Though cruelly hampered by the absence of Fokine,[1] Legat and all the leading Maryinsky dancers, Volynsky and Lopukhov did what they could with the material at their disposal. Fortunately the work of Ponomaryev and Vaganova eventually bore fruit in the shape of a number of talented artists—notably the danseurs Yermolayev (graduation of 1926), Chabukiani (1929) and Sergueyev (1931), and the danseuses Semyonova (1925) and Ulanova (1928).

Though Semyonova made a sensation at her début in 1925, she was considerably over-rated for exactly the same reason that Markova was over-rated in England. She was in fact the very first Soviet ballerina. But, like many other Vaganova pupils, she developed a rather hard, almost acrobatic style, with certain serious faults of line: though Vaganova had been a distinguished participant in Legat's *Classe de Perfection*,[2] and gave her pupils a considerable number of admirable qualities (above all great strength in the back), she introduced into her training certain ugly positions, and her pupils were inevitably influenced by the prevailing trend towards acrobatic expressionism.

Ulanova, however, stood out in a very marked manner from all her contemporaries, and revived in her dancing the glories of the pre-Revolutionary Russian school. This may partly be attributed to her exceptional talent, but no less important was the fact that she was in effect a child of the Maryinsky: her mother, her father and her uncle were all Maryinsky dancers, and she began to watch performances at the Maryinsky in 1916 (when she was only six), so that

---

[1] According to Anatole Chujoy (*Dance Encyclopedia*, p. 190), Fokine made an attempt to return to Russia in 1923: Chujoy suggests that this proposal by Fokine was foiled by the Soviet envoy Exkuzovich for personal reasons. Another possible explanation is Volynsky's violent antipathy to Fokine's ballets.

[2] Legat mentions Vaganova three times in his book *The Story of the Russian School*. She did not reach the rank of ballerina until 1915: according to Anatole Chujoy (*Ballet Encyclopedia*, p. 489) intrigues held up her promotion. She retired from the stage in 1916, at the age of thirty-seven.

she had the chance of seeing dancers like Karsavina before they left Russia for good. Moreover her mother was one of the teachers at the Maryinsky school, and watched over her development. Like many great dancers before her Ulanova had to fight against grave handicaps: in her case a rather awkward stance, a temperament which enabled her to tackle successfully only a very narrow range of parts, raised shoulders and a tendency to rely too heavily on continuity of movement without sharp accents. Nevertheless her triumph in the rôle of Odette (in *Le Lac des Cygnes*) in 1929, in the year following her début, prepared the way for a major change in Soviet ballet; and her achievements since then have caused her dancing to be regarded (quite rightly) as one of the main achievements of post-revolutionary Russian culture. She succeeded admirably in building a bridge over the years of expressionism to the glories of the past.

Though Lopukhov was regarded by the young men of Balanchine's generation as an old fogy, because he was not prepared to throw the baby out with the bath-water, he did in fact attempt to remedy obvious gaps in the Maryinsky repertoire: Leontiev having produced *Petrouchka* in 1920, Lopukhov followed this in 1921 with *L'Oiseau de Feu*. In later years Lopukhov found it desirable to produce ballets introducing all the fashionable expressionist trends of the day—acrobatics, movements taken from sport, machine-imitation, dancing without music, the introduction into ballet of speech and song, and so on. At the same time, however, he continued to produce the old ballets with a minimum of changes, and kept the standard of classical dancing as high as possible.

By the middle of the twenties Russian ballet inside Russia and Diaghilev Ballet-Russe had converged to such an extent that attempts were even made by the Soviet Government to induce Diaghilev to return as Director of the State Theatres. A good many features of Soviet expressionism had been carried into the Diaghilev Ballet by Nijinska and Balanchine, and in 1927 Diaghilev produced a constructivist ballet (*Le Pas d'Acier*) with the help of the Soviet designer Yakulov which might well have been staged in Leningrad or Moscow. At this time the differences between Diaghilev's artistic policy and the policy of the Soviet State ballet companies were of small importance: the deliberate breaking of the *Gesamtkunstwerk* by Diaghilev found a close parallel in Russia in constructivist productions of old ballets and much new work by expressionist choreographers and dramatic producers.

Early in the thirties there was a strong reaction against expressionism and constructivism in Russia; as in the West this reaction took the form of a return to the pseudo-classicism of Petipa, with the retention of a number of expressionist elements—in particular a strong element of acrobatics. Ballets were once again composed in several acts, lasting a whole evening, and classical dancing was rehabilitated. As in the West at this time the art of ballet increased enormously in popularity; many new companies were founded in big cities all over the Soviet Union, and there was a great increase in the number of schools and the number of dancers trained.

By general consent the triumph of the new trend in ballet was sealed by the production of *Romeo and Juliet* in Leningrad in 1940, with choreography by Lavrovsky, music by Prokofiev, and Ulanova admirably cast as Juliet. This ballet had a good deal in common with the Helpmann ballet *Hamlet*, produced by the Sadlers Wells Ballet in 1942. Both choreographers took their inspiration from Shakespeare, translating the action of a play into naturalistic rather than conventional mime, and adding academic dance-movements from time to time. There were of course important differences: Helpmann confined himself to certain episodes important for the exposition of various psychological theories about the play, and made very sparing use of dance-movements, whereas Lavrovsky produced the whole play with many academic solos, pas de deux, etc. Fundamentally, however, the two choreographers tackled their theme in the same archaic way, achieving no real harmony between the dancing and the mime. Both choreographers showed a strong feeling for dramatic effect, and Lavrovsky in particular made the duelling scene really exciting—but this same scene could quite well have been inserted into a spoken production of the play.

The most disturbing feature about Lavrovsky's ballet was the Petipa-like lack of harmony between the various elements in the production. The cushion dance in the ballroom scene, for example, was produced by Lavrovsky with admirable understanding of the dancing of the period, and gave an impression of complete authenticity down to the smallest details of the costumes; but this was followed by other dances with ballerinas on pointe which had nothing to do with the period, and whenever Juliet danced with Romeo she continued to use a tiny vocabulary of arabesques and quite inappropriately acrobatic lifts which in themselves were almost expressionless: Ulanova managed to pour meaning into them, but the best that could be said of the choreographic imagery was that it was neutral enough not to get in her way.

Unfortunately Soviet choreographers seemed to show the same uncritical reverence for Petipa as their pseudo-classical contemporaries in the West. The same was true of Soviet critics and historians: even the outstanding historian Yuri Slonimsky ended his sharply critical analysis of the career of Petipa[1] with a eulogy of Petipa's methods of composition. The full significance of the work of Fokine had been lost to sight, in spite of the fact that some of his best compositions (notably *Le Cygne* and *Chopiniana*) were kept in the repertoire. Here we can see the cumulative effect of the breaks in tradition caused by the de-

---

[1] *Marius Petipa* (Dance Index): translation by A. Chujoy of the section on Petipa in Slonimsky's important book *Peterburgian Maîtres de Ballet of the Nineteenth Century*.

parture of all the great dancers and also Fokine and Legat, the years of concentration on acrobatic expressionism, the isolation of Soviet choreographers from the best work of men like Massine and Tudor, and other similar factors.

Nevertheless a ballet like *Romeo and Juliet* demands criticism at the highest level, and is in a very different class from e.g. Soviet painting. The artists working in the field of ballet have been spared most of the political interference which has adversely affected other arts. There have been propaganda ballets such as *The Red Poppy*, and ballets of contemporary life such as *Svetlana*; in 1938 there was a rather unfortunate attempt by Vaganova to give the story of *Le Lac des Cygnes* more "realism" by transferring it to the first quarter of the nineteenth century and transforming the wicked magician into a ruined landowner; and in 1944 *Giselle* was taken out of the repertoire for a time as being too "mystical".[1] To a considerable extent, however, Soviet ballet has been allowed to develop in its own way.

One field in which Soviet choreographers and dancers have made big strides forward is in the balletizing of national dances. Here they were not troubled by a break in tradition (for there was a continuous tradition among the performers of the dances) nor by political directives, and they tackled the problems involved with admirable élan, imagination and good taste. This was true not only of the national dances in ballets like *The Fountain of Bakhchisaraï* (Zakharov, 1934) and *Taras Bulba* (Lopukhov, 1940) but also of the folk-dances from all over the Soviet Union produced by Moiseyev with his Folk-Dance Ensemble (the members of which were highly trained ballet dancers). In the dramatic ballets the total artistic effect was liable to be damaged from time to time by such lapses of taste as the performance by the Georgian girl Zarema (in *The Fountain of Bakhchisaraï*) of a dance on pointe in the harem, surrounded by odalisques in Oriental slippers; but in ballets like *Taras Bulba* (based almost entirely on Ukrainian dances) and in the Moiseyev items such lapses could not arise.

[1] *Cf.* Iris Morley, *Soviet Ballet*, p. 34.

H

India

(a) Classical Styles

THE SURVIVING classical styles of India are almost as important to the West as they are to India, for they represent a living tradition which has survived without a break for at least 2,500 years, and probably dates back to the very dawn of civilization some 5,000 years ago. (In the West the classical tradition was completely lost in the Dark Ages, and Western ballet in the modern sense of the term is only 250 years old.) Except during the unhappy period which is just ending, classical dancing was regarded in India as the mother of the arts and was honoured accordingly. Of all the ancient traditional arts of India classical dancing and music are the only ones to survive as a living tradition. In fact a contemporary performance by classical Indian dancers is almost the exact equivalent of the performance of an ancient Greek drama which by some miracle reproduces all the essential features of the original production.

In the Indian classical tradition there is no dichotomy between dance-technique and the expression of mood or emotion, and the training of arms and heads is just as highly developed as that of legs. In these respects the Western tradition is far inferior to the various Indian classical styles and the other Oriental classical styles derived from the Indian styles. This is probably the main reason why Oriental dancing had such profound influence on the main architects of the renaissance of ballet in the twentieth century (Fokine, Pavlova, Nijinsky and Tudor) and on the main pioneers of the free dance (Dalcroze, Laban, Wigman, Ruth St. Denis, and perhaps also Delsarte).

Too few dancing statues from the ancient Indus civilization (which lasted from about 3,000 B.C. to about 2,000 B.C.) have come to light to enable us to form a clear idea of the oldest Indian classical technique, but they show that dancing already had a very important place in Indian life, and give a definite indication of the probable origin of the Indian style. From about 300 B.C. onwards sculptured figures of dancers enable us to trace a steady evolution in the classical technique: the style remains basically the same, but the angles become more and more emphasized, the knees turn out, and mudras (symbolic gestures of the hands) become prominent. We can also trace a simultaneous spread of classical Indian dancing to the countries of South-East Asia as far as Japan, along with the Buddhist and Hindu religions. (From a choreographic point of view Mahayana Buddhism and Hinduism are almost indistinguishable: the technique is the same, and so are the themes, which are drawn from the ancient Hindu epics.)

The Gupta period (A.D. 320 to A.D. 647) was the golden age of classical Indian dancing and drama (which were in fact inseparable). We can form a fairly clear idea of the classical dancing of this period by comparing *all* the surviving classical styles of Indian origin with the detailed description of classical dancing in various ancient treatises (*sastras*) on dramatic art, and with ancient sculptured images of dancing figures from temples in India and the countries of South-East Asia.[1] The classical styles surviving in the various countries of South-East Asia are far less rich in movement and rhythm than the classical styles surviving in India, but they preserve certain poses described in the ancient *sastras* and not to be found in the classical styles surviving in India.

Each of the three principal classical styles[2] surviving in India maintains with remarkable fidelity some aspects of the classical style of the *sastras*. Bharata Natyam,[3] the solo dance of the devadasis (temple courtesans) of the Tamil country in South India, retains all the noble angularity of line of the ancient style, and a large number of the standard poses. At any moment the dancer looks as if she had just stepped down from the walls of a temple. Kathakali—the ritual dance-drama of Kerala[4] in South India—is unique in retaining the full range of ancient *abhinaya* (rhythmic mime in which the dancer represents the meanings of the sung words by means of mudras, stylized facial expressions, foot movements, etc.); in fact Kathakali *abhinaya* goes beyond ancient *abhinaya*, having mudras for every word in a sentence and even for punctuation. Kathak— the court dance of North India—goes beyond the other surviving Indian styles in the rhythmic complexity, power and range of tempo of its foot-beats; it probably goes even beyond the ancient style of the *sastras* in these respects. Kathak is unique among the surviving classical styles in preserving as an integral part of its tradition the ancient practice of having both sexes dance; Bharata Natyam is traditionally danced only by women, while Kathakali is traditionally danced only by men and boys.

All three styles have kept their vitality through centuries of violent social change because they are handed on by the gurus as a living tradition: each great

[1] The most valuable sources of information on the ancient classical style is the Nataraja temple at Chidambaram, which has a large number of sculptured illustrations to the *Bharata Natya Sastra*—one of the two most important of the ancient *sastras* dealing with dramatic art. (The other is *Abhinaya Darpana*.)

[2] There are in fact several others in remote parts of South India.

[3] This is the name given to the style in recent years by Tamil pundits, presumably to help its acceptance in respectable circles. Devadasis and their teachers use quite different names.

[4] Malabar, Cochin and Travancore—the Western coastal strip in the far South.

guru is a creative artist, devising new standard patterns of dance-movement and *abhinaya* and passing them on to chosen pupils along with the vast corpus of standard patterns he received from his guru. In Indian classical music one can make no distinction between composer and performer: the musician composes the music as he performs it, working within strict rules; and much the same is true of classical dancing. In fact the dance-guru is the equivalent of the maître de ballet of Europe in the eighteenth and nineteenth centuries. In Bharata Natyam the devadasi performs under the supervision of her *nattuvan* (who is a man and does not dance), but in Kathakali and Kathak the great gurus are also dancers, and when they perform they are able to give rein to their fancy, within the strict rules of their respective styles.

Manipuri is generally regarded as another classical style, and is taught as such in the dance-schools of Bombay, Calcutta and other cities. There is much to be said for this, for Manipuri has a fine variety of beautiful and complex dance-movements, with a lyrical fluidity and sweetness not to be found in the other styles. Rhythmically it is very complex; the training in real Manipuri (as distinct from the simplified variety popular at girls' schools) is long and exacting; and though it has absorbed many elements from the folk-dances of Manipur State, Manipuri can undoubtedly be traced back to the classical style of the *sastras*. On the other hand the *abhinaya* aspect of Manipuri is very weak; the few mudras are used decoratively rather than expressively, and the face remains impassive. For this reason it is perhaps best to place Manipuri in a separate category, along with the classical Kandyan dances of Ceylon.[1] Experts in Manipuri and Kandyan can explain the meaning of each movement, but through the passage of centuries this meaning has become so obscure that it has little existence for the average spectator.[2]

In Hindu and Buddhist society religion permeated every aspect of life; looking at the matter in another way one might regard these two great closely related religions as the characteristic expression of Indian customs, sentiments

---

[1] Though superficially Manipuri and Kandyan seem poles apart—Manipuri lyrical, soft and feminine, Kandyan angular, violent and masculine—there are important bonds of resemblance between the two. Resemblances are particularly obvious between the spins and the rhythms of male Manipuri dancing and the corresponding aspects of Kandyan. The drum dances of Kandy and Manipur show resemblances which are particularly striking. The early Indian settlers of Ceylon came from North-Eastern India, and it is possible that Manipuri and Kandyan have descended from a common ancestor, the ancient classical style of the region now known as Bengal.

[2] The relationship between Bharata Natyam, Kathakali and Kathak on the one hand and Manipuri and Kandyan on the other has many parallels in the countries of South-East Asia where the classical dances are derived from those of India. This relationship is particularly clear in Indonesia. The old classical Javanese style survives in Hindu Bali (where the dance-dramas are highly dramatic, and demand in the artists a good command of stylized facial expressions); in Moslem Java, on the other hand, the dance-dramas are still based on the Hindu epics Ramayana and Mahabharata, but the dancers keep impassive faces, and the tempo is rather slow. (Traditionally, the classical Javanese dramas were performed only by princes, and it was considered ungentlemanly to show emotion or move quickly.)

and ideals. All classical dancing was religious, and there was no fundamental difference between temple dancing and court dancing. In the temples the classical styles tended to be preserved without any changes, like religious ritual, whereas at the courts the gurus tended to adapt the classical styles (or at least the manner of presenting the dances) to changes in the taste of patrons and changing social conditions; in due course the new developments at the courts were incorporated into the temple performances. In general it seems that dance traditions were transmitted in the same way as the Hindu epics Ramayana and Mahabharata, which refer to events at a very early stage in Indian history, though in their surviving form they do not date back beyond the first few centuries A.D. (The Vedas, in contrast, were transmitted orally for about 3,000 years with only infinitesimal changes, in spite of the fact that their language became very hard to interpret.)

Though none of the surviving classical styles preserves the full range of the ancient classical style, this does not necessarily mean that taken as a whole Indian classical dancing is less rich and varied than it was a millenium ago. Each style has moved in a certain direction, absorbing certain influences and developing considerably those aspects in which it specializes. Much has been lost, but much has been gained.

Each of the three main classical styles conforms to classical Hindu aesthetic doctrines about *rasas* (moods), though the different styles emphasize certain *rasas* at the expense of others. (Kathakali, being a form of dance-drama, has the greatest variety of moods.) The three styles also retain the classical unity of *samgit* (dancing, singing and instrumental music) and the classical balance between *natya* (dramatic dancing) and *nrtta* (abstract or pure dancing).

Each of the Indian classical styles can best be understood by the Western spectator in relation to corresponding traditions in Western ballet. Bharata Natyam, for example, shows a relationship between the dancers and their gurus which in some respects is like the relationship between the classical ballerinas and their teachers and choreographers. Since the guru does not dance himself he is judged by the work of his pupils: one of the latter cannot dance properly unless he stands at the back of the stage and sets the time for her with small cymbals.

A Kathakali dance-drama is the nearest thing within the Indian classical tradition to a Western ballet, and accordingly Kathakali has had more influence on modern Indian ballet than the other classical styles. The greatest dancers (who are also gurus) form troupes which are capable of performing any one of a large number of traditional dramas on demand from a patron. The troupes vary widely in prestige and quality of performance, and dancers move about to some extent from one troupe to another; famous dancers are in demand as "guest artists" for special occasions. The finest troupes sometimes go on tour outside Kerala, but Kathakali is not properly appreciated outside its home.

Certain standard characters (gods, heroes, demons, witches, seductive demi-goddesses, etc.) appear in each drama, though the stories (drawn from various episodes in the two Hindu epics) differ widely. The dancers are to the last degree professionals, for any one of them must be prepared to take any rôle in a large repertoire of dramas, and each drama lasts a whole night. The specially constructed stage, the curtain, and the artificial illumination of Kathakali are just as important to the building up of atmosphere as they are in Western ballet. Like ballet, Kathakali is a popular art, attracting audiences which may amount to several thousands. There is no choreographer in the Western sense of the word: the guru teaches his pupils a precise manner of translating almost any word into mudras, facial expressions and foot movements, and also a large number of *kalasams* (standard passages of pure dancing) for use at the end of verses. For much of the performance the dancer is tied rigidly to the script (which is sung by members of the "orchestra"), but there are some passages without singing when the dancer must think for himself, as in the Commedia dell'Arte: he then improvises according to his fancy, with the drummers following him, and he must be prepared to answer questions from other players relating to his rôle and the action of the drama. The dancers do not work for regular salaries: the leader of the troupe is commissioned by a patron (who may be the artistic director of a temple or a wealthy private person) to put on a show with a certain number of dancers, and pays the dancers, drummers, singers, make-up artist and porters out of a lump sum provided by the patron for a specific performance. The make-up artist is sometimes the most highly paid member of the troupe.

From the point of view of dance-technique Kathak is by far the closest to ballet of the classical styles: Europeans seeing Kathak for the first time tend to imagine that Kathak has been influenced by ballet, though in fact Kathak took roughly its present form at least a thousand years before the ballet technique was developed. Pirouettes play the same important rôle in both techniques, and the specialized technique of head-movement to prevent dizziness in the spins is remarkably similar in the two styles.[1] Like the Western ballet dancer the

[1] Certain aspects of the Kathak technique, such as the parallel position of the feet, show close affinities to the classical style depicted in the oldest Buddhist bas-reliefs: it is possible that Kathak preserves aspects of the classical technique older than any preserved in the other classical styles. This would not be surprising, for Kathak belongs to North India, and it was in North India that Indian civilization originated. Such survivals from the remote past are by no means rare in India; not long ago, in Benares, an illiterate Hindu priest appeared who dictated a long religious work which was previously unknown and dated back to the Middle Ages, since when it had been transmitted orally by a line of priests. The Kathaks (a sub-caste of musicians and dancers) were in fact Brahmans, wearing the sacred cord and giving a blessing instead of the usual gesture of greeting: it would have been quite possible for a line of Kathaks to transmit to modern times traditions of dancing older than the style of the *sastras*. The common practice in books on Indian dancing of describing Kathak as a style of relatively recent origin, originating at the Mogul courts from a mixture of Hindu and Moslem elements, shows a lamentable ignorance of both Kathak and the cultural history of the Moslem world in the

Kathak dancer combines extremely powerful foot movements with light and graceful arm-movements. (It is possible that Kathak has had some influence on the development of the Western ballet technique via the traditional dances of Spain.)

Within each of the main classical styles of India there are schools corresponding roughly to the Italian and French schools of ballet: some schools stress purity of line and clear-cut rhythms, others grace, personality, individuality and expressiveness. Even within one school there are some gurus who specialize in *abhinaya* and others in pure dance; and the gap between the dancing taught by the greatest gurus of the best schools and the most corrupt gurus of the worst schools is if possible even wider than that between the best and the worst of ballet training.

During the nineteenth century the great classical dances of India fell under a cloud because of the importation from England into India of Victorian prudery and the development of an indigenous type of prudery associated with the rise of an Indian middle class.[1] The classical dances had already suffered considerably from the iconoclasm of some Moslem rulers,[2] and the wave of prudery nearly destroyed classical dancing entirely. All professional dancing came to be despised in India because of its association with prostitution, in exactly the same way that ballet dancing came to be despised in England in the late-Victorian period. For the first time in history a large number of Indians lost their traditional respect for the classical dances of their country, and could no longer understand the ancient Hindu tradition which had led

Middle Ages. In fact there is hardly a single element in Kathak (apart from the *salami tola* with which the dancer greets a Moslem patron and which has its exact equivalent in Bharata Natyam) which can be traced unmistakably to a source outside India: where Kathak has elements in common with the dances of Moslem countries to the West and North of India, these can usually be traced back in India to times much earlier than the rise of Islam, and one must assume a diffusion from India rather than to India. There were of course some counter-influences on Kathak from other parts of the Moslem world: one can perhaps trace an influence from Persian calligraphy on the arm-movements of Kathak (which are less angular and staccato than those of Bharata Natyam and Kathakali), and Mogul paintings suggest that the hand-clapper (ancient Greek crotale—Spanish castanet) was introduced into Kathak in the Mogul period from Persia. Nevertheless it is significant that the hand-clapper had very little lasting influence on Kathak—it interfered with the execution of mudras—and the basic technique of Kathak is just as Indian as the closely related techniques of the classical styles of South India.

[1] For a discussion of the relationship between prudery and the middle class, *see* Erich Fromm, *The Fear of Freedom*, p. 82, and Ranulf, *Moral Indignation and Middle Class Psychology*, p. 66 *ff*.

[2] Some of the early Moslem invaders set out to destroy every aspect of Hindu culture with puritanical zeal, but other Moslem rulers (such as the great Mogul Emperors) were great patrons of all the arts. Unfortunately Aurangzeb, the last of the powerful Mogul Emperors, was a highly neurotic religious bigot: there is a tradition that he was shocked by the fact that the devadasis of the Tamil-Nad danced almost nude, in the classical Indian manner, and forced them to adopt the cumbersome costumes which are now standard for Bharata Natyam. Prudery in sexual matters is quite foreign to Hindu traditions: in Hindu sculpture the sexual act is normally used to symbolize the highest religious conceptions, and a number of temples are decorated with erotic sculpture.

to the maintenance of courtesan dancers by Hindu temples.[1] Respectable Indian women considered themselves insulted if even the word devadasi was uttered in their presence. (One reason why Hindu women were so fanatical in their outcry against devadasis was that only devadasis were educated and taught music: this gave devadasis an unfair advantage over other women in winning the affections of men.) The fact that the "Nautch-dances" were in fact classical dances of ancient origin—one of the greatest glories of India's cultural heritage—was lost to sight by the mass of the middle-class population, though not by the dance-gurus (who preserved their ancient books and paid no attention to the stupid attacks by middle-class prudes, whether English or Indian). As early as 1917 the great art-historian Ananda Coomaraswamy emphasized the enormous artistic importance of "Nautch-dancing" in his introduction to his translation of certain chapters of the sastra Abhinaya Darpana,[2] making quite clear that it was a living tradition descended from the ancient classical style; but the outcry against "Nautch-dancing" was now at its height, and continued with unabated vigour well into the twenties. All classical dancing suffered from this campaign; Kathakali was partially exempt, being performed only by male dancers, but the Kerala equivalent of Bharata Natyam (Mohini Attam) almost disappeared during the first two decades of this century.

A number of books on Indian dancing speak of a renaissance of classical dancing in recent years. The word "renaissance" is badly chosen, and gives a false impression of what actually happened. The gurus continued to teach their pupils in the traditional way right through the period when classical dancing was under a cloud, and traditional patrons continued to support classical dancing in the districts where these dances were at home (Kathakali in Kerala, Bharata Natyam in the Tamil-Nad, and Kathak in Lucknow, Jaipur, Bikaner, Benares and a few other cities of North India). The dancers were professionals, being normally trained by the guru free of charge and maintained at his expense during training, later paying the guru back out of their earnings.

---

[1] Up to Victorian times Hindu temples had associated with them considerable numbers of devadasis in all predominantly Hindu areas; but the outcry against the devadasis caused the institution to be abolished everywhere except in the Tamil-Nad in South India, where it survived in spite of violent attacks. The higher-grade devadasis were very far from being prostitutes in the Western sense of the word: they were professional dancers whose marriage customs (as regulated by Hindu law) were different from those of other women, the normal marriage laws being quite incompatible with the profession of dancing. A Hindu wife had no more reason to object to her husband undertaking the support of a devadasi than to his taking a second wife, and a high-grade devadasi was normally loyal to the man of her choice while she lived with him. (A low-grade devadasi was, however, promiscuous.) The children of all devadasis were legitimate, the devadasi having been married to the god in the temple before making her début as a dancer. Things were different in North India, where e.g. the famous dancer-courtesans of Lucknow (who were expert Kathak dancers) had no connection with temples—though their song-dances dealt with religious themes (Krishna and Radha).

[2] Nandikesvara, The Mirror of Gesture (tr. A. Coomaraswamy and G. K. Duggirala).

What actually happened in the second, third and fourth decades of this century was a gradual rehabilitation of the classical styles all over India. These were taken up by middle-class girls and were no longer automatically despised by the middle-class public as prostitute-dancing. Pavlova herself did much to expedite this process of rehabilitation by showing the classical dancing of the West: inspired by her example Indian middle-class girls began to learn European ballet (both in India and in Europe) and in due course moved on to Indian classical dancing. Another very important influence was that of Tagore's school Santiniketan, where he introduced training in Manipuri as a normal part of the curriculum: Tagore's prestige was so great that he was able to defy the taboo against female dancing. Writers too began to play their part: in 1917 Coomaraswamy's voice was a lonely one, but gradually other writers began to take an interest in the various classical styles and write about them. The Kerala poet Vallathol drew attention to the Cochin style of Kathakali by bringing a troupe from his Kathakali school (the Kerala-Kalamandalam) to the great cities of India, and Guru Shankaran Nambudri did the same for the Travancorean school with his troupe. The distinguished theosophist Rukmini Devi defied convention and became an outstanding exponent of certain aspects of Bharata Natyam; she also started a school at Adyar (near Madras) where Bharata Natyam was taught.[1] Middle-class girls all over India began to learn dancing (simplified Manipuri or Bharata Natyam) at their schools, just as English girls learned Revived Greek or ballet, and eventually Bharata Natyam became highly fashionable—particularly in Tamil areas, of course, but also in other parts of India. In 1938 Shankar returned to India and opened a school where all the classical styles were taught, and Menaka followed his example a year later. Traditional gurus began to teach in the big cities, giving lessons for fees in the same way as European teachers.

One effect of all this was that a large number of semi-trained dancers began to perform the classical styles without any grasp of their essential features, and there was a great deal of bad dancing: unfortunately the relatively rare public performances by professional traditional dancers or talented and well-trained middle-class dancers were to some extent swamped, by innumerable performances by second-rate dancers who could not do a single step correctly, and mixed together the different styles in such a way that their characteristic features were lost. Even more disastrous were the attempts by these dancers to improve on the classical styles and adapt them to "modern taste": gurus had been doing this for thousands of years, but it was a very different process when carried out by semi-trained dancers with no understanding of the classical tradition. In fact their efforts at "modernization" had roughly the same aesthetic

[1] Her niece Radha was trained at this school and became a fine Bharata Natyam dancer: the beautiful solo performed by Radha in the film *The River* is in pure Bharata Natyam style.

Taras Bulba (Lopukhov, Leningrad, 1940) with Konstantin Sergueyev as Ostap

Romeo and Juliet (Lavrovsky, Leningrad, 1940) with Galina Ulanova as Juliet and Konstantin Sergueyev as Romeo. *Special production for the film Gala Festival*

Mrinalini (Marianne Balchin) in a Kathak dance. (Guru, Radhelal Misra; Jaipuri school)

Below: Guru Krishna Kutty in *The Art of Kathakali*, showing the pose "Riding in a Chariot". Commentary by Shirin Vajifdar

value as the moustaches we sometimes see scrawled on portraits of beautiful women. None of the stage dancing, however, was quite as appallingly bad as the dances in films: these were normally composed by dance-directors with almost no knowledge of any of the classical styles, for performance by actresses with only a few months' (or weeks') training, and managed to compete in sentimental triviality with the corresponding sequences in "Oriental" films made in Hollywood and London.

In spite of all the bad dancing, however, there were some traditional gurus in the remote regions where the classical styles belonged, and others in the big cities, who maintained the finest traditions of their art. The best of their pupils showed to them and their teachings the respect which is traditional in India, and so acquired the essence of Indian classical dancing. Even today professional dancing still carries for a large number of middle-class Indians the stigma of prostitution, and highly trained middle-class girls still take pride in describing themselves as "amateurs"; but undoubtedly this is only a transitional phase.

(b) FOLK DANCES

In India the gap between classical dances and folk dances is just as wide as in Europe. Among the four million inhabitants of the Indo-Pakistan sub-continent there are countless different types of dances among the various races, religions, castes and language groups, and each group normally has different dances for different occasions. Indian choreographers have had considerable success in transferring a few examples of this enormous mass of material to the stage, though they have had to take account of the laws of the theatre and adapt the dances in a number of ways—e.g. by bringing together steps from a number of related dances to build up one synthetic dance capable of holding the attention of an audience. (Indian folk dances, like those of Europe, tend to be very monotonous: Santhals, for example, like to dance all night performing only one or two simple steps.)

(c) MODERN INDIAN BALLET

The origins of modern Indian ballet can be traced back to the beginning of this century (long before the rehabilitation of the classical Indian styles), and for many years it was more European than Indian. Though the themes were

A.A.O.B—S

Indian, the structure of the dances and ballets was based on Western models, and the technique was derived partly from the Western classical technique and partly from the Western free dance. The pioneers of modern Indian ballet were mainly Western dancers and Europeanized Indians who composed "Indian" dances and ballets for performances to Western audiences, adapting themselves to a long-established Western myth about the mysterious, alluring and exotic East. Since the inhabitants of the great cities of India often had no knowledge of the classical styles of India these modern "Indian" ballets were welcomed with enthusiasm when they were shown in India, but they were originally designed for Western audiences.

When the classical styles emerged from obscurity the pioneers of modern Indian ballet found it desirable to come to terms with them as best they could, and with the rising interest in dancing in India they found it possible to get some sort of a foothold in the Indian "live" theatre—which is still very immature in comparison with that of Western countries. Their example was followed by a number of Indian dancers and choreographers with no direct contact with the West. In this way Indian ballet became Indianized, though its development continued to be powerfully influenced by its heritage from the West. (Much the same is true of Indian films, modern Indian literature, etc.)

The emergence of modern Indian ballets making use of the classical Indian styles, but distinct from them, is of the highest importance; for in India the absence of a continuous tradition of drama and opera has caused modern Indian ballet to attract to itself creative impulses which in the West would have found an outlet in other branches of the theatre. There is nothing provincial or immature about the best of modern Indian ballet: unlike other branches of the Indian theatre it can stand comparison with the best of the Western professional theatre.

Modern Indian ballet belongs essentially to the Western type of theatre, and at its best uses the full resources of modern theatrical technique. Its home is the big cities of India, where the millions of inhabitants are engaged on much the same occupations (in industry and commerce) as the populations of the big cities of the West; but companies from the big cities are beginning to go on tour through the smaller cities and towns. Its exponents get a living as best they can, teaching and working on films as well as dancing and doing choreography, and have much the same problems as their opposite numbers in the West.

Fortunately the classical dances of India lend themselves very well to theatrical presentation, and can be combined together with modern Indian ballets and theatricalized folk-dances to make up a well-balanced programme. They answer the same need that is provided for in Western programmes by old ballets like *Giselle* and *Le Lac des Cygnes*.

Ruth St. Denis (b. 1877)

Like the other pioneers of the free dance Ruth St. Denis was powerfully influenced during her formative years by the teachings of Delsarte. While still a young child, at the family home in New Jersey, she had lessons in Delsarte exercises from her mother, who herself had had lessons from "a Madame Poté, who was a seventh attenuation of a pupil of François Delsarte".[1] She then had training at several dancing schools, and at the age of sixteen managed to secure her first variety engagement in New York as an acrobatic dancer: thanks to her Delsarte exercises she was able to perform certain stunts beyond the power of other acrobatic dancers. This variety engagement led to a number of others, and with tremendous determination she managed to make a living in the extremely tough world of the American commercial theatre.

In 1898 she secured an engagement in *The Ballet Girl*, in which she did a short ballet solo on pointe: at this time she was very interested in "toe dancing", but later came to regard this as a shameful episode in her career.[2] She next danced in another musical, *The Runaway Girl*, and then auditioned successfully for a dancing rôle (The White Ballet Girl) in *Zaza*, directed by David Belasco.

She toured with Belasco for five years, first in *Zaza* and then in *Dubarry*, and learned a great deal from him. When she began to dance on her own she presented herself at the centre of a slick professional production, taking care to build up a spectacular show with the aid of elaborate décor, lighting effects and a number of supers: in fact each of her big numbers cost a lot of money to produce, requiring tons of scenery and many expensive costumes. In this respect she differed profoundly from Duncan, who was content to dance in front of plain blue curtains with a minimum of costume.

It was while on tour with the Dubarry company (in Buffalo, N.Y.) that she saw the cigarette poster with the semi-nude Egyptian goddess which inspired her to set up on her own as an Oriental dancer. In fact this poster was only the spark which ignited an explosion which had been building up for some time. By now she had seen a fair amount of Oriental dancing—notably the Japanese dancer-actress Sadi Yaco, whom she saw sharing a theatre with Loie Fuller at the Paris Exposition when she was on tour with *Zaza*. Sadi Yaco made a profound impression on her: "Her performance haunted me for years, and filled my soul with such a longing for the subtle and elusive in art that it became my chief ambition as an artist."[3] Characteristically she was just as impressed by the colours of Sadi Yaco's costumes as by her dancing; and when the cigarette poster inspired her to prepare a project for an evocation of ancient Egypt (*Egypta*) she planned décors, costumes, head-dresses and properties which

[1] Ruth St. Denis, *An Unfinished Life*, p. 7.
[2] "To my intense shame I did a toe dance." (*Ibid.*, p. 30.)
[3] *Ibid.*, p. 40.

would have cost several thousand dollars. The expenses proved to be beyond her capacity; she then saw a number of snake charmers, holy men and Nautch dancers at the "East Indian Village" at Coney Island (the great amusement park of New York), and altered her plans so as to produce an "Indian" number. From then on she devoted herself mainly to "Indian" numbers, though she also produced dances inspired by other Eastern countries.

Her first independent production was *The Dance of the Five Senses*, in which she impersonated the "goddess" Radha in an elaborate temple setting, with her small company of Indian supers taking the part of priests.[1] She produced this number with such a fine feeling for atmosphere that it went over well even with the rowdy variety audience of the "Sunday Night Smoking Concerts" at which it was first performed, and from then on she never looked back. Soon she produced a number of other Indian numbers—notably *The Cobras*, in which she played the part of a dirty and ragged snake charmer, using her arms to represent snakes; *Incense*, in which she carried a tray of incense and did a *puja* (ceremony of worship), then made her arms ripple to suggest the spirit of the incense smoke; and *Nautch Dance*, inspired by the Nautch dances she had seen at Coney Island.

The technique used by her in these "Indian" dances was very limited. The tempo was almost always slow, and foot-movements very simple, consisting for the most part of a slow rhythmic walk. From time to time she stopped to hold a striking pose: in general she relied much more on striking poses and the atmosphere produced by music, singing, lighting effects, décor, costumes, etc., than on dance-movements. As accompaniment she used mainly Western music with an exotic flavour: *The Dance of the Five Senses*, for example, was performed to music from the opera *Lakmé*.

She came to England in 1906, and continued to tour across Europe for the

---

[1] This dance set the style for the whole of Ruth St. Denis' later development as a choreographer. "The dance was comprised of three figures, the first being performed in five circles, one within the other, each circle representing one of the five senses. The senses were symbolised by different objects: jewels for sight, bells for hearing, garlands for smell, a bowl of wine for taste, and, for touch, kisses on her own hands. The second figure was danced on a square, representing, according to Buddhist theology, the fourfold miseries of life, and was done with writhings and twistings of the body to portray the despair of unfulfilment. At the end of this figure Radha sank to the ground in darkness. After a short interval a light disclosed her in an attitude of prayer and meditation. She now rose and, holding a lotus flower, began the third figure of the dance, which followed the lines of an open lotus flower. . . . She danced on the balls of the feet, thus typifying the ecstasy and joy which follow renunciation of the senses and freedom from their illusion. At the close of this figure, which finished the message, Radha slowly danced backward to the shrine, followed by the priest, and the doors of her shrine were closed." (*An Unfinished Life*, p. 70.) The whole number was intensely characteristic of Ruth St. Denis in its combination of shrewd feeling for atmosphere and dramatic effect with somewhat muddled religious ideas. (Radha is the beloved of Krishna, and has nothing to do with Buddhism.) Ruth St. Denis was far more concerned with making certain theatrical effects by every possible device of staging than with authenticity of theology or dance-technique. The "writhings and twistings of the body" to suggest despair and the movements "on the balls of the feet" to suggest ecstasy and joy are purely Delsartian, and could scarcely be more un-Indian.

next three years. Though she was well received in most countries it was in Germany she created the greatest furore: her success there rivalled even that of Duncan. In Berlin she was so popular that she came back over and over again. She returned to the United States in 1909, and from then on remained almost entirely in America, gradually becoming very famous and popular.

Her enormous success was due mainly to the fact that her productions gave accurate expression to the long-established Western myth about the mysterious and alluring Orient: no dancer showing the real dances of the Orient could have had anything like her impact on America and Europe. Because she represented the Western myth about the East so effectively her dances were generally accepted as being fairly close to the real thing, and she established the idea that all Oriental countries have much the same style of dancing—the style used by her. She had little interest in dance-technique in general, and made no effort to come to grips with real Indian dance-techniques—though on one occasion she spent several months in an effort to master the technique of Japanese geisha dances.

Even if the Western myth about Eastern dances existed before Ruth St. Denis, she strengthened it considerably. The nature of this influence can be seen clearly in the long chapter on Oriental Dancing in the book *The Dance* (1914) by the American writers Troy and M. W. Kinney. They cite her "Indian" dances as typical examples of the dances of India, and describe them as "wholly consistent with the originals in point of character" even though "only a part of the whole". They describe all Oriental art as being essentially similar, with the same characteristics as the dances of Ruth St. Denis: "To the Occidental, unused to Oriental art, the absence of crescendo and climax, and the substituted iteration carried on endlessly, is uninteresting. The Oriental art idea. . . . is to soothe, not to stimulate. . . . The rhythmic repetition of the tile designs on the wall, the decorative repetition of the beats of music, produce a spell of dreamy visioning comparable only to the effect of some potent but harmless narcotic." It is hard to imagine what the Kinneys would have thought of the terrifying climax of a Kathakali dance-drama, or one of the more advanced *tolas*[1] of the Jaipur school of Kathak in which the foot-beats reach a climax of virtuosity at a tempo so fast that the ear can hardly separate them: presumably they would not have regarded such dancing as authentically Oriental.

The influence of Ruth St. Denis was naturally very great in the United States, and her ideas have been taken over and further developed by La Meri, the leading American teacher of "ethnological dance". Though La Meri spent some time in India and learned authentic examples of dances in the three classical styles, she remained so much under the spell of Ruth St. Denis that in

---

[1] A *tola* (also spelled in English *toda* and *torah*) is a standard enchaînement of dance movements, with or without a dramatic element.

her book *The Gesture Language of the Hindu Dance* (1941) and in her article on "Oriental Dance" in *The Dance Encyclopedia* (1949) she wrote about Oriental dance in almost the same vein as the Kinneys.[1]

Though Ruth St. Denis herself was unable to make much headway in Paris before the First World War because of intrigues against her by the leading Parisian impresario of the day, her indirect influence on the development of "Oriental" dancing in Paris after the War was considerable. In fact Paris became the home of a number of European, Eurasian and Asiatic dancers who developed "Oriental" styles of their own, the most important of them being Uday Shankar and Nyota Inyoka. (Nyota Inyoka has remained in Paris ever since, continuing to produce "Indian" ballets in her own style.) A number of traditionally trained exponents of the classical dances of Bali, Java and Cambodia also appeared in Paris at this time; but they had relatively little influence on the "Oriental" dancers who continued in the Ruth St. Denis tradition.

Rabindranath Tagore (1861–1941)

Tagore was a pioneer of the highest importance in both the rehabilitation of the classical styles and the development of modern Indian ballet.

In 1917 he saw Manipuri dancers performing for the first time,[2] and was so impressed that he invited the distinguished Manipuri guru Naba Kumar to come and teach at his school Santiniketan, near Calcutta. This was a very bold step, for at this time the outcry against Nautch dancing was at its height. But Tagore succeeded in establishing dancing as a normal part of the Santiniketan curriculum, along with painting, music and so on. It was no part of his aim to produce professional danseuses: at that time "professional danseuse" (i.e. Nautch girl) was synonymous with "prostitute". The aim of Santiniketan was rather to enlarge the minds of the pupils through contact with many branches of art and science. Tagore knew very well that at one time dancing had been an important aspect of Indian culture, and was determined to re-establish its prestige.

Inspired by the Manipuri training at Santiniketan, Tagore began to produce dance-dramas with the Santiniketan pupils in which the words were sung by musicians while dancers enacted the meaning of the words. Tagore not only wrote the words and music: though no dancer himself he also devised the choreography. The style he evolved was mainly based on a simplified form of Manipuri, to which he added certain mudras taken from Kathakali, movements

---

[1] *Cf. The Gesture Language of the Hindu Dance*, p. 5: "The occidental dances from the waist down; the oriental from the waist up. . . . The occidental dance aims to excite; the oriental dance, to soothe. Choreography in the Occident is built like the drama, with a fast crescendo to a brilliant and exciting climax; in the Orient choreography seeks to maintain an emotional level which increases only in intensity."

[2] Manipur State is in Assam, on the border of Burma, but is relatively close to Tagore's home in Bengal.

from Bengali folk-dances and ideas from Western dancing. (Tagore had lived in Europe and was familiar with the Western theatre.) From time to time Tagore took a group of students on tour across India performing his dance-dramas (of which the stories were based on Hindu mythology).

The artistic value of these dance-dramas was limited by the poverty of their technical basis, the amateur status of their performers, and Tagore's determination to make the dancing as refined as possible: inevitably they were rather insipid compared with the great classical dance-dramas of Kerala and the best ballets of the West. Nevertheless they were of the highest importance in breaking down the prejudices against dancing and paving the way for the development of modern Indian ballet *in India*: the middle-class public was forced to realize that a girl could dance in public without being necessarily a prostitute. Moreover a considerable number of girls who came to study at Santiniketan absorbed Tagore's respectful attitude to dancing, and carried this attitude with them to their homes all over India.

Anna Pavlova (1881–1931)

The visit of the Royal Siamese dancers to St. Petersburg in 1900 made a strong impression on all the most sensitive of the Maryinsky artists, and perhaps one may trace Pavlova's intense and persistent interest in Indian dancing to this event. Fokine found the same sort of stimulus in the strange mudras and head movements of the Siamese dancers that Debussy found in the music of the Javanese gamelan orchestra which played at the Paris Exhibition of 1889, and he used ideas taken from the Siamese dancers in many of his compositions: as one might expect he was more successful when he used these ideas in a subtle way in items like *Le Cygne* (arranged for Pavlova) than in his rather naïve Oriental ballets such as *Schéhérazade* and *Le Dieu Bleu*.

In 1909 Pavlova showed her interest in Indian dancing by choosing to celebrate the tenth anniversary of her entry into the Maryinsky with a performance of *La Bayadère*, the only "Indian" ballet in the Maryinsky repertoire. A year later, on her first English tour, she included in her company an English girl, Roshanara, who had been trained in Indian dances in India and performed Indian dances in Pavlova's programme, including a snake-charmer's dance. When Pavlova enlarged her company in 1913 she commissioned two new ballets from Fokine, one of them being the Oriental ballet *The Seven Daughters* with a rôle for Pavlova which included voluptuous poses and undulations of the body: in this ballet (as in *Schéhérazade*) Fokine gave expression of the Western myth about the languorous and voluptuous East.

The Seven Daughters did not stay long in the repertoire, but Pavlova brought into her repertoire a considerable number of Oriental solos and ballets—notably

The Egyptian Mummy (a condensed version of the Petipa ballet *La Fille du Pharaon*), *La Peri* (a new version of the Coralli ballet), *Syrian Dance* (in which Pavlova portrayed an Oriental courtesan waiting for a rich man), and *Ajanta Frescoes* (a succession of poses derived from paintings in the Ajanta Caves worked out by Pavlova and her maître de ballet Clustine in collaboration).

On her two visits to India (in 1922 and 1928) Pavlova did her best to see the temple dances of the "bayadères", of which she had heard so much; but she was unlucky. In Calcutta the management of the theatre collected together 40 dancers to put on a show for her, but the result was very disappointing: "What we saw was a parody of Oriental dance, or so it seemed to us, with an obvious admixture of contemporary Western influence, the whole without even the redeeming feature of good taste."[1] She also saw two female soloists—one in Calcutta, the other in Bombay. Neither was very impressive. She was told that there were temples in faraway places where bayadères could still be found, but had no time to go in search of them.

It was Pavlova's interest in the Ajanta frescoes which brought her into contact with Uday Shankar. She wanted a painter to copy the frescoes for her, and Sir William Rothenstein recommended to her Uday Shankar, then an art student in London. Pavlova was already preparing a ballet *Oriental Impressions*, based on her 1922 Eastern tour: the final ballet (first produced at Covent Garden in 1923) consisted of three Japanese dances taught to Pavlova and her dancers by two Tokyo teachers of dancing, and two short Hindu ballets, *A Hindu Wedding* and *Krishna and Radha*. The music for the Hindu items was composed for European instruments by Comolata Banerji on the basis of Indian *ragas* and *talas*. Pavlova had already purchased the music from Miss Banerji, and was planning to put the two Hindu ballets into production, when she saw Shankar dance in London and decided to entrust the choreography to him, in spite of his youth and inexperience. In the Krishna-Radha ballet Radha was danced by Pavlova, Krishna by "M. F. Uday Shankar" and "The Goppies" by "Mlles Stuart, Coles, Friede, Glynde, Lake, Faber, Faucheux, Gervis".

Undoubtedly Pavlova was aware of the fact that the free-style choreography of the Indian items was on a different plane from the simplified traditional choreography of the Japanese items. Though Pavlova did not dance in the Japanese items, the programme note for *Oriental Impressions* almost ignored the Indian items, concentrating on the Japanese items and explaining the value of the great Japanese tradition of classical dancing: "Whereas in Europe the traditions of dancing schools go back at most a few decades and seldom extend

---

[1] V. Dandré, *Anna Pavlova*, p. 287. Dandré adds that "There are no schools of dancing in India, and it is an art in which nobody is interested". (He was writing in 1932.) Ruth St. Denis was more fortunate than Pavlova: in Calcutta she saw a "Nautch girl" (Kathak courtesan dancer).

more than a few hundred years, in Japan, on the contrary, uninterrupted traditions have been handed down from generation to generation, for six, seven, or even eight centuries, and in some cases can be traced back over a thousand years." The programme note ended with a sad little comment on Pavlova's failure to make contact with the classical dances of India: "If Japan displays with pride the richness of her treasures of artistic culture and shows an exceptional readiness in facilitating the knowledge and study of it, India, the mysterious, secretes with almost jealous care her works of art, and one must live a long time in the country and have an opportunity of visiting out-of-the-way places, far distant from the chief centres, to form an appreciation of what remains of the true art of dancing in the land of the nautch girl." Pavlova never had the time to go to the out-of-the-way places. Had she done so the history of Indian dancing in recent years might have been rather different: the rehabilitation of the Indian classical styles would certainly have come much sooner than it did.

Uday Shankar (b. 1902)

Uday Shankar had his first training from his father, Dr. Shyam Shankar Chowdhury, and first danced in public in shows produced by his father in London for the benefit of Indian soldiers wounded in the First World War. (Uday Shankar came to London in 1920 to study at the Royal College of Art.)

When Ruth St. Denis came to England in 1922, and began to stage a dramatization of one of Tagore's poems, she arranged with Uday Shankar's father to use a group of English girls which he had trained; Uday Shankar must have seen the productions of Ruth St. Denis for the first time at this period. Undoubtedly they had great influence on him: one of Ruth St. Denis's most characteristic movements (the rippling arms she used in *Incense*) became an important feature of Shankar's style in later years.

Shankar joined Pavlova in 1923 to compose two small ballets and dance in them as the male soloist. He stayed with Pavlova for one and a half years, travelling all over the world. In this way he learned the whole craft of touring a ballet company and innumerable devices of showmanship, as well as the methods of composition used by Western choreographers.[1] Above all he became very familiar with the taste of Western audiences and their reactions to "Oriental dancing". Time hung heavy on his hands, for the ballets in which he appeared were included on the programme only about once every week or ten days, and he offered to help Pavlova by learning some ballet steps and taking small parts in the other ballets; though he was anxious to learn the ballet technique of the

---

[1] *Cf.* article by Uday Shankar in 1951 Puja Number of *Amrita Bazar Patrika* ("My Remembrances with Gratitude"): "Being in her [Pavlova's] troupe I learned discipline, punctuality, co-operation, stage-craft, observation, sense of balance and proportion, sense of duty, responsibility, diligence and above all showmanship."

West Pavlova refused to permit this, telling him that by doing so he would spoil the beauty of his finger, hand and body movements.

He found little scope for developing his individuality in the Pavlova company, and so in 1925 he went to Paris to try to establish himself as a solo dancer. He studied a great deal in the libraries, museums and dance-studios of Paris, keeping himself alive by dancing in cabarets to the music of a piano, and gradually evolved a style of his own which exactly suited his physique and temperament and corresponded to the Western myth about the East even more accurately than the productions of Ruth St. Denis. Many different elements went to the making of this style—Bengali folk-dances, the dances of Ruth St. Denis, the Oriental ballets of Pavlova, a few simple mudras, poses from classical Indian paintings and sculpture, Santiniketan Manipuri, Yoga, European styles of the free dance, and a few movements from the classical styles of various countries of South-East Asia (which were to be seen in Paris from time to time).

Though Shankar belonged to a family which was highly musical even by Bengali standards, he made use of only the most simple and monotonous rhythms in his compositions, and his footwork did not go beyond the degree of complexity to be found in Indian folk-dances: the rhythmic complexity characteristic of the Indian classical styles would have been far beyond the understanding of the Western audiences for whom his dances were designed, and did not suit his synthetic style in any way.

Shankar's most important pupil[1] was the French girl Simkie (Simone Barbière), who was a pianist before she joined him. (She met him through playing the piano for his rehearsals, and begged him to teach her to dance.) Simkie mastered Shankar's style perfectly: though the limitations of Shankar's choreography prevented her from developing a strong personality or securing any striking effects, she danced with delightful simplicity and sincerity, and won the hearts of audiences wherever she appeared, both in the West and in India. Shankar owed a great deal of his success to his partner Simkie.

Shankar was just as much a pioneer in the field of Indian orchestral music as in choreography. The type of music used as accompaniment to the classical styles of India would have been quite unsatisfactory for Shankar's ballets, for such accompaniment mainly takes the form of drumming with extremely complex rhythms and songs in which the words are important. Shankar's ballets and dances, on the other hand, demanded music of a fairly light character which could be readily appreciated by Western audiences with no knowledge of the complexities of Indian *talas* and *ragas* and no understanding of any Indian language. He therefore took on a number of first-rate Indian musicians (includ-

---

[1] Other fine dancers joined his company from time to time—notably Zohra and the traditionally trained Kathakali dancers Madhavan and Sivaram—but they cannot be regarded as his pupils, and usually did not stay for long.

ing his own brothers) and commissioned the great Bengali musician Timirbaran to orchestrate the music of his ballets. The task he set Timirbaran in 1930 was very difficult, for up to now Indian orchestral music was almost unknown. (Indian classical music is extemporized by a single instrumentalist or singer to the accompaniment of a drummer and a drone.) Timirbaran rose to the occasion, providing changes in the instrumentation to agree with changes in the mood of the ballets, and providing music that was exactly in harmony with the choreography—understandable to Western ears and yet not offensive to Indian connoisseurs. By Indian classical standards this was "light music", but it had the merit of being exactly right for its purpose, and many of the greatest Indian instrumentalists played for Shankar at one time or another.

As the classical styles of Indian dancing emerged from obscurity Shankar took a keen interest in them, and added some elements from them to his dancing, though he did not change the fundamental technical basis of the free style he had evolved. Kathakali made a strong impression on him: from this style he took a number of mudras, one or two eye and eyebrow movements, and the idea for his most important composition, the dance-drama *Tandava Nritya* (1931). This was insipid compared with real Kathakali, but it had a definite dramatic structure and characterization, and accordingly it stood head and shoulders above his other compositions. His choreography was at its best when it was nearest to Kathakali—i.e. in the battle between Siva and Gajasura.

Though Shankar could assimilate only a few elements of the classical styles, he showed remarkable skill and sensitivity in adapting Indian folk-dances to the stage. Their simple rhythms were of exactly the same type that he used in his more ambitious compositions, and their naïve patterns of repetition also agreed well with his free style. Thanks to the financial support of Alice Boner (who also financed his Europen tours) he was able to go from village to village collecting material for his folk-dance compositions.

In 1931 Shankar returned to Paris with a large number of musical instruments, his musical director Vishnudas Shirali (a versatile instrumentalist who composed the music for all his items) and a company which included three of Shankar's brothers. Apart from Simkie none of the members of the company had had any previous training in dancing, and for some time Shankar trained them in supporting rôles in his ballets and theatricalized folk-dances. Then he rented a Paris theatre and presented himself at the head of his new company. The Paris season was a great success, and he followed it with a long international tour which brought him to London and also across America under the management of Hurok. He made a big impression in London, where Oriental dancing was almost unknown. In the United States audiences were familiar with the Denishawn Oriental style, but there too Shankar did amazingly well: he fitted the myth even better than Ruth St. Denis, for he had the face and body of a

Hindu god, his style and his themes were obviously more exotic than those of
Ruth St. Denis, and his music (though close enough to Western music to be
easily followed by Western audiences) sounded impressively exotic. Shankar
surprised Hurok by playing to twenty-five sold-out performances in New
York: as Hurok says,

> Shankar was good—but not that good. . . . There was no apparent virtuosity, no
> sensational technical feat which would make people gasp. It was all very beautiful
> but it was even-toned, serene, soothing rather than exciting.[1]

Hurok suggests that Shankar's surprising success was due to his sex-appeal
which attracted a large feminine audience; but Shankar's personality was not
strong enough to make his sex-appeal carry much beyond the first few rows. In
fact Shankar's extraordinary appeal came from the fact that he gave a far more
accurate representation than any predecessor of the Western myth about
Oriental dancing.

Shankar now made his headquarters at Dartington Hall, at the invitation
of Mr. and Mrs. Elmhirst. Thanks to their patronage he was able to spend long
periods between tours[2] training his dancers and rehearsing new items. He was
also able to go to the East to collect material from India, Java and many other
countries with his cine-camera. During his periods at Dartington he came into
close contact with two other important dance-groups—first the Dance Drama
Group (using a style adapted from that of Martha Graham) and later the Ballets
Jooss. The influence of these groups was not obvious while he was still working
in the West, but it emerged very strongly when he returned to India in 1938 to
start his dance centre at Almora with funds provided by Mr. and Mrs. Elmhirst
and Mrs. Beatrice Straight (of New York), the land being provided free by
the United Provinces Government.

Shankar's dance centre was constructed on the model of the Dartington
Hall cultural centre, and it is possible that he chose a remote spot like
Almora, up in the foothills of the Himalayas away from any major centres of
population, in imitation of Dartington Hall (which is near Totnes in Devon).
Once the dance centre was ready he opened a school, and students flocked to
Almora from all over India. The training at this school was shown in Shankar's
film *Kalpana*: much of it was derived from certain aspects of the Central Euro-
pean free dances, and had very little to do with Indian dancing. The students
spent a great deal of time practising walking: they walked with a typically
Central European impulse in the shoulders and hips, moving at different tempi

---

[1] *Impresario*, p. 162.
[2] Shankar toured even more widely than the Ballets Jooss, visiting France, Germany,
Italy, Spain, Hungary, Austria, Czechoslovakia, Switzerland, Belgium, Holland, Denmark,
Norway, Sweden, Esthonia, Lithuania, Latvia, Finland, Poland, etc.

and in different rhythms. They also had many periods in Yoga-like subjects such as "Concentration" and "Harmony". Shankar brought some very fine classical teachers to Almora—notably the great Kathakali guru Shankaran Nambudri, Kandapa (Bharata Natyam master of the famous devadasi Balasaraswati), and Ustad Alauddin Khan, most famous of living Indian musicians—but he planned the classical courses so that the pupils would spend a long time in the elementary stages and would have to stay at least five years before beginning to master the elements of even one of the classical styles. This led to bitter disputes in the school, and eventually Shankar was forced to disband it.

Shankar's tours with his company in India made a profound impression. Up to then the technical standard of Indian theatrical performances had been distinguished by happy-go-lucky amateurishness: at a Shankar performance, however, the curtain went up dead on time, there were no waits between items, the lighting was adequate, the background to the dances was in good taste (the musicians with their instruments), and every detail of the dancing was so polished that it moved like clockwork: if two girls danced a pas de deux they looked like mirror images of each other.

In India Shankar began to produce a number of expressionist ballets like *Labour and Industry*, inspired by the expressionist free-dance productions of Central Europe and of America. He used a few Indian steps and arm movements, but the atmosphere was completely expressionist. By the time Shankar began to work in this field, however, expressionist devices such as the imitation of machines by dancers were already worn out, and his work in this genre was derivative and insipid: it was accepted in India, where it seemed highly original, but it showed little of the technical skill that Shankar achieved in his normal free style. His attempts at expressionist satire were particularly naïve. Nevertheless his introduction of expressionism and constructivism into India was of considerable importance, opening new doors to young Indian choreographers and helping them to come to terms with life in modern India.

After the break-up of the school Shankar concentrated on the semi-autobiographical film *Kalpana*, which occupied him for five years. He included in this film extracts from almost every dance and ballet he had ever composed. Unfortunately for Shankar this film, on which he spent an enormous amount of time and money, did harm to his prestige in India. He would have done better to plump either for a purely fictional film or a straightforward documentary on his life: in fact *Kalpana* was an unhappy compromise between the two. (The film contained no hint that he had ever left India, and the rôle of Simkie in his career was distorted out of recognition.)

After the end of the War Shankar began visiting Europe and America once again. His repertoire was very similar to what it had been before the War: very wisely he excluded all the expressionist items which would have shattered the myth he had taken such pains to build up in the West. His craftsmanship was more polished than ever, and every item was rehearsed to the last millimetre, but the impact of his performances was much weaker than before the War. No one who had seen classical Indian dancing could fully accept the insipid and monotonous quality of Shankar's choreography and the childish simplicity of his rhythms, while his attempts at Kathakali eye-movements were very unimpressive compared with the real thing. Another major drawback was that the style used by Shankar was devised for performance by a young dancer with a slender and flexible body: classically trained Kathakali dancers can give superb performances even in their seventies, but Indian free dancers without a powerful technique to sustain them are at a great disadvantage when their body loses the slender lines of youth. Moreover Shankar's new partner Amala was a poor substitute for Simkie: though she had had considerable training in Bharata Natyam, her performances in this style were unsatisfactory (she did the movements in a languorous Shankarian manner which destroyed their essential quality), and in every item she treated the dancing as something completely physical. (Simkie, in contrast, managed to show both charm and spirituality in her dancing, and she was exactly the right height to make Shankar look like a demi-god—whereas Amala was almost as tall as Shankar.)

To some extent the disappointing post-War tours of Uday Shankar and his rapidly changing troupe have obscured the significance of his pioneer work in the twenties and thirties, just as happened with the post-War tours of the Ballet Rambert. In fact his work as a pioneer of modern Indian ballet was of the highest importance: all the artists who carried on from the point where he left off in such fields as mythological ballets, expressionist ballets, theatricalized folk-dances, orchestral music, stage lighting, costumes, head-dresses and programme construction owe him an incalculable debt. It is impossible to imagine the shape which modern Indian ballet would have taken without Shankar.

Menaka

Though Menaka never became world-famous like her contemporary Uday Shankar, her pioneer work was just as important as his: the rapid growth to maturity of modern Indian ballet would have been impossible without her bold pioneering in the thirties and early forties.

Like many other Indian girls who grew up in the twenties Menaka came to Europe to have training in European dancing: thanks to Pavlova European dancing had enormous prestige in India, and was considered suitable for respectable girls—unlike the "Nautch dances" of India. In Paris she came into contact with the type of "Oriental" dancing of which Ruth St. Denis had been the leading exponent, and began to compose dances of this sort for herself. After a while, however, she began to realize the limitations of this sort of dancing, and returned to India to study Kathak seriously under Sundaram Prasad and other leading teachers. She never mastered the full range of the pure-dance aspects of Kathak and was rather lacking in personality, but she showed real talent for *gaths* (passages of dramatic expression).

In 1936 she came to Europe to participate in the Berlin Olympiad, bringing with her two professional Kathak danseurs—her partner Ramnarayan and Gauri Shankar. Menaka won a prize at the Olympiad, and made a powerful impression: this was the first time that Indian classical dancing had been seen in Europe for generations. Subsequently Menaka took her company on long tours of Central Europe, under the able management of the Dutch impresario Ernst Krauss, giving hundreds of performances which had great influence on the free dancers of the countries she visited. She in turn was influenced by the free dance of Central Europe, breaking away from Indian tradition in such matters as costume.

After returning to India she began to compose ambitious ballets. Though in constructing these ballets she was considerably influenced by her experience of Western ballet and free dance, she took her themes from Indian mythology and Indian classical drama. The pure dances in her ballets were nearly all in Kathak style; but the dramatic aspects of Kathak are not very suitable for ballet (as distinct from solo performances)[1] and eventually she found it best to bring Kathakali dancers into her company and ask them to put the dramatic episodes of her ballets into Kathakali mime-language. Unfortunately the mixture of Kathak *tolas* and Kathakali *abhinaya* was not fully satisfactory, and there was a marked difference between the Kathakali style of the Kathakali dancers and of the other members of the troupe. An even more serious flaw in her ballets was due to her lack of feeling for dramatic construction: her ballets did not build up in a convincing way, and for this reason one ballet seemed much like another. In fact her artistic policy as a whole had the defects characteristic of the rich dancer's company.[2] Nevertheless her ideas were original and intelligent, and her initiative in bringing together various classical styles in their pure form was of the highest importance in the development of modern Indian ballet.

In 1939 she followed the example of Shankar and founded a school; like Shankar she chose a hill-station as the site of her school—Khandala, eighty miles from Bombay. (The advantage of a hill-station is that training is possible even in the hot months.) To this school she managed to attract first-rate Kathakali, Kathak and Manipuri gurus; unfortunately she was unable to attract a good

---

[1] The various dramatic aspects of Kathak are very subtle and sophisticated. The dancer assumes that the spectator is familiar with the story and represents only a few incidents from it, changing from one character to another without warning.

[2] *See* below, p. 352.

Bharata Natyam guru. At the school the pupils were given the chance of studying all the classical styles and making reasonably rapid progress: the gurus could not teach as freely as in their own homes, but restrictions were very much less than in Shankar's school at Almora.

The great advantage of this school to Menaka was that it produced dancers who were trained in three different styles and were therefore capable of doing justice to technically exacting choreography when they joined the company. In fact the school and the company were almost identical, and Menaka allowed talented pupils to train free of charge if they could not afford to pay fees. (This was true of most of the pupils.) Strangely enough her school did not attract many pupils, though it provided far more thorough training than any other school of its kind in India.

During the forties Bombay rose rapidly in importance as a centre of dancing, and in 1944 Menaka moved her school there. This brought to Bombay two important gurus—Krishna Kutty (Kathakali) and Bipin Sinha (Manipuri)—and did much to expedite the next important stage in the development of modern Indian ballet, even though Menaka's untimely death prevented her from taking a decisive part in it.

Ballet in Bombay

Up to the beginning of the forties Bombay was of little importance as a centre of dancing. During the forties, however, it became an important centre of classical dancing and the main centre of Indian ballet. There were several reasons for this. One important reason was the fact that Bombay was the centre of the Indian film industry, which had expanded so rapidly that it was second only to Hollywood in quantity of output: nearly all Indian films had dancing in them, and this provided Indian choreographers, dancers and musicians with occasional opportunities for making the money needed for enterprises of some artistic importance. (In the films the standard of dancing was very low, opportunities for artistic expression were very limited, and jobs were usually given to the wrong people; but sometimes it was possible for good artists to make money in them—whereas this was almost impossible in theatrical work.)

Another reason for the development of modern Indian ballet in Bombay was the cosmopolitan nature of the population and the existence of an audience for live theatre: the Bombay audience was prepared to take an interest in any theatrical novelty. The modern Indian ballets had a strong appeal in a great city with a population that included people speaking many different languages, including a considerable number of English people: the ballets appealed across the barriers of race, religion and language more effectively than dramas could do. Moreover, the existence of a living tradition of classical dancing made it

Ruth St. Denis in Berlin *ca.* 1908

Pavlova as Radha in *Krishna and Radha* (Shankar, London, 1923)

ay Shankar and Simkie in Paris *ca.* 1927

Menaka in Berlin in 1936

The Boon (Kutty, Bombay, 1950) with Guru Krishna Kutty as the demon-king
Bhasmasura and Roshan Vajifdar as Mohini. *Special production for B.B.C. Television
by Christian Simpson and Fernau Hall (1952)*

possible for them to reach a high professional standard of performance and composition much more easily than spoken plays.

A striking symptom of the rising interest in dancing in Bombay was the All-India Dance Festival held there in 1945, which attracted all the greatest Indian dancers of the day.

Towards the middle of the forties a number of different organizations began to present ballets on an amateur or semi-professional basis. (The high rentals of theatres, the undeveloped state of the ballet audience outside Bombay, and the long distances between the big cities inhibited the formation of permanent touring professional companies, just as in the United States two decades earlier.) One producing organization was the Bombay branch of the Indian People's Theatre Association, a left-wing group which presented expressionist ballets such as *The Spirit of India* and *India Immortal* in a style much influenced by Shankar's expressionist ballets. But the propagandist tendencies of this body were hostile to artistic progress, and the leading artists (dancers, choreographers and musicians) broke away in 1946. They joined forces in that year with the members of another theatrical organization, Indian National Theatre, to produce a large-scale ballet *The Discovery of India*, based on Pandit Nehru's book of the same name. This historical ballet (the Indian equivalent of the Elizabethan chronicle play) gave expression to the rapidly growing nationalist feelings of India, together with a growing awareness of the value and complexity of Indian cultural heritage, and was a great success both in Bombay and on tour. The choreography was by Shanti Burdhan and his assistants Sachin Shankar and Naarendra Sharma. It had many successors of a similar type, among them *Rhythm of Culture*, produced by I.N.T. in 1951.

Fortunately the production of ballets with contemporary and historical themes did not cause the neglect of mythological ballets. New Stage (an independent company formed by the same artists who left I.P.T.A. in 1946) had great success in 1950 with a *Ram Leela* ballet, based (like many of the Kathakali dance dramas) on the Ramayana: the epic character of the drama was suggested by specially composed ballads (based on folk-songs) which were sung between the scenes to link the latter together. Another large-scale mythological ballet was *Usha*, presented by I.N.T. in 1951; this was staged entirely in Manipuri[1] technique, and had choreography by Bipin and Surendra Sinha.

At the beginning of 1953 Shanti Burdhan presented a new group, the Little Ballet Company (including some of the same artists as New Stage) in a "puppet ballet" condensing the whole Ramayana story into three-quarters of an hour. This production was a popular success in Bombay, for he showed even more

---

[1] The Manipuri style taught by Bipin Sinha in Bombay has absorbed influences from other styles, notably Bharata Natyam. Pure Manipuri is not very suitable as a basis for complex ballets.

A.A.O.B—T

than his usual skill in disguising the deficiencies in training and facial appearance of his dancers: the dancers wore masks, and moved their limbs in a jerky manner as if pulled by strings.

Guru Krishna Kutty (b. 1924)

Krishna Kutty entered the world of Bombay ballet with the inestimable advantage of being a Kathakali guru with the full resources of this great traditional ballet at his finger-tips, and fifteen years of professional experience as a star soloist. In some respects his position was rather like that of Fokine at the beginning of the twentieth century: though his work broke away from tradition, it represented a renewal of the tradition rather than its destruction.

Krishna Kutty made his début[1] in Kathakali at the age of seven, only six months after beginning training, and was immediately cast in the important role of Krishna. Though the dancer playing Krishna wears only a light crown, and this rôle is therefore less exhausting than most other male rôles, this casting was evidence of extraordinary precocity in Krishna Kutty. By temperament he was an ideal Krishna, mischievous and with a highly developed sense of humour; from then on he was almost always cast as Krishna in Kerala, and very rarely danced the straight female rôles which normally fall to the boys in the troupes.

Five years later Krishna Kutty's fame was such that he was one of five dancers invited to dance with the troupe of the great guru Shankaran Nambudri as guest artists at a special performance. He made a strong impression on Shankaran Nambudri, who invited him to join his troupe for an all-India tour. Krishna Kutty's family opposed this very strongly, but eventually he was able to win their permission, and thus acquired fame as a boy prodigy all over India. As a pupil of the great Shankaran Nambudri he now commanded great respect in Travancore, in spite of his youth.

In 1938, at the age of fourteen, he joined the palace Kathakali company of the Maharajah of Travancore, after the usual long and exacting audition (three nights of performances with the palace troupe).

In 1939 Menaka saw him dancing in the palace company, and was so impressed that she invited him to join her school and company. It proved just as difficult to secure his release as the corresponding release of Imperial Russian dancers, but eventually she succeeded, and put Krishna Kutty under a five-year contract. For this period he was a leading soloist in her company and chief Kathakali guru in her school; he also helped her when she needed passages of Kathakali *abhinaya* in her ballets.

Though Krishna Kutty was only fiftten when he joined Menaka he was

---

[1] The début of a Kathakali dancer is a very solemn occasion, accompanied by elaborate ritual.

already a soloist of long experience, and had developed considerable independence of outlook. This emerged very clearly in his bold decision to study the other classical styles under his brother gurus. Up to then such a thing had been unimaginable: gurus stood very much on their dignity, and would not dream of putting themselves on a level with the beginners in another style—quite apart from the fact that they tended to despise all styles except their own. But Krishna Kutty persisted in his plan, and eventually his example was followed by the other gurus. The consequences of his action were far-reaching: when Krishna Kutty began to compose ballets in Bombay he was able to use all the Indian classical styles with understanding, employing each style where it fitted the dramatic situation—though he naturally relied largely on Kathakali for the dramatic passages in his ballets.

As already mentioned Menaka brought her school to Bombay in 1944; Krishna Kutty left when his contract expired, set up a school of his own in Bombay, and eventually began to compose ballets making use of his pupils.

In 1946, at the age of twenty-two, he was commissioned by Hima Kesarcodi to compose a ballet lasting a whole evening, *Chitra*. Krishna Kutty based this ballet (his first major composition) on a dance-drama by Tagore: he retained Tagore's script, having it spoken in English in synchronism with the mudras, but composed new choreography. This was the first time this technique was used: it proved very suited to the polyglot audiences of modern India, and Krishna Kutty retained it for all his later productions. Hima Kesarcodi was an actress rather than a dancer (she had had only a few months' training from Krishna Kutty), but Krishna Kutty skilfully concealed her deficiencies by giving her a purely mimed rôle and surrounding her with twenty talented dancers (including himself).

The success of *Chitra* was so great that Krishna Kutty was able to follow it with a number of other large-scale ballets in the next three years, notably the historical ballet *Birth of Our Nation*, based on the life of Gandhi, in which he danced the central rôle. But Hima Kesarcodi's ideas on artistic policy made continued collaboration impossible, and in due course Krishna Kutty was driven to leave her. After his departure the company went to pieces and eventually disbanded.

Krishna Kutty's next major production, *False Pride* (1949), had a mythological theme, and was composed by him working in complete independence. The leading female rôle was taken by the talented Kathak dancer Sitara. This ballet, lasting a whole evening (with a cast of no less that 45), was a great success in Bombay; it was performed every Sunday morning for three months—a very long run for this period in Bombay, when ballet was in much the same state as English ballet in the early thirties.

In 1950 he composed a mythological ballet *The Boon* which was distinguished by its powerful dramatic structure and his remarkable interpretation of the central rôle of Bhasmasura, the Demon-King. Without neglecting the ferocious aspect of the demon, he imbued this character with a Chaplinesque blend of humour and pathos which was irresistible. The climax of the ballet, in which Bhasmasura was lured to his doom by the wiles of the seductive temptress Mohini, was a masterly piece of choreography worthy of the finest Kathakali traditions. Mohini was intended for Shirin Vajifdar, but she fell ill, and the rôle was danced so well by Roshan Vajifdar that the latter was allowed to retain it from then on. As a Kathakali guru Krishna Kutty was familiar with the whole of Hindu mythology, and so had no difficulty in selecting a theme suitable for treatment in a one-act ballet; in the same way he had no difficulty in adapting the dramatic structure characteristic of Kathakali to the laws of the theatre.

In 1951 the distinguished Indian writer and editor Mulk Raj Anand succeeded in bringing together Krishna Kutty and Shirin Vajifdar as co-directors of a ballet company Nritya Darpana, with himself acting as something between a director-general and an artistic director. Shirin Vajifdar (one of the pioneers of classical dancing and modern Indian ballet in Bombay) had had some training at Shankar's school at Almora, but had received her main training at Menaka's school, and so was well able to collaborate on choreography with Krishna Kutty. Mulk Raj Anand made a valuable contribution to the work of the company, for he combined familiarity with the Western theatre (gained during twenty years of residence in London) with profound knowledge of Indian cultural traditions, and had many contacts with Indian painters.

In 1951 Nritya Darpana presented a new version of *The Boon* and two new ballets—the mythological ballet *The Birth of Urvashi* and the contemporary expressionist ballet *The Triumph of Life*, both with scripts by Mulk Raj Anand. *The Birth of Urvashi* was distinguished by superbly colourful costumes (inspired by the costumes of the figures in the Ajanta frescoes) designed by the distinguished Indian artist Shiavax Chavda.

In 1952 the directors of Nritya Darpana decided to take a small group to Europe, giving lecture-demonstrations on the classical styles and investigating the possibilities of a visit at a later date by a larger group presenting programmes of ballet. The small group consisted of Krishna Kutty, Shirin Vajifdar, the two younger sisters of Shirin Vajifdar (Khurshed and Roshan), the distinguished flautist and composer Sushil Das Gupta (normally associated with New Stage), and the versatile drummer-dancer Krishna Panicker (who had been with Krishna Kutty in the Trivandrum palace company and Menaka's school, and played for Krishna Kutty's classes).

Just before sailing for England the directors of the company were told that English audiences were already familiar with the classical styles, and would take relatively little interest in the lecture-demonstrations which had been planned. They accordingly decided to make an effort to present the two mythological ballets in the company's repertoire, taking on the necessary additional dancers and musicians in England.

Fortunately they were able to take on some excellent artists—notably the English dancer Mrinalini (Marianne Balchin, the first non-Indian to achieve mastery of several classical Indian styles), the Sinhalese dancer-drummer Anura (who like Mrinalini had made a name for himself in Ram Gopal's company) and the choreographer Yogin Desai (one of the pioneers of Bombay ballet, distinguished by his remarkable flair for the adaptation of folk-dances to the theatre). With the help of these artists and certain Indian instrumentalists and singers resident in London, Krishna Kutty and Shirin Vajifdar were able to stage admirable performances in England, showing for the first time outside India the latest developments in modern Indian ballet. Up to this time Indian ballet had been thought of in England as charming and exotic but rather insipid and monotonous, with only a very limited appeal. The ballets shown by Nritya Darpana, however, were full of contrasts of technique, tempo, rhythm, mood and characterization, and had the same solidity of construction and wide appeal as good Western ballets.

Spain

(a) FLAMENCO

THE HIGHLY developed forms of traditional Spanish dancing and music cannot be understood without some knowledge of the golden age of Andalusian civilization which began with the defeat of the Visigothic (German) rulers of South Spain in A.D. 711 by the Arab leader Tariq. Arab civilization reached extraordinary heights very quickly because the Arabs brought together the finest achievements of Greek philosophy, physics, chemistry and medicine, Persian painting, architecture and literature, Indian astronomy, mathematics, music and dancing, and so on. Islam had as one of its basic doctrines the idea that one Believer is as good as another, whatever his race or the colour of his skin, and no nationalistic barriers held back the diffusion of culture from one end of the Arab world to another. What is more, the greatest Arab rulers were tolerant of other faiths, and gave their patronage to talented Christians, Jews, Hindus and others.

The Arab rulers were accustomed to send long distances for distinguished exponents of the arts and sciences, and there was nothing unusual in the despatch by the great Caliph Haroun-al-Rashid of Baghdad of the famous Persian singer Ziryab to Abd-al-Rahman II, Sultan of Cordoba, in the first quarter of the eighth century A.D. The Arab-Persian style used by Ziryab and taught by him in his school at Cordoba was closely related to the North Indian style of singing practised in Sindh, and even today the similarities between cante jondo (the modern descendant of the style established in Cordoba by Ziryab and other Arab-Persian singers) and North Indian singing are very striking. Cante jondo has very little to do with other European music: it is improvised in the Indian way by a singer working within strict rules corresponding to the *ragas* of North Indian music.[1]

There is a classical style of Andalusian guitar-playing (*guitarra morisca*) based on melody, which is quite distinct from the guitar style based on harmony (*guitarra latina*). Like cante jondo, *guitarra morisca* can be traced back to the importation into Andalusia from the eighth century onwards of musicians from Baghdad; ivory caskets made at Cordoba in the tenth century show musicians

[1] *Cf.* Aziz Baluch, "Cante Jondo or Spanish Flamenco", *The Sufi*, January, 1952.

whose costumes and instruments are very similar to those shown on Baghdad coins of the same period. The analogies between the best *guitarra morisca* and the sitar-playing of North India are very striking; the guitarist even gives some suggestion of the drum-accompaniment of Indian instrumental music by striking the sound-board of his guitar with his fingers.

The analogies between Kathak and Flamenco dancing are even more striking. A Kathak guru can recognize many fragments of typical Kathak *bōls* (rhythmic patterns) in the *taconeo* (foot-beats) of Flamenco dancers; the finger movements curving away from the face characteristic of Flamenco are similar in many ways to the hand-movements which come at the beginning of many Kathak *tolas*; and the *vueltas quebradas* of Flamenco are similar in many ways to the Kathak pirouettes. Even the spiral kiss-curl plastered on the cheek of the Flamenco danseuse has its exact equivalent on the cheek of the Kathak danseuse. Apart from these similarities of detail, the fundamental basis of the two styles is identical: both styles are based on the combination of violent and complex foot-beats (with the feet parallel to each other) and delicate fluid movements of the hands, arms and head; in both styles the tempo is changed instantaneously; and in both styles there is a striking contrast between the masculine and feminine aspects, with provision for pas de deux as well as solos.

In Flamenco, as in Kathak, there is close association between dancing, singing and instrumental music; and this close association supports the presumption that an Arab-Persian version of the mediaeval ancestor of modern Kathak reached Andalusia at roughly the same time as the corresponding styles of singing and instrumental music.[1] The Caliph al-Amin, son of Haroun-al-Rashid, was very fond of dancing as well as singing, and himself arranged all-night ballets on specially constructed barges floating on the Tigris;[2] it is certain that Arab rulers in Andalusia copied his patronage of dancing, even if they did not construct special barges on the Guadalquivir.

Andalusian music and dancing during the Moorish period was not just a provincial copy of Indian and Arab-Persian models. Dancing was very popular in Andalusia long before the Arabs arrived, in Carthaginian and Roman times, and local styles influenced the development of the classical style imported from abroad, just as they did in the countries of South-East Asia. In North Africa Andalusian singing and dancing was recognized as having a character of its own and was highly regarded.

The Moslem civilization of Andalusia reached its peak between the ninth and twelfth centuries. At this time Cordoba was the most highly civilized city

---

[1] Documents surviving from the golden age of Arab civilization suggest that classical Arab music was derived from the music of Persia and that of Byzantium as well as that of India. In the field of dancing the position is very obscure, and much research is needed before we can say anything definite about the nature of classical Arab dancing.

[2] Such a ballet was described by the poet abu-Nawas in his poem *al-Aghani*.

of Europe; Paris and London were primitive and provincial by comparison. During the first centuries of Arab rule Spanish savants journeyed to the Eastern parts of the Moslem Empire in search of knowledge, but in the eleventh century the current was reversed, and Andalusia played a major part in transmitting Arab civilization to Europe. Moslem Spain was highly prosperous, producing enough agricultural and industrial products to export its surplus to countries as far away as India and Central Asia, and this prosperity was reflected in lavish patronage of the arts, including music and dancing. The Christian rulers of Leon, Navarre and Barcelona depended on Cordoba for professional experts of all kinds—surgeons, architects, singing teachers, even dressmakers—and only Moslem money circulated in North Spain. Seville was the main centre of music and dancing in Andalusia: Triana, a district of Seville famous in Moorish times for its singers and dancers, is still famous for them.

The conquest of Andalusia by the feudal lords of Christian North Spain was held up for a long time by quarrels between them, but it was accelerated by the final union of Castile and Leon in 1230. With the fall of Cordoba in 1231 and Seville in 1248 most of Andalusia (with the important exception of Granada) came under Christian rule. At this time the Christian rulers were barbarians compared with their Moslem subjects, and sensibly allowed the latter (the Mudejars) to retain their own language, religion and customs. Gradually the Mudejars lost their Arabic and began to speak a Romance dialect,[1] but they retained a good deal of their own customs, and some of these were taken over by the Christians. In Granada Moslem culture remained much as before.

The conquest of Granada by the Christians was delayed by the fact that the Christian territories were divided into two kingdoms, Castile and Aragon. The union of these two kingdoms in 1469 led to the conquest of Granada in 1492. Under the terms of the capitulation the Moslems were to be allowed to retain their religion and customs, but Ferdinand and Isabella failed to keep to the terms of the capitulation, and in the bitter persecutions of the Moslems which followed a great deal of Moslem culture was destroyed. The expulsion of the Moors from North Spain began in 1501; in 1556 a law was passed compelling all Moslems remaining in Spain to renounce their language, religion, institutions and manner of life; and in 1609 a decree expelled nearly all the remaining Moslems (some half a million). The loss to Spain resulting from the expulsion of the Moors and the Jews, the destruction of Moorish institutions, and the burning of Arab manuscripts was incalculable and irreparable—like the destruction by Arabs of Hindu culture in India and Hellenic culture in Alexandria during the violently aggressive phase of Islam some centuries earlier, and the destruction of the Aztec and Inca civilizations of the New World by the Spanish conquistadors a few years later.

[1] It is probable that they were bi-lingual from the start.

Fortunately traditions of music and dancing are less easily destroyed than manuscripts, and the classical Andalusian music and dancing were taken over by the gypsies who began to arrive in Spain about 1440. By about 1620 nearly all the Moors had been expelled, and from now on it was mainly the gypsies who preserved the classical Andalusian traditions of music and dancing. They picked up these styles very easily, for they preserved a great many customs and patterns of thought and feeling belonging to their ancestral home in India.

The Flamenco style of dancing is difficult to analyse, for its contains two distinct Indian elements—the classical style brought to Spain by the Arabs and the popular style brought by the gypsies—and these two Indian elements are themselves related to each other. In India the various gypsy tribes in different parts of the country have many different styles of dancing related to other Indian folk-dance styles, and the tribes that emigrated from India have in each country adopted to a large extent the dances of the country, so that it is difficult to establish what elements of dancing are specifically gypsy. (A certain seductive manner of shaking the shoulders is to be found in most European gypsy dances, but it is also to be found in Kathakali!)

What is clear is that the Spanish gypsies modified and simplified the classical Moorish style of Andalusia to adapt it to their temperament and primitive way of life; they discarded some of its subtlety and restraint and added to it characteristically gypsy elements of expressionist violence, arrogance and grotesque humour.[1] They also adapted the footwork to performance in heeled shoes instead of in bare feet or soft slippers, with bells round the ankles, in the Indian-Moorish manner. Being a primitive nomadic race,[2] specializing in fortune-telling, tavern entertainment and horse-trading (not to mention horse-stealing), they could not possibly preserve the full complexity of a classical court art; but they did manage to retain the basic features of the classical tradition with extraordinary fidelity: a great gypsy artist singing cante jondo or dancing a Farruca evokes the glories of Andalusia's golden age almost as vividly as the Alcazar of Seville and the Alhambra of Granada. In the nineteenth and twentieth centuries the very primitiveness of the gypsies was of the utmost importance in enabling them to preserve their classical traditions uncorrupted by ballet and Western harmony, both of which are fatal to the classical Andalusian styles. (It is no accident that the poet Garcia Lorca found the key to the Spanish soul—not just the gypsy soul—in the songs of the Spanish gypsies.)

Like cante jondo and *guitarra morisca* on the one hand, and like Kathak

[1] It is possible that Flamenco dancing was also influenced by the strong expressionist tendencies which appeared in most branches of Spanish art in the seventeenth century. Quevedo's strange book *Los Sueños*, for example, shows much the same combination of fantasy, satire, nonsense and buffoonery as the lighter aspects of Flamenco dancing.

[2] Later a considerable number of gypsies took up permanent residence in the main centres of Moorish culture—particularly Granada and Seville; but they still tended to live in caves and keep their traditional way of life.

dancing and Indian classical music on the other, Flamenco dancing is improvised within strict rules: the steps and arm-movements are standardized, and so are the rhythmic patterns, but the dancer works as a creative artist in putting together the steps, arm-movements and rhythmic patterns, and never does the same dance twice in the same way. The name of a dance does not imply a rigidly fixed choreography; it merely implies a certain type of song, a certain mood and basic rhythm, and perhaps a few characteristic steps or details of costume. The Farruca, for example, is a virile male dance,[1] distinguished by a savage mood and violent contrasts in the tempo and breadth of the movements, together with some characteristic lunges to the ground; the Zapateado consists entirely of foot-beats, and is allied to the *tat-kar* of Kathak; the Alegrías is a gay dance performed by the Flamenco danseuse in a dress with a long train which limits considerably the range of her foot-movements; the Bulerías is full of grotesque humour. As new dance-forms become popular older forms fall into oblivion, but the basic technique remains the same, and to a large extent the same steps, arm-movements, finger-movements, and rhythms of foot-beats and finger-snaps come into each dance. Flamenco mime is completely spontaneous, and does not differ much from the gestures and facial expressions used by the gypsies in normal conversation—which is usually very spirited by North European standards. (Kathak mime lies roughly half-way between the relatively standardized *abhinaya* that one finds in Bharata Natyam *padams* and the completely spontaneous mime of Flamenco.) Flamenco mime is rarely serious: generally it has strong elements of mockery and parody.

The typical café entertainment provided by gypsies is the Cuadro Flamenco, made of a series of songs and dances by different members of a small troupe of singers, dancers and guitarists; the members of the troupe not actually performing help those who are by shouting encouragement and clapping counter-rhythms. (Such entertainments are also provided by gypsies to the visitors to the lower caves of the Sacromonte of Granada.) These shows vary widely in quality, and there is nearly always a certain element of commercialization (the gypsies tending to cater to what they imagine to be the taste of the patrons); but at its best the Cuadro Flamenco has tremendous vitality and expressiveness. Gypsy troupes provide such shows in cafés cantantes in most parts of Spain.

For hundreds of years Spanish gypsies have taken real Flamenco from time to time outside Spain, but the expressionist violence of this style prevented it from becoming really popular in its pure state outside Spain until the rise of expressionism early in the twentieth century prepared the way for it. In 1900 Pepe Amayo brought a Flamenco troupe to the Exposition Universale in Paris, and during the next few years Flamenco artists began to appear in music-halls

---

[1] Flamenco danseuses sometimes perform a Farruca wearing men's clothes, but the dance is too violent to be fully suitable for the female physique.

inside and outside Spain: Amalia Molina and Pastora Imperio made names for themselves in this way. In 1921 Diaghilev very intelligently took advantage of the change in the Zeitgeist to present a real Cuadro Flamenco by a troupe of Spanish gypsies, as part of his programme of ballet; the only change he made in the traditional entertainment was to present it in a décor by Picasso. The dancers performed a typical series of Flamenco dances—Tango Gitano, Farruca, Alegrías, Garrotín Grotesco, and Garrotín Comico. Like many another gypsy troupe they also included in their programme a Jota Aragonesa, much to the detriment of the latter. (Gypsies have no feeling for the noble simplicity of the folk-dances of Central and North Spain, and even in the relatively Moorish Sevillanas of Andalusia they are usually too flamboyant.) The Cuadro Flamenco presented by Diaghilev helped to stimulate interest in real Flamenco outside Spain (though audiences were somewhat taken aback by the violence and grotesque humour of the show, just as they were by *Le Renard*), and since then a number of different gypsy dancers have brought real Flamenco to the great cities of Europe and America.

The outstanding Flamenco danseuse and singer of modern times was unquestionably Pastora Imperio: she gave her movements a nobility which made quite clear the classical origins of Flamenco, and she showed the vivid personality which only emerges when an artist is able to draw strength from an old tradition and a complex technique. Being more of a singer than a dancer, Pastora Imperio toured only in Spanish-speaking countries, and so her art unfortunately remained unknown outside these countries.

The first great gypsy dancer to win something like world fame was Vicente Escudero. He toured with a small company consisting of two gypsy danseuses, a guitarist and a pianist, and gave superb performances of Flamenco dances. In the Farruca—the supreme test of all male Flamenco dancers—he never failed to bring the house down. He achieved fame both in Europe and in America, and was hailed as the greatest male dancer in the world; this was an exaggeration, for Flamenco has not the technical and emotional range of the great classical styles of Europe, India, Bali, China and Japan—but he was certainly in a class by himself among male Flamenco dancers.

Hurok, being unaware of the fact that Escudero continued a professional tradition of dancing much older than ballet, was surprised to find that the gypsy Escudero was one of the steadiest, most reliable performers he ever managed:[1] like professional performers with a long tradition in every country, he was superstitious and temperamental, but he did not allow anything to injure the standard of his show.

Antonio, though not a gypsy, continued in the same path as Escudero, and was also hailed as "the greatest male dancer in the world". Antonio (an Anda-

[1] *Impresario*, p. 158.

lusian born in Seville) had training under the best Flamenco teachers (notably La Quica), and mastered not only the full technique of Flamenco but also its creative aspect—the ability of the Flamenco dancer to improvise in collaboration with his guitarist. Antonio was by no means the first non-gypsy dancer to become expert in Flamenco, but he distinguished himself by becoming a virtuoso in all the separate aspects of Flamenco technique, achieving remarkable clarity and power in his finger-snaps and foot-beats, variety in his rhythms, speed and precision in his *vueltas quebradas*, purity in his line, expressiveness in his mime, and so on. Like other non-gypsy Flamenco dancers he played down the grotesque humour of Flamenco, concentrating on virtuosity and violence rather than on a wide range of moods; nevertheless his achievements in the field of pure Flamenco were very impressive. No less impressive was the fact that though he spent the War years in America, performing to audiences unversed in the niceties of Flamenco, he did not allow his Flamenco style to be corrupted; and when he returned to Spain after the War he scored a triumph.

Unfortunately he was so much under the influence of the fashionable Spanish ballet of his day that in any one programme he included only one or two pure Flamenco dances: most of his dances were in free style, or else in a corrupt form of Flamenco performed to pre-existing piano music. (Though the gypsies themselves often do this, the practice of performing Flamenco to a piano or orchestra is as destructive of the real character of the art as the playing of jazz by large bands from scores, or the singing of blues in an operatic voice.[1]) Antonio also crippled himself by having as his partner his cousin Rosario, who is a competent singer and dancer but has little idea of the nature of Flamenco.[2] In spite of these self-imposed limitations, however, Antonio managed to win for himself a unique position among the internationally touring Spanish dancers of the forties and fifties: his Farruca and Zapateado were enough to make up for a great deal of banal and tedious choreography in free style, and invariably brought the house down.

From time to time other fine Flamenco dancers could be glimpsed in the Spanish ballet companies; and among these Teresa Maya (in José Greco's company) was outstanding. She appeared quite low in the billing of this company, and had only one solo; but when her chance came she seized it as only a great traditional artist can, walking down to the footlights and taking over the theatre with the warm and friendly arrogance characteristic of female Flamenco. (The great Flamenco danseuse seems to dance for herself alone,

---

[1] Alan Lomax and others have drawn attention to certain analogies between cante jondo and the blues singing of American Negroes. But cante jondo is very much older than the blues, which is a folk art originating in the nineteenth century.

[2] In 1952 bitter disputes between Antonio and Rosario came to a head, and they parted company. Antonio replaced Rosario with Mariemma, who made an even less satisfactory partner. (*See* below, p. 304.)

scowling at the ground, but her eyes and her expression carry to every person within view.) Teresa Maya's grotesque, violent and witty Bulerías (danced with her talented brother Juanele Maya) was as perfect in its own genre as Escudero's Farruca. Another fine gipsy artist to be seen outside Spain is Rosandro: though he and his ravishing partner Margarita lack virtuosity they have the same ability to turn the simplest movements into poetry as good dancers in any classical style.

Not all gypsies are artists: Carmen Amaya has shown that a pure-bred gypsy can transform Flamenco into the most tawdry sensationalism. Her commercialized music-hall dancing stands in much the same relationship to classical Flamenco that the commercialized "swing" or "bop" of certain American Negro performers stands to the classical jazz of the great Negro musicians. She performs every dance as fast as possible and makes every foot-beat as loud as possible, showing no interest in the subtleties by which good Flamenco artists build up to their striking effects, and ignores the differences in mood, tension and tempo between one dance and another. Her idea of showing "temperament" is to bury her head almost permanently in a shock of hair. These crude tactics have proved successful at the box office, just like similar tactics in film and ballet, and unfortunately have had a good deal of influence on other dancers. Like other traditional arts Flamenco has shown a strong tendency to degenerate in the twentieth century, and the misuse of her talents by Carmen Amaya has made it more difficult for the great Flamenco artists to arrest this decline.

(b) REGIONAL DANCES

Spanish-Arabic culture was dominant in the southern half of the Iberian peninsula for over six hundred years, and though a great deal of this was deliberately destroyed it persisted in the songs and dances (which, as already mentioned, resist destruction better than solid objects such as manuscripts); even today the traditional songs and dances of Andalusia, South Portugal, the Canary Islands and the Balearic Islands show a considerable amount of Spanish-Arabic influence. As one might expect Flamenco has certain arm-positions and steps in common with the folk-dances and social dances of these regions; but it is essentially a professional art, and differs fundamentally from them.[1]

The most highly developed of the regional dances of Spain are those of the Andalusian Seguidillas type, notably the Seguidillas[2] of Seville, which is per-

[1] This fundamental distinction is not well understood in Spain: the government-sponsored group *Coros y Danzas de España* includes in its repertoire a ludicrous synthetic folk-dance made up out of fragments of Flamenco.

[2] Its full name is the Seguidillas Sevillanas. Songs and dances called Seguidillas are also known outside Andalusia: the name merely implies a suite, and is normally followed by a geographical qualification.

formed in many parts of Andalusia under the name Sevillanas. One can hardly regard these dances as folk-dances, for they are taught by dancing-teachers, and the question of authenticity does not arise; they used to form part of the education of every Andalusian, and may be compared to the Highland dances of Scotland, which they resemble in many ways. They are normally performed by couples, with the man and the woman performing the same steps; sometimes a number of couples join together to perform them as a social dance, when they represent the Andalusian equivalent of Scottish ballroom dances. A Seguidillas moves through a series of coplas, corresponding to verses of the accompanying song; each copla ends in a standard position which is held for a moment. A good Sevillanas consists of a series of up to seven coplas of increasing complexity; such dances are performed at parties to the accompaniment of the same sort of *jaleo* (hand-clapping, shouts of encouragement, etc.) that the gypsies use. The castanets are played in the Andalusian way, suspended from the thumb. The technique used in the Sevillanas and other dances of a similar type is more complex than that of most of the regional dances of Spain, though very simple compared with that of Flamenco. The standard of Sevillanas dancing has degenerated in recent years; no big company touring outside Spain includes a good Sevillanas in its repertoire.

In Central and North Spain, in North Portugal, in Catalonia, and in the Basque country (which stretches into France) there are a large number of folk-dances of the same general character as those of other parts of Europe: in these dances Moorish-Indian influence is either faint or non-existent.

The regional dances of Spain can be and are adapted to the theatre in the same way as the folk-dances of India. Solo dances with a highly developed technique, such as the Sevillanas and Basque dances, need no adaptation.

(c) SPANISH BALLET

Spanish ballet has a very long history. It dates back to the beginnings of ballet in Spain (toward the middle of the seventeenth century) in the entertainments at the court of Philip IV: dances such as Seguidillas, Fandangos and Boleros were performed between the acts of plays. When a Royal Ballet was established as part of the Royal Opera the dance-training was based on the classical ballet technique imported from France and Italy, but considerable prominence was given to the performance of balletized versions of Spanish regional dances, and dancing teachers began to teach a hybrid style (the so-called *baile clasico español*) which brought together the international ballet technique and steps, arm-movements and rhythms from a number of different regional Spanish dances. This style (which continued to exist alongside the standard ballet technique) excluded all elements of Flamenco, which was despised as a vulgar gypsy dance, just as in India Bharata Natyam and Kathak were despised as prostitute dancing.

Dolores Serral created a sensation when she appeared in Paris in the 1830's performing dances such as the Bolero and the Cachuca in the *baile clasico español* style. These dances seemed to Parisians to be excitingly abandoned and voluptuous because Dolores Serral bent her body at the waist, stamped her feet, and tilted her head in the Sevillanas manner—movements quite unknown in the rather stilted ballets of the period. This strongly balletized style was accepted as authentically Spanish, and became very popular; it was taken up by ballet dancers such as the Noblet sisters, and Fanny Elssler had her greatest triumphs in the Cachuca. In later years other balletized national dances such as the Cancan and the Polka created much the same furore as the Bolero and the Cachuca; the movements used in the ballet of the period were so limited that almost any new style seemed exciting.

Spanish ballet degenerated in the second half of the nineteenth century much as did the ballet of other European countries. Its revival began as one aspect of the renaissance in Spanish music, and took shape under the inspiration of the great Spanish composer Manuel de Falla (1876–1946). Falla was a pupil of the nationalist Spanish composer Pedrell, and under the guidance of Pedrell he studied Spanish folklore very deeply. He was born in Cadiz (in Andalusia) and was strongly influenced by Flamenco dancing; intuitively he realized the remote origins of Flamenco dancing in religious ritual, and during the whole of his first period he devoted himself to the writing of dances based mainly on the dance-music of the Andalusian gypsies. He was well able to appreciate the talents of the great gypsy artist Pastora Imperio, and wrote the fine ballet *El Amor Brujo* in which she created the principal rôle. He then wrote the "pantomime" *El Corregidor y la molinara*, which was performed in a small theatre in Madrid by a group of folk-dancers; he later expanded this work into the ballet *Le Tricorne*, which Diaghilev produced with choreography by Massine; as mentioned above, Massine based his own rôle (that of the Miller) almost entirely on the dancing of the gypsy Felix.[1]

The next important pioneer in the revival of Spanish ballet was Argentina (Antonia Mercé, 1888–1936). She was stimulated by the renaissance in Russian ballet and the rise of the European free dance to devise a new Spanish free style more in harmony with the Zeitgeist of the twentieth century than the old *baile clasico español*. She began training in ballet at the age of four under her father Manuel Mercé, *primero bailarin* of the Madrid Opera, and joined the Opera in 1910 at the age of twelve. But she found the work at the Opera much too

[1] *See* p. 128 above.

dreary for her taste, and left two years later to continue her training under her mother, who was also a professional dancer. (By this time her father had died.) She worked out dances which differed from the old *baile clasico español* in that the Spanish steps and arm-movements were more prominent than the ballet technique; but her principal innovation was to study Flamenco and introduce refined versions of Flamenco dances into her recitals.[1] She did not balletize the technique of the Flamenco items to any marked extent, but she changed their character by taking out all the elements of violence, passion and grotesque humour, and abolishing the element of improvisation. (She danced to piano music.) She also made lavish use of castanets, which do not properly belong to Flamenco. (Gypsies sometimes use castanets, but these make it impossible for the dancer to use the characteristic Flamenco finger-movements: the Flamenco equivalent of castanets is finger-snapping.) Argentina was exceptionally musical and made considerable advances in the art of castanet-playing.

Argentina had the same devastating success as Dolores Serral, and for much the same reason: her dances were far enough from ballet to seem delightfully exotic, but not so far away as to present any difficulties in assimilation. Her influence was enormous, for she toured very widely.

Argentina obeyed a sound instinct in attempting to derive from Flamenco a classical style; some hundreds of years ago Moslem Andalusia must have possessed a classical court dance which was closely related to Kathak and was the choreographic equivalent of the architecture of the Alcazar and the Alhambra. But Argentina went astray in seeking to classicize Flamenco by altering it in the direction of European ballet. Flamenco belongs to the Indian family of dances, and attempts to balletize it are inevitably as sterile in the long run as the parallel attempts to introduce major and minor harmonies into cante jondo. Though Argentina's free style had validity when used by her it became stiff and arid when continued by Mariemma—who plays the castanets beautifully, but is lacking in personality and expression.

For many years Argentina followed in the tradition of Dolores Serral and other exponents of *baile clasico español*, confining herself to the composition of solos for herself and pas de deux for herself and her partner. Then, in 1929, she formed a troupe in Paris and gave a show in which she showed ballets as well as solos and pas de deux. She was unable to cope with the problems involved in taking the troupe on tour, and disbanded it after the Paris season; but in 1936 (the last year of her life) she formed another troupe in Paris (including Escudero) and produced at the Opéra, in collaboration with Falla, a new version of *El Amor Brujo*.

---

[1] The Cachuca popularized by Dolores Serral was based on a Flamenco dance that still exists in Granada; the version shown in Paris was considerably balletized.

Above: Antonio performing Flamenco dance in Barcelona, 1951

Argentina in 1924

Yugoslav national dance "Oro" in *The Legend of Ohrid* (Harmoš, Zagreb, 1949)

The Fountain of Bakhchisaraï (Harmoš, Zagreb, 1946) with Zlata Lanović as Zarema,
Oscar Harmoš as Khan Ghireï and Ana Roje as Maria

Argentina took some important steps toward the creation of modern Spanish ballet with her new version of *El Amor Brujo*, but she did not live long enough to bring Spanish ballet to maturity, and in any case it is probable that her personal style was too limited for this purpose. Though her successors have moved a certain distance along the path she opened up, they have by no means brought Spanish ballet to a point where it can stand comparison with the best modern Indian ballets or the best ballets based on the international classical technique of the West.

The most important and influential of Argentina's successors in this genre was Argentinita (Encarnacion Lopez, 1898–1945). Ten years younger than Argentina, she was able to profit by Argentina's example, studying all the different styles available in Spain—*baile clasico español*, regional dances, Flamenco, ballet, etc. In 1932 she returned from a long foreign tour and founded in Madrid the Madrid Ballet in collaboration with the great poet García Lorca. From then on she continued to dance at the head of fair-sized ballet companies, and composed a considerable number of ballets, though her programmes naturally included many solos and pas de deux as well. Perhaps owing to the influence of Lorca (who was a great lover of cante jondo and Flamenco dancing, and understood the arts of the Spanish gypsies more profoundly than anyone else of his generation),[1] Argentinita included far more Flamenco in her choreography than Argentina, and preserved the characteristic harshness and vigour of Flamenco much better. Unlike Lorca, however, she never quite succeeded in reconciling the sharply contrasted materials she used as the basis for her compositions—the stylized virtuosity and Oriental poetry of Flamenco, the noble simplicity of regional steps, and the cosmopolitan sophistication of Western ballet. Only a genius like Lorca could accomplish a task of this magnitude, and Argentinita was no genius. (Her task was much harder than that of her Indian contemporaries, for the techniques on which she built her ballets were much less closely related to each other than the classical styles of Indian dancing.) Nevertheless Argentinita's work was intelligent, and pointed the way to the future. Many of her ballets have been preserved in the repertoires of the companies directed respectively by her sister Pilar Lopez and her *primero bailarin* José Greco; and at some future date they may provide the basis for another major step forward in Spanish ballet. One cannot expect any major advances from Pilar Lopez or José Greco, neither of whom show much originality or imagination, though the latter (an American of mixed Italian-Greek parentage) has been well trained and has considerable charm as a dancer—even if his Flamenco style is somewhat lacking in the authentic gypsy *élan*.

[1] Lorca's understanding of cante jondo was so profound that some of his poems in this style are sung by cante jondo singers, and transmitted orally in the traditional way, their origin forgotten.

The deficiencies of modern Spanish ballet can be seen with particular clarity in the comedy number originally created by Argentina under the name *Lagarterana*; in this number she showed an ingenuous half-witted village yokel and a village girl of similar intellectual attainments. Both were dressed in the colourful costumes of the village of Lagartera, near Madrid, and performed steps from the folk-dances of this region, but the whole point of the number was the half-witted clowning of the two yokels. This number has been repeated with variations by almost every Spanish company: Antonio, for example, produced both *Los Lagarteranos* and a Peruvian adaptation of it, *Danza Incaica*. The humour in such numbers is pathetically insipid in comparison with gypsy Flamenco humour, and is quite unworthy of the land of Cervantes.

Yugoslavia

NO-ONE who saw the Yugoslav folk dancers when they first appeared in Western Europe in 1951–52 is likely to forget the impression they made. Here was something really new. The dances were in an extraordinary variety of moods and tempi, some of the rhythms were astonishingly complex, and the movements ranged in style from some which were completely Occidental to others which were completely Oriental; but all the dances were performed with the same strange compelling force that seemed to derive from a combination of passion, sincerity, spontaneity, restraint and abandon. It was obvious that if these people took to ballet they were capable of achieving something really impressive in this art.

One reason why the Yugoslavs are so good at national dances is that for the five hundred years that their country was under Turkish and Austro-Hungarian rule dancing was one of the few ways in which they could hang on to their national existence. In fact Yugoslavia has today, in proportion to its population, greater richness and variety in its national dances than any other country. Ballet is still a very young art in Yugoslavia, but the Yugoslavs have indeed brought to ballet the same qualities that make their national dances so exciting, and the achievements of Yugoslav ballet are already very promising.

In so far as Yugoslavia has any old traditions of ballet they are to be found in those parts of the country previously occupied by Austria-Hungary—Croatia, Slovenia and Dalmatia. These parts were in contact with Vienna and North Italy, and were occasionally visited by theatrical companies that included ballet dancers. Yugoslav ballet began in a very small way in Zagreb (the chief city of Croatia) about 1911, when the Viennese teacher Josephine Weiss began to give classes. Soon she began to present divertissements and small ballets at the Zagreb Opera House, her principal danseuses being Stephania Kraljeva, Draga Spoljar and Paula Hudi; she had no male pupils, and used danseuses *en travesti* for the male parts. The first Yugoslav male ballet dancer was Oscar Harmoš, who joined her classes in 1915 at the age of four-and-a-half. Within a year he and another infant prodigy (Zlata Lanović) were going on recital tours in Yugoslavia.

Soon after the Russian revolution of 1917 the small beginnings of Yugoslav ballet were swamped in a flood of refugees from Russia. One group of Moscow dancers led by Margarita Froman gave some performances in Zagreb (on its way to the West), and made such a strong impression that it was invited to join the Zagreb Ballet. The result was that ballet in Zagreb became almost entirely Russian and was completely dominated by Margarita Froman: she taught in the school, and began to produce a large number of Maryinsky and Diaghilev ballets—*Schéhérazade, Coppélia, Carnaval, Petrouchka, Les Papillons, Prince Igor, Chopiniana*[1] and so on. Like many other Russians in a similar position at this time she achieved reasonably correct reproductions of the originals; and her work as a régisseur was of the utmost value to Yugoslav ballet, for it enabled the latter to start off on the basis of some of the finest achievements of Russian ballet.

A number of talented Yugoslav dancers attended her classes, which were very much better than those of her Viennese predecessor, though her Moscow school was in turn far inferior to the great Legat school of St. Petersburg. Margarita Froman gave relatively few opportunities to the rising young Yugoslav dancers, and the best of them left Yugoslavia to seek careers elsewhere—notably Ana Roje, Mia Slavenska and later Oscar Harmoš. This was a very fortunate circumstance, for these dancers made contact with aspects of ballet tradition which otherwise might never have reached Yugoslavia and might even have been lost entirely.

In 1924 the first Yugoslav national ballet *Licitarsko Srce* (*The Gingerbread Heart*) was produced in Zagreb. It was based on a Croatian folk-tale, the music was by the Croatian composer Kresimir Baranović, and the décor was by the Croatian painter Maximilian Vanko; in fact the ballet was entirely Yugoslav in origin except for the choreography (which was by Margarita Froman), and even this had a certain national flavour through the inclusion of balletized versions of national dances.

Meanwhile the directorate of the National Theatre of Belgrade was making determined efforts to establish a strong ballet company in the capital of the country. There was no tradition of ballet in Serbia, and the new company was inevitably even more Russian than that in Zagreb. Employment was given to a large number of Russian artists—notably Poliakova, Kirsanova, Romanovsky, Pianowsky,[2] Kniasev, Vassiliev and Fortunato. These artists provided the Belgrade Ballet with a Russian repertoire fairly similar to that of the Zagreb Ballet—*The Sleeping Beauty, Le Lac des Cygnes, Schéhérazade, Giselle*, etc. Poliakova had some very talented pupils, among them Igor Youskevitch—who like so many others of the best Yugoslav-trained

---

[1] The original version, not the second version usually known as *Les Sylphides*.
[2] Romanovsky and Pianowsky were actually Polish, but had worked in Russian companies.

dancers found it desirable to go abroad for a career. Apart from the Russian dancers and the Belgrade-trained dancers some of the best Zagreb dancers (including Ana Roje and Oscar Harmoš, 1930–33) danced for a time in Belgrade.

One of the most important landmarks in the history of Yugoslav ballet was the arrival of Ana Roje in London in 1933 to study with Nicolas Legat. She intended to stay only a few months to acquire a final polish at Legat's *classe de perfection*—by this time she was the most promising of the young Yugoslav ballerinas—but Legat insisted on rebuilding her technique from its foundations. In fact he was so impressed with her that he made her his assistant, and kept her at his side right up to his death four years later. He knew that he did not have long to live, and decided to take advantage of her receptiveness to even the most subtle aspects of his system to pass on to her the whole of his vast knowledge and experience. The fact that Ana Roje could speak Russian was of great importance; Legat's English was very poor, and in the public classes he found it impossible to explain more than a small number of the things he had in mind, whereas in the Legat system progress is impossible unless the pupil understands the reason for everything. It was heartbreaking for Ana Roje to have to abandon her career for such a long time, watching dancers with no more talent than herself making great names for themselves; but Nicolas Legat knew very well what he was doing. By the time he died he had ensured that his system would be preserved without degeneration, in spite of its extreme subtlety and flexibility.

After Legat's death Ana Roje found herself in the same strange position that Legat had occupied in his youth: she was employed as teacher by the two leading Ballet-Russe companies in turn, and gave lessons to famous dancers like Massine, Danilova and Markova, who were older than her.

Oscar Harmoš remained in Yugoslavia for some time after Ana Roje's departure, but eventually he too came to London to study with Legat. By this time his main interest was choreography, and after Legat's death he joined the Ballets Jooss in order to gain experience with the most advanced European type of free-dance choreography.

Ana Roje and Oscar Harmoš joined forces once again in 1939 and began work in Split on the Dalmatian coast (Ana Roje's birthplace). Margarita Froman then wrote an article attacking them for deserting Yugoslavia. Oscar Harmoš replied to this article, explaining how it was that Ana Roje, himself and many other Yugoslav dancers had been forced to go abroad. The polemic went on for two years, and ended up by bringing about the return of Ana Roje and Oscar Harmoš to Zagreb under much more favourable conditions than before: Ana Roje was prima ballerina and chief teacher, Oscar Harmoš was chief choreographer and the leading character dancer, and Margarita Froman was employed in the rôle of régisseur, for which she had in fact exceptional qualifications.

This change made it possible once again for Yugoslav ballet to make progress. By this time Ana Roje was one of the greatest ballerinas in the world, as well as being in a class by herself as a teacher, and Oscar Harmoš had acquired the international background he needed to come to grips with the problems involved in creating Yugoslav ballets of more than local interest. He devoted himself partly to ballets with a cosmopolitan basis (e.g. *Night on a Bare Mountain* to the music of Mussorgsky, and *Life* to the music of Tchaikovsky, both composed in 1941) and partly to national Yugoslav ballets such as *Devil in the Village* (1942). The latter ballet was based on a folk-tale and had been originally produced in 1937, in Zurich, Munich and Ljubljana (capital of Slovenia), by the dancers Pia and Pino Mlakar, who had been trained in the free dance in Germany. Oscar Harmoš used a considerable number of expressionist ideas in his choreography, but because his background was largely classical he was able to use ballet-trained dancers effectively, and give the movements more subtlety than was normal among free dancers.

In 1946 Oscar Harmoš followed the example set by Soviet choreographers and began to produce ballets in several acts, lasting an entire evening. The first full-length ballet he produced was *The Fountain of Bakhchisaraï*, based on the Pushkin poem and the score written by Asafiev for Zakharov's Leningrad production. (The Leningrad production was unknown in Yugoslavia.) This ballet was admirably suited to the talents of Oscar Harmoš himself and of the dancers at his disposal. Ana Roje gave a performance as Maria which was fully worthy of the great tradition of noble and poetic simplicity established by the great Russian ballerinas (under the leadership of Legat) in ballets like *Le Lac des Cygnes* and *Giselle*, and continued by them in Fokine ballets like *Le Spectre de la Rose*. The other rôles gave fine opportunities to Oscar Harmoš (as Khan Ghireï), Zlata Lanović (Zarema), Nenad Lhotka (Nurali), Frane Jelinčić (Vaslav), and a number of talented young dancers who were beginning to emerge from Ana Roje's classes: the complex Yugoslav national traditions provided a good basis for their interpretations both of Polish national dances and the Oriental dances of the Tartars.

In 1951 Ana Roje and Oscar Harmoš, feeling the same need for stimulus from outside their country as Birgit Åkesson, went on a visit to England. There they spent several months teaching and studying the achievements of English ballet during the twelve years since their departure in 1939; and they returned to England for six months in 1952–53.

In 1953 the Yugoslav Government, recognizing that Ana Roje's work as a teacher was of considerably more than national significance, provided her and Oscar Harmoš with an independent school of their own in Split which provided training not only for the best Yugoslav dancers but also for dancers from foreign countries; in effect this school represented a continuation of that directed by Nicolas Legat in London with Ana Roje as his assistant. At the same time Ana Roje and Oscar Harmoš began to form a company of their own, to perform in split and also on tour.

By this time Yugoslav dancers, teachers and choreographers (many of them trained by Ana Roje and Oscar Harmoš) were beginning to build up ballet in the capitals of the various republics into which Yugoslavia was now divided. Interest in ballet had grown very rapidly after the liberation and the formation of a federal republic, and the Government responded to this interest by making arrangements for the formation of ballet companies in each capital, and State ballet schools in all the cities and large towns.

In many respects Yugoslav ballet reminds one of modern English, Indian and Spanish ballet: into each of these countries the international ballet tradition has been introduced or re-introduced during the twentieth century and has become enriched from old and powerful national traditions. The Yugoslavs are fortunate in having not only an extremely lively and varied folk-culture but also a direct link with the finest traditions of European classical dancing; and for this reason the potentialities of Yugoslav ballet are enormous.

PART III

Types of Ballet Company in the Twentieth Century

A

Old-established State Ballets Surviving into the Twentieth Century

THE ACHIEVEMENTS of Duke Carl Eugen in Stuttgart and Count Durazzo in Vienna were very exceptional; normally a State ballet has much the same characteristics as any other government department, and generates a climate wholly destructive to creative activity. Like other government departments, the State ballet is a complex permanent organization with an elaborate hierarchy of officials and the virtues and defects normal to such organizations. There is an inevitable emphasis on technical efficiency, precision, continuity, discipline and discretion. So far as possible problems are solved by fitting them into categories and applying the appropriate rule or precedent. The officials develop an outlook in harmony with their daily routine of work; all relationships between the members of the organization and with the outside world are kept as impersonal and mechanical as possible, and rules and precedents are given an almost sacred value independent of their original function—so much so that the efficiency of the individual tends to be judged by the accuracy with which he keeps to the rules, no matter how arbitrary and out-of-date these rules may be. There are invariably bitter intrigues within the organization, but these are temporarily laid aside to oppose any new development which might lead to changes in the existing hierarchy of power and patterns of intrigue. Under favourable conditions a good tradition can be preserved once it is solidly established, but only under exceptional circumstances can such a tradition be established; and such conditions are normally only present when the company is fairly young, before the patterns are completely rigid. In most cases the organization operates with great efficiency to preserve bad traditions.

In default of good new ballets produced by the staff choreographers, State ballets tend to rely on the commissioning of ballets by famous *foreign* choreographers who lie outside the circle of local intrigues. Sometimes this has made possible fine artistic achievements for a time, but eventually the foreign choreographer is certain to break his heart in his attempts to cope with intrigue and sabotage.

In theory the State ballet should be able to maintain a high standard of dancing even if not of choreography; ballet training is a lengthy and complex process, and lends itself to the systematization which is normal in all State schools. In fact, however, dancing is also a creative process, and it is not possible to keep dancing and choreography in watertight compartments. In Russia, for example, the standard of dancing declined in the sixties and seventies of the nineteenth century step by step with the decline in choreography, and the later renaissance in dancing formed part of a general balletic renaissance which culminated in the choreography of Fokine and the performances in Fokine ballets of great dancers like Pavlova, Karsavina, Spessivsteva and Nijinsky. The State ballets have a pressing need for great ballerinas, yet are normally no more able to create them from their own dancers than they are of bringing to maturity home-grown choreographers. Often the individuality which is essential to soloists gets crushed out of the dancers during their years in the lower ranks; and even if soloists manage to preserve some individuality they are likely to be defeated by the patterns of intrigue which ensure that promotion bears little relation to talent.

A great teacher can transform the atmosphere of a State ballet to some extent, but such teachers are liable to encounter much the same intrigue and sabotage as great choreographers, and rarely stay for long. Normally the State-employed dancers who wish to make real progress have to avoid the company classes and pay out of their meagre earnings for classes from great teachers outside the company; and often this practice is frowned on by the directors of the State ballets. (The latter make company classes compulsory, or arrange rehearsals at such times that the dancers cannot get off to attend the public classes.)

In this section we are concerned only with old-established State ballets surviving into the twentieth century. Private companies such as the Sadlers Wells Ballet and the New York City Ballet, which have acquired official or semi-official status in recent years, show a number of the characteristic features of State ballets; but they can best be understood in relation to their previous history as private companies.

The old-established State ballets were inevitably affected to some extent by the renaissance of ballet in the twentieth century, but the effects were only superficial. These State ballets have retained their essential characteristics so faithfully that by studying typical State ballets as they exist today we can understand many aspects of ballet history that would otherwise remain obscure. (The reverse is also true: the history of State ballets in the eighteenth and nine-teenth centuries helps us to understand the characteristics of State ballets in the twentieth century.)

Paris Opéra

The Paris Opéra of today presents a bewildering mixture of ancient traditions and relatively recent importations. The organization of the company, with its official hierarchy of ranks and its unofficial system of liaisons between danseuses and politicians, is of great antiquity. The repertoire, on the other hand, is for the most part of relatively recent origin, though it does contain one interesting old ballet, *Coppélia*,[1] with the part of Franz performed by a danseuse *en travesti* as in the original Saint Léon production of 1870. Unfortunately the break in tradition at the middle of the nineteenth century caused the loss of all the major ballets of the first half of the century (notably *Zéphire et Flore* and *Giselle*).

The school of dancing taught at the Opéra has almost nothing to do with the great French school of Vestris, Didelot and Perrot. Because of the degeneration of the French school the danseuses-étoiles were invariably Russian or Italian from the middle of the nineteenth century onwards, and the school in use after 1870 was a version of the contemporary Milanese school. The school taught today is still Milanese, in spite of the fact that for decades great Russian teachers in Paris have been teaching a style which retains the best features of the old French school, while the Milanese school has been degenerating for more than half a century.[2] There is no freedom of movement or length of line in the Milanese school: the necks of the dancers look short because the shoulders are hunched, the turn-out is from the feet rather than from the hips, the thighs are thick because the knees are not pulled properly, the arms are held in a slack and affected manner, and the hands are full of mannerisms. The phrasing is jerky and unmusical; to quote Edwin Denby:

> The Opéra dancer likes to put the dance stress where the shape of the musical phrase gives it no support; so it gets a petulant look. She likes to begin a shade behind the beat as if prettily taken unaware, and end a little ahead as if in confusion; then she adds a vigorous flip of the wrist on the last note.[3]

The male dancers are more vigorous than the danseuses, but have the same winsome affectations.

One common defect of English and American dancers which is not to be found among the Opéra dancers is lack of individuality: it is rare for any French dancer to perform in a dull mechanical manner. On the other hand the

---

[1] The repertoire also includes the second Delibes ballet *Sylvia*, but this ballet has new choreography by Lifar.

[2] The style commonly taught in Italy today has little in common with the Cecchetti method taught in England, the British Commonwealth and the United States, though English-trained Cecchetti teachers are beginning to teach in Italy.

[3] Article entitled "A letter from Florence about the Paris Opéra Ballet" in *Ballet*, July-August, 1950. This article is devoted to a penetrating analysis of the Opéra style.

Opéra dancers show little or no understanding of ballet as something more than the sum of its parts—a work of art produced by the disciplined collaboration of a number of artists. They treat their own rôles simply as a means of gaining applause for themselves, and think nothing of glancing at each other and at the conductor in a way which shatters the theatrical illusion. Since they have no feeling for breadth, nobility or continuity of movement they strive to outdo each other with affected movements of the head, shoulders and hands. Though they have the individuality which is the birthright of every French person, this individuality is confined to externals, and they are sadly lacking in personality: Sallé would have felt just as alone among the Opéra dancers of the twentieth century as she did among their eighteenth-century predecessors.

Casting is determined largely by rank and seniority: once a dancer reaches a certain rank she is entitled to certain rôles, and continues to dance them no matter how dull her performance. In theory promotion from rank to rank is determined solely by competitive examinations, but in practice the careers of the dancers depend to a considerable extent on the influence exerted by their protectors. Talent is helpful, but not essential; some dancers have gone to the top with such little talent that they could hardly rise out of the corps de ballet in a good company. This system has existed from time immemorial—from the very beginning the court ballet was deeply involved in politics, and was in fact used as an instrument of State policy—and it is taken for granted by Parisians, though sometimes newspaper critics appeal to the politicians not to interfere quite so much with the internal affairs of the Opéra ballet.

On several occasions in recent years there seemed to be a real chance of a major improvement in the artistic standard of the Opéra. In 1913, after the dismissal of Nijinsky by Diaghilev, Jaques Rouché (Director of the Opéra) offered Nijinsky the handsome yearly salary of 100,000 gold francs to join the Opéra as maître de ballet and premier danseur. Unfortunately Nijinsky felt obliged to refuse the offer when he saw the dancers he would have to use. Rouché deserves credit for trying to secure the services of Nijinsky, but the latter had quite the wrong temperament for coping with intrigue, and we can be certain that Diaghilev would have used all his influence to make Nijinsky's life at the Opéra unbearable. Nijinsky was probably wise to refuse Rouché's offer.

In 1921 Rouché brought Fokine from America to revive *Daphnis et Chloë* at the Opéra; this ballet appealed to the Opéra because of its music by Ravel for choir and orchestra—the first important ballet score by a French composer for generations. It is tempting to imagine what might have happened to Fokine and to the Opéra if the opportunity had been taken to appoint him maître de ballet. No doubt he would have encountered the same sort of intrigues as Noverre, but the prestige of the dowdy and provincial Opéra at this time was so low in comparison with that of Russian ballet that he would have been in a relatively strong position, and he had had many years of experience of intrigue at the Maryinsky. With the help of some of the Maryinsky stars who had left Russia after the Revolution Fokine might well have done wonders at the Opéra, reviving not only his own St. Petersburg "charity" ballets but the best of the old Maryinsky repertoire and reorganizing the training at the school. But the chance was missed: Rouché made no offer to Fokine, and the latter went back to frustration in America.

In 1924 Olga Spessivsteva, one of the greatest classical dancers of all time, was appointed "étoile" of the Opéra. (The appointment as "étoile" of a great foreign danseuse was in accordance with long-established tradition, but for several generations the appointments had gone to Italian ballerinas.) Spessivsteva's presence at the head of the Opéra company made almost no difference to the style of dancing of the other artists: she lived in a world of her own, and the atmosphere of intrigue which surrounded her was hostile to the diffusion of Russian ideas about nobility and simplicity in dancing. As Pierre Michaut points out, a great mistake was made in omitting to supplement her appointment with the engagement of a great Russian teacher.[1] Spessivsteva stayed at the Opéra until 1932, though she also danced in other cities as a guest artist during the period.

One important result of Spessivsteva's appointment was the production at the Opéra of the Russian version of *Giselle* for her benefit.[2] In this way the Opéra recovered its greatest ballet.

Rouché's appointment of Lifar in 1930 as premier danseur and maître de ballet had an immediate effect on the Opéra: Lifar brought with him the sophisticated public to which Diaghilev catered in his cocktail period, and the Opéra suddenly became fashionable again. This gave a fillip to the morale of the dancers in the company, though in his ballets Lifar gave no good opportunities for anyone but himself for a long time. As already mentioned, his ballets seemed avant-garde at the Opéra, though in fact they showed a distressing absence of real originality or imagination, and were really arrière-garde.

Lifar was not in the least interested in reforming the Opéra, which he used simply as a background for his own dancing; he soon found his feet among the complex intrigues of the Opéra, and left the system as he found it. Certain weaknesses already existing (such as the bad phrasing) were exaggerated by his unmusical choreography, and the dancers showed a tendency to pick up his personal mannerisms as a dancer, but in most respects the Opéra continued on exactly the same lines as before.

In 1940 something of great importance occurred. The French dancer

[1] *Le Ballet Contemporain*, p. 36.
[2] The revival was produced by Nicolas Sergueyev on the basis of his notes of Petipa's final revision of Perrot's choreography.

Yvette Chauviré began to emerge as a ballerina of the highest quality, able to challenge comparison with the best of the Russian ballerinas. She was in fact the first great French dancer since Beaugrand. She had been trained in the Opéra school, and had acquired the usual dry and clipped manner characteristic of the Milanese school taught there. But she had the intelligence and sensitivity to realize the inadequacy of this style, and began intensive training with the Russian teacher Boris Kniasev. Pierre Michaut has admirably described how Kniasev corrected her lack of turn-out, pulled down her shoulders, stretched her neck, straightened her legs and back, improved the placing of her hips, gave nobility and extension to her arm-movements, and communicated to her the fire and devotion to dancing characteristic of the Russian school.[1]

Chauviré first showed her extraordinary talents in the Kniasev ballet *Berioska*; at the Opéra she was given her first chance to show her remarkable talents in Lifar's new version of *Istar* in 1941. From now on her performances stood out from those of all the others at the Opéra, and eventually she was appointed étoile. Her performances represented the beginnings of a renaissance in French ballet. Other Opéra dancers followed her example in undertaking serious and lengthy training under Preobazhenskaya, Kniasev, Yegorova, Volinine and other Russian teachers—among them Renée Jeanmaire, Colette Marchand and Roland Petit. In due course most of these artists found it impossible to continue working at the Opéra, and with their departure the Opéra returned to normal, though a few of the young dancers continued to follow the lead given by Chauviré.

In 1951 Chauviré was suspended from the Opéra by the Director, M. Hirsch. The explanation given to the Press was that she had danced in London (without obtaining permission from the Opéra) in a show of poor quality, thus lowering the prestige of the Opéra. But there was more to this than met the eye, for another Opéra dancer taking part in this show (Kalioujny) was not suspended. Chauviré was only suspended for a year, but she chose not to return until 1953 (when she began to dance again at the Opéra as a guest artist).

M. Hirsch replaced Chauviré with Nina Vyroubova, a fine dancer of Russian origin who had been trained in Paris by Preobazhenskaya and Trefilova. Vyroubova was no Spessivsteva, but she stood out from the other Opéra dancers just as her predecessors had done.

Perhaps the most curious feature of the post-war Opéra was the toleration by its Directorate of Lifar's policy of continuing to dance in exacting male rôles which were far beyond his powers, and which were in any case totally unsuited to his thickened physique. One would have thought that Lifar himself would have wished to prevent the memory of his triumphs as a young man from being destroyed in this fashion.

[1] Pierre Michaut, *Le Ballet Contemporain*, p. 275.

Royal Danish Ballet

The Danes are fortunate, for in the Royal Danish Ballet they possess the only surviving court ballet of international stature and the only long-established ballet company in which the heritage from the past has not been affected by a sharp break in tradition.[1] The Royal Danish Ballet suffered a good deal in the second half of the nineteenth century from the destructive aspects of the Victorian Zeitgeist, but it preserves much of the Bournonville tradition with admirable fidelity.

This preservation of tradition is no accident: it is achieved by extremely careful attention to detail. Old dancers and maîtres de ballet have been encouraged to continue to take an interest in the company after their retirement, and lend a hand when old ballets are revived after being dropped from the repertoire. By far the most important of these guardians of tradition was Hans Beck (1861–1952), who began to dance in the company in 1879, only two years after Bournonville's retirement, when the latter was still alive and the tradition very strong. Hans Beck was maître de ballet from 1894 to 1915, and devoted himself to the preservation of the Bournonville ballets with all their original quality. After his retirement he continued to keep an eagle eye on the quality of performances of Bournonville ballets in the current repertoire, and collaborated with his successors from time to time on the revival of Bournonville ballets which had been allowed to drop out of the repertoire. As late as 1949, when he was eighty-eight, he collaborated with Harald Lander on the production of *Homage to Bournonville*, which included extracts from many Bournonville ballets.

About ten Bournonville ballets survive in the memory of dancers and maîtres de ballet, and can be revived when required; the Bournonville classes and the maintenance of the Bournonville system of training in mime makes it possible for the revivals to be faithful to the originals even if many years have gone by without a performance. Particular care is taken in the preservation of the Galeotti ballet *Les Caprices du Cupidon et du Maître de Ballet*,[2] for this is the oldest European ballet to survive with the original choreography; this ballet is never allowed to drop out of the repertoire for more than twenty years, and arrangements are always made to include in the new cast some members of the previous cast.

[1] The Warsaw State Ballet is one of the oldest in the world, dating back to the beginning of the sixteenth century. But its development was crippled when Warsaw was occupied by the Russians at the end of the eighteenth century: from then up to 1917 the Warsaw company was administered as one of the three Imperial Russian companies. During the second half of the nineteenth century the Poles were allowed to produce some fine character ballets based on Polish national dances, and they preserved two ballets of considerable historical interest—the Taglioni ballet *La Sylphide* and the Blasis ballet *Faust*; but unfortunately there was a sharp break in tradition when the Germans destroyed most of Warsaw (including the opera-house) during the Second World War. What did survive in Warsaw was a fine tradition of male classical dancing: during the twenties the "Russian" danseurs in both the Diaghilev and Pavlova companies were in fact mainly Polish.

[2] Known in Copenhagen as *Amors og Balletmesteren Luner*.

The Vestris-Bournonville style is enshrined in a number of standard classes of which every detail was originally laid down by Bournonville. Standard Bournonville classes are given two or three times a week, and this style is also preserved by the maintenance in the repertoire of a scene from the Bournonville ballet *Conservatoire* which is a stylized version of a Vestris class.

Those aspects of the Bournonville tradition which survive naturally reflect certain changes in taste during his lifetime and his efforts to cope with these changes. A number of his most interesting ballets have been lost, and the Danish female dancing of today shows the typical defects of the period when Bournonville retired (1877). Their movements lack extension and elasticity, their *port de bras* (style of arm-movement) is stiff, they do not pull up their knees properly, their pirouettes are slow and laboured, and they rely too much on broad smiles and affected movement of their hands—though their Franco-Danish style is far superior to the Milanese style of the Paris Opéra.

The Danish male dancers, on the other hand, have wonderful simplicity and nobility: their strength enables them to overcome certain technical weaknesses of the school. Though their pirouettes are laboured and they lack *épaulement*, they have splendid elevation and poise in the air, and their beats are superb. They bring to the interpretation of their rôles a fine understanding of the great traditions of the ballet d'action, building them up in a sincere and imaginative way and avoiding mannerisms and melodramatic exaggeration.

The repertoire of the Royal Danish Ballet contains a number of different elements of widely different value. The most important element is of course the Bournonville heritage; the solitary Galeotti ballet is of great historic interest, but its artistic value is slight, for it is no more than a suite of divertissements.

The new ballets composed by Bournonville's Danish successors fell a very long way below the Bournonville standard. Since the renaissance of ballet in the twentieth century the new Danish ballets have usually represented a sentimental, melodramatic and provincial imitation of the fashionable cosmopolitan style of the period preceding the one in which they were composed. A good example of such provincialism was *Qarrtsiluni* (1942), the most ambitious ballet of Harald Lander (maitre de ballet 1921–52). This attempt at a Greenlandian imitation of *Le Sacre du Printemps* was clumsily constructed (with inordinate repetition of a few simple steps) and showed little feeling for either expressionism or Eskimo dances. On the other hand it had all the typical expressionist faults such as hysterical over-emphasis.

Danish versions of famous foreign ballets have been more successful. Bournonville himself gave a lead by producing a new version of *La Sylphide* which was better than the original, making the hero's rôle as important as that of the heroine. In 1896 Hans Beck produced a new version of *Coppélia* in which the rôle of Dr. Coppélius was built up with mime until he became a real character instead of the familiar cardboard figure, and in successive productions of this ballet Harald Lander continued to strengthen its few Bournonvillean aspects.

By far the most important group of foreign ballets in the Royal Danish repertoire are the three Fokine ballets (*Petrouchka, Prince Igor* and *Chopiniana*) which Fokine himself produced in 1924 and which the Danes have carefully preserved ever since. Fokine was inspired by the fine male dancers at his disposal and the strong Danish mime tradition to produce a good version of *Petrouchka*; in his production of *Chopiniana*, however, he was hampered by the sentimental mannerisms of the ballerinas, and was unable to bring out the poetry of his choreography.

Another important foreign ballet in the repertoire is *Giselle*. The rôle of Albrecht is superbly danced by the Danish premiers danseurs (notably Børge Ralov), even though the Pavlova version of this ballet (reproduced for the Royal Danish Ballet by Volinine) gives less opportunity to the male soloist than the Maryinsky version. The Danish ballerinas show their usual winsome and dainty charm in the rôle of Giselle.

The Royal Danish Ballet has not shown much imagination in its choice of foreign ballets of recent origin. Massine's sentimental and derivative ballet *Le Beau Danube* falls far below the standard achieved by him in his best ballets, and the ballets commissioned from Balanchine and Lichine are scarcely worthy of the great traditions of the company.

In spite of the importation of a few foreign ballets the Royal Danish Ballet has remained to a very great extent cut off from the rest of the ballet world. The entertainment tax on ballet has largely prevented foreign classical ballet companies from visiting Copenhagen. The Royal Danish Ballet has very rarely gone to foreign countries, and the long summer holidays of the company have prevented visitors coming to Denmark during the tourist season from seeing any ballet. Finally in 1950 the Royal Danish Ballet began to do something to promote the international recognition of Danish ballet, arranging the first of a series of Annual Ballet Festivals at the beginning of June, in which the theatre was given up for a whole week to a selection of ballets from the repertoire; and in the Summer of 1953 the company visited London for the first time.

Though the Bournonville ballets have remained almost unknown outside Denmark, a number of highly talented Danish male dancers spread a knowledge of Danish male dancing soon after the end of the Second World War. So many fine male dancers emerged from the school at this time that the Royal Danish Ballet took the unusual step of appointing no less than six premiers danseurs, and gave a number of them long periods of leave so that they could gain experience in foreign countries. Through working with Russian-trained dancers and studying under Russian teachers these Danish dancers overcame certain deficiencies of the Vestris–Bournonville style and returned to Denmark to add new lustre to their own theatre. But the deficiencies in the Danish style of male dancing were of minor importance compared with those in the female dancing, and in 1952 a Russian teacher (Vera Volkova) was brought in to improve the standard of the Danish danseuses.

In this same year the maître de ballet Harald Lander left the Royal Ballet to join the Paris Opéra, where he was commissioned to produce several ballets, and the Danish authorities subsequently permitted Niels Bjørn Larsen to make a serious breach in the Bournonville heritage by producing a new version of the Bournonville ballet *Et Folkesagn* (*A Folk Legend*) which lacked some of the atmosphere and continuity of the original. But the Copenhagen ballet critics understand very well the importance of the Bournonville heritage; this production was sharply criticized, and one may hope that this iconoclastic tendency will not be allowed to gather momentum.

Ballet Companies Formed in the Twentieth Century

UNTIL ABOUT the middle of the nineteenth century, tours by complete ballet companies, with the elaborate décors and costumes needed for the presentation of a repertoire of ballets, were made impossible by the limited carrying capacity of the railways; and ballet was carried from country to country by individual maîtres de ballet and star dancers. There was a period in the fifties when small touring companies flourished in Italy, and also went on tour outside Italy to some extent; costumes were taken on tour, but normally the companies used scenery available in the theatres and took on local dancers for the corps de ballet. Subsequent changes in popular taste crippled these companies, and though they did not die out completely their artistic importance became slight.

Things were very different in the twentieth century, when it became normal for almost all ballet companies to tour; in fact the renaissance of ballet would scarcely have been possible if ballet companies had not been able to go on tour in search of the support and recognition they could not find in their native cities. The new touring companies were naturally of a type very different from the static companies characteristic of the eighteenth and nineteenth centuries. Even when the enthusiasm aroused by the visits of the touring companies led to the formation in various countries of ballet companies with permanent homes, these companies showed powerful influences from the cosmopolitan touring companies which dominated world ballet in the second, third and fourth decades of this century. Nearly all the new companies spent part of the year on tour, and some of the new companies were formed entirely for touring.

As mentioned above (in the Preface), the enormous expansion of ballet in the twentieth century led to a considerable diversification in the types of ballet company. Within each country the different companies showed certain common characteristics reflecting the national character and cultural traditions, but in general these were much less important than the characteristics which the various companies shared with other companies of the same type, whether belonging to the same country or to foreign countries.

So many companies have been formed in the twentieth century that discussion of all or even most of them would be intolerably tedious. I have therefore limited myself to those companies which show most clearly the characteristics of the international type to which they belong, and which have lasted long enough to exert an appreciable influence on ballet history.

I must emphasize at this point that the sections devoted to English companies and the Ballets Jooss are intended to supplement the corresponding sections of *Modern English Ballet*, not to replace them; instead of attempting to give a balanced account of the achievements of these companies I have concentrated mainly on analysing the factors limiting their development.

1. THE DANCER'S COMPANY

(a) The Individualistic Classical Dancer's Company

At every period of ballet history great dancers have tended to find themselves frustrated by the intrigues and the lack of good rôles in the companies they adorn. Until recently, however, their only method of dealing with this situation was to leave and join another company—where conditions might well be just as bad, but for a time at least they could have the comforting illusion of having better opportunities. In the twentieth century dancers had the alternative possibility of forming companies of their own, in which they could regulate every detail so as to show themselves off to best advantage. The apparent advantages of such a company are delusive, for the strain and worry involved in running a ballet company without a subsidy and without a home theatre are so great that no dancer persists in this course of action unless he or she is fanatically determined to win independence at all costs. Such fanaticism is highly characteristic of expressionism, and, as one might expect, the great expressionist dancers tend to form their own companies. This is not true of great classical dancers: only the most individualistic of them form their own companies, and it is no accident that all the great classical dancers who do form their own companies show some expressionist tendencies in their dancing. (When Diaghilev began to destroy his own artistic policy, certain great classical dancers with no expressionist tendencies in their performances—notably Karsavina and Spessivsteva—preferred to give up dancing for considerable periods rather than maintain companies of their own.[1])

The artistic policy of companies directed by solo dancers suffers from the fact that such directors combine the rôles of star dancer, artistic director and (very often) choreographer as well. Their interests in these different rôles tend to lead them in different directions, and they are much too bound up in their own neuroses to be able to work out a policy which is a reasonable compromise between these conflicting interests. Having formed the company primarily as a background to their own dancing, they can no more be objective and sensible about the running of the company than a woman can be objective and sensible about the love-affairs of her husband. Almost always the dancer-directors can

---

[1] It was a very different matter when Victor Dandré invited Spessivsteva to dance at the head of the Pavlova company in 1931–32, after the death of Pavlova.

recognize this flaw in the administration of other similar companies, but defend with the utmost conviction and many plausible arguments their own complete impartiality.[1]

Anna Pavlova (1881–1931)

From May 1 to September 1 the Imperial Russian Theatres were closed. Wealthy dancers were able to take a vacation during this period, but there were many who could not afford to remain out of work for four months,[2] and such dancers were accustomed to form themselves into groups of about fifteen to twenty artists to tour the smaller towns of Russia. These companies normally consisted of two or three experienced soloists and a corps de ballet consisting of recent graduates from the school (whose tiny salary from the school was not sufficient to enable them to keep body and soul together until the Imperial Theatres reopened in the Autumn). The programmes consisted mainly of short items extracted from ballets in the repertoire of the Imperial Theatres, and usually there was no décor; the musical accompaniment was provided by a pianist.

In 1907 the Maryinsky soloist Adolph Bolm organized a company on similar lines but with a far more ambitious programme, arranging to perform during the Imperial Ballet season and to visit foreign countries; for this he had of course to obtain special permission from the Director of the Imperial Theatres. The company organized by him consisted of twelve danseuses and eight danseurs; its prima ballerina was Anna Pavlova, and the female soloists were Yegorova and Vil, while the male soloists were Bolm himself, Obukhov, Nicolas Legat and Shiryaev. The repertoire consisted of cut-down versions of *Coppélia*, *The Enchanted Flute* and *Paquita*: these were all ballets in which Pavlova had distinguished herself at the Maryinsky. The company took on tour a conductor-musical director (Otto Bolm, Adolph Bolm's brother) and played in large theatres with proper orchestras in a number of European capitals, giving four performances in Helsingfors, six in Stockholm, two in Copenhagen and two in Prague. The tour was enormously successful, for the standard of performance was far above that to which audiences in these cities were accustomed, and Bolm and Pavlova decided to repeat it the following year; they added Berlin and Vienna to the itinerary and enlarged the repertoire

---

[1] *Cf.* Victor Dandré's admirable exposition of Pavlova's view of her own artistic policy as it affected her company. (*Anna Pavlova*, pp. 66–92.)

[2] Salaries were low at the Imperial Theatres, even for the stars. For seven years the State maintained and trained the dancers free of charge in the Imperial School, and then the dancers were expected to justify this training by dancing in the company for relatively low salaries. It was considered a great honour to belong to the Imperial Ballet, even as a corps-de-ballet dancer, and for this reason dancers put up with the low salaries. The position is much the same in all State ballets, though in some of them the honour is largely imaginary.

to include cut-down versions of several other ballets in which Pavlova had distinguished herself—*Harlequinade, La Fille Mal Gardée, Le Lac des Cygnes* and *Giselle.*

Pavlova took part in the Diaghilevian invasion of Paris in the Summer of 1909, but she arrived after the season had started, and unlike Bolm she refused to cast in her lot with the Diaghilev company and become a member of his team.

After leaving Paris she toured very widely with a small company led by her and Mordkin (the leading Moscow danseur), once again obtaining permission from Teliakovsky to be absent from Russia during part of the Maryinsky season. She first appeared in London in May, 1910, at the Palace Theatre, as part of a variety bill; at this time the company consisted of four soloists (Pavlova, Mordkin, Edwardova and Monakhov) and eight corps-de-ballets dancers. Pavlova and Mordkin had such fabulous success at the Palace that they arranged to return later in the year with an enlarged company, and for the first time the Pavlova-Mordkin company presented a ballet—*La Fille mal Gardée.* (Up to now its programme had consisted only of divertissements, and when the company appeared on its own in a theatre the programme included 'cello solos and ballads: usually it appeared to audiences that had never attended an evening of pure ballet, and it was thought that they would not consider a programme of pure dancing sufficient entertainment for an evening.)

After a long tour in the United States in 1911 Pavlova quarrelled with Mordkin, and the two dancers went separate ways. Up to now Pavlova had shared the limelight with her partner; from now on, however, she took care to keep her partner in a subordinate position.

After dancing in the miraculous Diaghilev season in London in the Autumn of 1911, Pavlova took such a liking to England and the English audiences that she decided to settle down there; in 1912 she bought Ivy House in London and in 1913 she resigned from the Maryinsky. Up to then she had continued to meet her obligations at the Maryinsky by visiting St. Petersburg for one or two months each year and cramming into a short period the ten performances which she was obliged to give each year. (By this time she had reached the second highest rank at the Maryinsky, and enjoyed the great privileges attached to this rank.) In 1913, however, she signed a contract to take to America a full-scale ballet company, complete with the costumes, scenery, etc., needed to present a repertoire of complete ballets, and from now on she maintained a permanent organization. In theory there was no reason why she should not have made London her headquarters and continued to fulfil her obligations in St. Petersburg, where she was idolized to such an extent that she could do almost as she pleased, and had the advantage of appearing with the support of a great company. Like Diaghilev, however, she was driven by her daemon to take advantage of the solid support for ballet in England to make herself completely independent of the Imperial Theatres: in fact she and Diaghilev together made London the centre of the ballet world.

Pavlova went even further than Diaghilev in her drive for independence; whereas Diaghilev continued to rely on dancers on leave from the Imperial Theatres, Pavlova brought into her company more and more English girls until she made herself almost completely independent of the Imperial Theatres.

It is possible that Pavlova was influenced in her decision to leave the Maryinsky by the fact that the Maryinsky ballerinas who did not tour during the Maryinsky season were able to prepare very carefully for each appearance, whereas Pavlova had to fit her appearances in as a part of a world tour based to a large extent on one-night stands. By leaving when she did Pavlova avoided any serious competition. Almost any other dancer would have been faced with stern official disapproval if she left the Maryinsky without good cause, but Pavlova's genius was so much respected that no official reprisals were taken, and in 1914 she was even commanded to give a performance at the Imperial Residence in Pavlovsk.

She was caught by the War in Berlin, but managed to escape to London, where she formed a new company. From now on she continued to tour right up to her death in 1931, with only a few weeks of holiday each year.

Pavlova was generally regarded as a traditionalist because of her preference for the choreography, music and décor characteristic of the Petipa era, and her indifference to the new developments in ballet in the last years of the Diaghilev company. In fact, however, she was a daring innovator who used those elements of the tradition which happened to suit her requirements, but did not hesitate to make the most ruthless changes when she felt them to be necessary.

It is important to remember that the culmination of the Russian renaissance in the Fokine ballets would scarcely have been possible without Pavlova. Fokine's first important composition, Le Cygne, was designed for her, and the whole of Les Sylphides was inspired by her performance in the romantic pas de deux of the first version of Chopiniana. Even Le Pavillon d'Armide could never have been produced at the Maryinsky but for her. The relationship between Pavlova and Fokine was much the same as that between Grisi and Perrot: the dancer came to maturity performing the compositions of the choreographer, while the choreographer for his part depended for inspiration on the dancing of his favourite ballerina. Fokine was so much under the spell of Pavlova's dancing that when it became obvious that she would not be available for the Diaghilev seasons, Benois and Diaghilev had great difficulty in convincing Fokine that Karsavina also had great talent and could do justice to his ideas. Pavlova, for her part, understood better than anyone Fokine's genius. To quote Victor Dandré:

How Pavlova used to dream of working with Fokine! Not only did she regard him as a ballet-master of genius, one before whom she was ready to bow her head, but he was infinitely dear to her as a great Russian of lofty ideals, who had uttered a new word, a living and beautiful word in her beloved art.[1]

Unlike Grisi, however, Pavlova did not make a point of dancing whenever possible in the ballets composed by the choreographer she inspired. In 1913 (the year in which Fokine resigned his position as maître de ballet of the Diaghilev ballet and Pavlova resigned from the Maryinsky) she commissioned two new ballets from Fokine, *Les Préludes* and *The Seven Daughters*; but she soon dropped them from her repertoire, and she commissioned no further ballets from Fokine.[2] In fact she included in her permanent repertoire only two Fokine items—*Le Cygne* and *Chopiniana* (*Les Sylphides*). Characteristically, she had her tame maître de ballet Clustin make a new version of the latter ballet, retaining Fokine's choreography only in her own solos. Since *Chopiniana* became part of the Maryinsky repertoire in 1909, before Pavlova left this company, her treatment of this ballet must be considered iconoclastic.

Her attitude to the Perrot tradition surviving at the Maryinsky was much the same as her attitude to the Fokine tradition. She excluded from her repertoire the Perrot ballets *Catarina*, *Ondine* and *Esmeralda*,[3] and cut down Albrecht's rôle in *Giselle*, so that he was little more than a cavalier (as in the Petipa ballets).

In modifying *Giselle* she showed herself far less of a traditionalist than Karsavina, the star of the Diaghilev Ballet. (In her autobiography *Theatre Street* Karsavina emphasizes that at the Maryinsky *Giselle* was considered as something sacred, and that the slightest alteration in it was unthinkable.)

From Pavlova's point of view the Perrot and Fokine ballets had two grave defects: they did not concentrate all attention on one ballerina, and the choreography was so strong that a dancer could make it effective simply by dancing it in a sincere and straightforward manner. She preferred to use shoddy choreography put together for her by Clustin, Shiryaev and others, because only her own rôle was given prominence and she could alter the choreography as

---

[1] *Anna Pavlova*, p. 30.

[2] According to Victor Dandré Pavlova could not commission further ballets from Fokine because of the "size and peculiar conditions of the Pavlova organisation. In order to unite the work of Pavlova and Fokine and give them the right atmosphere, either the old Imperial Theatres would have been necessary or some heavily subsidised theatre like the Metropolitan in New York." (*Anna Pavlova*, p. 30.) It is impossible to accept this explanation: nearly all the great works created by Fokine for Pavlova in St. Petersburg were rehearsed by him in great haste for charity performances, with costumes and décor borrowed from the Maryinsky. By far the greater part of the ballets composed by Fokine after his break with Diaghilev were rehearsed by him in very unhappy circumstances—often with half-trained dancers and never once with a ballerina worthy of his powers. Compared with most of the companies with which he worked after 1918 the Pavlova Ballet was an admirable body.

[3] Her neglect of *Esmeralda* was particularly striking, for all the great Russian ballerinas liked to dance the title rôle in this ballet and it was one of Pavlova's best rôles at the Maryinsky. But *Esmeralda* demanded a large company and elaborate décor.

much as she liked without compunction, finding an outlet for her own creative gifts in transforming it into something that gave the illusion of good ballet: the more feeble the raw material the more satisfying the transformation. In some respects her attitude to choreography reminds one of Irving's attitude to poetic drama; but Irving used the profits on plays like *The Bells* to stage all the Shakespeare plays which had parts within his range, whereas Pavlova concentrated mainly on the balletic equivalent of *The Bells*. In her completely subjective attitude to choreography she showed clear affinities to the expressionist dramatic producers who were her contemporaries. (In Pavlova's dancing one could trace influences of expressionism in such details as the quivering of her fingers in *Le Cygne* and the impulse she used in getting up from the sofa in *Christmas Eve*—though, being a great classical dancer, she never allowed these admirably expressive details to affect the classical harmony and economy of her performance as a whole.)

Her attitude to music was exactly parallel to her attitude to choreography. Though some of her greatest triumphs were achieved with the inspiration of fine music (e.g. in *Le Cygne*, *Chopiniana* and *Le Lac des Cygnes*), she used for preference the music of Minkus, Drigo and other composers of similar calibre. The latter type of music had for Pavlova the supreme merit of making no strong impact on the ear, thus ensuring that all attention was concentrated on the dancing. For the same reason she chose dreary naturalistic décor, in spite of the fact that a good tradition of décor had been established at the Maryinsky by Golovin, Korovin, Bakst and Benois in the early years of her career at the Maryinsky.

Her attitude to her company showed the same extreme subjectivism. Though in some ways she was extremely kind and considerate, she dominated the girls in such a way that none of them showed much personality or feeling on the stage; apart from her psychological domination she worked them so hard that they were always too tired to dance with freshness and vitality. (She worked twice as hard as anyone herself, but she had a fund of energy such as no dancer has probably ever had before or since.) One reason why she included a high proportion of English dancers in her company was that English dancers have a very highly developed sense of discipline and are capable of going on from year to year giving consistent but dull performances. (In justice to Pavlova and her dancers I must add that she also found in English dancers a sensitive understanding of the Russian tradition: though her dancers lacked individuality their performances were always in key with the mood of the ballets.)

Pavlova showed great care in her choice of a second ballerina; since she could not dance the lead in all the ballets she had to give good opportunities to another danseuse, and she therefore needed a danseuse who had a technique strong enough to enable her to perform the most exacting rôles but lacked the personality to take any of the limelight away from Pavlova. The English dancer Hilda Butsova (*née* Boot) exactly filled these requirements: Pavlova had no need to worry about competition from her even when she was feeling off-colour and was not dancing at her best.

Though Pavlova's artistic policy was based on her actual needs as a dancer at the head of her own company—it was in fact typical of all companies run by dancer-managers—her detailed application of this policy was fantastically out of proportion with her talents. Beginning in dire poverty, not even knowing who her father was, she won her way to the top by the sheer force of her genius until she was able to do almost as she liked at the Maryinsky—this at a time when the Maryinsky had more great dancers than probably any company has had at any other time. Such a dancer had no need to emphasize her talent by showing it against a drab background; she dominated any stage as soon as she stepped on it. (Even if she slipped on unobtrusively at the back her presence made itself felt at once.) But she persisted in her fanatical application of her policy in spite of everything, and was quite incapable of listening to advice. Walford Hyden had many opportunities to study this aspect of her temperament:

> She regarded herself as infallible. She was structurally incapable of understanding that other people could not see things from her point of view—or, indeed, that there could possibly be any other point of view than her own. She would become almost hysterical when contradicted and would suffer from depression afterwards.[1]

In this respect Pavlova was typical of all artists possessed by a daemon. Pavlova's daemon was so insatiable in its demands that she felt uneasy if she had a holiday lasting more than about a fortnight, and she kept her company continually on the move. No matter how small the town or how inadequate the theatre, Pavlova would go there if an audience could be collected.

Walford Hyden suggests that Pavlova's artistic policy was forced on her by the bad taste of the public:

> She was a missionary, spreading the very idea of ballet in remote parts of the earth. Naturally, the themes which she chose were those which would have the widest popular or sentimental appeal.[2]

This was undoubtedly true to some extent, but it does not account for the fact that she tended to use material which was bad *of its kind*—e.g. Clustin's choreography for *Chopiniana* in place of Fokine's original choreography, or

---

[1] *Pavlova*, p. 113.
[2] *Ibid.*, p. 148.

the music of Minkus and Drigo in place of equivalent music by Tchaikovsky or Glazunov.[1] In view of the enormous popularity of items like *Giselle* and *Le Cygne* (which were excellent of their kind) one cannot attribute the defects of Pavlova's artistic policy entirely to the bad taste of the public: they arose rather from the inner conflicts within Pavlova, and are to be found in the artistic policies of all companies of this type.

Anton Dolin (b. 1904)

Anton Dolin and Alicia Markova (*b*. 1910) started with much the same background: both were English dancers trained by Astafieva in London, and both joined the Diaghilev company in the early twenties. But their temperaments were quite different, and they reacted in almost opposite ways to the artistic climate of the Diaghilev company in its cocktail period.

Dolin joined the company in 1921 for the production of *The Sleeping Princess*, and became a star overnight in 1924 as the Beau Gosse in *Le Train Bleu* —a ballet arranged by Nijinska as a background to his acrobatic stunts. He was then only twenty, and the experience had a profound effect on him; he continued to use these tricks in various solos he composed for himself, and performed these solos both in variety programmes and as part of ballet programmes. Nevertheless he also developed into a fine partner of classical ballerinas in the "classics". There seemed to be no link between the two aspects of his nature: he incorporated into his own dancing the dichotomy which was characteristic of Diaghilev's artistic policy at this period.

Being very much of an individualist, Dolin left Diaghilev in 1925 to seek a career for himself on his own, dancing mainly in revues. In 1927 he returned to ballet, dancing with Nemchinova at the head of the Nemchinova-Dolin ballet, and joining Diaghilev once again in 1929 for the last tour of the Diaghilev company. After the death of Diaghilev Dolin returned to revue, then danced in Camargo Society productions, and then joined the Vic-Wells company. But he never stayed in the Vic-Wells for very long at a time, preferring to spend most of his time dancing in revue and variety, and appearing at Sadlers Wells and the Old Vic only for isolated performances. (On one occasion he persuaded Markova to join him in a variety show.) Dolin was an asset to the Vic-Wells as a partner for Markova, but it was in violent expressionist rôles that he showed to best advantage—notably in his magnificently arrogant performance as Satan in *Job*. Since he left the company only one dancer (Helpmann) has approached his interpretation of the rôle, which was created for him and gave full scope to his gift for acrobatics and his expressionist temperament.

Markova, in contrast to Dolin, joined the Diaghilev company in 1923 (at

---

[1] In *Amerilla*, for example, she used music by both Glazunov and Drigo.

the age of thirteen) and stayed with it until its dissolution, showing no interest in establishing a company of her own. She was a soloist in the Diaghilev company, but by no means a star; like Sokolova, she absorbed the outlook of the best Russian dancers (with their humility and devotion to the art of ballet), and somehow she managed to avoid being corrupted by the cocktail atmosphere of the company. (Though the company suffered severely from the lack of great ballerinas at its head, the dancers did their best to maintain the fine traditions of dancing established at the Maryinsky after 1890, and did not take the cocktail ballets very seriously.) Markova had her first chance to shine as a star after the dissolution of the Diaghilev company, when she became the prima ballerina of the Vic-Wells company and tackled a number of the most important Maryinsky rôles (such as Odette-Odile and Giselle). Her performances in these exacting rôles were unsatisfactory by comparison with those of the greatest Maryinsky ballerinas—her arms and hands, for example, sometimes showed a flabby line, she was somewhat turned in, she did not point her feet properly when they left the ground,[1] and her personality was weak—but she had acquired typically Russian qualities of simplicity, idealism and nobility, her lightness was outstanding, and her performances compared very well with any others to be seen in the early thirties (except those of the great Spessivsteva). The Vic-Wells Ballet owed a great deal of its success to Markova's performances in the classical rôles in the first critical half-decade of its existence.

Markova seemed fairly happy with the Vic-Wells, which provided her with golden opportunities, but left the company in 1935 (presumably in response to persuasion from Dolin) and joined Dolin as co-star of the Markova-Dolin Ballet. This company had as its backer and patron Mrs. Laura Henderson,[2] owner of the Windmill Theatre, and it was managed by Vivian van Damm, who was also manager of the Windmill Theatre on behalf of Mrs. Henderson.

Mrs. Henderson provided enough capital for the company to be launched on an impressive scale, with a large corps de ballet, a repertoire of considerable size and a good-sized orchestra. By this time Markova and Dolin were by far the most famous English dancers, and the seasons of the Ballets Russes de Monte Carlo had proved that ballet could make money in England; to Mrs. Henderson the prospects of the company must have seemed bright. Unfortunately the company had none of the qualities which made the performances of the Ballets Russes de Monte Carlo so exciting; its artistic policy was banal in the extreme, and only a Pavlova could have transformed the programme into

[1] Action photos by John Gabriel in his book *Ballet School* give a clear idea of the good qualities and technical deficiencies of Markova's style in the thirties.

[2] As Vivian van Damm pointed out in *Tonight and Every Night*, Mrs. Henderson was one of the most generous patrons of English ballet. She provided the money for the most important Vic-Wells production, *The Rake's Progress*, and took the Vic-Wells on tour in the English provinces at a time when it was impossible for this company to afford the loss inevitably involved in touring. For two years she made up the heavy losses of the Markova-Dolin Ballet.

something that would grip an audience. (The revivals of Maryinsky ballets were the same as those in the Vic-Wells repertoire, while the numerous new ballets were commissioned from English choreographers of very limited talent—Anton Dolin, Keith Lester and Susan Salaman.)

Dolin was not a director of the company when it was formed, but his strong personality and wide experience naturally gave him great influence on artistic policy, and eventually he was officially appointed one of the directors.

Early in 1936 the company appeared in the West End of London for a twelve-week season at the Duke of York's Theatre. At this time the de Basil-Massine company was at its peak of vitality, and both the Ballet Club and the Vic-Wells were maintaining a high level of originality and imagination in their new ballets. The Markova-Dolin company could not stand comparison with these companies, and the season was not a success. The company was a success in the Provinces (where ballet was almost unknown, and audiences had had no chance to build up standards), but it was not possible to put up prices to meet the heavy cost of ballet performances—according to Vivian van Damm,[1] the top price was 5s. 9d.—and Mrs. Henderson lost a great deal of money in spite of good houses. This would not have mattered if the company had been able to make a profit during long West-End seasons, but this was not possible, and losses continued to mount up.

In 1937 Dolin was able to arrange something he had hoped to do from the time of the formation of the Markova-Dolin Ballet: he arranged for Nijinska to be invited to produce some ballets for the company. (While in the Diaghilev company Dolin had continued his training under Nijinska, and it was she who gave him his first big chance in Le Train Bleu.) Unfortunately Nijinska was now firmly set in the pseudo-classical style she originated for Diaghilev's cocktail ballets, and though the ballets she created or revived for the Markova-Dolin Ballet were far superior in craftsmanship to the other modern ballets in the repertoire, they were not good enough to save the company. It continued to run at a loss, and during the 1937 season at the King's Theatre, Hammersmith, the board of directors decided to dissolve it.

During the War Markova and Dolin danced in America in Ballet Theatre and various American Ballet-Russe companies. During 1947–48 they headed a company of their own, the Markova-Dolin Ballet, which toured in Central America, Mexico and the United States.

They returned to England in the summer of 1948 and appeared as guest artists with the Sadlers Wells Ballet. In January, 1949, they appeared as the stars of five special performances at the Empress Hall, supported by a corps de ballet rehearsed by Grace Cone and mainly drawn from senior students of the Arts Educational School (directed by Grace Cone and Olive Ripman). There

---

[1] Tonight and Every Night, p. 96.

The Royal Danish Ballet, *ca.* 1885: Bournonville's version of *La Sylphide* (Copenhagen, 1836) with Anna Tychsen as the Sylphide and Hans Beck as James

The Paris Opéra, *ca.* 1925: Carlotta Zambelli (étoile) and Albert Aveline (premier danseur and choreographer)

The Festival Balle
Symphony for Fi
(Charnley, Londo
1952) with Noël Ro
sana, John Gilpin an
Anita Landa

Pavlova and Mordki
in 1910

was little connection between the items performed by the corps de ballet and the solos of the two stars. The Empress Hall is designed for sport, not for theatrical activities which must be seen from the front, and though 30,000 people were attracted by the opportunity of seeing Markova and Dolin, arena ballet proved to be very unsatisfactory artistically: there was no atmosphere, the distance between the dancers and even the most expensive seats was enormous, and many of the spectators saw the dancers from the side or even from the back. In fact arena ballet could never have succeeded except under the very unusual conditions prevailing at this time, when the War had brought about an enormous expansion in the ballet audience, and any sort of ballet had such glamour that massive audiences were prepared to tolerate almost any deficiencies in presentation to see famous stars.

The most interesting feature of this season was the revelation of a Markova very different from the one who had left England before the War. She had trained hard with good teachers while in the United States, and had enormously improved her style, while avoiding all the characteristic defects of American ballerinas; the line of her arms was now better, she pointed her feet, she was adequately turned out, and—above all—she had developed some warmth of personality. Unfortunately she was debarred from the highest achievements by her lack of strength: her arabesques, for example, were so low that at times she seemed to be "marking" the steps rather than dancing them, and her ideal of classicism seemed very insipid.

Dolin, on the other hand, showed all his pre-War faults in exaggerated form. He rarely pointed his feet at all, he hurled himself into the air with a visible effort, he failed to pull up his knees, and his line was so bad that at times it was difficult to recognize the steps.

Markova and Dolin went on a provincial tour with their corps de ballet. Having learned from bitter experience in the old Markova-Dolin company the danger of a premature attempt at breaking into the West End of London, Dolin very sensibly kept the group on tour in the Provinces for two years, waiting until the corps de ballet had reached a certain degree of professional assurance and he had acquired the capital needed to transform the group into a full-sized ballet company. (According to rumour, he started with a capital of only £2,000; if this is correct his success in making the group lift itself by its own bootstraps was very creditable, even though the times were exceptionally propitious for such an enterprise.)

In August, 1950, Dolin transformed the group into a ballet company by taking on a number of soloists and producing a number of ballets, complete with décor. (Up to this time Markova and Dolin had mainly appeared in solos and pas de deux on a neutral stage.)

The new company reached the Stoll Theatre in London in October, 1950,

A.A.O.B.—Y

when it was given the name Festival Ballet. This company was similar in many ways to the old Markova-Dolin company; but the new Markova-Dolin company had the financial success denied to the old company. In fact it played to good houses at one of the largest theatres of Europe from the beginning of October, 1950, to the end of January, 1951, with only a short break. This extraordinary difference in box-office takings as compared with the Duke of York's season in 1936 was not due to any marked improvement in the quality of the ballets or the dancing: though Markova's style was much better, she danced relatively seldom; Dolin's dancing was worse; the other soloists were on the average no better than before; and the new corps de ballet was still very immature. The main reason for the vast increase in the box-office takings as compared with 1936 was the change in English ballet as a whole during the intervening period: the audience had increased many times in size, other English companies had become so ossified that audiences were glad to have the chance of seeing some new faces, and there was no longer any competition from the de Basil company.

Dolin's artistic policy at this time can best be described as an anglicized version of American Ballet-Russe.[1] Great emphasis was given to the familiar Maryinsky ballets which now formed the basis of the repertoire of most ballet companies, and the new ballets were commissioned from Massine and Lichine (apart from a suite of character dances arranged by Grace Cone). The most important additions to the pre-War Markova-Dolin repertoire were *Petrouchka* and *Prince Igor*: these two ballets had been extremely popular in the Diaghilev repertoire and the repertoires of the various Ballet-Russe companies, but had never been taken into the Sadlers Wells repertoire, and so were new to the greater part of the post-War English ballet public.

By producing these two Fokine ballets (later also *Schéhérazade*) Dolin gave proof of some independence of outlook, and made his company stand out from all other English companies. The production of *Petrouchka*, in particular, illustrated with the utmost clarity both the positive and negative sides of Dolin's artistic policy. He himself danced Petrouchka, in spite of being hopelessly miscast in the rôle: he made all the movements crude and melodramatic, changing the poetry and tragedy into bathos. Most of the other soloists were little better, though Beriosov (who had worked with Fokine in 1936–37 in the Blum company) gave a workmanlike performance as the Moor. Markova showed real understanding of the rôle of the Ballerina, but the ethereal quality of her dancing made her unsuitable for the rôle; Anita Landa was completely doll-like as the Ballerina, showing no understanding of the fact that the puppets in *Petrouchka* are not ordinary dolls but figures of myth. Beriosov's production followed closely Fokine's rather unsatisfactory production of 1936, but missed

---

[1] *See* p. 414 ff., below.

out a considerable number of nuances of choreography, and the corps-de-ballet dancers showed little feeling for the style of the ballet. The colours of the costumes and décors were almost all just wrong, and the lighting was almost unbelievably lacking in atmosphere; such extraordinary lapses of taste suggested that Dolin was more at home in the variety world than in classical ballet. With all these defects, however, the great ballet managed to hold the stage as only a masterpiece can, and made its effects with an economy and speed that showed up very clearly the deficiencies of most subsequent ballets.

By inviting Massine and Chauviré to dance in *Petrouchka* Dolin made clear exactly what was wrong with the production as a whole: it was as if a curtain had been drawn back and the original *Petrouchka* revealed for a few moments in its true colours. Massine's interpretation of the rôle of Petrouchka was never as good as that of Nijinsky, for by temperament he lacked any feeling for tragedy, and could only suggest a man playing a puppet rather than a puppet trying to be a man: nevertheless he showed in his performance complete intellectual understanding of the rôle, and perfect respect for the genius of Fokine's original choreography. Instead of Dolin's clumsy and melodramatic interpretation, one saw the real thing, and the result was electrifying. Though Massine was by now over fifty, and though his technique had never been strong, he made no effort to fake the part to suit his capacities (as he was accustomed to do when he revived for himself any of the rôles he had composed for himself in the twenties); somehow he found the strength and control to perform the movements with all their nuances of technique and expression.

In spite of the fact that Chauviré (unlike Massine) had never been rehearsed by Fokine, she danced the rôle of the Ballerina with such devastating wit and imagination that her performance challenged comparison with those of the great Diaghilev ballerinas. Her performances of classical rôles had been losing some of their power for several years, but she seemed to find in the rôle of the Ballerina something of the same personal meaning that Nijinsky found in the rôle of Petrouchka. She gave the doll a vacuous triviality that was completely doll-like and yet disturbingly human: though French in its elegance, her doll had the terrifying myth-like and superhuman quality of the characters in Gogol's short stories.

It was characteristic of the Festival Ballet that it presented these wonderful performances (as no other English company of the day would have done), and yet was not in the least affected by them: after the departure of Massine and Chauviré the production returned to normal.

Dolin's artistic outlook had been formed in the Diaghilev Ballet in its cocktail period, and his artistic policy showed much the same glaring discrepancies as Diaghilev's policy at that time. His ideas were sometimes excellent, but his execution of them tended to be crippled by what one might call his

cocktail outlook. A good example of this was his "revival" of the Perrot ballet
Le Pas de Quatre. Though it is possible to form a very good idea of the style of
this period from *Giselle* and the Bournonville ballets in the Royal Danish
repertoire, Dolin ignored these models and made only a few crude attempts to
suggest period flavour by introducing poses from contemporary lithographs
and an exaggerated version of the Cecchetti *assemblé* (in which the feet are
snatched together in the air); he took little account of the sharp differences
which Perrot is known to have made in his choreography for the different
ballerinas, and drew attention to the characteristic Taglioni arabesque by
having the dancer hold this position for some time balanced on pointe in the
modern manner, in spite of the fact that the unblocked shoes of the period
would have made such a feat impossible.

During 1951 the dancers of the corps de ballet improved noticeably in stage
presence and assurance, and showed less of the familiar stodginess than the old-
established English companies; even if Dolin's artistic policy had many faults,
he clearly did not demand of his corps de ballet that it should become a set of
robots. He also employed two fine male dancers, John Gilpin and Oleg Briansky;
but he employed no danseuses of similar calibre, and Markova reigned in
solitary glory. Nathalie Krassovska (also known as Nathalie Leslie) danced
with the same stolid, rather hard, and quite unmusical competence she had
shown in the Blum company, while Anita Landa remained precise but
insipid, and Noël Rossana was quite lacking in personality. Apart from
Markova only Sonia Arova could really be called a ballerina, and she did not
stay for long.

At the beginning of 1952 the future of the company became clouded over.
The boom in ballet had subsided, the Fokine ballets had lost the charm of
novelty, and so had the dancing of Markova and Dolin. Being a big company
the Festival Ballet could not keep going without losses unless it continued to
play in large theatres with nearly full houses—and this was no longer easy to
achieve.

In March, 1952, the company received a body-blow: Markova announced
that she was leaving it. For some time there had been rumours that she was
dissatisfied with the way Dolin treated her, and in her Press announcement she
gave some slight hint of the nature of her grievances: "I am not going back to
his ballet company in London, and I don't think I shall ever be dancing with him
again. A row? Just a matter of Mr. Dolin wanting what he wants—and I
wanting something else. I couldn't even go to the places I wanted, like Paris
and South America."[1]

When this statement was reported to Dolin, he retaliated with a statement
which cast light on an aspect of artistic policy which is normally carefully

[1] *Daily Express*, March 6, 1952.

concealed from the public—the attitude of the prima ballerina of a company to her possible rivals: "Markova is one of the great ballerinas. But in a company everyone must have a chance. My company is fresh and eager."[1] He added that he would replace Markova with Belinda Wright: "She will have the qualities of Markova—lightness, effortless style. I will make her a star. She will have me as a partner."

Belinda Wright (a typical Rambert dancer) was very unlike Markova, but Dolin was quite right in asserting that the departure of Markova would not cripple the company. In fact it seemed to stimulate the company to dance better than ever before.

The summer of 1952 was critical for the company. The whole of the English theatre was in the doldrums, and the company could no longer rely on long and financially profitable seasons in ordinary London theatres. At this juncture the L.C.C. made the Royal Festival Hall available, a special stage being constructed to transform it into a theatre suitable for ballet.[2] (Presumably the L.C.C. found it desirable to let the Festival Hall for ballet to avoid competition with the Promenade Concerts at the Albert Hall.)

The transformation of the Festival Hall cost a lot of money (the expenses presumably being shared by the L.C.C. and the Festival Ballet), and the season could easily have lost a lot of money if audiences had been as slack as they were in most of London's theatres at this time. In fact the company danced better than ever, audiences were consistently good, and the L.C.C. was encouraged to make plans for converting the Hall in a semi-permanent manner, with regular seasons by the Festival Ballet during the Promenade seasons. This ensured the continuance of the company, which otherwise might have had to disband.

Though the performances were not different in any fundamental way from preceding ones, the soloists were stimulated by the opportunities given to them by the departure of Markova and Dolin's knee injury, while the company as a whole still had a certain freshness and spontaneity which was lacking in most of the Sadlers Wells dancers. Dolin even commissioned a new ballet from a talented young English choreographer, Michael Charnley; Symphony for Fun was clearly inspired by Interplay, but Charnley brought together ideas from the Jooss-Leeder style, Martha Graham, Antony Tudor and other unlikely sources with considerable intelligence. Obviously the Festival Ballet, in spite of the many weaknesses of its artistic policy and its lack of good ballerinas, had something positive to contribute, and its continuing existence was of real importance to English ballet—if only because it offered strong competition to the two Sadlers

[1] Daily Express, March 6, 1952
[2] Ballet demands the picture-frame stage with proscenium and wings. Previous seasons of ballet at the Festival Hall had suffered from lack of atmosphere.

Wells companies. (In fact the Sadlers Wells Ballet found itself in the rather odd position of being haunted by the ghost of its own youth.)

Unlike his contemporary Lifar, Dolin was sensible enough as he approached the age of fifty to cease allotting to himself rôles far beyond his technical capacity. On the other hand the fact that he danced much less often had little or no effect on his artistic policy: by this time his temperament and his outlook were much too firmly established to change. Curiously enough his artistic policy (which permitted the employment of two good male soloists but not one ballerina of similar quality) was exactly what one might expect in a company like the Pavlova Ballet, directed by a ballerina.

In the Summer of 1953 Dolin made a bold attempt to establish the Festival Ballet as a company of major importance: the company came to the Royal Festival Hall for a "Coronation Season" of ten weeks during which it presented no less than five new productions, two of them being world premières.

The company was seen at its best in three Fokine ballets (*Petrouchka*, *Prince Igor* and *Schéhérazade*) which were not in the repertoire of any other English company, and gave good opportunities to its fine male dancers. Vassili Trunoff was in fact so stimulated by these opportunities that he matured into one of the finest living character dancers, challenging comparison even with the pre-War Shabelevsky. He was outstanding as the Chief Warrior in *Prince Igor*, and encouraged by him the whole company danced well in this ballet, doing credit to Beriosov's intelligent production: this was obviously a ballet which Beriosov liked and understood.

But the fine dancing of the men in these Fokine ballets made the defects of the rest of the repertoire show up very clearly. The company's own female soloists were as neat and insipid as ever, and Marina Svetlova—a ballerina brought over "from the Metropolitan Opera in New York" to appear as guest artist—danced with such archness and affectation that she reduced every ballet in which she appeared into tawdry melodrama: her facial expressions were exactly those of a tap dancer of the thirties.

The new ballets showed that Dolin's judgment in matters of choreography had not improved noticeably since the days of the pre-War Markova-Dolin Ballet. The principal new production was a ballet in two acts, *Alice in Wonderland*, with choreography by Michael Charnley: Dolin clearly considered this production of great importance, for in the programme it was labelled "under the Artistic Direction of ANTON DOLIN"; but in the immensely long ballet there were hardly more than a few moments of wit or fantasy, and in fact the humour had the same repetitive woodenness as that of Jooss ballets like *A Spring Tale*; the stodgy quality of the choreography was brought out clearly by the delightful wit and fantasy of the costumes, designed by Kenneth Rowell.

Michael Charnley considerably improved the ballet by cutting it severely after the première, but it still remained a long way from the book by Lewis Carroll. (Charnley was unwise in agreeing to do this ballet, so unsuited to his talents.)

Ruth Page's ballet *Vilia* was even more inadequate as a choreographic version of *The Merry Widow*: she used every cliché of musical comedy and the variety stage with such clumsiness that the unfortunate dancers had no chance to show any gaiety or charm. Seeing that the repertoire already included Massine's sentimental but enormously skilful operetta-ballet *Le Beau Danube*, Dolin's acceptance of the Ruth Page ballet for production was very disturbing. It was obvious that in one aspect of ballet—male dancing—he had flair and discrimination, and the fine results he achieved showed what was wrong with the artistic policies of other English companies; but in other aspects of ballet his artistic policy was very unsatisfactory.

Ram Gopal

It was only with the utmost difficulty that Ram Gopal managed to take up dancing as a career. His father considered dancing totally unsuitable as an occupation for his son, and there were no good teachers in Ram Gopal's native town (Bangalore). Nevertheless he managed to study Kathakali for a short time at Vallathol's Kerala-Kalamandalam; he rapidly learned enough to give his remarkable personality a chance to shine out on the stage, and made such an impression on La Meri (when she visited Bangalore with her troupe) that she took him into her company. He toured with this company as far as Japan, where he left La Meri and began to give recitals on his own. He was fortunate enough to attract the attention of Aleksander Janta, a Polish journalist, who became his manager and presented him in successful recitals in Hollywood, New York, Warsaw and Paris.

These recitals were given by him alone, with music on gramophone records. In London, however, solo recitals of this character have never been successful, and before presenting him in London Aleksander Janta sensibly made arrangements for Ram Gopal to collect a small company of dancers and musicians— notably the talented Javanese dancer Retna Mohini, who had also had some training in Kathakali at the Kalamandalam and lived in Paris. This group was not a company in the same sense as e.g. Shankar's company: the programme consisted almost entirely of a series of solos, each dancer performing his or her own items. (Ram Gopal did, however, dance one pas de deux with Retna Mohini—a scene from a Javanese dance-drama in a simplified Javanese classical technique.)

Though Ram Gopal's technique at this time was limited compared with that of the other members of his company, he had no difficulty in dominating the show completely.[1] The most striking item in the show was *Tandava Nrittya* (Dance of Siva), in which he did little more than walk around the stage, extending first one arm and then another in front of him. In another item, almost equally successful, he did nothing except perform a few mudras at the back of the stage in dim lighting while his music director (Kheshan Dhorda) played a flute solo. He had a face and body of unearthly beauty, and seemed able to magnetize audiences with movements and rhythms which would have seemed childish if used by almost any other dancer. Most of his dances at this time were very much in the Ruth St. Denis tradition, though one of them (*Garuda, the Golden Eagle*) owed more to Ted Shawn than to Ruth St. Denis.

The London season was a great success, being extended by popular demand to a month, and he returned to a different London theatre a few months later for another successful season. The War then made it necessary for Ram Gopal to disband his company; he thereupon returned to India and began a serious study of Bharata Natyam.

He made rapid progress in Bharata Natyam, and soon began to give solo recitals in this style. He started a school of his own at Bangalore, and from time to time took a company on tour, performing both Bharata Natyam items and also his pre-War compositions in free style. He was a great success at the All-India Dance Festival in Bombay in 1945. His great achievement both as dancer and teacher in the Bharata Natyam style was to add to the pure line and strong foot-rhythms of the Tanjore school certain subtle elements of expressiveness, individuality and grace from the Conjeevaram school. (His work in the field of Bharata Natyam was analogous to that of Russian dancers and teachers who added Franco-Russian poetry and expressiveness to the powerful technique of the Italian school.)

After the War he returned to London, the scene of his greatest pre-War triumph, and made his home there. After a long period of waiting and rehearsal (during which he presented a few lecture-demonstrations) he appeared at the head of a new company in a remarkable show at the Playhouse, Oxford, in November, 1947. From a structural point of view the show was much the same as his pre-War shows—a series of solo items, each dancer performing his or her own items—but it was enormously strengthened in quality and variety by the inclusion of a considerable number of classical and near-classical items.

The core of the show was a fine selection of the shorter standard Bharata Natyam items of pure dancing—*Alarippu, Jethisvaram* and *Thillana*—and the song-dances *Madura Nagarilo* and *Natanam Adinar*; each of these was skilfully

---

[1] The company included the traditionally trained Kathak dancer Sohan Lal, a pupil of the great Jaipuri guru Pandit Jailal. But at this time Sohan Lal had had (by professional Kathak standards) relatively little training, and danced in a rough and acrobatic manner.

composed by Ram Gopal and performed or produced by him with careful attention to the tenets of classical Bharata Natyam.[1] (These items were highly successful, thus re-establishing the fact that good Indian classical dancing could become a box-office draw in Europe.) Next in importance were a group of items in simplified Manipuri (with some elements of Lucknowi Kathak) performed by the highly talented artists Lakshmi and Shevanti; at this time Shevanti (Menaka's favourite pupil) was lacking in personality and power of projection, but her artistry was already clearly apparent. Ram Gopal performed his *Dance of the Setting Sun*—a much improved version of his pre-War dance, and now one of the strongest items in his repertoire—together with some other pre-War items of relatively minor interest.

The only really weak number among the new items was *Rajput Serenade of Love*. This was presumably inspired by Menaka compositions such as *Mogul Serenade*, but its Kathak choreography (fragments of elementary *tolas* put together without any regard for *tala*[2]) was very insipid. This item was labelled "Kathakali" in the programme, and from now on Ram Gopal continued to permit the labelling of items in his show "Kathak", "Manipuri" or "Kathakali" with surprisingly little concern for their actual nature. (On no occasion, however, did he permit any misuse of the label "Bharata Natyam".)

When the show reached London, some weeks later, the programme was much less satisfying, and from now on there was a slow and interrupted but progressive decline in both quality and variety. Good dancers joined the company from time to time, but they rarely stayed for long, while Kumudini (who established a record of duration as Ram Gopal's partner during the period 1949–52) showed only a tiny fragment of her Kathak training. (She was by far the most highly trained Kathak dancer[3] to reach Europe since Gauri Shankar and Ramnarayan came with Menaka in 1936.) There were several attempts at the productions of ballets (e.g. *The Legend of Rama* and *The Cloud Messengers*), but these were much closer in style and construction to the most feeble and conventional type of Western ballets than to the new type of ballet being composed in Bombay at the time, and it was hard to believe that Ram Gopal had any share in their composition.

Though he showed real creative ability in composing *Dance of the Setting Sun* and the pure Bharata Natyam items, it was clear that he had little interest in

[1] Some were performed by Ram Gopal, Shevanti and Rajeshwar as solos, others as pas de deux and pas de trois.

[2] The rhythms and phrasing of classical Indian music and dancing are based on *talas*—standard rhythmic phrases which may contain a large number of accented and unaccented beats.

[3] Kumudini had had five years of intensive training under Pandit Jailal's favourite pupil Radhelal Misra. The latter accompanied Kumudini to Europe, and played the drums for her. (All Kathak gurus are expert drummers, and in fact the more complex aspects of Kathak dancing cannot be shown unless the dancer and drummer are equally virtuosic; the same is true of the more complex aspects of Bharata Natyam, Kathakali and Kandyan.)

group choreography. He relied on his own performances and those of one or two other outstanding soloists to carry the show.

Even if Ram Gopal's achievements in the field of classical dancing were in range of technique and expression less than those of Pavlova, his career was like hers in surprisingly many respects. Like Pavlova he brought something new to the classical dancing of his own country, and introduced it to a large number of people in many different countries. Though his treatment of Katha-kali and Kathak was open to criticism, he did his best to maintain high standards of technique and expression in Bharata Natyam, both in his own dancing and in that of his pupils, and three of his pupils—Shevanti, Kumudini and Mrinalini (Marianne Balchin)—reached a very high standard of technique, expression and personality in the pure-dance aspects of this style. (Unfortunately for Ram Gopal, his own Bharata Natyam dancing suffered during his long separation from his teachers.) Like Pavlova he was apparently content to dance in ballets with choreography quite unworthy of his talents, relying on his personality and stage presence to put the dancing over to the audience. His *Dance of the Setting Sun* occupied much the same place in his programmes as Pavlova's Dying Swan in hers, and in fact seemed to be partly inspired by this item. Unlike *Le Cygne*, *Dance of the Setting Sun* suffered from a certain looseness of construction and the inclusion of certain passages (such as the Shankarian rolling of the shoulders) which were out of key with the rest of the dance. Nevertheless Ram Gopal's achievements in this dance gave some hint of what he might achieve in ballets suited to his talents.

(b) THE EXPRESSIONIST FREE DANCER'S COMPANY

The division of the expressionist free dance into a cerebral wing and an ecstatic wing was repeated in a corresponding division between the expressionist dance groups. The cerebral wing was dominated by choreographers who showed relatively little interest in appearing themselves on the stage, whereas the ecstatic wing was dominated by dancers who normally started their careers by giving recitals, and continued to think in terms of their own dancing throughout their careers; if they founded a dance group they treated this simply as a background to their own dancing.

We are here concerned with the latter type of company.

Isadora Duncan (1878–1927)

Though Duncan began her career working in companies (Jane May's mime company performing *L'Enfant Prodigue* and a dramatic company performing

A Midsummer Night's Dream), she found no outlet for her ideas in such companies, and accordingly devised a new type of programme in which she appeared on her own in a series of solos, performed to the music of a piano. She was able to perform these solos in London in the drawing-rooms of wealthy people, but no-one appreciated the full significance of her work under these conditions, nor was she herself able to come to maturity without contact with a theatre audience under good conditions. This did not happen until a remarkable Hungarian impresario, Alexander Gross, saw her dancing for a small audience of artists at the Künstler Haus in Vienna. Realizing that her appeal was not limited to small specialized audiences, he offered her a contract to appear for thirty evenings at the Urania Theatre in Budapest. This proposal frightened Duncan—she insisted that her dancing was for an élite audience, not for the general public—but Gross overcame her objections, and his expectations were fully justified. Duncan was a tremendous success appearing on her own in a full-sized theatre with an orchestra, and played to capacity for the entire season. This season represented a turning-point in her career, and indeed in the history of the dance. Gross then presented Duncan at the huge Kroll Opera House in Berlin, with a full symphony orchestra and the finest conductor in Berlin; her success was so great that she was nearly crushed to death by her adoring audience.

Duncan then moved forward very gradually towards the formation of a group. Undoubtedly she took the idea of a group to some extent from the group maintained by Loie Fuller,[1] with whom she travelled for some weeks before making contact with Gross in Vienna. She was probably also influenced to some extent by her contact with Pavlova and the Imperial Russian Ballet: though she hated the ballet technique, she was deeply impressed by the performance of Pavlova in *Giselle*, and could see that Pavlova owed much to the support of the other dancers.

After returning from Russia, Duncan pushed ahead enthusiastically with the formation of a school in Berlin, where she had made a more powerful impression than anywhere else. At first she took some of the classes herself, but later she left the school entirely in the hands of her sister, Elizabeth. The training of the children was based on Duncan's own dancing: simple walking, running and leaping rhythms, movements to suggest the swaying of trees, the flight of birds, and so on. Duncan now began to dream about vast group dances:

If I had only visioned the dance as a solo, my way would have been quite simple. Already famous, sought after in every country, I had only to pursue a triumphal

[1] Loie Fuller made a sensation in the first two decades of this century by waving lengths of drapery in the coloured beams of powerful spotlights: she was the first person to show the possibilities of electrical stage lighting in this way.

career. But, alas! I was possessed by the idea of . . . a vast ensemble dancing in the Ninth Symphony of Beethoven. At night, I had only to shut my eyes and these figures danced through my brain in mighty array, calling on me to bring them to life. . . . With these dreams I returned to Grunewald to teach the little group who were already learning to dance with such beauty as to strengthen my faith in the ultimate perfection of an orchestra of dancers—an orchestra which would be to sight what great symphonies were to sound.[1]

The pupils were still very young, but she needed money badly for the school, and she therefore took twenty of them with her on tour, presenting them dancing on the stage and appealing for financial support. She was unsuccessful in her efforts, and eventually she had to abandon the school. Later she started another school in Paris with the help of her wealthy patron whom she called Lohengrin, and as soon as possible she began to present them on the stage with her. During the War she was forced to disband the school, but she was able to retain the six best pupils, and took them to America with her. When she went to Moscow at the invitation of the Soviet Government, she started another school. When she went on tour to the United States in 1922 she was unable to bring her pupils, but she missed them very much, and made Hurok promise to bring them from Moscow; he was eventually able to do so in 1928, after Duncan's death.

Duncan composed only the simplest choreography for her pupils—e.g. long lines of girls making simultaneous movements evoking the ancient Greek chorus; in fact she used them mainly as background to her own dancing rather than as instruments in a visual symphony. Duncan was debarred by her own outlook from giving the dancing of her pupils any independent value; they learned only her own habits of movement (one might almost call them mannerisms) and these movements could not come to life except when executed by her. Her approach to choreography was so subjective that she could not imagine movements except in terms of her own physique and temperament. To her the simple walks, runs, skips and leaps she performed were natural and inevitable—the only possible way of representing the themes she had in mind. Her dance-groups consisted only of girls; the movements Duncan imagined for her students to perform were concerned so much in terms of herself that performance by a man would have been unthinkable. In this (as in many other respects) she established a precedent followed by a large number of free dancers.

Duncan's attitude to décor and costume was perfectly in harmony with her attitude to her dance-group. She broke away from existing ideas of décor, dancing invariably in front of the blue curtains which she took with her everywhere. All that mattered to her was the music and the dancing body—her

---

[1] *My Life*, p. 151.

dancing body, clothed just enough to satisfy the prudishness of the general public. The effects of her ideas on décor and costumes were almost as widespread and profound as her choreographic ideas. She did not originate the idea of dancing in Grecian robes against a plain dark background—Ruth St. Denis saw Genevieve Stebbens performing Delsartian "plastiques" (with poses drawn from Greek statuary) against a dark green background several years before Duncan began to dance[1]—but it was Duncan who popularized these new ideas of costume and décor.

Mary Wigman (b. 1886)

Wigman had considerable experience of group work at the Dalcroze Institute at Hellerau and later at Laban's school, and in 1918, while recovering from a nervous breakdown brought on by overwork, she devised on paper (using Laban's Dance Notation) her first group composition *The Seven Dances of Life*. Laban succeeded in securing appointments as Director of Movement at various State and municipal opera-houses, and devoted himself to the production of complex group dances; but Wigman had no success in obtaining such appointments. Like Duncan she moved on to the composition of group items with the pupils of her school, but (as with Duncan) these items were completely subordinated to her own dancing; she used the dancers almost as she used costumes and percussion music.

Because of her enormous success as a solo dancer she attracted pupils to her school in Dresden from all over Central Europe, from Scandinavia, and even from countries as far away as the United States and Japan. The pupils were mainly (though not entirely) female; when she formed a dance-group out of the best of the senior pupils she used only girls. The Wigman-Tanzgruppe was something very different from a ballet company, with its corps de ballet and soloists of both sexes; some of the girls were given small solos, but Wigman made sure that none of them developed any qualities of individuality and personality while they worked for her. The Wigman cult at Dresden was completely hostile to original work among the pupils.

As often happens with expressionists, Wigman's practice was completely at variance with her principles. The training at her school laid great stress on improvisation and individual creative work, and she herself declared that she considered the most wonderful thing of all to be "collective work leading to the larger structural forms".[2] In theory her group dances took shape as the result of a process of collective improvisation, with each dancer taking part in the process of creation. Even in class she claimed to teach nothing, confining

[1] Ruth St. Denis, *An Unfinished Life*, p. 16.
[2] S. Enkelmann, *Tänzer unserer Zeit*, appendix.

herself to encouraging each dancer to create for herself. In practice, however, her technique was to a large extent a collection of her mannerisms, and she dominated her dancers with her personality so completely that they inevitably developed into pale imitations of herself. Under such circumstances collective composition was a fiction; the movements in the group dances were pure Wigman, whether composed directly by her or not.

Though the collective impulse toward idolatry was very strong at the Wigman school, it did happen that pupils with exceptional strength of character and creative power would begin to develop in their own way—as did Birgit Åkesson. Wigman tended to treat the development of such independence as treachery. Her instinct in this matter was perfectly sound; such pupils were likely to develop into dancers able to compete with her and even to supplant her. She had no need to worry about the little Wigmans.

Unlike the choreographers of the Laban wing of expressionism, Wigman showed little interest in building up a team of designers and composers. She remained faithful to a percussion accompaniment long after the Labanist choreographers had broken away from this type of accompaniment, and she used costumes which were distressingly drab in colour and unimaginative in cut. Like Duncan, she gave the whole of her attention to dancing.

Martha Graham (b. ca. 1903)

In contrast to Wigman, Martha Graham began to teach even before she gave her first recital, and used her pupils in her recitals during the whole of her independent career. At first she used only six girls, but by 1930 she was using as many as twenty. Like Wigman, however, she exercised a spell over her dancers; they idolized her and were quite incapable of developing any personality of their own while they were in her group. In any case her productions were devised as solo dances for herself, accompanied by a kind of chorus of group movements, and gave no scope to members of the group to come to maturity as interpretative artists with ideas and feelings of their own.

But for the extraordinary spell which Graham cast over her pupils she could scarcely have held the group together. The girls were not paid like a ballet company: they worked during the day to earn a living, and came almost every evening and every Sunday for classes and rehearsals. Martha Graham herself earned a living teaching in various institutions, and arranged her annual New York concerts and tours to fit in with the college holidays.

For many years the Graham dance-group (like the Wigman dance-group) was entirely feminine, but in 1938 Martha Graham took the important step of adding men to her group. This widened considerably the range of moods covered by her work—not only because she was forced to think to some extent in terms of physiques and temperaments different from her own, but also because the men in her group were less inclined to idolatry than the girls, and developed some individuality.

Though Martha Graham was like Duncan and Wigman in basing all her compositions on her own dancing, she showed affinities with the Laban wing of expressionism in making her theatre pieces into genuine *Gesamtkunstwerke* with complete harmony between theme, choreography, costumes, décor, lighting and music. She designed all the costumes herself in her early years, showing great originality and an extraordinary flair for the textures and draping qualities of different materials. (Her influence on the costuming of the American free dance has been as profound as her influence on technique and choreography.) Originally she worked against the usual dark curtains, but as her theatre pieces became more complex in their themes she began to feel the need to make the whole expanse of the stage part of the dance; she therefore commissioned a new type of semi-abstract décor in harmony with her choreography, and adjusted the patterns of her dances to fit the décors. (She was not always successful in her use of properties and small items of décor, but her pioneer work in this direction was of great importance.)

In her music she was greatly helped by her music director Louis Horst, who wrote the music for most of her early compositions and helped her with advice on commissioning music from other American composers. In her work with Louis Horst (e.g. on *El Penitente* and *Primitive Mysteries*) she followed in the same path as her contemporaries in Central Europe, working out each phrase of the music and the dancing in close collaboration in the dance-studio. Things were more difficult when she commissioned music from composers like Aaron Copland (*Appalachian Spring*), Gian-Carlo Menotti (*Errand into the Maze*) and Paul Hindemith (*Herodiade*), for they naturally could not collaborate with her as closely as Louis Horst; nevertheless she showed herself well able to adapt herself to their patterns of musical thought. (Occasionally her experimentation in musical matters led her astray; but mistakes are inevitable in all pioneer work of this nature.)

Though she widened her range considerably in the forties, her creative powers still found their natural expression in terms of her own body and her own temperament, and the other dancers on the stage remained shadows of her. (When she hurt her knee at the beginning of her Paris season in the Summer of 1951 an attempt was made to continue with the season without her, but the attempt had to be abandoned after two performances: without her the compositions were quite dead.) She also hampered herself by commissioning theatre pieces from her partner Erick Hawkins which were pretentious and unconvincing commentaries on spoken poetry—perhaps the most dangerous genre which an unimaginative choreographer can tackle, for the words enable him to dispense with the need of making his ideas clear in dance-imagery.

Though Martha Graham's theatre pieces showed all the limitations typical of this genre of expressionism, they were far in advance of nearly all other works in this genre, and represented a major contribution to twentieth-century choreography. Perhaps her most striking achievement was to win nation-wide recognition without sacrificing any of her integrity, continuing from one decade to the next to use the themes and the styles which she felt to be right at any time, irrespective of their popular appeal. All important American choreographers have been profoundly influenced by her work, whether they use the classical technique or a free-dance technique, and it is greatly to be regretted that her work is little known on the Eastern side of the Atlantic.

(c) The Rich Dancer's Company

Not all rich dancers form their own companies: many of them find that they can secure satisfactory opportunities for themselves by providing the director of the company in which they are dancing with financial support at one of the inevitable crises when such support is essential if the company is to continue; far more dancers become stars in this way than is generally realized.[1] Sometimes such dancers provide the whole of the backing, but prefer to hand over management to someone else, taking little interest in artistic policy except to ensure that they get good parts and to suppress dangerous competition within the company. They have good reason to avoid the responsibilities of direct management, for this can be a heavy burden, and is certain to take up time in which they might be having private lessons or special rehearsals; in any case the critics and the public are always liable to be prejudiced against wealthy dancer-managers, feeling that they use their wealth to secure themselves rôles which they could not achieve by their talent. The existence of this prejudice acts as a deterrent against direct management of a ballet company by a rich dancer unless he or she is extremely ambitious or has a strong urge to power. (It is nearly always "she".)

In many respects the artistic policy of the rich dancer is similar to that of the great individualistic dancer: every detail is arranged to give prominence to the star and suppress dangerous rivals. But the artistic policy of the former differs from that of the latter in breeding a characteristic insipid quality in the pro-

[1] The reverse is also true: many promising careers have been cut short because the director expected a poor but talented dancer to provide the same financial support that was forthcoming from the rich soloists.

Isadora Duncan dancing with her pupils in 1910

Mary Wigman with her dance-group in *Prayer* (Dresden, *ca.* 1930)

Above: the Internationa[l] Ballet, *ca.* 1948: *Gisel[le]* (Perrot–Coralli, Pari[s] 1841) with Mon[a] Inglesby as Giselle

Ida Rubinstein as Cleo[-] patra at the Londo[n] Coliseum in 1909

grammes. The rich dancer does not need to make contact with the audience, and can afford to ignore adverse reviews by critics and mediocre box-office returns. Her own staff are not so foolish as to endanger their jobs by giving her frank criticisms, even if she asks for them. In fact the rich dancer lives in a well-upholstered vacuum, and invariably fails to make the best of her talents. Her lack of contact with the public tends to prevent her from developing the feeling of responsibility to the public characteristic of all great dancers. Even if she has the resources to keep her company permanently in existence she is liable to get tired of the strain of continuous touring after a year or two, and to disband the permanent company in favour of occasional performances with scratch companies. If she does maintain a permanent company she is liable to put on someone else in her place at a moment's notice if she does not feel in the mood for dancing. Such policies have very serious repercussions on the morale of the dancers in the company, and tend to create a barrier between the rich dancer-manager and the public.

In the same way the rich dancer-manager is debarred from real appreciation of the talents of the members of her company. The great dancer who has made his or her way to the top by a combination of talent, drive and good luck (all three are in fact indispensable) retains some degree of fellow-feeling for the talented young dancer struggling for an opening; the great dancer has enough humility to learn from the work of rivals while he or she is on the way up, and even after reaching the top he or she is capable of appreciating and showing respect for real talent wherever it appears (though this does not mean that he or she will allow it a place in his or her company). The rich dancer-manager, on the other hand, usually has no chance of developing this humility towards good dancing in others, and is inclined to be quite ruthless in suppressing it; the other dancers in her company soon learn that it is fatal to dance really well or get good notices. In this way the rich dancer-manager is driven inescapably to deprive herself of real competition very early in her career, and her dancing suffers accordingly.

Ida Rubinstein (b. ca. 1880)

Ida Rubinstein had enormous success in the first season of the Diaghilev company in 1909, when she played the title rôle in *Cléopâtre*. Though she had had a few lessons from Fokine, she was by no means a dancer; on the other hand, she had real talent as a mime, and with her slender body, almond eyes and Oriental profile she was ideally cast as Cléopâtre. At this time the general public in Paris knew very little about dancing, and Ida Rubinstein's miming made just as strong an impression as the incomparably more important achievements of Pavlova, Karsavina and Nijinsky. The following year, Ida Rubinstein made an equally strong impression as Zobeide in *Schéhérazade*—another mimed rôle which suited her to perfection. She then began to imagine that she was a great artist: becoming tired of her mimed rôles, she tried to persuade Diaghilev to let her dance. He refused, knowing her to have no ability as a dancer, and she left him in disgust. She then began to stage productions in Paris, employing the same artists as Diaghilev (Bakst, Benois, Debussy, Florent Schmitt, Stravinsky, Golovin, etc.) and also some famous artists of the day not used by Diaghilev (e.g. d'Annunzio, Verhaeren, André Gide, Déodat de Severac, Pizzetti, Honegger, etc.) Though with her own money and the large fortune of her husband she was able to pay her artists well, and staged her productions with the utmost luxury, their artistic importance as *Gesamtkunstwerke* was slight, no matter how high the quality of the individual contributions; having little feeling for the important trends in art, she remained faithful to productions of the same type as *Cléopâtre* and *Schéhérazade*, though these were rather old-fashioned even when first produced. Quite apart from this fundamental artistic weakness the artists employed by her had to subordinate their ideas to the task of providing a good part for her—and her powers were much too limited to give them much inspiration.

During 1928 and 1929 she maintained a permanent ballet company, and produced a considerable number of new ballets with choreography by Nijinska and Massine, décor by Benois, and music by the leading Parisian composers of the day—Honegger, Milhaud, Poulenc, Auric and Sauguet. With the exception of Honegger all these artists had already been employed by Diaghilev; but the results of their labours were ephemeral, even in comparison with the Diaghilev ballets of the cocktail period.

From 1931 onwards Ida Rubinstein attempted to break fresh ground with spectacular productions uniting instrumental music, choral singing, spoken words, mime and dancing. A typical production of this type was *Amphion* (1934), with text by Paul Valéry, music by Honegger, choreography by Massine, and décor and costumes by Benois. The whole production revolved around Ida Rubinstein, who spoke lines, mimed and danced. She spent an enormous amount of money on the production, but the results were only of ephemeral interest, and were totally out of proportion with the talents of the artists involved.

Mona Inglesby (b. 1918)

The most striking feature about Mona Inglesby's career is the contrast between her early experiences as a dancer and the artistic policy she adopted as director of her own company. Many dancers (Pavlova included) have reacted away from their early experiences, but few as violently as Mona Inglesby.

She was fortunate enough to be sent to the Rambert School in 1930, at the age of twelve, and stayed there for five years—thus participating in the golden age of the Ballet Club; the artistic climate at the Mercury Theatre at this time was quite astonishingly stimulating to every sort of creative and interpretative ability. Nevertheless Mona Inglesby was given relatively few parts—she created no rôles at all, and danced only five solo rôles, most of these being minor ones— and it was perhaps as a reaction to this unhappy experience that when she founded her own company she established an artistic policy which was almost the exact opposite of that of the Ballet Club at this period. (She plumped for the dreariest aspects of the Petipa tradition.)

After leaving the Rambert School, Mona Inglesby went for training to many of the best teachers available—Margaret Craske and Nicolas Legat in London, Yegorova and Kshessinskaya in Paris. (She was unfortunate in having no training from Preobazhenskaya).

She formed her first company, the Inglesby Ballet, in 1940, at the age of twenty-two. This was only a small group, performing short items in small theatres to the music of two pianos. Such a group could not hope to appear in large theatres nor give Mona Inglesby a chance to dance the standard classical rôles under good conditions, and so in 1941 she formed a full-sized company, the International Ballet. She composed a number of ballets for this company (in a style closely related to Andrée Howard's version of Ashton's pseudo-classical style) and also followed the example set by Ninette de Valois in commissioning Nicolas Sergueyev to stage a number of productions of the familiar Maryinsky "classics".

In its early years the International Ballet had a certain amount of vitality. The corps de ballet had the suffocating stodginess which English danseuses always acquire when conditions are unfavourable for the development of individuality, but there were a number of soloists who managed to show real talent in spite of the dreary repertoire and the unstimulating artistic climate— notably Harold Turner, Anna Marinova, Nina Tarakanova, Joyce Graeme, Anne Negus, Sonia Arova, Moira Shearer, Angela Bailey, Muriel Harding and Joan Tucker. The most sensitive of these soloists were considerably helped by Stanislas Idzikovsky, who was maître de ballet, though the artistic climate of the company prevented Idzikovsky from making much impact on the general stodginess. The stimulating war-time atmosphere also contributed to keeping some measure of spontaneity in the performances of the soloists.

One by one, however, all the good dancers without exception left the company; they were replaced by others with less individuality and personality, and these in turn were replaced by others whose performances were, if possible, even less exciting.

Idzikovsky's departure in 1943 also represented a very serious loss to the company.

In fact the rate of turnover (both of soloists and corps-de-ballet dancers) was so high that in 1946 Mona Inglesby found it essential to form a school (the International School) and link the students of the school to the company by means of contracts; she also took the extraordinary step of introducing five-year and even seven-year contracts with the company dancers. The students of the school were trained mainly in the R.A.D. style, and this became in due course the style of the company. Here again we can see Mona Inglesby reacting away from the experiences of her youth, when she had training in the Cecchetti and Russian styles.

In 1941, when the company was formed, there was a shortage of trained dancers in England, and the technical standard of the corps-de-ballet dancers was very erratic. In later years the technical standard of the corps de ballet became much more consistent, but on the other hand its dancing reached such a degree of stodginess that one would have welcomed a few technical lapses to vary the monotony.

Mona Inglesby's own dancing developed in a complex way. She did not dance well in the early years of the company, being too plump and showing little vitality or personality. But she worked hard with Judith Espinosa, and by 1945 was dancing very much better; the plumpness had gone, and she showed real lightness and fluidity. In one rôle, Giselle, she gave a very interesting performance, bringing out well the dramatic aspects of the rôle and showing considerable feeling for the character she portrayed. In all her other rôles, however, her dancing was insipid, and was exactly the same whatever the character she was supposed to portray. If she had worked hard on her portrait of Giselle, and looked around for other rôles which gave similar scope to her dramatic abilities, she might have confounded the critics and justified her position as prima ballerina of the company. In fact her policy was almost the reverse of this; she very rarely included Giselle in the programme, and narrowed her range of parts instead of widening it. The result was that her dancing tended to become more and more insipid and monotonous.

Evidently she was more interested in dancing than in choreography, for she allowed all her own ballets to drop out of the repertoire, and limited the repertoire almost entirely to the ballets with the biggest box-office appeal— Le Lac des Cygnes, The Sleeping Beauty and Coppélia. The few new ballets commissioned by Mona Inglesby were of paralysing banality, being far inferior even to her own ballets. (Having worked at the Ballet Club during its best period she had at least some feeling for composition.) In spite of the fact that there were a number of poor choreographers available in England, she went to considerable trouble to commission bad ballets from overseas choreographers— notably Sea Legend from the Australian choreographer Dorothy Stevenson and Visions from the cosmopolitan choreographer Julian Algo. It looked as if she wished to prevent invidious comparisons even with the memory of her own ballets.

It was typical of the International Ballet that having the honour of playing at the Royal Festival Hall during the Festival of Britain in 1951 it presented a new ballet by Algeranov, *For Love or Money*, which was clearly based on Algeranov's memories of the dreariest ballets in Pavlova's repertoire; this ballet had much the same sort of sentimental and conventional story (concerned with a gypsy girl and some haughty aristocrats) as the Clustin ballet *Amarilla*, and the choreography was even more banal than that of Clustin, while the specially commissioned music was as noisy and meaningless as Drigo at his worst.

London critics have often tried to make some impression on the stodgy complacency of the International Ballet's artistic policy: on one occasion Richard Buckle even began a review with the biting remark that "There is something for everyone to dislike in the programmes of the International Ballet". But like all companies of this type it remained completely impervious to criticism; presumably nothing short of an atom bomb could have any effect on its artistic policy.

At the end of 1952 the International Ballet reached a critical position. It had no immediate English bookings, and disbanded for several weeks before re-forming for a long Italian tour. By this time it was clear that the company was going to have somewhat greater difficulty in booking tours in England. Its weakened position in England was generally ascribed to the competition of the Festival Ballet. In a sense this was true: the Festival Ballet had a fairly similar repertoire, and in spite of severe deficiencies its performances were never as dull as those of the International Ballet. But a company with vitality and spontaneity is not damaged by competition: it is stimulated by it, just like an individual dancer. Even if the Festival Ballet had never come into existence it is hard to imagine that the International Ballet would have continued to attract English audiences in the fifties quite as strongly as it did in the forties.

Mrinalini Sarabhai

Mrinalini Sarabhai was born in South India, but was sent by her parents at the age of twelve to complete her education in Switzerland. At her Swiss school she studied not only classical ballet (Cecchetti method) but also Dalcroze "moving plastic". After returning to India she spent several years at Santini-ketan, where she included dancing in her studies, and toured all over India appearing in the plays and dance-dramas of Tagore. In 1938 she studied Javanese dancing in Java for some months, and then went on to New York, where she studied acting at the American Academy of Dramatic Art. After giving some recitals in the United States she returned to India, studying Bharata Natyam at Ram Gopal's school at Bangalore and touring with him as his partner.

She then started a school of her own (Darpana) in South India, providing training in the two South Indian styles (Bharata Natyam and Kathakali), and followed the example set by Menaka and the Bombay choreographers of composing ambitious ballets making use of both the styles taught at her school, using as dancers mainly the staff and pupils of her school. Her work as a choreographer was facilitated by the fact that she employed two highly trained traditional Kathakali dancers, able to translate anything into Kathakali mime on demand.

In 1949 she brought her company to the West, visiting England and several other countries of Western Europe. Her programmes aroused considerable interest for a number of reasons. The achievements of the Bombay companies were still unknown; her programme differed in many ways from the familiar programmes of Ram Gopal and Uday Shankar; her principal male dancer, Chatunni Panicker, was a Kathakali dancer of strong personality, ideal in heroic rôles; and she brought a fine group of instrumentalists and singers to perform the classical Carnatic music of South India. On the other hand her programmes had severe weaknesses which limited their popular appeal.

One major weakness was her own dancing, for she took the leading rôle in nearly all the ballets: throughout the evening she danced in exactly the same manner, irrespective of the classical technique she was using, the nature of the rôle, and the dramatic situation. This manner seemed to arise from a mixture of the various styles she had learned. She gave all her movements a soft, languid, almost sentimental quality which would have been appropriate at Santiniketan but destroyed the flavour of Bharata Natyam and Kathakali; she followed through with her gestures in the manner of Western ballet instead of giving them the accent which is typical of the South Indian styles; and she used her eyes in the spontaneous naturalistic manner of the West which goes very badly with the stylized mudras of India.

Like Mona Inglesby she failed to make the most of her very real talents; her usual soft and smiling manner did not suit her temperament at all, and it came as a surprise to spectators when she suddenly showed marked dramatic ability in the first scene of the Chitrangada (a new version of a dance-drama by Tagore). In this scene the Princess Chitrangada goes hunting in the forest, dressed as a man; characteristically, Mrinalini Sarabhai did not dress as a man, but she gave the rôle vivid actuality by adopting a stern, aloof manner and making her movements crisp and determined. The result was excellent; one could only regret that Chitrangada very soon fell in love with Arjuna and began to dance in the familiar languid manner.

This ballet showed a good example of the type of miscasting which is common in companies run by a dancer-manager. Chatunni Panicker is a fine artist, though rather limited in his range; whatever the rôle he invariably dances it in a swashbuckling manner suited to the hero Arjuna. Shivashankar is another fine artist who lacks the striking personality of Chatunni Panicker but has a superb technique, a perfect sense of line, and a delicacy of feeling which one hardly expects in a Kathakali dancer. In *Chitrangada* Mrinalini Sarabhai crippled both these fine artists by casting Chatunni Panicker as the God of Love and Shivashankar as Arjuna.

None of the ballets showed much feeling for construction. Scene followed scene in a curiously casual way, and there was little attempt to establish character or build up toward some sort of a satisfying conclusion. This absence of dramatic sense was exceptionally obvious in *Manushya*, an attempt at an Indian equivalent of the expressionist drama of Central Europe. At the end of the ballet "Man" suddenly dropped dead, for no apparent reason except that the ballet had gone on long enough. There were certain charming scenes in these ballets (notably the Kathakali dance-class and the game of hop-scotch in *Manushya*) which proved that Mrinalini Sarabhai had real talent as a choreographer, but she did not seem to have much feeling for the laws of the theatre and the needs of audiences.

Her lack of dramatic instinct was equally clear in *Matsya Kanya*, an attempt at an Indian equivalent of *Le Lac des Cygnes*. (In spite of living in the home of Kathakali, Mrinalini Sarabhai showed little interest in the wonderful mythological stories of the Ramayana and Mahabharata.) Ignoring the example of the Petipa-Ivanov ballet, Mrinalini Sarabhai made no effort to establish the fish-like nature of the fish-maidens (corresponding to the Swan maidens of *Le Lac des Cygnes*): it was only after the maidens had gone away that the companions of the Prince suddenly made the mudra for fish. The ending of this ballet was typically inconclusive: the fish-maidens went back to their celestial abode, and the Prince and his companions pursued their way.

Between her first and second European tours Mrinalini Sarabhai took the important step of commissioning décors for her ballets from Jayantkumar Desai. Mrinalini Sarabhai's company was in fact the very first Indian company to take décors on tour in Europe. Its décors were gay and colourful, in a stylized manner that married well with the stylized character of Indian dancing. These décors gave a hint of what Mrinalini Sarabhai could achieve; with her international background, her lavish financial resources, and her training in both styles of South Indian classical dancing, she was in a strong position to do important pioneer work in modern Indian ballet. Unfortunately, however, the limitations inherent in all companies of this type prevented her from taking full advantage of these assets.

2. THE CHOREOGRAPHER'S COMPANY

Choreographers, like dancers, are normally frustrated artistically, and therefore have a strong inducement to form their own companies in order to achieve freedom of action. Like dancers, they almost invariably fail to make the best of their talents when they do this. Their ballets tend to be disappointing, and their administration to show severe defects.

There are many reasons for this. One is that a ballet company usually exists in a state of recurrent catastrophe. Every week brings at least one devastating problem that at the time seems insoluble, and demands the most feverish attention from the director. Dancers hurt their feet, throw temperaments, or miss train calls; skips full of costumes go astray; scenery gets damaged by rain; the theatre lighting proves to be quite inadequate; drapes cannot be hired for love or money; trains are late and connections are missed; fine weather keeps people away from the theatre; bad weather keeps people away from the theatre; "weeks out" with no theatre bookings loom ahead; bills come in and there is no money to pay for them; a printers' strike holds up the posters; all lodgings and hotels are booked up and there is nowhere for the company to stay; and so on. Such things happen to all theatrical companies, but somehow they seem to happen much more often to ballet companies than to other types of company.[1] Under the circumstances a choreographer rarely achieves the peace of mind needed for artistic creation, and cannot undertake an ambitious pioneer work needing months or years of single-minded preparation.

Another reason for the unsatisfactory results which usually follow the formation of a company by a choreographer is that twentieth-century audiences expect a balanced repertoire with ballets in various styles by several good choreographers. Choreographers are usually no more capable than other artists of cultivating a balanced judgment of the works of their contemporaries: the more they have developed their own ideas, the more likely they are to see the ballets of other choreographers in terms of the relationship of these ballets to their own ideas. When they do select another choreographer as associate they are likely to choose one whose works seem likely to provide a suitable foil to their own ballets, irrespective of the artistic merit of the former, and they are unlikely to choose a choreographer good enough to compete seriously with

---

[1] The picture of a ballet company in the delightful "whodunit" *A Bullet in the Ballet*, by Caryl Brahms and S. J. Simon, is not in the least exaggerated. This book is more of a documentary than a satire.

them; if by force of circumstances they are driven to commission a ballet from such a choreographer, they must be expected to lay down conditions which prevent the guest choreographer from doing justice to himself. These things are liable to happen even if the choreographer-manager has the greatest artistic integrity and is genuinely anxious to secure the best possible repertoire; for all good artists are driven by a daemon, and unconsciously take care to defend their own interests as creators (which in the short run may well be different from their long-term interests as company directors). When the choreographer is a cynical opportunist these things are certain to happen.

A choreographer inevitably chooses dancers and arranges training so as to produce a company best suited to do justice to his own ballets; and this may well mean that the dancers are not suitable for any other style. This does not matter if the choreographer is a genius, and has the resources to keep the company going; when Vigano was directing the ballet company of La Scala no one had any reason to complain that the dancers would not do justice to the ballets of some other choreographer. But geniuses are rare, and so is patronage: the chances of their being joined together are so small that one can almost (but not quite) ignore the possibility.

In this century almost all the leading choreographers have formed companies of their own at least once, but usually they failed to keep these companies going for long, for the reasons mentioned above.

There were, however, certain very important exceptions. A few choreographers were fortunate enough to receive adequate and permanent financial support, so that they were able to carry on their companies indefinitely, in spite of serious faults in their artistic policies. In due course these companies became as much a projection of the personality and neuroses of their directors as the latter's handwriting and choreography. A company formed by any one expressionist choreographer shows profound resemblances with the companies formed by other expressionist choreographers, in spite of great differences in dance-technique and national character. Much the same is true of companies formed by the pseudo-classical choreographers (closely related to the expressionist choreographers in temperament and outlook). Unfortunately other types of choreographer have not received the financial support needed to maintain independent companies for any length of time, and in these companies it is hard to distinguish between the results of the basic artistic policy and the deficiencies caused by lack of money and rehearsal time.

(a) Subsidized Companies

Kurt Jooss (b. 1901)

As we have seen, Jooss was not to any great extent a pioneer as a choreographer: his experimental work in the early twenties was based on that of Laban, and other German choreographers were before him in producing free-dance versions of Diaghilev ballets and mixing the free dance and the classical technique. The unique position attained by Jooss was due to the fact that he achieved a reasonably satisfactory synthesis out of a large number of elements: almost at the beginning of his career as a choreographer he formed a strong team of collaborators, and held this team together through two decades of violent changes.

By far the most important of Jooss' colleagues was Sigurd Leeder. Their talents were admirably complementary: Jooss had the qualities of leadership needed to run a company and creative ability as a choreography, but relatively limited ability as practical teacher, while Leeder had outstanding creative ability as a teacher but was unable to give this creative stream the continuity and precision needed for choreography.

Other important collaborators were the designer Hein Heckroth and the composer F. A. Cohen. In addition to keeping this team of collaborators together, Jooss was able to arouse great devotion in his dancers, who stuck to him for long periods in spite of great hardships. It is noteworthy that the whole company followed him into exile in 1934.

Jooss formed his first company at the Stadttheater, Munster (1924–26). His second group, formed at Essen in 1927, was in many ways a continuation of the first. When this group was made official dance-group to the two muncipal theatres of Essen, Jooss benefited by the lavish subsidy granted to these theatres in the usual German manner.

In 1934 Jooss reorganized his company and its associated school at Dartington Hall at Totnes, Devon, receiving a subsidy from Mr. and Mrs. Elmhirst and enjoying all the facilities of this admirable cultural centre (rehearsal rooms, dormitories, Barn Theatre, etc.). He was now in the happy position of being able to take his company on tour across the world for about five months of each year without worrying much about box-office returns, giving his whole attention to achieving the highest possible artistic standard.

In fact his position was so exceptional that the subsequent development of the Ballets Jooss can be regarded almost as a pure laboratory experiment. Here was one of the greatest expressionist choreographers, provided with complete freedom to put his theories into practice without interference from governments or patrons, and without having to worry about the taste of the public in different countries. As the years went by the experiment became even more significant, for the element of nationality became less prominent. (The Jooss-Leeder school at Dartington Hall attracted students from all over the world, and the best of these naturally joined the company.)

From a technical point of view results were admirable. At a time when the average level of dance-technique in English companies was very erratic the Ballets Jooss defied criticism in even the smallest details of the minor rôles. The same was true of stage technique: the lighting plots used by Jooss were more complex than those of almost any other theatrical company, yet everything went smoothly at every performance. As a result certain scenes admirably composed by Joos in a pure expressionist style—notably the Peace Conference scenes in *The Green Table*—never failed to make a strong effect on audiences. Here there was no need for individuality in the dancers, who wore masks and took their parts in the overall pattern with superb precision.

Such scenes, however, made up only a small part of an evening's performance: in fact a whole evening in this style would have been intolerable. In the scenes where dancers were called on to interpret individual rôles the results were much less satisfying. Hans Zullig danced with fire and personality, but he was exceptional. Nearly all the others gave the impression of being very skilfully operated marionettes, an illusion heightened by the extraordinary precision with which they repeated their performances every night. Changes of cast made no difference: the performance remained the same to within a millimetre. This impression of mechanical soulless precision was further emphasized by the fact that the programmes remained much the same from year to year; the new ballets lacked the imaginative vitality of *The Green Table* and *Big City*, and in them the faults of expressionism were distressingly obvious, so that they seldom lasted long in the repertoire. *The Green Table* and *Big City* were necessarily performed *ad nauseam*.

The mechanical quality of performance corresponded to a fundamental element in German expressionism. As in other German companies, every detail in the lives of the Jooss dancers was closely regulated, and in rehearsal Jooss worked with fanatical intensity for months to get every tiny detail as he wanted it. Though in theory the dancers brought their own creative ideas to the building up of their rôles, there was no sign of this in the finished product. The dancers did not worship Jooss in quite the same manner that the members of Wigman's group worshipped her, but the psychological climate was in many respects similar, and so were the effects of this climate on the dancers. This suppression of individuality in the dancers of a company is an inevitable corollary to the over-emphasis of individuality in the leader of the company, and is just as characteristic of a company led by an expressionist choreographer as of one led by an expressionist dancer.

Fortunately for Jooss the War brought many difficulties which made it impossible for him to run the company with the same meticulous perfectionism as in the thirties. He had to recruit classically trained dancers who had not been conditioned in the Jooss-Leeder school to accept the Jooss way of doing things as the only one consistent with high artistic ideals, and the necessity of constant touring cut down the amount of rehearsal time which could be allocated to new ballets and the maintenance of old ballets in their previous state of mathematical precision. The result was that some of the dancers were able to develop real individuality.

In harmony with the rest of Jooss' expressionist artistic policy he gave no opportunities to other choreographers for a long time. This was not because of any lack of talent among his dancers: in fact both Yoma Sasburgh and Michael Charnley later gave evidence of choreographic talent. But it is significant that neither of those dancers stayed long in the company. The atmosphere in the Jooss company was in fact hostile to the development of anything but a feeble imitation of Jooss' own ideas. In 1945 Jooss took the important step of commissioning a ballet from his principal dancer (Hans Zullig), but the resultant ballet was extremely insipid, and showed no spark of originality. The ballets composed for Jooss by Sigurd Leeder had the usual weaknesses of ballets composed by outstanding teachers.

When Jooss re-formed his company in 1950 at Essen he took into it the soloists of the old company and also the best of the young dancers trained in the Jooss-Leeder style in England, Chile and Switzerland. Rolf Alexander danced very well as Death in *The Green Table*, and the young English dancer Joan Turner (a Leeder pupil) showed a powerful technique and a strong personality as The Woman: in fact the company as a whole danced admirably in this ballet. But in the rest of the repertoire it showed exactly the same deficiencies as before.

After a long period of rehearsal the company began to go on tour in Germany, and reached England once again in the Spring of 1953. As re-organized by Jooss, however, the company proved very expensive to the Essen municipality—even though it gave relatively few performances in Essen—and the municipality accordingly withdrew its support of the company. Jooss was therefore forced to disband it.

Ninette de Valois (b. 1898)

It is impossible to exaggerate the importance to the Vic-Wells Ballet of Lilian Baylis and the Vic-Wells organization. When Lilian Baylis had the Sadlers Wells theatre reconstructed in 1931 she did not work out the consequences of controlling two theatres, and suddenly found herself in a position where she was obliged to put on opera every night of the week, either at the

Wells or the Old Vic. This was in fact impossible, and so she was more or less forced to found a ballet company. The Vic-Wells Ballet thus had from the very beginning the inestimable advantage of a highly experienced administrative staff, a small but adequate orchestra, and two theatres with old-established reputations which were out of the West End and so could draw popular audiences at cheap prices. Though from the point of view of general artistic policy the Vic-Wells Ballet was inferior to the Ballet Club, the former company was in the fortunate position of being able to operate on a professional basis, and grave defects in artistic policy which would have destroyed the Ballet Club were not in fact fatal to the growth of the Vic-Wells.

The artistic policy of the Vic-Wells Ballet in its early stages represented a mixture of a number of disparate elements. The company as a whole was clearly the creation of an expressionist choreographer, having many characteristics in common with the Ballets Jooss; but because of its position as one branch of the Vic-Wells organization, largely dependent on box-office receipts for its continued existence, it could not develop in a purely expressionist way in a country where expressionism makes a relatively small appeal.

At the school the dancers had classical training in Ninette de Valois' version of the Cecchetti Method and also in "moving plastic". Few showed any real feeling for the classical tradition, and there was a wide gap between the corps de ballet and minor soloists on the one hand and on the other hand the small group of leading soloists who were brought into the company from the outside in 1932–33 — notably Markova from the Diaghilev company and the Ballet Club, Harold Turner from the Ballet Club, and Stanislas Idzikovsky, one of the greatest classical dancers of the period, who danced some of his finest parts with the Vic-Wells in 1933. (It was in many ways characteristic of the Vic-Wells Ballet that it employed Idzikovsky as dancer and teacher for only a relatively short time.)

The repertoire showed just as pronounced a dichotomy as the dancing. The ballets composed by Ninette de Valois, like those composed by Jooss at this same period, were of two kinds: uncompromisingly avant-garde expressionist ballets such as *La Création du Monde* and *Job* (corresponding to Jooss ballets like *The Green Table*), and insipid pseudo-classical ballets like *Nursery Suite* and *Douanes* (corresponding to Jooss ballets like *Ball in Old Vienna*). The proportion of Kitsch to avant-garde in the Vic-Wells repertoire was much higher than in the Jooss repertoire, but this did not indicate any fundamental difference in temperament between the two choreographers: it merely reflected the relatively small appeal of expressionism in England.

During the next few years Ninette de Valois' production policy brought about considerable changes in the repertoire, though her artistic policy remained fundamentally the same. She devoted a high proportion of the available time and money to the production of a series of Maryinsky ballets (treating these as "classics"—the essential foundation of a ballet company's repertoire, the equivalent of Shakespeare and Verdi). English ballets were gradually dropped as their appeal faded, but the Maryinsky "classics" were kept in the repertoire, and in due course the latter came to take up more than half the total performing time.

She herself composed one major expressionist ballet (*The Rake's Progress*, 1935), but devoted herself mainly to Kitsch from 1933 onwards. At the same time she gave increasing prominence to new ballets composed by Frederick Ashton, whom she appointed staff choreographer; his facile pseudo-classicism had far more popular appeal than her own rather laboured efforts in this genre. After 1935 the Zeitgeist was hostile to thoroughgoing expressionism, and since Ashton was much better than Ninette de Valois at Kitsch she reduced her own rate of output considerably, abandoning choreography almost completely after 1938. Like Jooss she was an organizer rather than an innovator and could find an outlet for her expressionism in administration as well as in choreography.

The fact that her policy continued to be basically expressionist was clearly apparent in many of its details—notably her preference for Petipa rather than Fokine. In the early years of the company, when it was necessary to build up the repertoire quickly, she staged three Fokine ballets—*Le Spectre de la Rose* (1932), *Les Sylphides* (1932) and *Carnaval* (1933)—but Fokine had no hand in these productions, and they were distressingly deficient in poetry and atmosphere, apart from a few brilliant individual performances such as Idzikovsky's Harlequin in *Carnaval*. (The whole climate of the company was strongly opposed to any real understanding of Fokine.) After 1933 Ninette de Valois staged no further ballets by Fokine, ignoring such masterpieces as *Petrouchka* and *Prince Igor*.

Her choice of Petipa rather than Fokine, and of Ashton rather than Tudor, was characteristically expressionist. To most expressionists the pseudo-classicism of Petipa and its post-expressionist equivalent in the work of men like Balanchine and Ashton seemed the essence of classicism—which expressionists regard as something essentially formal and lacking in emotional content.

Like the Jooss company (and for rather similar reasons) the Vic-Wells School and the Vic-Wells company failed to develop soloists with individuality and personality, and developed no choreographers. In its early years the company depended heavily on Markova and Dolin; in its later years it depended even more heavily on soloists imported from outside—chiefly from the Ballet Club. In the 1937–38 season, for example, the leading female soloists (in the order of precedence in the publicity) were Pearl Argyle, Margot Fonteyn, Mary Honer, Elizabeth Miller and June Brae. The leading male soloists (again in order of precedence) were Robert Helpmann, Harold Turner, Frederick

Ashton and William Chappell. Out of these nine dancers no less than four—Pearl Argyle, Harold Turner, Frederick Ashton and William Chappell—came from the Ballet Club, while all the dancers with the technique, style and personality needed for classical rôles—Margot Fonteyn, June Brae, Pearl Argyle and Harold Turner—had had their basic training elsewhere and supplemented this with intensive work under Nicolas Legat. Robert Helpmann (whose technique was inadequate for exacting classical rôles) had had considerable stage experience before taking up dancing seriously. In fact only Mary Honer and Elizabeth Miller could be considered products of the Vic-Wells: and both had a limited range of feeling and a rather brittle prosaic style which fitted them for demi-caractère rôles in *Les Patineurs* but for little else—though Elizabeth Miller gave a hint of remarkable potentialities in her performance of the leading female rôle of the expressionist ballet *The Rake's Progress*.

Notwithstanding the enormous gap between the leading soloists and the rest of the dancers, the former were very much in evidence[1] at each of the twice-weekly performances, and for this reason the Vic-Wells Ballet was well able to stand comparison with the de Basil company (which gave eight performances a week) when the latter company began to degenerate after 1936. For one thing the de Basil company had no classical ballerina to compare with Margot Fonteyn, who by this time was in a class by herself as an interpreter of Odette-Odile and Giselle, in spite of certain technical deficiencies; as I pointed out in an article in *The Dancing Times* of November, 1937,[2] Danilova, though incomparable in her own demi-caractère rôles, was little suited to the classical rôles in which Margot Fonteyn excelled. In this same issue, however, Arnold Haskell drew attention to very significant deficiencies in the dancing of the Vic-Wells corps de ballet:

> Watching Russian and English dancers as I have been on alternate evenings, I am struck not by the difference in general technique but by the lack of life in the English corps de ballet. It is competent enough, but Oh! so stodgy. Each girl looks as if she is doing a routine job, which in a sense she is, but she should keep it a secret. . . . The corps de ballet has inevitably a problem, the disciplining of personality, yet not to the point where the dancer becomes merely a piece of animated scenery. . . . These same artists can each act magnificently in the small rôles in *The Rake's Progress*, they can be animated, yet every trace of life is left behind in *The Swan Lake*. The movements it is true are at times maddeningly mechanical, but there must be a marked difference between the rendering on the stage and in the class-rooms, a difference that the Russians show. They are often slipshod, but that is a fault that jars less than deadness.[3]

[1] When a company performs every night, it has to rest its stars as much as possible, and have alternative dancers for leading rôles.
[2] "De Basil and Vic-Wells: Three Comparisons".
[3] "Balletomane's Log-Book", *The Dancing Times*, November, 1937.

At the Maryinsky every dancer on the stage, though highly disciplined, was expected to be an individual and full of the spirit of the ballet; and some of this outlook remained even in the degenerate de Basil company. Ninette de Valois took care to achieve strong characterization in all the rôles of her expressionist ballet *The Rake's Progress*, but her expressionist outlook prevented her from solving the basic problem of reconciling discipline with the development of personality and individuality in classical-romantic dancing.

This expressionist artistic policy was perhaps also responsible for the fact that only a very small number of dancers developed into satisfactory soloists, in spite of the fact that a considerable number of highly talented children were sent by their parents and teachers to the Vic-Wells School after the company became well known in the early thirties; though Margot Fonteyn was given every encouragement, very few opportunities were given to other highly talented dancers in the company.

Outstanding among these other talented dancers was June Brae. Like Margot Fonteyn, she had her early training in Shanghai under the Russian teacher Goncharov, and worked hard under Legat in London up to the latter's death in 1937; in style and technique she excelled Margot Fonteyn in certain respects,[1] though by temperament she was suited for strong dramatic rôles rather than the lyrical rôles which suited Margot Fonteyn. In 1937 she made a sensation as the diabolically seductive Black Queen in *Checkmate*—a rôle far outside Margot Fonteyn's range at the time. She also did very well in major rôles in Tudor ballets on tour with the Ballet Rambert and at the Mercury—notably as Caroline in *Jardin aux Lilas* and as The Mortal Born under Neptune in *The Planets* (though in the latter rôle her passionate temperament made it difficult for her to achieve the appropriate quality of mysterious inhumanity). She left the Sadlers Wells Ballet for a time during the War, but after her return Helpmann cast her in the leading female rôle (or rather series of rôles) in *Adam Zero* (1946); she danced so brilliantly in these rôles that she made the same sort of sensation as in 1937. But she was given no further rôles of any consequence, and even her own rôle of the Black Queen was taken away from her and given to Pamela May—who could make little of it. Some years later she left the company (as was only to be expected under the circumstances) and her remarkable talents were lost to English ballet.

In all theatrical companies with an expressionist policy we find the same tendencies: the company provides scope for the individuality of the director, and perhaps for one or two leading soloists as well, but not for the mass of the

---

[1] John Gabriel's book *Ballet School* has a large number of action photographs of all the best dancers attending Legat's classes in London in the middle thirties—Danilova, Markova, Ana Roje, Margot Fonteyn, June Brae, Harold Turner, Peggy van Praagh, etc. The differences in technique and style between Margot Fonteyn and June Brae at this time emerge clearly in the photographs.

Opposite: Margot Fonteyn as Odette in *Le Lac des Cygnes*, as produced by the Sadlers Wells Ballet in 1953

The Vic-Wells Ballet in 1937: *Checkmate* (de Valois, Paris, 1937) with June Brae as the Black Queen and Harold Turner as the Red Knight

The London Ballet in 1938: Peggy van Praagh dancing the Bolero in *Soirée Musicale* (Tudor, London, 1938)

artists. In general the first signs of the development of real individuality and independence of outlook are liable to arouse hostility, and may even lead to the departure of the artist. Such tendencies were very clear in Meyerhold's dramatic company in Moscow in the twenties and thirties. His artistic policy made it impossible for him to train actors, and so he drew his actors from other theatre schools, where they had been trained by the Stanislavsky method. No matter what talents they had when they arrived, they were given no chance to develop their full powers at Meyerhold's theatre; Meyerhold achieved dazzling results by imposing his own personal interpretations on second-rate plays (teaching his actors every detail of intonation and mime), but he was incapable of bringing out the full meaning of great plays, and eventually he lost his hold on his public (which was never a wide one at the best of times).

The regrettable decline in the artistic standard of the Vic-Wells Ballet in 1938 and 1939, and the renaissance brought about by the challenge of the War, have already been described in detail in *Modern English Ballet*. Instead of progressing smoothly towards the stodgiest kind of State ballet the company was flung into the stimulating hurly-burly of war-time touring (giving nightly performances in a different town each week), and the increased strain on the stars (together with the loss of many dancers) made necessary profound changes in the company. A number of fine soloists were brought in from the defunct London-Rambert Ballet, the International Ballet and the Anglo-Polish Ballet; moreover Helpmann was allowed to compose ballets. In fact a much-needed draught of fresh air blew through the company. The corps de ballet was still stodgy and the company itself still failed to produce soloists with individuality, but the new soloists who came in were experienced artists who (with the help of the stimulating war-time atmosphere) were able to resist the deadening effect of an expressionist artistic policy.

Significantly enough, the company showed unsuspected reserves of talent in Helpmann's expressionist mime-melodramas *Hamlet* and *Miracle in the Gorbals*: though the atmosphere of the company made it impossible for the corps-de-ballet dancers to get the feel of poetic ballets like *Les Sylphides*, they were quite capable of coming to terms with expressionism, and acted as well in Helpmann's expressionist mime-plays as they had done in *The Rake's Progress*. As mentioned above, June Brae (returning to the company after a long absence) had an enormous personal success in the central female rôle of *Adam Zero* (1946), in spite of the serious defects of the ballet as a whole. Another dancer who did extremely well during the forties was Gordon Hamilton (who joined the company in 1941 after dancing in the Ballet Rambert and the Anglo-Polish Ballet): he showed admirable vitality and virility in a variety of leading rôles.

The Sadlers Wells Ballet moved to Covent Garden under very happy auspices. The Arts Council provided a handsome capital allowance and annual subsidy; the tide of popular interest in ballet was in full flood; the fine dancers who had joined during the War still remained in the company; men who had fought in the War were rapidly returning; the prestige of the great opera-house helped to pull in the "carriage trade"; Ashton (returning from the wars) put together all his best ideas of the last ten years in one ballet *Symphonic Variations*; and Massine revived two of his best Diaghilev ballets for the company. At this time the Sadlers Wells Ballet had no competition; the touring Ballet-Russe companies had degenerated during the War so far that they could not be taken seriously, and the Sadlers Wells Ballet was now regarded (with much justice) as the finest in the Western world.

Before very long, however, the company settled into a rut which was in effect a continuation of the rut which it occupied in 1938–39, and the expressionist policy exerted its inevitable effect. One by one the soloists with the most individuality and personality left the company—Gordon Hamilton, Celia Franca, Robert Helpmann, June Brae, Gillian Lynne and many others—and the dancers promoted to take their place were not in fact able to do so. It was not that they lacked talent; the South African dancer Nadia Nerina, for example, showed a strong personality and admirable joie de vivre as soon as she was given solo rôles in the junior company, but then she was moved to the senior company and kept for a long time in the corps de ballet there. When she began to dance solo rôles again she showed some of her previous gaiety and personality, but usually she was severely miscast in rôles such as Odette-Odile and the Prélude in *Les Sylphides*; she accordingly lost some of her animation, and failed to mature artistically.

Like the Vic-Wells Ballet, the Sadlers Wells Ballet remained almost completely dependent on imported ballerinas; but even the ballerinas who came in from outside (such as Violetta Elvin from the Bolshoy in Moscow and Moira Shearer from the International Ballet) showed a disappointing failure to mature artistically; the shining exception was Beriosova from the Grand Ballet de Monte Carlo and the Metropolitan Ballet. In contrast to their opposite numbers in the Vic-Wells Ballet (June Brae, Pearl Argyle and Margot Fonteyn) the post-war dancers suffered from the fact that there was in London no Nicolas Legat to help them to tackle the problems involved in the interpretation of the major classical rôles; but their failure to mature was also due in considerable measure to the unstimulating quality of the artistic climate at Covent Garden. The corps de ballet showed exactly the same stodginess as before the War, though the technical standard was very much higher.

The shortage of real ballerinas became very apparent after 1950, during the long periods when Margot Fonteyn was unable to dance because of injuries or ill-health; her absence, combined with the poor quality of the new ballets and the general decline in interest in theatre in England, caused the box-office takings to slip considerably. Now, for the first time in many years, it was sometimes possible to obtain the cheaper seats for the Sadlers Wells Ballet without booking them a long time in advance.

The successive returns of Margot Fonteyn to the company did not make as much difference as one might have expected. By this time her dancing showed clearly the long-term effects of an expressionist artistic policy. There was never any pressure on her to conform to a mechanical ideal of uniformity, as there was on the others: as the prima ballerina on whom the fortunes of the company largely depended she was in a privileged position. Year by year she worked hard with the best available teachers, and her dancing improved steadily in line, breadth of movement, fluidity and musicality, but at the same time it declined in personality and emotional expressiveness; this had the paradoxical result that her prestige continued to grow while she gradually lost a great deal of her power to move audiences. This was not apparent to those who saw her for the first time during and after the War, but it was distressingly clear to those who had witnessed her pre-War triumphs as Odette-Odile and Giselle; even such great admirers of her work as Caryl Brahms and P. W. Manchester regretfully admitted that her post-War dancing failed to move them. Her talent was clearly outstanding, she had had training under a series of distinguished Russian teachers (including Astafieva, Legat and Preobazhenskaya), and she had the chance of dancing all the big classical rôles under good conditions; but she was misled by the artistic climate of the company into putting all her energy into perfecting her technique, and did not seem to realize the decline in the more subtle aspects of her interpretations. (It was not until 1953 that she came to grips with this problem—and then results were electrifying.)

One of the most striking features of the post-War period of the Sadlers Wells Ballet was the series of unexpectedly brilliant performances by various dancers in ballets arranged for the company by guest choreographers. Two such performances were those given by Harold Turner in the leading male character rôles in *La Boutique Fantasque* and *Le Tricorne*. No less devastating was the performance given by Margaret Dale in the central comic rôle in Roland Petit's ballet *Ballabile*; this rôle was created for Anne Negus (who amazed audiences by suddenly showing an admirable sense of humour), but Margaret Dale (who took it over from Anne Negus) was even more delightful. Such performances as these made it clear that there was a great deal of talent in the company which in normal circumstances had no chance of making itself visible.

The developments within the Sadlers Wells Ballet after the end of the War can best be understood against the background of parallel developments in the junior company, formed in 1946 to perform at the Sadlers Wells Theatre. Here the effects of an expressionist policy were unmistakable, for they were not obscured by any reserve of artistic vitality carried forward from the stimulating war-time period. This company was formed very largely from senior pupils of the Sadlers Wells School with little or no previous stage experience. For several years the junior company had exactly the same difficulty in building up an audience that the Vic-Wells Ballet had had in the early thirties; the new company had the advantage of reflected glory from the main company and a theatre now solidly established as a home of ballet, but it had no Markova, and showed no capacity for developing a Margot Fonteyn. Moreover it was crippled by the new ballets commissioned for it by Ninette de Valois, for nearly all of these were little more than insipid suites of divertissements, and gave the young dancers no chance to mature artistically. Though they gradually learned stage presence and professional slickness, and some gave hints of outstanding talent, they made no apparent artistic progress, and at times even slipped back. (Quite a number of the most independent-minded of the dancers left in 1947, when the junior company was reorganized.)

Because of the great post-War prestige of the Sadlers Wells company the Sadlers Wells School attracted many of the best dancers from all over England and the Commonwealth, and the best of these were quickly taken into the junior company. Though one must assume that dancers entering the school possessed many varieties of temperament, the school and the company seemed capable of fostering the development of only one type of dancer—the bright, perky, demi-caractère type of danseuse represented before the War by Mary Honer and Elizabeth Miller and now by Elaine Fifield (who became the prima ballerina of the junior company).

One danseuse, however, managed to retain some qualities of lyricism and nobility which she had brought with her from South Africa. This was Patricia Miller, who clearly had the talent to become a great classical dancer; but she lacked a great teacher, fine models to copy and the stimulus of suitable parts, so that her progress was inevitably very slow.

Much the same was true of the male dancers, a number of whom showed outstanding talent—notably Pirmin Trecu (who showed from time to time that he was capable of developing into a great classical dancer), the brilliant comedian Stanley Holden, and the versatile dramatic dancer David Blair. These men would have been ornaments to any ballet company in the world, and were in fact better than their opposite numbers in the main company. This was made plain when Ninette de Valois produced *The Rake's Progress* for the junior company in 1952: this was the first modern ballet of real stature which was staged for the junior company, and all the male dancers took full advantage of their opportunities; David Blair, in the title rôle, failed to achieve the same elegance in the first scene as Helpmann, but in the mad scene he was better than any dancer yet seen in the part. Unfortunately he had little support from the sentimental and insipid dancing of various ballerinas in the rôle of the Betrayed Girl.

With the gradual strengthening in the repertoire of the junior company, and the parallel weakening in the standard of new choreography and performance in the main company, the differences between the two companies became much less marked. In 1952–53, however, the transfer of the two best dancers of the Theatre Ballet (Beriosova and David Blair) to the senior company, and the sudden flowering in the art of Margot Fonteyn, made the differences as prominent as ever.

By this time the Sadlers Wells organization was very solidly established with the help of most of the money allotted to ballet by the Arts Council, and possessed two fine theatres and a flourishing school: it was in effect the British State Ballet, and had developed a style of its own so distinct that even when dancers joined it after considerable experience in other companies they were profoundly influenced by it. (Moira Shearer, however, retained her own style, and so did Beriosova.)

Compared with the styles used in some other State Ballets the Sadlers Wells style is distinguished by its relative freedom from mannerisms and the very high average level of neatness and precision: the dancers perform exactly as they have been rehearsed, adding none of the sentimental flicks of the wrist typical of the Paris Opéra. Not even the Jooss dancers show more meticulous attention to detail: lines intended to be straight are exactly straight, feet all come down in time to the music, and heads all incline at the same angle. This extreme precision is characteristic of the troupes of Tiller and Bluebell girls, who have had great success on the Continent for generations, and in fact English girls with their strong sense of discipline seem better at precision dancing than those of any other nationality: it is completely unattainable with, for example, French girls. English critics often criticize the Sadlers Wells Ballet severely for the raggedness of its corps de ballet, but their standards in this matter have been formed by the Sadlers Wells Ballet itself, and are in fact very high.

From a technical point of view the Sadlers Wells style represents a mixture of the three most important styles taught in England—R.A.D., Cecchetti and Russian; all three styles are taught at the Sadlers Well School.

The most striking feature of the Sadlers Wells style in the forties was that the line was pushed as far as possible in the direction of virtuosity, even though a certain restraint prevented the dancing from seeming acrobatic in the American manner. In the arabesque the raised leg was pulled up as high as possible, and the toe was bent upwards so hard that it made a definite angle with the leg; at the same time the torso was bent up sharply at the waist, and the front arm was raised so high that it nearly touched the face. There was an enormous emphasis on neatness in knees and feet: the knee was pulled back so strongly that the leg seemed likely to break in two, while toes were pointed so hard that the instep bulged out and the toe nearly bent back the wrong way. The effect of all this was to produce a line made up of a variety of angles with no overall rhythm: this line might even be called expressionist, by contrast with the classical harmony of the line of a great dancer like Spessivsteva.

Towards the end of the forties and in the early fifties the line improved enormously (perhaps because of contemporary changes in R.A.D. training); but in its dynamic qualities the Sadlers Wells style remained much as before. All emphasis was concentrated on the big spectacular steps, and on a bright brittle quality of movement. The small connecting-up steps (such as the *glissade*, the *pas-de-bourrée* and the *temps lié*) were performed in a desultory manner, the *plié* was shallow, heels were rarely put down even when this was essential for proper *ballon* and elevation, and arm-movements were lacking in subtlety and expressiveness. These faults did not prevent dancers from achieving the brittle quality which was clearly in demand, and in fact they helped the dancers to give an impression of neatness with the least possible effort; but they made quite impossible the achievements of the subtleties of phrasing necessary in poetic rôles, and slow sustained movements became dull and meaningless. In the same way the dancers seemed to find it difficult to achieve real brilliance in footwork (as distinct from neatness): the *élan* which derives from the elastic snap of the foot into a stretched position as the foot leaves the floor was rarely visible, and when the choreography made really exacting demands on footwork (e.g. towards the end of the pas de quatre of the Cygnets in Act II of *Le Lac des Cygnes*) the characteristic Sadlers Wells neatness was noticeably absent. Though the phrasing was usually far better than at the Paris Opéra, the dancers rarely filled out the music or made full use of the stage; even in big steps of elevation they remained neat and clipped, never achieving the nobility and freedom characteristic of the Russian school at its best. For this reason the typical Sadlers Wells danseuse did fairly well in *Coppélia*, but she was hopelessly at sea in *Les Sylphides*: even Margot Fonteyn was dull in the latter ballet.

The male dancer suffered much less from the defects of the style, counteracting them with his natural vigour, and was in fact far more troubled by the lack of good male rôles. Neither the Petipa ballets nor Ashton's pseudo-classical ballets provided much scope for the danseur, and the main company particularly remained weak in good male soloists. It was characteristic of the artistic policy of this company that Harold Turner was retired in 1951, when he had established himself (in the rôles of the Cancan Dancer in *La Boutique Fantasque* and the Miller in *Le Tricorne*) as one of the finest living character dancers, and was in fact dancing better than ever: there was no one in the company capable of replacing him.

The danseuses have of course also been affected by the lack of stimulating rôles in new ballets, but the Sadlers Wells repertoire has always included a number of ballets such as *Giselle*, *Le Lac des Cygnes* and *Les Sylphides* which give fine opportunities to the ballerina. The tragedy for the Sadlers Wells ballerinas was that all these ballets demanded qualities of romantic mystery and poetry which they could not hope to achieve in the artistic climate in which they lived.

In theory this climate should have fostered a high standard of performance in expressionist ballets, whatever the deficiencies in the performances of the classical-romantic ballets. For some reason, however, Ninette de Valois gave very little prominence to expressionist ballets at Covent Garden, in spite of her deep understanding of this genre and the great popularity of the best of them. Though she regarded Massine as a genius she dropped *La Boutique Fantasque* from the repertoire in 1950 and presented *Le Tricorne* very seldom after 1949, while she declined to add to the repertoire such major expressionist ballets as *Le Sacre du Printemps*, *Les Noces* and *La Symphonie Fantastique*. Moreover the artistic climate inhibited the emergence of artists capable of taking the place of Harold Turner, June Brae and Robert Helpmann in the leading rôles of expressionist ballets; the revival of *Checkmate* at Covent Garden with e.g. Philip Chatfield as the Red Knight and Pamela May or Beryl Grey as the Black Queen was painfully insipid compared with the original production.

The basic weaknesses in the Sadlers Wells artistic policy were shown exceptionally clearly in the new production of *Le Lac des Cygnes*, mounted early in 1953 for the main company by Ninette de Valois herself. This production was excellent in many ways, and represented a major interruption in the steady progress of the company toward ossification. The décors and costumes designed by Leslie Hurry were quite free from the incongruous surrealist devices which had disfigured his earlier work on this ballet, and his superbly colourful costumes for Act III were worthy of Bakst. The lighting was entrusted to a specialist (John Sullivan), and though it was rather lacking in mystery it had the great merit of concentrating light exactly where it was needed (i.e. on the dancers). The small changes made by Ninette de Valois in the choreography showed both intelligence and good taste: she mainly devoted herself to elaborating the stage patterns in order to make effective use of an enlarged corps de ballet, following the example set by Balanchine. But this new production had two defects. One of these defects—the pas de six added by Ashton to Act I, with its laboured attempt at a climax of virtuosity in the Petipa manner—was of small importance. The other defect—desperately inadequate performances in the main rôles—was of the utmost gravity, for it is precisely in ballets like *Le Lac des Cygnes* and *Giselle* that one must expect the dancers of a State ballet to show to best advantage. Nadia Nerina was seriously miscast in the rôle of Odette-Odile, while Beryl Grey was graceful but dull, showing little dramatic ability or feeling for the mysterious poetry of the rôle. The company's leading male dancer, Michael Somes, suggested as usual that he would be much happier dancing Prince Siegfried if his arms had been amputated. But the most astonishing performance was that given by Rowena Jackson, suddenly promoted to stardom over the head of Beriosova: to all appearances the only qualification this clumsy dancer had for the rôle of Odette-Odile was a fabulous gift for turning to the right. The contrast between her and Beriosova (dancing with her usual lyricism and nobility in the rôle of a Swan Leader) could scarcely have been more violent or more characteristic of the Sadlers Wells Ballet at this stage in its development.

But even this contrast paled beside those which appeared when Margot Fonteyn began to dance Odette-Odile once again in May, 1953, after a long absence followed by some weeks in light rôles. Each of the three performances which she gave as Odette-Odile was rightly regarded by the public as an artistic event of outstanding importance; after each final curtain she received the prolonged and thunderous ovation which the London public accords the supreme artist in a great part. In these performances Margot Fonteyn broke clean away from the remote and enigmatic mask which she had adopted during the War and perfected at Covent Garden. In fact she danced with all the warmth, humanity, spontaneity and vitality which she had shown in the late thirties; but the effect she created was much richer than before, since she was able to base her interpretation on a far more highly developed technique and a more subtle musicality, and she brought out innumerable nuances of characterization which had been outside the range of the teen-age Margot Fonteyn of the Vic-Wells Ballet. Here, for once, was an artist able to make Odile just as convincing as Odette: it was hard to believe that the hard and vicious but infinitely sensual and alluring Odile of Act III was performed by the same artist that danced the tragic, mysterious and disturbingly vulnerable Odette of Acts II and IV.

Between Margot Fonteyn and the rest of the company (apart from Beriosova) the gap was just as immense and unbridgeable as that which separated Spessivsteva from the other dancers of the Paris Opéra. If the Sadlers Wells Ballet had any dancers able to do justice to the smaller solo rôles of *Lac*, the casting was so consistently bad that this was not apparent to the public. Michael Somes (though a fine solid partner) gave no sign that he had ever had any contact with the great Russian tradition; when he performed the *grands jetés* of his solo he lifted his shoulders and strained his arms and neck like a bad acrobat, and he managed to go through all four acts without making any change in his facial expression—apart from occasionally giving a heightened suggestion of vacuousness by leaving his mouth open.[1] (Even when Odile directed at him, from a distance of a few inches, glances of overpowering seductiveness, he remained as wooden as ever.) Pauline Clayden and Avril Navarre were almost equally badly miscast in the pas de trois: though this is probably the most rewarding item of its kind in the entire classical repertoire, they made very little of it, and at the end of the coda their dancing was no more than a desperate scurry to keep up with the music. The pas de quatre of the Cygnets was just as clumsy as ever: not one of the eight feet involved in this bravura number seemed to make much effort to point when in the air, and the standard achieved would have disgraced the end-of-term show of a good ballet school.

In 1937 the defects of the company as a whole seemed of small importance when Margot Fonteyn was on the stage, and the same was true in 1953. In both years, however, these defects were of profound significance: they showed the fundamental contradiction between an expressionist artistic policy and a repertoire based largely on a classical-romantic tradition.

George Balanchine (b. 1904)

The first company joined by Balanchine after leaving Blum (Les Ballets 1933) did not give full expression to his own temperament and ideas, for this company had been formed by Edward James as a peace-offering to his wife Tilly Losch, being intended to give her the chance to star as a dancer. (Tilly Losch was a Viennese artist with some experience in mime and a certain amount of training in ballet and the free dance; she had "danced" in a number of Hollywood films, but in fact she was no more of a dancer than Ida Rubinstein.)

Balanchine brought with him from the Monte Carlo company his associates Kokhno and Bérard, and together they devised six ballets which faithfully continued the late-Diaghilev tradition of pretentious triviality. *L'Errante*, for example, had semi-transparent décor and special lighting effects devised by Chelichev, and was in the same genre as *Ode*; Nabokov, the composer of *Ode*, provided choral music for another ballet *Job*. Without Diaghilev's genius the cocktail ballets had little success, and the company disbanded after seasons in Paris and London.

Nevertheless the performances of this company made a strong impression on Lincoln Kirstein, a wealthy young American balletomane who became so fired with enthusiasm for what he considered to be Balanchine's genius that he decided to bring him to America and put him at the head of both a ballet school

---

[1] This artist was obviously doing his best; but by temperament he was quite unsuited to the *danseur noble* rôles almost invariably allotted to him. (He showed remarkable *élan* and sense of character as the Cossack Chief in *La Boutique Fantasque*.) Another artist consistently miscast was Pauline Clayden: she danced brilliantly on the rare occasions that she received rôles giving scope to her dramatic gifts.

and a ballet company. He therefore joined together with a wealthy friend (Edward M. M. Warburg[1]) to found the School of American Ballet at Hartford, Connecticut,[2] in 1934; and as soon as the school was launched he and his associates began to make plans for the formation of a ballet company out of the students of the school. Kirstein announced that the aim of the school was "to further the tradition of classical theatrical dancing in order to provide adequate material for the growth of a new art in America". It was clear that Kirstein saw both "classical theatrical dancing" and "a new art in America" entirely in terms of Balanchine's style, and in fact Balanchine had as much of a free hand in America as Jooss at Dartington Hall. Though Balanchine's productions received a cool reception for some time, Kirstein stuck to his friend with unbounded loyalty, and his faith in him never seemed to slacken. Seldom in ballet history has a choreographer had such a loyal patron, manager and publicist. But for Kirstein, Balanchine might easily have fallen into obscurity after the break-up of the Diaghilev Ballet.

The American Ballet (with Balanchine as artistic director, maître de ballet and sole choreographer) gave its first performance at Hartford, Connecticut, in December, 1944, only a few months after the formation of the school; clearly neither Balanchine nor Kirstein felt under any compulsion to make haste slowly. In the Spring of 1935 the company gave a two-week season in New York; half the repertoire consisted of ballets from the repertoire of Les Ballets 1933, but it also included *Serenade* (the model for innumerable later "classic ballets") and a rather feeble college-boy comedy *Alma Mater*. The New York critics—who had recently seen the Blum-de Basil-Massine company in its youthful prime—gave a cool reception to the new Balanchine company. Over a year later Irving Deakin wrote:

> It is too early to pass anything like a final judgment on the School of the American Ballet. Dancers cannot be made in a year or two or three. But when the American Ballet Company bids for public favour on a professional basis, competes with professional companies on the same stages, charges the public the same prices that are charged by professionals, then one must, perforce, judge them by professional standards. . . . Judged by any professional standards the American Ballet Company, in the public performances I have seen, has been, for the most part, woefully amateurish.[3]

Balanchine and his associates were not disheartened by the cool reception in New York, and made plans for a coast-to-coast tour. Unfortunately the

---

[1] Both Lincoln Kirstein and Edward Warburg belonged to wealthy American merchant and banking families. According to Anatole Chujoy, Edward Warburg left the organization three years later for personal reasons which had nothing to do with ballet. ("New York City Ballet—a Chronology"—article in *Ballet Today*, July, 1950.)

[2] The school later moved to New York.

[3] *Ballet Profile*, p. 147.

managing agency left the company stranded almost at the start of the tour, and the company had to return home. Losses had been heavy, and the directors gladly accepted an offer from the Metropolitan Opera in New York to provide the ballets in the opera seasons.

The offer came to Balanchine and his associates because of a recent change in the management of the Metropolitan Opera, which had become extremely fusty. No doubt the American Ballet seemed to Edward Johnson (the new director) as likely to help in establishing a less dreary atmosphere in the Metropolitan, and its grave deficiencies as a self-sufficient professional ballet company were not of great importance at the Metropolitan, where ballet played only a small part in the opera seasons.

The association between the American Ballet and the Metropolitan Opera did not work well, and was unsatisfactory to both parties. Balanchine and his associates wanted to stage a number of ballets and gradually build up a repertoire, whereas the management of the Metropolitan wanted only dances in the operas, and refused to give facilities for the staging of independent ballets. The association with the Metropolitan lasted for three years, but it began to show obvious signs of wear in 1936: in this year Balanchine produced a choreographic version of Gluck's opera *Orpheus* (using the most wildly iconoclastic costumes and décor by Chelichev) which was clearly intended as a gesture of defiance. In the Spring of 1937 the ballet company produced a Stravinsky festival in which Balanchine presented three Stravinsky ballets—*Apollon Musagète, Le Baiser de la Fée* and *Jeu de Cartes*—and then the Metropolitan Opera decided not to renew its contract with the American Ballet. The latter thereupon ceased to exist.

Meanwhile Kirstein had begun work with a small company, Ballet Caravan, which he first organized in the Spring of 1936. This semi-permanent group consisted at first of twelve dancers, but was later expanded to fifteen dancers, drawn partly from the ranks of the American Ballet and partly from the senior students of the school. This company was revived each year until 1939, performing in Summer theatres in small towns and in colleges each Summer in between the opera seasons; clearly it had been inspired by the small groups which go on tour in Russia during the Summer holidays of the Maryinsky and Bolshoy dancers. After the dissolution of the American Ballet in 1937 it expanded its tours and even appeared briefly in New York; it made its last appearance in 1940 at the New York World's Fair in a dancing "commercial" for the Ford Motor Company.

The artistic policy of this company reflected clearly Kirstein's own personal taste: most of the ballets had books by him, and several of the ballets had décor and costumes by the "symbolist-realist" painters whose works he collected and publicized.

By far the most important of the Ballet Caravan productions was *Billy the Kid*, produced in 1938 with book by Kirstein, choreography by Eugene Loring, music by the fine American composer Aaron Copland, and décor and costumes by the "symbolist-realist" painter Jared French. Though *Billy the Kid* was regarded in its day as a pioneer ballet, the frontier as a subject had been done to death by the American free dancers long before 1938; and though the title rôle gave its interpreters an opportunity for a fine display of masculine virtuosity, the rest of the ballet showed much the same blend of painstaking naturalism and pretentious symbolism as the "symbolist-realist" paintings. (Balanchine composed no ballets for this company.)

In the Spring of 1941 Kirstein and Balanchine brought together what remained of both the American Ballet and Ballet Caravan in a new company for the purposes of a goodwill tour of Latin America under official auspices— the U.S. Office for Co-ordination of Commercial and Cultural Relations between the American Republics; this tour formed part of a broad campaign to counter the danger of a German invasion of Dakar. The company (the second American Ballet) visited twelve countries in seven months; half its repertoire consisted of Balanchine ballets and half of Ballet Caravan ballets.

It was at this time that Balanchine first began to specialize in "classic ballets" (i.e. abstract music-interpretations); both the new ballets he composed for the company (*Ballet Imperial* and *Concerto Barocco*) were of this character, and so were two of his three revivals (*Apollon* and *Serenade*).

After the end of the South American tour Kirstein and Balanchine intended to take the company on tour across America, but once again they were disappointed—this time by the entry of the United States into the War. The excitements of the War distracted attention from ballet; male dancers were rapidly being called up, and there were already two companies permanently on tour. In order to preserve the Balanchine ballets in the repertoire of the American Ballet, Kirstein offered them to Lucia Chase for incorporation in the Ballet Theatre repertoire. But she and her managing director (J. Alden Talbot) refused the offer, and so Balanchine took his ballets to the Ballet Russe de Monte Carlo, which was badly in need of new productions. Balanchine continued to direct the School of American Ballet, but now he was also chief choreographer to the Ballet Russe de Monte Carlo and in effect its artistic director. It was at this time that he really established himself in the United States as an important choreographer. He continued the policy he had already begun with the American Ballet, reviving all the "classic ballets" he had produced up to then, and composing a new one—*Danses Concertantes*. He also staged new versions of one of his productions for Les Ballets 1933, *Mozartiana*, and of the two Stravinsky ballets he had composed while at the Metropolitan.

Kirstein was drafted into the army in 1942. As soon as he was released in 1946 he began to make plans with Balanchine for the formation of still another company—Ballet Society. This was not intended to compete with the two long-established professional touring companies, Ballet Russe de Monte Carlo and Ballet Theatre: instead, it conformed to the pattern of semi-professional local companies to be found all over the United States and Canada. (These companies are usually formed out of the pupils of the local school, and present short seasons at long intervals.) Though only semi-professional, Ballet Society had the great advantage of operating in New York, and so could call on the services of a certain number of experienced professionals. In fact it was rather like the pre-War London Ballet Club, except that it worked on a much larger scale and disposed of much larger funds. One of the aims of Ballet Society was the encouragement of young choreographers, but nearly all the ballets were composed by Balanchine, and the organization was in effect a revival of the American Ballet on a new basis.

There was no intention that Ballet Society should meet its expenses from the sale of tickets. Its aim was the production of ballets, and Kirstein kept his losses down to a reasonable figure by limiting the number of performances in each season. The original plan was for the performances to be open only to those who subscribed to the entire series, but this proved to be unsatisfactory, for the audience was a very narrow one, and in 1948 a series of performances was given at the New York City Center for which seats were sold to the public in the normal way.

The following season Ballet Society was attached to the New York City Opera, providing dances in the operas and giving performances of pure ballet twice a week. The City of New York had come into possession of the City Center through a tax default by a masonic lodge. Finding themselves in possession of a large building with a number of offices and a large auditorium, the New York authorities decided to operate the building as a centre of popular-priced entertainment, making arrangements with appropriate organizations to make their home at the City Center, add "New York City" to their names, and present seasons of opera and drama. The success of the performances of Ballet Society as part of the opera company induced the New York authorities to invite Kirstein and Balanchine to establish the ballet company as an independent organization with the title New York City Ballet, with seasons of its own at intervals through the year.

The various City Center companies received no direct cash subsidy, but indirectly they were subsidized by having at their disposal the City Center theatre and escaping the enormous rents characteristic of Broadway; in this way they were able to charge cheap prices and so build up a steady audience. Moreover the various companies worked together, so that the losses on one season could be made up by the profits on another. In fact conditions were similar in many ways to those enjoyed by the various sections of the Vic-Wells organization before the War,[1] and the New York City Ballet flourished like the Vic-Wells company for precisely the same reasons. In spite of severe flaws in its artistic policy (which was clearly inspired to a considerable extent by that of the Sadlers Wells Ballet) it had a tremendous advantage over its rivals, and flourished accordingly. The two companies were in fact blood-brothers, and their directors made an agreement for reciprocal visits and the exchange of choreographers.

In exactly the same way that the Vic-Wells Ballet drew strength from the Ballet Club, the New York City Ballet (with Balanchine as artistic director and Kirstein as Director General[2]) absorbed nearly all the finest artists in Ballet Theatre—notably Nora Kaye, Jerome Robbins, Hugh Laing and Diana Adams. There were two reasons why the New York City Ballet was able to do this: one was the rapid degeneration in the artistic standard of Ballet Theatre, and the other was the fact that the New York City Ballet could offer a reasonably settled life for part of the year in New York, instead of a killing existence of constant touring. Though the New York City Ballet was very far from being a paradise for the dancers, it looked like paradise to anyone in other American companies.

Unlike Ninette de Valois, the directors of the New York City Ballet commissioned ballets from Antony Tudor. There was exactly the same violent conflict between his ideals and outlook and those of the company directors as there had been when he was employed by Ninette de Valois as a dancer, but now he was world-famous, and under the circumstances it would have been difficult to ignore him; on the other hand the ballets commissioned from him gave very little scope to his talents—*Camille*, for example, was given to him at the last minute after another choreographer had abandoned it—and he was unable to do much with the company, in spite of the fact that he had three of the best Ballet Theatre artists at his disposal.

One cannot regard the style of dancing in the New York City Ballet as belonging specifically to this company, in the same way that the Sadlers Wells style belongs to the two Sadlers Wells companies. Ever since the beginning of American ballet the dancers have moved rapidly from one company to another, with an almost complete change in the corps de ballet each year, and there is a distinctive American style which is common to all the American companies. Nevertheless Balanchine has played a large part in the evolution of this style

---

[1] It seems likely that the New York City authorities were to some extent inspired by the example of the pre-War Vic-Wells, as well as by the municipal theatres of the continent of Europe.

[2] It is typical of Kirstein that in the "billing" at the head of the programme he put Balanchine's name first as artistic director, followed by that of Jerome Robbins (associate artistic director) and Leon Barzin (musical director); then came his own name, and finally that of Jean Rosenthal (technical director). Very few men in his position would have shown such modesty.

(at the same time being powerfully influenced by it) and it is in his company that it has achieved its most clear-cut expression.

The style is seen at its best in the dancing of Tanaquil Leclercq in humorous rôles. This dancer, who was trained in the School of American Ballet and joined Ballet Theatre in 1946, is the American equivalent of Nadia Nerina and Elaine Fifield. In the comedy rôles which suit her, she dances superbly, with irresistible assurance and joie de vivre, and a gay, inconsequent, lightly satirical quality that reminds one of Danny Kaye at his best. Her dancing has a strong element of acrobatics—movements are done in such a way as to emphasize their technical difficulty rather than disguise it—but in comedy rôles this acrobatic quality is not at all objectionable, and in fact is an essential element in the humour. Tanaquil Leclercq is such a fine comedienne that in comedy rôles she is invariably under-parted: no choreographer takes full advantage of her superb sense of humour, and she has to make bricks without straw. In serious rôles, on the other hand, the defects of her style are clearly apparent: the athleticism gets in the way of any depth of interpretation.

The American style is also seen to very good advantage in the dancing of men like Jerome Robbins, Michael Kidd and Paul Godkin in the comedy ballets of Jerome Robbins. This dancing has much the same insouciant brio as that of Tanaquil Leclercq, though naturally it has a more virile and violent quality. It is sad to see such admirable dancers decline into embarrassed dummies when adorned with ridiculous berets and marshalled in long lines in Balanchine's "classic ballets"; and in exacting serious rôles like Petrouchka even a highly intelligent dancer like Jerome Robbins gives a mechanical and insensitive performance. In any rôles which give no scope to athleticism the American dancer (whether male or female) is at a great disadvantage.

The trouble with this athleticism is that it suppresses all light-and-shade in dancing. There is little attempt to retain the characteristic flavour of each type of movement: all that seems to matter to the dancer is the achievement of the highest possible speed, the greatest possible elevation and the raising of the leg as high as possible in the air. Little attention is paid to severe faults such as stiff arms, twisted hips and fussy hand movements, and little use is made of épaulement (shoulder-work) and head-movements. The range of moods and emotions which the typical American dancer can tackle with success is accordingly limited.

Balanchine is not to be held wholly or even mainly responsible for these aspects of American ballet. Tendencies in this direction were present long before he arrived—the American ballerina Augusta Maywood showed very similar tendencies in the hey-day of the Romantic Ballet; but his own expressionist variety of pseudo-classicism fitted in well with these tendencies, and helped to steer American ballet in this direction. It is conceivable that if Fokine or Tudor had had the same support as Balanchine they might have succeeded in making the development of American classical dancing rather more diversified. (We must not forget that Isadora Duncan with her noble and poetic simplicity was very much an American.) American ballerinas are undoubtedly aware of certain deficiencies in their performances in classical parts, and have worked hard in an attempt to remedy them: unfortunately they have often taken Markova as a model, and have copied her worst faults—notably her poked-forward head and hunched shoulders.

It is no accident that after Nora Kaye entered the New York City Ballet she lost many of the fine qualities which had been fostered in her by Tudor, in spite of the fact that *Lilac Garden* was revived by the New York City Ballet for her, and Tudor composed several new ballets for the New York City Ballet in which she had the principal parts. This decline in the quality of her dancing took a different form from the corresponding decline in the quality of the dancing of Margot Fonteyn at Covent Garden; instead of a loss of vitality and individuality there was a loss of subtlety and a great increase in melodramatic exaggeration. Clearly Balanchine's artistic policy was not as firmly opposed to the development of individuality as the expressionist policy across the Atlantic; nevertheless it gave dancers no encouragement to develop subtlety, grace or poetry.

Though on the whole the New York City Ballet dancers showed more individuality than the Sadlers Wells dancers, it was obvious that the performance of a relatively large number of Balanchine ballets (in which the stress was entirely on precision) tended to develop a certain monotony and dullness in their dancing.

Fortunately this tendency was counteracted by the fact that the company was able to attract the best American dancers, and also by the fact that they were not tired out by continual touring like those in other American companies. (The New York City Ballet also went on tour, but had a number of relatively long seasons in New York each year.) For these two reasons the general standard of technique increased with astonishing speed: by 1952 the company looked quite polished, whereas in 1950 there was little discipline and the corps de ballet was ragged.

It was noticeable that the men shone with much dimmer lustre than the women: the company included a number of ballerinas that would have done credit to almost any ballet company, but the men (barring Hugh Laing and Michael Maule) were sadly lacking in personality and dramatic ability. This was presumably due to the fact that Balanchine ballets made little use of men, and gave them no opportunity to mature artistically.

Because of their monotony and sentimentality the "classic ballets" of Balanchine gave little stimulus to designers, and in fact most of them were

The Ballets-Suédois in 1920: *La Maison des Fous* (Borlin, Paris, 1920).
Décor by Nils Dardel

The Marie Rambert Dancers having a class from Marie Rambert in
the studio beside the Mercury Theatre (London) in 1930: Pearl Argyle,
Harold Turner, Andrée Howard, Frederick Ashton, Prudence Hyman,
William Chappell and Robert Stuart

The de Basil-Massine company in the United States in 1936 after a rehearsal of
Le Beau Danube (Massine, Paris, 1924). *On the ground:* Borovansky, Toumanova.
Sitting: Morosova, Massine, Riabouchinska, Col. de Basil, Zorina, Shabelevsky.
Standing: Lichine, Psota, Hoyer, S. Hurok

René Blum and Léonide Massine in 1938

danced in front of curtains[1]—much to their advantage, for when they did have décor it was in a pompous baroque style that had little to do with the dancing. The costumes worn by the dancers in these ballets were alarmingly tasteless in their cut and their colour schemes; it was obvious that Balanchine's idea of the classical tradition did not exclude costumes that were inept in a typically Hollywood manner.

(b) UNSUBSIDIZED COMPANIES

We can learn relatively little from the achievements and failures of unsubsidized choreographer's companies, for such companies rarely last long, and are so crippled by financial difficulties that their leaders can show only a small proportion of their talents as company directors and choreographers. Nevertheless one cannot ignore such companies entirely, for concentration on the subsidized companies formed by expressionist and pseudo-classical choreographers gives a very inadequate idea of the potentialities of the choreographer's company.

Michel Fokine (1880–1942)

Fokine went to the United States in 1919, and lived there almost continuously from then on; at first he gave a number of solo recitals with his wife Vera Fokina, but later he occupied himself mainly with teaching. Unfortunately for him, ballet was very little developed in the United States at this time, and he was given no satisfactory opportunities of showing his talent as a choreographer: from 1919 to 1936 he frittered away his talents in New York on a succession of musical comedies and revues.

His two attempts at the production of "straight" ballet with companies formed from his students were profoundly disappointing. In 1924 he made an ambitious attempt at establishing a permanent company by founding the American Ballet; he composed a number of new ballets for this company, and presented them at the Metropolitan in New York and on tour. This enterprise ended in disaster: Fokine had no support from impresarios, he lacked the capital to rehearse his ballets properly and engage first-rate soloists, his wife Vera Fokina was far from being an ideal prima ballerina, and the romanticism of his ballets did not suit either his pupils or the public. But it was the undeveloped

---

[1] According to John Martin (*World Book of Modern Ballet*, p. 128) the advantages of curtain-staging for the "classic ballets" were discovered accidentally when Balanchine revived *Concerto Barocco* for the Ballet Russe de Monte Carlo and was unable to make use of the costumes and décor designed for the original production.

state of the American ballet public which was his worst enemy; even the Diaghilev company, with a large and varied repertoire and the powerful support of Otto Kahn and the Metropolitan Opera, did not succeed in covering its expenses, and Fokine's enterprise was doomed from the start.

In 1926–27 Fokine once again staged productions of "straight" ballet with a company he called the "Fokine Ballet". He presented this company at the Lewisohn Stadium of the College of the City of New York, and also in various auditoriums and cinema theatres on tour. Once again, however, he was crippled by lack of money, shortage of time for rehearsals, the limitations of his accustomed prima ballerina, and the fact that the dancers consisted mainly of semi-trained pupils. Tudor managed to do fine work in London under conditions almost equally unpropitious, but he had the great advantage of working in his own country with dancers who could understand all the nuances of feeling which a choreographer can only suggest by metaphor. Things were very different for Fokine in the United States: he had formed his style of choreography working in Russia with great Russian dancers, and was unable to devise a new style suited to the artists at his disposal. American audiences were well able to appreciate Fokine's classical romanticism when interpreted by Pavlova in *Le Cygne* and *Chopiniana*, but American dancers could make little of this style, which was almost as remote from them as the dances of ancient Egypt.

Antony Tudor (b. 1908)

The performances of the London Ballet, founded by Tudor in 1938 at Toynbee Hall, were admirably polished, with few of the inadequacies that were taken for granted at the semi-amateur Ballet Club; the London Ballet was a professional company, of which every member was chosen by Tudor on the basis of talent and personality, irrespective of the school at which he or she had been trained. Moreover, Tudor himself had had extensive experience as a stage manager, and was able to deal effectively with all technical problems of staging. The standard of décor, of costume, of lighting and of music was impeccably high.

Unfortunately this professional polish was achieved at the cost of disproportionate efforts by a small number of enthusiasts, for Tudor never had the backing he needed to build up a satisfactory repertoire, and it was impossible to draw a large audience to a theatre in such an inaccessible part of the East End. The décors were painted by the designer Hugh Stevenson on the floor of a hired rehearsal room. The theatre itself was not available except on the day of the show, and in order to cut down the cost of hiring rehearsal rooms Tudor often took rehearsals in his tiny flat.

The most striking feature of the performances at Toynbee Hall (and later at the Arts Theatre, after Tudor had gone to New York) was the high standard of individuality, intelligence and imagination in the performances of the whole company. In this respect Tudor's artistic policy was a natural development of that pursued by Marie Rambert at the Ballet Club—but it was also implicit in his choreographic style, which demanded this individuality in all the dancers. Like all the great choreographers of the past, from Noverre to Fokine, Tudor had no use for a corps de ballet of robots, and his professed objective was a company consisting entirely of soloists or potential soloists. Not all the dancers in the London Ballet reached this ideal; Legat was dead, and though there were many ballet teachers in England, very few taught a style that was acceptable to Tudor, so that he had to take into the company a certain number of dancers who were unable to do justice to the solo rôles given to them. Nevertheless the general standard was high from the very start; Peggy van Praagh showed the full range of a remarkable talent which had received relatively little scope at the Ballet Club, another Craske pupil Gerd Larsen showed admirable depth of feeling in the first solo of *Dark Elegies*, and the Nesta Brooking pupil Sylvia Hayden (the company's "baby ballerina") matured with the same astonishing speed as Baronova in the Blum-de Basil-Massine company in the early thirties.

Tudor aroused such loyalty in his dancers that they stuck by him in spite of the fact that he was able to pay them only starvation wages: they all had a clear appreciation of the honour of belonging to the London Ballet. For this reason he was able to keep up a high average standard of performance in female rôles. In male rôles he was not so fortunate: English male dancers with solid techniques were very rare at this time.

The company achieved a particularly high standard in typical Tudor ballets such as *The Planets*, *Jardin aux Lilas* and *Dark Elegies*: these demanded sincerity and imagination rather than a virtuosic technique, and the dancers responded magnificently to the demands made on them. But in *Gala Performance* (with its satire on pseudo-classicism) and in the naturalistic expressionist ballet *Judgment of Paris* they were rather out of their element. Whereas at Sadlers Wells the dancers were consistently under-parted, the Toynbee Hall dancers were constantly being expected to master new styles and nuances of mood and emotion. Since Tudor knew very well what he wanted from the dancers, it is likely that if he had been able to continue with the company he would eventually have educated his dancers to take ballets like *Gala Performance* and *Judgment of Paris* in their stride.

Tudor suffered very much from the strain of running a professional ballet company without adequate capital in a theatre where it was impossible to avoid running into debt. *Pillar of Fire* was not the only project which he had to postpone until it was too late: C. W. Beaumont published in *Design for the Ballet* some sketches by Hugh Stevenson of décor and costumes for a Tudor ballet

Kalevala, described as "in preparation". The London Ballet achieved fine things between its début at Toynbee Hall in December, 1938, and Tudor's departure for New York in the Autumn of 1939, but it is likely that these were only a small fraction of what Tudor had in mind.

Though the London Ballet inevitably ceased to progress artistically after the departure of Tudor, the remarkable success of the seasons presented by the combined London and Rambert companies at the Arts Theatre during the London blitz of 1940–41 proved that Tudor's ideas in founding this company had been basically sound, and that his ballets when adequately performed in a reasonably accessible theatre were capable of attracting and holding a broad popular audience. It was no accident that the Arts Theatre (presenting the London-Rambert company in "Lunch-Time Ballet") was one of the three theatres which alone kept open during the blitz of 1940–41: the others were the Windmill (with a variety show including nudes) and the Ambassador (with a brilliant satirical revue).

Ironically enough it was Tudor himself who arranged for the transfer of his company to the management of the impresario Harold Rubin, lessee of the Arts Theatre; after Tudor's departure for America this transfer to the West End of London provided just those conditions of permanent employment whose absence had crippled Tudor's work at Toynbee Hall.

The dissolution of the London-Rambert Ballet in 1941 had disastrous consequences. English ballet had already suffered a heavy blow at the death of Nicolas Legat early in 1937. The departure of both Tudor and Craske in 1939 dealt English ballet a second heavy blow; and the dissolution of the London-Rambert company in 1941 dissipated much of the remaining creative vitality. The extraordinary conditions prevailing during the War concealed the cumulative force of these three blows, but quite soon after the end of the War their full significance became unmistakable, in spite of the enormous expansion in the ballet audience brought about by the War, the corresponding expansion in the quantity of English ballet, the fine work done by various Cecchetti teachers (notably Idzikovsky, Nesta Brooking, Margaret Marsh and Pat Hardy) and the miraculous performances in classical rôles of Margot Fonteyn.

Roland Petit (b. 1924)

At the time when Roland Petit founded the Ballets de Paris (the Spring of 1948) he was fortunate in having a reasonably high degree of freedom of action: his backer provided him with enough capital to produce a repertoire of ballets with very expensive décors and costumes, and with his established name and his contacts in the major cities of Europe he had little difficulty in getting bookings. Within fairly wide limits he could introduce any artistic policy he liked.

Very sensibly he selected a small company of highly talented soloists: he took on a few dancers who hardly knew one foot from the other, but his principals included a number of the finest French and Franco-Russian dancers (Renée Jeanmaire, Vladimir Skouratov, Colette Marchand and Serge Perrault) and also the fine Australian dancer Gordon Hamilton, now completely cosmopolitan in style.

In Roland Petit's first production for his new company, *Les Demoiselles de la Nuit*, he broke away very definitely from the artistic policy of the Champs-Élysées company. The ballet had a strong dramatic script by the experienced dramatist Anouilh, and the various elements in the production were in harmony with the theme and each other. In the rôle of Agathe, Petit suddenly showed himself a choreographer with much more than a slick superficial talent: he could never have composed this rôle in the artistic climate of the earlier company, and it fully justified his decision to found his own company.

This decision was also justified by *Carmen*, composed by Roland Petit nine months later; with all its faults *Carmen* had one immensely vital rôle that could never have come into existence in the Champs-Élysées company.

Colette Marchand and Renée Jeanmaire both came to maturity in the leading female rôles in these two ballets: their achievements and those of Roland Petit were interdependent. It is even possible that Jeanmaire's achievements in the rôle of Carmen went beyond anything intended by Roland Petit.

Roland Petit gave no such wonderful opportunities to his male dancers—this was hardly to be expected, since he was the leading male dancer as well as the sole choreographer—and it was noticeable that Skouratov left after a few months, whereas Renée Jeanmaire and Colette Marchand stayed with Roland Petit right up to the disintegration of the company.[1] (A dancer's whole existence as an artist depends on being given the opportunity of dancing rôles which give real scope to his or her talents, and for this reason he or she is prepared to stand a great deal of hardship.)

The most disturbing feature of *Les Demoiselles de la Nuit* and *Carmen* was the extraordinary gap between the two main female rôles and the rest of the choreography: Petit seemed to have none of the powers of self-criticism which are essential in a choreographer-manager. His judgment in matters of décor was no less unsatisfactory: both his major ballets were crippled by décors so elaborate that the intervals between scenes were as long as or longer than the scenes themselves, and this caused the tension to evaporate in the intervals. Though Clavé's sets for *Carmen* were brilliantly effective, a good artistic director would have insisted that he design them in such a way as to permit quick changes, as Benois

---

[1] Jeanmaire stayed with him right up to the end of the film *Hans Christian Andersen* (1952), and then told the Press that she was leaving him. On being asked her reason she said that "Ballet dancers are sometimes rather difficult people"—a masterly understatement.

did for *Petrouchka*; *Les Demoiselles de la Nuit* failed to build up to a climax, partly because of the long intervals and partly because Petit allowed the designer (Léonor Fini) to devise a setting for the final scene which made dancing impossible. (The dancing area was covered with slanting rostrums, representing a sloping roof.) This setting belonged to the same genre as Diaghilev's cocktail settings, such as the talc stage-cloth of *La Chatte*.

The other new ballets composed by Petit and commissioned by him from other choreographers belonged so completely to the cocktail style of the Champs-Élysées company that he might just as well not have broken away from it. Typical of the ballets commissioned by him was *'Adame Miroir* (1948), with a very obscure book by Jean Genet (Cocteau's favourite poet) and choreography by Janine Charrat. This was danced by three men, and there was a great deal of pretentious but deliberately obscure symbolism associated with mirror reflections, together with some vague attempts at the suggestion of naughty perversions in the late-Diaghilev manner. This ballet belonged with *Ode* in a museum of the arty-craftiness of the twenties at its most futile. Choreographically the ballet had almost no existence.

Though *Carmen* and *Les Demoiselles de la Nuit* became for the Ballets de Paris what *The Green Table* and *Big City* were to the Ballets Jooss, they were not strong enough to keep the company going indefinitely. In 1951 Petit took his company to the United States, and after reaching Hollywood he waited for such a long time to make a film (which was constantly postponed) that his company disintegrated. It deserved a better fate, for with all its faults it was by far the most important French company. Fortunately Petit was able to re-organize his company in the Summer of 1953 under the name Les Ballets de Paris de Roland Petit: the re-organized company had Colette Marchand as its female star, but suffered from the absence of Renée Jeanmaire and Gordon Hamilton and the casting of Colette Marchand in the rôle of Carmen (and many other similar rôles in new ballets) for which she was totally unsuited —but not in her own rôle of Agathe, *Les Demoiselles de la Nuit* being excluded from the repertoire. The new company was a large one, and a few of the dancers showed real promise; but the pretentious and superficial new ballets included no rôles giving them a chance to mature as artists.

3. THE CREATIVE COMPANY

By "creative company" I mean one of which the artistic policy is primarily directed toward the production of the best possible ballets: in other words, the director is not primarily a dancer or choreographer with powerful creative needs in one of these directions, and is more interested in artistic achievement than in making money or exercising power. Such companies are very rare—not so much because a creative artistic director needs an unusual combination of qualities, but because the organization of a ballet company needs a great deal of money, and commercial backers are very disinclined to trust the judgment and administrative ability of a person who has not established himself or herself as a dancer or choreographer. (In fact they are little inclined to back even the most famous dancers and choreographers, for ballet is a risky investment which does not promise quick returns.) Non-commercial patrons are potentially more enterprising, but such patrons have almost ceased to exist since the early days of Diaghilev.

There never has been a company in which the artistic policy was ideal—i.e. it gave the maximum scope to the creative ability of the best available artists. Directors of ballet companies are fallible human beings, equipped with their fair share of obsessions and neuroses, and are always liable to have their judgment corrupted by falling in love with untalented members of their companies.[1] Moreover they have to cope with the psychological peculiarities of their artistic collaborators (who are often extremely difficult people to deal with, so obsessed with their own problems that they cannot take account of those of other people), and also with intrigues among the dancers. Intrigues tend to be less vicious in a creative company than in other types of company, for in such a company a good dancer can have some hope of advancement simply by dancing well—whereas in most companies outstanding talent is more of a hindrance than a help, for it causes jealousy; but even in creative companies at their hey-day there is a good deal of intrigue, for no company is made up entirely of dedicated artists with the outlook of a Karsavina. The creative director seeks to keep intrigue within reasonable dimensions by making a point of seeking out hidden talent and giving it a chance to flourish; some other types of director are liable to encourage intrigue, on the principle of "divide and rule".

Though the conditions in which a company operates as a creative company

[1] On the other hand they are equally likely to be inspired to bold pioneering efforts by falling in love with talented artists, as Diaghilev did when he fell in love with Nijinsky. Love provides a powerful driving force in ballet, as in every artistic enterprise.

come together very rarely and never seem to last for long, these periods are of the utmost importance in ballet history, for it is during them that nearly all the great ballets are composed: to a very large extent ballet depends for its continuing hold on the public on the heritage of these creative periods in the life of a few creative companies.

The Diaghilev company during the period 1909–13 is the supreme example of a creative company. As we have seen, Diaghilev's artistic policy was by no means flawless at this period: he often behaved badly to his artistic collaborators, and his treatment of Fokine was shameful. Nevertheless the defects of his administration were far outweighed by its merits, and the achievements of this period are of enormous importance. After 1921 the reverse was true: the defects far outweighed the merits, and the ballets of the cocktail period are with few exceptions forgotten. The history of the Diaghilev company has already been dealt with, and needs no further discussion at this point.

Rolf de Maré's Ballets-Suédois

The Diaghilev ballets of the twenties brought together some of the finest painters and composers of the day, and seemed to be in step with the latest movements in art. In fact, however, they reflected only the superficial trends of the period. This was not only the period of Elinor Glyn, Clara Bow and short skirts: it was also the period which saw the publication of *The Waste Land*, *Ulysses*, the last volumes of *À la Recherche du Temps Perdu* and Kafka's best novels, the maturity of the silent film, the flowering of modern architecture, the major achievements in music of Alban Berg and Bartok, and the hey-day of the École de Paris painters. In reality it was one of the most creative periods in the history of the world.

The isolation of the Diaghilev company from the main artistic trends of the day gave an opportunity to other avant-garde companies; but there was only one man with the resources and the understanding to seize this opportunity. This was Rolf de Maré, a wealthy Swedish connoisseur and art-collector, who established his company (the Ballets-Suédois) in 1920, at the very moment when Massine's neo-classical expressionism was beginning to flag.

If we allow for the fact that Diaghilev was Russian, beginning work in the field of ballet in the flood-tide of the Russian renaissance in ballet, whereas Rolf de Maré was Swedish, beginning work at a time when there were very few Swedish dancers and no Swedish ballet of any stature, we can see that the two men had much in common. Both belonged to well-to-do landowning families, and in some ways were typical *grands seigneurs* of their respective countries. Both were men of wide culture, profoundly interested in the latest developments in theatrical technique, who became professionally expert in such complex crafts as stage lighting. Unlike Diaghilev, however, Rolf de Maré had interests extending beyond theatrical dancing to the national dances of many countries, including the Far East, and built up a collection of dance-films (shot by himself) which was of considerable archaeological value. After disbanding his company he continued to take a keen interest in all kinds of dancing, establishing in Paris the Archives Internationales de la Danse (a combination of museum, library and dance-studio) and from time to time organizing international ballet competitions.

Though Rolf de Maré's achievements were limited by the inadequacy of the Swedish dancers at his disposal—very few Swedish dancers could stand comparison with even the second rank of Russian solo dancers—he had one great advantage over the post-War Diaghilev: nothing in his previous experiences acted to prevent him from encouraging his collaborators to come to grips with themes which gave full opportunities to their creative powers.

It is characteristic of the relationship between the Ballets-Suédois and the Diaghilev Ballet that Rolf de Maré accepted for production in 1921 *L'Homme et son Désir*, a ballet which Paul Claudel and Darius Milhaud had devised in Brazil. This ballet had an abstract expressionist theme of great interest, akin to that of Joyce's novel *Finnegans Wake*. They offered it to Nijinsky when he came to Brazil in 1917 with the Diaghilev company; it appealed strongly to Nijinsky, and no doubt he would have staged it if fate had been more kind to him. On the other hand Diaghilev had no inducement to use such a theme after 1920, except in a cynical way which would have infuriated Claudel and Milhaud; though he staged *Le Renard* in 1922 and *Les Noces* in 1923 it was only with great reluctance after many years of delay. (As soon as he perfected his cocktail policy he would have nothing to do with serious projects like *L'Homme et son Désir*.)

In certain important respects Rolf de Maré's artistic policy represented a development out of Diaghilev's pre-War policy. Being a rich man Rolf de Maré was able to provide whatever was called for in the way of décor, costumes, properties, lighting and orchestra, even if these were unconventional and expensive. All that mattered to him was that the final production should represent the ideas of its originators as perfectly as possible, and he persisted in this policy in spite of the fact that the expressionist style favoured by him and his chosen collaborators was bitterly attacked by the Parisian critics of the day. In the same way he persisted in his plan of keeping the company as Swedish as possible,[1] in spite of the isolation of his company from Sweden[2] and the

---

[1] The company included some Danish male dancers, some Finns, and even one English dancer (Rupert Doone), but most of the dancers were Swedish, as was the choreographer-maître de ballet Jean Borlin.

[2] In its first year (1920) the company visited only Paris and London. In its second year it went on a tour of cities in France, Spain and Belgium. It did not reach Sweden until 1923, in the midst of a long tour of cities in France, Germany, Austria, Hungary, Switzerland, Norway and Great Britain.

weaknesses of his Swedish dancers as compared with the best of the Russian émigrés. Though one must respect his patriotic determination to build a Swedish company of international stature, his integrity in this matter was perhaps somewhat ill-advised.

Another related defect of the company was its limitation to one choreographer—the only talented Swedish choreographer of the day. Rolf de Maré used a great variety of musicians, designers and writers of several different nationalities, but he remained faithful to Jean Borlin, who was not equally talented in all types of choreography.

All ballet companies are complex organizations which tend to escape through the meshes of any classification. The Ballets-Suédois in particular departed in many respects from the specifications of an ideal creative company which we might draft on the model of the Diaghilev company in its hey-day. When Rolf de Maré staged *Iberia*, for example, he arranged for Jean Borlin to have Spanish lessons from José Otero, instead of commissioning the choreography from Otero himself, and when he staged *Chopiniana* he commissioned new choreography from Borlin instead of bringing in Fokine to revive the original ballet: in this way he deprived the dancers of valuable chances of widening their range and maturing artistically. When it was no longer practicable for him to commission ballets from Borlin he dissolved the company rather than continue with other choreographers. In some respects his relationship with Borlin was akin to that of Kirstein with Balanchine. On the other hand Rolf de Maré was beyond question artistic director of the Ballets-Suédois as well as general director, and his policy of limiting himself to one choreographer, in spite of the great advantages to be derived from a more eclectic policy, might be considered a typical expression of the expressionist Zeitgeist of the early twenties.

Marie Rambert's Ballet Club

Anyone seeing the Rambert Ballet for the first time in the fifties could hardly believe that this second-rate company, performing fairly often in small theatres in provincial towns, was the origin of nearly all the creative impulses in English ballet, and that Marie Rambert was almost alone in carrying on in the thirties from the point where Diaghilev left off in the early twenties. Like Diaghilev, Marie Rambert was eventually driven to destroy what she had built up, but her creative period lasted long enough to change the face of world ballet.

In comparison with the facilities available, Marie Rambert's achievements were in some ways more impressive than Diaghilev's. In his creative period Diaghilev had enormous subsidies at his disposal; he was able to select dancers from a remarkable generation of great artists emerging in all three of the

Imperial companies, and he was able to take advantage of the fact that a choreographer of genius (Fokine) had already come to maturity. Marie Rambert, in contrast, began in England at a time when there were almost no English dancers capable of doing justice to good choreography and no choreographers at all; she had to train dancers from the elementary stage, and to work on a shoe-string in a shoe-box of a theatre without wings or flies and hardly space for a piano, not to mention the orchestra which she could not have afforded.

Though the Ballet Club was not able to afford wages for its dancers (except during the rare West-End seasons), and the smaller rôles were taken by the students of the school, it was fundamentally far more professional than the Vic-Wells Ballet. The latter company had some outstanding soloists (many of whom had started at the Ballet Club), but the minor soloists and the corps de ballet danced in a dull amateurish way, with little or no stage presence and no contact with the audience, while the décors and costumes in early Vic-Wells productions (apart from those taken over from Camargo Society productions) were dowdy and provincial until Ninette de Valois began to take advantage of the talents discovered and fostered by Marie Rambert in Sophie Fedorovitch, William Chappell and Hugh Stevenson.

As a teacher Marie Rambert had certain weaknesses and blind spots. Students trained entirely by her had technical deficiencies which held them back unless they remedied them by going to other teachers; on the other hand she had worked in the Diaghilev Ballet in its best period, collaborating with Nijinsky at the height of his creative powers, and was familiar with the Russian tradition of noble and expressive dancing. Moreover she had a fiery Polish temperament, and could not stand dullness in a dancer: she stormed at the dancers with indefatigable energy until even the most puddingy English girls developed a certain amount of stage presence and dramatic ability. The most talented of the Ballet Club dancers—notably Harold Turner, Pearl Argyle and the Craske pupil Peggy van Praagh—had the sense to go to the *classe de perfection* of Nicolas Legat, and the combination of this wonderful training and the stimulating rôles they received in the Ballet Club ballets enabled them to mature as artists, within the limits of their respective talents.

Marie Rambert had an extraordinary capacity for taking it for granted that any dancer could if necessary tackle anything; sometimes this confidence was misplaced, but on balance it gave good results. This is not to say that she did not on occasion play favourites and ignore outstanding talent because of prejudices such as an objection to the shape of a dancer's legs; nevertheless the fact that she did not suppress individuality (and indeed demanded it in everybody) made the company for a time a wonderful nursery of talent—not only in dancing, but also in choreography and décor.

Because of the creative atmosphere at the Ballet Club, fresh talent continued to emerge, and though dancers kept coming and going as they found paying jobs Marie Rambert was able to keep up an astonishingly high artistic standard; even the youngest students acquitted themselves well, apart from technical deficiencies. Whereas the Vic-Wells of the late thirties would have been unimaginable without Pearl Argyle, Margot Fonteyn, Harold Turner and Robert Helpmann, and the departure of Pearl Argyle in 1937 left a serious gap, the Ballet Club suffered losses quite as serious as this without disaster. (Pearl Argyle and Harold Turner were in fact stars of the Ballet Club who were rarely seen there after joining the Wells.)

We may doubt whether Marie Rambert had any intention of breaking away from the fashionable late-Diaghilev style when she began to present ballets: she encouraged Frederick Ashton to model himself on Balanchine and Nijinska, and later encouraged Andrée Howard to move in the same direction. On the other hand she was sufficiently catholic in her outlook to tolerate work in a quite different vein from Antony Tudor, and created an artistic climate in which new ideas could not only originate but develop steadily over a period of years. She sometimes infuriated choreographers by interfering in their work, particularly in the matter of casting, and her flair was by no means infallible, but she really did care deeply for artistic achievement, and the results of this attitude were apparent in a long series of interesting ballets—some of them masterpieces.

Unfortunately Marie Rambert had the defects of her qualities, and a time came when the latter overshadowed the former. The production of *Dark Elegies* during a West-End season in 1937 represented a turning-point in the history of the Ballet Club. Agnes de Mille in her book *Dance to the Piper* describes how Marie Rambert's interference with Tudor, and the bitter disputes which resulted, finally led Tudor to leave after this season, taking with him the best of the Ballet Club dancers. This action by Tudor was in fact long overdue, and probably it was only lack of capital which prevented him from doing it before. *Dark Elegies* was a large-scale tragic ballet that would have been completely out of place on the tiny Mercury Stage, in the midst of a repertoire consisting mainly of pseudo-classical ballets by Ashton and Andrée Howard. Moreover work of this quality was quite impossible with a semi-professional company in which most of the dancers were students in training. The organization of the Ballet Club was now obsolete: further progress demanded the maintenance of a permanent professional company—a task for which Marie Rambert was quite unfitted by temperament. (She might have succeeded with the help of a good business man as administrator and someone like Margaret Craske as ballet mistress, but it was in her nature to want to run everything herself.)

The Ballet Club was a very different institution after the departure of its best dancers and its greatest choreographer. Marie Rambert continued to encourage new talent—e.g. the choreographer Frank Staff and the dancer Sally Gilmour—but the atmosphere was rather different, and the quality of the new work was very much much lower. The Ballet Club was now in somewhat the same position as the Diaghilev Ballet after the departure of Fokine, Nijinsky, Massine and Karsavina.

The Ballet Club could no longer exist on a semi-professional basis after the outbreak of war, and continued for a time on a professional basis as one of three ballet companies controlled by Harold Rubin and centred on the Arts Theatre. When the Rambert company fused with the London Ballet of Antony Tudor, artistic leadership passed to the latter company, which had absorbed the major creative impulse of the old Ballet Club; even without Tudor the London Ballet led by Peggy van Praagh had far more sense of direction than the Ballet Rambert of this period.

The renaissance of the Ballet Rambert under the direct management of C.E.M.A., at the darkest period of the War, is one of the most extraordinary events in ballet history. The revived company had everything against it: only a few dancers of the London-Rambert company were still available, fully trained male dancers were not to be had for love or money, and the company spent its whole time on tour in the smaller towns, often playing one-night stands in hostels. In spite of every difficulty, however, the company—stimulated by the war-time atmosphere and goaded on by Marie Rambert—quickly developed tremendous esprit-de-corps and individuality. It was inferior to the London-Rambert company, and technically it could not compare with the Sadlers Wells Ballet; but it could teach the Sadlers Wells Ballet a good deal about the combination of discipline with individuality.

It is to be hoped that at least one of the versatile and intelligent dancers who danced in the Rambert company at this time will write an account of their experiences. Any book with the title *Life with Mim* would be entertaining, but the experiences of the dancers of this period represented a remarkable combination of epic and farce. Very sensibly C.E.M.A. employed Marie Rambert only as artistic director, putting the company under the management of professional administrators who (together with the dancers) preserved it from the disasters which threatened it on more than one occasion.

The revived company reached its peak in 1944 in two important London seasons at the Mercury and at the Lyric, Hammersmith, respectively. During these seasons Marie Rambert revived all the best ballets in the repertoire of the Ballet Club and the London Ballet (including all the major Tudor ballets). In many respects the performances fell below the standard achieved by the London-Rambert Ballet at the Arts Theatre in 1940–41, but in view of the distance in time since the ballets had last been performed Marie Rambert's achievement was highly creditable. There were a number of good soloists in the company at this time—among them Joan McClelland, Sally Gilmour, Sonia Arova, Paula Hinton, Sara Luzita, Elizabeth Schooling, Joyce Graeme, Annette Chappell, Frank Staff, Walter Gore, Michael Bayston, Michael Holmes and John Gilpin; some had been in the London-Rambert Ballet, and all were rehearsed by dancers who preserved a good memory of the original ballets. It was not just the steps which were revived: the dancers brought to life much of the spirit.

These seasons were of the highest historical interest, for they showed that under favourable conditions State control is not incompatible with high artistic standards. It is true that the revived Ballet Rambert did not produce any *new* ballets of any interest; but in the world of ballet degeneration is so normal that even the revival of something outstanding with a fair proportion of its original quality demands an artistic policy which is to some extent creative: this is proved by the complete failure of nearly all ballet companies during the past two decades to revive adequately such ballets as *Les Sylphides* and *Petrouchka*.

The high level achieved at this season did not last for long. Marie Rambert took over direct management of the company. The good dancers left, until not a single dancer of the war-time company remained. At the same time the best ballets were dropped (for lack of anyone to dance them), the technical standard slumped, and the company became a parody of itself.

It is easy to understand a decline in the quality of the company's performances after the stimulus of the War was no longer present. A company either progresses or slips back, and once the dancers ceased to be buoyed up by the War effort they no longer felt inclined to stand up to the strain and frustration involved in working in the Rambert company; nevertheless the speed with which the company slid downhill was very distressing to those who had seen it at its best. Once it got well under way the decline gathered momentum like a snowball: the new ballets were appallingly bad, and by 1950 there was no one in the company with much idea of how the older ballets should be danced. The satirical Tudor ballet *Gala Performance* retained some of its original quality, but on the rare occasions they were revived the serious Tudor ballets went for very little.

In 1951 and 1952 the technical standard improved to some extent, and one dancer (Noreen Sopwith, from the Sadlers Wells Theatre Ballet) showed quite a solid technique; but none of the dancers developed any real personality to back up their characteristic Rambertian stage presence, and their interpretations of their rôles remained superficial. Marie Rambert made desperate efforts to produce stars, using the same tactics that had proved successful before the War: she pushed Margaret Hill, for example, into every possible leading rôle, in spite of the fact that this dancer had a faulty technique and only a minor talent. But in the absence of classes from Legat or Craske and rehearsals from Tudor the old tactics gave very different results: the dancers showed no signs of developing into artists of the calibre of Pearl Argyle, Harold Turner and Peggy van Praagh. The contrast with pre-War conditions was shown very clearly when the prima ballerina Margaret Hill left the company in 1952 (in spite of the fact that she was given wonderful opportunities) to join the Sadlers Wells Theatre Ballet: there she danced for some time in the corps de ballet, before being promoted to minor solo rôles.

Margaret Barr's Dance Drama Group

It has often been said that a theatrical company must have a single dictator at its head: if there is a division of authority among several directors this is bound to give rise to conflicts which absorb all the energy which should go into creative work. This is certainly true if the directors have opposing artistic ideals or are more interested in power than in artistic achievement; but under favourable circumstances a partnership can achieve admirable results, with the talents of one partner complementing those of another. This is exactly what happened when Konstantin Stanislavsky joined with Nemirovich-Danchenko to found the Moscow Art Theatre, and the latter persuaded his partner that they should attempt a play by Chekhov (*The Sea-Gull*) which had failed at another theatre. Such partnerships have been rare in ballet history, but when they occurred they have been of great importance—notably the Sallé-Rich partnership and that of Durazzo, Calzabigi, Gluck and Angiolini. The Diaghilev company in its most creative period (1910–13) was to a considerable extent directed by a partnership—that of Diaghilev, Benois, Bakst and Stravinsky. A recent example of such a creative and complementary partnership is that of Ana Roje and Oscar Harmoš.

One English company, the Dance Drama Group which Mr. and Mrs. Elmhirst commissioned Margaret Barr to form at Dartington Hall in 1930, operated as a creative company during the period 1932–35, when it was directed not by Margaret Barr alone but by a team consisting of Margaret Barr herself (general director and director of movement), the composer Edmund Rubbra (director of music) and the designer Peter Goffin (director of décor, costumes and lighting). The dancers also had some say in artistic policy—notably Teda de Moor, who was principal dancer after Margaret Barr and assistant teacher. The artistic policy which resulted had many fine characteristics, and made possible a series of productions which were of great interest, in spite of certain serious deficiencies in the training and choreography. (Margaret Barr's style was based on that of Martha Graham at the end of the twenties.)

In theory this collective responsibility was characteristic of all the free-dance groups, but in practice it was very rare, for it conflicted with the expressionist Zeitgeist and the natural tendency of expressionist dancers towards hero-worship. Though Margaret Barr had exactly the type of personality which aroused hero-worship in the free-dance groups of Central Europe and the United States at this time, there were two things which prevented hero-worship from developing at Dartington Hall. One was the English habit of moderation and balance, which persisted in this group in spite of its expressionist style; the other was the fact that Edmund Rubbra and Peter Goffin had both developed strong creative individualities before joining Margaret Barr, and were not in the least inclined to be dominated by her.

As a result of the stimulating artistic climate the group failed to settle into a rut, and developed as one of its most striking characteristics a remarkable flexibility in its choice of themes and its treatment of the chosen themes. Almost every new production represented an attempt at a new genre: satirical drama in *The Three Sisters*, psychological abstraction in *Epithalamium*, symbolism in *The Mothers*, a religious theme in *The Three Marys*, and so on. In this respect the Dance Drama Group did not differ fundamentally from other free-dance groups such as that of Martha Graham; but it did show a rare capacity for coming to grips with the problems involved, for bringing every aspect of a new production into harmony with the theme, and above all for encouraging the dancers to keep their individuality and spontaneity. Margaret Barr's individuality was not allowed to flourish at the expense of that of the others.

The conflicts of view which developed between the members of the Dance Drama Group and the members of the Ballets Jooss, when the latter arrived as guests at Dartington Hall in 1934, brought out clearly the differences between the English group and most other free-dance groups. The Jooss dancers took themselves very seriously indeed, and were dumbfounded by the habit of the English dancers of laughing at themselves and the work of their Central European colleagues; they could not understand that such laughter was compatible with high artistic ideals. When Mr. and Mrs. Elmhirst tried to organize a fusion of the two groups (with Jooss as general director of the combined group), the negotiations broke down over the fact that Jooss and his artists were unable to see that their outlook was not the only possible one, and that some problems could be tackled better if they absorbed ideas from the English artists; the latter were prepared to make important concessions and to learn from their Central European colleagues, but not to abandon their independence of outlook and flexible approach to the problems of composition. Jooss had no wish to drive the Dartington group out of their home; on the other hand he could not, after over a decade of experimental work, make basic changes in his habits of thought and work; and the major differences in outlook between the two groups led to the departure of the Dance Drama Group and its eventual

The Blum-de Basil-Massine company on its first visit to London in 1933: *Les Présages* (Massine, Monte Carlo, 1932) with Baronova as Passion and Lichine as The Hero

Below: the de Basil-Massine company in 1937: the end of *Schéhérazade* (Fokine, Paris, 1910) with Shabelevsky performing the death-somersault of the Favourite Slave

The Blum company in 1936: *L'Épreuve d'Amour* (Fokine, Monte Carlo, 1936)

The Denham Ballet Russe de Monte Carlo in 1945: *Danses Concertantes* (Balanchine, New York, 1945), with Danilova and Frederick Franklin (*couple in front*)

dissolution. Technically the Jooss dancers were superior to the English dancers, but as interpretative artists the English dancers had many advantages over the Jooss dancers.

As with other free-dance groups of the period the most effective compositions of the Dance Drama Group were those in a satirical expressionist genre: Margaret Barr herself was excellent in vicious dramatic rôles, and other members of the group gave her strong competition. The expressionist style of dancing of the group was unsuited to the creation of semi-abstract works like *Epithalamium*, but its pioneer work in abstraction was of great interest, and suggested that this is a genre in which English choreographers and dancers may some day do work of considerable importance.

4. THE HYBRID COMPANY

Most companies become in due course an extension of the personalities of their director, reflecting all his limitations and inner conflicts. As we have seen, this does not happen in a creative company, whether directed by an individual or a complementary partnership. It does not even happen in a certain type of hybrid company in which authority is effectively divided between two or more ill-matched directors, but the conflicts between these people provide some scope for creative work by the artists of the company. In such companies artistic policy is liable to change suddenly and violently, for it is the resultant of a network of opposing forces, and any change in the magnitude of one of them is almost certain to cause marked changes in the direction and magnitude of the resultant.

One cannot expect hybrid companies to foster pioneer work of major importance, but under favourable conditions they can develop an artistic climate which is less oppressive than that of most other companies; this makes possible a high standard of freshness, vitality and individuality in the dancing, while talented choreographers can put into production projects which they have had to shelve while working in other companies.

Unfortunately the favourable artistic climate of the hybrid company depends on a delicate balance of power within the company. Sooner or later one of the directors is certain to squeeze out the others and secure absolute power for himself. The company then ceases to be a hybrid, and its artistic standard degenerates with disconcerting speed and irrevocability.

Ballets Russes de Monte Carlo No. 2[1]

Monte Carlo was an important annual port of call for the Diaghilev Ballet from 1913 onwards, and from 1924 onwards the company depended for its existence on its contract with the Societé des Bains de Mer de Monaco. Under this contract the company was provided with winter quarters and the opportunity to rehearse new ballets free of charge under ideal conditions. Though the company did not earn much money in Monte Carlo, it had a much-needed rest and plenty of time for rehearsal. (Some of the dancers appeared during the opera season, and the whole company appeared during the ballet season, but there were only a limited number of performances each week.)

[1] The Diaghilev company was the first Ballets Russes de Monte Carlo.

During the last years of the Diaghilev company the "Directeur des Spectacles" at Monte Carlo was the sensitive, intelligent and cultured René Blum (1878–1944). He was occupied chiefly with plays and operettas, but he was deeply interested in all the arts, and his work brought him into close contact with Diaghilev and the Diaghilev Ballet. After Diaghilev died Blum was given his job of director of the ballet season, and did his best to revive the Diaghilev company, carrying on negotiations with Massine, Balanchine, Lifar, Kokhno and Grigoriev (Diaghilev's stage director). According to Pierre Michaut,[1] each of these (except Grigoriev) insisted on being Blum's sole associate director. (This was perhaps the basic reason why the Diaghilev Ballet did not survive the death of Diaghilev.) For this reason Blum broke off negotiations. He was also influenced by the fact that the directors of the Societé des Bains de Mer were not much interested in continuing the Diaghilev Ballet, of which the new productions since *Le Train Bleu* had had only a very limited and ephemeral appeal. The Diaghilev décors and costumes, saddled with mortgages, were offered to the Societé des Bains de Mer, but this offer was refused, and they were bought by an American named Gertz who planned to form a new company with the collaboration of Massine. (There were a great many abortive projects of this nature during the years 1929–33.)

For the next few years René Blum kept the Monte Carlo ballet season going with many different types of company—Uday Shankar, Argentina, the Paris Opéra company, Boris Kniasev, etc.

Toward the end of 1931 Blum began once again to form a ballet company of his own. He brought together all the available dancers of the Diaghilev Ballet, together with some young dancers trained in Paris. He took on Balanchine as maître de ballet and choreographer, Massine as guest choreographer, and Grigoriev as stage director; Boris Kokhno and Christian Bérard accompanied Balanchine, these three having resolved to work together. Blum kept his independence as director of the company by having two choreographers. He would have liked to employ other choreographers as well, to make the repertoire as varied as possible, but found this impossible. (Fokine in particular was bound by contract in the United States at this time.)

Blum had remarkable *expertise* in music, opera, drama and literature, and in these arts he showed much the same flair as Diaghilev for what was new and important: in fact he made possible the publication of the first volume of Proust's novel *À la Recherche du Temps Perdu* at a time when its author was generally considered a wealthy dilettante. In choreography, however, he showed no such *expertise* or flair: he failed to discover any important new choreographer, though he directed ballet companies from 1931 to 1939, and he failed to see the importance of a return from Diaghilev's cocktail policy to one

---

[1] *Le Ballet Contemporain*, p. 62.

the new company appealed to the general public. The Diaghilevians came of course, and so did the Pavlovians, but a large number of people came who had never been to the ballet before. From now on right up to the War the Summer visits of this company represented one of the most important features of the London theatre.

In his publicity de Basil laid great stress on the "baby ballerinas"[1] of the company, and indeed they provided very good publicity material. But spectators would not have come over and over again[2] for four months just to see children dancing, no matter how brilliant their performances. What kept the house filled after the first few days was the high average standard of the performances and the variety of the repertoire. The programme was changed at each performance, and every evening there was at least one good ballet admirably performed. The directors had been very wise in reviving the early Diaghilev ballets, for these provided a solid core for the repertoire, and went on earning money long after the cocktail ballets were forgotten.

Considering the strain under which the company worked (with eight performances a week, and the stars dancing principal rôles in several ballets each evening) the standard of performance was very creditable. The preservation of the Russo-Polish tradition of dancing was ensured by the presence in the company of a number of Diaghilev soloists (Danilova, Massine, Woizikovsky and Tchernicheva) and also several lesser-known Diaghilev dancers (Jan Hoyer, Maryan Ladre, Nathalia Branitza and Tatiana Chamié) who helped to build a tradition of expressive dancing in minor rôles and the corps de ballet. Much of the fine quality of the dancing was due to the work of Massine as maître de ballet: when he rehearsed the ballets he took care to explain every detail to the dancers, and worked patiently until he achieved a satisfactory result. (He could not always remember the details of choreography—a common failing with choreographers—but he was greatly helped by Woizikovsky, who had a photographic memory.)

The weakest items in the repertoire were the new cocktail ballets and the early Diaghilev ballets with lyrical feeling (*Le Lac des Cygnes, Carnaval, Les Sylphides, Le Spectre de la Rose*). These suffered from the lack of dancers with a feeling for lyricism, and also from Massine's lack of sympathy with romanticism. On the other hand the dancers achieved wonderful results in the highly dramatic Diaghilev ballets (such as *Prince Igor, Petrouchka* and *Schéhérazade*) and in Massine's own expressionist ballets.

Massine himself was now dancing better than ever, and so was Danilova. In rôles which suited them these two dancers gave performances of the highest quality, filling the theatre with their personalities.

---

[1] Baronova and Riabouchinska; Toumanova did not appear until later.
[2] Some came every evening.

The young soloists in the company were helped by the favourable artistic climate in the company and the stimulus of the London public to mature with amazing speed. Three of them—Verchinina, Shabelevsky and Baronova—developed into artists of the highest quality, continuing the finest traditions of the Maryinsky and the early years of the Diaghilev ballet. Verchinina's range was limited, but within that range—rôles in Massine symphonic ballets showing strong influence from the free dance—she was incomparable. The Polish dancer Shabelevsky developed remarkable fire and versatility, being equally outstanding as Petrouchka, the chief warrior in *Prince Igor*, the Favourite Slave in *Schéhérazade* and the Snob in *La Boutique Fantasque*. Baronova showed fine sensitivity and imagination even in the first season (when she was only thirteen), and then developed so rapidly that she was soon able to take over Danilova's soubrette rôles when required, as well as triumphing in a demoniacal rôle in the last scene of *La Symphonie Fantastique* and in several other exacting rôles.

On the other hand an essential weakness in the artistic policy was suggested by the failure of the company to foster any good young choreographers. The only young choreographer to be given a chance was Lichine: he devoted himself to clever-clever stunts of the type already done to death by Balanchine and Lifar.

The success of the 1933 season in London led to an American tour under the management of the famous impresario S. Hurok. This tour (like the two Diaghilev tours) was financially unsuccessful: modern ballet was still a novelty in the United States. (Pavlova had been financially successful, but her company was a relatively small one, and she was able to appear in theatres and halls unsuitable for a large company with elaborate décor.) Hurok, however, had confidence in the future of Ballet-Russe in the United States; he booked the company for return visits in the following years, and receipts gradually improved from year to year until the company was making a handsome profit. In the fourth season (1936–37) Hurok announced a gross of a million dollars. By this time Ballet-Russe had proved itself to be a sound commercial proposition. Ballet had in fact become Big Business.

As soon as it was clear that the company was going to prosper a bitter struggle for power developed within the company. In this struggle de Basil had every advantage over Blum: he was completely ruthless in his tactics, and a master of intrigue: no artistic consideration deterred him from taking any action he thought best to get rid of Blum. (Though he picked up considerable knowledge about ballet from the others and could talk in the most fluent manner about his plans and artistic policy,[1] he had in fact very little understanding of artistic matters, and artistic integrity was a meaningless concept to him.)

---

[1] He claimed, for example, that he brought together the best ballets produced by all the best choreographers in their best periods, thus building up an incomparable repertoire of over a hundred ballets. In fact most of this repertoire existed only on paper, and the main lines of the artistic policy of the company were established by Blum, not by him.

In 1934, after the company had been in existence for two years, Blum was unwise enough to renounce his position as general director, and was described in the programmes as artistic director. Since de Basil (as general director) was in charge of all day-to-day administration he was able to interfere very effectively in the execution of the artistic policy laid down by Blum, and there were many disputes between the two. By the end of 1935 the disagreements between the two had become so bitter that Blum left in despair. By this time he must have realized that the dice were loaded against him.

The departure of Blum meant that de Basil's position was very much stronger. Nevertheless he still had to share power to some extent with Massine (now described in the programme as "maître de ballet et collaborateur artistique"), and there was little apparent change in the artistic policy of the company in 1936. In fact this was the peak year of the company from the artistic point of view: the young dancers now had the style and personality to match their dazzling technique, and Massine finally completed his masterpiece *La Symphonie Fantastique* (after three years of hard work).

De Basil, having tasted the delight of getting rid of the founder of the company, now became set on obtaining absolute power, and allowed himself the disastrous luxury of quarrelling with Massine. It was one of de Basil's tenets that no one is indispensable: he was fond of encouraging intrigue (because any internecine conflicts strengthened his own position) and did not worry if such conflicts caused artists to leave. In the same way he liked to surround himself with nonentities, knowing that they would be unlikely to dispute his power, and remained oblivious to the artistic weaknesses this policy entailed. Fundamentally he cared nothing about the artistic value of productions: all that mattered to him was power, and he failed to understand that the whole success of the company had been based on genuine artistic achievement; this is the only thing that pays in the long run, for this alone keeps on drawing the mass public. Like Diaghilev, de Basil believed that he could replace choreographers and maîtres de ballet just as he could replace other members of the company: like Diaghilev he was fatally wrong in this belief. Even before Massine left the standard began to fall, and after his departure it fell catastrophically.

Even if Blum and Massine had not left when they did it is likely that the standard of the company would have declined after 1936. By 1936 the company had exhausted all its possibilities of development. Nearly all the Diaghilev ballets worth reviving had been revived, and Massine could not find any more inspiration in Labanist expressionism. Failing good new productions the company would undoubtedly have lost some of its spirit. But the standard need not have fallen nearly as rapidly as it did. The company now suffered from the fact that it had no one to rehearse the ballets properly: Grigoriev knew the steps, but he could not teach style or expression. To make things worse, Blum set up a rival company and eventually attracted away a number of the best dancers.

One of the main reasons why Massine left was that de Basil invited Fokine (who had been attracting attention by his work as artistic director of the new Blum company) to become artistic director of the de Basil company. This was a good example of the sort of intrigue in which de Basil delighted; if he could entice Fokine away from Blum he could damage his rival and greatly strengthen himself. This invitation to Fokine to become artistic director was of course a bitter affront to Massine, who had been associated with the company from the beginning, and as "maître de ballet et collaborateur artistique" had a considerable amount of responsibility for artistic policy.

Massine's final appearance with the company was in January, 1938, but long before this date he had been engaged in bitter disputes with de Basil, and the company was split into rival factions. The Massine faction (including Danilova and Toumanova) left de Basil along with Massine and joined Blum.

De Basil did not profit much from his success in obtaining Fokine. The latter composed one very dreary new ballet *Cendrillon* which was old-fashioned in style and was badly received, and a rather embarrassing attempt at expressionism (*Paganini*). His most important achievement was to compose for Riabouchinska a new version of the Prélude in *Les Sylphides* which suited her very well, and which she preserved for many years exactly as rehearsed by him; this one solo was almost the only performance to show some of the original *Sylphides* atmosphere for a long time.

In 1938 the famous war broke out between the rival companies. This was fought out with great bitterness in the English law-courts: the battle took place in England, for the London season was by far the richest prize for any touring ballet company. The backers of the Blum–Massine company brought an action to restrain de Basil from performing certain Massine ballets in London. To keep within the letter of the law de Basil resigned his position as head of the company, and so the company was able to open at Covent Garden under the name Covent Garden Ballets Russes, performing the ballets in question without breaking the law.

Though the war aroused great interest, there was not much difference between the companies, and it made relatively little difference which side won. The wonderful quality which made the Blum–de Basil–Massine company of 1932–36 so entrancing was not to be found in either company. Cosmopolitan Ballet-Russe was dead, and it was beyond the power of either company to revive it.

One result of the split between the companies was that Hurok refused to book the Covent Garden company, which went to Australia. De Basil joined it there, and once again took control. The outbreak of War in September made it impossible for the company to return to Europe, and so de Basil took it to New York, where Hurok presented it in succession to the Blum company. After the New York season de Basil started his company on a tour of Latin America, but in Cuba eighteen of the dancers went on strike because of various grievances, including the payment of salaries in arrears. The tour had therefore to be cancelled. To make things worse, de Basil finally lost his connection with Hurok: the standard of the company was now so low that Hurok was no longer interested in it.

After an abortive tour in the United States de Basil took the company back to Latin America, where standards in ballet were low, and the company managed to keep going somehow for the next four years. By the end of this period it bore very little resemblance to the original Blum-de Basil-Massine company: all the good soloists had left, and the mass of the company consisted of Latin-American dancers.

In 1946 the company was reorganized by Hurok. He had just ended his relationship with Ballet Theatre, and decided to form what was in effect a new Ballet-Russe company in order to present a season in New York. He therefore brought to New York the small surviving Russian nucleus of the de Basil company, along with its décors, costumes and scores, and arranged with de Basil for the presentation of the company's ballets with soloists comprising many of the most popular stars working in the United States—notably Markova, Dolin, Rosella Hightower, Eglevsky and Skibine. Hurok appointed the Marquis de Cuevas artistic director, and the Marquis brought with him the surviving remnants of his Ballet International.[1] The corps de ballet was drawn mainly from the senior pupils of the ballet schools of New York. In spite of the galaxy of stars the season was not a success because of the slipshod production of the ballets: audiences and critics remembered pre-War performances, and were not taken in.

De Basil then somehow managed to get a booking for his company at Covent Garden for the summer of 1947. As a business man he had lost none of his skill and effrontery, even if the goods he had to sell were now rather shoddy. The company that performed in London was even worse than the one that appeared in New York, for Hurok's stars were left behind, and many solo rôles were taken by dancers who were scarcely worthy of a place in the corps de ballet. De Basil took on some first-rate soloists from Paris (notably Renée Jeanmaire and Vladimir Skouratov) but hopelessly misused their talents. The majority of the dancers brought by de Basil from New York showed no feeling for the different styles of the various ballets, dancing everything in a wooden acrobatic style which made nonsense of the steps.

It was not that they were without talent. They did reasonably well in one

[1] *See* below, p. 429.

ballet, *Graduation Ball*; this ballet, strongly American in style and feeling, had been composed by Lichine in 1940 to suit the talents of the somewhat Americanized de Basil company of that period. *Graduation Ball* was by no means a good ballet, but it had a certain brash exuberance which was within the understanding of the dancers; and they also did reasonably well in the best scenes of the expressionist ballets *Les Présages* and *La Symphonie Fantastique*. These ballets, however, bulked rather small in the repertoire as a whole.

Apart from the enormous decline in the quality of the dancing and the choreography, the technical details of the productions were hopelessly inferior to the originals. The colours of the backcloths, for example, were quite different from the original colours, and bore little relation to each other. The lighting was drab and monotonous, bearing no apparent relationship to the choreography. The dancers could scarcely have shown more self-assurance if they had come straight from the Maryinsky, and yet their ignorance of even such things as ballet make-up was unfathomable. The season was by no means a failure from a financial point of view: very large numbers of people who had vivid memories of the old de Basil company came at least once to see what the new one was like, while the enormous new audiences that had grown up during the War also visited the theatre to see for themselves the company about which such a legend had gathered. But the general impression made by the company was very bad, and it was clear that de Basil could never again come to Covent Garden, once the Summer home of the company.

It was typical of de Basil that he brought to Covent Garden an enormous company—no less than seventy dancers: evidently he was now living in a dream world, and thought that he could once again make a large amount of money playing the capitals of Europe, in spite of the shoddy quality of the performances. He had bluffed audiences and critics in the past, and presumably expected to go on doing so. In this he miscalculated badly. After a short season in Paris in October, 1947, he could get bookings only in Spain and Portugal, where audiences had few standards in ballet. There were long periods without bookings, and most of his dancers left. By 1949 the company was reduced once again to a small nucleus of Russians—de Basil himself, his wife Morosova, the stage director Grigoriev, the ballet mistress Tchernicheva, the premier danseur Dokoudovsky, Dokoudovsky's Danish wife Nina Stroganova, and a few others.

In 1951 de Basil completed negotiations with Universal Ballet (London) Ltd. for the formation of a new company composed mainly of English dancers. De Basil's backers had ample capital to launch the company in a satisfactory way; but de Basil died before the company was launched, and the backers were not prepared to go ahead with the enterprise without him to run it. In fact de Basil's staff went ahead with this company as best they could with almost no capital, and with George Kirsta as director. The company appeared for a week at Wimbledon (a remote London suburb) after a very short period of rehearsal, there being no funds for adequate rehearsals. Then came a season at the Royal Festival Hall (Dec. 1951–Jan. 1952) with the première of dreary new ballet arranged by Dokoudovsky, *Femmes d'Alger*. The company met its Waterloo at a subsequent West-End season at the Adelphi Theatre.

Ballets Russes de Monte Carlo No. 3

At the end of 1935 Blum left the company he had formed. He was still director of the Monte Carlo ballet season, and in 1936 he formed a small new company at Monte Carlo with the Diaghilev dancers Nemchinova and Obukhov as stars and Zverev as choreographer; the rest of the company consisted of inexperienced dancers brought from Paris or locally engaged. Zverev's own ballets were of little interest, and his revivals of Fokine ballets were unsatisfactory. The new company would probably never have amounted to much if Blum had not managed to make contact with Fokine, who had been brought to France to arrange some ballets for Ida Rubinstein. Fokine agreed to stay with Blum for a month, but actually stayed for six months, coming to London in 1937 with the company to complete his extended contract.

For Blum Fokine composed four new ballets, revived two ballets which he had composed in the United States, and revived a number of the great ballets which had formed the core of both the Diaghilev and Blum-de Basil-Massine repertoires—*Petrouchka*, *Les Sylphides*, *Prince Igor*, *Carnaval*, *Spectre de la Rose* and *Schéhérazade*.

Fokine took rehearsals with fire and enthusiasm—after years of frustration in the United States he was delighted to have the chance of working with a strong professional company again—but he was cruelly hampered by the lack of soloists capable of doing justice to his choreography.[1] When he produced *Les Sylphides*, for example, he did not have a single soloist with the appropriate qualities of lyricism and imagination.[2] He altered the choreography in many different ways in an attempt to give some hint of the right atmosphere, but with little success.

The most successful of his new ballets was *L'Épreuve d'Amour*: as mentioned above, he concentrated on the use of group movements and theatrical effects rather than solos, and so concealed the deficiencies of the soloists. Though *Épreuve* was highly praised at the time, this was rather because of the low level of the other new Russian ballets than for its intrinsic merits.

In spite of its serious deficiencies the new Blum company, as reorganized

[1] Obukhov, Nemchinova and Zverev left the company soon after Fokine joined it.
[2] The Danish dancer Hélène Kirsova was greatly praised at the time, and indeed had a typically Danish charm; but she was out of her depth in the great Fokine ballets.

by Fokine, was well able to challenge comparison with the degenerate de Basil company, and had considerable success on tour.

The Blum company was transformed in 1938 when Massine left de Basil and brought to the Blum company wealthy backers which he had found in the United States: a group of backers had joined together to found World Art Inc.,[1] with Julius Fleischmann (of the great yeast corporation) as president and Sergei Denham (of New York financial circles) as vice-president. Blum became co-director[2] with Sergei Denham of the reorganized Ballet Russe de Monte Carlo, with Massine as artistic director. The company was strengthened by the addition of a number of dancers who had sided with Massine in his disputes with de Basil, and it visited London in the Summer of 1938, when the ballet war took place. It then went to the United States for the usual Hurok tour which up to then had been the prerogative of the de Basil company. It was due to open at Covent Garden in September, 1939, for a slightly delayed Summer season, but the outbreak of war caused this season to be cancelled. It has remained in the United States from then on, gradually becoming almost completely American.

The type of ballet performed by this company—American Ballet-Russe—demands analysis by an American anthropologist of the school of Ruth Benedict and Margaret Mead rather than by a ballet historian. There is material here for any number of doctoral theses; I can only give some suggestions as to the nature of the problems involved.

In some respects American Ballet-Russe developed in the same way as Chinese institutions in Japan in the early stage of Japanese civilization. The Japanese who set out to reproduce Chinese institutions unwittingly distorted these almost out of recognition because their background of culture was quite different from that of the Chinese, and they completely misunderstood what they saw. Much the same thing happened in the United States when Ballet-Russe became established there. In fact the American cultural patterns were so strong, and so different from those of Russia, that they had a powerful influence on Russian choreographers like Massine and Balanchine and on the dancing of artists of Russian origin trained in the United States by Russian teachers. The Americans who moved into American Ballet-Russe in large numbers naturally translated every aspect of Ballet-Russe into its nearest American equivalent.

As already mentioned, the de Basil company became to some extent Americanized in the middle thirties, when de Basil took into the company a number of American and Canadian dancers. At this time, however, the traditions of the

[1] Later Universal Art. Inc.

[2] Blum remained in theory co-director until 1942, but he did not tour with the company to any extent, and after the occupation of France he was completely cut off from the company. He died in a German concentration camp in 1944.

de Basil company were so strong that the style of the company changed relatively little; the Americans and Canadians picked up much of the Russian style, and it was not always possible to pick them out from the Russian-trained Russians, the Poles, the second-generation Russians trained in Paris, and the Russian-trained English dancers.

Things were very different in the second Blum company reorganized by Massine. This company had only very feeble contacts with the old Russian traditions, and no contact at all with European audiences and ballet schools. The tail now wagged the dog: the company gradually adapted itself to a life of continuous touring in America, and evolved a type of ballet which was essentially American in spite of its exotic trappings. It was perhaps most American in its somewhat phoney exoticism: at this stage in the evolution of American ballet, audiences in the United States expected ballet to be Russian, just as English audiences in the eighteenth century expected opera to be Italian, even when composed by a German resident in England.

One of the main factors which determined the nature of the development of American Ballet-Russe was the organization of the American theatre. There were very few cities where the ballet audience was large enough to permit a stay of more than a few days, and in order to keep its head above water the company had to keep constantly on the move. The strain of continuous touring (with the dancers normally sleeping on the train between towns) was very great, and even the strongest dancers tended to crack up after a time. The soloists had the stimulus of publicity and the chance to appear on the stage by themselves, and also enjoyed special concessions such as private bedrooms on the company trains. On the other hand they suffered bitterly from the practice of employing guest artists to take principal rôles when the company came to New York; and this caused a steady drift of soloists away from the company to New York, even though this meant that the dancers appeared very rarely on the stage.

The star system was exploited to the limit, and accordingly the life of the corps-de-ballet dancers was almost unbearably hard and frustrating: they had no stimulus from publicity or solo dancing, and almost no prospect of rising to be soloists. Under these conditions the strain of constant touring knocked all individuality and personality out of them. The turnover in the corps de ballet was very rapid; normally the entire corps de ballet was renewed every year.

Because of the constant changes in personnel a great deal of the company's time was spent in rehearsing fresh dancers in the old ballets; there was little time for the production of new ballets, and choreographers were forced to make use only of movements familiar to the dancers in class. Even if they managed to bring in unconventional movements, these inevitably became transformed into the nearest classroom movements on being transmitted to another dancer.

In the same way all the standard ballets of the Ballet-Russe repertoire came to be danced in exactly the same somewhat mechanical general-purpose style.

American Ballet-Russe developed mainly within the Blum-Denham company, though other companies of a similar type were founded from time to time. The development of American Ballet-Russe within the Blum-Denham company took place in a number of definite stages.

During the first period (1938-42) Massine was artistic director both in name and in fact, and the company was in effect a choreographer's company. As one might expect, Massine devoted all his energy to the production of a series of large-scale ballets. Now, at last, he had complete freedom of action, and was working in a country where expressionism was fully appreciated. Unfortunately the opportunity came too late: he continued to use the mixture of neo-classicism and Central European free-dance which he had used for the first time in *Les Présages*, but by now this style had no more stimulus for him. His ballets became more and more cerebral, and their bewildering complexity prevented them from winning much popularity, in spite of his skilful craftsmanship.

Massine did his best to come to terms with his audience by arranging ballets with American themes—e.g. *The New Yorker* and *Saratoga*—but these were no more American than his earlier effort in the same direction (*Union Pacific*), and made a similarly slight impression. Americans were surprised by his complete failure to assimilate American types and customs, when he had assimilated those of Spain and Italy so well; but he had produced Spanish and Italian ballets at a much earlier period, when his expressionism was still viable: his attempt at a Spanish ballet in 1939 (*Capriccio Espagnol*) was sadly inferior to *Le Tricorne*.

In 1942, discontented with the poor results of years of enormous effort, Massine left the company. His departure was in fact the culmination of a long series of bitter conflicts within the company. The fact that he used the company merely as a platform for the expression of his own ideas would not have mattered so much if he still had had the creative fire of the years 1932-36, or even if his ballets had been bad in ways which would have made them seem to American eyes classical (like the Balanchine "classic ballets"). Unfortunately for Massine his ballets fell between two stools, being neither artistically good nor phoney in a slick and impressive way,[1] and the success of Ballet Theatre with the public made clear that something was badly wrong. Hurok realized this very well, and abandoned the Monte Carlo company for Ballet Theatre. This meant that the Monte Carlo company was deprived of its best dates, including the Metropolitan Opera House in New York; its earning power was very

[1] The American view of the Massine ballets of this period is admirably summarized by George Amberg: "Massine's serious substantial compositions did not touch the general American public in a profound emotional sense. There was always a mutual detachment of feeling, breeding respect rather than affection." (*Ballet in America*, p. 46.)

seriously reduced, and the company had to suffer a decline in numbers to about forty.

After the departure of Massine no-one was appointed to take his place as artistic director, and Denham took over responsibility for all the activities of the company. With the departure of Massine and the severance of the connection with Hurok, Denham was in much the same position as de Basil after 1938, and in fact his policy was like de Basil's in many respects. Though the dancers developed a characteristic Ballet-Russe arrogance, the standard of performance was erratic because of the extremely onerous touring conditions described above; according to Agnes de Mille (whose book *Dance to the Piper* evokes the atmosphere in this company with remarkable skill), dancers sometimes went on the stage with no rehearsal at all, and only a "verbal briefing" in their rôle.[1] In spite of everything, however, Denham managed to keep the company going, driving hard bargains with everyone (the dancers were paid so badly that they could hardly afford enough to eat) and managing to extract a flow of patronage from rich old ladies.[2]

As already explained,[3] Denham was driven by his desperate need for a new ballet to commission an American ballet *Rodeo* from Agnes de Mille in 1942. This was by far the most important achievement of the third Monte Carlo company, but Denham made no effort to continue in this direction, preferring to rely on Russian choreographers. No doubt he was afraid of endangering the exotic quality of the company—which now needed careful nursing, since by this time only a minority of the danseurs were Slavs, and hardly any of the danseuses. (Danilova was a tower of strength, a great Russian dancer in her prime; unfortunately, however, she had to spend most of her time dancing the classical rôles such as Odette which did not suit her exuberant temperament.)

Between 1942 and 1944 Denham commissioned three pseudo-classical revivals from Nijinska—the abstract ballets *Chopin Concerto* and *Étude* and the insipid dramatic ballet *Snow Maiden* (*Le Baiser de la Fée*). These were closer to American taste than the extremely complicated expressionist ballets of Massine, and helped to keep the company solvent during a difficult time.

The period 1944–48 was dominated by Balanchine, who became in effect associate artistic director. The company was now much the same sort of hybrid as the de Basil company after the departure of Blum and before the departure of Massine, and it won a good deal of prestige because of the success of Balanchine's "classic ballets"—now seen for the first time by the broad public. It was during this period that Balanchine perfected the abstract style which became habitual to him, and came to be regarded by many Americans

[1] *Dance to the Piper*, p. 247.
[2] *Ibid*, p. 255.
[3] *See* p. 235, above.

Ballet Theatre in 1946: *Pillar of Fire* (Tudor, New York, 1942) with Lucia Chase as
The Elder Sister and Nora Kaye as Hagar

Ballet Theatre in 1946: *Undertow* (Tudor, New York, 1946) with Nora Kaye as
Medusa and Hugh Laing as The Transgressor

Above: the Ballets des Champs-Élysées in 1946: *Le Jeune Homme et la Mort* (Petit, Paris, 1946) with Jean Babilée as the Young Man and Nathalie Philippart as Death

The Grand Ballet du Marquis de Cuevas in 1949: *Night Shadow* (Balanchine, New York, 1946) with Éthery Pagava as the Somnambulist and George Skibine as the Poet

as the greatest living choreographer. These "classic ballets" established more clearly than ever before the pattern of American Ballet-Russe, which now became unmistakably Balanchinian, whatever the choreographer and whatever the company; to a large extent the New York City Ballet represented a slight adaptation of American Ballet-Russe without the exotic trappings.

The success of Balanchine's ballets enabled the Massine ballets to be dropped from the repertoire, and the company acquired fresh momentum which enabled it to continue after the departure of Balanchine. On the other hand the turnover of dancers continued to be very high, and after April, 1950, Denham seemed to abandon the idea of New York seasons in competition with the New York City Ballet, Ballet Theatre and visiting Sadlers Wells companies, concentrating on coast-to-coast tours from September to early April each year. This naturally made the company unattractive to its stars, and the departure of both Danilova and Frederick Franklin in 1952 dealt it a heavy blow. Somehow Denham managed to keep the company going, but only with great difficulty.

Ballet Theatre

The Mordkin Ballet, a professional company formed by Mordkin in 1937 with backing provided by Lucia Chase, was a company of the same general type as the International Ballet. Lucia Chase, who had just completed her training at the Mordkin School, was the prima ballerina of the company, and most of the other danseuses in the company were also drawn from the Mordkin School; in addition two experienced male soloists were brought in from outside.

In 1938 Richard Pleasant was appointed general manager, and the company was considerably enlarged, a number of experienced soloists being engaged. It now attempted, without success, to compete with the Ballet Russe de Monte Carlo—a cosmopolitan company with a large repertoire and many of the greatest stars of the day (Massine, Danilova, Markova, Toumanova, etc.). The Mordkin Ballet had no stars of this magnitude, and its repertoire was unimpressive: inevitably it lost a great deal of money, and was disbanded in 1939.

Richard Pleasant then devised a project for a new company which would avoid the mistakes made by the Mordkin Ballet and other American companies, and have a distinct character of its own; only a company very different from the Mordkin Ballet could hope to compete effectively with the Ballet Russe de Monte Carlo and keep its head above water in the very difficult conditions of the American commercial theatre. Pleasant learned much from the failure of the Mordkin Ballet, but his scheme was by no means sudden improvisation; he had been dreaming of such a scheme as early as 1935 when he had been employed as secretary in Mordkin's studio.

The grandiose scale of Pleasant's project commands admiration, and so does Lucia Chase's courage in accepting it: she had to be prepared to spend a million dollars or more before any money could be taken at the box-office. Only in America could such a gigantic scheme have been conceived, much less put into action, at this stage of world history.

In scale the new company challenged comparison with the old-established and heavily subsidized State Ballets of Europe. It began with eleven choreographers (including two men of genius—Fokine and Tudor), ninety-two dancers (twenty "principal dancers", fifteen "soloists", a corps de ballet of twenty-four, nineteen Spanish dancers and fourteen Negro dancers), eleven designers, and music by eighteen composers. Preparations lasted a year, and nearly half this time was spent on rehearsals—a number of different ballets being rehearsed simultaneously. Eighteen ballets were made ready for the opening season, yet this represented only a small part of the plans for the future.

Though this project demanded enormous sums of money, these sums were, as John Martin says, "not in the least out of proportion with the amounts that were accepted as perfectly reasonable for similar institutions in the other arts".[1] One of Pleasant's most important achievements was to acclimatize in the United States the idea that ballet is a major art, as worthy of lavish financial support as e.g. painting and orchestral music.

From the point of view of general artistic policy Pleasant's project was highly original, breaking away violently from the various types of American Ballet-Russe and also from the self-conscious folksy Americanism of Kirstein's Ballet Caravan. Pleasant's idea was to bring together in one company the best ballets of all periods and all countries, and at the same time to provide for the production of new American ballets which would draw strength from the contact made by their creators with the greatest possible variety of older traditions. He considered—quite rightly—that with very lavish financial backing and enormous publicity such a company would be able to carve a place for itself in the American theatrical world.

One essential element in Pleasant's project was the creation of a number of different wings—old Russian, Diaghilev-Russian, American, English, Negro and Spanish: each of these wings was to be under the control of an expert in the style in question.[2] Later Pleasant planned to add an American free-dance wing.

Lucia Chase provided the enormous capital required, and Pleasant was made director of the new company, which they decided to call Ballet Theatre. Lucia Chase was not officially co-director, preferring to keep in the background, but presumably she took an important share in preparing the plan and deter-

---

[1] *World Book of Modern Ballet*, p. 62

[2] In due course Anton Dolin was made régisseur of the classic wing, Eugene Loring of the American wing and Antony Tudor of the new English wing. Fokine, of course, supervised the Fokine ballets in the repertoire.

mining the artistic policy. Though the company grew out of the Mordkin Ballet, Mordkin seemed to have very little importance in the new enterprise: only one of his ballets was included in the repertoire.

The company made its début at the beginning of 1940 in a four-week season at the Center Theatre in the Rockefeller Center in New York—an enormous theatre with a seating capacity of no less than 3,200. A great many people prophesied failure, but these dismal prophecies were counteracted by lavish advertising, and the new company made a good impression on both critics and the public. Just as Pleasant had planned, it struck a new note, providing a type of repertoire that was new in the United States and in fact anywhere. In spite of its cosmopolitan character—in fact largely because of it—Ballet Theatre was unmistakably American. (Its motto might well have been *E Pluribus Unum.*)

Though Pleasant's project was sound in theory, he lacked the judgment and knowledge needed to put it into practice with the necessary discrimination, and the enormous size of the project did not compensate for grave defects in quality, as might well have happened in an industrial project of similar magnitude. (In art, as in surgery, differences in quality are a matter of life and death.) Fokine, for example, was commissioned to produce two of his most delicate and poetic works (*Les Sylphides* and *Le Spectre de la Rose*), even though the company included no dancers capable of doing justice to them—and the bad performances in these ballets gave people a quite false impression of their real nature; on the other hand Pleasant did not commission from Fokine *Prince Igor*, though Fokine might well have achieved quite good results in this ballet with the dancers at his disposal. The main attempt at an important American ballet in the opening season (*The Great American Goof*, with book by Saroyan and choreography by Eugene Loring) had no chance of success because Saroyan's script, with its mass of sentimental and arbitrary symbolism, and the lines provided for the dancers to speak, was quite unsuitable for choreographic treatment. Antony Tudor—whose ballet *Lilac Garden* (*Jardin aux Lilas*) was the sensation of the opening season, and became one of the main pillars of the repertoire—was only taken on because of the persistent urging of Agnes de Mille; Pleasant was trying to get Ashton, and in fact commissioned two ballets from Ashton's epigone Andrée Howard.

These mistakes, though serious, were simply errors of judgment, and in theory could have been corrected with increased experience. But the treatment of Agnes de Mille fell into a different category, arising as it did from the hybrid nature of the company. To judge from Agnes de Mille's account of events in *Dance to the Piper*, Pleasant was quite well aware of her importance as a choreographer, but (as mentioned above) he was forced to lay down conditions for her employment which made it impossible for her to do justice to her abilities: she could choose any subject, but she might not dance in her ballets. Agnes de

Mille had the misfortune to have outstanding talent as a dancer in the same sort of character rôles that suited Lucia Chase: the latter also cast herself in rôles like Giselle, but she must have known that her talents in this direction were some-what limited. The eventual result was that Ballet Theatre's opening repertoire included no important American ballet; *Rodeo* was produced by the Monte Carlo company, not by Ballet Theatre, and Agnes de Mille's talent never flowered as it might have done under happier circumstances. She did not even receive opportunities to dance in other ballets in the repertoire: in *Dark Elegies* the rôle she had created went to Lucia Chase.

In spite of the weaknesses of the repertoire, Pleasant's original plan was so imaginative that the company's programmes created a fine impression of freshness and enterprise, and the company established itself overnight as one of the most important ballet companies in the world. If Richard Pleasant and Lucia Chase had been able to cut away the dead wood and adapt the company to the hard realities of the American theatre the company might well have made rapid progress. Unfortunately, however, this particular variety of hybrid company was ill equipped to stand the violent stresses of the period that followed. Though the New York season had been artistically successful, much money was lost; subsequent bookings were very scattered, and losses continued to be heavy, probably amounting eventually to several million dollars. Not even the greatest American fortune could stand losses at this rate, and the situation was complicated by the emergence of factions and bitter intrigues within the company.

Differences between Lucia Chase and Pleasant became more and more acute; finally, at the end of the 1941 season in New York, Pleasant left the company, and Ballet Theatre underwent a complete reorganization. German Sevastianov, who had been de Basil's Executive Secretary (1934–37) and Hurok's Promotion Manager (1940), was appointed Managing Director of Ballet Theatre, and a few months later Hurok began to book Ballet Theatre, having abandoned the Monte Carlo company.

The artistic policy of Ballet Theatre was now determined to a large extent by Hurok. He did his best to transform Ballet Theatre into a company of the same general type as the Ballet Russe de Monte Carlo—billing it as "The Best in Russian Ballet", exploiting the star system to the limit, and sending the company on a long series of back-breaking transcontinental tours. Since Massine had left the Ballet Russe de Monte Carlo, Hurok invited him to compose ballets for Ballet Theatre, and he introduced so many "Ballet-Russe" stars into the company (Markova, Baronova, Osato, Dolin, Lazovsky, etc.) that it had more of them than the Ballet Russe de Monte Carlo. (The stars did not always tour with the company, but the New York seasons were invariably star-studded.) By this time Ballet Theatre had shed all its various wings, and

conformed very closely to the pattern of American Ballet-Russe established by
the Monte Carlo company. Hurok's policy was of course based on commercial
calculations: he had found that this "Ballet-Russe" policy could be made to
pay, and he therefore adapted Ballet Theatre to the Ballet-Russe formula. It
seemed strange that he should transform Ballet Theatre into the image of the
Ballet Russe de Monte Carlo, when he might easily have hung on to the older
company; but Ballet Theatre had a freshness and sparkle lacking in the older
company.

Though on the face of it Hurok's policy was artistically retrograde, it did
save the company from extinction and made it into a going concern. Moreover
Pleasant's original project had such vitality that it continued to influence the
development of the company even after this reorganization. The company now
became a very complex hybrid, combining together elements of the original
Mordkin-Chase company, the grandiose Pleasant project, and the Hurokian
Ballet-Russe company. It was accordingly pulled in several directions at the
same time, and its artistic policy showed some curious zig-zags. Fortunately,
however, the erratic character of the artistic policy gave a certain amount of
freedom to creative artists inside the company; two of them (Antony Tudor
and Jerome Robbins) were able to develop their own ideas and put them into
practice without excessive interference from above.

Tudor's position in Ballet Theatre was very difficult. Because of the enormous success of *Lilac Garden* he enjoyed great prestige in the United States,
and this gave him some opportunity to secure a hearing for his ideas within the
company; on the other hand he suffered from the fact that his ballets demanded
dancers of a completely different type from those already existing in America,
and before he could put his ideas into execution he had to create at least a few
dancers with the maturity and sensitivity to do justice to his choreography:
in other words he had to do within Ballet Theatre what he had done inside the
Ballet Club a decade earlier. His success was relatively less than in London, for the
whole pattern of American life was opposed to the emergence of the classical
maturity his choreography demanded, and he had outstanding success with
only one American dancer, Nora Kaye. (This dancer joined Ballet Theatre at
its inception, but danced only minor rôles until Tudor took her in hand and
transformed her into the greatest American dramatic ballerina.) Tudor also
effected a transformation in himself and in Hugh Laing which in its own way
was just as impressive as that in Nora Kaye: he overcame many of his own
technical limitations and transformed his self-consciousness into a stage presence
almost without equal at the time, while Hugh Laing under his guidance realized
all the potentialities which had been latent in England.

The sensitivity, power and maturity of the dancing of Nora Kaye, Hugh
Laing and Antony Tudor in *Pillar of Fire* (1942) was an artistic achievement of

the very highest order, comparable with anything achieved by the Diaghilev Ballet at its best, and fully justified all the money and effort that had been poured into Ballet Theatre. Nevertheless this was achieved by Tudor against great odds: these remarkable performances stood out not only from the rest of the repertoire but from the rest of *Pillar of Fire*, and the production of this masterpiece had no lasting effect on the artistic policy of the company.

Most of the other new ballets were very disappointing. Fokine composed two clumsy comedy ballets, *Bluebeard* and *Helen of Troy*,[1] with much the same banality as the *Cendrillon* he composed in 1939; Massine showed the decline of his powers in *Mlle Angot*; and Agnes de Mille devoted herself to crude slapstick in *Three Virgins and the Devil* and *Tally-Ho*. Lacking American ballets of any consequence, the company commissioned a revival of *Billy the Kid*. (Many years later *Rodeo* was also taken into the repertoire.)

In 1943 Sevastianov joined the U.S. Army, and his place was taken by J. Alden Talbot. Hurok continued to book the company, and there was no apparent change in artistic policy.

In 1944 Jerome Robbins leaped into fame by composing *Fancy Free*. Though far less in stature than *Pillar of Fire*, this American ballet was of the utmost importance in the development of American ballet; along with *Interplay* it greatly strengthened the artistic importance of Ballet Theatre.

Though the hybrid nature of the company during the period 1941–44 permitted the production of some very fine ballets, the artistic climate of the company was opposed to any continuing development in its choreographers and dancers. Jerome Robbins profited by the publicity he received from *Fancy Free* to leave the company and set up as a free-lance. Tudor remained with the company, but it was evident that he found conditions in it more and more frustrating. In *Romeo and Juliet* he tackled a theme which could easily have stimulated him, but treated it in such a way that it gave him little opportunity to use his gifts to good advantage, and his next major ballet, *Undertow*, was crippled by inappropriate music and décor. (In England he had shown himself a master of all aspects of theatrical technique, and invariably managed to achieve poetic décor, costumes and music suited to the themes of his ballets: the failure of *Undertow* as a *Gesamtkunstwerk* must be attributed to the artistic policy of Ballet Theatre.)

Undertow was attacked by critics in exactly the same way as *L'Après-Midi d'un Faune* and *Le Sacre du Printemps*, but the directors of Ballet Theatre reacted very differently from Diaghilev. Whereas Diaghilev delighted in the attacks (taking them as a sign of vitality in his artistic policy), and fought back effectively to establish the ballets as important additions to his repertoire, Ballet

---

[1] This was left unfinished at his death, and was revised by Lichine before presentation to the public.

Theatre dropped *Undertow* almost at once. At the time of *Faune* and *Sacre*, Diaghilev's policy was a positive one, directed toward achieving artistic progress in spite of opposition, and he even managed to exploit the publicity value of the opposition; Ballet Theatre's policy, being merely the resultant of a network of forces, was incapable of supporting such bold tactics.

In 1945 J. Alden Talbot resigned, and his place was taken by Lucia Chase and Oliver Smith (co-directors). At this time Oliver Smith was only twenty-seven. He had designed the décor for the Massine ballet *Saratoga*, but first made his name when Agnes de Mille chose him as designer for *Rodeo*. He then became the chief designer working for Ballet Theatre. At this time disputes with Hurok were growing in intensity, and a breach was obviously approaching: presumably Lucia Chase felt it desirable to take over direct control, while at the same time securing as collaborator a man who would relieve her of some of the responsibilities of direct management.

In 1946 Lucia Chase finally took the bold step of breaking with Hurok. This made the future of the company uncertain, for Hurok had at this time the monopoly of the Metropolitan Opera (the only New York theatre where a ballet season could be made to show a profit), and also controlled most of the best touring dates.

For two months, however, in July–August, 1946, the company enjoyed a glorious Indian summer in London. It was no longer tied to the Hurokian system of guest stars, and the company's own stars gave the performances of their lives working under almost ideal conditions in a beautiful old theatre, before the warmly appreciative and stimulating London audiences. London gave Ballet Theatre the same tumultuous reception that it had once given to the Diaghilev Ballet and the Blum–de Basil companies in their best periods: in fact Ballet Theatre could have stayed almost indefinitely if the theatre had been free. (Productions such as Ballet Theatre's appalling *Giselle* had a cool reception, but this did not damp the enthusiasm of the public for fine productions like *Pillar of Fire*, *Undertow*, *Fancy Free* and *Interplay*.)

After this brief Indian summer Ballet Theatre continued to lose ground both artistically and financially. Tudor was described in the billing as "artistic administrator", but he did not seem to have much share in the determination of artistic policy—which veered in an apparently haphazard way. (In addition to appointing Oliver Smith as co-director Lucia Chase appointed an artistic committee of seven, and a board of eight directors: presumably all of these people offered advice on artistic policy.) Like Mona Inglesby, Lucia Chase did not even manage to make the best of her own limited talents, casting herself for preference in rôles, such as a soloist in *Les Sylphides* and the Ballerina in *Petrouchka*, for which she was quite unsuited. The heritage of Pleasant's original project and the survival in the repertoire of good ballets by Tudor and Robbins prevented the company from becoming merely an American equivalent of the International Ballet, but it was no longer a hybrid company, and was no longer capable of artistic progress.

In the middle of 1948 Ballet Theatre reached a critical situation. Engagements for 1948–49 were cancelled, and the company suspended its activities until the Spring of 1949.[1] It then re-formed with much the same personnel as before, but its vitality had almost disappeared. One by one the finest artists left; by the time Hugh Laing, Diana Adams, Antony Tudor, Nora Kaye and a few others had left the company was almost as unrecognizable as the de Basil company of the same period. (Of all the scores of dancers that joined Ballet Theatre in 1939 only one or two remained.) A number of star dancers were taken on to replace the emigrants, and the company continued to give fine performances of the four unmistakably American ballets in its repertoire— *Billy the Kid*, *Rodeo*, *Fancy Free* and *Interplay*; but it was obvious that no further progress was possible in this direction, and that the creative spirit which animated the company in 1939–44 was irrevocably lost.

Ballets des Champs-Élysées

The Ballets des Champs-Élysées had their origin in Roland Petit's first full-scale ballet *Les Forains*, produced by him at the beginning of 1945 (for a single "recital" performance) with book by Boris Kokhno, décor by Christian Bérard and music by Henri Saugeut; in addition Jean Cocteau helped with the costumes.

The success of *Les Forains* encouraged Petit to prepare for a short season of four performances at the Théâtre Sarah Bernhardt, with a repertoire including *Les Forains* and several new ballets, notably *Le Rendezvous* with book by Jacques Prévert. This season was a great success, and Roland Petit's father, confident in his son's future, provided the necessary capital for the formation of a permanent company. Together they made arrangements with Roger Eudes (then director of the Théâtre des Champs-Élysées) for the projected company to have its headquarters at the Champs-Élysées theatre; Boris Kokhno was asked to become artistic director of the company.

As described above,[2] Kokhno, Bérard and Cocteau set themselves to revive the Diaghilev cocktail policy, and succeeded all to well. For a time, however, the company had remarkable success in spite of great deficiencies in its policy and repertoire. There was no evidence of any marked conflict of view between Petit on the one hand and Kokhno and his associates on the other. Petit was

---

[1] According to John Martin (*World Book of Modern Ballet*, p. 98) the suspension of activities of Ballet Theatre was made necessary by new tax laws concerning enterprises operating at a continual loss.

[2] *See* p. 248.

very young, with no experience of managing a permanent company, while the others (notably Kokhno) had had many years of experience with Diaghilev and were much older; inevitably Petit came largely under their influence. On the other hand he had established quite a name for himself as a recital dancer before he met them, and had a very strong individuality, while the fact that the company had been formed around his ballets (it was quite rightly spoken of as the "Roland Petit company") put him in a strong position.

A third element in the company was its fine young solo dancers. There was nothing that could be called a corps de ballet, and the tail of the company consisted of dancers who were scarcely worthy of the name,[1] but the leading soloists—including Vyroubova, Jean Babilée, Nathalie Philippart, Ana Nevada, Éthery Pagava, and Roland Petit himself—had irresistible freshness and individuality. Their dancing, product of a highly stimulating period in French history, had little to do with the cocktail policy of Kokhno, and to some extent transformed the ballets in which they appeared. Though Petit's choreography had few positive merits, it did not hamper the expression of this exuberant vitality as Lifar's choreography would have done, and the new company was very well received in Paris and London.

The most typical and also the most successful of the new works produced by the Ballets des Champs-Élysées was Le Jeune Homme et la Mort (June, 1946), a "ballet" devised by Cocteau in which the major effects were obtained by changes of décor, kicks in the face and a very realistic hanging; there was little place for choreography in this work.

After Le Jeune Homme et la Mort the company almost ceased to produce new ballets. It had become clear that Kokhno and his associates were little interested in choreography: to them a ballet was a visual spectacle in which (as in the Diaghilev cocktail ballets) décor was paramount, dancing was of relatively little importance, and incongruity between the elements of the ballets was indispensable.

Though Roland Petit had clearly been considerably influenced by his collaboration with Kokhno, Bérard and Cocteau, he was driven eventually to revolt against their neglect of choreography, and left the company in January, 1948.

After the departure of Roland Petit the company was no longer a hybrid, and lost its capacity for artistic development. Kokhno ran the company on

---

[1] This was not entirely the fault of the directors of the company. The great Russian teachers at this time were turning out some wonderful solo dancers out of the best talent coming to their classes, but the number of students in the whole of France was very small, and consequently the average standard of a company was liable to suffer from the totally inadequate technique of the minor dancers. This was just as true of the Opéra as of private companies. On the other hand even the worst dancers showed an individuality which is characteristically French, and is sadly lacking in the minor members of English companies with incomparably better techniques.

completely "cocktail" lines, employing a number of different choreographers —Lichine, Janine Charrat, Jean Babilée, Massine and John Taras. The departure of Roland Petit left the company with several talented dancers—notably Jean Babilée, Nathalie Philippart and Éthery Pagava—but they were not provided with any real opportunities. Nathalie Philippart, for example, showed herself a dancer with an extraordinary feeling for nuances of style and feeling in rôles as diverse as La Mort in *Le Jeune Homme et la Mort* and Effie in *La Sylphide*, while Babilée (appearing as guest artist at the Nijinsky Gala at the Empress Hall in London) showed himself an ideal Faun in Nijinsky's famous ballet, in spite of the fact that he had had only one rehearsal. The company was kept in existence for a time by the remarkable performances of these and other soloists, but in the long run the complete sterility of its late-Diaghilevian artistic policy caused it to lose contact with audiences, just as all other companies with similar policies had done in the past. Finally it was disbanded. Various attempts were made to revive it, but these had only temporary and limited success. The cocktail policy, moribund even before Diaghilev's death, was by now as unsuitable for revival as the bathing costumes of *Le Train Bleu*.

5. THE PATRON-MANAGER'S COMPANY: GRAND BALLET DU MARQUIS DE CUEVAS

The wealthy patron has always been of great importance in ballet history, and wealthy Americans such as Otto Kahn, Edward Warburg and Lincoln Kirstein are the exact twentieth-century equivalents of eighteenth-century patrons such as Duke Carl Eugen of Württemberg and nineteenth-century patrons such as the Tsars of Russia.

At every period the wealthy patron of ballet has found it difficult to spend his money to good advantage, and things were particularly difficult for him in the confused aftermath of the Diaghilev cocktail period. The American million-aire who bought Old-Master paintings from Duveen was investing in names which had stood the test of centuries, and he had guarantees of authenticity from men like Berenson. With a living art like ballet no such guarantees were possible, and this is probably the main reason why relatively few rich Americans have become patrons of ballet, in spite of the enormous increase in the prestige of ballet in the United States in recent years.

The patron does not normally determine the artistic policy of a ballet company. He selects the artist whose work impresses him the most, and gives this artist the money he needs to apply whatever artistic policy he considers desirable. The Marquis de Cuevas, however, followed the example of Rolf de Maré in forming his own company instead of giving someone else the money to do this, though he differed fundamentally from Rolf de Maré in having nothing that could be described as a positive artistic policy. The company formed by the Marquis was in fact unique of its kind in the twentieth century, though one may compare it in some respects to the serf ballets maintained by certain Russian nobles in the eighteenth and nineteenth centuries in imitation of the Imperial Russian ballet. In other respects it reminds one of the rich dancers' companies.

The origins of the Grand Ballet du Marquis de Cuevas can be traced back to the fifth[1] of the Monte Carlo companies. In 1946, following the Liberation, the impresario Eugene Grunberg began to form a company at Monte Carlo to revive the traditional ballet season. Lifar had left the Opéra in Paris two years previously and now he was fortunate enough to be invited to become artistic director of the Nouveau Ballet de Monte Carlo. This company attracted the best French and Franco-Russian dancers of the day—among them Yvette

[1] The fourth Monte Carlo company was formed during the German occupation.

427

Chauviré, Renée Jeanmaire, Vladimir Skouratov, Janine Charrat, Alexandre Kalioujny and Youly Algarov. The star of the company was beyond question Yvette Chauviré, then at the height of her achievements as a classical ballerina.

The company began with performances of solos and pas de deux composed by Lifar for the soloists of the company. During the next few months he staged a number of large-scale ballets—including *Dramma per Musica* and the enormous *Chota Roustaveli*. The company then came to London, where it was booked at the Cambridge Theatre for an indefinite run; its directors presumably hoped that the fifth Monte Carlo company would have the same success in London as the first three. (Lifar's work as a choreographer since 1929 was practically unknown in London at this time.)

The season started well, for Londoners had been confined to English ballet and English dancers throughout the War, and were delighted at the prospect of seeing something fresh. Very soon, however, audiences realized that Lifar's style of choreography made it impossible for even the greatest artists to dance well, and that *all* the ballets were composed by him. (Even *Giselle* was presented in a Lifarian version.) Though some of the dancers (Chauviré in particular) had a personal success, they could not make English audiences tolerate the almost unbelievable deficiencies of Lifar's choreography; after a week audiences faded away almost to nothing, and the season ended in disaster.

Each of the previous Monte Carlo companies (including the Diaghilev Ballet) had depended heavily on their annual London seasons, and it was now clear that the Nouveau Ballet de Monte Carlo could not survive without a wealthy patron. According to Pierre Michaut[1] Lifar made contact with a number of rich men, including the Aga Khan: they all declined the honour of becoming the Maecenas of the new company. Finally the Marquis de Cuevas was approached in New York; he showed great interest, coming at once to Monte Carlo, and the deal went through very quickly. The Marquis de Cuevas now took over the company, adding to it a number of American dancers and choreographers from the Ballet International founded by him in New York in 1944. Lifar, invited to return to the Opéra, then left the company, and so did most of the French and Franco-Russian dancers. The reorganized company lost its connection with Monte Carlo, and became in effect an American Ballet-Russe company touring in Europe from a base in Paris, with occasional visits to North and South America.

Though the Marquis de Cuevas belonged to an ancient line of European nobility, his background was completely American. He was born in Chile (of a Spanish father and a Danish mother), married Margaret Strong (grand-daughter of John D. Rockefeller), and became an American citizen in 1940.

[1] *Le Ballet Contemporain*, p. 158.

The Marquis de Cuevas first moved into the ballet world by founding in 1943 the Ballet Institute "for the advancement of the art of ballet and its allied arts; for the education and instruction of students in these arts; and for the furtherance of public appreciation of ballet".

He then bought the International Theatre in New York as a home for a school and a company, making the Vilzak-Schollar School part of the Ballet Institute and appointing Anatole Vilzak maître de ballet of the company (which the Marquis called Ballet International). Rehearsals went on for six months, and then the company presented eleven ballets by ten different choreographers.

The repertoire had almost exactly the same weaknesses as that of Ballet Theatre (which had obviously inspired it). The Marquis commissioned ballets from all the available Russian choreographers—Massine, Nijinska, Boris Romanov, Simon Simeonov and Anatole Vilzak—and also from some American choreographers—Edward Caton, William Dollar, Antonia Cobos and André Eglevsky. The ballets showed a desperate attempt at novelty at all costs: clearly the Marquis wanted his company to establish itself as an important artistic enterprise in competition with the Ballet Russe de Monte Carlo and Ballet Theatre; but the quality he achieved was much too low for such an ambitious aim. The pièce de résistance of the repertoire was Massine's *Tristan Fou*, the worst ballet by a great choreographer since *Cendrillon*: the choreography of Massine's ballet could hardly have been more trite if it had been improvised by the dancers, and the Marquis de Cuevas showed lack of judgment in allowing it to be seen by the public.

Though the new company had lavish financial resources, it was crippled by the fact that its home theatre was unsuitable for ballet. The seating capacity was too small to enable expenses to be covered even if all seats were sold, and the stage was too small; losses were accordingly heavy,[1] and the Marquis was forced to disband the company.

As mentioned above, Hurok arranged a merger of the remnants of the de Basil company and Ballet International in New York in 1946, with the Marquis de Cuevas as artistic director of the new company; but this arrangement did not continue after the end of the New York season.

The offer from the Nouveau Ballet de Monte Carlo provided the Marquis with an attractive means of reviving Ballet International. In Europe theatrical conditions were far more flexible than in the United States, for a great many cities had theatres suitable for ballet and available for hire; moreover the American Ballet-Russe formula used by the Cuevas company, though only too familiar in the United States, was something of a novelty in Europe at this time, after a long war-time period when there had been no tours by ballet companies.

[1] According to Anatole Chujoy (*Ballet Encyclopedia*, p. 45) the Marquis lost about $800,000 during the New York season (which lasted from October 30 to December 23, 1944).

It was therefore possible for the Marquis to maintain his company in Europe at a cost far below what would have been necessary in the United States.

When the Marquis took over the Nouveau Ballet de Monte Carlo he brought with him Skibine, Eglevsky, Rosella Hightower, Marjorie Tallchief and a number of other dancers; gradually more and more Americans arrived until they amounted to well over half the company. At the same time the repertoire was completely transformed: the Lifar ballets were abandoned, and were replaced by revivals of Balanchine ballets and new compositions by two American disciples of Balanchine, William Dollar and John Taras. The Balanchine style of dancing was carefully nurtured in the company by John Taras, whom the Marquis appointed maître de ballet. The repertoire also included the inevitable ballets blancs (*Giselle, Le Lac des Cygnes* and *Les Sylphides*) and the inevitable Massine revival (*Le Beau Danube*), together with the ballets composed by Massine and Nijinska for Ballet International. The new ballets were all more or less Balanchinian: Taras copied his style so closely that the Taras ballet *Design with Strings* was in effect a new version of Balanchine's ballet *Serenade* (very familiar to American audiences, but little known in Europe at this time).

In the early years after its reorganization the corps de ballet was very ragged, but the soloists showed an interesting mixture of Franco-Russian and American elements. There were two excellent Franco-Russian dancers—Éthery Pagava, very young but showing fine promise of poetry and nobility, and the superb French character dancer René Bon. The American dancers included three talented artists whose style showed a blend of Russo-American and Franco-Russian qualities—Rosella Hightower, Marjorie Tallchief and George Skibine.

By 1951 the company had settled into a rut and almost all its freshness had gone. Taras had achieved a high degree of discipline and uniformity in the corps de ballet, but at the cost of nearly all personality and individuality. Éthery Pagava and René Bon had left, and Rosella Hightower had changed into a frigid technician, devoting all her remarkable talents to the execution of difficult stunts. In fact the whole tendency of the company was in the direction of technique for its own sake: the Marquis was clearly able to pay high salaries and attract some of the finest technicians in the world (notably the brilliant danseur Serge Golovine), but he did not seem to appreciate the importance of giving them opportunities to develop into artists.

Conclusion

If our Art, all imperfect as it is, seduces & captivates the Spectator; if dancing stripped of charms of expression sometimes disturbs us, causes us emotion, & throws our soul into a pleasing disorder; what force & what sovereignty would it not have over our senses, if the movements were regulated by esprit & the Pictures drawn by feeling! It is not to be doubted that Ballets will have the preference over Painting when those who perform them are less like Automatons, & those who compose them are better organized.

NOVERRE (Letter IV—1760)

UP TO NOW I have made considerable use of the metaphorical expression "artistic climate" (in connection with ballet companies) without discussing the origin and significance of this phenomenon. The time has now come for such a discussion.

This is a very complex matter, and it may be a long time before we arrive at a reasonably satisfactory explanation for the differences between the artistic climates of the various types of company and the effects of these climates on dancing and choreography. In the meantime, however, we can find valuable suggestions in the work of a number of post-Freudian psycho-analysts and social psychologists—notably C. G. Jung, Otto Rank, and three pioneers in the field of interpersonal relations who have been working in the United States (Eric Fromm, Karen Horney and Harry Stack Sullivan).

It is not necessary at first for us to consider dancers separately from choreographers, for both need creative ability, and the choreographer invariably starts as a dancer.

Normally a dancer enters a company by going through the school attached to the company, and his experiences in the school and the company are in many respects similar to those of a child in its family circle. Dancing involves the whole of the personality, and is very far from being a purely physical activity (as it is regarded in most schools and companies). By some mysterious process of empathy we become aware of emotional and symbolic aspects of the dancer's movements—aspects originally imagined by the choreographer and re-created by the dancer in terms of his own personality. The re-creative process in the dancer (like the creative process in the choreographer) is crippled unless the artist has matured as an individual and become what Rank calls "creative" and Fromm "productive" or "spontaneous". The processes of individuation and maturation are as all-important in the field of ballet as they are in social life in general.

431

The life of the dancer is one long continuous process of education—physical, emotional and mental. Throughout his career the dancer must continue with his daily classes and fit into his existing patterns of thought and feeling the new experiences he has while in contact with other people—teachers, company directors, choreographers and other dancers. (One may almost exclude the dancer's relations with people outside the ballet world, for these are usually of small importance.)

Dancers are strongly affected by the attitudes to them of the teacher and the company director: the more talented and imaginative the dancer the more sensitive he is likely to be to these attitudes. Being by aptitude and training particularly sensitive to gestures, facial expressions and bodily postures, dancers react powerfully to the attitudes to them of their superiors even when these find no expression in words: in fact dancers show the same power of empathy as infants who have not yet learned the meaning of words.

The extent to which a dancer develops his artistic capacities depends very largely on the way he is treated in school and in the company. All education involves some frustration and prohibition: it is the kind of frustration and prohibition, and the attitude to the dancers of teachers and the company director, which is all-important. If this attitude is warm and constructive, the dancer develops his capacities to their full extent within the limits set by the style of dancing, the ballets in the repertoire, the quality of the models available for study, and so on. As the various aspects of his being (physical, emotional and mental) gradually become more and more integrated, he ceases to copy others, develops spontaneity, and begins to do things in his own way, within the limits set by the style of choreography and the theme of the ballet.

Things are very different when the dancer works in the usual atmosphere of hostility: his ventures in individual expression are then treated as attacks on discipline, and attempts are made to break the dancer's spirit. The dancer accordingly loses self-confidence and self-respect and ceases to mature. Instead, he seeks various ways of escape from the pervading atmosphere of hostility and anxiety; he develops inner conflicts, loses all spontaneity, and wastes his creative powers in various neurotic mechanisms for coping with these conflicts. It is precisely the most sensitive and imaginative artists who suffer the most in this way.

Dancers react in various manners according to their temperaments and childhood experiences, but certain reactions are far more common than others. The most common reaction of girls is the development of what Fromm calls "automaton conformity" and Horney "neurotic submissiveness". This takes slightly different forms in England and the United States, in harmony with national patterns of culture. In England the danseuse tends to adopt an attitude of compliance to those in authority, allowing herself to be badly treated for years without protest, and eventually (when the strain becomes unbearable) leaving the company without fuss or demonstration. In the United States the danseuse is apparently rather more vital and independent, but in fact she is just as stunted and regimented as her English colleague; in the words of Fromm, she "becomes exactly as all others are and as they expect [her] to be".[1] Such dancers aim to think, feel, imagine and act in exactly the same way as all the other dancers in the company, and accept an ideal which is extremely limiting. "In other words they substitute a pseudo-self for their own real self."[2]

Male dancers also show these escape mechanisms, but (perhaps because they normally take up dancing much later than girls) they show these mechanisms less prominently than two others—cynicism and homosexuality. Cynicism finds its characteristic expression in "camp" talk: the dancer tries to cover up the frustration he suffers by talking as if artistic ideals did not exist, and making every aspect of ballet into a rather feeble joke, until he reaches a point where he cannot talk seriously about anything for long without feeling embarrassed.[3]

Homosexuality is another very important neurotic mechanism. We may regard all men as being composed of a mixture of masculine and feminine elements: by no means all homosexuality represents a neurotic escape mechanism, and boys in whom feminine elements are dominant are often attracted to ballet because it has been considered a characteristically feminine art ever since the middle of the nineteenth century. On the other hand the existence and importance of virile male dancing has been widely recognized since the arrival of the Diaghilev Ballet in the West before the First World War, and dancing has a broad appeal which cuts across all categories of sexuality. We should therefore expect, in the absence of neurotic complications, that the proportion of homosexuality in the ballet world would be higher than that in the general population, but that the difference between the two proportions would be of moderate size. In fact the difference is enormous: whereas in the general population men who are predominantly heterosexual considerably outnumber those who are bisexual or predominantly homosexual, one may guess (in the absence of a Kinsey survey) that in the ballet world the reverse is probably true; and a good part of the difference between the two proportions is probably of neurotic origin.[4]

[1] Eric Fromm, *Escape from Freedom*, p. 186.
[2] Patrick Mullahy, *Oedipus Myth and Complex*, p. 257.
[3] Nijinsky showed in his early career all three of the neurotic mechanisms described here. In his day, however, the Diaghilev Ballet preserved the great Russian tradition of the dedicated artist, and cynical talk would have been unthinkable: Nijinsky's inane small-talk was the contemporary equivalent of the cynical conversation which later became characteristic of the ballet world in the cocktail period. Diaghilev's description of himself as a purveyor of cocktails was typically "camp" in its combination of bitterness, cynicism and truth.
[4] The relationship between the various kinds of homosexuality and the problem of effeminacy in male dancing is much too complex for discussion here: a homosexual or bisexual male dancer does not necessarily dance in an effeminate manner.

The attitude of the company director to the dancer makes itself felt in a hundred different ways, both directly and indirectly; even if the dancer rarely sees the director, he comes into contact with the latter's attitude as transmitted by teachers, maîtres de ballets, choreographers and star dancers. In some companies there is a very distinctive atmosphere of mutual suspicion and intrigue: dancers fear to say what they really think, for a careless remark may have terrible consequences. (In the Diaghilev company in the twenties this atmosphere was very strong, some dancers being suspected by the others of being Diaghilev's spies.)[1] Most dancers have had experience of this horrible atmosphere at some time or another.

Very often the experiences of the dancer in school set narrow limits to his potentialities of development. Great teachers like Auguste Vestris, Didelot, Blasis and Nicolas Legat turn out great dancers not only because they have profound understanding of technique and expression, but also because they have respect for the individuality of their various pupils and foster this in every way. Being or having been great dancers themselves they have intuitive understanding of the patterns of thought and feeling of those highly sensitive and imaginative pupils who are capable of developing into great dancers, and so are able to help these pupils to discover what sort of persons they really are.[2] (The personality of the dancer and his style of dancing are inseparable: the teacher trains the whole of the pupil, not just the limbs.) There are many teachers, however, who for one reason or another do not help their pupils to progress beyond a certain point, and distort the natural development of the pupil to such an extent that even if he later comes into contact with good teachers he may not be able to profit by their teaching. It is no accident that the really great teachers sometimes have fewer pupils than have second-rate teachers; the great teacher makes what one might call spiritual demands on the pupil—demands to which only those with a certain amount of nobility, integrity and maturity are able to respond. (The others feel uneasy, and soon go off to less exacting teachers.)

Few directors of ballet companies are capable of feeling humility toward great teachers, and it is rare for a great teacher to be associated with a ballet company school for any length of time. Important exceptions were of course the Maryinsky (Johannsen, Cecchetti, Legat, etc.) and the Diaghilev Ballet (Cecchetti, Legat and Nijinska). Other exceptions were the Ida Rubinstein Ballet (Nijinska, 1927–28), the de Basil company (Ana Roje, 1939), the Ballets

[1] *Cf.* Ninette de Valois, *Invitation to the Ballet*, p. 60.
[2] *Cf.* Nicolas Legat, "What is Élan in Dancing?" *The Dancing Times*, February, 1937: "How profound, how sympathetic must be the understanding of the spiritual guide in art (I use the expression deliberately) whose task it is slowly to unfold the hidden possibilities of the aspirant's artistic soul. How far-reaching must be his knowledge of technique, how wide must be his experience. . . . No opportunity should be missed to evoke . . . the co-operative imagination in young students, and make them grasp the vital fact that the movements of ballet are natural movements, idealized and woven into an artistic picture."

Russes de Monte Carlo No. 3 (Ana Roje, 1938, and Nijinska, 1943–4), the London Ballet (Craske, 1938–9), Ballet Theatre (Craske, 1947), the Ram Gopal company (Radhelal Misra, 1949–52) and the José Greco company (La Quica). But it is quite normal for an institution like the Paris Opéra to make no use as teachers or régisseurs of Parisians like Preobazhenskaya, Trefilova, Yegorova, Kshessinshaya, Volinine and Kniasev. In the same way we find the Vic-Wells Ballet making no use as teachers or régisseurs of Londoners like Nicolas Legat, Karsavina, Lopukhova and Sokolova, and employing Idzikovsky as teacher for only two years.[1]

The impoverishment of tradition which has resulted from the lack of contact between the great Maryinsky and Diaghilev dancers and the big ballet companies of today is so great that it is hard to take its measure. It emerges clearly, however, in the gesture of Preobazhenskaya as she corrects the angle of an arm or the slope of a head; in the miming of Karsavina as she shows how she used to perform the beginning of Le Spectre de la Rose; in the dancing of Idzikovsky in street shoes and a lounge suit at the front of his class, as precise and controlled as ever; and in revivals by ballet clubs of tattered old films of Pavlova and Spessivsteva in their prime. It also emerges clearly in the dancing of those younger artists who had the good fortune to make contact with the Russian tradition at its best and the sensitivity to absorb it: Margot Fonteyn as Giselle, Odette-Odile and Aurora; Ulanova as Odette; Ana Roje as Maria; Beriosova as the Lilac Fairy. It is equally clear in good performances of Fokine and Tudor ballets in which the great tradition is both preserved and extended: Massine and Chauviré in Petrouchka; Kaye, Tudor and Laing in Pillar of Fire.

From the point of view of the dancer, the most important aspect of artistic policy is casting. If a dancer receives one or two good rôles, he can find some sort of relief from his inner conflicts in creative work, and is thus able to put up with many other types of frustration for years on end. But it is only in creative companies, hybrid companies in their creative phase, and some types of choreographer's company that good casting is the rule rather than the exception: very often casting is determined by other considerations than the dancer's talent and suitability for the rôle. Sometimes a combination of circumstances forces the director to break through the usual pattern of casting and give a rôle to a dancer who richly deserves it: to the public and the critics it then seems that this dancer has made enormous progress and developed new qualities, though in fact these qualities were there all the time—carefully hidden

---

[1] I must add that Craske did good work at the Vic-Wells school before the War, and much of the polish of the dancing of the Sadlers Wells Ballet in the period 1948–51 was due to the careful work of Mary Skeaping as ballet mistress: after her departure the general standard deteriorated seriously. Karsavina was commissioned to produce Le Spectre de la Rose for the Sadlers Wells Ballet in 1944, but this revival was disappointing: neither Margot Fonteyn nor Alexis Rassine seemed able to assimilate the Fokine style, so different from the styles to which they were accustomed.

under a bushel. This sudden flowering of a dancer is most likely to happen in the early stages of a company's existence, before it has sunk too far into a rut and before the most individual and imaginative of the dancers have left. As the years go by such events tend to become more and more rare until they cease entirely.

It is above all frustration over casting which causes dancers to take the drastic (and usually irrevocable) step of leaving a company. By this action they are almost certain to deprive themselves of the chance of dancing for long periods, and possibly for good; for it is very difficult to break into long-established companies. (In England things are made exceptionally difficult for the free-lance dancer by the fact that nearly all companies are associated with one school.) Dancers leave a company only when they reach a state where they feel they must do something even if it wrecks their career: the alternative to leaving the company (the virtual destruction of their creative powers and individuality) is even worse. When dancers continue to leave a company this is a sign that something is seriously wrong with its artistic policy: with any encouragement dancers develop feelings of loyalty very quickly, and are prepared to put up with great hardships to stay with a company which they feel will give them real opportunities, but they can feel no loyalty to a company which breaks their spirit.

Intrigues are to be found in most institutions, but they reach an exceptional degree of viciousness in ballet companies; the career of a dancer is relatively short, and the dancer who relies on talent alone is liable to get nowhere until it is too late. Willy-nilly he must learn to defend his interests—by financial, sexual or other means. The greater the talent of the dancer the more jealousy he arouses and the more he suffers from intrigue—as Nijinsky and Karsavina found to their cost in the Maryinsky.[1] Unfortunately the greatest dancers, with their high ideals and dedicated outlook, are the ones least able to cope with intrigue. When the artistic climate is healthy the great dancers at the top of the ladder take an interest in the fate of the talented young dancers on the way up, and give them invaluable assistance, but in normal circumstances the best young dancers waste years in frustration and misery until they learn to recognize intrigue and deal with it.

Though companies with a relatively expressionist artistic policy are likely to have climates hostile to the development of a high degree of personality and individuality among the dancers, we often find that one or two dancers in such companies receive every possible encouragement: the company-directors seem to regard these dancers as their alter egos, and take unalloyed pride in their achievements. But even such highly favoured dancers suffer indirectly from

[1] *Cf.* Anatole Bourman, *The Tragedy of Nijinsky*, p. 26; Tamara Karsavina, *Theatre Street*, p. 110. Nijinsky owed a great deal to the help given him by Kshessinskaya.

deficiencies in the artistic policies of the companies to which they belong, and tend eventually to reach an impasse in their development.

Choreographers can best be considered as a specialized type of dancer; some gifted dancers have no feeling for choreography, but a fair proportion of the best dancers have real potentialities as choreographers, and under favourable circumstances can develop these potentialities to a point where they can compose interesting ballets. Geniuses like Fokine are of course very rare, but there is no reason why we should not expect the same average level of imagination, sensitivity and technical skill among contemporary choreographers that we find among contemporary composers. In fact the average level of choreography cannot be compared in any way with that of musical composition: even moderate technical skill in choreography is so rare that it is liable to cause a new ballet to be hailed as a masterpiece, and in scarcely one new ballet out of a score does the choreographer show any understanding of how to begin tackling a theme. This is of course partly due to the confusion of styles to be found in the aftermath of expressionism; only the most original choreographers can do satisfactory work in such a period. But it is also due in large measure to the destructive artistic climate inside ballet companies; this prevents dancers from coming to maturity, and *a fortiori* choreographers.

Apart from the artistic climate, choreographers are injured by the distortion or cancellation of their projects, and by the warped development of the dancers at their disposal. There is in fact a close bond between the development of choreography and that of dancing: choreographers need sensitive and mature individuals to give satisfactory interpretations to the various rôles in their ballets, while dancers need exacting rôles in new ballets to come to full maturity. (The great ballets of the past become so impoverished in transmission from dancer to dancer that they cannot stimulate the dancer in the same way as good new ballets: this is not true of two great rôles—Odette-Odile and Giselle—in which there has been an apostolic succession, but relatively few dancers get the chance of tackling these rôles.)

Because of the frustration of talent in nearly all ballet companies, the dancers in these companies and the ballets in which they appear represent what Sullivan calls "inferior caricatures of what they might have been". The best dancers degenerate instead of making progress, or else are hardly ever seen by the public because they have left their parent company, and the great choreographers are deprived of any opportunity of doing creative work.

Even when great choreographers are brought in from outside the results are usually disappointing. Noverre broke his heart in the Paris Opéra at the end of the eighteenth century, and Fokine and Tudor had many similar experiences in the twentieth century.

Though it would be Utopian to expect a State Ballet to foster work of real originality, we are entitled to expect that an institution run with the help of the tax-payer's money should preserve the heritage of the past at least as well as the Royal Danish Ballet, providing the choreographic equivalent of a museum or public library. Unfortunately it is only under special circumstances and for relatively short periods that most State Ballets are capable of fostering the development of great solo dancers or even of a satisfactory corps de ballet, and they rarely preserve choreography intact.

From private companies we must of course accept whatever the director chooses to give us, and should be grateful for small mercies in the shape of brilliant individual performances. These are likely to be fairly common with most types of private company in their early stages, and are of the highest importance in keeping the great ballet tradition alive. At the same time they draw attention to the extremely wide gap between the resources available and the actual level of achievement—a gap which is probably greater now than at any time in the history of ballet; for, today, in spite of every kind of frustration, a surprisingly large number of dancers with great independence of outlook have managed to preserve their ideals and achieve an impressive degree of individuality. Though the chasm between resources and achievement appears unbridgeable, there is no reason to think that this problem is any more insoluble than many others which have been successfully tackled in recent years.

One of the most encouraging features of twentieth-century ballet is that the most artistically important companies—e.g. the Diaghilev company of 1909–13 and the Blum–de Basil–Massine company of 1932–36—were also the ones which drew the largest and most faithful audiences. The Diaghilev company established the self-sufficient touring company as an artistic enterprise of major importance; the Blum–de Basil–Massine company proved that a good company with a well-balanced repertoire can make money. No less encouraging was the enormous success of Tudor's ballets in attracting audiences new to ballet during the London blitz of 1940–41 and in helping to consolidate Ballet Theatre during the critical early years of its existence. When ballet is degenerate it attracts only a coterie audience, but good ballet has the same broad appeal as the Elizabethan drama as presented by Elizabethan actors.

Ballet history shows that no one country can claim persistent pre-eminence in all branches of this art. The Italians excel in the mechanical aspects of dance-technique and in powerful dramatic mime; the French and the English show outstanding talent for the composition of self-sufficient ballets d'action and for subtlety and restraint in expression; the Russians excel in these same qualities of subtlety and restraint and also have a flair for the most violent and exuberant type of character dances; the Danish male dancers delight us with their nobility and simplicity, the Poles with their elevation and *élan*, the Yugoslavs with their intelligence and fire, the Americans with their joie de vivre and sense of humour; and so on. Ballet has need of all these qualities, and that is one reason why ballet is perhaps the most international of the arts: though every good ballet draws strength from national traditions, it also has tap-roots in the ballet traditions of other countries. We have seen how elements from a number of different countries contributed to the renaissance of ballet in Russia towards the end of the nineteenth century. Such an international synthesis is just as important in the second half of the twentieth century, and can lead to quite as exciting a renaissance.

Ballet history also shows that this art cannot retain its vitality and make progress unless it is sustained by the imagination and enterprise of *both* patrons *and* theatrical managers (impresarios). Sallé was backed by the theatrical managers Moylin, John Rich and Monnet; Noverre was backed in turn by Monnet, Garrick, Carl Eugen of Württemberg, Durazzo (acting for the Emperor of Austria), Marie Antoinette (Queen of France), and several London theatrical managers; Didelot was backed by London theatrical managers and the Tsars of Russia; and so on. The twentieth century has seen the development of many new types of ballet and ballet company, and the pattern of commercial and non-commercial backing is far more complex than in previous centuries; but essentially the position is much the same as before. In some respects there has been a change for the worse: the fact that the cost of running a company has risen much more than the price of theatre seats has reduced the possible margin of profit and greatly increased the risk. In other respects, however, there has been a change for the better: the ballet audience is now far larger and more widespread than ever before, and ballet is one of the very few branches of the theatre which is helped rather than hindered by the competition of television—the small flat figures moving across a screen being unable to compete effectively with living dancers. On balance, therefore, it would appear that the opportunities available to contemporary successors of Rich, Monnet, Karl Eugen, Durazzo, Lumley, the Russian Tsars, Mamontov, Alexander Gross, Otto Kahn and Sir Oswald Stoll—not to mention a great many dynasties of Indian princes and Maecenas himself, patron of the pantomine Bathyllus— are as great as ever before: possibly even greater. The talent is there, and the future beckons strongly. There is room for any amount of enterprise and imagination in the ballet world of tomorrow.

BIOGRAPHICAL NOTE ON THE AUTHOR

FERNAU HALL's background is almost as cosmopolitan as the art of ballet. His father belongs to a family which emigrated to North America at the time of the Napoleonic Wars, whilst his mother (Elena Fernau) was born near Seville in Spain. His maternal grandmother was a well-known Andalusian dancer.

Fernau Hall was born in Victoria, British Columbia, on the West coast of Canada, and was educated in Victoria and Vancouver. At University he concentrated on the theatre: after travelling in various European countries he began work as an actor and stage manager in London. But he soon found himself powerfully attracted to ballet, and started serious training, studying both the Russian and the Cecchetti schools of classical ballet. Later he added the free dance, Spanish dancing and Indian dancing to his work and studies. After some years of intensive training he began to dance in ballet companies, taking part in the formative period of English ballet. His work left little time for writing, but in 1937 he began to write criticism for *The Dancing Times*.

He spent nearly six years in the British Army (1940–46), and during this period found opportunities—in many places—to further his research in ballet history. It was then that he began work on *Modern English Ballet* (published by Andrew Melrose Ltd. in 1950). This is the only comprehensive book on English ballet and is now regarded as the standard work: it has been reprinted several times.

After his Army service he danced in a variety of companies—English classical, cosmopolitan Ballet-Russe, "modern", Indian, Negro, etc., and was also in two ballet films. But his career as a dancer was inevitably limited by the fact that he began his training when already adult: he began then to concentrate on the production of ballet—which had always attracted him. He worked for a number of companies of a wide variety of types, usually as a stage director, but sometimes as lighting director, assistant maître-de-ballet, producer or business manager. He also worked in collaboration with B.B.C. producers on the production of dance-programmes for English Television. (It was here that his wartime experience on the experimental side of Radar proved very helpful.) He also lectured on ballet at the City Literary Institute— London's famous centre of adult education.

An Anatomy of Ballet was completed in three years' intensive work, but it represents the distillation of practical experience and sustained historical research extending over many years.

LINE DRAWINGS

Page

Colette Marchand as Agathe, the White Kitten, in *Les Demoiselles de la Nuit* (Petit, Paris, 1948)   *drawing by Milein Cosman*   43

Left: *cabriole*. Right: *grand jeté en avant*. The beginnings of the Blasis school.   Illustration drawn by Casartelli and engraved by Rados for Carlo Blasis, *Traité élémentaire, théorique et pratique de l'Art de la Danse* (Milan, 1820)   84

Markova as the Ballerina in *Petrouchka* (Fokine, Paris, 1911), as produced by the Festival Ballet in 1951   *drawing by Milein Cosman*   96

Marianne Balchin in class   *drawing by Milein Cosman*   219

Croisé position of the feet.   *Blasis illustration as above*   258

The Birth of Urvashi (Kutty-Vajifdar, Bombay, 1951) with Roshan Vajifdar (*left*) as the apsara Passion and Khurshed Vajifdar (*right*) as the apsara Longing   *drawings by Shiavax Chavda*   293

Rosario and Antonio in a Sevillanas   *drawing by Milein Cosman*   306

Ana Roje giving a private lesson   *drawing by Milein Cosman*   311

Maria Medina Vigano as Atalanta (choreography by Salvatore Vigano, ca. 1795)   *drawing by Schadow*   324

A Kandyan dancer (Ceylon)   *drawing by Shiavax Chavda*   326

Posé en arabesque: the dancers represent Diana and Apollo   401
Blasis illustration as above

A cat in *Les Demoiselles de la Nuit* (Petit, Paris, 1948)   426
drawing by Milein Cosman

ACKNOWLEDGEMENT

The author is very grateful to Milein Cosman (who made drawings specially for this book); to Raymond Mander and Joe Mitchenson (who ransacked their remarkable theatre collection in search of illustrations to this book); to Nan Spence and Olive Shewring (who helped with the index); and to a number of great teachers, choreographers and dancers (who taught him the meaning of tradition in the classical dancing of the West and the East).

INDEX OF BALLETS, DANCES, Etc.

This index covers original compositions for the theatre (ballets, dances, operas, films, plays, musicals, pantomimes, etc.); it excludes traditional dances. Figures in italics refer to pages opposite which, or on which, there are illustrations relating to the item in question.

Acis et Galathée, 88
'Adame Miroir, 390
Adam Zero, 158, 159, 368, 369
Adding Machine, The (Play), 144
Adieu, 253
Aeneas, 181
Age of Anxiety, The, 241, 245, 256, 257
Ajanta Frescoes, 280
Alcina, 23
Alexandre le Grand, 181
Alice in Wonderland, 342
Alma Mater, 378
Amarilla, 334n, 357
Amor, 42
Amor Brujo, El, 303, 304, 305
Amors og Balletmesteren Luner (see Caprices du Cupidon et du Maître de Ballet)
Amours de Jupiter, Les, 248
Amphion (Massine), 354
Amphion and Thalia (1791), 33
Apollo and Daphne, or The Burgomaster Tricked (Pantomime), 21
Apollon Musagète, 165, 167, 187, 379, 380
Appalachian Spring, 351
Apparitions, 189, 190
Après-Midi d'un Faune, L' (Lifar), 180
Après-Midi d'un Faune, L' (Nijinsky), 71, 97, 103, 104, 105, 112, 113, 113, 114, 137, 139, 140, 163, 179, 204, 422, 423
Arianna (Opera), 33
Art of Kathakali, The, 273
Astuzie Feminili, Le (Opera Ballet), 129
Atalanta of the East, 202, 203
Audition, 230, 234
Aurora's Wedding, 141, 187, 201

Bacchus et Ariane, 23, 176, 178
Baiser de la Fée, Le, 189, 190, 379, 416
Ballabile, 251, 252, 371
Ballade (Robbins), 246
Ballade (Staff), 241
Bal, Le (Balanchine), 166, 167, 188, 245, 404
Bal, Le (Jooss), 149
Ballet Chinois, 24
Ballet Class, 230
Ballet Girl, The (Musical), 275

Ballet Imperial, 257, 380
Ball in Old Vienna, 365
Barabau, 164
Bar aux Folies-Bergères, 156
Barbe-Bleu, 95
Bayadère, La, 279
Beach, 404
Beau Danube, Le, 130, 131, 158, 323, 343, 385, 430
Beautiful Joseph (see Légende de Joseph)
Beauty and the Beast, 254
Beggar's Opera, The (Opera by Weill), 210
Berioska, 320
Biches, Les, 160, 160, 161, 164, 166, 172, 186, 188
Big City, 138, 151, 363, 390
Billy the Kid, 236, 380, 422, 424
Birth of Our Nation, 291
Birth of Urvashi, The, 292, 293
Bluebeard, 242, 422
Bonne-Bouche, 256
Boon, The, 289, 291, 292
Boris Godunov (Opera), 66, 67
Bourrée Fantasque, 169
Boutique Fantasque, La (Jooss), 149
Boutique Fantasque, La (Massine), 128, 129, 134, 149, 151, 152, 156, 371, 374, 375, 377n., 407
Broken Bow (Play), 163
Brudefærden i Hardanger, 40, 49

Cabinet of Dr. Caligari, The (Film), 121
Cage, The, 246
Camille, 382
Cantique des Cantiques, Le, 181
Capriccio Espagnol, 415
Caprices du Cupidon et du Maître de Ballet, Les, 321
Carmen, 250, 251, 252, 256, 389, 390
Carmen et son Toreador, 48
Carnaval (Fokine), 68, 87, 90, 177, 214, 259, 366, 406, 412
Carnaval (Froman), 308
Casse-Noisette, 60, 61, 199, 260
Catarina, 38, 42, 50, 331
Cave of the Heart, 146

Cendrillon, 54, 95, 409, 422, 429
Chatte, La, 81, 160, 165, 166, 177, 188, 390
Cheats of Scapin, The; or, The Tavern Bilkers, 20
Checkmate, 157, 158, 191, 368, 369, 375
Children's Corner, 253, 256
Chitra (Kutty), 291
Chitrangada (Sarabhai), 358, 359
Chopin Concerto, 416
Chopiniana (Borlin), 138, 394
Chopiniana (Fokine–Clustine), 333, 386
Chopiniana (Fokine), 90, 259, 308, 323, 330, 331, 332 (see also *Sylphides, Les*)
Chopiniana (Froman), 308
Choreartium, 131, 132, 404
Chota Roustaveli, 183, 428
Chout, 77, 104
Christmas Eve, 332
Cimarosiana, 129n
Cinderella, 194, 198
Ciné-Bijou, 252
Cléopâtre, 67, 89, 135, 138, 259, 353, 354
Cleopatra (solo item by Rubinstein), 353
Clock Symphony, 133
Cloud Messengers, The, 345
Cobras, The, 276
Concerto Barocco, 380, 385n
Concurrence, La, 166, 170
Conservatoire, 322
Coppélia (Beck), 322
Coppélia (Froman), 308
Coppélia (Jooss), 149n
Coppélia (Petipa–Ivanov), frontispiece, 55, 328, 356, 374
Coppélia (Saint-Léon), 41, 317
Corregidor y la Molinara, El, 303
Corsaire, Le, 50, 62
Cotillon, 166, 167, 172, 188, 241, 245, 404
Création du Monde, La (Borlin), 137, 155, 234
Création du Monde, La (de Valois), 155, 191, 365
Créatures de Promethée, Les, 178
Cross-Gartered, 201
Cuadro Flamenco, 77, 299
Cupid and Psyche, 190, 191, 196
Cygne, Le, 87, 90, 263, 279, 330, 331, 332, 334, 346, 386
Czernyana, 240, 241, 254

Dance of the Five Senses, 276
Dance of the Setting Sun, 345, 346
Danses Caucasiennes, 90
Danses Concertantes, 380, 401

Dante Sonata, 190, 191
Danza Incaica, 306
Daphnis et Chloë (Ashton), 195, 196
Daphnis et Chloë (Fokine), 71, 88, 185, 318
Dark Elegies, 207, 208, 209, 209, 210, 211, 212, 213, 216, 217, 218, 224, 232, 254, 387, 396, 420
Dark Meadow, 146
David Triomphant, 181
Deaths and Entrances, 146
Débutante, La, 39
Déjeuner sur L'Herbe, Le, 248
Demoiselles de la Nuit, Les, 249, 250, 252, 257, 389, 390, 426
Départ pour une Corride, 48
Descent of Hebe, The, 204, 206
Design with Strings, 430
Deuil en 24 Heures, 252
Deux Mendiants, Les, 165
Devil in the Village, 310
Diable Amoureux, Le, 48
Diavolina, 41
Dido and Aeneas (Opera), 209
Dieu Bleu, Le, 89, 90, 279
Discovery of India, The, 289
Divertissement de Tchaikovsky, 179
Donald of the Burthens, 133, 134, 135
Don Juan (Angiolini), 25
Don Juan (Ashton), 194, 196, 199
Don Juan (Fokine), 95
Don Quixote (Gerhard), 158, 159
Don Quixote (Petipa), 48, 260
Douanes, 365
Dramma per Musica, 428
Dubarry (Musical), 275
Dying Swan, The (see Cygne, Le)

Earth-Spirit (Play), 98
Ecuyère, L', 183
Egypta, 275
Egyptian Mummy, The, 280
Éléments, Les, 199
Elfes, Les, 94
El Greco, 136, 153
El Penitente, 351
Elysian Fields, The, 101
Emperor Jones, The (Play), 144
Enchanted Flute, The, 328
Enfant Prodigue, L' (Mime Play), 346
Enigma, 163
Enigma Variations, 241
Epithalamium, 400, 401
Épreuve d'Amour, L', 95, 400, 412

Errand into the Maze, 351
Errante, L', 377
Erwartung (Monodrama), 98
Esmeralda, 37, 38, 42, 48, 50, 259, 260, 331 *and n*
Étude de Bach, 162, 416
Eugene Onegin, 29
Eunice, 88
Every Soul is a Circus, 146
Excelsior, 42

Façade, *177*, 187, 188, 189, 190, 197, 240
Facheux, Les, 161
Facsimile, 238n, 245
Fall River Legend, 237, 238
False Pride, 291
Fanciulla delle Rose, 241
Fancy Free, *241*, 242, 243, 244, 251, 255, 422, 423, 424
Faune (see *Après-Midi d'un Faune, L'*)
Faust (Blasis), 321n
Faust (Perrot), 37, 42, 48, 50
Feather of the Dawn, The, 143
Femmes D'Alger, 412
Femmes de Bonne Humeur, Les, 127, 128, 129, 130, 152, 156, 404
Festin, Le, 67
Fête Etrange, La, 239
Fiancée du Diable, La, 248
Fille du Pharaon, La, 49, 280
Fille Mal Gardée, La, 27, 36, 260 *and n*, 329
Fils Prodigue, Le (Balanchine) (see *Prodigal Son*)
Fils Prodigue, Le (Jooss), 149
Firebird (Balanchine), *161*, 173
Firebird, The (see *Oiseau de Feu, L'*)
Folkesagn, Et, 40, 324
Folk Legend, A (see *Folkesagn, Et*)
Forains, Les, 183, 247, 248, 251, 424
For Love or Money, 357
Fountain of Bakhchisaraï, The (Harmoš), *305*, 310
Fountain of Bakhchisaraï, The (Zakharov), 264, 310
Fra Sibirien til Moskou, 40

Gaieté Parisienne, 133
Gala Festival (Film), 272
Gala Performance, 211, 387
Gallant Assembly, 209, 210
Garuda, the Golden Eagle, 344
Ghosts (Play), 99

Gingerbread Heart, The (see *Licitarsko Srce*)
Giselle (Lifar), 428
Giselle (Perrot-Coralli), 35, 36, 42, 48, *49*, 50, 77, 141, 179, 184, 190, 201, 241, 259, 260, 264, 274, 308, 310, 317, 319, 323, 329, 331, 334, 340, 347, *353*, 356, 375, 376, 420, 423, 430
Gloire, La, 218
Good Humoured Ladies, The (see *Femmes de Bonne Humeur, Les*)
Graduation Ball, 411
Great American Goof, The, 419
Green Table, The, *145*, 150, 151, 152, 156, 157, 181, 203, 363, 364, 365, 390
Guests, The, 245

Hairy Ape, The (Play), 144
Hamlet, 158, 263, 369
Hans Christian Andersen (Film), 252, 389n
Harlem Incident, 242
Harlequinade, 329
Harlequin in April, 256, 257
Harvest According, The, 238
Helen of Troy, 242, 422
Herodiade, 351
Hexentanz, 119
High Button Shoes (Musical), 244
Hindu Wedding, A, 280
Histoire du Soldat, L' (Musical tale), 79, 109n
Homage to Bournonville, 321
Homage to the Queen, *177*, 199
Homme et Son Désir, L', 137, *144*, 393
Hooray for What (Musical), 233
Horoscope, 189
Hunch-Backed Horse, The, 260

Iberia, 136, 394
Icare, *176*, 180, 181, 185
Illuminations, 195
Incense, 276, 281
India Immortal, 289
Interplay, 244, 246, 341, 422, 423, 424
Intolerance (Film), 142n
Islamey, 89
Istar, 320

Jardin aux Lilas, 205, 206, 207, 208, *208*, 211, 212, 213, 215, 216, 234, 241, 257, 368, 384, 387, 419, 421
Jeu de Cartes, 379
Jeune Homme et la Mort, Le, 248, *417*, 425, 426

Jeux (Borlin), 136
Jeux d'Enfants, 404
Jeux, Les (Nijinsky), 105, 106, 107, 108, 113,
    114, 115, 136, 140, 160
Job (Balanchine), 377
Job (De Valois), 155, 156, 191, 334, 365
Journey in the Fog, 152
Judgment of Paris, 210, 211, 213, 215, 216,
    234, 387

Kalevala, 388
Kalpana (Film), 284, 285
Krishna and Radha, 280

Labour and Industry, 285
Labyrinth, 146
Lac des Cygnes, Le, 54, 57, 58, 60, 61, 62, 64,
    66, 77, 84, 90, 174, 175, 177, 187, 198,
    199, 201, 257, 259, 260, 262, 264, 274,
    308, 310, 329, 332, 356, 359, 367, 368,
    374, 375, 376, 406, 430
Lady in the Ice, The, 252
Lagarterana, 306
Lagarteranos, Los, 306
Lakmé (Opera), 276
Légende de Joseph, La (Fokine), 89
Légende de Joseph, La (Goleizovsky), 261
Legend of Ohrid, The (Harmoš), 305
Legend of Rama, The, 345
Letter to the World, 146
Licitarsko Srce, 308
Life, 310
Lilac Garden (see Jardin aux Lilas)
Livjægerne paa Amager, 40
Loup, Le, 252
Lovers' Gallery, 241
Loves of Mars and Venus, The, 21
Lucifer, 185
Lysistrata, 202, 206, 210

Macbeth, 30
Mad Tristan (see Tristan Fou)
Magic Mirror, The, 135
Maison des Fous, La, 136, 156, 384
Mam'zelle Angot, 133, 422
Manushya, 359
Masques, Les, 188
Matelots, Les, 161, 164
Matsya Kanya, 359
Medée et Jason, 25, 28, 30
Mephisto Valse (Nijinsky), 74, 109

Mercury, 188
Merry Widow, The (Operetta), 343
Metamorphoses, 169
Midsummer Night's Dream, A (Play), 347
Miracle in the Gorbals, 158, 369
Mogul Serenade, 345
Moon and Rain, 223
Morceaux Enfantins, 253
Mothers, The, 400
Movement, 223, 224, 224, 225
Mozartiana, 188, 380
Muse s' Amuse, La, 239

Naïade and the Fisherman, The (see Ondine)
Namouna, 182
Narcisse, 88, 89, 144
Nautch Dance, 276
New Yorker, The, 415
Night Journey, 146
Night on a Bare Mountain, 310
Night Shadow, 172, 173, 417
Nina ou la Folle par Amour, 36
Noces, Les, 79, 81, 98, 140, 141, 153n, 162,
    177, 211, 375, 393
Nocturne, 189, 190
Nuit D'Égypte, Une (see Cléopâtre)
Nuit de St. Jean, La, 136
Nuit, La, 138, 151
Nursery Suite, 365

Ode, 82, 83, 377, 390
Oeuf à la Coque, L', 251, 252
Offerlunden, 137
Öga: sömn i dröm, 225, 226
Oiseau de Feu, L' (Balanchine), 173, 174, 179
Oiseau de Feu, L' (Fokine), 68, 88, 89, 95,
    97, 107, 177, 179, 259
Oiseau de Feu, L' (Lopukhov), 262
Oiseau de Feu, L' (Maudrik), 149
Oklahoma! (Musical), 225, 236, 237, 242
Ondine, 50, 331
On the Town (Musical), 244
Orfeo (Opera), 101n
Oriane et le Prince d'Amour, 185
Oriental Impressions, 280
Orphée et Euridice (Opera with Choreographic
    Production by Balanchine), 172, 379
Orpheus, 172, 173

Paganini, 95, 409
Palais de Cristal, Le, 170
Papillons, Les (Fokine), 90, 259

Papillons, Les (Froman), 308
Paquita, 48, 328
Parade, 128
Pas d'Acier, Le, 177, 262
Pas de Quatre, Le (Dolin), 340
Pas de Quatre, Le (Perrot), 57, 91, 199
Pastorale, 255, 257
Patineurs, Les, 190, 197, 255, 367
Pavillon d'Armide, Le, 64, 65, 65, 66, 67, 69, 92, 330
Peri, La (Pavlova), 280
Perle de Seville, La, 48
Perseus and Andromeda, 21
Peter and the Wolf, 240, 240, 241, 251, 254
Petrouchka (Fokine), 70, 71, 72, 80, 81, 84, 88, 90, 92, 93, 95, 96, 96, 98, 104, 107, 108, 110, 112, 113, 114, 115, 132, 134, 139, 144, 149, 152, 166, 177, 185, 208, 242, 259, 323, 338, 339, 342, 366, 390, 398, 406, 412, 423, 435
Petrouchka (Froman), 308
Petrouchka (Georgi), 150
Petrouchka (Jooss), 149
Petrouchka (Leontiev), 262
Pied Piper, The, 246
Pillar of Fire, 207n, 209, 211, 212, 213, 214, 215, 216, 225, 238, 257, 387, 416, 421, 422, 423, 435
Pineapple Poll, 255, 256, 257
Planets, The, 203, 204, 208, 208, 210, 211, 217, 368, 387
Polovtsian Dances from Prince Igor (see Prince Igor)
Pomona, 187, 191
Prayer, 352
Préludes, Les, 331
Présages, Les, 129, 131, 132, 167, 400, 404, 411, 415
Pride, 154
Primitive Mysteries, 208, 351
Prince Igor (Fokine), 67, 84, 87, 88, 90, 174, 177, 196, 323, 338, 342, 366, 406, 407, 412, 419
Prince Igor (Froman), 308
Prince Igor (Jooss), 149
Prodigal Son, The (Balanchine), 166, 172, 173
Promenade, 158
Provençale, La, 43
Pulcinella (Georgi), 150
Pulcinella (Jooss), 149
Pulcinella (Massine), 129, 149
Punch and the Judy, 146
Puppenfee, Die, 128
Pygmalion, 22

A.A.O.B.—2F

Qarrtsiluni, 322

Rajput Serenade of Love, 345
Rake's Progress, The, 145, 156, 157, 191, 335n, 366, 367, 368, 369, 372
Ram Leela, 289
Raymonda, 198, 260
Red Poppy, The, 264
Reflection, 257
Relâche, 82, 138
Renard, Le, 78, 81, 98, 139, 177, 179, 299, 393
Rendezvous, Les (Ashton), 188, 189
Rendezvous, Le (Petit), 248, 424
Rhythm of Culture, 289
Robert le Diable (Opera), 33
Rodeo, 225, 233, 234, 235, 236, 237, 242, 243, 251, 416, 420, 422, 423, 424
Roger Bloomer (Play), 144
Romeo and Juliet (Lavrovsky), 263, 264, 272
Romeo and Juliet (Tudor), 422
Romeo and Juliet (Film), 233
Romeo and Juliet (Shakespeare Play), 161
Roméo et Juliette (Nijinska), 82, 161, 164
Rose, la Violette et le Papillon, La, 39
Runaway Girl, The, 275
Ruy Blas (Play), 35

Sacre du Printemps, Le (Massine), 129, 130, 137, 179, 203
Sacre du Printemps, Le (Nijinsky), 70, 72, 76, 78, 81, 98, 105, 106, 107, 108, 109, 110, 113, 113, 114, 115, 127, 130, 135, 137, 139, 140, 179, 185, 208, 209, 217, 224, 322, 375, 422, 423
Salem Shore, 146
Salome, 163
Saratoga, 415, 423
Scènes de Ballet, 193, 194, 196, 199
Schéhérazade (Fokine), 68, 69, 70, 87, 89, 90, 96, 144, 174, 196, 214, 279, 308, 338, 342, 354, 400, 406, 407, 412
Schéhérazade (Froman), 308
Schuhplattltanz, 230
Sculpture Nègre, 136, 137
Scuolo di Ballo, 404
Sea Change, 254
Sea-Gull, The (Play), 399
Sea Legend, 356
Semiramide, 25
Serenade, 161, 167, 257, 378, 380, 430
Seven Dances of Life, The, 349

Seven Daughters, The, 279, 331
Shadow, The, 257
Shadow of the Wind, 217
Sieba, 42
Skating Rink, 138
Sleeping Beauty, The, 58–60, 61, 62, 77, 78, 135, 139, 141, 179, 260, 308, 334, 356
Sleeping Princess, The (see Sleeping Beauty, The)
Snow Maiden (see Baiser de la Fée)
Soir Bleu, 222, 223, 224
Soirée Musicale, 211, 369
Soleil de Nuit, 127
Songe, Un, 241
Sonnambula, La (Opera), 172
Spectre de la Rose, Le, 87, 149, 177, 179, 214, 310, 366, 406, 412, 419, 435 and n
Spirit of India, The, 289
Sport, 42
Spring Tale, A, 342
Stagefright, 230
Suite en Blanc, 182, 183
Svetlana, 264
Swan Lake, The (see Lac des Cygnes)
Sylphide, La (Bournonville), 40, 322, 336
Sylphide, La (Gsovsky), 426
Sylphide, La (Taglioni), 34, 91, 321n
Sylphides, Les, 67, 84, 87, 90, 91, 92, 94, 96, 97, 149, 153, 170, 177, 179, 187, 201, 204, 214, 241, 259, 263, 308n, 323, 330, 331, 332, 366, 369, 370, 374, 375, 398, 406, 409, 412, 419, 423, 430 (see also Chopiniana)
Sylvia (Ashton), 198
Sylvia (Legat), 63
Sylvia (Lifar), 317n
Sylvia (Mérante), 41
Symphonic Variations, 191, 192, 193, 197, 198, 370
Symphonie Fantastique, La, 38, 95, 132, 375, 404, 408, 411
Symphony for Fun, 337, 341
Symphony in C, 170n
Syrian Dance, 280

Tales of Hoffman (Film), 197
Tally-Ho, 422
Tandava Nrittya (Gopal), 344
Tandava Nritya (Shankar), 283
Tannhaüser (Opera), 104
Taras Bulba, 264, 272
Tartans, The, 239
Tentations de la Bergère, Les, 161

Thamar, 89, 90
Three-Cornered Hat, The, (see Tricorne, Le)
Three Gopi Maidens, 145
Three Ivans, The, 141
Three Marys, The, 400
Three Sisters, The, 209, 400
Three Virgins and a Devil, 234, 235, 242, 422
Tiresias, 196, 197
Titan, 120
Train Bleu, Le, 81, 161, 334, 336, 403, 426
Tricorne, Le, 128, 129, 133, 152, 303, 371, 374, 375, 415
Tristan Fou, 133, 429
Tritsch-Tratsch, 253
Triumph of Life, The, 292
Triumph of Neptune, The, 165, 187
Trumpet Concerto, 170
Turandot (Play), 99
Tyl Eulenspiegel (Nijinsky), 74, 75, 76, 78, 79, 109, 110, 115, 144, 217

Undertow, 214, 215, 216, 217, 250, 255, 257, 416, 422, 423
Union Pacific, 415
Usha, 289

Vain Precautions (see Fille Mal Gardée)
Valentine's Eve, 193, 239
Valse, La, 162
Valses Nobles et Sentimentales, 190, 193
Variations de Beethoven, 162
Vierges Folles, Les, 153
Vilia, 343
Visions, 356

Wanderer, The, 191
Wedding Bouquet, A, 190
Wedding Voyage in Hardanger (see Brudefærden i Hardanger)
Wise and Foolish Virgins, The, 156
Witch, The, 254, 255
Wozzeck (Opera), 98

Xochitl, 143

Zaza (Musical), 275
Zéphire et Flore (Didelot), 28, 30, 317
Zéphire et Flore (Massine), 177
Zingaro, Le (Opera-ballet), 35

GENERAL INDEX

This index excludes original compositions for the theatre, but includes traditional dances. Figures in italics refer to pages opposite which, or on which, there are illustrations relating to the item in question.

ABBEY Theatre, Dublin, 154
Abd-Al-Rahman II, 294
Abhinaya, 117, 222, 266, 267, 290, 298
Abstraction, expressionist, 97, 106, 123, 130, 131–2, 140, 203, 393, 400–1
——, music-interpretation (Duncan-Dalcroze), 101–2, 116–17, 143
——, neo-classical (Nijinsky), 109
——, post-expressionist classical (Tudor), 203, 208, 212
——, post-expressionist free dance (Åkesson), 220–6
——, pseudo-classical, 162, 165–6, 167–71, 182, 183, 191–2, 193–4, 199, 241, 244, 246, 255, 416–17
——, romantic (Fokine), 92
Abstract-Surrealist décor, costumes and properties, 173, 351
Abu-Nawas, 295
Academy of Choreographic Art, 154
Acrobatics, 155, 161, 165, 169, 177, 178, 184, 223, 260, 262, 275, 334, 383
Adagio (see Double-work)
Adams, Diana, 161, 217, 218, 382, 424
Adelphi Theatre, 412
Adler, Alfred, 257
Aga Khan, 428
Ajanta Cave paintings, 280, 292
Åkesson, Birgit, 220–6, 224, 310, 350
Al-Amin, Caliph, 295
Alarippu, 344
Alegrías, 298, 299
Alexander, Rolf, 364
Algarov, Youly, 428
Algeranov, Harcourt, 357
Algo, Julian, 356
Almora (Shankar School), 284, 292
Amala, 286
Amateur ballet, 289
Amaya, Carmen, 301
Ambassador's Theatre, 388
Amberg, George, 236, 242n, 415n
America (see United States of America)
American Academy of Dramatic Art, 357
—— audiences, 171, 385, 410, 414
—— Ballet-Russe, 336, 338, 407, 410, 413, 414–17, 418, 420, 421, 428, 429–30

American Ballet, The (Balanchine), 167, 378, 379, 380, 381
—— Ballet, The (Fokine), 94, 385–6
—— dancers, 235, 317, 337, 382–4, 438
—— folk-dances, 142
—— Indian dances, 142
Anand, Mulk Raj, 292
Andalusia, 294–8, 301
Andersen, Hans Christian, 257
Angiolini, Gasparo, 25, 27, 30, 399
Anglo-Polish Ballet, 369
Anouilh, 249, 252, 389
Anthropology, 413
Antonio, 299–300, 304, 306
Anura, 293
Appia, Adolphe, 116
Arab folk-dances, 117
Arab-Persian classical dancing, 295
Architecture, use of dancers as living, 140, 260
Archives Internationales de la Danse, 393
Arena ballet, 337
Arensky, Anton, 67
Argentina (Antonia Mercé), 303–5, 304, 403
Argentinita (Encarnación Lopez), 305
Argyle, Pearl, 366, 367, 370, 384, 395, 396, 399
Arnell, Richard, 256
Arnold, Malcolm, 199
Arova, Sonia, 340, 355, 398
Artistic climate of companies, 355, 363, 364, 370, 396, 407, 422, 431–9
—— policy, Determination of, 327, 334, 339, 352, 384, 391, 392, 398, 399, 402, 408, 422, 423
Art of Movement Studio, 121
Arts Council, The, 370, 373
—— Educational School, 336
—— Theatre, London, 387, 388, 397
Asafiev, 310
Ashton, Frederick, 158, 185–99, 227, 239, 240, 241, 242, 249, 251, 253, 254, 258, 355, 366, 367, 370, 374, 375, 384, 396, 419
Astafieva, Serafina, 58n, 334, 371
Astaire, Fred, 243
Astruc, Gabriel, 69

Athleticism (*see* Acrobatics)
Auden, W. H., 218, 245, 246
Audiences, American, 171, 385, 410, 414
——, Copenhagen, 40
——, English Provincial, 336
—— in general, 439
——, London, 23, 24, 26, 37, 69–71, 209, 255, 338, 370, 371, 376, 406–7, 411, 414
——, Petrograd, 259–60
Auguste, 28
Aurangzeb, 270
Auric, 354
Austria, Emperor of, 439
Austria-Hungary, 25–6, 117, 122, 307
Aveline, Albert, *336*
Aztec dances, 143

BABILÉE, Jean, 248, 249, 251, 425, 426
Bach, Johann Sebastian, 109, 118, 134, 167, 199, 222, 225, 249
Backers, 391, 439
Baile clasico español, 302–4
Bailey, Angela, 355
Bakst, Leon, 67, 68, 73, 77, 81, 88, 103, 104, 105, 112, 128, 332, 354, 375, 399
Balanchine, George, *81*, 82, 131, 152, *161*, 162, 176, 178, 180, 184, 185, 186, 187, 188, 189, 190, 193, 194, 195, 227, 241, 242, 244, 245, 247, 254, 255, 257, 262, 323, 366, 375, 377–85, 394, 396, *401*, 403, 404, 405, 407, 413, 415, 416, 417, *417*, 430
Balasaraswati, 285
Balchin, Marianne (Mrinalini), *219*, *273*, 293, 346
Balearic Islands, dances of, 301
Balinese classical dances, 125, 221, 222, 267n
Ballerina, privileges attaching to rank of, 329
Ballet Caravan, 379, 380, 418
—— Club (London), 188, 201, 202, 208n, 209, 232, 239, 336, 355, 356, 365, 366, 367, 381, 382, 386, 387, 395–7, 421
—— d'action, 20–30, 35, 39, 42, 322, 438
—— Institute, 429
—— International, 410, 428, 429, 430
—— Rambert, 188n, 205n, 208, 210, 232, 240, 286, 368, 369, 394, 397–9
Ballet-Russe, American, 336, 338, 407, 410, 413, 414–17, 418, 420, 421, 428, 429–30
——, Cosmopolitan, 402–13
Ballet Russe de Monte Carlo (U.S.A.– Denham company), 235, 380, 381, 385n, *401*, 416, 417, 420, 421, 429

Ballet Society, 381
Ballet Theatre, 95, 133, 205n, 207n, 211, 212, 217, 218, 234, 235, 238, 242, 244, 245, 336, 380, 381, 382, 383, 410, 415, *416*, 417–24, 429, 435, 438
—— War (1938), 409
Ballets de Paris, 249, 388–90
—— de Paris de Roland Petit, 390
—— des Champs-Élysées, 248, 249, 251, 389, 390, *417*, 424–6
—— Jooss, 149–52, 284 *and n*, 309, 326, 362–4, 365, 366, 390, 400
—— 1933, Les, 166, 188, 377, 378, 380, 405
Ballets Russes de Monte Carlo No. 1 (*see* Diaghilev Ballet)
—— Russes de Monte Carlo No. 2 (Blum-de Basil-Massine), 131, 167, 181, 201, 309, 335, 367, 378, *385*, 387, *400*, 402–12, 423
—— Russes de Monte Carlo No. 3 (Blum-Massine-Denham), 94, 170, 182, 184, 235, 309, 380, 381, 385, 412–17, 423, 435
—— Suédois, 136, 138, 156, *384*, 392–4
Baluch, Aziz, 294n
Banerji, Comolata, 280
Baranović, Kresimir, 308
Barbière, Simone (*see* Simkie)
Barea, Arturo, 216n
Barlach, 150
Baronova, Irina, 387, *400*, 406n, 407, 420
Barr, Margaret (*see also* Dance Drama Group), 299, 399, 400, 401
Bartok, Bela, 225, 392
Barzin, Leon, 382n
Basil, de (*see* de Basil)
Basque folk-dances, 302
Bathyllus, 439
Baton, René, 109
Bauhaus, 177
Bayadères (*see* Devadasis)
Baylis, Lilian, 154, 364
Bayston, Michael, 398
Beaugrand, Léontine, 41, 320
Beaumont, Count Etienne de, 130
——, Cyril W., 35, 54, 57, 62, 81, 112, 138, 188, 257, 387
Beck, Hans, 321, 322, *336*
Beethoven, 348
Belasco, David, 275
Belgrade, 308–9
Belgrade National Theatre, 308, 309
Bellini, Vincenzo, 172
Benedict, Ruth, 413
Bengali folk-dances, 279, 282

Benney, Mark, 178
Benois, Alexandre, 58, 63, 65, 67, 68, 69, 70, 71, 72, 79, 81, 82, 92, 109, 127, 164, 214, 330, 332, 354, 389, 399
Benthall, Michael, 158n
Bérard, Christian, 166, 247, 248, 250, 377, 403, 424, 425
Berenson, Bernard, 427
Beretta, Cattarina, 42, 55, 56
Berg, Alban, 98, 392
Bergson, Henri, 205, 206, 210, 214
Beriosov, Nicolas, 338, 342
Beriosova, Svetlana, *frontispiece*, 241, 257, 370, 373, 376, 435
Berlin, 100, 150, 277, 287, 328, 347
——, Irving, 228
—— State Opera, 150
Berlioz, Hector, 38, 132
Bernstein, Leonard, 245
Bharata Natyam, 266–73, 285, 286, 288, 289n, 303, 344, 345 and n, 346, 358
Bio-mechanics, 260
Bizet, 167, 170, 250
Blair, David, *frontispiece*, 157, 372, 373
Blake, William, 155, 185, 222
Blasis, Carlo, 32, 42, 54, *84*, *258*, *401*, 434
Blasis-Cecchetti school, 32–3, 42, 55–8, *84*, *258*, 344, *401*
Blasis-Lepri-Cecchetti school (*see* Blasis-Cecchetti school)
Blasis school (*see* Blasis-Cecchetti school)
Bliss, Arthur, 157
Bloch, Ernest, 204
Blomdahl, Karl-Birger, 225
Bluebell Girls, 373
Blues, 300 *and n*
Blum, René, 94, *385*, 403, 404 *and n*, 405, 407 *and n*, 408, 409, 412, 413n
—— company (1936–38), 94, 95, 167, 338, *401*, 412
Blum-de Basil-Massine company (1932–35), 131, 167, 181, 182, 201, 378, 387, *400*, 402–8, 409, 410, 412, 413, 414, 438
Blum-Massine company (1938–40), 309, 409, 410, 413, 414, 415
Bolender, Todd, 169, 227
Bolero, 303
Bolm, Adolph, 58n, 74, 75, *80*, *97*, 165, 328, 329
——, Otto, 328
Bolshoy school, 126
—— Theatre and company (Moscow), 54, 65 *and n*, 126, 136, 195, 260, 261, 370, 379

Bombay ballet, 267, 288–93, 345
Bon, René, 127, 430
Boner, Alice, 283
Boquet, 25
Bordeaux, 27, 48
Borlin, Jean, 135–8, 143, *144*, 153, 157, 226, *384*, 393n, 394
Borovansky, Edouard, *385*
Bosch, Hieronymus, 97, 110
Boucher, 24
Boulanger, Nadia, 233
Bourman, Anatole, 69, 110, 114, 115, 436n
Bournonville, Antoine, 39–40, 47, 50
——, Auguste, 39–40, *49*, 50, 56, 71, 321, 322, 323, 324, *336*, 340
—— school (*see* Franco-Danish school)
Bow, Clara, 392
Bozacchi, Giuseppina, 41
Brae, June, 158, 366, 367, 368 *and n, 369*, 369, 370, 375
Brahms, Caryl, 360n, 371
Branitza, Nathalia, 406
Braque, 161
Bratislava, 117
Breughel, 110
Briansky, Oleg, 340
Brianza, Carlotta, 56, 58
British Dance Theatre, 121
Britten, Benjamin, 195
Broadway, 230, 231, 242, 244
Brooking, Nesta, 387, 388
Bruhn, Erik, 252
Buckle, Richard, 357
Buddhist religion, 266, 267, 268, 276
Bulerías, 298
Bummel-Vigano, Maria, 32
Burdhan, Shanti, 289
Burke, Anthony, 253
Butsova, Hilda, 333

Cachuca, 250, 303
Calcutta, 267
Callot, 127
Calmette, 97
Calzabigi, 25, 399
Camargo, Marie, 22
—— Society, 154, 155, 187, 188n, 334, 395
Cambridge Theatre (London), 428
"Camp" talk, 433
Canary Islands, Dances of, 301
Cante jondo, 294, 297, 305 *and n*
Cape Town, 239, 252
——, Town Ballet, 252

Carl Eugen, Duke of Württemberg, 25, 315, 427, 439
Carné, 248
Carner, Mosco, 98
Carroll, Lewis, 343
Carter, Alan, 253
Carter, Huntley, 260n
Casartelli, 84, 258, 401
Castanets, 270n, 304
Casting, 318, 358–9, 370, 376, 377 and n, 435
Catalan folk-dances, 302
Caton, Edward, 429
Caucasian folk-dances, 90
Cecchetti, Enrico, 55, 56, 57, 58, 60, 150n, 176, 179, 317n, 434
—— method, 57, 356, 357, 365, 373, 388
—— school (see Blasis-Cecchetti school)
Cendrars, Blaise, 155
Center Theatre (New York), 419
Central Europe, 99–100, 102, 116–26, 131, 164, 191, 347, 362, 364, 400
Cerito, Fanny, 34, 48
Ceylon, classical dances of (Kandyan), 267, 293
Cézanne, 106, 185
Chabrier, Alexis, 188
Chabukiani, Vakhtang, 261
Chaliapine, Feodor, 66, 67
Chamié, Tatiana, 406
Champs-Élysées, Ballets des (see Ballets des Champs-Élysées)
Chaplin, Charlie, 110, 229, 238, 292
Chappell, Annette, 398
——, William, 192, 193, 367, 384, 395
Charnley, Michael, 341, 342, 343, 364
Charrat, Janine, 227, 247, 390, 426, 428
Chase, Lucia, 380, 416, 417, 418, 420, 423
Chatfield, Philip, 375
Chausson, 206, 213
Chauviré, Yvette, 320, 339, 428, 435
Chavda, Shiavax, 292, 293, 326
Chekhov, 99, 399
Chelichev, Pavel, 82, 83, 172, 377, 379
Cherepnin, Alexander, 66, 68, 89, 183
Chladek, Rosalia, 122
Chopin, Frédéric, 91
Choreographers (see Table of Contents, Parts I and II, for list of those discussed in detail)
Choreographer's Company, The, 360–90, 435
Choreography, aspects of composition in, 31, 48, 50–3, 186–7, 189, 192, 204, 208, 213, 225, 233–4, 249, 256, 287, 319, 345, 348, 359, 437

Choreography, relationship of dancing to music in (see Music, relationship to dancing)
Chowdhury, Dr. Shyam Shankar, 281
Chrimes, Pamela, 252
Chujoy, Anatole, 261n, 263n, 378n, 429n
Circus, 260
Classe de Perfection, 52, 261, 309, 395
Classical-romantic tradition in conflict with expressionism, 306–77
Classical romanticism, 86, 87–96, 386
Classical technique, ancient Arab-Persian, 295, 304
—— technique, Balinese, 125, 221, 222, 267n
—— technique, Cambodian, 222
—— technique, Chinese, 299
—— technique, European, 30, 32–3, 42, 50, 55–8, 124, 125, 142, 146, 201, 222, 229, 299, 311, 320, 335, 344, 356, 374
—— technique, Japanese (see also Kabuki), 109, 125, 201, 222, 266, 280, 299
—— technique, Javanese, 222, 267n, 343, 357
—— technique, Siamese, 90, 222
—— technique, Sinhalese (Kandyan), 267 and n, 293, 345n
—— technique, Spanish (Flamenco), 297–9, 304
—— techniques, Indian (see also Bharata Natyam, Kathak, Kathakali, Manipuri and Mohini Attam), 125, 222, 224, 265–73, 282, 283, 287, 291, 299, 304, 346
—— tradition as seen by post-expressionist pseudo-classicists, 168 and n, 179, 192, 385
"Classic ballets" (Balanchine), 167–70, 244, 255, 380, 415–7
Classicism, 92, 101, 109, 124, 125, 141, 168, 200–19, 221, 222, 233, 366
——, as seen by expressionists, 230, 366
——, post-expressionist, 200–19
Claudel, Paul, 137, 393
Clavé, Antoni, 252, 389
Clayden, Pauline, 377 and n
Clustine, Ivan, 280, 331, 333, 357
Cobos, Antonia, 429
Cochin school of Kathakali, 272
Cocktail ballets, 79–84, 141, 160, 164, 166, 177, 186, 188, 195, 200, 240, 247, 249, 336, 339, 340, 377, 390, 392, 393, 403, 404, 406, 424, 425, 426, 427, 433n
Cocteau, Jean, 128, 194, 248, 250, 390, 424, 425
Cohen, F. A., 362

Coleridge, 148n
Colin, Paul, 136
Collective creation in free dance, 349, 399–400
Comédie Française, 22, 35
Commedia dell' Arte, 21, 22, 269
Compagnie des Champs-Élysées (*see* Ballets des Champs-Élysées)
Companies (*see* Table of Contents (Part III, pp. 13–14, for list of companies discussed in detail)
Companies formed in the Twentieth Century, 325–439
Complementary partnership of directors, 399
Composition, methods of (*see* Choreography, aspects of composition in)
Cone, Grace, 336, 338
Conjeevaram school of Bharata Natyam, 344
Consciousness, 8, 205
Constructivism, 120, 140n, 169, 177, 260, 262, 285
Coolidge, Elizabeth Sprague, 165
Coomaraswamy, Ananda, 271
Copenhagen, 30, 39–40, 136, 321–4, 328
—— audience, 40
Copland, Aaron, 235, 246, 351, 380
Coralli, Jean, 36, *49*, 280
Cordoba, 294
Coreodramma, 31–2, 92
Coronation ballet, 199
Coros y Danzas de España, 301
Cosman, Milein, *96, 219, 306, 311, 426*, 441
Costumes, 69, 105, 136, 162, 178, 255, 270n, 292, 339, 342, 348, 350, 351, 385, 386, 388, 393, 395, 399, 422
Council for the Encouragement of Music and Art (C.E.M.A.), 397
Court ballet, 19, 28, 33, 39, 47–66, 321–4
Cowboy ballets, 235–6, 380, 422, 424
Cranko, John, 252–8
Craske, Margaret, 57, 355, 387, 388, 395, 396, 399, 435 *and* n
Creative Company, The, 391–401, 435
Creative process in dancing and choreography, 8, 431
Crete, ancient, 196–7
Crises in ballet companies, 360, 422
Critics, 175, 324, 410
Croatia, 307, 308
Cuadro Flamenco, 298, 299
Cuevas, Marquis de (*see* de Cuevas)
Curtains, use as décor of, 348, 385

Cynicism in male dancers, 433
Czerny, 240

DACIER, Émile, 22, 23
Dada, 128, 138
Daemon, artists possessed by, 329–30, 333, 361
Dalcroze, Émile Jaques-, 105, 106, 108, 116–26, 131, 140, 145, 154, 162, 171n, 176, 204, 265, 349, 357
Dale, Margaret, 251, 371
Dali, Salvador, 133
Dalmatia, 307, 309–10
Dance Center of Gluck-Sandor and Felicia Sorel, 242
Dance Drama Group, 284, 399–401
Dance-images, 172, 197, 205, 208, 209, 211, 212, 213, 223, 237–8, 249
Dance notation, 20, 114, 121, 349
Dance Theatre (Tudor), 209, 232, 233, 239
Dandré, Victor, 280n, 327n, 328n, 330, 331n
Danilova, Alexandra, 80, *129*, 164, 309, 367, 368n, *401*, 406, 407, 409, 416, 417
Danish dancers, 322–4, 438
Danish Royal ballet, Copenhagen, 30, 39, 252, 321–4, *336*, 340, 438
d'Annunzio, 354
Dardel, Nils, *384*
Darlu, 214
Darpana (Mrinalini Sarabhai school), 358
——, Nritya, 292, 293
Dartington Hall, 284, 362, 378, 399, 400
Darwin, Charles, 214
Dauberval, Jean, 27, 28
Daumier, 132
Deakin, Irving, 94n, 163, 378
de Basil, Col. W., 95, 130, *385*, 404 *and* n, 405, 406, 407 *and* n, 408, 409, 410, 413, 416
——, Company (1938–52), 127, 309, 336, 338, 340, 368, 408–412, 424, 429, 434
de Basil-Massine company (1936–38), 367 *and* n, 368, *385, 400*, 408, 413, 414, 416
Debussy, Claude, 104, 105, 279, 354
Décor, 32, 49, 51, 58, 63, 64, 65, 67, 77, 78, 81, 82, 98, 99, 100, 104, 106, 133, 157, 252, 332, 348, 351, 359, 385 *and* n, 386, 388, 389, 390, 393, 395, 399, 411, 422, 423, 425
de Cuevas company, 127, 427–30
——, Marquis, 410, 427, 428, 429–30
Degas, Edgar, 230
Degeneration, 40–53, 398
Delibes, 198, 317n

Dell' Era, Antonietta, 56
Delsarte, François, 117, 118, 119, 120, 142,
    145, 148, 208, 265, 275, 276*n*
Delsartism (*see* Delsarte)
de Maré, Rolf, 136, 155, 392–4, 427
de Mille, Agnes, 146, 208, *209*, 210, 216,
    217, 221*n*, *225*, 228–39, 241, 242, 244,
    245, 251, 396, 416, 419, 420, 422, 423
——, Cecil B., 229
de Moor, Teda, 399
Denby, Edwin, 317
Denham company (*see* Ballet Russe de
    Monte Carlo)
——, Sergei, 235, 413, 416, 417
Denishawn, 142, 143, 144, 145, 230, 283
Denmark, 39–40, 321–4
Depression, American (1929), 146
Desai, Jayantkumar, 359
——, Yogin, 293
de Severac, Déodat, 354
Designers, stage (*see* Décor *and* Costumes)
Detachment of creative artist, 207, 223,
    226
Devadasis, 266 *and n*, 285
de Valois, Ninette, 152–9, 190, 191, 192,
    201, 252, 355, 364–77, *369*, 382, 395, 434*n*
de Vos, Audrey, 134
Dhorda, Kheshan, 344
Diaghilev Ballet, 48, *65*, 72, 95, *97*, 106, 109,
    110, 115, 139, 144, 149, 150, 152, 153*n*,
    186, 187, 201, 259, 262, 329, 330, 331,
    334, 335, 336, 338, 339, 353, 365, 378,
    386, 392, 393, 394, 395, 397, 399, 402
    and n, 403, 405, 407, 422, 423, 428, 433
    and n, 434, 435, 438
——, Sergei, 63, 65–84, *65*, 87, 88, 89, 90,
    102, 103, 104, 105, 106, 108, 109, 110,
    111, 112, 113, 114, 115, 116, 126, 127,
    128, 129, 130, 131, 135, 139, 140, 141,
    149, 154, 160, 161, 162, 164, 165, 175,
    176, 177, 178, 185, 186, 188, 200, 201,
    202, 209, 239, 248, 251, 259, 262, 308,
    318, 319, 327, 329, 330, 331*n*, 334, 339,
    354, 370, 377, 390, 391 *and n*, 392, 393,
    394, 396, 399, 403, 404, 408, 422, 423,
    425, 426, 434
Didelot, Charles, 27–30, *33*, 53, 87, 92, 317,
    434, 439
Directors of State Theatres with ballet
    companies (*see* Durazzo, Guédéonov,
    Hirsch, Lopukhov, Pillet, Rouché,
    Saburov, Teliakovsky, Tufiakin, Vaga-
    nova, Véron, Volkonsky, Volynsky,
    Vsevolozhky

Discipline, 368, 397
Diversification in types of ballet and
    ballet company, 7, 325
Divertissement, 161*n*
Dmitriev, V., 163
Dohrn, Wolf and Harald, 116
Dokoudovsky, Vladimir, 411, 412
Dolgarukov-Argutinky, Prince, 67
Dolin, Anton, *81*, 155, 161, 334–43, 366,
    410, 418*n*, 420
Dollar, William, 227, 429, 430
Donne, John, 222
Doone, Rupert, 393*n*
Dostoyevsky, Fyodor, 84
Double-work, 194 *and n*
Dresden, 116, 349
Drigo, Richard, 51, 60, 61, 332, 334 *and n*,
    357
Drumming, 123, 180, 282, 345*n*
Drury Lane Theatre (London), 26
Dublin, 154
Duke of York's Theatre (London), 336,
    338
Dukes, Lulu, *225*, *240*
Duncan, Elizabeth, 347
—— Group, 346–9
——, Isadora, 86, 87, 88, 91, 97, 101, 102,
    112, 117, 119, 122, 123, 126, 131, 141,
    142, 143, 146*n*, 154, 176, 185, 200, 204,
    221, 222, 224, 229, 238, 275, 277, 346–9,
    350, 351, *352*, 384
—— School, 347–8
Dupré, Louis, 22, 24
Durazzo, Count, 25, 315, 399, 439
Duveen, Lord, 427

EAST and West, synthesis of, 202–3, 273–93,
    303–6
East, Western myth about the, 277, 279,
    282, 284, 286
Eastern School of Music, 145
École de Paris (Painters), 83, 161, 177
Edwardova, Eugenia, 329
Effeminacy in male dancers, 433*n*
Eglevsky, André, 410, 429, 430
Egorova, Lubov (*see* Yegorova, Lubov)
Elgar, Edward, 241
El Greco, 97, 106, 136
Eliot, T. S., 219, 256
Elmhirst, Mr. and Mrs., 284, 362, 399,
    400
Elssler, Fanny, 34, 38, 48, 250
Elvin, Violetta, *177*, 199, 370

Empress Hall (London), 336–7, 426

Enchaînements, carrying forward of favourite, 187, 189, 191

England, 20–3, 24, 26, 27, 35, 37–8, 69–70, 77–8, 80, 102, 152–9, 185–219, 231–4, 239–41, 252–8, 293, 344–5, 354–7, 386–8, 394–401

English audiences, 370, 371, 376, 406–7, 411

—— dancers, 235, 317, 330, 332, 355–6, 387, 388, 438

Enkelmann, S., 349*n*

Eroticism, 163, 173, 195, 197, 248, 260

Escudero, Vicente, 299

Eskimo dances, 322

Espinosa, Judith, 356

Essen, 149–50, 364

Ethnological dance (U.S.A.), 277

Eurhythmics, Dalcroze, 105, 142, 154

European folk-dances, 167, 302

Exkuzovich, 261*n*

Expertise, 68, 392, 403, 405

Expressionism, abstract, 97, 106, 123, 130, 131–2, 140, 203, 393, 400–1

—— based on classical technique, 72, 73, 92, 103–15, 126–40, 152–9, 160, 163, 165, 169, 172, 184, 190, 191, 201, 204, 215, 261–2, 322, 327, 332, 334, 365, 368, 374, 375, 406, 415

——, cerebral (*see* Expressionist free dance, cerebral wing of, and Expressionism based on classical technique)

——, hysterical, 99, 122–3, 191, 246, 322

—— in general, 97–102, 297, 298

——, naturalistic, 123, 210, 215, 387

——, neo-classical, 127, 129, 136, 140, 152, 392, 406

——, satirical, 105, 120, 127–9, 132, 139, 146, 150–2, 156–7, 160, 164, 203, 210, 213, 215–16, 218, 285, 289, 400

Expressionist artistic policy, 349–51, 362–77, 392–3, 436

—— choreography, 102–59

—— companies, repression of individuality in, 368–9, 436

—— drama, 99–100, 137, 144, 256, 359

—— free dance, cerebral wing of, 120–2, 149–52, 153, 156, 170, 346, 350, 351, 362–4

—— free dance, ecstatic wing of, 122–3, 143–9, 220–1, 346, 349, 350–2, 399–401

—— free dancer's company, 346–52, 399–401

A.A.O.B.—2G

FABERGÉ, Carl, 260

Facial expression, 122, 221, 249

Fair theatre, 24

Falla, Manuel de, 129, 303, 304, 305

Farruca, 128, 297, 299, 300

Fauré, Gabriel, 241

Favart, 24

Favourite enchaînements (*see* Enchaînements)

Fedorovitch, Sophie, 186, 188, 395

Fehling, 100

Felix (gypsy dancer), 128

Ferdinand and Isabella, 296

Ferran, José, 252

Festival Ballet, *96, 337, 338–43,* 357

—— Hall, Royal (*see* Royal Festiva Hall)

Fifield, Elaine, 255, *257,* 372, 383

Film, 7, 197, 223, 229, 233, 242, 243, 244, 252, 288, 377, 392

—— ballet, 197, 233, 244, 252, 288, 390

Fini, Léonor, 390

Firbank, Ronald, 161

Flair, 68, 395, 403

Flamenco, 128–9, 294–301, 304, 305

Fleischmann, Julius, 413

Fokina, Vera, 385

Fokine Ballet, 386

Fokine, Michel, 58*n*, 65–6, *65,* 67, 68, 70, 71, 72, 80, 86, 87–96, *96,* 97, 102, 103, 104, 105, 107, 108, 112, 114, 119, 127, 129, 135, 136, 138, 143, 149, 152, 153, 163, 171, 173, 174, 176, 177, 179, 180, 185, 196, 200, 201, 202, 204, 210, 214, 259, 260, 261 *and n,* 263, 264, 265, 279, 290, 316, 318, 319, 323, 330, 331 *and n,* 333, 338, 339, 340, 342, 353, 366, 383, 385–6, 387, 392, 394, 395, 397, *400,* 403, 409, 412 *and n,* 413, 418 *and n,* 419, 422, 435 *and n,* 437

Folk-dances (*see* American, American Indian, Basque, Catalan, English, Eskimo, European, German-Austrian, Indian, Norwegian, Polish, Portuguese, Russian, Scottish, Spanish, Swedish, Tartar, Ukrainian, and Yugoslav folk-dances)

Fontenelle, 22

Fonteyn, Margot, *177,* 185, 189, 198, 199, 249, 366, 367, 368 *and n, 368,* 370, 371, 372, 373, 376, 377, 384, 388, 396, 435 *and n*

Forain, 132

Fortunato, 308

Franca, Celia, *240,* 253, 370

France, 21–4, 27, 28, 33–7, 41, 48, 66–7, 102, 176–84, 228, 246–52, 317–21, 353–4, 388–90

Franck, César, 191

Franco-Danish school (Vestris-Bournonville-Johannsen), 39, 43, 57, 322, 323

Franco-Italian school, 32–3, 42, 55–8, *84*, *258*, 344, *401*

Franco-Russian dancers, 427, 430

Franklin, Frederick, *401*, 417

Frederick, 48

Free dance, American, 86, 101–2, 126, 141–9, *144*, 153, 173, 175, 208, 220, 225, 229, 230, 231, 232, 237, 238, 243, 245, 275–9, 284, 341, 350–2, 399, 400

—— dance, Central European, 116–26, 131, 134, 143–52, 153, 156, 170, 175, 180, 186, 220–2, 265, 274, 282, 284, 309, 310, 346, 349–52, 362–4, 399–401, 415

—— dance—Duncan, 86, 101–2

—— dance, Indian, 275–9, 281–6, 289

—— dance, post-expressionist (Akesson), 220–6

—— dance, Russian, 260

—— dance, Spanish, 304–5

French dancers, 317–20, 389, 425, 438

——, Jared, 380

—— Revolution, 19

—— school, 23, 32, 39, 41, 42, 317 (*see also* Franco-Danish school)

Freud, Sigmund, 214, 257

Froman, Margarita, 308, 309

Fromm, Eric, 431, 432, 433 *and n*

Frontier, American, 233

Fuller, Loie, 275, 347*n*

Gabo, Naum, 82, 120, 165

Gabriel, John, 335*n*, 368*n*

Gagarin, Prince, 29

Galeotti, Vincenzo, 30, 321, 322

Gandhi, Mahatma, 291

Gardel, Maximilien, 26

Garfield, Constance, 241

Garrick, David, 24, 118, 439

Garrotín, 299

Gath (passage of dramatic expression in Kathak), 287 *and n*

Gauguin, 97

Gautier, Théophile, 171*n*, 194

Gavrilov, Alexander, 58*n*, 104

Geltser, V. F., 54

Genet, Jean, 390

Georgi, 150

Gerdt, Paul, 88

Gerhardt, Roberto, 158, 159

German-Austrian folk-dances, 218

Germany, 24–5, 119, 122, 149–50, 152, 277

Gertz, 403

Gesamtkunstwerk, 31, 70, 79, 262, 404, 422

Geva, Tamara, 164

Gevergeva (*see* Geva)

Gide, André, 354

Gilbert, W. S., 255, 256

Gilmour, Sally, 397, 398

Gilpin, John, *337*, 340, 398

Gimmick, 80, 177, 195, 249, 257

Ginner, Ruby, 102

Giraud, Claude, 247

Glazunov, Alexander, 334 *and n*

Glinka, Michael, 92

Gluck, 25, 101, 172, 379, 399

Glyn, Elinor, 392

Godkin, Paul, 383

Goffin, Peter, 225, 399, 400

Gogol, 228, 339

Goldoni, 127

Goleizovsky, Kasyan, 140*n*, 163, 166, 176, 260, 261

Golovin, Serge, 63, 64, 332, 354, 430

Goncharov, George, 368

Goncharova, Nathalie, 79, 81, 164

Gopal company, Ram, 343–6, 435

Gopal, Ram, 293, 343–6, 358

Gore, Walter, *209*, 210, 227, 239, *240*, 398

Gorelik, Mordecai, 100*n*

Gorky, Maxim, 99

Gorsky, Alexander, 65

Gowing, Lawrence, 226

Goya, 97

Graeme, Joyce, 210, 355, 398

Graham Dance Group, Martha, 350–2, 400

Graham, Martha, 141–9, *144*, 153, 173, 175, 208, 220, 225, 229, 231, 232, 237, 238, 243, 245, 284, 341, 350–2, 399, 400

Grahn, Lucile, 34, 39

Grand Ballet du Marquis de Cuevas, *417*, 427–30

Grant, Alexander, 196, 198

Grantsova, Adèle, 36, 41

Gray, Terence, 154

Greco company, José, 435

——, El, 97, 106, 136

——, José, 305

"Greek" dancing, 88, 89, 101–2, 142, 195

Grey, Beryl, 134, 375, 376

Grigoriev, Serge, 403, 404, 408, 411

Gris, Juan, 161

Grisi, Carlotta, 34, 35, 36, 38, *49*, 91, 330, 331
Gross, Alexander, 347, 439
Grosz, Georg, 150
Grotesk, 164
Group movements, 40, 91, 120, 174, 412
Grunberg, Eugene, 427
Grunewald, 97
Guédéonov, 38, 39
Guest choreographers, 371
Guitar-playing, Spanish, 294, 295, 297
Gunsbourg, Baron, 70
Gupta, Sushil Das, 292
Gurus (Indian teachers), 266, 267, 268, 271, 272, 273
Gypsy dances, Indian, 297
—— dances, Russian, 90
—— dances, Spanish (*see* Flamenco)

HABIMA, 99
Hamilton, Gordon, 251, 369, 370, 389, 390
Hammerstein II, Oscar, 236
Handel, 23
Hands, 122, 148, 151, 221
Hanover, 150
Hansen, Olaf, 54
Harding, Muriel, 355
Hardy, Pat, 388
Harmony of movement, 221
Harmoš, Oscar, *305*, 307, 308, 309, 310, 311, 399
Haroun-al-Rashid, Caliph, 294
Harsanyi, 183
Hart, John, *177*
Haskell, Arnold, 92, 104*n*, 255, 367
Hawkins, Erick, 351
Hayden, Melissa, *161*
——, Sylvia, 241, 387
Hazlitt, 148*n*
Heckroth, Hein, 362
Hellerau Institute (Dalcroze), 116, 349
Hellerau-Laxenburg school, 122
Helpmann, Robert, 158, 191, 194, 256, 263, 334, 366, 367, 368, 369, 370, 372, 375, 396
Helsingfors, 328
Henderson, Mrs. Laura, 335 *and n*
Her Majesty's Theatre (London), 37, *48*
Hermitage Theatre (St. Petersburg), 66
Hightower, Rosella, 410, 430
Hill, Aaron, 117, 118
——, John, 118
——, Margaret, 398, 399
Hilverding, 27

Hindemith, Paul, 169, 225, 351
Hindu religion, 267-8, 276
Hinton, Paula, 210, 398
Hirsch, 320
Hogarth, William, 156
Hoggart, Richard, 218
Holden, Stanley, 372
Holidays, tours by groups of dancers during Summer, 328, 379
Hollywood, 80, 173, 377
Holm, Hanya, 145
Holmes, Michael, 398
Holst, Gustav, 203
Homosexuality, 110, 161, 433
Honegger, 183, 354
Honer, Mary, 366, 367, 372
Horney, Karen, 431, 432
Horst, Louis, 144, 231, 351
Howard, Andrée, 227, 239, 355, *384*, 396, 419
Hoyer, Jan, *385*, 406
Hudi, Paula, 307
Humour in Flamenco, 300, 301, 306
——, satirical expressionist (*see* Expressionism, satirical)
Humphrey, Doris, 143, 237
Hurok, S., 235, 283, 284, 299, 348, *385*, 407, 409, 410, 413, 415, 416, 420, 421, 422, 423, 429
Hurry, Leslie, 375
Huxley, Julian, 126
Hybrid Company, The, 402-26, 435
Hyden, Walford, 333
Hyman, Prudence, *384*

IBSEN, 98, 99
Idzikovsky, Stanislas, 57, *177*, 355, 365, 366, 388, 435
Images, dance (*see* Dance-images)
Imperial and Royal Academy of Dancing and Mime (Milan), 32-3
—— Russian Ballet (*see under* Bolshoy, Maryinsky and Warsaw)
—— Society of Teachers of Dancing (England), 168*n*
—— Theatre school, St. Petersburg (*see also* Maryinsky school), 28
—— Theatres, Directorate of Russian, 29, 38, 50, 63, 64, 68, 73, 88, 119, 259, 329
—— Theatres, Russian (*see* Bolshoy, Maryinsky and Warsaw State Ballet)
Imperio, Pastora, 299, 303
Impersonality, classical, 207, 223

Impresario (*see* Theatrical manager)
Improvisation, 101, 122, 221, 349
Impulses (in free dance), 145
India, 265–93, 343
Indian ballet, modern, 273–93
—— classical styles (*see also* Bharata Natyam, Kathak, Kathakali, Manipuri and Mohini Attam), 125, 222, 224, 265–73, 282, 283, 287, 291, 299, 304, 346
—— folk-dances, 273, 282, 283
—— music, 267, 282–3
—— National Theatre, 289
—— People's Theatre Association, 289
Individualistic Classical Dancers' Company, The, 327–46
Individuality in dancers, 190, 223, 316, 317, 318, 364, 366, 384, 395, 397, 400, 425, 430, 431, 434, 438
Inglesby Ballet (*see* International Ballet)
——, Mona, *353*, 354–7, 358, 423
Ingres, 127
Innocent eye, 227–58
International Ballet, *353*, 355–7, 369, 417, 424
—— Ballet School (Split), 310–11
—— School of Ballet (London), 355
—— Theatre, 429
Intrigue, 22, 25, 26, 27, 28–9, 29–30, 31, 33, 35, 38, 48, 66, 318, 319, 327, 391, 408, 434
Inyoka, Nyota, 278
Ireland, 154
Irving, Sir Henry, 332
Istomina, Anna, 29
Italian dancers, 30–3, 42–3, 55–6, 57, 58, 438
—— school, 32, 42, 55–8, 317, 320, 322
Italy, 30–3, 42–3, 325
Ivanov, Lev, *frontispiece*, 52, 55, 60–1, 62, 64, 88, 90, 91, 171, 174, 177, 199, 359, *368*

Jackson, Rowena, 376
Jailal, Pandit, 344n, 345n
Jaipuri school of Kathak, *273*, 277
Jaleo, 298, 302
James, Edward, 377
——, Henry, 219
Janta, Aleksander, 343
Japanese classical dances (*see also* Kabuki), 266, 280
Jaques-Dalcroze, Émile (*see* Dalcroze)
Javanese classical dances, 222, 267n, 343, 357
Jazz, 300 *and* n, 248
Jazz dancing, 252

Jeanmaire, Renée, 247, 250, 252, *256*, 320, 389 *and* n, 390, 410, 428
Jelinčič, Frane, 310
Jessner, 100, 137
Jethisvaram, 344
Jig, Elizabethan, 20
Johannsen, Christian, 50, 56, 434
Johnson, Edward, 379
Joly, Anténor, 35
Jommelli, Niccolo, 25
Jones, Robert Edmund, 144
Jooss, Kurt, 121, 138, *145*, 148, 149–52, 153, 159, 181, 201, 203, 341, 342, 362–4, 365, 366, 373, 378, 400, 401
Jooss-Leeder school, 149, 363–4
José Greco company, 435
Jota Aragonesa, 128, 299
Joyce, James, 98, 393
Jung, C. G., 246, 257, 431

Kabuki, 201, 209, 222, 266
Kahn, Otto, 73, 74, 75, 386, 427, 439
Kaiser, Georg, 100
Kalasams (standard Kathakali enchaînements), 269
Kalioujny, Alexandre, 320, 428
Kandapa, 285
Kandyan dances, 267 *and* n, 345n
Karpakova, 54
Karsavina, Tamara, 58n, 65, 69, *80*, 88, 89, 92n, 94, *96*, 97, 101, 102, 104, 177, 201, 262, 316, 327, 330, 331, 353, 391, 397, 435 *and* n, 436 *and* n
Kathak, 266–73, *273*, 277, 287n, 291, 295, 303, 344n, 345 *and* n, 346
Kathakali, 129, 222, 266–73, *273*, 277, 278, 282n, 283, 285, 286, 287, 288, 289, 290 *and* n, 291, 292, 343, 345n, 346, 358, 359
Kauffer, McKnight, 157
Kaye, Danny, 252, 383
——, Nora, *209*, 211, 212, 217, 218, 238, 245, 246, 382, 384, *416*, 421, 424, 435
Kean, Edmund, 147, 148
Kelly, Gene, 244
Kerala, 266, 268, 290, 343
Kerala-Kalamandalam, 272, 343
Kersley, Leo, *240*
Kesarcodi, Hima, 291
Keynes, Geoffrey, 155, 156
Keystone comedies, 244
Khan, Ustad Alauddin, 285
Khandala, 287
Kidd, Michael, 383

Kiev, 30, 139
Kinetographie (Laban Dance Notation), 121, 175
King's Theatre, Hammersmith, 336
—— Theatre (London), 26, 28
Kinney, M. W., 277, 278
——, Troy, 277, 278
Kinsey, 433
Kirsanova, 308
Kirsova, Hélène, 95, 412*n*
Kirsta, George, 412
Kirstein, Lincoln, 218, 255, 377–85, 394, 418, 427
Kitsch, 158 *and n*, 235, 246, 248, 365, 366, 419
Klementovich, Loda, 115
Kniasev, Boris, 170, 308, 320, 403, 435
Kochno, Boris (*see* Kokhno)
Kokhno, Boris, 81, 82, 83, 166, 194, 247, 248, 250, 377, 403, 424, 425
Kokoschka, 100
Kollwitz, Käthe, 150
Komisarjevsky, 64
Korovin, 63, 64, 332
Koslov, 58*n*, 229
—— School, 229
Kraljeva, Stephania, 307
Krassovska, Nathalie (*see* Leslie)
Kratina, Valeria, 122
Krauss, Ernst, 287
Kreutzberg, Harald, 145, 150
Kriza, John, 243
Krotkov, 60
Kshessinskaya, Mathilde, 49, 58*n*, 64, 66, 69, 88, 355, 435, 436*n*
Kumar, Naba, 278
Kumudini, 345 *and n*, 346
Kuprensky, 66
Kutty, Krishna, *273*, 288, *289*, 290–3, *293*
Kyaksht, George, 58*n*
——, Lydia, 49, 58*n*, 259

LABAN, Rudolf von, 116–26, *128*, 131, 138, 143, 145, 149, 150, 151, 154, 170, 171*n*, 175, 176, 180, 224, 265, 349, 350, 351, 362, 404
—— school (*see also* Art of Movement Studio), 119, 349
Labarre, Théodore, 91
Ladre, Maryan, 406
Laing, Hugh, 206, *208*, 210, 211, 212, 213, 216, 217, 218, 232, 239, 382, 384, *416*, 421, 424, 435

Lakshmi, 345
Lal, Sohan, 344*n*
Lalo, Victor, 182
Lambert, Constant, 82, 190, 196
La Meri, 277, 343
Lancaster, Osbert, 255, 256
Lancret, *32*
Landa, Anita, *337*, 338, 340
Lander, Harald, 321 *and n*, 322, 323, 324
Lang, Harold, 243
Lanović, Zlata, *305*, 307, 310
Lany, 24
La Quica, 435
Larionov, Michel, 77, 78, 81, 82, 104, 127, 139, 164
Larsen, Gerd, 212 *and n*, 387
——, Niels Bjørn, 324
La Scala, Milan, 30, 31, 32, 42, 362
Lasiná brothers, 42
Lavrovsky, 263
Lawson, John Howard, 144
Lazovsky, Yurek, 420
LeClercq, Tanaquil, 169, 246, 383
Lecocq, 133
Leeder, Sigurd, 149, 150, 341, 362, 363, 364
Legat, Nicolas, 52, 55, 56–7, 58*n*, 60, *64*, 128, 171*n*, 201, 259, 261 *and n*, 264, 309, 310, 311, 328, 355, 367, 368 *and n*, 370, 371, 387, 388, 395, 399, 434 *and n*, 435
——, Serge, 58*n*, 128
—— system, 57, 171*n*, 308, 309
Léger, Fernand, 137, 138, 155
Legnani, Pierina, 56, 57
Leitmotives (*see* Motto steps)
Leningrad (*see also* St. Petersburg and Petrograd), 261–4
Leontiev, 262
Lepri, Giovanni, 42, 55
Leslie, Nathalie, 340
Lessing, 118
Lester, Keith, 336
Lévier, Nancy, 25
Levinson, André, 80
Lhotka, Nenad, 310
Liberation of Paris, 182, 247
Lichine, David, 323, 338, *385*, *400*, 407, 411, 422*n*, 426
Lidova, Irène, 247
Lifar, Serge, 80, 81, *81*, 103, 104, *160*, 164, 176–85, *176*, 186, 189, 190, 193, 194, 196, 227, 242, 247, 248, 249, 251, 317*n*, 319, 320, 342, 403, 407, 425, 427, 428, 430
Lighting, stage, 137, 256, 285, 339, 363, 375, 386, 393, 399

Limido, Giovannina, 55, 56
Lincoln's Inn Fields Theatre (London), 21
Lindegren, Erik, 226
Li Po, 217
Liszt, Franz, 118
Little Ballet Company, 289
Little Tich, 110
Lloyd, Maude, *208, 209*, 232, 239
Lohengrin, 348
Lomax, Alan, 300*n*
Lomonosov, 83
London, 20–3, 24, 26, 27, 35, 37–8, 69–70, 77–8, 80, 152–9, 185–219, 232–9, 252–8, 309, 329, 354–7, 365–77, 386–8
—— audiences (*see* Audiences, London)
—— Ballet, 205, 207*n*, 209, 210, 211, 218 *369*, 386–8, 397, 435
—— Ballet Circle, 167*n*, 168*n*
—— public (*see* Audiences, London), 338
London-Rambert company, 369, 388, 397,
Lopez, Pilar, 305
—— company, Pilar, 305
Lopukhov, Fyodor, 260, 261, 262, 264
Lopukhova, Lydia, 58*n*, 74, 77, 79, 177, 187, 435
Lorca, Federico García, 216, 297, 305
Loring, Eugene, 236, 380, 418*n*, 419
Losch, Tilly, 377
Louis Phillippe, French monarch, 33
Love, effect on directors of ballet companies of falling in, 391 *and n*
Lucknowi school of Kathak, 287, 345
Lumley, Benjamin, 37, 439
Lunacharsky, 102, 260
Lunch-time ballet, 388
Luzita, Sara, 398
Lynne, Gillian, 370
Lyons, 24
Lyric Theatre, Hammersmith, 397
Lyricism, romantic, 91, 94, 179, 229, 406 412

McCLELLAND, Joan, 398
Macedonian folk-dances, 197
Machinery imitation, 260, 262, 285
McLerie, Allyn, *225*
McNaught, Nancy, 253
Madhavan, 282*n*
Madrid Ballet (Argentinita-Lorca), 305
—— Opera Ballet, 48, 307
Madura Nagarilo, 344
Maecenas, 428, 439
Magallanes, Nicolas, *161*
Magriel, Paul, 109, 110*n*

Mahabharata, 289
Mahler, Gustav, 209*n*, 213, 217, 218
Maître de ballet, 19, 406
Make-up, 147*n*, 269
Malabar, Old (*see* Kerala)
Mallarmé, 104, 112
Malter, 22
Mamontov, Savva, 63, 439
Mamoulian, Rouben, 236
Manchester, P. W., 371
Mander, Raymond, 441
Manipuri, 267, 272, 278, 282, 287, 288, 289 *and n*, 345
Mannerisms in free dance, 122, 350
Manzotti, Luigi, 42, 55
Marchand, Colette, *43*, 249, 320, 389, 390
Margarita, 301
Maria Teresa, Empress of Austria, 30
Marie Antoinette, Queen of France, 26, 439
Mariemma, 300*n*
Marie Rambert Dancers (*see also* Ballet Club and Ballet Rambert), 187, *384*
Marinova, Anna, 355
Markova, Alicia, *96, 145*, 261, 309, 334–43, 365, 366, 368*n*, 372, 384, 410, 417, 420
Markova-Dolin Ballet (America), 336
Markova-Dolin Ballet (England), 335 *and n*, 336, 337, 338, 342
Marsh, Margaret, 388
Martha Graham Dance Group, 350–2, 400
Martin, John, 207*n*, 215*n*, 385*n*, 418, 424*n*
Marx Brothers, 257
Maryinsky school, 28, 56, 111, 138, 139, 162, 176, 259, 261, 328
Maryinsky Theatre and company, 47–66, 67, 69, 87–8, 259–64, 279, 308, 319, 323, 328, 329, 330, 331 *and n*, 332, 333, 335, 336, 338, 355, 366, 368, 379, 407, 411, 434, 435, 436
Massine-Denham company (1940–42), 415
Massine, Leonide, 74, 75, 76, 77, 78, 83, 95, 126–35, *129*, 136, 139, 140, 149, 151, 152, 153, 156, 157, 158, 159, 161, 164, 165, 167, 170, 171, 177, 184, 187, 188, 191, 197, 201, 210, 235, 240, 264, 309, 323, 338, 339, 343, 354, 370, 375, *385*, 392, 397, *400*, 403, 404, 405, 406, 408, 409, 413, 415 *and n*, 416, 417, 420, 422, 423, 426, 429, 430, 435
Masson, André, 404 *and n*
Maturity, dancers' development to artistic, 342, 370, 371, 372, 376, 383–4, 387, 389–90, 395, 398, 407, 421, 425, 430, 432, 437

Maudrik, 149
Maule, Michael, 384
Maurepas, 22
May, Jane, 346
——, Pamela, 368, 375
Maya, Juanele, 301
——, Teresa, 300-1
Maywood, Augusta, 42, 383
Mazilier, 38
Mead, Margaret, 413
Medina, Maria, *33, 324*
Menaka, 286-8, *288*, 290, 291, 292, 345, 358
Mendelssohn, Felix, 94, 134
Menotti, Gian-Carlo, 351
Mérante, 198
Mercé, Manuel, 303
Mercury Theatre, 231, 232, 355, 368, 396, 397
Meri, La (*see* La Meri)
Metropolitan Ballet, 74, 241, 370
—— Opera, New York, 172, 379, 385, 386, 415, 423
Meyerbeer, 33, 190
Meyerhold Theatre, 369
——, Vsevolod, 64, 66, 99, 128, 164, 260, 369
Michaut, Pierre, 180n, 250, 251, 319, 320 *and n*, 403, 428
Mikhailovsky Theatre, 163
Milan, 30-3, 35, 142
Milanese school (*see* Italian school)
Milhaud, Darius, 137, 155, 354, 393
Mille, Agnes de (*see* de Mille)
Miller, Antonia, 32
Miller, Elizabeth, 366, 367, 372
——, Patricia, 252, 254, 372
Milon, Louis, 36
Mime (*see also* Abhinaya), 123, 167, 193, 194, 212, 248, 263, 298, 354, 358, 360, 377
Mime-plays, expressionist, 368, 369
Minkus, L., 51, 332, 334
Mir Iskustva, 63, 64
Miro, Joan, 404
Miscasting (*see* Casting)
Misra, Radhelal, 345n, 435
Mitchenson, Joe, 441
Mlakar, Pia and Pino, 310
Modern dance (*see* Free dance)
Modern English Ballet (book by Fernau Hall), 8, 36
Modern Indian ballet, 273-93
Mogul Emperors, 270n
Mohini Attam, 271
——, Retna, 343

Moiseyev, 264
—— folk-dance ensemble, 264
Molière, 161
Monakhov, 329
Moncion, Francisco, *161*
Monnet, Jean, 24, 439
Monte Carlo, 78, 183, 402, 403, 404, 412, 427
Montéclair, 161
Montesquieu, 22
Moore, Lillian, 169n
Moorish classical dancing in Spain, 294-7, 304
Moors, Spanish, 296-7
Mordkin Ballet, 417, 419
——, Mikhail, 74, 329, *337*, 417, 419
—— School, 417
Morosova, Olga, *385*, 411
Moscow, 53-4, 65 *and n*, 126, 136, 195, 260, 261, 308, 370, 379
—— Art Theatre, 209, 399
—— Imperial Theatres (*see* Bolshoy)
—— Kamerny Ballet, 260
Moslem civilization in Middle Ages, 295-6
—— countries, dances in, 270n
Motto steps, 151, 157
Movement, 171
Movement-studies, 225
Moving plastic (Dalcroze), 116-17, 357
Moylin, Francisque, 22, 439
Mozart, 95, 107, 253
Mrinalini (Marianne Balchin), *273*, 293, 346
Mrinalini Sarabhai (*see* Sarabhai, Mrinalini)
Mudras (Indian symbolic gestures), 265, 266, 358
Mullahy, Patrick, 433n
Munch, Edvard, 99, 122, 148, 150
Munich, 35
Munnings, Hilda (*see* Sokolova, Lydia)
Munster Stadttheater, 362
Muravieva, Martha, 36, 41
Music, Arab-Persian, 294
—— hall, 188, 251, 260
——, Indian, 267, 294, 295
—— interpretation (*see* Abstraction)
——, relationship of dancing to, 50-1, 59-60, 91-2, 107-8, 115, 116-17, 130, 162, 168, 180, 192, 194, 198, 204, 213, 256, 317, 319, 351
Musical films, 243
—— (musical comedy), 236-7, 242, 244, 385
Mussorgsky, 310

Myth, 93, 101, 115, 134, 166, 172, 181, 195, 196, 210, 254, 268, 282, 289, 291–3, 339

Myth about the East, Western, 277, 279, 284, 286

Mythological ballets, Indian, 283, 289, 291–3

NABOKOV, Nicolas, 82, 377

Naïveté and sophistication, balance between, 228, 243, 244

Nambudri, Guru Shankaran, 285, 290

Nantes, 48

Naples, 35

Natanam Adinar, 344

Natya, 224, 268

Nautch dancing (classical Indian dancing), 271, 286 (*see also* Bharata Natyam and Kathak)

—— dancing (degenerate Indian dancing), 276

Navarre, Avril, 377

Negro dances, 135, 136, 142

Negus, Anne, 251, 355, 371

Nehru, Pandit Jawaharlal, 289

Nemchinova-Dolin ballet, 334

Nemchinova, Vera, 161, 334, 412 *and n*

Nemirovich-Danchenko, 399

Neo-classical expressionism (*see* Expressionism, neo-classical)

Nerina, Nadia, 199, 252, 370, 376, 383

Neurotic escape mechanisms in dancers, 432–3

Nevada, Ana, 425

New-Ballet company, 241

New Dance League, 242

—— Stage, 289, 292

—— York, 74–5, 141–9, 167–76, 195, 230, 234–9, 350–2, 378–85, 410, 417, 424, 428

—— York City Ballet, 170n, 205, 217, 218, 245 254, 316, 378n, 381, 382, 384, 417

—— York City Center, 381

—— York City Opera, 381

—— York World's Fair, 379

New Yorker, The (magazine), 244

Nijinska, Bronislava, 58n, 81, 89, 108, 129, 131, 138–41, 152, 160–2, 160, 164, 165, 166, 167, 171n, 176, 177, 184, 186, 187, 188, 201, 259, 262, 334, 336, 354, 396, 416, 429, 430, 434, 435

——, Kyra, 208

——, Romola, 103, 109, 112, 115

Nijinsky, Vaslav, 58n, 65, 69, 71, 72, 73, 75, 76, 78, 88, 89, 92, 93, 94, 96, 102, 103–16, 113, 119, 126, 127, 129, 130, 131, 135, 136, 137, 139, 140, 144, 160, 162, 171, 176, 177, 201, 209, 210, 217, 229, 259, 265, 316, 318, 339, 353, 391n, 393, 395, 397, 426, 433n, 436 *and n*

Nikitina, Alice, 80, 160

Noblet sisters, 303

Noguchi, Isamo, 173

Nolde, 119

Norwegian dances, 40

Nouveau Ballet de Monte Carlo, 182, 427, 428, 429, 430

Noverre, Jean Georges, 23–7, 28, 30, 58n, 117, 177, 185, 214, 318, 387, 431, 437, 439

Nrtta, 224, 268

Nude dancing, 260

Nuitter, Charles, 41

OBUKHOV, Anatole, 58n, 91, 95, 328, 412 *and n*

Old Vic, 154, 365

Olympic Games, Berlin, 287

O'Neill, Eugene, 144

——, Rose Meller, 119n

Opera-ballet, 35, 129, 172

Opéra Comique, Paris, 24

——, Paris (*see* Paris Opéra)

Opera seria, 47

Operas, ballets based on, 129, 172

Operettas, ballets based on, 130, 133, 161, 343

O'Reilly, 26

"Oriental" dancing, 89, 90, 145, 201, 275–8

Osato, Sono, 420

Otero, José, 394

Ovid, 248

Oxford, 232

PADAM (Bharata Natyam song dance), 298

Padua, 30

Pagava, Éthery, 417, 425, 426, 430

Page, Ruth, 343

Palace Theatre, London, 139, 329

Palestrina, 118

Pallerini, Antonia, 32

Panicker, Chatunni, 358, 359

——, Krishna, 292

Pantomime ballet, 20–3

—— (English Christmas), 21, 52, 53, 194

——, Graeco-Roman, 21n, 23

Paris, 33, 35, 67, 104, 177–85, 231, 246–52, 282, 317–21, 328, 353–4, 388–91, 392–4, 424–7, 430
—— Opéra Ballet, 26, 27, 33, 35–6, 38, 149*n*, 170, 183, 198, 247, 248, 317–20, 322 324, *336*, 373, 374, 376, 403, 425*n*, 427, 428, 435, 437
Parr, Andrée, 137
Partnership, complementary, of directors of companies, 399
Pas d'action, 60, 172, 173, 198
Passions, 18th century theories on the, 117
Patent theatres (London), 22*n*
Patron-Manager's Company, The, 427–30
Patrons (*see under* Astruc, Austria (Emperor of), de Cuevas, Dolgarukov-Argutinsky, Gunsbourg, Kahn, Karl Eugen, Kirstein, Maecenas, Mamontov, Marie Antoinette, Mogul Emperors, Sert, Societé des Bains de Mer, Tenishev, Travancore (Maharajah of), Tsars of Russia, Warburg)
Pavlova, Anna, 58*n*, *64*, 66, 69, 75, 87, 88, 90, 91, 94, 102, 135, 141, 171*n*, 198, 201, 229, 230, 238, 259, 265, 272, 279–81, 282, 286, *288*, 316, 323, 327*n*, 328–34, *337*, 346, 347, 353, 354, 357, 386, 407, 435
—— Ballet, 48, 149*n*, 279–82, 327*n*, 328–34, 342
Pavlova-Bolm company, 328–9
Pavlova-Mordkin company, 329
Pedrell, Felipe, 303
Percussion music, 123, 180, 282
Perfection class (*see* Classe de Perfection)
Perrault, Serge, 251, 252, 389
Perrot, Jules, 35–9, 40, 42, 48, *49*, 53, 71, 87, 89, 91, 176, 179, 180, 198, 199, 201, 317, 319*n*, 330, 331, 340
Personality in dancers, 8, 223, 318, 366, 386, 430, 431, 434
Petipa, Jean, 48
——, Marius, *frontispiece*, 47, 55, 59, 61, *64*, 65, 89, 90, 123, 128, 134, 135, 152, 160, 165, 167, 168, 169, 170, 171, 174, 177, 178, 179, 180, 184, 198, 212, 259, 262, 263 *and n*, 280, 319*n*, 330, 331, 355, 359, 366, *368*, 374, 375
Petit, Roland, 183, 184, 246–52, *256*, *257*, 320, 371, 388–90, *417*, 424, 425, 426, *426*
Petrograd (*see also* St. Petersburg and Leningrad), 259–62
—— audience, 259–60
Pevsner, Antoine, 82, 120
Philippart, Nathalie, 248, *417*, 425, 426
Pianowsky, 308 *and n*

Picabia, 138
Picasso, Pablo, 97, 106, 127, 128, 136, 226
Pilar Lopez company, 305
Pillet, Léon, 36
Piltz, Marie, 108, 130, 139
Piper, John, 256
Pizzetti, 354
Playful satire, 227–8, 233, 240–1, 242–4, 249–52, 253, 255–7
Pleasant, Richard, 234, 417, 418, 419, 420, 421, 423
Poliakova, 308
Polish dancers, 235, 321*n*, 406, 438
—— folk-dances, 321*n*
Ponomaryev, 261
Poole, David, 252, *257*
Porter, Cole, 228
Portuguese dances, 301
Post-expressionist classicism, 200–19
Post-expressionist free dance, 220–5
Post-expressionist pseudo-classicism, 160–99, 200, 201, 227–58, 377–85, 388–90, 414–7, 419, 424–30
Poulenc, 354
Praagh, Peggy van (*see* van Praagh)
Prague, 328
Prasad, Sundaram, 287
Preobazhenskaya, Olga, 58*n*, 170, 320, 355, 371, 435
Prévert, 248, 424
Prévost, Françoise, 21, 22
Prikhunova, Alexandra, 38
Production (*see* Régisseur)
Prokofiev, 195, 240, 263
Propert, W. A., 92, 106, 107*n*
Properties, stage, 148, 393
Prostitution, association of professional dancing with, 41, 279
Proust, Marcel, 203, 205, 206, 207, 214, 215, 217, 218, 403
Pseudo-classicism (19th century), 49, 132
Pseudo-classicism, post-expressionist, 160–99, 200, 201, 227–58, 377–85, 388–90, 414–17, 419, 424–30
Pseudo-classicism, Soviet, 262
Psota, Vania, *385*
Psycho-analysis, 431
Psychological themes, 146, 211–16, 245–6, 256–7
Public (*see* Audiences)
Pugni, Cesare, 37, 51
Pulszky, Romola (*see* Nijinska, Romola)
Purcell, Henry, 209
Pushkin, 29, 92, 310

QUICA, La, 435

R.A.D. PRODUCTION Club, 253 and n
—— style, 359, 373, 374
Radha, 272
Rados, *84, 258, 401*
Ragas (Indian modes), 280, 282, 294
Rajeshwar, 345n
Ralov, Børge, 323
Ram Gopal company, 343–6, 435
Ramayana, 268, 289
Rambert Ballet (see Ballet Rambert)
—— Dancers, Marie (see Marie Rambert
    Dancers)
——, Marie, 105n, 114, 186, 187, 208n, 209,
    221n, 232, 239, 387, 394–9
—— School, 232, 239, 354, 355
Rameau, 24
Ramnarayan, 287, 345
Rank, Otto, 431
Rasas, 117n, 268
Rassine, Alexis, 435n
Ravel, Maurice, 89, 162, 195, 196, 254,
    318
Read, Herbert, 120n
Recitals, solo dance, 347
Recording of dancing (see Dance notation)
Régisseur, 19, 308, 310, 406, 408–9
Reinhardt, Max, 99, 100
Reisinger, 54
René Blum's Monte Carlo Opera Ballet
    (see Ballets Russe de Monte Carlo No. 2)
Repetitiousness in pseudo-classical ballets,
    169
Revival of old ballet, 398, 406, 408–9 (see
    also Régisseur)
Revived Greek, 102
Revue, 334, 385
Riabouchinska, Tatiana, *385*, 406n, 409
Riccoboni, 118
Rice, Elmer, 144
Rich, John, 21, 399, 439
—— dancers' company, 352–9, 417
Richard, Zina, 36
Rimbaud, 185, 195
Rimsky-Korsakov, Nicholas Andreievich,
    98, 107
Ripman, Olive, 336
Ripon, Lady, 73
Robbins, Jerome, 238n, 241–6, *241*, 251,
    256, 257, 382 and n, 383, 421, 422, 423
Roberts, Grace, 54
Rockefeller, John D., 428

Rodgers, Richard, 236, 256
Rodin, 97
Roerich, Nicholas, 106
Rogers, Ginger, 243
Roje, Ana, 57, *305*, 308, 309, 310, 311, *311*,
    368n, 399, 434, 435
Rolf de Mare's Swedish Ballet (see Ballets-
    Suédois)
Romanov, Boris, 58n, 429
Romanovsky, 308 and n
Romantic ballet, The (mid-19th century),
    33–40, 383
Romanticism, 34, 49, 62, 71, 97, 101, 147,
    165, 406
Rosandro, 301
Rosario, 300, *306*
Rosenthal, Jean, 382n
Roshanara, 279
Rossana, Noël, *337*, 340
Rothenstein, Sir William, 280
Rouché, Jaques, 178, 318, 319
Rowell, Kenneth, 342
Rowlandson, *33*
Royal Academy of Dancing (see R.A.D.)
—— Danish Ballet (see Danish Royal
    Ballet)
—— Festival Hall, 341 and n, 342, 357
—— Siamese dancers, 89, 279
—— Swedish Ballet (see Swedish Royal
    Ballet)
Rubbra, Edmund, 399, 400
Rubin, Harold, 388, 397
Rubinstein Ballet, 186, 189, 353–4
——, Ida, 94, 162, 167, 186, 187, 353–4,
    353, 377, 412, 434
Russia, 28–30, 38, 42, 47–66, 98–9, 102, 162–4,
    259–64
Russian dancers, 235, 438
—— folk-dances, 90, 127, 264
—— school, 55–8, 201, 229, 320, 335, 356,
    374
Russo-American dancers, 430
Russo-Polish tradition of dancing, 406

SABUROV, 39
Sadlers Wells Ballet, 133, 156, 157, 188n,
    196, 197, 212n, 251, 254, 255, 256, 257,
    263, 316, 336, 338, 341, 342, 369–77,
    368, 382, 384, 397, 417, 435n
—— Wells Opera Ballet (see Sadlers Wells
    Theatre Ballet)
—— Wells organization, 253n, 254, 258,
    373

Sadlers Wells School, 252, 372, 376 (*see also* Vic-Wells School)
—— Wells style, 373, 374, 382
—— Wells Theatre, 364, 371, 373
—— Wells Theatre Ballet, 188*n*, 252, 253, 254, 255, 256, 257, 258, 342, 372, 382, 398, 399, 417
Saint-Albine, 118
St. Denis, Ruth, 119, 142, 143, 146*n*, 220, 229, 265, 275–8, 280, 281, 282, 283, 284, 286, *288*, 344, 349
Saint-Georges, 36
Saint-Léon, *frontispiece*, 41, 47, 48, 55, 317
St. Petersburg, 25, 28, 38, 40, 47–53, 55–66, 135, 139, 259 (*see also* Petrograd and Leningrad)
Saint-Saëns, Charles Camille, 90
Salaman, Susan, 336
Salaries in State ballets, 328*n*
Sallé, Marie, 21–3, 24, *32*, 318, 399, 439
Sangalli, Rita, 41
Sanquirico, 32
Santhals, 273
Santiniketan, 278, 279, 282, 357, 358
Sarabhai company, 357–9
——, Mrinalini, 357–9
Sarah Bernhardt, Théâtre, 247, 424
Saroyan, William, 419
Sasburgh, Yoma, 364
Sastras (ancient Indian treatises), 266
Satie, Erik, 128
Satire, playful (*see* Playful satire)
Sauguet, 247, 354, 424
Scala, La (*see* La Scala)
Scandinavian folk-dances, 137
Schadow, *33*, *324*
Schmitt, Florent, 354
Schneitzhoeffer, Jean, 91
Schollar, Ludmila, 429
Schönberg, Arnold, 97, 98, 213
School of American Ballet, 378, 380, 383
Schooling, Elizabeth, 398
Schumann, Robert Alexander, 118
Scott, Margaret, 210
Scottish dances, 40, 133–4, 239, 302
Scribe, 34
Searle, Ronald, 255
Seats, prices of, 336, 439
Sedova, 58*n*
Seguidillas, 299, 301 *and n*
Semi-amateur ballet (*see* Semi-professional ballet)
Semi-commercial State ballet, 19, 33

Semi-professional ballet, 289, 381, 386, 394–6
Semyonova, Marina, 261
Sentimentality (*see* Kitsch)
Serbia, 308
Serf ballets, 427
Sergueyev, Konstantin, 261, *272*, 319*n*, 355
Serral, Dolores, 303
Sert, Misia, 67
Servandoni, 25
Sevastianov, German, 420, 422
Sevillanas, 301–2, *306*
Seville, 296, 300
Sex, ballet and, 216, 230, 284
Shabelevsky, Yurek, 201, 342, *385*, *400*, 407
Shakespeare, 148*n*, 212, 227, 263, 332, 366
Shanghai, 368
Shankar, Gauri, 287, 345
——, Sachin, 289
——, Uday, 201, 202, 278, 280, 281–6, 287, *288*, 288, 289, 292, 358, 403
Sharma, Naarendra, 289
Shawn, Ted, 142, 143, 145, 220, 344
Shearer, Moira, 355, 370, 373
Shevanti, 345 *and n*, 346
Shewring, Olive, 441
Shirali, Vishnudas, 283
Shiryaev, M., 328, 331
Shivashankar, 359
Shore, Jane, 253
Siamese dancers, Royal, 89
Sibelius, Jean, 254
Silence, dancing in, 123, 222–3, 262
Simeonov, Simon, 429
Simkie, 282, 283, 285, *288*
Simon, S. J., 360*n*
Sinha, Bipin, 288, 289 *and n*
——, Surendra, 289 *and n*
Sinhalese classical dances, 267 *and n*, 293, 345*n*
Sitara, 291
Sitwell, Edith, 187, 188
Sivaram, 282*n*
Skeaping, Mary, 435*n*
Skibine, George, 410, *417*, 430
Skouratov, Vladimir, 389, 410, 428
Slavenska, Mia, 308
Slavinsky, Tadeo, 77, 104
Slonimsky, Yuri, 263 *and n*
Slovenia, 307
Smith, Oliver, 423
Social psychology, 431
—— significance, 146, 245
Societé des Bains de Mer, Monaco, 402, 403

Sokolova, Lydia, *81*, 130, 177, 335, 435
Somes, Michael, 376, 377 *and* n
Sophistication, balance between naïveté and, 228, 243, 244
Sopwith, Noreen, 398
Sounds uttered by dancers, 238
South Africa, 227, 239
Soviet ballet, 259–64
Spanish ballet, 302–6, 415
—— dancing (*see also* Flamenco), 129, 136, 142, 250, 294–306
—— Royal Ballet, 302, 303
Speech, use of in connection with dancing, 146 *and* n, 262, 351
Spence, Nan, 441
Spessivsteva, Olga, *58*n, 78, 84, *176*, 177, 178, 179, 190, 201, 316, 319, 320, 327 *and* n, 335, 374, 376, 435
Spirit, breaking of, in dancers, 436
Split Ballet company, 311
Spoljar, Draga, 307
Spontaneity, 233, 240, 242, 243–4, 248, 251, 357, 400, 431, 432
Sport, 161, 262
Staff, Frank, 239–41, *240*, 245, 251, 254, 397, 398
Stage lighting (*see* Lighting, stage)
Stage-patterns, 40, 91, 120, 174
Stage presence, 395, 398 421,
Stanislavsky, Konstantin, 98, 99, 100, 102, 369, 399
Star system, 414
State ballet, 19, 182, 315–24, 328n, 373, 418
Stebbens, Genevieve, 349
Stendhal, 32, 207
Stevenson, Dorothy, 356
——, Hugh, 386, 387, 395
Stewart, Marguerite, *225*
Stiller, 226
Stockholm, 40, 50, 135, 223–4, 225, 328
—— Royal Opera House, 225
Stodginess in corps de ballet dancers, 340, 355, 363, 367, 370, 387, 395
Stoll, Sir Oswald, 76, 77, 78, 439
—— Theatre, 337
Stormbühne, 100
Straight, Mrs. Beatrice, 284
Strain (*see* Tension)
Strauss, Richard, 89n
Stravinsky, Igor, *65*, 68, 70, 71, 78, 81, 82, 83, 88, 89, 92, 93, 97, 98, 103, 104, 106, 107, 108, 109n, 114, 139, 140, 164, 165, 166, 167, 172, 173, 174, 194, 259, 354, 379, 380, 399

Strindberg, August, 98, 148, 226
Stroganova, Nina, 411
Strong, Margaret, 428
Stuart, Robert, *384*
Stuttgart, 24, 25
Sullivan, Arthur, 255, 256
——, Harry Stack, 431, 437
——, John, 375
Suprematists, 120
Surrealism, 83, 133, 244, 404
Svetlova, Marina, 342
Sweden, 40, 135, 150, 205n, 223–4, 225, 328
Swedish Ballet (*see* Ballets-Suédois)
Swedish dancers, 393
Swedish folk-dances, 137, 153
Swedish Royal Ballet, 135, 205n
Symbolist-realist painters, 379–80
Szyfer, J. E., 180

TAGLIONI, Fillippo, 34, 40, 91n, 321n
——, Marie, 34, 90, 91
——, Salvatore, 32, 34
Tagore, Rabindranath, 278–9, 281, 291, 357, 358
Tairov, 164, 260
Talas (Indian rhythmic patterns), 280, 282, 345 *and* n
Talbot, J. Alden, 380, 422, 423
Tallchief, Maria, *161*, 174
——, Marjorie, 430
Tango Gitano, 299
Tanjore school of Bharata Natyam, 344
Tarakanova, Nina, 355
Taras, John, 227, 426, 430
Tariq, 294
Tartar folk-dances, 310
Tat-kar, 298
Taylor, 26
Tchaikovsky, 167, 310, 334
Tchelitcheff, Pavel (*see* Chelichev)
Tcherepnine (*see* Cherepnin)
Tchernicheva, Lubov, 406, 411
Teachers, European classical ballet (*see under* Astafieva, Beck, Beretta, Blasis, Bournonville, Brooking, Cecchetti, Craske, Didelot, Dupré, Gardel, Goncharov, Guillet, Hardy, Idzikovsky, Johannsen, Karsavina, Kniasev, Kshessinshaya, Koslov, Legat, Lepri, Marsh, Noverre, Obukhov, Preobazhenskaya, Prevost, Roje, Salle, Schollar, Skeaping, Trefilova, Tudor, Vestris, Vigano, Vilzak, Volinin, Volkova)

Teachers, free dance (*see under* Åkesson, de Vos, Dalcroze, Delsarte, Duncan, Graham, Kratina, Laban, Leeder, St. Denis, Shawn, Wigman)
——, Indian classical (*see under* Gopal, Kandapa, Kutty, Jailal, Misra, Nambudri, Prasad, Sinha)
—— in companies, 434–5
Teatro Ducale, Milan, 30
Television, 7, 439
Teliakovsky, 64, 66, 68, 73, 259, 329
Temple dancing, 266
Tenishev, Princess, 63
Tension, 124, 148, 221, 245
Théâtre de la Renaissance, Paris, 35
Théâtre des Champs-Elysées, 424
Theatre Guild, 236
Théâtre Sarah Bernhardt, 247, 424
Theatrical managers (impresarios), *see under* Garrick, Gross, Handel, Hurok, Kahn, Krauss, Joly, Lumley, Monnet, Moylin, O'Reilly, Rich, Rubin, Taylor
Théodore, Mlle, *33*
Thillana, 344
Tich, Little, 110
Tiller Girls, 170, 373
Timirbaran, 283
Toda (*see* Tola)
Todd, Arthur, 175
Tola (standard Kathak enchaînements), 287, 295, 345
Toller, Ernst, 100, 148, 163
Torah (*see* Tola)
Toulouse-Lautrec, 97, 156
Toumanova, Tamara, 166, *385*, 406*n*, 409, 417
Tours by companies, 325, 382, 414, 429, 438
Toynbee Hall, 211, 386–8
Tradition, break in, 218, 317, 321, 435
——, influence of, 206, 218, 220
——, preservation of, 315, 317, 321
Training of dancers (*see also* French school, Italian school and Russian school), 432, 434
Travancore, palace company of Maharaja of, 290, 292
Travancorean school of Kathakali, 272, *273*
Trecu, Pirmin, 372
Trefilova, Vera, 78, 320, 435
Trilling, Lionel, 111
Trivandrum palace company, 292
Trunoff, Vassili, 342
Tsars of Russia, 427, 439
Tucker, Joan, 355

Tudor, Antony, 172, 186, 200–19, *208*, *209*, 220, 224, 225, 228, 232, 233, 234, 237, 238, 239, 241, 244, 245, 257, 258, 264, 265, 341, 366, 368, *369*, 382, 384, 386–8, 396, 397, 399, *416*, 418 *and n*, 419, 421, 422, 423, 424, 435, 437, 438
Tufiakin, Prince, 29
Turin, 42
Turner, Harold, *145*, 157, 190, 239, 355, 365, 366, 367, 368*n*, *369*, 371, 374, 375, *384*, 395, 396, 399
——, Joan, 364
Tychsen, Anna, *336*

Ukrainian folk-dances, 90, 264, *272*
Ulanova, Galina, 261, 262, 263, *272*, 435
Umemoto, Rikuhei, 201
Underparting of dancers, 383, 387
United States of America, 42, 74–6, 101, 102, 126, 141–9, 167–76, 195, 230, 234–9, 350–2, 378–85, 410, 417, 424, 428
University Ballet (Cape Town), 252
Unsubsidized choreographers companies, 385–90
Urania Theatre, Budapest, 347

Vacations, tours by groups of dancers during Summer, 328, 379
Vaganova, Agrippina, *58n*, 261 *and n*, 264
—— school, 261
Vajifdar, Khurshed, 292, *293*
——, Roshan, *289*, 292, *293*
——, Shirin, *273*, 292, 293
Vakhtangov, 99, 260
—— Theatre, 99
Valberg, 28
Valéry, Paul, 354
Vallathol, 272, 343
van Damm, Vivian, 335 *and n̄*, 336
van Gogh, V., 97, 148
van Praagh, Peggy, 206, *208*, 209, *209*, 212, 216, 232, 233, 368*n*, *369*, 387, 395, 397, 399
van Vechten, Carl, 110, 144
Vanko, Maximilian, 308
Variety, 143, 253, 275, 334, 339
Vassiliev, 308
Vaudeville (*see* Variety)
Vendredis de la Danse, 247
Venice, 30
Verchinina, Nina, *129*, 131, 132, 133, 407
Verdi, 31, 366

Verhaeren, 354
Vermeer, 226
Véron, Dr. Louis, 33
Versailles, royal theatre at, 24
Vestris, Auguste, 27, 28, 54, 317, 322, 323, 434
Vestris-Bournonville-Johannsen school (*see* Franco-Danish school)
Victorian age, 40
Vic-Wells Ballet, 154, 155, 156, 157, 187, 188, 189, 239, 334, 335 *and* n, 336, 364, 365, 366, 367, 369, *369*, 370, 372, 376, 382, 387, 395, 396, 435
Vic-Wells organization, 364–5, 382 *and* n
Vic-Wells School, 365, 366, 367, 368, 435n (*see also* Sadlers Wells School)
Vienna, 25, 35, 40, 328
Vigano, Giulia, 32
——, Salvatore, 27, 31–2, *33*, 87, 92, 114, 361
Vil, Elsa, 58n, 328
Vilzak, Anatole, 429
Vilzak-Schollar School, 429
Virile male dancing, 433
Vladimirov, 58n
Volinine, Alexandre, 320, 323, 435
Volkonsky, Prince, 63–4, 73, 119
Volkova, Vera, 324
Volynsky, Akim, 163, 260, 261 *and* n
Vsevolozhky, I. A., 54, 55, 58, 59, 61
Vueltas quebradas, 300
Vuillermoz, E., 108, 130n
Vyroubova, Nina, 247, 320, 425

Wagner, Richard, 54, 58n, 118, 185
Wahlberg, 28
Wallman, Margaret, 143n
Walton, William, 188
Warburg, Edward M. M., 378 *and* n, 427
Warsaw State Ballet, 321n
Weaver, John, 20–1
Webb, Helen, 239
Wedekind, 98, 100
Weill, Kurt, 210

Weiss, Josephine, 307
Westminster Theatre, 234
Whistler, Rex, 157
Wigman Dance Group, 220, 349–50, 363
——, Mary, 116–26, *128*, 143, 145, 149, 153, 175, 180, 186, 220, 221, 222, 265, 349–50, 351, *352*, 363
—— school, 122, 220
Williams, Vaughan, 155, 156
Windmill Theatre, 335, 388
Woizikovsky, Leon, 77, 177, 201, 406
Wolfe, E., 155
Wood, Christopher, 82
Wright, Belinda, 341
Württemberg, Carl Eugen, Duke of, 24
Wycherly, Margaret, 144

Yaco, Sadi, 275
Yakulov, 262
Yeats, W. B., 154
Yegorova, Lubov, 58n, 78, 170, 320, 328, 355, 435
Yermolayev, Alexei, 261
Yiddish Art Theatre, 242
Yoga, 282, 285
Youskevich, Igor, 308
Yugoslav dancers (classical), 438
—— folk-dancers, 196, *305*, 307
Yugoslavia, 307–11

Zagreb Ballet, 307, 308, 309, 311
—— Opera House, 307
Zakharov, 264
Zambelli, Carlotta, *336*
Zapateado, 298, 300
Zeitgeist, 87, 124, 132, 366, 394, 400
Zeretelli, Prince, 405
Ziryab, 294
Zohra, 282
Zorina, *385*
Zucchi, Virginia, 56
Zullig, Hans, 363, 364
Zverev, 412 *and* n